Guy de Maupassant was a master of brevity. Born in 1850, he turned everyday moments into unforgettable stories. Whether delving into romance, greed, or human folly, Maupassant had a gift for bringing characters to life with a few well-chosen words. His works remain timeless snapshots of human nature, perfect for when you need a little wisdom or a lot of heart.

Maupassant Complete Short Stories I

Guy de Maupassant

Om Books International

This edition first published in 2025 by

Om Books International

Corporate & Editorial Office
A-12, Sector 64, Noida 201 301
Uttar Pradesh, India
Phone: +91 120 477 4100
Email: editorial@ombooks.com
Website: www.ombooksinternational.com

Sales Office
107, Ansari Road, Darya Ganj,
New Delhi 110 002, India
Phone: +91 11 4000 9000
Email: sales@ombooks.com
Website: www.ombooks.com

ISBN: 978-93-6395-955-2

Printed in India

10 9 8 7 6 5 4 3 2 1

Table of Contents

VOLUME I

A STUDY BY POL. NEVEUX

"I entered literary life as a meteor, and I shall leave it like a thunderbolt." These words of Maupassant to Jose Maria de Heredia on the occasion of a memorable meeting are, in spite of their morbid solemnity, not an inexact summing up of the brief career during which, for ten years, the writer, by turns undaunted and sorrowful, with the fertility of a master hand produced poetry, novels, romances and travels, only to sink prematurely into the abyss of madness and death. . . . .

In the month of April, 1880, an article appeared in the "Le Gaulois" announcing the publication of the Soirees de Medan. It was signed by a name as yet unknown: Guy de Maupassant. After a juvenile diatribe against romanticism and a passionate attack on languorous literature, the writer extolled the study of real life, and announced the publication of the new work. It was picturesque and charming. In the quiet of evening, on an island, in the Seine, beneath poplars instead of the Neapolitan cypresses dear to the friends of Boccaccio, amid the continuous murmur of the valley, and no longer to the sound of the Pyrennean streams that murmured a faint accompaniment to the tales of Marguerite's cavaliers, the master and his disciples took turns in narrating some striking or pathetic episode of the war. And the issue, in collaboration, of these tales in one volume, in which the master jostled elbows with his pupils, took on the appearance of a manifesto, the tone of a challenge, or the utterance of a creed.

In fact, however, the beginnings had been much more simple, and they had confined themselves, beneath the trees of Medan, to deciding on a general title for the work. Zola had contributed the manuscript of the "Attaque du Moulin," and it was at Maupassant's house that the five young men gave in their contributions. Each one read his story, Maupassant being the last. When he had finished Boule de Suif, with a spontaneous impulse, with an emotion they never forgot, filled with enthusiasm at this revelation, they all rose and, without superfluous words, acclaimed him as a master.

He undertook to write the article for the Gaulois and, in cooperation with his friends, he worded it in the terms with which we are familiar, amplifying and embellishing it, yielding to an inborn taste for mystification which his youth rendered excusable. The essential point, he said, is to "unmoor" criticism.

It was unmoored. The following day Wolff wrote a polemical dissertation in the Figaro and carried away his colleagues. The volume was a brilliant success, thanks to Boule de Suif. Despite the novelty, the honesty of effort, on the part of all, no mention was made of the other stories. Relegated to the second rank, they passed without notice. From his first battle, Maupassant was master of the field in literature.

At once the entire press took him up and said what was appropriate regarding the budding celebrity. Biographers and reporters sought information concerning his life. As it was very simple and perfectly straightforward, they resorted to invention. And thus it is that at the present day Maupassant appears to us like one of those ancient heroes whose origin and death are veiled in mystery.

I will not dwell on Guy de Maupassant's younger days. His relatives, his old friends, he himself, here and there in his works, have furnished us in their letters enough valuable revelations and touching remembrances of the years preceding his literary debut. His worthy biographer, H. Edouard Maynial, after collecting intelligently all the writings, condensing and comparing them, has been able to give us some definite information regarding that early period.

I will simply recall that he was born on the 5th of August, 1850, near Dieppe, in the castle of Miromesnil which he describes in Une Vie. . . .

Maupassant, like Flaubert, was a Norman, through his mother, and through his place of birth he belonged to that strange and adventurous race, whose heroic and long voyages on tramp trading ships he liked to recall. And just as the author of "Education sentimentale" seems to have inherited in the paternal line the shrewd realism of Champagne, so de Maupassant appears to have inherited from his Lorraine ancestors their indestructible discipline and cold lucidity.

His childhood was passed at Etretat, his beautiful childhood; it was there that his instincts were awakened in the unfoldment of his prehistoric soul. Years went by in an ecstasy of physical happiness. The delight of running at full speed through fields of gorse, the charm of voyages of discovery in hollows and ravines, games beneath the dark hedges, a passion for going to sea with the fishermen and, on nights when there was no moon, for dreaming on their boats of imaginary voyages.

Mme. de Maupassant, who had guided her son's early reading, and had gazed with him at the sublime spectacle of nature, put, off as long as possible the hour of separation. One day, however, she had to take the child to the little seminary at Yvetot. Later, he became a student at the college at Rouen, and became a literary correspondent of Louis Bouilhet. It was at the latter's house on those Sundays in winter when the Norman rain drowned the sound of the bells and dashed against the window panes that the school boy learned to write poetry.

Vacation took the rhetorician back to the north of Normandy. Now it was shooting at Saint Julien l'Hospitalier, across fields, bogs, and through the woods. From that time on he sealed his pact with the earth, and those "deep and delicate roots" which attached him to his native soil began to grow. It was of Normandy, broad, fresh and virile, that he would presently demand his inspiration, fervent and eager as a boy's love; it was in her that he would take refuge when, weary of life, he would implore a truce, or when he simply wished to work and revive his energies in old-time joys. It was at this time that was born in him that voluptuous love of the sea, which in later days could alone withdraw him from the world, calm him, console him.

In 1870 he lived in the country, then he came to Paris to live; for, the family fortunes having dwindled, he had to look for a position.

For several years he was a clerk in the Ministry of Marine, where he turned over musty papers, in the uninteresting company of the clerks of the admiralty.

Then he went into the department of Public Instruction, where bureaucratic servility is less intolerable. The daily duties are certainly scarcely more onerous and he had as chiefs, or colleagues, Xavier Charmes and Leon Dierx, Henry Roujon and Rene Billotte, but his office looked out on a beautiful melancholy garden with immense plane trees around which black circles of crows gathered in winter.

Maupassant made two divisions of his spare hours, one for boating, and the other for literature. Every evening in spring, every free day, he ran down to the river whose mysterious current veiled in fog or sparkling in the sun called to him and bewitched him. In the islands in the Seine between Chatou and Port-Marly, on the banks of Sartrouville and Triel he was long noted among the population of boatmen, who have now vanished, for his unwearying biceps, his cynical gaiety of good-fellowship, his unfailing practical jokes, his broad witticisms. Sometimes he would row with frantic speed, free and joyous, through the glowing sunlight on the stream; sometimes, he would wander along the coast, questioning the sailors, chatting with the ravageurs, or junk gatherers, or stretched at full length amid the irises and tansy he would lie for hours watching the frail insects that play on the surface of the stream, water spiders, or white butterflies, dragon flies, chasing each other amid the willow leaves, or frogs asleep on the lily-pads.

The rest of his life was taken up by his work. Without ever becoming despondent, silent and persistent, he accumulated manuscripts, poetry, criticisms, plays, romances and novels. Every week he docilely submitted his work to the great Flaubert, the childhood friend of his mother and his uncle Alfred Le Poittevin. The master had consented to assist the young man, to reveal to him the secrets that make chefs-d'oeuvre immortal. It was he who compelled him to make copious research and to use direct observation and who inculcated in him a horror of vulgarity and a contempt for facility.

Maupassant himself tells us of those severe initiations in the Rue Murillo, or in the tent at Croisset; he has recalled the implacable didactics of his old master, his tender brutality, the paternal advice of his generous and candid heart. For seven years Flaubert slashed, pulverized, the awkward attempts of his pupil whose success remained uncertain.

Suddenly, in a flight of spontaneous perfection, he wrote Boule de Suif. His master's joy was great and overwhelming. He died two months later.

Until the end Maupassant remained illuminated by the reflection of the good, vanished giant, by that touching reflection that comes from the dead to those souls they have so profoundly stirred. The worship of Flaubert was a religion from which nothing could distract him, neither work, nor glory, nor slow moving waves, nor balmy nights.

At the end of his short life, while his mind was still clear: he wrote to a friend: "I am always thinking of my poor Flaubert, and I say to myself that I should like to die if I were sure that anyone would think of me in the same manner."

During these long years of his novitiate Maupassant had entered the social literary circles. He would remain silent, preoccupied; and if anyone, astonished at his silence, asked him about his plans he answered simply: "I am learning my trade." However, under the pseudonym of Guy de Valmont, he had sent some articles to the newspapers, and, later, with the approval and by the advice of Flaubert, he published, in the "Republique des Lettres," poems signed by his name.

These poems, overflowing with sensuality, where the hymn to the Earth describes the transports of physical possession, where the impatience of love expresses itself in loud melancholy appeals like the calls of animals in the spring nights, are valuable chiefly inasmuch as they reveal the creature of instinct, the fawn escaped from his native forests, that Maupassant was in his early youth. But they add nothing to his glory. They are the "rhymes of a prose writer" as Jules Lemaitre said. To mould the expression of his thought according to the strictest laws, and to "narrow it down" to some extent, such was his aim. Following the example of one of his comrades of Medan, being readily carried away by precision of style and the rhythm of sentences, by the imperious rule of the ballad, of the pantoum or the chant royal, Maupassant also desired to write in metrical lines. However, he never liked this collection that he often regretted having published. His encounters with prosody had left him with that monotonous weariness that the horseman and the fencer feel after a period in the riding school, or a bout with the foils.

Such, in very broad lines, is the story of Maupassant's literary apprenticeship.

The day following the publication of "Boule de Suif," his reputation began to grow rapidly. The quality of his story was unrivalled, but at the same time it must be acknowledged that there were some who, for the sake of discussion, desired to place a young reputation in opposition to the triumphant brutality of Zola.

From this time on, Maupassant, at the solicitation of the entire press, set to work and wrote story after story. His talent, free from all influences, his individuality, are not disputed for a moment. With a quick step, steady and alert, he advanced to fame, a fame of which he himself was not aware, but which was so universal, that no contemporary author during his life ever experienced the same. The "meteor" sent out its light and its rays were prolonged without limit, in article after article, volume on volume.

He was now rich and famous . . . . He is esteemed all the more as they believe him to be rich and happy. But they do not know that this young fellow with the sunburnt face, thick neck and salient muscles whom they invariably compare to a young bull at liberty, and whose love affairs they whisper, is ill, very ill. At the very moment that success came to him, the malady that never afterwards left him came also, and, seated motionless at his side, gazed at him with its threatening countenance. He suffered from terrible headaches, followed by nights of insomnia. He had nervous attacks, which he soothed with narcotics and anesthetics, which he used freely. His sight, which had troubled him at intervals, became affected, and a celebrated oculist spoke of abnormality, asymetry of the pupils. The famous young man trembled in secret and was haunted by all kinds of terrors.

The reader is charmed at the saneness of this revived art and yet, here and there, he is surprised to discover, amid descriptions of nature that are full of humanity, disquieting flights towards the supernatural, distressing conjurations, veiled at first, of the most commonplace, the most vertiginous shuddering fits of fear, as old as the world and as eternal as the unknown. But, instead of being alarmed, he thinks that the author must be gifted with infallible intuition to follow out thus the taints in his characters, even through their most dangerous mazes. The reader does not know that these hallucinations which he describes so minutely were experienced by Maupassant himself; he does not know that the fear is in himself, the anguish of fear "which is not caused by the presence of danger, or of inevitable death, but by certain abnormal conditions, by certain mysterious influences in presence of vague dangers," the "fear of fear, the dread of that horrible sensation of incomprehensible terror."

How can one explain these physical sufferings and this morbid distress that were known for some time to his intimates alone? Alas! the explanation is only too simple. All his life, consciously or unconsciously, Maupassant fought this malady, hidden as yet, which was latent in him.

As his malady began to take a more definite form, he turned his steps towards the south, only visiting Paris to see his physicians and publishers. In the old port of Antibes beyond the causeway of Cannes, his yacht, Bel Ami, which he cherished as a brother, lay at anchor and awaited him. He took it to the white cities of the Genoese Gulf, towards the palm trees of Hyeres, or the red bay trees of Antheor.

After several tragic weeks in which, from instinct, he made a desperate fight, on the 1st of January, 1892, he felt he was hopelessly vanquished, and in a moment of supreme clearness of intellect, like Gerard de Nerval, he attempted suicide. Less fortunate than the author of Sylvia, he was unsuccessful. But his mind, henceforth "indifferent to all unhappiness," had entered into eternal darkness.

He was taken back to Paris and placed in Dr. Meuriot's sanatorium, where, after eighteen months of mechanical existence, the "meteor" quietly passed away.

BOULE DE SUIF

For several days in succession fragments of a defeated army had passed through the town. They were mere disorganized bands, not disciplined forces. The men wore long, dirty beards and tattered uniforms; they advanced in listless fashion, without a flag, without a leader. All seemed exhausted, worn out, incapable of thought or resolve, marching onward merely by force of habit, and dropping to the ground with fatigue the moment they halted. One saw, in particular, many enlisted men, peaceful citizens, men who lived quietly on their income, bending beneath the weight of their rifles; and little active volunteers, easily frightened but full of enthusiasm, as eager to attack as they were ready to take to flight; and amid these, a sprinkling of red-breeched soldiers, the pitiful remnant of a division cut down in a great battle; somber artillerymen, side by side with nondescript foot-soldiers; and, here and there, the gleaming helmet of a heavy-footed dragoon who had difficulty in keeping up with the quicker pace of the soldiers of the line. Legions of irregulars with high-sounding names "Avengers of Defeat," "Citizens of the Tomb," "Brethren in Death"—passed in their turn, looking like banditti. Their leaders, former drapers or grain merchants, or tallow or soap chandlers—warriors by force of circumstances, officers by reason of their mustachios or their money—covered with weapons, flannel and gold lace, spoke in an impressive manner, discussed plans of campaign, and behaved as though they alone bore the fortunes of dying France on their braggart shoulders; though, in truth, they frequently were afraid of their own men—scoundrels often brave beyond measure, but pillagers and debauchees.

Rumor had it that the Prussians were about to enter Rouen.

The members of the National Guard, who for the past two months had been reconnoitering with the utmost caution in the neighboring woods, occasionally shooting their own sentinels, and making ready for fight whenever a rabbit rustled in the undergrowth, had now returned to their homes. Their arms, their uniforms, all the death-dealing paraphernalia with which they had terrified all the milestones along the highroad for eight miles round, had suddenly and marvellously disappeared.

The last of the French soldiers had just crossed the Seine on their way to Pont-Audemer, through Saint-Sever and Bourg-Achard, and in their rear the vanquished general, powerless to do aught with the forlorn remnants of his army, himself dismayed at the final overthrow of a nation accustomed to victory and disastrously beaten despite its legendary bravery, walked between two orderlies.

Then a profound calm, a shuddering, silent dread, settled on the city. Many a round-paunched citizen, emasculated by years devoted to business, anxiously awaited the conquerors, trembling lest his roasting-jacks or kitchen knives should be looked upon as weapons.

Life seemed to have stopped short; the shops were shut, the streets deserted. Now and then an inhabitant, awed by the silence, glided swiftly by in the shadow of the walls. The anguish of suspense made men even desire the arrival of the enemy.

In the afternoon of the day following the departure of the French troops, a number of uhlans, coming no one knew whence, passed rapidly through the town. A little later on, a black mass descended St. Catherine's Hill, while two other invading bodies appeared respectively on the Darnetal and the Boisguillaume roads. The advance guards of the three corps arrived at precisely the same moment at the Square of the Hotel de Ville, and the German army poured through all the adjacent streets, its battalions making the pavement ring with their firm, measured tread.

Orders shouted in an unknown, guttural tongue rose to the windows of the seemingly dead, deserted houses; while behind the fast-closed shutters eager eyes peered forth at the victors-masters now of the city, its fortunes, and its lives, by "right of war." The inhabitants, in their darkened rooms, were possessed by that terror which follows in the wake of cataclysms, of deadly upheavals of the earth, against which all human skill and strength are vain. For the same thing happens whenever the established order of things is upset, when security no longer exists, when all those rights usually protected by the law of man or of Nature are at the mercy of unreasoning, savage force. The earthquake crushing a whole nation under falling roofs; the flood let loose, and engulfing in its swirling depths the corpses of drowned peasants, along with dead oxen and beams torn from shattered houses; or the army, covered with glory, murdering those who defend themselves, making prisoners of the rest, pillaging in the name of the Sword, and giving thanks to God to the thunder of cannon—all these are appalling scourges, which destroy all belief in eternal justice, all that confidence we have been taught to feel in the protection of Heaven and the reason of man.

Small detachments of soldiers knocked at each door, and then disappeared within the houses; for the vanquished saw they would have to be civil to their conquerors.

At the end of a short time, once the first terror had subsided, calm was again restored. In many houses the Prussian officer ate at the same table with the family. He was often well-bred, and, out of politeness, expressed sympathy with France and repugnance at being compelled to take part in the war. This sentiment was received with gratitude; besides, his protection might be needful some day or other. By the exercise of tact the number of men quartered in one's house might be reduced; and why should one provoke the hostility of a person on whom one's whole welfare depended? Such conduct would savor less of bravery than of foolhardiness. And foolhardiness is no longer a failing of the citizens of Rouen as it was in the days when their city earned renown by its heroic defenses. Last of all-final argument based on the national politeness—the folk of Rouen said to one another that it was only right to be civil in one's own house, provided there was no public exhibition of familiarity with the foreigner. Out of doors, therefore, citizen and soldier did not know each other; but in the house both chatted freely, and each evening the German remained a little longer warming himself at the hospitable hearth.

Even the town itself resumed by degrees its ordinary aspect. The French seldom walked abroad, but the streets swarmed with Prussian soldiers. Moreover, the officers of the Blue Hussars, who arrogantly dragged their instruments of death along the pavements, seemed to hold the simple townsmen in but little more contempt than did the French cavalry officers who had drunk at the same cafes the year before.

But there was something in the air, a something strange and subtle, an intolerable foreign atmosphere like a penetrating odor—the odor of invasion. It permeated dwellings and places of public resort, changed the taste of food, made one imagine one's self in far-distant lands, amid dangerous, barbaric tribes.

The conquerors exacted money, much money. The inhabitants paid what was asked; they were rich. But, the wealthier a Norman tradesman becomes, the more he suffers at having to part with anything that belongs to him, at having to see any portion of his substance pass into the hands of another.

Nevertheless, within six or seven miles of the town, along the course of the river as it flows onward to Croisset, Dieppedalle and Biessart, boat-men and fishermen often hauled to the surface of the water the body of a German, bloated in his uniform, killed by a blow from knife or club, his head crushed by a stone, or perchance pushed from some bridge into the stream below. The mud of the river-bed swallowed up these obscure acts of vengeance—savage, yet legitimate; these unrecorded deeds of bravery; these silent attacks fraught with greater danger than battles fought in broad day, and surrounded, moreover, with no halo of romance. For hatred of the foreigner ever arms a few intrepid souls, ready to die for an idea.

At last, as the invaders, though subjecting the town to the strictest discipline, had not committed any of the deeds of horror with which they had been credited while on their triumphal march, the people grew bolder, and the necessities of business again animated the breasts of the local merchants. Some of these had important commercial interests at Havre —occupied at present by the French army—and wished to attempt to reach that port by overland route to Dieppe, taking the boat from there.

Through the influence of the German officers whose acquaintance they had made, they obtained a permit to leave town from the general in command.

A large four-horse coach having, therefore, been engaged for the journey, and ten passengers having given in their names to the proprietor, they decided to start on a certain Tuesday morning before daybreak, to avoid attracting a crowd.

The ground had been frozen hard for some time-past, and about three o'clock on Monday afternoon—large black clouds from the north shed their burden of snow uninterruptedly all through that evening and night.

At half-past four in the morning the travellers met in the courtyard of the Hotel de Normandie, where they were to take their seats in the coach.

They were still half asleep, and shivering with cold under their wraps. They could see one another but indistinctly in the darkness, and the mountain of heavy winter wraps in which each was swathed made them look like a gathering of obese priests in their long cassocks. But two men recognized each other, a third accosted them, and the three began to talk. "I am bringing my wife," said one. "So am I." "And I, too." The first speaker added: "We shall not return to Rouen, and if the Prussians approach Havre we will cross to England." All three, it turned out, had made the same plans, being of similar disposition and temperament.

Still the horses were not harnessed. A small lantern carried by a stable-boy emerged now and then from one dark doorway to disappear immediately in another. The stamping of horses' hoofs, deadened by the dung and straw of the stable, was heard from time to time, and from inside the building issued a man's voice, talking to the animals and swearing at them. A faint tinkle of bells showed that the harness was being got ready; this tinkle soon developed into a continuous jingling, louder or softer according to the movements of the horse, sometimes stopping altogether, then breaking out in a sudden peal accompanied by a pawing of the ground by an iron-shod hoof.

The door suddenly closed. All noise ceased.

The frozen townsmen were silent; they remained motionless, stiff with cold.

A thick curtain of glistening white flakes fell ceaselessly to the ground; it obliterated all outlines, enveloped all objects in an icy mantle of foam; nothing was to be heard throughout the length and breadth of the silent, winter-bound city save the vague, nameless rustle of falling snow—a sensation rather than a sound—the gentle mingling of light atoms which seemed to fill all space, to cover the whole world.

The man reappeared with his lantern, leading by a rope a melancholy-looking horse, evidently being led out against his inclination. The hostler placed him beside the pole, fastened the traces, and spent some time in walking round him to make sure that the harness was all right; for he could use only one hand, the other being engaged in holding the lantern. As he was about to fetch the second horse he noticed the motionless group of travellers, already white with snow, and said to them: "Why don't you get inside the coach? You'd be under shelter, at least."

This did not seem to have occurred to them, and they at once took his advice. The three men seated their wives at the far end of the coach, then got in themselves; lastly the other vague, snow-shrouded forms clambered to the remaining places without a word.

The floor was covered with straw, into which the feet sank. The ladies at the far end, having brought with them little copper foot-warmers heated by means of a kind of chemical fuel, proceeded to light these, and spent some time in expatiating in low tones on their advantages, saying over and over again things which they had all known for a long time.

At last, six horses instead of four having been harnessed to the diligence, on account of the heavy roads, a voice outside asked: "Is every one there?" To which a voice from the interior replied: "Yes," and they set out.

The vehicle moved slowly, slowly, at a snail's pace; the wheels sank into the snow; the entire body of the coach creaked and groaned; the horses slipped, puffed, steamed, and the coachman's long whip cracked incessantly, flying hither and thither, coiling up, then flinging out its length like a slender serpent, as it lashed some rounded flank, which instantly grew tense as it strained in further effort.

But the day grew apace. Those light flakes which one traveller, a native of Rouen, had compared to a rain of cotton fell no longer. A murky light filtered through dark, heavy clouds, which made the country more dazzlingly white by contrast, a whiteness broken sometimes by a row of tall trees spangled with hoarfrost, or by a cottage roof hooded in snow.

Within the coach the passengers eyed one another curiously in the dim light of dawn.

Right at the back, in the best seats of all, Monsieur and Madame Loiseau, wholesale wine merchants of the Rue Grand-Pont, slumbered opposite each other. Formerly clerk to a merchant who had failed in business, Loiseau had bought his master's interest, and made a fortune for himself. He sold very bad wine at a very low price to the retail-dealers in the country, and had the reputation, among his friends and acquaintances, of being a shrewd rascal a true Norman, full of quips and wiles. So well established was his character as a cheat that, in the mouths of the citizens of Rouen, the very name of Loiseau became a byword for sharp practice.

Above and beyond this, Loiseau was noted for his practical jokes of every description—his tricks, good or ill-natured; and no one could mention his name without adding at once: "He's an extraordinary man—Loiseau." He was undersized and potbellied, had a florid face with grayish whiskers.

His wife-tall, strong, determined, with a loud voice and decided manner —represented the spirit of order and arithmetic in the business house which Loiseau enlivened by his jovial activity.

Beside them, dignified in bearing, belonging to a superior caste, sat Monsieur Carre-Lamadon, a man of considerable importance, a king in the cotton trade, proprietor of three spinning-mills, officer of the Legion of Honor, and member of the General Council. During the whole time the Empire was in the ascendancy he remained the chief of the well-disposed Opposition, merely in order to command a higher value for his devotion when he should rally to the cause which he meanwhile opposed with "courteous weapons," to use his own expression.

Madame Carre-Lamadon, much younger than her husband, was the consolation of all the officers of good family quartered at Rouen. Pretty, slender, graceful, she sat opposite her husband, curled up in her furs, and gazing mournfully at the sorry interior of the coach.

Her neighbors, the Comte and Comtesse Hubert de Breville, bore one of the noblest and most ancient names in Normandy. The count, a nobleman advanced in years and of aristocratic bearing, strove to enhance by every artifice of the toilet, his natural resemblance to King Henry IV, who, according to a legend of which the family were inordinately proud, had been the favored lover of a De Breville lady, and father of her child—the frail one's husband having, in recognition of this fact, been made a count and governor of a province.

A colleague of Monsieur Carre-Lamadon in the General Council, Count Hubert represented the Orleanist party in his department. The story of his marriage with the daughter of a small shipowner at Nantes had always remained more or less of a mystery. But as the countess had an air of unmistakable breeding, entertained faultlessly, and was even supposed to have been loved by a son of Louis-Philippe, the nobility vied with one another in doing her honor, and her drawing-room remained the most select in the whole countryside—the only one which retained the old spirit of gallantry, and to which access was not easy.

The fortune of the Brevilles, all in real estate, amounted, it was said, to five hundred thousand francs a year.

These six people occupied the farther end of the coach, and represented Society—with an income—the strong, established society of good people with religion and principle.

It happened by chance that all the women were seated on the same side; and the countess had, moreover, as neighbors two nuns, who spent the time in fingering their long rosaries and murmuring paternosters and aves. One of them was old, and so deeply pitted with smallpox that she looked for all the world as if she had received a charge of shot full in the face. The other, of sickly appearance, had a pretty but wasted countenance, and a narrow, consumptive chest, sapped by that devouring faith which is the making of martyrs and visionaries.

A man and woman, sitting opposite the two nuns, attracted all eyes.

The man—a well-known character—was Cornudet, the democrat, the terror of all respectable people. For the past twenty years his big red beard had been on terms of intimate acquaintance with the tankards of all the republican cafes. With the help of his comrades and brethren he had dissipated a respectable fortune left him by his father, an old-established confectioner, and he now impatiently awaited the Republic, that he might at last be rewarded with the post he had earned by his revolutionary orgies. On the fourth of September—possibly as the result of a practical joke—he was led to believe that he had been appointed prefect; but when he attempted to take up the duties of the position the clerks in charge of the office refused to recognize his authority, and he was compelled in consequence to retire. A good sort of fellow in other respects, inoffensive and obliging, he had thrown himself zealously into the work of making an organized defence of the town. He had had pits dug in the level country, young forest trees felled, and traps set on all the roads; then at the approach of the enemy, thoroughly satisfied with his preparations, he had hastily returned to the town. He thought he might now do more good at Havre, where new intrenchments would soon be necessary.

The woman, who belonged to the courtesan class, was celebrated for an embonpoint unusual for her age, which had earned for her the sobriquet of "Boule de Suif" (Tallow Ball). Short and round, fat as a pig, with puffy fingers constricted at the joints, looking like rows of short sausages; with a shiny, tightly-stretched skin and an enormous bust filling out the bodice of her dress, she was yet attractive and much sought after, owing to her fresh and pleasing appearance. Her face was like a crimson apple, a peony-bud just bursting into bloom; she had two magnificent dark eyes, fringed with thick, heavy lashes, which cast a shadow into their depths; her mouth was small, ripe, kissable, and was furnished with the tiniest of white teeth.

As soon as she was recognized the respectable matrons of the party began to whisper among themselves, and the words "hussy" and "public scandal" were uttered so loudly that Boule de Suif raised her head. She forthwith cast such a challenging, bold look at her neighbors that a sudden silence fell on the company, and all lowered their eyes, with the exception of Loiseau, who watched her with evident interest.

But conversation was soon resumed among the three ladies, whom the presence of this girl had suddenly drawn together in the bonds of friendship—one might almost say in those of intimacy. They decided that they ought to combine, as it were, in their dignity as wives in face of this shameless hussy; for legitimized love always despises its easygoing brother.

The three men, also, brought together by a certain conservative instinct awakened by the presence of Cornudet, spoke of money matters in a tone expressive of contempt for the poor. Count Hubert related the losses he had sustained at the hands of the Prussians, spoke of the cattle which had been stolen from him, the crops which had been ruined, with the easy manner of a nobleman who was also a tenfold millionaire, and whom such reverses would scarcely inconvenience for a single year. Monsieur Carre-Lamadon, a man of wide experience in the cotton industry, had taken care to send six hundred thousand francs to England as provision against the rainy day he was always anticipating. As for Loiseau, he had managed to sell to the French commissariat department all the wines he had in stock, so that the state now owed him a considerable sum, which he hoped to receive at Havre.

And all three eyed one another in friendly, well-disposed fashion. Although of varying social status, they were united in the brotherhood of money—in that vast freemasonry made up of those who possess, who can jingle gold wherever they choose to put their hands into their breeches' pockets.

The coach went along so slowly that at ten o'clock in the morning it had not covered twelve miles. Three times the men of the party got out and climbed the hills on foot. The passengers were becoming uneasy, for they had counted on lunching at Totes, and it seemed now as if they would hardly arrive there before nightfall. Every one was eagerly looking out for an inn by the roadside, when, suddenly, the coach foundered in a snowdrift, and it took two hours to extricate it.

As appetites increased, their spirits fell; no inn, no wine shop could be discovered, the approach of the Prussians and the transit of the starving French troops having frightened away all business.

The men sought food in the farmhouses beside the road, but could not find so much as a crust of bread; for the suspicious peasant invariably hid his stores for fear of being pillaged by the soldiers, who, being entirely without food, would take violent possession of everything they found.

About one o'clock Loiseau announced that he positively had a big hollow in his stomach. They had all been suffering in the same way for some time, and the increasing gnawings of hunger had put an end to all conversation.

Now and then some one yawned, another followed his example, and each in turn, according to his character, breeding and social position, yawned either quietly or noisily, placing his hand before the gaping void whence issued breath condensed into vapor.

Several times Boule de Suif stooped, as if searching for something under her petticoats. She would hesitate a moment, look at her neighbors, and then quietly sit upright again. All faces were pale and drawn. Loiseau declared he would give a thousand francs for a knuckle of ham. His wife made an involuntary and quickly checked gesture of protest. It always hurt her to hear of money being squandered, and she could not even understand jokes on such a subject.

"As a matter of fact, I don't feel well," said the count. "Why did I not think of bringing provisions?" Each one reproached himself in similar fashion.

Cornudet, however, had a bottle of rum, which he offered to his neighbors. They all coldly refused except Loiseau, who took a sip, and returned the bottle with thanks, saying: "That's good stuff; it warms one up, and cheats the appetite." The alcohol put him in good humor, and he proposed they should do as the sailors did in the song: eat the fattest of the passengers. This indirect allusion to Boule de Suif shocked the respectable members of the party. No one replied; only Cornudet smiled. The two good sisters had ceased to mumble their rosary, and, with hands enfolded in their wide sleeves, sat motionless, their eyes steadfastly cast down, doubtless offering up as a sacrifice to Heaven the suffering it had sent them.

At last, at three o'clock, as they were in the midst of an apparently limitless plain, with not a single village in sight, Boule de Suif stooped quickly, and drew from underneath the seat a large basket covered with a white napkin.

From this she extracted first of all a small earthenware plate and a silver drinking cup, then an enormous dish containing two whole chickens cut into joints and imbedded in jelly. The basket was seen to contain other good things: pies, fruit, dainties of all sorts-provisions, in fine, for a three days' journey, rendering their owner independent of wayside inns. The necks of four bottles protruded from among the food. She took a chicken wing, and began to eat it daintily, together with one of those rolls called in Normandy "Regence."

All looks were directed toward her. An odor of food filled the air, causing nostrils to dilate, mouths to water, and jaws to contract painfully. The scorn of the ladies for this disreputable female grew positively ferocious; they would have liked to kill her, or throw, her and her drinking cup, her basket, and her provisions, out of the coach into the snow of the road below.

But Loiseau's gaze was fixed greedily on the dish of chicken. He said:

"Well, well, this lady had more forethought than the rest of us. Some people think of everything."

She looked up at him.

"Would you like some, sir? It is hard to go on fasting all day."

He bowed.

"Upon my soul, I can't refuse; I cannot hold out another minute. All is fair in war time, is it not, madame?" And, casting a glance on those around, he added:

"At times like this it is very pleasant to meet with obliging people."

He spread a newspaper over his knees to avoid soiling his trousers, and, with a pocketknife he always carried, helped himself to a chicken leg coated with jelly, which he thereupon proceeded to devour.

Then Boule le Suif, in low, humble tones, invited the nuns to partake of her repast. They both accepted the offer unhesitatingly, and after a few stammered words of thanks began to eat quickly, without raising their eyes. Neither did Cornudet refuse his neighbor's offer, and, in combination with the nuns, a sort of table was formed by opening out the newspaper over the four pairs of knees.

Mouths kept opening and shutting, ferociously masticating and devouring the food. Loiseau, in his corner, was hard at work, and in low tones urged his wife to follow his example. She held out for a long time, but overstrained Nature gave way at last. Her husband, assuming his politest manner, asked their "charming companion" if he might be allowed to offer Madame Loiseau a small helping.

"Why, certainly, sir," she replied, with an amiable smile, holding out the dish.

When the first bottle of claret was opened some embarrassment was caused by the fact that there was only one drinking cup, but this was passed from one to another, after being wiped. Cornudet alone, doubtless in a spirit of gallantry, raised to his own lips that part of the rim which was still moist from those of his fair neighbor.

Then, surrounded by people who were eating, and well-nigh suffocated by the odor of food, the Comte and Comtesse de Breville and Monsieur and Madame Carre-Lamadon endured that hateful form of torture which has perpetuated the name of Tantalus. All at once the manufacturer's young wife heaved a sigh which made every one turn and look at her; she was white as the snow without; her eyes closed, her head fell forward; she had fainted. Her husband, beside himself, implored the help of his neighbors. No one seemed to know what to do until the elder of the two nuns, raising the patient's head, placed Boule de Suif's drinking cup to her lips, and made her swallow a few drops of wine. The pretty invalid moved, opened her eyes, smiled, and declared in a feeble voice that she was all right again. But, to prevent a recurrence of the catastrophe, the nun made her drink a cupful of claret, adding: "It's just hunger—that's what is wrong with you."

Then Boule de Suif, blushing and embarrassed, stammered, looking at the four passengers who were still fasting:

"'Mon Dieu', if I might offer these ladies and gentlemen——"

She stopped short, fearing a snub. But Loiseau continued:

"Hang it all, in such a case as this we are all brothers and sisters and ought to assist each other. Come, come, ladies, don't stand on ceremony, for goodness' sake! Do we even know whether we shall find a house in which to pass the night? At our present rate of going we sha'n't be at Totes till midday to-morrow."

They hesitated, no one daring to be the first to accept. But the count settled the question. He turned toward the abashed girl, and in his most distinguished manner said:

"We accept gratefully, madame."

As usual, it was only the first step that cost. This Rubicon once crossed, they set to work with a will. The basket was emptied. It still contained a pate de foie gras, a lark pie, a piece of smoked tongue, Crassane pears, Pont-Leveque gingerbread, fancy cakes, and a cup full of pickled gherkins and onions—Boule de Suif, like all women, being very fond of indigestible things.

They could not eat this girl's provisions without speaking to her. So they began to talk, stiffly at first; then, as she seemed by no means forward, with greater freedom. Mesdames de Breville and

Carre-Lamadon, who were accomplished women of the world, were gracious and tactful. The countess especially displayed that amiable condescension characteristic of great ladies whom no contact with baser mortals can sully, and was absolutely charming. But the sturdy Madame Loiseau, who had the soul of a gendarme, continued morose, speaking little and eating much.

Conversation naturally turned on the war. Terrible stories were told about the Prussians, deeds of bravery were recounted of the French; and all these people who were fleeing themselves were ready to pay homage to the courage of their compatriots. Personal experiences soon followed, and Boule le Suif related with genuine emotion, and with that warmth of language not uncommon in women of her class and temperament, how it came about that she had left Rouen.

"I thought at first that I should be able to stay," she said. "My house was well stocked with provisions, and it seemed better to put up with feeding a few soldiers than to banish myself goodness knows where. But when I saw these Prussians it was too much for me! My blood boiled with rage; I wept the whole day for very shame. Oh, if only I had been a man! I looked at them from my window—the fat swine, with their pointed helmets!—and my maid held my hands to keep me from throwing my furniture down on them. Then some of them were quartered on me; I flew at the throat of the first one who entered. They are just as easy to strangle as other men! And I'd have been the death of that one if I hadn't been dragged away from him by my hair. I had to hide after that. And as soon as I could get an opportunity I left the place, and here I am."

She was warmly congratulated. She rose in the estimation of her companions, who had not been so brave; and Cornudet listened to her with the approving and benevolent smile of an apostle, the smile a priest might wear in listening to a devotee praising God; for long-bearded democrats of his type have a monopoly of patriotism, just as priests have a monopoly of religion. He held forth in turn, with dogmatic self-assurance, in the style of the proclamations daily pasted on the walls of the town, winding up with a specimen of stump oratory in which he reviled "that besotted fool of a Louis-Napoleon."

But Boule de Suif was indignant, for she was an ardent Bonapartist. She turned as red as a cherry, and stammered in her wrath: "I'd just like to have seen you in his place—you and your sort! There would have been a nice mix-up. Oh, yes! It was you who betrayed that man. It would be impossible to live in France if we were governed by such rascals as you!"

Cornudet, unmoved by this tirade, still smiled a superior, contemptuous smile; and one felt that high words were impending, when the count interposed, and, not without difficulty, succeeded in calming the exasperated woman, saying that all sincere opinions ought to be respected. But the countess and the manufacturer's wife, imbued with the unreasoning hatred of the upper classes for the Republic, and instinct, moreover, with the affection felt by all women for the pomp and circumstance of despotic government, were drawn, in spite of themselves, toward this dignified young woman, whose opinions coincided so closely with their own.

The basket was empty. The ten people had finished its contents without difficulty amid general regret that it did not hold more. Conversation went on a little longer, though it flagged somewhat after the passengers had finished eating.

Night fell, the darkness grew deeper and deeper, and the cold made Boule de Suif shiver, in spite of her plumpness. So Madame de Breville offered her her foot-warmer, the fuel of which had been several times renewed since the morning, and she accepted the offer at once, for her feet were icy cold. Mesdames Carre-Lamadon and Loiseau gave theirs to the nuns.

The driver lighted his lanterns. They cast a bright gleam on a cloud of vapor which hovered over the sweating flanks of the horses, and on the roadside snow, which seemed to unroll as they went along in the changing light of the lamps.

All was now indistinguishable in the coach; but suddenly a movement occurred in the corner occupied by Boule de Suif and Cornudet; and Loiseau, peering into the gloom, fancied he saw the big, bearded democrat move hastily to one side, as if he had received a well-directed, though noiseless, blow in the dark.

Tiny lights glimmered ahead. It was Totes. The coach had been on the road eleven hours, which, with the three hours allotted the horses in four periods for feeding and breathing, made fourteen. It entered the town, and stopped before the Hotel du Commerce.

The coach door opened; a well-known noise made all the travellers start; it was the clanging of a scabbard, on the pavement; then a voice called out something in German.

Although the coach had come to a standstill, no one got out; it looked as if they were afraid of being murdered the moment they left their seats. Thereupon the driver appeared, holding in his hand one of his lanterns, which cast a sudden glow on the interior of the coach, lighting up the double row of startled faces, mouths agape, and eyes wide open in surprise and terror.

Beside the driver stood in the full light a German officer, a tall young man, fair and slender, tightly encased in his uniform like a woman in her corset, his flat shiny cap, tilted to one side of his head, making him look like an English hotel runner. His exaggerated mustache, long and straight and tapering to a point at either end in a single blond hair that could hardly be seen, seemed to weigh down the corners of his mouth and give a droop to his lips.

In Alsatian French he requested the travellers to alight, saying stiffly:

"Kindly get down, ladies and gentlemen."

The two nuns were the first to obey, manifesting the docility of holy women accustomed to submission on every occasion. Next appeared the count and countess, followed by the manufacturer and his wife, after whom came Loiseau, pushing his larger and better half before him.

"Good-day, sir," he said to the officer as he put his foot to the ground, acting on an impulse born of prudence rather than of politeness. The other, insolent like all in authority, merely stared without replying.

Boule de Suif and Cornudet, though near the door, were the last to alight, grave and dignified before the enemy. The stout girl tried to control herself and appear calm; the democrat stroked his long russet beard with a somewhat trembling hand. Both strove to maintain their dignity, knowing well that at such a time each individual is always looked upon as more or less typical of his nation; and, also, resenting the complaisant attitude of their companions, Boule de Suif tried to wear a bolder front than her neighbors, the virtuous women, while he, feeling that it was incumbent on him to set a good example, kept up the attitude of resistance which he had first assumed when he undertook to mine the high roads round Rouen.

They entered the spacious kitchen of the inn, and the German, having demanded the passports signed by the general in command, in which were mentioned the name, description and profession of each traveller, inspected them all minutely, comparing their appearance with the written particulars.

Then he said brusquely: "All right," and turned on his heel.

They breathed freely, All were still hungry; so supper was ordered. Half an hour was required for its preparation, and while two servants were apparently engaged in getting it ready the travellers went to look at their rooms. These all opened off a long corridor, at the end of which was a glazed door with a number on it.

They were just about to take their seats at table when the innkeeper appeared in person. He was a former horse dealer—a large, asthmatic individual, always wheezing, coughing, and clearing his throat. Follenvie was his patronymic.

He called:

"Mademoiselle Elisabeth Rousset?"

Boule de Suif started, and turned round.

"That is my name."

"Mademoiselle, the Prussian officer wishes to speak to you immediately."

"To me?"

"Yes; if you are Mademoiselle Elisabeth Rousset."

She hesitated, reflected a moment, and then declared roundly:

"That may be; but I'm not going."

They moved restlessly around her; every one wondered and speculated as to the cause of this order. The count approached:

"You are wrong, madame, for your refusal may bring trouble not only on yourself but also on all your companions. It never pays to resist those in authority. Your compliance with this request cannot possibly be fraught with any danger; it has probably been made because some formality or other was forgotten."

All added their voices to that of the count; Boule de Suif was begged, urged, lectured, and at last convinced; every one was afraid of the complications which might result from headstrong action on her part. She said finally:

"I am doing it for your sakes, remember that!"

The countess took her hand.

"And we are grateful to you."

She left the room. All waited for her return before commencing the meal. Each was distressed that he or she had not been sent for rather than this impulsive, quick-tempered girl, and each mentally rehearsed platitudes in case of being summoned also.

But at the end of ten minutes she reappeared breathing hard, crimson with indignation.

"Oh! the scoundrel! the scoundrel!" she stammered.

All were anxious to know what had happened; but she declined to enlighten them, and when the count pressed the point, she silenced him with much dignity, saying:

"No; the matter has nothing to do with you, and I cannot speak of it."

Then they took their places round a high soup tureen, from which issued an odor of cabbage. In spite of this coincidence, the supper was cheerful. The cider was good; the Loiseaus and the nuns drank it from motives of economy. The others ordered wine; Cornudet demanded beer. He had his own fashion of uncorking the bottle and making the beer foam, gazing at it as he inclined his glass and then raised it to a position between the lamp and his eye that he might judge of its color. When he drank, his great beard, which matched the color of his favorite beverage, seemed to tremble with affection; his eyes positively squinted in the endeavor not to lose sight of the beloved glass, and he looked for all the world as if he were fulfilling the only function for which he was born. He seemed to have established in his mind an affinity between the two great passions of his life—pale ale and revolution—and assuredly he could not taste the one without dreaming of the other.

Monsieur and Madame Follenvie dined at the end of the table. The man, wheezing like a broken-down locomotive, was too short-winded to talk when he was eating. But the wife was not silent a moment; she told how the Prussians had impressed her on their arrival, what they did, what they said; execrating them in the first place because they cost her money, and in the second because she had two sons in the army. She addressed herself principally to the countess, flattered at the opportunity of talking to a lady of quality.

Then she lowered her voice, and began to broach delicate subjects. Her husband interrupted her from time to time, saying:

"You would do well to hold your tongue, Madame Follenvie."

But she took no notice of him, and went on:

"Yes, madame, these Germans do nothing but eat potatoes and pork, and then pork and potatoes. And don't imagine for a moment that they are clean! No, indeed! And if only you saw them drilling for hours, indeed for days, together; they all collect in a field, then they do nothing but march backward and forward, and wheel this way and that. If only they would cultivate the land, or remain at home and work on their high roads! Really, madame, these soldiers are of no earthly use! Poor people have to feed and keep them, only in order that they may learn how to kill! True, I am only an old woman with no education, but when I see them wearing themselves out marching about from morning till night, I say to myself: When there are people who make discoveries that are of use to people, why should others take so much trouble to do harm? Really, now, isn't it a terrible thing to kill people, whether they are Prussians, or English, or Poles, or French? If we revenge ourselves on any one who injures us we do wrong, and are punished for it; but when our sons are shot down like partridges, that is all right, and decorations are given to the man who kills the most. No, indeed, I shall never be able to understand it."

Cornudet raised his voice:

"War is a barbarous proceeding when we attack a peaceful neighbor, but it is a sacred duty when undertaken in defence of one's country."

The old woman looked down:

"Yes; it's another matter when one acts in self-defence; but would it not be better to kill all the kings, seeing that they make war just to amuse themselves?"

Cornudet's eyes kindled.

"Bravo, citizens!" he said.

Monsieur Carre-Lamadon was reflecting profoundly. Although an ardent admirer of great generals, the peasant woman's sturdy common sense made him reflect on the wealth which might accrue to a country by the employment of so many idle hands now maintained at a great expense, of so much unproductive force, if they were employed in those great industrial enterprises which it will take centuries to complete.

But Loiseau, leaving his seat, went over to the innkeeper and began chatting in a low voice. The big man chuckled, coughed, sputtered; his enormous carcass shook with merriment at the pleasantries of the other; and he ended by buying six casks of claret from Loiseau to be delivered in spring, after the departure of the Prussians.

The moment supper was over every one went to bed, worn out with fatigue.

But Loiseau, who had been making his observations on the sly, sent his wife to bed, and amused himself by placing first his ear, and then his eye, to the bedroom keyhole, in order to discover what he called "the mysteries of the corridor."

At the end of about an hour he heard a rustling, peeped out quickly, and caught sight of Boule de Suif, looking more rotund than ever in a dressing-gown of blue cashmere trimmed with white lace. She held a candle in her hand, and directed her steps to the numbered door at the end of the corridor. But one of the side doors was partly opened, and when, at the end of a few minutes, she returned, Cornudet, in his shirt-sleeves, followed her. They spoke in low tones, then stopped short. Boule de Suif seemed to be stoutly denying him admission to her room. Unfortunately, Loiseau could not at first hear what they said; but toward the end of the conversation they raised their voices, and he caught a few words. Cornudet was loudly insistent.

"How silly you are! What does it matter to you?" he said.

She seemed indignant, and replied:

"No, my good man, there are times when one does not do that sort of thing; besides, in this place it would be shameful."

Apparently he did not understand, and asked the reason. Then she lost her temper and her caution, and, raising her voice still higher, said:

"Why? Can't you understand why? When there are Prussians in the house! Perhaps even in the very next room!"

He was silent. The patriotic shame of this wanton, who would not suffer herself to be caressed in the neighborhood of the enemy, must have roused his dormant dignity, for after bestowing on her a simple kiss he crept softly back to his room. Loiseau, much edified, capered round the bedroom before taking his place beside his slumbering spouse.

Then silence reigned throughout the house. But soon there arose from some remote part—it might easily have been either cellar or attic—a stertorous, monotonous, regular snoring, a dull, prolonged rumbling, varied by tremors like those of a boiler under pressure of steam. Monsieur Follenvie had gone to sleep.

As they had decided on starting at eight o'clock the next morning, every one was in the kitchen at that hour; but the coach, its roof covered with snow, stood by itself in the middle of the yard, without either horses or driver. They sought the latter in the stables, coach-houses and barns —but in vain. So the men of the party resolved to scour the country for him, and sallied forth. They found themselves in the square, with the church at the farther side, and to right and left low-roofed houses where there were some Prussian soldiers. The first soldier they saw was peeling potatoes. The second, farther on, was washing out a barber's shop. Another, bearded to the eyes, was fondling a crying infant, and dandling it on his knees to quiet it; and the stout peasant women, whose menfolk were for the most part at the war, were, by means of signs, telling their obedient conquerors what work they were to do: chop wood, prepare soup, grind coffee; one of them even was doing the washing for his hostess, an infirm old grandmother.

The count, astonished at what he saw, questioned the beadle who was coming out of the presbytery. The old man answered:

"Oh, those men are not at all a bad sort; they are not Prussians, I am told; they come from somewhere farther off, I don't exactly know where. And they have all left wives and children behind them; they are not fond of war either, you may be sure! I am sure they are mourning for the men where they come from, just as we do here; and the war causes them just as much unhappiness as it does us. As a matter of fact, things are not so very bad here just now, because the soldiers do no harm, and work just as if they were in their own homes. You see, sir, poor folk always help one another; it is the great ones of this world who make war."

Cornudet indignant at the friendly understanding established between conquerors and conquered, withdrew, preferring to shut himself up in the inn.

"They are repeopling the country," jested Loiseau.

"They are undoing the harm they have done," said Monsieur Carre-Lamadon gravely.

But they could not find the coach driver. At last he was discovered in the village cafe, fraternizing cordially with the officer's orderly.

"Were you not told to harness the horses at eight o'clock?" demanded the count.

"Oh, yes; but I've had different orders since."

"What orders?"

"Not to harness at all."

"Who gave you such orders?"

"Why, the Prussian officer."

"But why?"

"I don't know. Go and ask him. I am forbidden to harness the horses, so I don't harness them—that's all."

"Did he tell you so himself?"

"No, sir; the innkeeper gave me the order from him."

"When?"

"Last evening, just as I was going to bed."

The three men returned in a very uneasy frame of mind.

They asked for Monsieur Follenvie, but the servant replied that on account of his asthma he never got up before ten o'clock. They were strictly forbidden to rouse him earlier, except in case of fire.

They wished to see the officer, but that also was impossible, although he lodged in the inn. Monsieur Follenvie alone was authorized to interview him on civil matters. So they waited. The women returned to their rooms, and occupied themselves with trivial matters.

Cornudet settled down beside the tall kitchen fireplace, before a blazing fire. He had a small table and a jug of beer placed beside him, and he smoked his pipe—a pipe which enjoyed among democrats a consideration almost equal to his own, as though it had served its country in serving Cornudet. It was a fine meerschaum, admirably colored to a black the shade of its owner's teeth, but sweet-smelling, gracefully curved, at home in its master's hand, and completing his physiognomy. And Cornudet sat motionless, his eyes fixed now on the dancing flames, now on the froth which crowned his beer; and after each draught he passed his long, thin fingers with an air of satisfaction through his long, greasy hair, as he sucked the foam from his mustache.

Loiseau, under pretence of stretching his legs, went out to see if he could sell wine to the country dealers. The count and the manufacturer began to talk politics. They forecast the future of France. One believed in the Orleans dynasty, the other in an unknown savior—a hero who should rise up in the last extremity: a Du Guesclin, perhaps a Joan of Arc? or another Napoleon the First? Ah! if only the Prince Imperial were not so young! Cornudet, listening to them, smiled like a man who holds the keys of destiny in his hands. His pipe perfumed the whole kitchen.

As the clock struck ten, Monsieur Follenvie appeared. He was immediately surrounded and questioned, but could only repeat, three or four times in succession, and without variation, the words:

"The officer said to me, just like this: 'Monsieur Follenvie, you will forbid them to harness up the coach for those travellers tomorrow. They are not to start without an order from me. You hear? That is sufficient.'"

Then they asked to see the officer. The count sent him his card, on which Monsieur Carre-Lamadon also inscribed his name and titles. The Prussian sent word that the two men would be admitted to see him after his luncheon—that is to say, about one o'clock.

The ladies reappeared, and they all ate a little, in spite of their anxiety. Boule de Suif appeared ill and very much worried.

They were finishing their coffee when the orderly came to fetch the gentlemen.

Loiseau joined the other two; but when they tried to get Cornudet to accompany them, by way of adding greater solemnity to the occasion, he declared proudly that he would never have anything to do with the Germans, and, resuming his seat in the chimney corner, he called for another jug of beer.

The three men went upstairs, and were ushered into the best room in the inn, where the officer received them lolling at his ease in an armchair, his feet on the mantelpiece, smoking a long porcelain pipe, and enveloped in a gorgeous dressing-gown, doubtless stolen from the deserted dwelling of some citizen destitute of taste in dress. He neither rose, greeted them, nor even glanced in their direction. He afforded a fine example of that insolence of bearing which seems natural to the victorious soldier.

After the lapse of a few moments he said in his halting French:

"What do you want?"

"We wish to start on our journey," said the count.

"No."

"May I ask the reason of your refusal?"

"Because I don't choose."

"I would respectfully call your attention, monsieur, to the fact that your general in command gave us a permit to proceed to Dieppe; and I do not think we have done anything to deserve this harshness at your hands."

"I don't choose—that's all. You may go."

They bowed, and retired.

The afternoon was wretched. They could not understand the caprice of this German, and the strangest ideas came into their heads. They all congregated in the kitchen, and talked the subject to death, imagining all kinds of unlikely things. Perhaps they were to be kept as hostages—but for what reason? or to be extradited as prisoners of war? or possibly they were to be held for ransom? They were panic-stricken at this last supposition. The richest among them were the most alarmed, seeing themselves forced to empty bags of gold into the insolent soldier's hands in order to buy back their lives. They racked their brains for plausible lies whereby they might conceal the fact that they were rich, and pass themselves off as poor—very poor. Loiseau took off his watch chain, and put it in his pocket. The approach of night increased their apprehension. The lamp was lighted, and as it wanted yet two hours to dinner Madame Loiseau proposed a game of trente et un. It would distract their thoughts. The rest agreed, and Cornudet himself joined the party, first putting out his pipe for politeness' sake.

The count shuffled the cards—dealt—and Boule de Suif had thirty-one to start with; soon the interest of the game assuaged the anxiety of the players. But Cornudet noticed that Loiseau and his wife were in league to cheat.

They were about to sit down to dinner when Monsieur Follenvie appeared, and in his grating voice announced:

"The Prussian officer sends to ask Mademoiselle Elisabeth Rousset if she has changed her mind yet."

Boule de Suif stood still, pale as death. Then, suddenly turning crimson with anger, she gasped out:

"Kindly tell that scoundrel, that cur, that carrion of a Prussian, that I will never consent—you understand?—never, never, never!"

The fat innkeeper left the room. Then Boule de Suif was surrounded, questioned, entreated on all sides to reveal the mystery of her visit to the officer. She refused at first; but her wrath soon got the better of her.

"What does he want? He wants to make me his mistress!" she cried.

No one was shocked at the word, so great was the general indignation. Cornudet broke his jug as he banged it down on the table. A loud outcry arose against this base soldier. All were furious. They drew together in common resistance against the foe, as if some part of the sacrifice exacted of Boule de Suif had been demanded of each. The count declared, with supreme disgust, that those people behaved like ancient barbarians. The women, above all, manifested a lively and tender sympathy for Boule de Suif. The nuns, who appeared only at meals, cast down their eyes, and said nothing.

They dined, however, as soon as the first indignant outburst had subsided; but they spoke little and thought much.

The ladies went to bed early; and the men, having lighted their pipes, proposed a game of ecarte, in which Monsieur Follenvie was invited to join, the travellers hoping to question him skillfully as to the best means of vanquishing the officer's obduracy. But he thought of nothing but his cards, would listen to nothing, reply to nothing, and repeated, time after time: "Attend to the game, gentlemen! attend to the game!" So absorbed was his attention that he even forgot to expectorate. The consequence was that his chest gave forth rumbling sounds like those of an organ. His wheezing lungs struck every note of the asthmatic scale, from deep, hollow tones to a shrill, hoarse piping resembling that of a young cock trying to crow.

He refused to go to bed when his wife, overcome with sleep, came to fetch him. So she went off alone, for she was an early bird, always up with the sun; while he was addicted to late hours, ever ready to spend the night with friends. He merely said: "Put my egg-nogg by the fire," and went on with the game. When the other men saw that nothing was to be got out of him they declared it was time to retire, and each sought his bed.

They rose fairly early the next morning, with a vague hope of being allowed to start, a greater desire than ever to do so, and a terror at having to spend another day in this wretched little inn.

Alas! the horses remained in the stable, the driver was invisible. They spent their time, for want of something better to do, in wandering round the coach.

Luncheon was a gloomy affair; and there was a general coolness toward Boule de Suif, for night, which brings counsel, had somewhat modified the judgment of her companions. In the cold light of the morning they almost bore a grudge against the girl for not having secretly sought out the Prussian, that the rest of the party might receive a joyful surprise when they awoke. What more simple?

Besides, who would have been the wiser? She might have saved appearances by telling the officer that she had taken pity on their distress. Such a step would be of so little consequence to her.

But no one as yet confessed to such thoughts.

In the afternoon, seeing that they were all bored to death, the count proposed a walk in the neighborhood of the village. Each one wrapped himself up well, and the little party set out, leaving behind only Cornudet, who preferred to sit over the fire, and the two nuns, who were in the habit of spending their day in the church or at the presbytery.

The cold, which grew more intense each day, almost froze the noses and ears of the pedestrians, their feet began to pain them so that each step was a penance, and when they reached the open country it looked so mournful and depressing in its limitless mantle of white that they all hastily retraced their steps, with bodies benumbed and hearts heavy.

The four women walked in front, and the three men followed a little in their rear.

Loiseau, who saw perfectly well how matters stood, asked suddenly "if that trollop were going to keep them waiting much longer in this Godforsaken spot." The count, always courteous, replied that they could not exact so painful a sacrifice from any woman, and that the first move must come from herself. Monsieur Carre-Lamadon remarked that if the French, as they talked of doing, made a counter attack by way of Dieppe, their encounter with the enemy must inevitably take place at Totes. This reflection made the other two anxious.

"Supposing we escape on foot?" said Loiseau.

The count shrugged his shoulders.

"How can you think of such a thing, in this snow? And with our wives? Besides, we should be pursued at once, overtaken in ten minutes, and brought back as prisoners at the mercy of the soldiery."

This was true enough; they were silent.

The ladies talked of dress, but a certain constraint seemed to prevail among them.

Suddenly, at the end of the street, the officer appeared. His tall, wasp-like, uniformed figure was outlined against the snow which bounded the horizon, and he walked, knees apart, with that motion peculiar to soldiers, who are always anxious not to soil their carefully polished boots.

He bowed as he passed the ladies, then glanced scornfully at the men, who had sufficient dignity not to raise their hats, though Loiseau made a movement to do so.

Boule de Suif flushed crimson to the ears, and the three married women felt unutterably humiliated at being met thus by the soldier in company with the girl whom he had treated with such scant ceremony.

Then they began to talk about him, his figure, and his face. Madame Carre-Lamadon, who had known many officers and judged them as a connoisseur, thought him not at all bad-looking; she even regretted that he was not a Frenchman, because in that case he would have made a very handsome hussar, with whom all the women would assuredly have fallen in love.

When they were once more within doors they did not know what to do with themselves. Sharp words even were exchanged apropos of the merest trifles. The silent dinner was quickly over, and each one went to bed early in the hope of sleeping, and thus killing time.

They came down next morning with tired faces and irritable tempers; the women scarcely spoke to Boule de Suif.

A church bell summoned the faithful to a baptism. Boule de Suif had a child being brought up by peasants at Yvetot. She did not see him once a year, and never thought of him; but the idea of the child who was about to be baptized induced a sudden wave of tenderness for her own, and she insisted on being present at the ceremony.

As soon as she had gone out, the rest of the company looked at one another and then drew their chairs together; for they realized that they must decide on some course of action. Loiseau had an inspiration: he proposed that they should ask the officer to detain Boule de Suif only, and to let the rest depart on their way.

Monsieur Follenvie was intrusted with this commission, but he returned to them almost immediately. The German, who knew human nature, had shown him the door. He intended to keep all the travellers until his condition had been complied with.

Whereupon Madame Loiseau's vulgar temperament broke bounds.

"We're not going to die of old age here!" she cried. "Since it's that vixen's trade to behave so with men I don't see that she has any right to refuse one more than another. I may as well tell you she took any lovers she could get at Rouen—even coachmen! Yes, indeed, madame—the coachman at the prefecture! I know it for a fact, for he buys his wine of us. And now that it is a question of getting us out of a difficulty she puts on virtuous airs, the drab! For my part, I think this officer has behaved very well. Why, there were three others of us, any one of whom he would undoubtedly have preferred. But no, he contents himself with the girl who is common property. He respects married women. Just think. He is master here. He had only to say: 'I wish it!' and he might have taken us by force, with the help of his soldiers."

The two other women shuddered; the eyes of pretty Madame Carre-Lamadon glistened, and she grew pale, as if the officer were indeed in the act of laying violent hands on her.

The men, who had been discussing the subject among themselves, drew near. Loiseau, in a state of furious resentment, was for delivering up "that miserable woman," bound hand and foot, into the enemy's power. But the count, descended from three generations of ambassadors, and endowed, moreover, with the lineaments of a diplomat, was in favor of more tactful measures.

"We must persuade her," he said.

Then they laid their plans.

The women drew together; they lowered their voices, and the discussion became general, each giving his or her opinion. But the conversation was not in the least coarse. The ladies, in particular, were adepts at delicate phrases and charming subtleties of expression to describe the most improper things. A stranger would have understood none of their allusions, so guarded was the language they employed. But, seeing that the thin veneer of modesty with which every woman of the world is furnished goes but a very little way below the surface, they began rather to enjoy this unedifying episode, and at bottom were hugely delighted—feeling themselves in their element, furthering the schemes of lawless love with the gusto of a gourmand cook who prepares supper for another.

Their gaiety returned of itself, so amusing at last did the whole business seem to them. The count uttered several rather risky witticisms, but so tactfully were they said that his audience could not help smiling. Loiseau in turn made some considerably broader jokes, but no one took offence; and the thought expressed with such brutal directness by his wife was uppermost in the minds of all: "Since it's the girl's trade, why should she refuse this man more than another?" Dainty Madame Carre-Lamadon seemed to think even that in Boule de Suif's place she would be less inclined to refuse him than another.

The blockade was as carefully arranged as if they were investing a fortress. Each agreed on the role which he or she was to play, the arguments to be used, the maneuvers to be executed. They decided on the plan of campaign, the stratagems they were to employ, and the surprise attacks which were to reduce this human citadel and force it to receive the enemy within its walls.

But Cornudet remained apart from the rest, taking no share in the plot.

So absorbed was the attention of all that Boule de Suif's entrance was almost unnoticed. But the count whispered a gentle "Hush!" which made the others look up. She was there. They suddenly stopped talking, and a vague embarrassment prevented them for a few moments from addressing her. But the countess, more practiced than the others in the wiles of the drawing-room, asked her:

"Was the baptism interesting?"

The girl, still under the stress of emotion, told what she had seen and heard, described the faces, the attitudes of those present, and even the appearance of the church. She concluded with the words:

"It does one good to pray sometimes."

Until lunch time the ladies contented themselves with being pleasant to her, so as to increase her confidence and make her amenable to their advice.

As soon as they took their seats at table the attack began. First they opened a vague conversation on the subject of self-sacrifice.

Ancient examples were quoted: Judith and Holofernes; then, irrationally enough, Lucrece and Sextus; Cleopatra and the hostile generals whom she reduced to abject slavery by a surrender of her charms. Next was recounted an extraordinary story, born of the imagination of these ignorant millionaires, which told how the matrons of Rome seduced Hannibal, his lieutenants, and all his mercenaries at Capua. They held up to admiration all those women who from time to time have arrested the victorious progress of conquerors, made of their bodies a field of battle, a means of ruling, a weapon; who have vanquished by their heroic caresses hideous or detested beings, and sacrificed their chastity to vengeance and devotion.

All was said with due restraint and regard for propriety, the effect heightened now and then by an outburst of forced enthusiasm calculated to excite emulation.

A listener would have thought at last that the one role of woman on earth was a perpetual sacrifice of her person, a continual abandonment of herself to the caprices of a hostile soldiery.

The two nuns seemed to hear nothing, and to be lost in thought. Boule de Suif also was silent.

During the whole afternoon she was left to her reflections. But instead of calling her "madame" as they had done hitherto, her companions addressed her simply as "mademoiselle," without exactly knowing why, but as if desirous of making her descend a step in the esteem she had won, and forcing her to realize her degraded position.

Just as soup was served, Monsieur Follenvie reappeared, repeating his phrase of the evening before:

"The Prussian officer sends to ask if Mademoiselle Elisabeth Rousset has changed her mind."

Boule de Suif answered briefly:

"No, monsieur."

But at dinner the coalition weakened. Loiseau made three unfortunate remarks. Each was cudgeling his brains for further examples of self-sacrifice, and could find none, when the countess, possibly without ulterior motive, and moved simply by a vague desire to do homage to religion, began to question the elder of the two nuns on the most striking facts in the lives of the saints. Now, it fell out that many of these had committed acts which would be crimes in our eyes, but the Church readily pardons such deeds when they are accomplished for the glory of God or the good of mankind. This was a powerful argument, and the countess made the most of it. Then, whether by reason of a tacit understanding, a thinly veiled act of complaisance such as those who wear the ecclesiastical habit excel in, or whether merely as the result of sheer stupidity—a stupidity admirably adapted to further their designs—the old nun rendered formidable aid to the conspirator. They had thought her timid; she proved herself bold, talkative, bigoted. She was not troubled by the ins and outs of casuistry; her doctrines were as iron bars; her faith knew no doubt; her conscience no scruples. She looked on Abraham's sacrifice as natural enough, for she herself would not have hesitated to kill both father and mother if she had received a divine order to that effect; and nothing, in her opinion, could displease our Lord, provided the motive were praiseworthy. The countess, putting to good use the consecrated authority of her unexpected ally, led her on to make a lengthy and edifying paraphrase of that axiom enunciated by a certain school of moralists: "The end justifies the means."

"Then, sister," she asked, "you think God accepts all methods, and pardons the act when the motive is pure?"

"Undoubtedly, madame. An action reprehensible in itself often derives merit from the thought which inspires it."

And in this wise they talked on, fathoming the wishes of God, predicting His judgments, describing Him as interested in matters which assuredly concern Him but little.

All was said with the utmost care and discretion, but every word uttered by the holy woman in her nun's garb weakened the indignant resistance of the courtesan. Then the conversation drifted somewhat, and the nun began to talk of the convents of her order, of her Superior, of herself, and of her fragile little neighbor, Sister St. Nicephore. They had been sent for from Havre to nurse the hundreds of soldiers who were in hospitals, stricken with smallpox. She described these wretched invalids and their malady. And, while they themselves were detained on their way by the caprices of the Prussian officer, scores of Frenchmen might be dying, whom they would otherwise have saved! For the nursing of soldiers was the old nun's specialty; she had been in the Crimea, in Italy, in Austria; and as she told the story of her campaigns she revealed herself as one of those holy sisters of the fife and drum who seem designed by nature to follow camps, to snatch the wounded from amid the strife of battle, and to quell with a word, more effectually than any general, the rough and insubordinate troopers—a masterful woman, her seamed and pitted face itself an image of the devastations of war.

No one spoke when she had finished for fear of spoiling the excellent effect of her words.

As soon as the meal was over the travellers retired to their rooms, whence they emerged the following day at a late hour of the morning.

Luncheon passed off quietly. The seed sown the preceding evening was being given time to germinate and bring forth fruit.

In the afternoon the countess proposed a walk; then the count, as had been arranged beforehand, took Boule de Suif's arm, and walked with her at some distance behind the rest.

He began talking to her in that familiar, paternal, slightly contemptuous tone which men of his class adopt in speaking to women like her, calling her "my dear child," and talking down to her from the height of his exalted social position and stainless reputation. He came straight to the point.

"So you prefer to leave us here, exposed like yourself to all the violence which would follow on a repulse of the Prussian troops, rather than consent to surrender yourself, as you have done so many times in your life?"

The girl did not reply.

He tried kindness, argument, sentiment. He still bore himself as count, even while adopting, when desirable, an attitude of gallantry, and making pretty—nay, even tender—speeches. He exalted the service she would render them, spoke of their gratitude; then, suddenly, using the familiar "thou":

"And you know, my dear, he could boast then of having made a conquest of a pretty girl such as he won't often find in his own country."

Boule de Suif did not answer, and joined the rest of the party.

As soon as they returned she went to her room, and was seen no more. The general anxiety was at its height. What would she do? If she still resisted, how awkward for them all!

The dinner hour struck; they waited for her in vain. At last Monsieur Follenvie entered, announcing that Mademoiselle Rousset was not well, and that they might sit down to table. They all pricked up their ears. The count drew near the innkeeper, and whispered:

"Is it all right?"

"Yes."

Out of regard for propriety he said nothing to his companions, but merely nodded slightly toward them. A great sigh of relief went up from all breasts; every face was lighted up with joy.

"By Gad!" shouted Loiseau, "I'll stand champagne all round if there's any to be found in this place." And great was Madame Loiseau's dismay when the proprietor came back with four bottles in his hands. They had all suddenly become talkative and merry; a lively joy filled all hearts. The count seemed to perceive for the first time that Madame Carre-Lamadon was charming; the manufacturer paid compliments to the countess. The conversation was animated, sprightly, witty, and, although many of the jokes were in the worst possible taste, all the company were amused by them, and none offended—indignation being dependent, like other emotions, on surroundings. And the mental atmosphere had gradually become filled with gross imaginings and unclean thoughts.

At dessert even the women indulged in discreetly worded allusions. Their glances were full of meaning; they had drunk much. The count, who even in his moments of relaxation preserved a dignified demeanor, hit on a much-appreciated comparison of the condition of things with the termination of a winter spent in the icy solitude of the North Pole and the joy of shipwrecked mariners who at last perceive a southward track opening out before their eyes.

Loiseau, fairly in his element, rose to his feet, holding aloft a glass of champagne.

"I drink to our deliverance!" he shouted.

All stood up, and greeted the toast with acclamation. Even the two good sisters yielded to the solicitations of the ladies, and consented to moisten their lips with the foaming wine, which they had never before tasted. They declared it was like effervescent lemonade, but with a pleasanter flavor.

"It is a pity," said Loiseau, "that we have no piano; we might have had a quadrille."

Cornudet had not spoken a word or made a movement; he seemed plunged in serious thought, and now and then tugged furiously at his great beard, as if trying to add still further to its length. At last, toward midnight, when they were about to separate, Loiseau, whose gait was far from steady, suddenly slapped him on the back, saying thickly:

"You're not jolly to-night; why are you so silent, old man?"

Cornudet threw back his head, cast one swift and scornful glance over the assemblage, and answered:

"I tell you all, you have done an infamous thing!"

He rose, reached the door, and repeating: "Infamous!" disappeared.

A chill fell on all. Loiseau himself looked foolish and disconcerted for a moment, but soon recovered his aplomb, and, writhing with laughter, exclaimed:

"Really, you are all too green for anything!"

Pressed for an explanation, he related the "mysteries of the corridor," whereat his listeners were hugely amused. The ladies could hardly contain their delight. The count and Monsieur Carre-Lamadon laughed till they cried. They could scarcely believe their ears.

"What! you are sure? He wanted——"

"I tell you I saw it with my own eyes."

"And she refused?"

"Because the Prussian was in the next room!"

"Surely you are mistaken?"

"I swear I'm telling you the truth."

The count was choking with laughter. The manufacturer held his sides. Loiseau continued:

"So you may well imagine he doesn't think this evening's business at all amusing."

And all three began to laugh again, choking, coughing, almost ill with merriment.

Then they separated. But Madame Loiseau, who was nothing if not spiteful, remarked to her husband as they were on the way to bed that "that stuck-up little minx of a Carre-Lamadon had laughed on the wrong side of her mouth all the evening."

"You know," she said, "when women run after uniforms it's all the same to them whether the men who wear them are French or Prussian. It's perfectly sickening!"

The next morning the snow showed dazzling white tinder a clear winter sun. The coach, ready at last, waited before the door; while a flock of white pigeons, with pink eyes spotted in the centres with black, puffed out their white feathers and walked sedately between the legs of the six horses, picking at the steaming manure.

The driver, wrapped in his sheepskin coat, was smoking a pipe on the box, and all the passengers, radiant with delight at their approaching departure, were putting up provisions for the remainder of the journey.

They were waiting only for Boule de Suif. At last she appeared.

She seemed rather shamefaced and embarrassed, and advanced with timid step toward her companions, who with one accord turned aside as if they had not seen her. The count, with much dignity, took his wife by the arm, and removed her from the unclean contact.

The girl stood still, stupefied with astonishment; then, plucking up courage, accosted the manufacturer's wife with a humble "Good-morning, madame," to which the other replied merely with a slight and insolent nod, accompanied by a look of outraged virtue. Every one suddenly appeared extremely busy, and kept as far from Boule de Suif as if her skirts had been infected with some deadly disease. Then they hurried to the coach, followed by the despised courtesan, who, arriving last of all, silently took the place she had occupied during the first part of the journey.

The rest seemed neither to see nor to know her—all save Madame Loiseau, who, glancing contemptuously in her direction, remarked, half aloud, to her husband:

"What a mercy I am not sitting beside that creature!"

The lumbering vehicle started on its way, and the journey began afresh.

At first no one spoke. Boule de Suif dared not even raise her eyes. She felt at once indignant with her neighbors, and humiliated at having yielded to the Prussian into whose arms they had so hypocritically cast her.

But the countess, turning toward Madame Carre-Lamadon, soon broke the painful silence:

"I think you know Madame d'Etrelles?"

"Yes; she is a friend of mine."

"Such a charming woman!"

"Delightful! Exceptionally talented, and an artist to the finger tips. She sings marvellously and draws to perfection."

The manufacturer was chatting with the count, and amid the clatter of the window-panes a word of their conversation was now and then distinguishable: "Shares—maturity—premium—time-limit."

Loiseau, who had abstracted from the inn the timeworn pack of cards, thick with the grease of five years' contact with half-wiped-off tables, started a game of bezique with his wife.

The good sisters, taking up simultaneously the long rosaries hanging from their waists, made the sign of the cross, and began to mutter in unison interminable prayers, their lips moving ever more and more swiftly, as if they sought which should outdistance the other in the race of orisons; from time to time they kissed a medal, and crossed themselves anew, then resumed their rapid and unintelligible murmur.

Cornudet sat still, lost in thought.

Ah the end of three hours Loiseau gathered up the cards, and remarked that he was hungry.

His wife thereupon produced a parcel tied with string, from which she extracted a piece of cold veal. This she cut into neat, thin slices, and both began to eat.

"We may as well do the same," said the countess. The rest agreed, and she unpacked the provisions which had been prepared for herself, the count, and the Carre-Lamadons. In one of those oval dishes, the lids of which are decorated with an earthenware hare, by way of showing that a game pie lies within, was a succulent delicacy consisting of the brown flesh of the game larded with streaks of bacon and flavored with other meats chopped fine. A solid wedge of Gruyere cheese, which had been wrapped in a newspaper, bore the imprint: "Items of News," on its rich, oily surface.

The two good sisters brought to light a hunk of sausage smelling strongly of garlic; and Cornudet, plunging both hands at once into the capacious pockets of his loose overcoat, produced from one four hard-boiled eggs and from the other a crust of bread. He removed the shells, threw them into the straw beneath his feet, and began to devour the eggs, letting morsels of the bright yellow yolk fall in his mighty beard, where they looked like stars.

Boule de Suif, in the haste and confusion of her departure, had not thought of anything, and, stifling with rage, she watched all these people placidly eating. At first, ill-suppressed wrath shook her whole person, and she opened her lips to shriek the truth at them, to overwhelm them with a volley of insults; but she could not utter a word, so choked was she with indignation.

No one looked at her, no one thought of her. She felt herself swallowed up in the scorn of these virtuous creatures, who had first sacrificed, then rejected her as a thing useless and unclean. Then she remembered her big basket full of the good things they had so greedily devoured: the two chickens coated in jelly, the pies, the pears, the four bottles of claret; and her fury broke forth like a cord that is overstrained, and she was on the verge of tears. She made terrible efforts at self-control, drew herself up, swallowed the sobs which choked her; but the tears rose nevertheless, shone at the brink of her eyelids, and soon two heavy drops coursed slowly down her cheeks. Others followed more quickly, like water filtering from a rock, and fell, one after another, on her rounded bosom. She sat upright, with a fixed expression, her face pale and rigid, hoping desperately that no one saw her give way.

But the countess noticed that she was weeping, and with a sign drew her husband's attention to the fact. He shrugged his shoulders, as if to say: "Well, what of it? It's not my fault." Madame Loiseau chuckled triumphantly, and murmured:

"She's weeping for shame."

The two nuns had betaken themselves once more to their prayers, first wrapping the remainder of their sausage in paper:

Then Cornudet, who was digesting his eggs, stretched his long legs under the opposite seat, threw himself back, folded his arms, smiled like a man who had just thought of a good joke, and began to whistle the Marseillaise.

The faces of his neighbors clouded; the popular air evidently did not find favor with them; they grew nervous and irritable, and seemed ready to howl as a dog does at the sound of a barrel-organ. Cornudet saw the discomfort he was creating, and whistled the louder; sometimes he even hummed the words:

Amour sacre de la patrie,
Conduis, soutiens, nos bras vengeurs,
Liberte, liberte cherie,
Combats avec tes defenseurs!

The coach progressed more swiftly, the snow being harder now; and all the way to Dieppe, during the long, dreary hours of the journey, first in the gathering dusk, then in the thick darkness, raising his voice above the rumbling of the vehicle, Cornudet continued with fierce obstinacy his vengeful and monotonous whistling, forcing his weary and exasperated-hearers to follow the song from end to end, to recall every word of every line, as each was repeated over and over again with untiring persistency.

And Boule de Suif still wept, and sometimes a sob she could not restrain was heard in the darkness between two verses of the song.

TWO FRIENDS

Besieged Paris was in the throes of famine. Even the sparrows on the roofs and the rats in the sewers were growing scarce. People were eating anything they could get.

As Monsieur Morissot, watchmaker by profession and idler for the nonce, was strolling along the boulevard one bright January morning, his hands in his trousers pockets and stomach empty, he suddenly came face to face with an acquaintance—Monsieur Sauvage, a fishing chum.

Before the war broke out Morissot had been in the habit, every Sunday morning, of setting forth with a bamboo rod in his hand and a tin box on his back. He took the Argenteuil train, got out at Colombes, and walked thence to the Ile Marante. The moment he arrived at this place of his dreams he began fishing, and fished till nightfall.

Every Sunday he met in this very spot Monsieur Sauvage, a stout, jolly, little man, a draper in the Rue Notre Dame de Lorette, and also an ardent fisherman. They often spent half the day side by side, rod in hand and feet dangling over the water, and a warm friendship had sprung up between the two.

Some days they did not speak; at other times they chatted; but they understood each other perfectly without the aid of words, having similar tastes and feelings.

In the spring, about ten o'clock in the morning, when the early sun caused a light mist to float on the water and gently warmed the backs of the two enthusiastic anglers, Morissot would occasionally remark to his neighbor:

"My, but it's pleasant here."

To which the other would reply:

"I can't imagine anything better!"

And these few words sufficed to make them understand and appreciate each other.

In the autumn, toward the close of day, when the setting sun shed a blood-red glow over the western sky, and the reflection of the crimson clouds tinged the whole river with red, brought a glow to the faces of the two friends, and gilded the trees, whose leaves were already turning at the first chill touch of winter, Monsieur Sauvage would sometimes smile at Morissot, and say:

"What a glorious spectacle!"

And Morissot would answer, without taking his eyes from his float:

"This is much better than the boulevard, isn't it?"

As soon as they recognized each other they shook hands cordially, affected at the thought of meeting under such changed circumstances.

Monsieur Sauvage, with a sigh, murmured:

"These are sad times!"

Morissot shook his head mournfully.

"And such weather! This is the first fine day of the year."

The sky was, in fact, of a bright, cloudless blue.

They walked along, side by side, reflective and sad.

"And to think of the fishing!" said Morissot. "What good times we used to have!"

"When shall we be able to fish again?" asked Monsieur Sauvage.

They entered a small cafe and took an absinthe together, then resumed their walk along the pavement.

Morissot stopped suddenly.

"Shall we have another absinthe?" he said.

"If you like," agreed Monsieur Sauvage.

And they entered another wine shop.

They were quite unsteady when they came out, owing to the effect of the alcohol on their empty stomachs. It was a fine, mild day, and a gentle breeze fanned their faces.

The fresh air completed the effect of the alcohol on Monsieur Sauvage. He stopped suddenly, saying:

"Suppose we go there?"

"Where?"

"Fishing."

"But where?"

"Why, to the old place. The French outposts are close to Colombes. I know Colonel Dumoulin, and we shall easily get leave to pass."

Morissot trembled with desire.

"Very well. I agree."

And they separated, to fetch their rods and lines.

An hour later they were walking side by side on the-highroad. Presently they reached the villa occupied by the colonel. He smiled at their request, and granted it. They resumed their walk, furnished with a password.

Soon they left the outposts behind them, made their way through deserted Colombes, and found themselves on the outskirts of the small vineyards which border the Seine. It was about eleven o'clock.

Before them lay the village of Argenteuil, apparently lifeless. The heights of Orgement and Sannois dominated the landscape. The great plain, extending as far as Nanterre, was empty, quite empty-a waste of dun-colored soil and bare cherry trees.

Monsieur Sauvage, pointing to the heights, murmured:

"The Prussians are up yonder!"

And the sight of the deserted country filled the two friends with vague misgivings.

The Prussians! They had never seen them as yet, but they had felt their presence in the neighborhood of Paris for months past—ruining France, pillaging, massacring, starving them. And a kind of superstitious terror mingled with the hatred they already felt toward this unknown, victorious nation.

"Suppose we were to meet any of them?" said Morissot.

"We'd offer them some fish," replied Monsieur Sauvage, with that Parisian light-heartedness which nothing can wholly quench.

Still, they hesitated to show themselves in the open country, overawed by the utter silence which reigned around them.

At last Monsieur Sauvage said boldly:

"Come, we'll make a start; only let us be careful!"

And they made their way through one of the vineyards, bent double, creeping along beneath the cover afforded by the vines, with eye and ear alert.

A strip of bare ground remained to be crossed before they could gain the river bank. They ran across this, and, as soon as they were at the water's edge, concealed themselves among the dry reeds.

Morissot placed his ear to the ground, to ascertain, if possible, whether footsteps were coming their way. He heard nothing. They seemed to be utterly alone.

Their confidence was restored, and they began to fish.

Before them the deserted Ile Marante hid them from the farther shore. The little restaurant was closed, and looked as if it had been deserted for years.

Monsieur Sauvage caught the first gudgeon, Monsieur Morissot the second, and almost every moment one or other raised his line with a little, glittering, silvery fish wriggling at the end; they were having excellent sport.

They slipped their catch gently into a close-meshed bag lying at their feet; they were filled with joy—the joy of once more indulging in a pastime of which they had long been deprived.

The sun poured its rays on their backs; they no longer heard anything or thought of anything. They ignored the rest of the world; they were fishing.

But suddenly a rumbling sound, which seemed to come from the bowels of the earth, shook the ground beneath them: the cannon were resuming their thunder.

Morissot turned his head and could see toward the left, beyond the banks of the river, the formidable outline of Mont-Valerien, from whose summit arose a white puff of smoke.

The next instant a second puff followed the first, and in a few moments a fresh detonation made the earth tremble.

Others followed, and minute by minute the mountain gave forth its deadly breath and a white puff of smoke, which rose slowly into the peaceful heaven and floated above the summit of the cliff.

Monsieur Sauvage shrugged his shoulders.

"They are at it again!" he said.

Morissot, who was anxiously watching his float bobbing up and down, was suddenly seized with the angry impatience of a peaceful man toward the madmen who were firing thus, and remarked indignantly:

"What fools they are to kill one another like that!"

"They're worse than animals," replied Monsieur Sauvage.

And Morissot, who had just caught a bleak, declared:

"And to think that it will be just the same so long as there are governments!"

"The Republic would not have declared war," interposed Monsieur Sauvage.

Morissot interrupted him:

"Under a king we have foreign wars; under a republic we have civil war."

And the two began placidly discussing political problems with the sound common sense of peaceful, matter-of-fact citizens—agreeing on one point: that they would never be free. And Mont-Valerien thundered ceaselessly, demolishing the houses of the French with its cannon balls, grinding lives of men to powder, destroying many a dream, many a cherished hope, many a prospective happiness; ruthlessly causing endless woe and suffering in the hearts of wives, of daughters, of mothers, in other lands.

"Such is life!" declared Monsieur Sauvage.

"Say, rather, such is death!" replied Morissot, laughing.

But they suddenly trembled with alarm at the sound of footsteps behind them, and, turning round, they perceived close at hand four tall, bearded men, dressed after the manner of livery servants and wearing flat caps on their heads. They were covering the two anglers with their rifles.

The rods slipped from their owners' grasp and floated away down the river.

In the space of a few seconds they were seized, bound, thrown into a boat, and taken across to the Ile Marante.

And behind the house they had thought deserted were about a score of German soldiers.

A shaggy-looking giant, who was bestriding a chair and smoking a long clay pipe, addressed them in excellent French with the words:

"Well, gentlemen, have you had good luck with your fishing?"

Then a soldier deposited at the officer's feet the bag full of fish, which he had taken care to bring away. The Prussian smiled.

"Not bad, I see. But we have something else to talk about. Listen to me, and don't be alarmed:

"You must know that, in my eyes, you are two spies sent to reconnoitre me and my movements. Naturally, I capture you and I shoot you. You pretended to be fishing, the better to disguise your real errand. You have fallen into my hands, and must take the consequences. Such is war.

"But as you came here through the outposts you must have a password for your return. Tell me that password and I will let you go."

The two friends, pale as death, stood silently side by side, a slight fluttering of the hands alone betraying their emotion.

"No one will ever know," continued the officer. "You will return peacefully to your homes, and the secret will disappear with you. If you refuse, it means death-instant death. Choose!"

They stood motionless, and did not open their lips.

The Prussian, perfectly calm, went on, with hand outstretched toward the river:

"Just think that in five minutes you will be at the bottom of that water. In five minutes! You have relations, I presume?"

Mont-Valerien still thundered.

The two fishermen remained silent. The German turned and gave an order in his own language. Then he moved his chair a little way off, that he might not be so near the prisoners, and a dozen men stepped forward, rifle in hand, and took up a position, twenty paces off.

"I give you one minute," said the officer; "not a second longer."

Then he rose quickly, went over to the two Frenchmen, took Morissot by the arm, led him a short distance off, and said in a low voice:

"Quick! the password! Your friend will know nothing. I will pretend to relent."

Morissot answered not a word.

Then the Prussian took Monsieur Sauvage aside in like manner, and made him the same proposal.

Monsieur Sauvage made no reply.

Again they stood side by side.

The officer issued his orders; the soldiers raised their rifles.

Then by chance Morissot's eyes fell on the bag full of gudgeon lying in the grass a few feet from him.

A ray of sunlight made the still quivering fish glisten like silver. And Morissot's heart sank. Despite his efforts at self-control his eyes filled with tears.

"Good-by, Monsieur Sauvage," he faltered.

"Good-by, Monsieur Morissot," replied Sauvage.

They shook hands, trembling from head to foot with a dread beyond their mastery.

The officer cried:

"Fire!"

The twelve shots were as one.

Monsieur Sauvage fell forward instantaneously. Morissot, being the taller, swayed slightly and fell across his friend with face turned skyward and blood oozing from a rent in the breast of his coat.

The German issued fresh orders.

His men dispersed, and presently returned with ropes and large stones, which they attached to the feet of the two friends; then they carried them to the river bank.

Mont-Valerien, its summit now enshrouded in smoke, still continued to thunder.

Two soldiers took Morissot by the head and the feet; two others did the same with Sauvage. The bodies, swung lustily by strong hands, were cast to a distance, and, describing a curve, fell feet foremost into the stream.

The water splashed high, foamed, eddied, then grew calm; tiny waves lapped the shore.

A few streaks of blood flecked the surface of the river.

The officer, calm throughout, remarked, with grim humor:

"It's the fishes' turn now!"

Then he retraced his way to the house.

Suddenly he caught sight of the net full of gudgeons, lying forgotten in the grass. He picked it up, examined it, smiled, and called:

"Wilhelm!"

A white-aproned soldier responded to the summons, and the Prussian, tossing him the catch of the two murdered men, said:

"Have these fish fried for me at once, while they are still alive; they'll make a tasty dish."

Then he resumed his pipe.

THE LANCER'S WIFE

I

It was after Bourbaki's defeat in the east of France. The army, broken up, decimated, and worn out, had been obliged to retreat into Switzerland after that terrible campaign, and it was only its short duration that saved a hundred and fifty thousand men from certain death. Hunger, the terrible cold, forced marches in the snow without boots, over bad mountain roads, had caused us 'francs-tireurs', especially, the greatest suffering, for we were without tents, and almost without food, always in the van when we were marching toward Belfort, and in the rear when returning by the Jura. Of our little band that had numbered twelve hundred men on the first of January, there remained only twenty-two pale, thin, ragged wretches, when we at length succeeded in reaching Swiss territory.

There we were safe, and could rest. Everybody knows what sympathy was shown to the unfortunate French army, and how well it was cared for. We all gained fresh life, and those who had been rich and happy before the war declared that they had never experienced a greater feeling of comfort than they did then. Just think. We actually had something to eat every day, and could sleep every night.

Meanwhile, the war continued in the east of France, which had been excluded from the armistice. Besancon still kept the enemy in check, and the latter had their revenge by ravaging Franche Comte. Sometimes we heard that they had approached quite close to the frontier, and we saw Swiss troops, who were to form a line of observation between us and them, set out on their march.

That pained us in the end, and, as we regained health and strength, the longing to fight took possession of us. It was disgraceful and irritating to know that within two or three leagues of us the Germans were victorious and insolent, to feel that we were protected by our captivity, and to feel that on that account we were powerless against them.

One day our captain took five or six of us aside, and spoke to us about it, long and furiously. He was a fine fellow, that captain. He had been a sublieutenant in the Zouaves, was tall and thin and as hard as steel, and during the whole campaign he had cut out their work for the Germans. He fretted in inactivity, and could not accustom himself to the idea of being a prisoner and of doing nothing.

"Confound it!" he said to us, "does it not pain you to know that there is a number of uhlans within two hours of us? Does it not almost drive you mad to know that those beggarly wretches are walking about as masters in our mountains, when six determined men might kill a whole spitful any day? I cannot endure it any longer, and I must go there."

"But how can you manage it, captain?"

"How? It is not very difficult! Just as if we had not done a thing or two within the last six months, and got out of woods that were guarded by very different men from the Swiss. The day that you wish to cross over into France, I will undertake to get you there."

"That may be; but what shall we do in France without any arms?"

"Without arms? We will get them over yonder, by Jove!"

"You are forgetting the treaty," another soldier said; "we shall run the risk of doing the Swiss an injury, if Manteuffel learns that they have allowed prisoners to return to France."

"Come," said the captain, "those are all bad reasons. I mean to go and kill some Prussians; that is all I care about. If you do not wish to do as I do, well and good; only say so at once. I can quite well go by myself; I do not require anybody's company."

Naturally we all protested, and, as it was quite impossible to make the captain alter his mind, we felt obliged to promise to go with him. We liked him too much to leave him in the lurch, as he never failed us in any extremity; and so the expedition was decided on.

II

The captain had a plan of his own, that he had been cogitating over for some time. A man in that part of the country whom he knew was going to lend him a cart and six suits of peasants' clothes. We could hide under some straw at the bottom of the wagon, which would be loaded with Gruyere cheese, which he was supposed to be going to sell in France. The captain told the sentinels that he was taking two friends with him to protect his goods, in case any one should try to rob him, which did not seem an extraordinary precaution. A Swiss officer seemed to look at the wagon in a knowing manner, but that was in order to impress his soldiers. In a word, neither officers nor men could make it out.

"Get up," the captain said to the horses, as he cracked his whip, while our three men quietly smoked their pipes. I was half suffocated in my box, which only admitted the air through those holes in front, and at the same time I was nearly frozen, for it was terribly cold.

"Get up," the captain said again, and the wagon loaded with Gruyere cheese entered France.

The Prussian lines were very badly guarded, as the enemy trusted to the watchfulness of the Swiss. The sergeant spoke North German, while our captain spoke the bad German of the Four Cantons, and so they could not understand each other. The sergeant, however, pretended to be very intelligent; and, in order to make us believe that he understood us, they allowed us to continue our journey; and, after travelling for seven hours, being continually stopped in the same manner, we arrived at a small village of the Jura in ruins, at nightfall.

What were we going to do? Our only arms were the captain's whip, our uniforms our peasants' blouses, and our food the Gruyere cheese. Our sole wealth consisted in our ammunition, packages of cartridges which we had stowed away inside some of the large cheeses. We had about a thousand of them, just two hundred each, but we needed rifles, and they must be chassepots. Luckily, however, the captain was a bold man of an inventive mind, and this was the plan that he hit upon:

While three of us remained hidden in a cellar in the abandoned village, he continued his journey as far as Besancon with the empty wagon and one man. The town was invested, but one can always make one's way into a town among the hills by crossing the tableland till within about ten miles of the walls, and then following paths and ravines on foot. They left their wagon at Omans, among the Germans, and escaped out of it at night on foot; so as to gain the heights which border the River Doubs; the next day they entered Besancon, where there were plenty of chassepots. There were nearly forty thousand of them left in the arsenal, and General Roland, a brave marine, laughed at the captain's daring project, but let him have six rifles and wished him "good luck." There he had also found his wife, who had been through all the war with us before the campaign in the East, and who had been only prevented by illness from continuing with Bourbaki's army. She had recovered, however, in spite of the cold, which was growing more and more intense, and in spite of the numberless privations that awaited her, she persisted in accompanying her husband. He was obliged to give way to her, and they all three, the captain, his wife, and our comrade, started on their expedition.

Going was nothing in comparison to returning. They were obliged to travel by night, so as to avoid meeting anybody, as the possession of six rifles would have made them liable to suspicion. But, in spite of everything, a week after leaving us, the captain and his two men were back with us again. The campaign was about to begin.

III

The first night of his arrival he began it himself, and, under pretext of examining the surrounding country, he went along the high road.

I must tell you that the little village which served as our fortress was a small collection of poor, badly built houses, which had been deserted long before. It lay on a steep slope, which terminated in a wooded plain. The country people sell the wood; they send it down the slopes, which are called coulees, locally, and which lead down to the plain, and there they stack it into piles, which they sell thrice a year to the wood merchants. The spot where this market is held in indicated by two small houses by the side of the highroad, which serve for public houses. The captain had gone down there by way of one of these coulees.

He had been gone about half an hour, and we were on the lookout at the top of the ravine, when we heard a shot. The captain had ordered us not to stir, and only to come to him when we heard him blow his trumpet. It was made of a goat's horn, and could be heard a league off; but it gave no sound, and, in spite of our cruel anxiety, we were obliged to wait in silence, with our rifles by our side.

It is nothing to go down these coulees; one just lets one's self slide down; but it is more difficult to get up again; one has to scramble up by catching hold of the hanging branches of the trees, and sometimes on all fours, by sheer strength. A whole mortal hour passed, and he did not come; nothing moved in the brushwood. The captain's wife began to grow impatient. What could he be doing? Why did he not call us? Did the shot that we had heard proceed from an enemy, and had he killed or wounded our leader, her husband? They did not know what to think, but I myself fancied either that he was dead or that his enterprise was successful; and I was merely anxious and curious to know what he had done.

Suddenly we heard the sound of his trumpet, and we were much surprised that instead of coming from below, as we had expected, it came from the village behind us. What did that mean? It was a mystery to us, but the same idea struck us all, that he had been killed, and that the Prussians were blowing the trumpet to draw us into an ambush. We therefore returned to the cottage, keeping a careful lookout with our fingers on the trigger, and hiding under the branches; but his wife, in spite of our entreaties, rushed on, leaping like a tigress. She thought that she had to avenge her husband, and had fixed the bayonet to her rifle, and we lost sight of her at the moment that we heard the trumpet again; and, a few moments later, we heard her calling out to us:

"Come on! come on! He is alive! It is he!"

We hastened on, and saw the captain smoking his pipe at the entrance of the village, but strangely enough, he was on horseback.

"Ah! ah!" he said to us, "you see that there is something to be done here. Here I am on horseback already; I knocked over an uhlan yonder, and took his horse; I suppose they were guarding the wood, but it was by drinking and swilling in clover. One of them, the sentry at the door, had not time to see me before I gave him a sugarplum in his stomach, and then, before the others could come out, I jumped on the horse and was off like a shot. Eight or ten of them followed me, I think; but I took the crossroads through the woods. I have got scratched and torn a bit, but here I am, and now, my good fellows, attention, and take care! Those brigands will not rest until they have caught us, and we must receive them with rifle bullets. Come along; let us take up our posts!"

We set out. One of us took up his position a good way from the village on the crossroads; I was posted at the entrance of the main street, where the road from the level country enters the village, while the two others, the captain and his wife, were in the middle of the village, near the church, whose tower served for an observatory and citadel.

We had not been in our places long before we heard a shot, followed by another, and then two, then three. The first was evidently a chassepot —one recognized it by the sharp report, which sounds like the crack of a whip—while the other three came from the lancers' carbines.

The captain was furious. He had given orders to the outpost to let the enemy pass and merely to follow them at a distance if they marched toward the village, and to join me when they had gone well between the houses. Then they were to appear suddenly, take the patrol between two fires, and not allow a single man to escape; for, posted as we were, the six of us could have hemmed in ten Prussians, if needful.

"That confounded Piedelot has roused them," the captain said, "and they will not venture to come on blindfolded any longer. And then I am quite sure that he has managed to get a shot into himself somewhere or other, for we hear nothing of him. It serves him right; why did he not obey orders?" And then, after a moment, he grumbled in his beard: "After all I am sorry for the poor fellow; he is so brave, and shoots so well!"

The captain was right in his conjectures. We waited until evening, without seeing the uhlans; they had retreated after the first attack; but unfortunately we had not seen Piedelot, either. Was he dead or a prisoner? When night came, the captain proposed that we should go out and look for him, and so the three of us started. At the crossroads we found a broken rifle and some blood, while the ground was trampled down; but we did not find either a wounded man or a dead body, although we searched every thicket, and at midnight we returned without having discovered anything of our unfortunate comrade.

"It is very strange," the captain growled. "They must have killed him and thrown him into the bushes somewhere; they cannot possibly have taken him prisoner, as he would have called out for help. I cannot understand it at all." Just as he said that, bright flames shot up in the direction of the inn on the high road, which illuminated the sky.

"Scoundrels! cowards!" he shouted. "I will bet that they have set fire to the two houses on the marketplace, in order to have their revenge, and then they will scuttle off without saying a word. They will be satisfied with having killed a man and set fire to two houses. All right. It shall not pass over like that. We must go for them; they will not like to leave their illuminations in order to fight."

"It would be a great stroke of luck if we could set Piedelot free at the same time," some one said.

The five of us set off, full of rage and hope. In twenty minutes we had got to the bottom of the coulee, and had not yet seen any one when we were within a hundred yards of the inn. The fire was behind the house, and all we saw of it was the reflection above the roof. However, we were walking rather slowly, as we were afraid of an ambush, when suddenly we heard Piedelot's well-known voice. It had a strange sound, however; for it was at the same time—dull and vibrating, stifled and clear, as if he were calling out as loud as he could with a bit of rag stuffed into his mouth. He seemed to be hoarse and gasping, and the unlucky fellow kept exclaiming: "Help! Help!"

We sent all thoughts of prudence to the devil, and in two bounds we were at the back of the inn, where a terrible sight met our eyes.

IV

Piedelot was being burned alive. He was writhing in the midst of a heap of fagots, tied to a stake, and the flames were licking him with their burning tongues. When he saw us, his tongue seemed to stick in his throat; he drooped his head, and seemed as if he were going to die. It was only the affair of a moment to upset the burning pile, to scatter the embers, and to cut the ropes that fastened him.

Poor fellow! In what a terrible state we found him. The evening before he had had his left arm broken, and it seemed as if he had been badly beaten since then, for his whole body was covered with wounds, bruises and blood. The flames had also begun their work on him, and he had two large burns, one on his loins and the other on his right thigh, and his beard and hair were scorched. Poor Piedelot!

No one knows the terrible rage we felt at this sight! We would have rushed headlong at a hundred thousand Prussians; our thirst for vengeance was intense. But the cowards had run away, leaving their crime behind them. Where could we find them now? Meanwhile, however, the captain's wife was looking after Piedelot, and dressing his wounds as best she could, while the captain himself shook hands with him excitedly, and in a few minutes he came to himself.

"Good-morning, captain; good-morning, all of you," he said. "Ah! the scoundrels, the wretches! Why, twenty of them came to surprise us."

"Twenty, do you say?"

"Yes; there was a whole band of them, and that is why I disobeyed orders, captain, and fired on them, for they would have killed you all, and I preferred to stop them. That frightened them, and they did not venture to go farther than the crossroads. They were such cowards. Four of them shot at me at twenty yards, as if I had been a target, and then they slashed me with their swords. My arm was broken, so that I could only use my bayonet with one hand."

"But why did you not call for help?"

"I took good care not to do that, for you would all have come; and you would neither have been able to defend me nor yourselves, being only five against twenty."

"You know that we should not have allowed you to have been taken, poor old fellow."

"I preferred to die by myself, don't you see! I did not want to bring you here, for it would have been a mere ambush."

"Well, we will not talk about it any more. Do you feel rather easier?"

"No, I am suffocating. I know that I cannot live much longer. The brutes! They tied me to a tree, and beat me till I was half dead, and then they shook my broken arm; but I did not make a sound. I would rather have bitten my tongue out than have called out before them. Now I can tell what I am suffering and shed tears; it does one good. Thank you, my kind friends."

"Poor Piedelot! But we will avenge you, you may be sure!"

"Yes, yes; I want you to do that. There is, in particular, a woman among them who passes as the wife of the lancer whom the captain killed yesterday. She is dressed like a lancer, and she tortured me the most yesterday, and suggested burning me; and it was she who set fire to the wood. Oh! the wretch, the brute! Ah! how I am suffering! My loins, my arms!" and he fell back gasping and exhausted, writhing in his terrible agony, while the captain's wife wiped the perspiration from his forehead, and we all shed tears of grief and rage, as if we had been children. I will not describe the end to you; he died half an hour later, previously telling us in what direction the enemy had gone. When he was dead we gave ourselves time to bury him, and then we set out in pursuit of them, with our hearts full of fury and hatred.

"We will throw ourselves on the whole Prussian army, if it be necessary," the captain said; "but we will avenge Piedelot. We must catch those scoundrels. Let us swear to die, rather than not to find them; and if I am killed first, these are my orders: All the prisoners that you take are to be shot immediately, and as for the lancer's wife, she is to be tortured before she is put to death."

"She must not be shot, because she is a woman," the captain's wife said. "If you survive, I am sure that you would not shoot a woman. Torturing her will be quite sufficient; but if you are killed in this pursuit, I want one thing, and that is to fight with her; I will kill her with my own hands, and the others can do what they like with her if she kills me."

"We will outrage her! We will burn her! We will tear her to pieces! Piedelot shall be avenged!

"An eye for an eye, a tooth for a tooth!"

V

The next morning we unexpectedly fell on an outpost of uhlans four leagues away. Surprised by our sudden attack, they were not able to mount their horses, nor even to defend themselves; and in a few moments we had five prisoner, corresponding to our own number. The captain questioned them, and from their answers we felt certain that they were the same whom we had encountered the previous day. Then a very curious operation took place. One of us was told off to ascertain their sex, and nothing can describe our joy when we discovered what we were seeking among them, the female executioner who had tortured our friend.

The four others were shot on the spot, with their backs to us and close to the muzzles of our rifles; and then we turned our attention to the woman. What were we going to do with her? I must acknowledge that we were all of us in favor of shooting her. Hatred, and the wish to avenge Piedelot, had extinguished all pity in us, and we had forgotten that we were going to shoot a woman, but a woman reminded us of it, the captain's wife; at her entreaties, therefore, we determined to keep her a prisoner.

The captain's poor wife was to be severely punished for this act of clemency.

The next day we heard that the armistice had been extended to the eastern part of France, and we had to put an end to our little campaign. Two of us, who belonged to the neighborhood, returned home, so there were only four of us, all told: the captain, his wife, and two men. We belonged to Besancon, which was still being besieged in spite of the armistice.

"Let us stop here," said the captain. "I cannot believe that the war is going to end like this. The devil take it! Surely there are men still left in France; and now is the time to prove what they are made of. The spring is coming on, and the armistice is only a trap laid for the Prussians. During the time that it lasts, a new army will be raised, and some fine morning we shall fall upon them again. We shall be ready, and we have a hostage—let us remain here."

We fixed our quarters there. It was terribly cold, and we did not go out much, and somebody had always to keep the female prisoner in sight.

She was sullen, and never said anything, or else spoke of her husband, whom the captain had killed. She looked at him continually with fierce eyes, and we felt that she was tortured by a wild longing for revenge. That seemed to us to be the most suitable punishment for the terrible torments that she had made Piedelot suffer, for impotent vengeance is such intense pain!

Alas! we who knew how to avenge our comrade ought to have thought that this woman would know how to avenge her husband, and have been on our guard. It is true that one of us kept watch every night, and that at first we tied her by a long rope to the great oak bench that was fastened to the wall. But, by and by, as she had never tried to escape, in spite of her hatred for us, we relaxed our extreme prudence, and allowed her to sleep somewhere else except on the bench, and without being tied. What had we to fear? She was at the end of the room, a man was on guard at the door, and between her and the sentinel the captain's wife and two other men used to lie. She was alone and unarmed against four, so there could be no danger.

One night when we were asleep, and the captain was on guard, the lancer's wife was lying more quietly in her corner than usual, and she had even smiled for the first time since she had been our prisoner during the evening. Suddenly, however, in the middle of the night, we were all awakened by a terrible cry. We got up, groping about, and at once stumbled over a furious couple who were rolling about and fighting on the ground. It was the captain and the lancer's wife. We threw ourselves on them, and separated them in a moment. She was shouting and laughing, and he seemed to have the death rattle. All this took place in the dark. Two of us held her, and when a light was struck a terrible sight met our eyes. The captain was lying on the floor in a pool of blood, with an enormous gash in his throat, and his sword bayonet, that had been taken from his rifle, was sticking in the red, gaping wound. A few minutes afterward he died, without having been able to utter a word.

His wife did not shed a tear. Her eyes were dry, her throat was contracted, and she looked at the lancer's wife steadfastly, and with a calm ferocity that inspired fear.

"This woman belongs to me," she said to us suddenly. "You swore to me not a week ago to let me kill her as I chose, if she killed my husband; and you must keep your oath. You must fasten her securely to the fireplace, upright against the back of it, and then you can go where you like, but far from here. I will take my revenge on her myself. Leave the captain's body, and we three, he, she and I, will remain here."

We obeyed, and went away. She promised to write to us to Geneva, as we were returning thither.

VI

Two days later I received the following letter, dated the day after we had left, that had been written at an inn on the high road:

"MY FRIEND: I am writing to you, according to my promise. For the moment I am at the inn, where I have just handed my prisoner over to a Prussian officer.

"I must tell you, my friend, that this poor woman has left two children in Germany. She had followed her husband, whom she adored, as she did not wish him to be exposed to the risks of war by himself, and as her children were with their grandparents. I have learned all this since yesterday, and it has turned my ideas of vengeance into more humane feelings. At the very moment when I felt pleasure in insulting this woman, and in threatening her with the most fearful torments, in recalling Piedelot, who had been burned alive, and in threatening her with a similar death, she looked at me coldly, and said:

"'What have you got to reproach me with, Frenchwoman? You think that you will do right in avenging your husband's death, is not that so?'

"'Yes,' I replied.

"'Very well, then; in killing him, I did what you are going to do in burning me. I avenged my husband, for your husband killed him.'

"'Well,' I replied, 'as you approve of this vengeance, prepare to endure it.'

"'I do not fear it.'

"And in fact she did not seem to have lost courage. Her face was calm, and she looked at me without trembling, while I brought wood and dried leaves together, and feverishly threw on to them the powder from some cartridges, which was to make her funeral pile the more cruel.

"I hesitated in my thoughts of persecution for a moment. But the captain was there, pale and covered with blood, and he seemed to be looking at me with his large, glassy eyes, and I applied myself to my work again after kissing his pale lips. Suddenly, however, on raising my head, I saw that she was crying, and I felt rather surprised.

"'So you are frightened?' I said to her.

"'No, but when I saw you kiss your husband, I thought of mine, of all whom I love.'

"She continued to sob, but stopping suddenly, she said to me in broken words and in a low voice:

"'Have you any children?'

"A shiver rare over me, for I guessed that this poor woman had some. She asked me to look in a pocketbook which was in her bosom, and in it I saw two photographs of quite young children, a boy and a girl, with those kind, gentle, chubby faces that German children have. In it there were also two locks of light hair and a letter in a large, childish hand, and beginning with German words which meant:

"'My dear little mother.

"'I could not restrain my tears, my dear friend, and so I untied her, and without venturing to look at the face of my poor dead husband, who was not to be avenged, I went with her as far as the inn. She is free; I have just left her, and she kissed me with tears. I am going upstairs to my husband; come as soon as possible, my dear friend, to look for our two bodies.'"

I set off with all speed, and when I arrived there was a Prussian patrol at the cottage; and when I asked what it all meant, I was told that there was a captain of francs-tireurs and his wife inside, both dead. I gave their names; they saw that I knew them, and I begged to be allowed to arrange their funeral.

"Somebody has already undertaken it," was the reply. "Go in if you wish to, as you know them. You can settle about their funeral with their friend."

I went in. The captain and his wife were lying side by side on a bed, and were covered by a sheet. I raised it, and saw that the woman had inflicted a similar wound in her throat to that from which her husband had died.

At the side of the bed there sat, watching and weeping, the woman who had been mentioned to me as their best friend. It was the lancer's wife.

THE PRISONERS

There was not a sound in the forest save the indistinct, fluttering sound of the snow falling on the trees. It had been snowing since noon; a little fine snow, that covered the branches as with frozen moss, and spread a silvery covering over the dead leaves in the ditches, and covered the roads with a white, yielding carpet, and made still more intense the boundless silence of this ocean of trees.

Before the door of the forester's dwelling a young woman, her arms bare to the elbow, was chopping wood with a hatchet on a block of stone. She was tall, slender, strong-a true girl of the woods, daughter and wife of a forester.

A voice called from within the house:

"We are alone to-night, Berthine; you must come in. It is getting dark, and there may be Prussians or wolves about."

"I've just finished, mother," replied the young woman, splitting as she spoke an immense log of wood with strong, deft blows, which expanded her chest each time she raised her arms to strike. "Here I am; there's no need to be afraid; it's quite light still."

Then she gathered up her sticks and logs, piled them in the chimney corner, went back to close the great oaken shutters, and finally came in, drawing behind her the heavy bolts of the door.

Her mother, a wrinkled old woman whom age had rendered timid, was spinning by the fireside.

"I am uneasy," she said, "when your father's not here. Two women are not much good."

"Oh," said the younger woman, "I'd cheerfully kill a wolf or a Prussian if it came to that."

And she glanced at a heavy revolver hanging above the hearth.

Her husband had been called upon to serve in the army at the beginning of the Prussian invasion, and the two women had remained alone with the old father, a keeper named Nicolas Pichon, sometimes called Long-legs, who refused obstinately to leave his home and take refuge in the town.

This town was Rethel, an ancient stronghold built on a rock. Its inhabitants were patriotic, and had made up their minds to resist the invaders, to fortify their native place, and, if need be, to stand a siege as in the good old days. Twice already, under Henri IV and under Louis XIV, the people of Rethel had distinguished themselves by their heroic defence of their town. They would do as much now, by gad! or else be slaughtered within their own walls.

They had, therefore, bought cannon and rifles, organized a militia, and formed themselves into battalions and companies, and now spent their time drilling all day long in the square. All-bakers, grocers, butchers, lawyers, carpenters, booksellers, chemists-took their turn at military training at regular hours of the day, under the auspices of Monsieur Lavigne, a former noncommissioned officer in the dragoons, now a draper, having married the daughter and inherited the business of Monsieur Ravaudan, Senior.

He had taken the rank of commanding officer in Rethel, and, seeing that all the young men had gone off to the war, he had enlisted all the others who were in favor of resisting an attack. Fat men now invariably walked the streets at a rapid pace, to reduce their weight and improve their breathing, and weak men carried weights to strengthen their muscles.

And they awaited the Prussians. But the Prussians did not appear. They were not far off, however, for twice already their scouts had penetrated as far as the forest dwelling of Nicolas Pichon, called Long-legs.

The old keeper, who could run like a fox, had come and warned the town. The guns had been got ready, but the enemy had not shown themselves.

Long-legs' dwelling served as an outpost in the Aveline forest. Twice a week the old man went to the town for provisions and brought the citizens news of the outlying district.

On this particular day he had gone to announce the fact that a small detachment of German infantry had halted at his house the day before, about two o'clock in the afternoon, and had left again almost immediately. The noncommissioned officer in charge spoke French.

When the old man set out like this he took with him his dogs—two powerful animals with the jaws of lions-as a safeguard against the wolves, which were beginning to get fierce, and he left directions with the two women to barricade themselves securely within their dwelling as soon as night fell.

The younger feared nothing, but her mother was always apprehensive, and repeated continually:

"We'll come to grief one of these days. You see if we don't!"

This evening she was, if possible, more nervous than ever.

"Do you know what time your father will be back?" she asked.

"Oh, not before eleven, for certain. When he dines with the commandant he's always late."

And Berthine was hanging her pot over the fire to warm the soup when she suddenly stood still, listening attentively to a sound that had reached her through the chimney.

"There are people walking in the wood," she said; "seven or eight men at least."

The terrified old woman stopped her spinning wheel, and gasped:

"Oh, my God! And your father not here!"

She had scarcely finished speaking when a succession of violent blows shook the door.

As the woman made no reply, a loud, guttural voice shouted:

"Open the door!"

After a brief silence the same voice repeated:

"Open the door or I'll break it down!"

Berthine took the heavy revolver from its hook, slipped it into the pocket of her skirt, and, putting her ear to the door, asked:

"Who are you?" demanded the young woman. "What do you want?".

"The detachment that came here the other day," replied the voice.

"My men and I have lost our way in the forest since morning. Open the door or I'll break it down!"

The forester's daughter had no choice; she shot back the heavy bolts, threw open the ponderous shutter, and perceived in the wan light of the snow six men, six Prussian soldiers, the same who had visited the house the day before.

"What are you doing here at this time of night?" she asked dauntlessly.

"I lost my bearings," replied the officer; "lost them completely. Then I recognized this house. I've eaten nothing since morning, nor my men either."

"But I'm quite alone with my mother this evening," said Berthine.

"Never mind," replied the soldier, who seemed a decent sort of fellow. "We won't do you any harm, but you must give us something to eat. We are nearly dead with hunger and fatigue."

Then the girl moved aside.

"Come in;" she said.

Then entered, covered with snow, their helmets sprinkled with a creamy-looking froth, which gave them the appearance of meringues. They seemed utterly worn out.

The young woman pointed to the wooden benches on either side of the large table.

"Sit down," she said, "and I'll make you some soup. You certainly look tired out, and no mistake."

Then she bolted the door afresh.

She put more water in the pot, added butter and potatoes; then, taking down a piece of bacon from a hook in the chimney earner, cut it in two and slipped half of it into the pot.

The six men watched her movements with hungry eyes. They had placed their rifles and helmets in a corner and waited for supper, as well behaved as children on a school bench.

The old mother had resumed her spinning, casting from time to time a furtive and uneasy glance at the soldiers. Nothing was to be heard save the humming of the wheel, the crackling of the fire, and the singing of the water in the pot.

But suddenly a strange noise—a sound like the harsh breathing of some wild animal sniffing under the door-startled the occupants of the room.

The German officer sprang toward the rifles. Berthine stopped him with a gesture, and said, smilingly:

"It's only the wolves. They are like you—prowling hungry through the forest."

The incredulous man wanted to see with his own eyes, and as soon as the door was opened he perceived two large grayish animals disappearing with long, swinging trot into the darkness.

He returned to his seat, muttering:

"I wouldn't have believed it!"

And he waited quietly till supper was ready.

The men devoured their meal voraciously, with mouths stretched to their ears that they might swallow the more. Their round eyes opened at the same time as their jaws, and as the soup coursed down their throats it made a noise like the gurgling of water in a rainpipe.

The two women watched in silence the movements of the big red beards. The potatoes seemed to be engulfed in these moving fleeces.

But, as they were thirsty, the forester's daughter went down to the cellar to draw them some cider. She was gone some time. The cellar was small, with an arched ceiling, and had served, so people said, both as prison and as hiding-place during the Revolution. It was approached by means of a narrow, winding staircase, closed by a trap-door at the farther end of the kitchen.

When Berthine returned she was smiling mysteriously to herself. She gave the Germans her jug of cider.

Then she and her mother supped apart, at the other end of the kitchen.

The soldiers had finished eating, and were all six falling asleep as they sat round the table. Every now and then a forehead fell with a thud on the board, and the man, awakened suddenly, sat upright again.

Berthine said to the officer:

"Go and lie down, all of you, round the fire. There's lots of room for six. I'm going up to my room with my mother."

And the two women went upstairs. They could be heard locking the door and walking about overhead for a time; then they were silent.

The Prussians lay down on the floor, with their feet to the fire and their heads resting on their rolled-up cloaks. Soon all six snored loudly and uninterruptedly in six different keys.

They had been sleeping for some time when a shot rang out so loudly that it seemed directed against the very walls of the house. The soldiers rose hastily. Two-then three-more shots were fired.

The door opened hastily, and Berthine appeared, barefooted and only half dressed, with her candle in her hand and a scared look on her face.

"There are the French," she stammered; "at least two hundred of them. If they find you here they'll burn the house down. For God's sake, hurry down into the cellar, and don't make a sound, whatever you do. If you make any noise we are lost."

"We'll go, we'll go," replied the terrified officer. "Which is the way?"

The young woman hurriedly raised the small, square trap-door, and the six men disappeared one after another down the narrow, winding staircase, feeling their way as they went.

But as soon as the spike of the last helmet was out of sight Berthine lowered the heavy oaken lid—thick as a wall, hard as steel, furnished with the hinges and bolts of a prison cell—shot the two heavy bolts, and began to laugh long and silently, possessed with a mad longing to dance above the heads of her prisoners.

They made no sound, inclosed in the cellar as in a strong-box, obtaining air only from a small, iron-barred vent-hole.

Berthine lighted her fire again, hung the pot over it, and prepared more soup, saying to herself:

"Father will be tired to-night."

Then she sat and waited. The heavy pendulum of the clock swung to and fro with a monotonous tick.

Every now and then the young woman cast an impatient glance at the dial-a glance which seemed to say:

"I wish he'd be quick!"

But soon there was a sound of voices beneath her feet. Low, confused words reached her through the masonry which roofed the cellar. The Prussians were beginning to suspect the trick she had played them, and presently the officer came up the narrow staircase, and knocked at the trap-door.

"Open the door!" he cried.

"What do you want?" she said, rising from her seat and approaching the cellarway.

"Open the door!"

"I won't do any such thing!"

"Open it or I'll break it down!" shouted the man angrily.

She laughed.

"Hammer away, my good man! Hammer away!"

He struck with the butt-end of his gun at the closed oaken door. But it would have resisted a battering-ram.

The forester's daughter heard him go down the stairs again. Then the soldiers came one after another and tried their strength against the trapdoor. But, finding their efforts useless, they all returned to the cellar and began to talk among themselves.

The young woman heard them for a short time, then she rose, opened the door of the house; looked out into the night, and listened.

A sound of distant barking reached her ear. She whistled just as a huntsman would, and almost immediately two great dogs emerged from the darkness, and bounded to her side. She held them tight, and shouted at the top of her voice:

"Hullo, father!"

A far-off voice replied:

"Hullo, Berthine!"

She waited a few seconds, then repeated:

"Hullo, father!"

The voice, nearer now, replied:

"Hullo, Berthine!"

"Don't go in front of the vent-hole!" shouted his daughter. "There are Prussians in the cellar!"

Suddenly the man's tall figure could be seen to the left, standing between two tree trunks.

"Prussians in the cellar?" he asked anxiously. "What are they doing?"

The young woman laughed.

"They are the same as were here yesterday. They lost their way, and I've given them free lodgings in the cellar."

She told the story of how she had alarmed them by firing the revolver, and had shut them up in the cellar.

The man, still serious, asked:

"But what am I to do with them at this time of night?"

"Go and fetch Monsieur Lavigne with his men," she replied. "He'll take them prisoners. He'll be delighted."

Her father smiled.

"So he will-delighted."

"Here's some soup for you," said his daughter. "Eat it quick, and then be off."

The old keeper sat down at the table, and began to eat his soup, having first filled two plates and put them on the floor for the dogs.

The Prussians, hearing voices, were silent.

Long-legs set off a quarter of an hour later, and Berthine, with her head between her hands, waited.

The prisoners began to make themselves heard again. They shouted, called, and beat furiously with the butts of their muskets against the rigid trap-door of the cellar.

Then they fired shots through the vent-hole, hoping, no doubt, to be heard by any German detachment which chanced to be passing that way.

The forester's daughter did not stir, but the noise irritated and unnerved her. Blind anger rose in her heart against the prisoners; she would have been only too glad to kill them all, and so silence them.

Then, as her impatience grew, she watched the clock, counting the minutes as they passed.

Her father had been gone an hour and a half. He must have reached the town by now. She conjured up a vision of him telling the story to Monsieur Lavigne, who grew pale with emotion, and rang for his servant to bring him his arms and uniform. She fancied she could bear the drum as it sounded the call to arms. Frightened faces appeared at the windows. The citizen-soldiers emerged from their houses half dressed, out of breath, buckling on their belts, and hurrying to the commandant's house.

Then the troop of soldiers, with Long-legs at its head, set forth through the night and the snow toward the forest.

She looked at the clock. "They may be here in an hour."

A nervous impatience possessed her. The minutes seemed interminable. Would the time never come?

At last the clock marked the moment she had fixed on for their arrival. And she opened the door to listen for their approach. She perceived a shadowy form creeping toward the house. She was afraid, and cried out. But it was her father.

"They have sent me," he said, "to see if there is any change in the state of affairs."

"No-none."

Then he gave a shrill whistle. Soon a dark mass loomed up under the trees; the advance guard, composed of ten men.

"Don't go in front of the vent-hole!" repeated Long-legs at intervals.

And the first arrivals pointed out the much-dreaded vent-hole to those who came after.

At last the main body of the troop arrived, in all two hundred men, each carrying two hundred cartridges.

Monsieur Lavigne, in a state of intense excitement, posted them in such a fashion as to surround the whole house, save for a large space left vacant in front of the little hole on a level with the ground, through which the cellar derived its supply of air.

Monsieur Lavigne struck the trap-door a blow with his foot, and called:

"I wish to speak to the Prussian officer!"

The German did not reply.

"The Prussian officer!" again shouted the commandant.

Still no response. For the space of twenty minutes Monsieur Lavigne called on this silent officer to surrender with bag and baggage, promising him that all lives should be spared, and that he and his men should be accorded military honors. But he could extort no sign, either of consent or of defiance. The situation became a puzzling one.

The citizen-soldiers kicked their heels in the snow, slapping their arms across their chest, as cabdrivers do, to warm themselves, and gazing at the vent-hole with a growing and childish desire to pass in front of it.

At last one of them took the risk-a man named Potdevin, who was fleet of limb. He ran like a deer across the zone of danger. The experiment succeeded. The prisoners gave no sign of life.

A voice cried:

"There's no one there!"

And another soldier crossed the open space before the dangerous vent-hole. Then this hazardous sport developed into a game. Every minute a man ran swiftly from one side to the other, like a boy playing baseball, kicking up the snow behind him as he ran. They had lighted big fires of dead wood at which to warm themselves, and the figures of the runners were illumined by the flames as they passed rapidly from the camp on the right to that on the left.

Some one shouted:

"It's your turn now, Maloison."

Maloison was a fat baker, whose corpulent person served to point many a joke among his comrades.

He hesitated. They chaffed him. Then, nerving himself to the effort, he set off at a little, waddling gait, which shook his fat paunch and made the whole detachment laugh till they cried.

"Bravo, bravo, Maloison!" they shouted for his encouragement.

He had accomplished about two-thirds of his journey when a long, crimson flame shot forth from the vent-hole. A loud report followed, and the fat baker fell face forward to the ground, uttering a frightful scream. No one went to his assistance. Then he was seen to drag himself, groaning, on all-fours through the snow until he was beyond danger, when he fainted.

He was shot in the upper part of the thigh.

After the first surprise and fright were over they laughed at him again. But Monsieur Lavigne appeared on the threshold of the forester's dwelling. He had formed his plan of attack. He called in a loud voice "I want Planchut, the plumber, and his workmen."

Three men approached.

"Take the eavestroughs from the roof."

In a quarter of an hour they brought the commandant thirty yards of pipes.

Next, with infinite precaution, he had a small round hole drilled in the trap-door; then, making a conduit with the troughs from the pump to this opening, he said, with an air of extreme satisfaction:

"Now we'll give these German gentlemen something to drink."

A shout of frenzied admiration, mingled with uproarious laughter, burst from his followers. And the commandant organized relays of men, who were to relieve one another every five minutes. Then he commanded:

"Pump!!!"

And, the pump handle having been set in motion, a stream of water trickled throughout the length of the piping, and flowed from step to step down the cellar stairs with a gentle, gurgling sound.

They waited.

An hour passed, then two, then three. The commandant, in a state of feverish agitation, walked up and down the kitchen, putting his ear to the ground every now and then to discover, if possible, what the enemy were doing and whether they would soon capitulate.

The enemy was astir now. They could be heard moving the casks about, talking, splashing through the water.

Then, about eight o'clock in the morning, a voice came from the vent-hole "I want to speak to the French officer."

Lavigne replied from the window, taking care not to put his head out too far:

"Do you surrender?"

"I surrender."

"Then put your rifles outside."

A rifle immediately protruded from the hole, and fell into the snow, then another and another, until all were disposed of. And the voice which had spoken before said:

"I have no more. Be quick! I am drowned."

"Stop pumping!" ordered the commandant.

And the pump handle hung motionless.

Then, having filled the kitchen with armed and waiting soldiers, he slowly raised the oaken trapdoor.

Four heads appeared, soaking wet, four fair heads with long, sandy hair, and one after another the six Germans emerged—scared, shivering and dripping from head to foot.

They were seized and bound. Then, as the French feared a surprise, they set off at once in two convoys, one in charge of the prisoners, and the other conducting Maloison on a mattress borne on poles.

They made a triumphal entry into Rethel.

Monsieur Lavigne was decorated as a reward for having captured a Prussian advance guard, and the fat baker received the military medal for wounds received at the hands of the enemy.

TWO LITTLE SOLDIERS

Every Sunday, as soon as they were free, the little soldiers would go for a walk. They turned to the right on leaving the barracks, crossed Courbevoie with rapid strides, as though on a forced march; then, as the houses grew scarcer, they slowed down and followed the dusty road which leads to Bezons.

They were small and thin, lost in their ill-fitting capes, too large and too long, whose sleeves covered their hands; their ample red trousers fell in folds around their ankles. Under the high, stiff shako one could just barely perceive two thin, hollow-cheeked Breton faces, with their calm, naive blue eyes. They never spoke during their journey, going straight before them, the same idea in each one's mind taking the place of conversation. For at the entrance of the little forest of Champioux they had found a spot which reminded them of home, and they did not feel happy anywhere else.

At the crossing of the Colombes and Chatou roads, when they arrived under the trees, they would take off their heavy, oppressive headgear and wipe their foreheads.

They always stopped for a while on the bridge at Bezons, and looked at the Seine. They stood there several minutes, bending over the railing, watching the white sails, which perhaps reminded them of their home, and of the fishing smacks leaving for the open.

As soon as they had crossed the Seine, they would purchase provisions at the delicatessen, the baker's, and the wine merchant's. A piece of bologna, four cents' worth of bread, and a quart of wine, made up the luncheon which they carried away, wrapped up in their handkerchiefs. But as soon as they were out of the village their gait would slacken and they would begin to talk.

Before them was a plain with a few clumps of trees, which led to the woods, a little forest which seemed to remind them of that other forest at Kermarivan. The wheat and oat fields bordered on the narrow path, and Jean Kerderen said each time to Luc Le Ganidec:

"It's just like home, just like Plounivon."

"Yes, it's just like home."

And they went on, side by side, their minds full of dim memories of home. They saw the fields, the hedges, the forests, and beaches.

Each time they stopped near a large stone on the edge of the private estate, because it reminded them of the dolmen of Locneuven.

As soon as they reached the first clump of trees, Luc Le Ganidec would cut off a small stick, and, whittling it slowly, would walk on, thinking of the folks at home.

Jean Kerderen carried the provisions.

From time to time Luc would mention a name, or allude to some boyish prank which would give them food for plenty of thought. And the home country, so dear and so distant, would little by little gain possession of their minds, sending them back through space, to the well-known forms and noises, to the familiar scenery, with the fragrance of its green fields and sea air. They no longer noticed the smells of the city. And in their dreams they saw their friends leaving, perhaps forever, for the dangerous fishing grounds.

They were walking slowly, Luc Le Ganidec and Jean Kerderen, contented and sad, haunted by a sweet sorrow, the slow and penetrating sorrow of a captive animal which remembers the days of its freedom.

And when Luc had finished whittling his stick, they came to a little nook, where every Sunday they took their meal. They found the two bricks, which they had hidden in a hedge, and they made a little fire of dry branches and roasted their sausages on the ends of their knives.

When their last crumb of bread had been eaten and the last drop of wine had been drunk, they stretched themselves out on the grass side by side, without speaking, their half-closed eyes looking away in the distance, their hands clasped as in prayer, their red-trousered legs mingling with the bright colors of the wild flowers.

Towards noon they glanced, from time to time, towards the village of Bezons, for the dairy maid would soon be coming. Every Sunday she would pass in front of them on the way to milk her cow, the only cow in the neighborhood which was sent out to pasture.

Soon they would see the girl, coming through the fields, and it pleased them to watch the sparkling sunbeams reflected from her shining pail. They never spoke of her. They were just glad to see her, without understanding why.

She was a tall, strapping girl, freckled and tanned by the open air—a girl typical of the Parisian suburbs.

Once, on noticing that they were always sitting in the same place, she said to them:

"Do you always come here?"

Luc Le Ganidec, more daring than his friend, stammered:

"Yes, we come here for our rest."

That was all. But the following Sunday, on seeing them, she smiled with the kindly smile of a woman who understood their shyness, and she asked:

"What are you doing here? Are you watching the grass grow?"

Luc, cheered up, smiled: "P'raps."

She continued: "It's not growing fast, is it?"

He answered, still laughing: "Not exactly."

She went on. But when she came back with her pail full of milk, she stopped before them and said:

"Want some? It will remind you of home."

She had, perhaps instinctively, guessed and touched the right spot.

Both were moved. Then not without difficulty, she poured some milk into the bottle in which they had brought their wine. Luc started to drink, carefully watching lest he should take more than his share. Then he passed the bottle to Jean. She stood before them, her hands on her hips, her pail at her feet, enjoying the pleasure that she was giving them. Then she went on, saying: "Well, bye-bye until next Sunday!"

For a long time they watched her tall form as it receded in the distance, blending with the background, and finally disappeared.

The following week as they left the barracks, Jean said to Luc:

"Don't you think we ought to buy her something good?"

They were sorely perplexed by the problem of choosing something to bring to the dairy maid. Luc was in favor of bringing her some chitterlings; but Jean, who had a sweet tooth, thought that candy would be the best thing. He won, and so they went to a grocery to buy two sous' worth, of red and white candies.

This time they ate more quickly than usual, excited by anticipation.

Jean was the first one to notice her. "There she is," he said; and Luc answered: "Yes, there she is."

She smiled when she saw them, and cried:

"Well, how are you to-day?"

They both answered together:

"All right! How's everything with you?"

Then she started to talk of simple things which might interest them; of the weather, of the crops, of her masters.

They didn't dare to offer their candies, which were slowly melting in Jean's pocket. Finally Luc, growing bolder, murmured:

"We have brought you something."

She asked: "Let's see it."

Then Jean, blushing to the tips of his ears, reached in his pocket, and drawing out the little paper bag, handed it to her.

She began to eat the little sweet dainties. The two soldiers sat in front of her, moved and delighted.

At last she went to do her milking, and when she came back she again gave them some milk.

They thought of her all through the week and often spoke of her: The following Sunday she sat beside them for a longer time.

The three of them sat there, side by side, their eyes looking far away in the distance, their hands clasped over their knees, and they told each other little incidents and little details of the villages where they were born, while the cow, waiting to be milked, stretched her heavy head toward the girl and mooed.

Soon the girl consented to eat with them and to take a sip of wine. Often she brought them plums pocket for plums were now ripe. Her presence enlivened the little Breton soldiers, who chattered away like two birds.

One Tuesday something unusual happened to Luc Le Ganidec; he asked for leave and did not return until ten o'clock at night.

Jean, worried and racked his brain to account for his friend's having obtained leave.

The following Friday, Luc borrowed ten sons from one of his friends, and once more asked and obtained leave for several hours.

When he started out with Jean on Sunday he seemed queer, disturbed, changed. Kerderen did not understand; he vaguely suspected something, but he could not guess what it might be.

They went straight to the usual place, and lunched slowly. Neither was hungry.

Soon the girl appeared. They watched her approach as they always did. When she was near, Luc arose and went towards her. She placed her pail on the ground and kissed him. She kissed him passionately, throwing her arms around his neck, without paying attention to Jean, without even noticing that he was there.

Poor Jean was dazed, so dazed that he could not understand. His mind was upset and his heart broken, without his even realizing why.

Then the girl sat down beside Luc, and they started to chat.

Jean was not looking at them. He understood now why his friend had gone out twice during the week. He felt the pain and the sting which treachery and deceit leave in their wake.

Luc and the girl went together to attend to the cow.

Jean followed them with his eyes. He saw them disappear side by side, the red trousers of his friend making a scarlet spot against the white road. It was Luc who sank the stake to which the cow was tethered. The girl stooped down to milk the cow, while he absent-mindedly stroked the animal's glossy neck. Then they left the pail in the grass and disappeared in the woods.

Jean could no longer see anything but the wall of leaves through which they had passed. He was unmanned so that he did not have strength to stand. He stayed there, motionless, bewildered and grieving-simple, passionate grief. He wanted to weep, to run away, to hide somewhere, never to see anyone again.

Then he saw them coming back again. They were walking slowly, hand in hand, as village lovers do. Luc was carrying the pail.

After kissing him again, the girl went on, nodding carelessly to Jean. She did not offer him any milk that day.

The two little soldiers sat side by side, motionless as always, silent and quiet, their calm faces in no way betraying the trouble in their hearts. The sun shone down on them. From time to time they could hear the plaintive lowing of the cow. At the usual time they arose to return.

Luc was whittling a stick. Jean carried the empty bottle. He left it at the wine merchant's in Bezons. Then they stopped on the bridge, as they did every Sunday, and watched the water flowing by.

Jean leaned over the railing, farther and farther, as though he had seen something in the stream which hypnotized him. Luc said to him:

"What's the matter? Do you want a drink?"

He had hardly said the last word when Jean's head carried away the rest of his body, and the little blue and red soldier fell like a shot and disappeared in the water.

Luc, paralyzed with horror, tried vainly to shout for help. In the distance he saw something move; then his friend's head bobbed up out of the water only to disappear again.

Farther down he again noticed a hand, just one hand, which appeared and again went out of sight. That was all.

The boatmen who had rushed to the scene found the body that day.

Luc ran back to the barracks, crazed, and with eyes and voice full of tears, he related the accident: "He leaned—he—he was leaning —so far over—that his head carried him away—and—he—fell —he fell——"

Emotion choked him so that he could say no more. If he had only known.

FATHER MILON

For a month the hot sun has been parching the fields. Nature is expanding beneath its rays; the fields are green as far as the eye can see. The big azure dome of the sky is unclouded. The farms of Normandy, scattered over the plains and surrounded by a belt of tall beeches, look, from a distance, like little woods. On closer view, after lowering the worm-eaten wooden bars, you imagine yourself in an immense garden, for all the ancient apple-trees, as gnarled as the peasants themselves, are in bloom. The sweet scent of their blossoms mingles with the heavy smell of the earth and the penetrating odor of the stables. It is noon. The family is eating under the shade of a pear tree planted in front of the door; father, mother, the four children, and the help—two women and three men are all there. All are silent. The soup is eaten and then a dish of potatoes fried with bacon is brought on.

From time to time one of the women gets up and takes a pitcher down to the cellar to fetch more cider.

The man, a big fellow about forty years old, is watching a grape vine, still bare, which is winding and twisting like a snake along the side of the house.

At last he says: "Father's vine is budding early this year. Perhaps we may get something from it."

The woman then turns round and looks, without saying a word.

This vine is planted on the spot where their father had been shot.

It was during the war of 1870. The Prussians were occupying the whole country. General Faidherbe, with the Northern Division of the army, was opposing them.

The Prussians had established their headquarters at this farm. The old farmer to whom it belonged, Father Pierre Milon, had received and quartered them to the best of his ability.

For a month the German vanguard had been in this village. The French remained motionless, ten leagues away; and yet, every night, some of the Uhlans disappeared.

Of all the isolated scouts, of all those who were sent to the outposts, in groups of not more than three, not one ever returned.

They were picked up the next morning in a field or in a ditch. Even their horses were found along the roads with their throats cut.

These murders seemed to be done by the same men, who could never be found.

The country was terrorized. Farmers were shot on suspicion, women were imprisoned; children were frightened in order to try and obtain information. Nothing could be ascertained.

But, one morning, Father Milon was found stretched out in the barn, with a sword gash across his face.

Two Uhlans were found dead about a mile and a half from the farm. One of them was still holding his bloody sword in his hand. He had fought, tried to defend himself. A court-martial was immediately held in the open air, in front of the farm. The old man was brought before it.

He was sixty-eight years old, small, thin, bent, with two big hands resembling the claws of a crab. His colorless hair was sparse and thin, like the down of a young duck, allowing patches of his scalp to be seen. The brown and wrinkled skin of his neck showed big veins which disappeared behind his jaws and came out again at the temples. He had the reputation of being miserly and hard to deal with.

They stood him up between four soldiers, in front of the kitchen table, which had been dragged outside. Five officers and the colonel seated themselves opposite him.

The colonel spoke in French:

"Father Milon, since we have been here we have only had praise for you. You have always been obliging and even attentive to us. But to-day a terrible accusation is hanging over you, and you must clear the matter up. How did you receive that wound on your face?"

The peasant answered nothing.

The colonel continued:

"Your silence accuses you, Father Milon. But I want you to answer me! Do you understand? Do you know who killed the two Uhlans who were found this morning near Calvaire?"

The old man answered clearly

"I did."

The colonel, surprised, was silent for a minute, looking straight at the prisoner. Father Milon stood impassive, with the stupid look of the peasant, his eyes lowered as though he were talking to the priest. Just one thing betrayed an uneasy mind; he was continually swallowing his saliva, with a visible effort, as though his throat were terribly contracted.

The man's family, his son Jean, his daughter-in-law and his two grandchildren were standing a few feet behind him, bewildered and affrighted.

The colonel went on:

"Do you also know who killed all the scouts who have been found dead, for a month, throughout the country, every morning?"

The old man answered with the same stupid look:

"I did."

"You killed them all?"

"Uh huh! I did."

"You alone? All alone?"

"Uh huh!"

"Tell me how you did it."

This time the man seemed moved; the necessity for talking any length of time annoyed him visibly. He stammered:

"I dunno! I simply did it."

The colonel continued:

"I warn you that you will have to tell me everything. You might as well make up your mind right away. How did you begin?"

The man cast a troubled look toward his family, standing close behind him. He hesitated a minute longer, and then suddenly made up his mind to obey the order.

"I was coming home one night at about ten o'clock, the night after you got here. You and your soldiers had taken more than fifty ecus worth of forage from me, as well as a cow and two sheep. I said to myself: 'As much as they take from you; just so much will you make them pay back.' And then I had other things on my mind which I will tell you. Just then I noticed one of your soldiers who was smoking his pipe by the ditch behind the barn. I went and got my scythe and crept up slowly behind him, so that he couldn't hear me. And I cut his head off with one single blow, just as I would a blade of grass, before he could say 'Booh!' If you should look at the bottom of the pond, you will find him tied up in a potato-sack, with a stone fastened to it.

"I got an idea. I took all his clothes, from his boots to his cap, and hid them away in the little wood behind the yard."

The old man stopped. The officers remained speechless, looking at each other. The questioning began again, and this is what they learned.

Once this murder committed, the man had lived with this one thought: "Kill the Prussians!" He hated them with the blind, fierce hate of the greedy yet patriotic peasant. He had his idea, as he said. He waited several days.

He was allowed to go and come as he pleased, because he had shown himself so humble, submissive and obliging to the invaders. Each night he saw the outposts leave. One night he followed them, having heard the name of the village to which the men were going, and having learned the few words of German which he needed for his plan through associating with the soldiers.

He left through the back yard, slipped into the woods, found the dead man's clothes and put them on. Then he began to crawl through the fields, following along the hedges in order to keep out of sight, listening to the slightest noises, as wary as a poacher.

As soon as he thought the time ripe, he approached the road and hid behind a bush. He waited for a while. Finally, toward midnight, he heard the sound of a galloping horse. The man put his ear to the ground in order to make sure that only one horseman was approaching, then he got ready.

An Uhlan came galloping along, carrying dispatches. As he went, he was all eyes and ears. When he was only a few feet away, Father Milon dragged himself across the road, moaning: "Hilfe! Hilfe!" (Help! Help!) The horseman stopped, and recognizing a German, he thought he was wounded and dismounted, coming nearer without any suspicion, and just as he was leaning over the unknown man, he received, in the pit of his stomach, a heavy thrust from the long curved blade of the sabre. He dropped without suffering pain, quivering only in the final throes. Then the farmer, radiant with the silent joy of an old peasant, got up again, and, for his own pleasure, cut the dead man's throat. He then dragged the body to the ditch and threw it in.

The horse quietly awaited its master. Father Milon mounted him and started galloping across the plains.

About an hour later he noticed two more Uhlans who were returning home, side by side. He rode straight for them, once more crying "Hilfe! Hilfe!"

The Prussians, recognizing the uniform, let him approach without distrust. The old man passed between them like a cannon-ball, felling them both, one with his sabre and the other with a revolver.

Then he killed the horses, German horses! After that he quickly returned to the woods and hid one of the horses. He left his uniform there and again put on his old clothes; then going back into bed, he slept until morning.

For four days he did not go out, waiting for the inquest to be terminated; but on the fifth day he went out again and killed two more soldiers by the same stratagem. From that time on he did not stop. Each night he wandered about in search of adventure, killing Prussians, sometimes here and sometimes there, galloping through deserted fields, in the moonlight, a lost Uhlan, a hunter of men. Then, his task accomplished, leaving behind him the bodies lying along the roads, the old farmer would return and hide his horse and uniform.

He went, toward noon, to carry oats and water quietly to his mount, and he fed it well as he required from it a great amount of work.

But one of those whom he had attacked the night before, in defending himself slashed the old peasant across the face with his sabre.

However, he had killed them both. He had come back and hidden the horse and put on his ordinary clothes again; but as he reached home he began to feel faint, and had dragged himself as far as the stable, being unable to reach the house.

They had found him there, bleeding, on the straw.

When he had finished his tale, he suddenly lifted up his head and looked proudly at the Prussian officers.

The colonel, who was gnawing at his mustache, asked:

"You have nothing else to say?"

"Nothing more; I have finished my task; I killed sixteen, not one more or less."

"Do you know that you are going to die?"

"I haven't asked for mercy."

"Have you been a soldier?"

"Yes, I served my time. And then, you had killed my father, who was a soldier of the first Emperor. And last month you killed my youngest son, Francois, near Evreux. I owed you one for that; I paid. We are quits."

The officers were looking at each other.

The old man continued:

"Eight for my father, eight for the boy—we are quits. I did not seek any quarrel with you. I don't know you. I don't even know where you come from. And here you are, ordering me about in my home as though it were your own. I took my revenge upon the others. I'm not sorry."

And, straightening up his bent back, the old man folded his arms in the attitude of a modest hero.

The Prussians talked in a low tone for a long time. One of them, a captain, who had also lost his son the previous month, was defending the poor wretch. Then the colonel arose and, approaching Father Milon, said in a low voice:

"Listen, old man, there is perhaps a way of saving your life, it is to—"

But the man was not listening, and, his eyes fixed on the hated officer, while the wind played with the downy hair on his head, he distorted his slashed face, giving it a truly terrible expression, and, swelling out his chest, he spat, as hard as he could, right in the Prussian's face.

The colonel, furious, raised his hand, and for the second time the man spat in his face.

All the officers had jumped up and were shrieking orders at the same time.

In less than a minute the old man, still impassive, was pushed up against the wall and shot, looking smilingly the while toward Jean, his eldest son, his daughter-in-law and his two grandchildren, who witnessed this scene in dumb terror.

A COUP D'ETAT

Paris had just heard of the disaster at Sedan. A republic had been declared. All France was wavering on the brink of this madness which lasted until after the Commune. From one end of the country to the other everybody was playing soldier.

Cap-makers became colonels, fulfilling the duties of generals; revolvers and swords were displayed around big, peaceful stomachs wrapped in flaming red belts; little tradesmen became warriors commanding battalions of brawling volunteers, and swearing like pirates in order to give themselves some prestige.

The sole fact of handling firearms crazed these people, who up to that time had only handled scales, and made them, without any reason, dangerous to all. Innocent people were shot to prove that they knew how to kill; in forests which had never seen a Prussian, stray dogs, grazing cows and browsing horses were killed.

Each one thought himself called upon to play a great part in military affairs. The cafes of the smallest villages, full of uniformed tradesmen, looked like barracks or hospitals.

The town of Canneville was still in ignorance of the maddening news from the army and the capital; nevertheless, great excitement had prevailed for the last month, the opposing parties finding themselves face to face.

The mayor, Viscount de Varnetot, a thin, little old man, a conservative, who had recently, from ambition, gone over to the Empire, had seen a determined opponent arise in Dr. Massarel, a big, full-blooded man, leader of the Republican party of the neighborhood, a high official in the local masonic lodge, president of the Agricultural Society and of the firemen's banquet and the organizer of the rural militia which was to save the country.

In two weeks, he had managed to gather together sixty-three volunteers, fathers of families, prudent farmers and town merchants, and every morning he would drill them in the square in front of the town-hall.

When, perchance, the mayor would come to the municipal building, Commander Massarel, girt with pistols, would pass proudly in front of his troop, his sword in his hand, and make all of them cry: "Long live the Fatherland!" And it had been noticed that this cry excited the little viscount, who probably saw in it a menace, a threat, as well as the odious memory of the great Revolution.

On the morning of the fifth of September, the doctor, in full uniform, his revolver on the table, was giving a consultation to an old couple, a farmer who had been suffering from varicose veins for the last seven years and had waited until his wife had them also, before he would consult the doctor, when the postman brought in the paper.

M. Massarel opened it, grew pale, suddenly rose, and lifting his hands to heaven in a gesture of exaltation, began to shout at the top of his voice before the two frightened country folks:

"Long live the Republic! long live the Republic! long live the Republic!"

Then he fell back in his chair, weak from emotion.

And as the peasant resumed: "It started with the ants, which began to run up and down my legs—-" Dr. Massarel exclaimed:

"Shut up! I haven't got time to bother with your nonsense. The Republic has been proclaimed, the emperor has been taken prisoner, France is saved! Long live the Republic!"

Running to the door, he howled:

"Celeste, quick, Celeste!"

The servant, affrighted, hastened in; he was trying to talk so rapidly, that he could only stammer:

"My boots, my sword, my cartridge-box and the Spanish dagger which is on my night-table! Hasten!"

As the persistent peasant, taking advantage of a moment's silence, continued, "I seemed to get big lumps which hurt me when I walk," the physician, exasperated, roared:

"Shut up and get out! If you had washed your feet it would not have happened!"

Then, grabbing him by the collar, he yelled at him:

"Can't you understand that we are a republic, you brass-plated idiot!"

But professional sentiment soon calmed him, and he pushed the bewildered couple out, saying:

"Come back to-morrow, come back to-morrow, my friends. I haven't any time to-day."

As he equipped himself from head to foot, he gave a series of important orders to his servant:

"Run over to Lieutenant Picart and to Second Lieutenant Pommel, and tell them that I am expecting them here immediately. Also send me Torchebeuf with his drum. Quick! quick!"

When Celeste had gone out, he sat down and thought over the situation and the difficulties which he would have to surmount.

The three men arrived together in their working clothes. The commandant, who expected to see them in uniform, felt a little shocked.

"Don't you people know anything? The emperor has been taken prisoner, the Republic has been proclaimed. We must act. My position is delicate, I might even say dangerous."

He reflected for a few moments before his bewildered subordinates, then he continued:

"We must act and not hesitate; minutes count as hours in times like these. All depends on the promptness of our decision. You, Picart, go to the cure and order him to ring the alarm-bell, in order to get together the people, to whom I am going to announce the news. You, Torchebeuf beat the tattoo throughout the whole neighborhood as far as the hamlets of Gerisaie and Salmare, in order to assemble the militia in the public square. You, Pommel, get your uniform on quickly, just the coat and cap. We are going to the town-hall to demand Monsieur de Varnetot to surrender his powers to me. Do you understand?"

"Yes."

"Now carry out those orders quickly. I will go over to your house with you, Pommel, since we shall act together."

Five minutes later, the commandant and his subordinates, armed to the teeth, appeared on the square, just as the little Viscount de Varnetot, his legs encased in gaiters as for a hunting party, his gun on his shoulder, was coming down the other street at double-quick time, followed by his three green-coated guards, their swords at their sides and their guns swung over their shoulders.

While the doctor stopped, bewildered, the four men entered the town-hall and closed the door behind them.

"They have outstripped us," muttered the physician, "we must now wait for reenforcements. There is nothing to do for the present."

Lieutenant Picart now appeared on the scene.

"The priest refuses to obey," he said. "He has even locked himself in the church with the sexton and beadle."

On the other side of the square, opposite the white, tightly closed town-hall, stood the church, silent and dark, with its massive oak door studded with iron.

But just as the perplexed inhabitants were sticking their heads out of the windows or coming out on their doorsteps, the drum suddenly began to be heard, and Torchebeuf appeared, furiously beating the tattoo. He crossed the square running, and disappeared along the road leading to the fields.

The commandant drew his sword, and advanced alone to half way between the two buildings behind which the enemy had intrenched itself, and, waving his sword over his head, he roared with all his might:

"Long live the Republic! Death to traitors!"

Then he returned to his officers.

The butcher, the baker and the druggist, much disturbed, were anxiously pulling down their shades and closing their shops. The grocer alone kept open.

However, the militia were arriving by degrees, each man in a different uniform, but all wearing a black cap with gold braid, the cap being the principal part of the outfit. They were armed with old rusty guns, the old guns which had hung for thirty years on the kitchen wall; and they looked a good deal like an army of tramps.

When he had about thirty men about him, the commandant, in a few words, outlined the situation to them. Then, turning to his staff: "Let us act," he said.

The villagers were gathering together and talking the matter over.

The doctor quickly decided on a plan of campaign.

"Lieutenant Picart, you will advance under the windows of this town-hall and summon Monsieur de Varnetot, in the name of the Republic, to hand the keys over to me."

But the lieutenant, a master mason, refused:

"You're smart, you are. I don't care to get killed, thank you. Those people in there shoot straight, don't you forget it. Do your errands yourself."

The commandant grew very red.

"I command you to go in the name of discipline!"

The lieutenant rebelled:

"I'm not going to have my beauty spoiled without knowing why."

All the notables, gathered in a group near by, began to laugh. One of them cried:

"You are right, Picart, this isn't the right time."

The doctor then muttered:

"Cowards!"

And, leaving his sword and his revolver in the hands of a soldier, he advanced slowly, his eye fastened on the windows, expecting any minute to see a gun trained on him.

When he was within a few feet of the building, the doors at both ends, leading into the two schools, opened and a flood of children ran out, boys from one side, girls from the ether, and began to play around the doctor, in the big empty square, screeching and screaming, and making so much noise that he could not make himself heard.

As soon as the last child was out of the building, the two doors closed again.

Most of the youngsters finally dispersed, and the commandant called in a loud voice:

"Monsieur de Varnetot!"

A window on the first floor opened and M. de Varnetot appeared.

The commandant continued:

"Monsieur, you know that great events have just taken place which have changed the entire aspect of the government. The one which you represented no longer exists. The one which I represent is taking control. Under these painful, but decisive circumstances, I come, in the name of the new Republic, to ask you to turn over to me the office which you held under the former government."

M. de Varnetot answered:

"Doctor, I am the mayor of Canneville, duly appointed, and I shall remain mayor of Canneville until I have been dismissed by a decree from my superiors. As mayor, I am in my place in the townhall, and here I stay. Anyhow, just try to get me out."

He closed the window.

The commandant returned to his troop. But before giving any information, eyeing Lieutenant Picart from head to foot, he exclaimed:

"You're a great one, you are! You're a fine specimen of manhood! You're a disgrace to the army! I degrade you."

"I don't give a——!"

He turned away and mingled with a group of townspeople.

Then the doctor hesitated. What could he do? Attack? But would his men obey orders? And then, did he have the right to do so?

An idea struck him. He ran to the telegraph office, opposite the town-hall, and sent off three telegrams:

To the new republican government in Paris.

To the new prefect of the Seine-Inferieure, at Rouen.

To the new republican sub-prefect at Dieppe.

He explained the situation, pointed out the danger which the town would run if it should remain in the hands of the royalist mayor; offered his faithful services, asked for orders and signed, putting all his titles after his name.

Then he returned to his battalion, and, drawing ten francs from his pocket, he cried: "Here, my friends, go eat and drink; only leave me a detachment of ten men to guard against anybody's leaving the town-hall."

But ex-Lieutenant Picart, who had been talking with the watchmaker, heard him; he began to laugh, and exclaimed: "By Jove, if they come out, it'll give you a chance to get in. Otherwise I can see you standing out there for the rest of your life!"

The doctor did not reply, and he went to luncheon.

In the afternoon, he disposed his men about the town as though they were in immediate danger of an ambush.

Several times he passed in front of the town-hall and of the church without noticing anything suspicious; the two buildings looked as though empty.

The butcher, the baker and the druggist once more opened up their stores.

Everybody was talking about the affair. If the emperor were a prisoner, there must have been some kind of treason. They did not know exactly which of the republics had returned to power.

Night fell.

Toward nine o'clock, the doctor, alone, noiselessly approached the entrance of the public building, persuaded that the enemy must have gone to bed; and, as he was preparing to batter down the door with a pick-axe, the deep voice of a sentry suddenly called:

"Who goes there?"

And M. Massarel retreated as fast as his legs could carry him.

Day broke without any change in the situation.

Armed militia occupied the square. All the citizens had gathered around this troop awaiting developments. Even neighboring villagers had come to look on.

Then the doctor, seeing that his reputation was at stake, resolved to put an end to the matter in one way or another; and he was about to take some measures, undoubtedly energetic ones, when the door of the telegraph station opened and the little servant of the postmistress appeared, holding in her hands two papers.

First she went to the commandant and gave him one of the despatches; then she crossed the empty square, confused at seeing the eyes of everyone on her, and lowering her head and running along with little quick steps, she went and knocked softly at the door of the barricaded house, as though ignorant of the fact that those behind it were armed.

The door opened wide enough to let a man's hand reach out and receive the message; and the young girl returned blushing, ready to cry at being thus stared at by the whole countryside.

In a clear voice, the doctor cried:

"Silence, if you please."

When the populace had quieted down, he continued proudly:

"Here is the communication which I have received from the government."

And lifting the telegram he read:

Former mayor dismissed. Inform him immediately, More orders following.

For the sub-prefect:

SAPIN, Councillor.

He was-triumphant; his heart was throbbing with joy and his hands were trembling; but Picart, his former subordinate, cried to him from a neighboring group:

"That's all right; but supposing the others don't come out, what good is the telegram going to do you?"

M. Massarel grew pale. He had not thought of that; if the others did not come out, he would now have to take some decisive step. It was not only his right, but his duty.

He looked anxiously at the town-hall, hoping to see the door open and his adversary give in.

The door remained closed. What could he do? The crowd was growing and closing around the militia. They were laughing.

One thought especially tortured the doctor. If he attacked, he would have to march at the head of his men; and as, with him dead, all strife would cease, it was at him and him only that M. de Varnetot and his three guards would aim. And they were good shots, very good shots, as Picart had just said. But an idea struck him and, turning to Pommel, he ordered:

"Run quickly to the druggist and ask him to lend me a towel and a stick."

The lieutenant hastened.

He would make a flag of truce, a white flag, at the sight of which the royalist heart of the mayor would perhaps rejoice.

Pommel returned with the cloth and a broom-stick. With some twine they completed the flag, and M. Massarel, grasping it in both hands and holding it in front of him, again advanced in the direction of the town-hall. When he was opposite the door, he once more called: "Monsieur de Varnetot!" The door suddenly opened and M. de Varnetot and his three guards appeared on the threshold.

Instinctively the doctor stepped back; then he bowed courteously to his enemy, and, choking with emotion, he announced: "I have come, monsieur, to make you acquainted with the orders which I have received."

The nobleman, without returning the bow, answered: "I resign, monsieur, but understand that it is neither through fear of, nor obedience to, the odious government which has usurped the power." And, emphasizing every word, he declared: "I do not wish to appear, for a single day, to serve the Republic. That's all."

Massarel, stunned, answered nothing; and M. de Varnetot, walking quickly, disappeared around the corner of the square, still followed by his escort.

The doctor, puffed up with pride, returned to the crowd. As soon as he was near enough to make himself heard, he cried: "Hurrah! hurrah! Victory crowns the Republic everywhere."

There was no outburst of joy.

The doctor continued: "We are free, you are free, independent! Be proud!"

The motionless villagers were looking at him without any signs of triumph shining in their eyes.

He looked at them, indignant at their indifference, thinking of what he could say or do in order to make an impression to electrify this calm peasantry, to fulfill his mission as a leader.

He had an inspiration and, turning to Pommel, he ordered: "Lieutenant, go get me the bust of the ex-emperor which is in the meeting room of the municipal council, and bring it here with a chair."

The man presently reappeared, carrying on his right shoulder the plaster Bonaparte, and holding in his left hand a cane-seated chair.

M. Massarel went towards him, took the chair, placed the white bust on it, then stepping back a few steps, he addressed it in a loud voice:

"Tyrant, tyrant, you have fallen down in the mud. The dying fatherland was in its death throes under your oppression. Vengeful Destiny has struck you. Defeat and shame have pursued you; you fall conquered, a prisoner of the Prussians; and from the ruins of your crumbling empire, the young and glorious Republic arises, lifting from the ground your broken sword——"

He waited for applause. Not a sound greeted his listening ear. The peasants, nonplussed, kept silent; and the white, placid, well-groomed statue seemed to look at M. Massarel with its plaster smile, ineffaceable and sarcastic.

Thus they stood, face to face, Napoleon on his chair, the physician standing three feet away. Anger seized the commandant.

What could he do to move this crowd and definitely to win over public opinion?

He happened to carry his hand to his stomach, and he felt, under his red belt, the butt of his revolver.

Not another inspiration, not another word cane to his mind. Then, he drew his weapon, stepped back a few steps and shot the former monarch.

The bullet made a little black hole: like a spot, in his forehead. No sensation was created. M. Massarel shot a second time and made a second hole, then a third time, then, without stopping, he shot off the three remaining shots. Napoleon's forehead was blown away in a white powder, but his eyes, nose and pointed mustache remained intact.

Then in exasperation, the doctor kicked the chair over, and placing one foot on what remained of the bust in the position of a conqueror, he turned to the amazed public and yelled: "Thus may all traitors die!"

As no enthusiasm was, as yet, visible, the spectators appearing to be dumb with astonishment, the commandant cried to the militia: "You may go home now." And he himself walked rapidly, almost ran, towards his house.

As soon as he appeared, the servant told him that some patients had been waiting in his office for over three hours. He hastened in. They were the same two peasants as a few days before, who had returned at daybreak, obstinate and patient.

The old man immediately began his explanation:

"It began with ants, which seemed to be crawling up and down my legs——"

LIEUTENANT LARE'S MARRIAGE

Since the beginning of the campaign Lieutenant Lare had taken two cannon from the Prussians. His general had said: "Thank you, lieutenant," and had given him the cross of honor.

As he was as cautious as he was brave, wary, inventive, wily and resourceful, he was entrusted with a hundred soldiers and he organized a company of scouts who saved the army on several occasions during a retreat.

But the invading army entered by every frontier like a surging sea. Great waves of men arrived one after the other, scattering all around them a scum of freebooters. General Carrel's brigade, separated from its division, retreated continually, fighting each day, but remaining almost intact, thanks to the vigilance and agility of Lieutenant Lare, who seemed to be everywhere at the same moment, baffling all the enemy's cunning, frustrating their plans, misleading their Uhlans and killing their vanguards.

One morning the general sent for him.

"Lieutenant," said he, "here is a dispatch from General de Lacere, who will be destroyed if we do not go to his aid by sunrise to-morrow. He is at Blainville, eight leagues from here. You will start at nightfall with three hundred men, whom you will echelon along the road. I will follow you two hours later. Study the road carefully; I fear we may meet a division of the enemy."

It had been freezing hard for a week. At two o'clock it began to snow, and by night the ground was covered and heavy white swirls concealed objects hard by.

At six o'clock the detachment set out.

Two men walked alone as scouts about three yards ahead. Then came a platoon of ten men commanded by the lieutenant himself. The rest followed them in two long columns. To the right and left of the little band, at a distance of about three hundred feet on either side, some soldiers marched in pairs.

The snow, which was still falling, covered them with a white powder in the darkness, and as it did not melt on their uniforms, they were hardly distinguishable in the night amid the dead whiteness of the landscape.

From time to time they halted. One heard nothing but that indescribable, nameless flutter of falling snow—a sensation rather than a sound, a vague, ominous murmur. A command was given in a low tone and when the troop resumed its march it left in its wake a sort of white phantom standing in the snow. It gradually grew fainter and finally disappeared. It was the echelons who were to lead the army.

The scouts slackened their pace. Something was ahead of them.

"Turn to the right," said the lieutenant; "it is the Ronfi wood; the chateau is more to the left."

Presently the command "Halt" was passed along. The detachment stopped and waited for the lieutenant, who, accompanied by only ten men, had undertaken a reconnoitering expedition to the chateau.

They advanced, creeping under the trees. Suddenly they all remained motionless. Around them was a dead silence. Then, quite near them, a little clear, musical young voice was heard amid the stillness of the wood.

"Father, we shall get lost in the snow. We shall never reach Blainville."

A deeper voice replied:

"Never fear, little daughter; I know the country as well as I know my pocket."

The lieutenant said a few words and four men moved away silently, like shadows.

All at once a woman's shrill cry was heard through the darkness. Two prisoners were brought back, an old man and a young girl. The lieutenant questioned them, still in a low tone:

"Your name?"

"Pierre Bernard."

"Your profession?"

"Butler to Comte de Ronfi."

"Is this your daughter?"

'Yes!'

"What does she do?"

"She is laundress at the chateau."

"Where are you going?"

"We are making our escape."

"Why?"

"Twelve Uhlans passed by this evening. They shot three keepers and hanged the gardener. I was alarmed on account of the little one."

"Whither are you bound?"

"To Blainville."

"Why?"

"Because there is a French army there."

"Do you know the way?"

"Perfectly."

"Well then, follow us."

They rejoined the column and resumed their march across country. The old man walked in silence beside the lieutenant, his daughter walking at his side. All at once she stopped.

"Father," she said, "I am so tired I cannot go any farther."

And she sat down. She was shaking with cold and seemed about to lose consciousness. Her father wanted to carry her, but he was too old and too weak.

"Lieutenant," said he, sobbing, "we shall only impede your march. France before all. Leave us here."

The officer had given a command. Some men had started off. They came back with branches they had cut, and in a minute a litter was ready. The whole detachment had joined them by this time.

"Here is a woman dying of cold," said the lieutenant. "Who will give his cape to cover her?"

Two hundred capes were taken off. The young girl was wrapped up in these warm soldiers' capes, gently laid in the litter, and then four' hardy shoulders lifted her up, and like an Eastern queen borne by her slaves she was placed in the center of the detachment of soldiers, who resumed their march with more energy, more courage, more cheerfulness, animated by the presence of a woman, that sovereign inspiration that has stirred the old French blood to so many deeds of valor.

At the end of an hour they halted again and every one lay down in the snow. Over yonder on the level country a big, dark shadow was moving. It looked like some weird monster stretching itself out like a serpent, then suddenly coiling itself into a mass, darting forth again, then back, and then forward again without ceasing. Some whispered orders were passed around among the soldiers, and an occasional little, dry, metallic click was heard. The moving object suddenly came nearer, and twelve Uhlans were seen approaching at a gallop, one behind the other, having lost their way in the darkness. A brilliant flash suddenly revealed to them two hundred men lying on the ground before them. A rapid fire was heard, which died away in the snowy silence, and all the twelve fell to the ground, their horses with them.

After a long rest the march was resumed. The old man whom they had captured acted as guide.

Presently a voice far off in the distance cried out: "Who goes there?"

Another voice nearer by gave the countersign.

They made another halt; some conferences took place. It had stopped snowing. A cold wind was driving the clouds, and innumerable stars were sparkling in the sky behind them, gradually paling in the rosy light of dawn.

A staff officer came forward to receive the detachment. But when he asked who was being carried in the litter, the form stirred; two little hands moved aside the big blue army capes and, rosy as the dawn, with two eyes that were brighter than the stars that had just faded from sight, and a smile as radiant as the morn, a dainty face appeared.

"It is I, monsieur."

The soldiers, wild with delight, clapped their hands and bore the young girl in triumph into the midst of the camp, that was just getting to arms. Presently General Carrel arrived on the scene. At nine o'clock the Prussians made an attack. They beat a retreat at noon.

That evening, as Lieutenant Lare, overcome by fatigue, was sleeping on a bundle of straw, he was sent for by the general. He found the commanding officer in his tent, chatting with the old man whom they had come across during the night. As soon as he entered the tent the general took his hand, and addressing the stranger, said:

"My dear comte, this is the young man of whom you were telling me just now; he is one of my best officers."

He smiled, lowered his tone, and added:

"The best."

Then, turning to the astonished lieutenant, he presented "Comte de Ronfi-Quedissac."

The old man took both his hands, saying:

"My dear lieutenant, you have saved my daughter's life. I have only one way of thanking you. You may come in a few months to tell me—if you like her."

One year later, on the very same day, Captain Lare and Miss Louise-Hortense-Genevieve de Ronfi-Quedissac were married in the church of St. Thomas Aquinas.

She brought a dowry of six thousand francs, and was said to be the prettiest bride that had been seen that year.

THE HORRIBLE

The shadows of a balmy night were slowly falling. The women remained in the drawing-room of the villa. The men, seated, or astride of garden chairs, were smoking outside the door of the house, around a table laden with cups and liqueur glasses.

Their lighted cigars shone like eyes in the darkness, which was gradually becoming more dense. They had been talking about a frightful accident which had occurred the night before—two men and three women drowned in the river before the eyes of the guests.

General de G——remarked:

"Yes, these things are affecting, but they are not horrible.

"Horrible, that well-known word, means much more than terrible. A frightful accident like this affects, upsets, terrifies; it does not horrify. In order that we should experience horror, something more is needed than emotion, something more than the spectacle of a dreadful death; there must be a shuddering sense of mystery, or a sensation of abnormal terror, more than natural. A man who dies, even under the most tragic circumstances, does not excite horror; a field of battle is not horrible; blood is not horrible; the vilest crimes are rarely horrible.

"Here are two personal examples which have shown me what is the meaning of horror.

"It was during the war of 1870. We were retreating toward Pont-Audemer, after having passed through Rouen. The army, consisting of about twenty thousand men, twenty thousand routed men, disbanded, demoralized, exhausted, were going to disband at Havre.

"The earth was covered with snow. The night was falling. They had not eaten anything since the day before. They were fleeing rapidly, the Prussians not being far off.

"All the Norman country, sombre, dotted with the shadows of the trees surrounding the farms, stretched out beneath a black, heavy, threatening sky.

"Nothing else could be heard in the wan twilight but the confused sound, undefined though rapid, of a marching throng, an endless tramping, mingled with the vague clink of tin bowls or swords. The men, bent, round-shouldered, dirty, in many cases even in rags, dragged themselves along, hurried through the snow, with a long, broken-backed stride.

"The skin of their hands froze to the butt ends of their muskets, for it was freezing hard that night. I frequently saw a little soldier take off his shoes in order to walk barefoot, as his shoes hurt his weary feet; and at every step he left a track of blood. Then, after some time, he would sit down in a field for a few minutes' rest, and he never got up again. Every man who sat down was a dead man.

"Should we have left behind us those poor, exhausted soldiers, who fondly counted on being able to start afresh as soon as they had somewhat refreshed their stiffened legs? But scarcely had they ceased to move, and to make their almost frozen blood circulate in their veins, than an unconquerable torpor congealed them, nailed them to the ground, closed their eyes, and paralyzed in one second this overworked human mechanism. And they gradually sank down, their foreheads on their knees, without, however, falling over, for their loins and their limbs became as hard and immovable as wood, impossible to bend or to stand upright.

"And the rest of us, more robust, kept straggling on, chilled to the marrow, advancing by a kind of inertia through the night, through the snow, through that cold and deadly country, crushed by pain, by defeat, by despair, above all overcome by the abominable sensation of abandonment, of the end, of death, of nothingness.

"I saw two gendarmes holding by the arm a curious-looking little man, old, beardless, of truly surprising aspect.

"They were looking for an officer, believing that they had caught a spy. The word 'spy' at once spread through the midst of the stragglers, and they gathered in a group round the prisoner. A voice exclaimed: 'He must be shot!' And all these soldiers who were falling from utter prostration, only holding themselves on their feet by leaning on their guns, felt all of a sudden that thrill of furious and bestial anger which urges on a mob to massacre.

"I wanted to speak. I was at that time in command of a battalion; but they no longer recognized the authority of their commanding officers; they would even have shot me.

"One of the gendarmes said: 'He has been following us for the three last days. He has been asking information from every one about the artillery.'"

I took it on myself to question this person.

"What are you doing? What do you want? Why are you accompanying the army?"

"He stammered out some words in some unintelligible dialect. He was, indeed, a strange being, with narrow shoulders, a sly look, and such an agitated air in my presence that I really no longer doubted that he was a spy. He seemed very aged and feeble. He kept looking at me from under his eyes with a humble, stupid, crafty air.

"The men all round us exclaimed.

"'To the wall! To the wall!'

"I said to the gendarmes:

"'Will you be responsible for the prisoner?'

"I had not ceased speaking when a terrible shove threw me on my back, and in a second I saw the man seized by the furious soldiers, thrown down, struck, dragged along the side of the road, and flung against a tree. He fell in the snow, nearly dead already.

"And immediately they shot him. The soldiers fired at him, reloaded their guns, fired again with the desperate energy of brutes. They fought with each other to have a shot at him, filed off in front of the corpse, and kept on firing at him, as people at a funeral keep sprinkling holy water in front of a coffin.

"But suddenly a cry arose of 'The Prussians! the Prussians!'

"And all along the horizon I heard the great noise of this panic-stricken army in full flight.

"A panic, the result of these shots fired at this vagabond, had filled his very executioners with terror; and, without realizing that they were themselves the originators of the scare, they fled and disappeared in the darkness.

"I remained alone with the corpse, except for the two gendarmes whose duty compelled them to stay with me.

"They lifted up the riddled mass of bruised and bleeding flesh.

"'He must be searched,' I said. And I handed them a box of taper matches which I had in my pocket. One of the soldiers had another box. I was standing between the two.

"The gendarme who was examining the body announced:

"'Clothed in a blue blouse, a white shirt, trousers, and a pair of shoes.'

"The first match went out; we lighted a second. The man continued, as he turned out his pockets:

"'A horn-handled pocketknife, check handkerchief, a snuffbox, a bit of pack thread, a piece of bread.'

"The second match went out; we lighted a third. The gendarme, after having felt the corpse for a long time, said:

"'That is all.'

"I said:

"'Strip him. We shall perhaps find something next his skin."

"And in order that the two soldiers might help each other in this task, I stood between them to hold the lighted match. By the rapid and speedily extinguished flame of the match, I saw them take off the garments one by one, and expose to view that bleeding bundle of flesh, still warm, though lifeless.

"And suddenly one of them exclaimed:

"'Good God, general, it is a woman!'

"I cannot describe to you the strange and poignant sensation of pain that moved my heart. I could not believe it, and I knelt down in the snow before this shapeless pulp of flesh to see for myself: it was a woman.

"The two gendarmes, speechless and stunned, waited for me to give my opinion on the matter. But I did not know what to think, what theory to adopt.

"Then the brigadier slowly drawled out:

"'Perhaps she came to look for a son of hers in the artillery, whom she had not heard from.'

"And the other chimed in:

"'Perhaps, indeed, that is so.'

"And I, who had seen some very terrible things in my time, began to cry. And I felt, in the presence of this corpse, on that icy cold night, in the midst of that gloomy plain; at the sight of this mystery, at the sight of this murdered stranger, the meaning of that word 'horror.'

"I had the same sensation last year, while interrogating one of the survivors of the Flatters Mission, an Algerian sharpshooter.

"You know the details of that atrocious drama. It is possible, however, that you are unacquainted with one of them.

"The colonel travelled through the desert into the Soudan, and passed through the immense territory of the Touaregs, who, in that great ocean of sand which stretches from the Atlantic to Egypt and from the Soudan to Algeria, are a kind of pirates, resembling those who ravaged the seas in former days.

"The guides who accompanied the column belonged to the tribe of the Chambaa, of Ouargla.

"Now, one day we encamped in the middle of the desert, and the Arabs declared that, as the spring was still some distance away, they would go with all their camels to look for water.

"One man alone warned the colonel that he had been betrayed. Flatters did not believe this, and accompanied the convoy with the engineers, the doctors, and nearly all his officers.

"They were massacred round the spring, and all the camels were captured.

"The captain of the Arab Intelligence Department at Ouargla, who had remained in the camp, took command of the survivors, spahis and sharpshooters, and they began to retreat, leaving behind them the baggage and provisions, for want of camels to carry them.

"Then they started on their journey through this solitude without shade and boundless, beneath the devouring sun, which burned them from morning till night.

"One tribe came to tender its submission and brought dates as a tribute. The dates were poisoned. Nearly all the Frenchmen died, and, among them, the last officer.

"There now only remained a few spahis with their quartermaster, Pobeguin, and some native sharpshooters of the Chambaa tribe. They had still two camels left. They disappeared one night, along with two, Arabs.

"Then the survivors understood that they would be obliged to eat each other, and as soon as they discovered the flight of the two men with the two camels, those who remained separated, and proceeded to march, one by one, through the soft sand, under the glare of a scorching sun, at a distance of more than a gunshot from each other.

"So they went on all day, and when they reached a spring each of them came to drink at it in turn, as soon as each solitary marcher had moved forward the number of yards arranged upon. And thus they continued marching the whole day, raising everywhere they passed, in that level, burnt up expanse, those little columns of dust which, from a distance, indicate those who are trudging through the desert.

"But one morning one of the travellers suddenly turned round and approached the man behind him. And they all stopped to look.

"The man toward whom the famished soldier drew near did not flee, but lay flat on the ground, and took aim at the one who was coming toward him. When he believed he was within gunshot, he fired. The other was not hit, and he continued then to advance, and levelling his gun, in turn, he killed his comrade.

"Then from all directions the others rushed to seek their share. And he who had killed the fallen man, cutting the corpse into pieces, distributed it.

"And they once more placed themselves at fixed distances, these irreconcilable allies, preparing for the next murder which would bring them together.

"For two days they lived on this human flesh which they divided between them. Then, becoming famished again, he who had killed the first man began killing afresh. And again, like a butcher, he cut up the corpse and offered it to his comrades, keeping only his own portion of it.

"And so this retreat of cannibals continued.

"The last Frenchman, Pobeguin, was massacred at the side of a well, the very night before the supplies arrived.

"Do you understand now what I mean by the horrible?"

This was the story told us a few nights ago by General de G——.

MADAME PARISSE

I was sitting on the pier of the small port of Obernon, near the village of Salis, looking at Antibes, bathed in the setting sun. I had never before seen anything so wonderful and so beautiful.

The small town, enclosed by its massive ramparts, built by Monsieur de Vauban, extended into the open sea, in the middle of the immense Gulf of Nice. The great waves, coming in from the ocean, broke at its feet, surrounding it with a wreath of foam; and beyond the ramparts the houses climbed up the hill, one after the other, as far as the two towers, which rose up into the sky, like the peaks of an ancient helmet. And these two towers were outlined against the milky whiteness of the Alps, that enormous distant wall of snow which enclosed the entire horizon.

Between the white foam at the foot of the walls and the white snow on the sky-line the little city, dazzling against the bluish background of the nearest mountain ranges, presented to the rays of the setting sun a pyramid of red-roofed houses, whose facades were also white, but so different one from another that they seemed to be of all tints.

And the sky above the Alps was itself of a blue that was almost white, as if the snow had tinted it; some silvery clouds were floating just over the pale summits, and on the other side of the gulf Nice, lying close to the water, stretched like a white thread between the sea and the mountain. Two great sails, driven by a strong breeze, seemed to skim over the waves. I looked upon all this, astounded.

This view was one of those sweet, rare, delightful things that seem to permeate you and are unforgettable, like the memory of a great happiness. One sees, thinks, suffers, is moved and loves with the eyes. He who can feel with the eye experiences the same keen, exquisite and deep pleasure in looking at men and things as the man with the delicate and sensitive ear, whose soul music overwhelms.

I turned to my companion, M. Martini, a pureblooded Southerner.

"This is certainly one of the rarest sights which it has been vouchsafed to me to admire.

"I have seen Mont Saint-Michel, that monstrous granite jewel, rise out of the sand at sunrise.

"I have seen, in the Sahara, Lake Raianechergui, fifty kilometers long, shining under a moon as brilliant as our sun and breathing up toward it a white cloud, like a mist of milk.

"I have seen, in the Lipari Islands, the weird sulphur crater of the Volcanello, a giant flower which smokes and burns, an enormous yellow flower, opening out in the midst of the sea, whose stem is a volcano.

"But I have seen nothing more wonderful than Antibes, standing against the Alps in the setting sun.

"And I know not how it is that memories of antiquity haunt me; verses of Homer come into my mind; this is a city of the ancient East, a city of the odyssey; this is Troy, although Troy was very far from the sea."

M. Martini drew the Sarty guide-book out of his pocket and read: "This city was originally a colony founded by the Phocians of Marseilles, about 340 B.C. They gave it the Greek name of Antipolis, meaning counter-city, city opposite another, because it is in fact opposite to Nice, another colony from Marseilles.

"After the Gauls were conquered, the Romans turned Antibes into a municipal city, its inhabitants receiving the rights of Roman citizenship.

"We know by an epigram of Martial that at this time——"

I interrupted him:

"I don't care what she was. I tell you that I see down there a city of the Odyssey. The coast of Asia and the coast of Europe resemble each other in their shores, and there is no city on the other coast of the Mediterranean which awakens in me the memories of the heroic age as this one does."

A footstep caused me to turn my head; a woman, a large, dark woman, was walking along the road which skirts the sea in going to the cape.

"That is Madame Parisse, you know," muttered Monsieur Martini, dwelling on the final syllable.

No, I did not know, but that name, mentioned carelessly, that name of the Trojan shepherd, confirmed me in my dream.

However, I asked: "Who is this Madame Parisse?"

He seemed astonished that I did not know the story.

I assured him that I did not know it, and I looked after the woman, who passed by without seeing us, dreaming, walking with steady and slow step, as doubtless the ladies of old walked.

She was perhaps thirty-five years old and still very beautiful, though a trifle stout.

And Monsieur Martini told me the following story:

Mademoiselle Combelombe was married, one year before the war of 1870, to Monsieur Parisse, a government official. She was then a handsome young girl, as slender and lively as she has now become stout and sad.

Unwillingly she had accepted Monsieur Parisse, one of those little fat men with short legs, who trip along, with trousers that are always too large.

After the war Antibes was garrisoned by a single battalion commanded by Monsieur Jean de Carmelin, a young officer decorated during the war, and who had just received his four stripes.

As he found life exceedingly tedious in this fortress this stuffy mole-hole enclosed by its enormous double walls, he often strolled out to the cape, a kind of park or pine wood shaken by all the winds from the sea.

There he met Madame Parisse, who also came out in the summer evenings to get the fresh air under the trees. How did they come to love each other? Who knows? They met, they looked at each other, and when out of sight they doubtless thought of each other. The image of the young woman with the brown eyes, the black hair, the pale skin, this fresh, handsome Southerner, who displayed her teeth in smiling, floated before the eyes of the officer as he continued his promenade, chewing his cigar instead of smoking it; and the image of the commanding officer, in his close-fitting coat, covered with gold lace, and his red trousers, and a little blond mustache, would pass before the eyes of Madame Parisse, when her husband, half shaven and ill-clad, short-legged and big-bellied, came home to supper in the evening.

As they met so often, they perhaps smiled at the next meeting; then, seeing each other again and again, they felt as if they knew each other. He certainly bowed to her. And she, surprised, bowed in return, but very, very slightly, just enough not to appear impolite. But after two weeks she returned his salutation from a distance, even before they were side by side.

He spoke to her. Of what? Doubtless of the setting sun. They admired it together, looking for it in each other's eyes more often than on the horizon. And every evening for two weeks this was the commonplace and persistent pretext for a few minutes' chat.

Then they ventured to take a few steps together, talking of anything that came into their minds, but their eyes were already saying to each other a thousand more intimate things, those secret, charming things that are reflected in the gentle emotion of the glance, and that cause the heart to beat, for they are a better revelation of the soul than the spoken ward.

And then he would take her hand, murmuring those words which the woman divines, without seeming to hear them.

And it was agreed between them that they would love each other without evidencing it by anything sensual or brutal.

She would have remained indefinitely at this stage of intimacy, but he wanted more. And every day he urged her more hotly to give in to his ardent desire.

She resisted, would not hear of it, seemed determined not to give way.

But one evening she said to him casually: "My husband has just gone to Marseilles. He will be away four days."

Jean de Carmelin threw himself at her feet, imploring her to open her door to him that very night at eleven o'clock. But she would not listen to him, and went home, appearing to be annoyed.

The commandant was in a bad humor all the evening, and the next morning at dawn he went out on the ramparts in a rage, going from one exercise field to the other, dealing out punishment to the officers and men as one might fling stones into a crowd,

On going in to breakfast he found an envelope under his napkin with these four words: "To-night at ten." And he gave one hundred sous without any reason to the waiter.

The day seemed endless to him. He passed part of it in curling his hair and perfuming himself.

As he was sitting down to the dinner-table another envelope was handed to him, and in it he found the following telegram:

"My Love: Business completed. I return this evening on the nine o'clock train.

PARISSE."

The commandant let loose such a vehement oath that the waiter dropped the soup-tureen on the floor.

What should he do? He certainly wanted her, that very, evening at whatever cost; and he would have her. He would resort to any means, even to arresting and imprisoning the husband. Then a mad thought struck him. Calling for paper, he wrote the following note:

MADAME: He will not come back this evening, I swear it to you,—and I shall be, you know where, at ten o'clock. Fear nothing. I will answer for everything, on my honor as an officer.

JEAN DE CARMELIN.

And having sent off this letter, he quietly ate his dinner.

Toward eight o'clock he sent for Captain Gribois, the second in command, and said, rolling between his fingers the crumpled telegram of Monsieur Parisse:

"Captain, I have just received a telegram of a very singular nature, which it is impossible for me to communicate to you. You will immediately have all the gates of the city closed and guarded, so that no one, mind me, no one, will either enter or leave before six in the morning. You will also have men patrol the streets, who will compel the inhabitants to retire to their houses at nine o'clock. Any one found outside beyond that time will be conducted to his home 'manu militari'. If your men meet me this night they will at once go out of my way, appearing not to know me. You understand me?"

"Yes, commandant."

"I hold you responsible for the execution of my orders, my dear captain."

"Yes, commandant."

"Would you like to have a glass of chartreuse?"

"With great pleasure, commandant."

They clinked glasses drank down the brown liquor and Captain Gribois left the room.

The train from Marseilles arrived at the station at nine o'clock sharp, left two passengers on the platform and went on toward Nice.

One of them, tall and thin, was Monsieur Saribe, the oil merchant, and the other, short and fat, was Monsieur Parisse.

Together they set out, with their valises, to reach the city, one kilometer distant.

But on arriving at the gate of the port the guards crossed their bayonets, commanding them to retire.

Frightened, surprised, cowed with astonishment, they retired to deliberate; then, after having taken counsel one with the other, they came back cautiously to parley, giving their names.

But the soldiers evidently had strict orders, for they threatened to shoot; and the two scared travellers ran off, throwing away their valises, which impeded their flight.

Making the tour of the ramparts, they presented themselves at the gate on the route to Cannes. This likewise was closed and guarded by a menacing sentinel. Messrs. Saribe and Parisse, like the prudent men they were, desisted from their efforts and went back to the station for shelter, since it was not safe to be near the fortifications after sundown.

The station agent, surprised and sleepy, permitted them to stay till morning in the waiting-room.

And they sat there side by side, in the dark, on the green velvet sofa, too scared to think of sleeping.

It was a long and weary night for them.

At half-past six in the morning they were informed that the gates were open and that people could now enter Antibes.

They set out for the city, but failed to find their abandoned valises on the road.

When they passed through the gates of the city, still somewhat anxious, the Commandant de Carmelin, with sly glance and mustache curled up, came himself to look at them and question them.

Then he bowed to them politely, excusing himself for having caused them a bad night. But he had to carry out orders.

The people of Antibes were scared to death. Some spoke of a surprise planned by the Italians, others of the landing of the prince imperial and others again believed that there was an Orleanist conspiracy. The truth was suspected only later, when it became known that the battalion of the commandant had been sent away, to a distance and that Monsieur de Carmelin had been severely punished.

Monsieur Martini had finished his story. Madame Parisse returned, her promenade being ended. She passed gravely near me, with her eyes fixed on the Alps, whose summits now gleamed rosy in the last rays of the setting sun.

I longed to speak to her, this poor, sad woman, who would ever be thinking of that night of love, now long past, and of the bold man who for the sake of a kiss from her had dared to put a city into a state of siege and to compromise his whole future.

And to-day he had probably forgotten her, if he did not relate this audacious, comical and tender farce to his comrades over their cups.

Had she seen him again? Did she still love him? And I thought: Here is an instance of modern love, grotesque and yet heroic. The Homer who should sing of this new Helen and the adventure of her Menelaus must be gifted with the soul of a Paul de Kock. And yet the hero of this deserted woman was brave, daring, handsome, strong as Achilles and more cunning than Ulysses.

MADEMOISELLE FIFI

Major Graf Von Farlsberg, the Prussian commandant, was reading his newspaper as he lay back in a great easy-chair, with his booted feet on the beautiful marble mantelpiece where his spurs had made two holes, which had grown deeper every day during the three months that he had been in the chateau of Uville.

A cup of coffee was smoking on a small inlaid table, which was stained with liqueur, burned by cigars, notched by the penknife of the victorious officer, who occasionally would stop while sharpening a pencil, to jot down figures, or to make a drawing on it, just as it took his fancy.

When he had read his letters and the German newspapers, which his orderly had brought him, he got up, and after throwing three or four enormous pieces of green wood on the fire, for these gentlemen were gradually cutting down the park in order to keep themselves warm, he went to the window. The rain was descending in torrents, a regular Normandy rain, which looked as if it were being poured out by some furious person, a slanting rain, opaque as a curtain, which formed a kind of wall with diagonal stripes, and which deluged everything, a rain such as one frequently experiences in the neighborhood of Rouen, which is the watering-pot of France.

For a long time the officer looked at the sodden turf and at the swollen Andelle beyond it, which was overflowing its banks; he was drumming a waltz with his fingers on the window-panes, when a noise made him turn round. It was his second in command, Captain Baron van Kelweinstein.

The major was a giant, with broad shoulders and a long, fan-like beard, which hung down like a curtain to his chest. His whole solemn person suggested the idea of a military peacock, a peacock who was carrying his tail spread out on his breast. He had cold, gentle blue eyes, and a scar from a swordcut, which he had received in the war with Austria; he was said to be an honorable man, as well as a brave officer.

The captain, a short, red-faced man, was tightly belted in at the waist, his red hair was cropped quite close to his head, and in certain lights he almost looked as if he had been rubbed over with phosphorus. He had lost two front teeth one night, though he could not quite remember how, and this sometimes made him speak unintelligibly, and he had a bald patch on top of his head surrounded by a fringe of curly, bright golden hair, which made him look like a monk.

The commandant shook hands with him and drank his cup of coffee (the sixth that morning), while he listened to his subordinate's report of what had occurred; and then they both went to the window and declared that it was a very unpleasant outlook. The major, who was a quiet man, with a wife at home, could accommodate himself to everything; but the captain, who led a fast life, who was in the habit of frequenting low resorts, and enjoying women's society, was angry at having to be shut up for three months in that wretched hole.

There was a knock at the door, and when the commandant said, "Come in," one of the orderlies appeared, and by his mere presence announced that breakfast was ready. In the dining-room they met three other officers of lower rank—a lieutenant, Otto von Grossling, and two sub-lieutenants, Fritz Scheuneberg and Baron von Eyrick, a very short, fair-haired man, who was proud and brutal toward men, harsh toward prisoners and as explosive as gunpowder.

Since he had been in France his comrades had called him nothing but Mademoiselle Fifi. They had given him that nickname on account of his dandified style and small waist, which looked as if he wore corsets; of his pale face, on which his budding mustache scarcely showed, and on account of the habit he had acquired of employing the French expression, 'Fi, fi donc', which he pronounced with a slight whistle when he wished to express his sovereign contempt for persons or things.

The dining-room of the chateau was a magnificent long room, whose fine old mirrors, that were cracked by pistol bullets, and whose Flemish tapestry, which was cut to ribbons, and hanging in rags in places from sword-cuts, told too well what Mademoiselle Fifi's occupation was during his spare time.

There were three family portraits on the walls a steel-clad knight, a cardinal and a judge, who were all smoking long porcelain pipes, which had been inserted into holes in the canvas, while a lady in a long, pointed waist proudly exhibited a pair of enormous mustaches, drawn with charcoal. The officers ate their breakfast almost in silence in that mutilated room, which looked dull in the rain and melancholy in its dilapidated condition, although its old oak floor had become as solid as the stone floor of an inn.

When they had finished eating and were smoking and drinking, they began, as usual, to berate the dull life they were leading. The bottles of brandy and of liqueur passed from hand to hand, and all sat back in their chairs and took repeated sips from their glasses, scarcely removing from their mouths the long, curved stems, which terminated in china bowls, painted in a manner to delight a Hottentot.

As soon as their glasses were empty they filled them again, with a gesture of resigned weariness, but Mademoiselle Fifi emptied his every minute, and a soldier immediately gave him another. They were enveloped in a cloud of strong tobacco smoke, and seemed to be sunk in a state of drowsy, stupid intoxication, that condition of stupid intoxication of men who have nothing to do, when suddenly the baron sat up and said: "Heavens! This cannot go on; we must think of something to do." And on hearing this, Lieutenant Otto and Sub-lieutenant Fritz, who preeminently possessed the serious, heavy German countenance, said: "What, captain?"

He thought for a few moments and then replied: "What? Why, we must get up some entertainment, if the commandant will allow us." "What sort of an entertainment, captain?" the major asked, taking his pipe out of his mouth. "I will arrange all that, commandant," the baron said. "I will send Le Devoir to Rouen, and he will bring back some ladies. I know where they can be found, We will have supper here, as all the materials are at hand and; at least, we shall have a jolly evening."

Graf von Farlsberg shrugged his shoulders with a smile: "You must surely be mad, my friend."

But all the other officers had risen and surrounded their chief, saying: "Let the captain have his way, commandant; it is terribly dull here." And the major ended by yielding. "Very well," he replied, and the baron immediately sent for Le Devoir. He was an old non-commissioned officer, who had never been seen to smile, but who carried out all the orders of his superiors to the letter, no matter what they might be. He stood there, with an impassive face, while he received the baron's instructions, and then went out, and five minutes later a large military wagon, covered with tarpaulin, galloped off as fast as four horses could draw it in the pouring rain. The officers all seemed to awaken from their lethargy, their looks brightened, and they began to talk.

Although it was raining as hard as ever, the major declared that it was not so dark, and Lieutenant von Grossling said with conviction that the sky was clearing up, while Mademoiselle Fifi did not seem to be able to keep still. He got up and sat down again, and his bright eyes seemed to be looking for something to destroy. Suddenly, looking at the lady with the mustaches, the young fellow pulled out his revolver and said: "You shall not see it." And without leaving his seat he aimed, and with two successive bullets cut out both the eyes of the portrait.

"Let us make a mine!" he then exclaimed, and the conversation was suddenly interrupted, as if they had found some fresh and powerful subject of interest. The mine was his invention, his method of destruction, and his favorite amusement.

When he left the chateau, the lawful owner, Comte Fernand d'Amoys d'Uville, had not had time to carry away or to hide anything except the plate, which had been stowed away in a hole made in one of the walls. As he was very rich and had good taste, the large drawing-room, which opened into the dining-room, looked like a gallery in a museum, before his precipitate flight.

Expensive oil paintings, water colors and drawings hung against the walls, while on the tables, on the hanging shelves and in elegant glass cupboards there were a thousand ornaments: small vases, statuettes, groups of Dresden china and grotesque Chinese figures, old ivory and Venetian glass, which filled the large room with their costly and fantastic array.

Scarcely anything was left now; not that the things had been stolen, for the major would not have allowed that, but Mademoiselle Fifi would every now and then have a mine, and on those occasions all the officers thoroughly enjoyed themselves for five minutes. The little marquis went into the drawing-room to get what he wanted, and he brought back a small, delicate china teapot, which he filled with gunpowder, and carefully introduced a piece of punk through the spout. This he lighted and took his infernal machine into the next room, but he came back immediately and shut the door. The Germans all stood expectant, their faces full of childish, smiling curiosity, and as soon as the explosion had shaken the chateau, they all rushed in at once.

Mademoiselle Fifi, who got in first, clapped his hands in delight at the sight of a terra-cotta Venus, whose head had been blown off, and each picked up pieces of porcelain and wondered at the strange shape of the fragments, while the major was looking with a paternal eye at the large drawing-room, which had been wrecked after the fashion of a Nero, and was strewn with the fragments of works of art. He went out first and said with a smile: "That was a great success this time."

But there was such a cloud of smoke in the dining-room, mingled with the tobacco smoke, that they could not breathe, so the commandant opened the window, and all the officers, who had returned for a last glass of cognac, went up to it.

The moist air blew into the room, bringing with it a sort of powdery spray, which sprinkled their beards. They looked at the tall trees which were dripping with rain, at the broad valley which was covered with mist, and at the church spire in the distance, which rose up like a gray point in the beating rain.

The bells had not rung since their arrival. That was the only resistance which the invaders had met with in the neighborhood. The parish priest had not refused to take in and to feed the Prussian soldiers; he had several times even drunk a bottle of beer or claret with the hostile commandant, who often employed him as a benevolent intermediary; but it was no use to ask him for a single stroke of the bells; he would sooner have allowed himself to be shot. That was his way of protesting against the invasion, a peaceful and silent protest, the only one, he said, which was suitable to a priest, who was a man of mildness, and not of blood; and every one, for twenty-five miles round, praised Abbe Chantavoine's firmness and heroism in venturing to proclaim the public mourning by the obstinate silence of his church bells.

The whole village, enthusiastic at his resistance, was ready to back up their pastor and to risk anything, for they looked upon that silent protest as the safeguard of the national honor. It seemed to the peasants that thus they deserved better of their country than Belfort and Strassburg, that they had set an equally valuable example, and that the name of their little village would become immortalized by that; but, with that exception, they refused their Prussian conquerors nothing.

The commandant and his officers laughed among themselves at this inoffensive courage, and as the people in the whole country round showed themselves obliging and compliant toward them, they willingly tolerated their silent patriotism. Little Baron Wilhelm alone would have liked to have forced them to ring the bells. He was very angry at his superior's politic compliance with the priest's scruples, and every day begged the commandant to allow him to sound "ding-dong, ding-dong," just once, only just once, just by way of a joke. And he asked it in the coaxing, tender voice of some loved woman who is bent on obtaining her wish, but the commandant would not yield, and to console himself, Mademoiselle Fifi made a mine in the Chateau d'Uville.

The five men stood there together for five minutes, breathing in the moist air, and at last Lieutenant Fritz said with a laugh: "The ladies will certainly not have fine weather for their drive." Then they separated, each to his duty, while the captain had plenty to do in arranging for the dinner.

When they met again toward evening they began to laugh at seeing each other as spick and span and smart as on the day of a grand review. The commandant's hair did not look so gray as it was in the morning, and the captain had shaved, leaving only his mustache, which made him look as if he had a streak of fire under his nose.

In spite of the rain, they left the window open, and one of them went to listen from time to time; and at a quarter past six the baron said he heard a rumbling in the distance. They all rushed down, and presently the wagon drove up at a gallop with its four horses steaming and blowing, and splashed with mud to their girths. Five women dismounted, five handsome girls whom a comrade of the captain, to whom Le Devoir had presented his card, had selected with care.

They had not required much pressing, as they had got to know the Prussians in the three months during which they had had to do with them, and so they resigned themselves to the men as they did to the state of affairs.

They went at once into the dining-room, which looked still more dismal in its dilapidated condition when it was lighted up; while the table covered with choice dishes, the beautiful china and glass, and the plate, which had been found in the hole in the wall where its owner had hidden it, gave it the appearance of a bandits' inn, where they were supping after committing a robbery in the place. The captain was radiant, and put his arm round the women as if he were familiar with them; and when the three young men wanted to appropriate one each, he opposed them authoritatively, reserving to himself the right to apportion them justly, according to their several ranks, so as not to offend the higher powers. Therefore, to avoid all discussion, jarring, and suspicion of partiality, he placed them all in a row according to height, and addressing the tallest, he said in a voice of command:

"What is your name?" "Pamela," she replied, raising her voice. And then he said: "Number One, called Pamela, is adjudged to the commandant." Then, having kissed Blondina, the second, as a sign of proprietorship, he proffered stout Amanda to Lieutenant Otto; Eva, "the Tomato," to Sub-lieutenant Fritz, and Rachel, the shortest of them all, a very young, dark girl, with eyes as black as ink, a Jewess, whose snub nose proved the rule which allots hooked noses to all her race, to the youngest officer, frail Count Wilhelm d'Eyrick.

They were all pretty and plump, without any distinctive features, and all had a similarity of complexion and figure.

The three young men wished to carry off their prizes immediately, under the pretext that they might wish to freshen their toilets; but the captain wisely opposed this, for he said they were quite fit to sit down to dinner, and his experience in such matters carried the day. There were only many kisses, expectant kisses.

Suddenly Rachel choked, and began to cough until the tears came into her eyes, while smoke came through her nostrils.

Under pretence of kissing her, the count had blown a whiff of tobacco into her mouth. She did not fly into a rage and did not say a word, but she looked at her tormentor with latent hatred in her dark eyes.

They sat down to dinner. The commandant seemed delighted; he made Pamela sit on his right, and Blondina on his left, and said, as he unfolded his table napkin: "That was a delightful idea of yours, captain."

Lieutenants Otto and Fritz, who were as polite as if they had been with fashionable ladies, rather intimidated their guests, but Baron von Kelweinstein beamed, made obscene remarks and seemed on fire with his crown of red hair. He paid the women compliments in French of the Rhine, and sputtered out gallant remarks, only fit for a low pothouse, from between his two broken teeth.

They did not understand him, however, and their intelligence did not seem to be awakened until he uttered foul words and broad expressions, which were mangled by his accent. Then they all began to laugh at once like crazy women and fell against each other, repeating the words, which the baron then began to say all wrong, in order that he might have the pleasure of hearing them say dirty things. They gave him as much of that stuff as he wanted, for they were drunk after the first bottle of wine, and resuming their usual habits and manners, they kissed the officers to right and left of them, pinched their arms, uttered wild cries, drank out of every glass and sang French couplets and bits of German songs which they had picked up in their daily intercourse with the enemy.

Soon the men themselves became very unrestrained, shouted and broke the plates and dishes, while the soldiers behind them waited on them stolidly. The commandant was the only one who kept any restraint upon himself.

Mademoiselle Fifi had taken Rachel on his knee, and, getting excited, at one moment he kissed the little black curls on her neck and at another he pinched her furiously and made her scream, for he was seized by a species of ferocity, and tormented by his desire to hurt her. He often held her close to him and pressed a long kiss on the Jewess' rosy mouth until she lost her breath, and at last he bit her until a stream of blood ran down her chin and on to her bodice.

For the second time she looked him full in the face, and as she bathed the wound, she said: "You will have to pay for, that!" But he merely laughed a hard laugh and said: "I will pay."

At dessert champagne was served, and the commandant rose, and in the same voice in which he would have drunk to the health of the Empress Augusta, he drank: "To our ladies!" And a series of toasts began, toasts worthy of the lowest soldiers and of drunkards, mingled with obscene jokes, which were made still more brutal by their ignorance of the language. They got up, one after the other, trying to say something witty, forcing themselves to be funny, and the women, who were so drunk that they almost fell off their chairs, with vacant looks and clammy tongues applauded madly each time.

The captain, who no doubt wished to impart an appearance of gallantry to the orgy, raised his glass again and said: "To our victories over hearts." and, thereupon Lieutenant Otto, who was a species of bear from the Black Forest, jumped up, inflamed and saturated with drink, and suddenly seized by an access of alcoholic patriotism, he cried: "To our victories over France!"

Drunk as they were, the women were silent, but Rachel turned round, trembling, and said: "See here, I know some Frenchmen in whose presence you would not dare say that." But the little count, still holding her on his knee, began to laugh, for the wine had made him very merry, and said: "Ha! ha! ha! I have never met any of them myself. As soon as we show ourselves, they run away!" The girl, who was in a terrible rage, shouted into his face: "You are lying, you dirty scoundrel!"

For a moment he looked at her steadily with his bright eyes upon her, as he had looked at the portrait before he destroyed it with bullets from his revolver, and then he began to laugh: "Ah! yes, talk about them, my dear! Should we be here now if they were brave?" And, getting excited, he exclaimed: "We are the masters! France belongs to us!" She made one spring from his knee and threw herself into her chair, while he arose, held out his glass over the table and repeated: "France and the French, the woods, the fields and the houses of France belong to us!"

The others, who were quite drunk, and who were suddenly seized by military enthusiasm, the enthusiasm of brutes, seized their glasses, and shouting, "Long live Prussia!" they emptied them at a draught.

The girls did not protest, for they were reduced to silence and were afraid. Even Rachel did not say a word, as she had no reply to make. Then the little marquis put his champagne glass, which had just been refilled, on the head of the Jewess and exclaimed: "All the women in France belong to us also!"

At that she got up so quickly that the glass upset, spilling the amber-colored wine on her black hair as if to baptize her, and broke into a hundred fragments, as it fell to the floor. Her lips trembling, she defied the looks of the officer, who was still laughing, and stammered out in a voice choked with rage:

"That—that—that—is not true—for you shall not have the women of France!"

He sat down again so as to laugh at his ease; and, trying to speak with the Parisian accent, he said: "She is good, very good! Then why did you come here, my dear?" She was thunderstruck and made no reply for a moment, for in her agitation she did not understand him at first, but as soon as she grasped his meaning she said to him indignantly and vehemently: "I! I! I am not a woman, I am only a strumpet, and that is all that Prussians want."

Almost before she had finished he slapped her full in the face; but as he was raising his hand again, as if to strike her, she seized a small dessert knife with a silver blade from the table and, almost mad with rage, stabbed him right in the hollow of his neck. Something that he was going to say was cut short in his throat, and he sat there with his mouth half open and a terrible look in his eyes.

All the officers shouted in horror and leaped up tumultuously; but, throwing her chair between the legs of Lieutenant Otto, who fell down at full length, she ran to the window, opened it before they could seize her and jumped out into the night and the pouring rain.

In two minutes Mademoiselle Fifi was dead, and Fritz and Otto drew their swords and wanted to kill the women, who threw themselves at their feet and clung to their knees. With some difficulty the major stopped the slaughter and had the four terrified girls locked up in a room under the care of two soldiers, and then he organized the pursuit of the fugitive as carefully as if he were about to engage in a skirmish, feeling quite sure that she would be caught.

The table, which had been cleared immediately, now served as a bed on which to lay out the lieutenant, and the four officers stood at the windows, rigid and sobered with the stern faces of soldiers on duty, and tried to pierce through the darkness of the night amid the steady torrent of rain. Suddenly a shot was heard and then another, a long way off; and for four hours they heard from time to time near or distant reports and rallying cries, strange words of challenge, uttered in guttural voices.

In the morning they all returned. Two soldiers had been killed and three others wounded by their comrades in the ardor of that chase and in the confusion of that nocturnal pursuit, but they had not caught Rachel.

Then the inhabitants of the district were terrorized, the houses were turned topsy-turvy, the country was scoured and beaten up, over and over again, but the Jewess did not seem to have left a single trace of her passage behind her.

When the general was told of it he gave orders to hush up the affair, so as not to set a bad example to the army, but he severely censured the commandant, who in turn punished his inferiors. The general had said: "One does not go to war in order to amuse one's self and to caress prostitutes." Graf von Farlsberg, in his exasperation, made up his mind to have his revenge on the district, but as he required a pretext for showing severity, he sent for the priest and ordered him to have the bell tolled at the funeral of Baron von Eyrick.

Contrary to all expectation, the priest showed himself humble and most respectful, and when Mademoiselle Fifi's body left the Chateau d'Uville on its way to the cemetery, carried by soldiers, preceded, surrounded and followed by soldiers who marched with loaded rifles, for the first time the bell sounded its funeral knell in a lively manner, as if a friendly hand were caressing it. At night it rang again, and the next day, and every day; it rang as much as any one could desire. Sometimes even it would start at night and sound gently through the darkness, seized with a strange joy, awakened one could not tell why. All the peasants in the neighborhood declared that it was bewitched, and nobody except the priest and the sacristan would now go near the church tower. And they went because a poor girl was living there in grief and solitude and provided for secretly by those two men.

She remained there until the German troops departed, and then one evening the priest borrowed the baker's cart and himself drove his prisoner to Rouen. When they got there he embraced her, and she quickly went back on foot to the establishment from which she had come, where the proprietress, who thought that she was dead, was very glad to see her.

A short time afterward a patriot who had no prejudices, and who liked her because of her bold deed, and who afterward loved her for herself, married her and made her a lady quite as good as many others.

A DUEL

The war was over. The Germans occupied France. The whole country was pulsating like a conquered wrestler beneath the knee of his victorious opponent.

The first trains from Paris, distracted, starving, despairing Paris, were making their way to the new frontiers, slowly passing through the country districts and the villages. The passengers gazed through the windows at the ravaged fields and burned hamlets. Prussian soldiers, in their black helmets with brass spikes, were smoking their pipes astride their chairs in front of the houses which were still left standing. Others were working or talking just as if they were members of the families. As you passed through the different towns you saw entire regiments drilling in the squares, and, in spite of the rumble of the carriage-wheels, you could every moment hear the hoarse words of command.

M. Dubuis, who during the entire siege had served as one of the National Guard in Paris, was going to join his wife and daughter, whom he had prudently sent away to Switzerland before the invasion.

Famine and hardship had not diminished his big paunch so characteristic of the rich, peace-loving merchant. He had gone through the terrible events of the past year with sorrowful resignation and bitter complaints at the savagery of men. Now that he was journeying to the frontier at the close of the war, he saw the Prussians for the first time, although he had done his duty on the ramparts and mounted guard on many a cold night.

He stared with mingled fear and anger at those bearded armed men, installed all over French soil as if they were at home, and he felt in his soul a kind of fever of impotent patriotism, at the same time also the great need of that new instinct of prudence which since then has, never left us. In the same railway carriage were two Englishmen, who had come to the country as sightseers and were gazing about them with looks of quiet curiosity. They were both also stout, and kept chatting in their own language, sometimes referring to their guidebook, and reading aloud the names of the places indicated.

Suddenly the train stopped at a little village station, and a Prussian officer jumped up with a great clatter of his sabre on the double footboard of the railway carriage. He was tall, wore a tight-fitting uniform, and had whiskers up to his eyes. His red hair seemed to be on fire, and his long mustache, of a paler hue, stuck out on both sides of his face, which it seemed to cut in two.

The Englishmen at once began staring at him, with smiles of newly awakened interest, while M. Dubuis made a show of reading a newspaper. He sat concealed in his corner like a thief in presence of a gendarme.

The train started again. The Englishmen went on chatting and looking out for the exact scene of different battles; and all of a sudden, as one of them stretched out his arm toward the horizon as he pointed out a village, the Prussian officer remarked in French, extending his long legs and lolling backward:

"I killed a dozen Frenchmen in that village and took more than a hundred prisoners."

The Englishmen, quite interested, immediately asked:

"Ha! and what is the name of this village?"

The Prussian replied:

"Pharsbourg." He added: "We caught those French scoundrels by the ears."

And he glanced toward M. Dubuis, laughing conceitedly into his mustache.

The train rolled on, still passing through hamlets occupied by the victorious army. German soldiers could be seen along the roads, on the edges of fields, standing in front of gates or chatting outside cafes. They covered the soil like African locusts.

The officer said, with a wave of his hand:

"If I had been in command, I'd have taken Paris, burned everything, killed everybody. No more France!"

The Englishman, through politeness, replied simply:

"Ah! yes."

He went on:

"In twenty years all Europe, all of it, will belong to us. Prussia is more than a match for all of them."

The Englishmen, getting uneasy, no longer replied. Their faces, which had become impassive, seemed made of wax behind their long whiskers. Then the Prussian officer began to laugh. And still, lolling back, he began to sneer. He sneered at the downfall of France, insulted the prostrate enemy; he sneered at Austria, which had been recently conquered; he sneered at the valiant but fruitless defence of the departments; he sneered at the Garde Mobile and at the useless artillery. He announced that Bismarck was going to build a city of iron with the captured cannon. And suddenly he placed his boots against the thigh of M. Dubuis, who turned away his eyes, reddening to the roots of his hair.

The Englishmen seemed to have become indifferent to all that was going on, as if they were suddenly shut up in their own island, far from the din of the world.

The officer took out his pipe, and looking fixedly at the Frenchman, said:

"You haven't any tobacco—have you?"

M. Dubuis replied:

"No, monsieur."

The German resumed:

"You might go and buy some for me when the train stops."

And he began laughing afresh as he added:

"I'll give you the price of a drink."

The train whistled, and slackened its pace. They passed a station that had been burned down; and then they stopped altogether.

The German opened the carriage door, and, catching M. Dubuis by the arm, said:

"Go and do what I told you—quick, quick!"

A Prussian detachment occupied the station. Other soldiers were standing behind wooden gratings, looking on. The engine was getting up steam before starting off again.

Then M. Dubuis hurriedly jumped on the platform, and, in spite of the warnings of the station master, dashed into the adjoining compartment.

He was alone! He tore open his waistcoat, his heart was beating so rapidly, and, gasping for breath, he wiped the perspiration from his forehead.

The train drew up at another station. And suddenly the officer appeared at the carriage door and jumped in, followed close behind by the two Englishmen, who were impelled by curiosity. The German sat facing the Frenchman, and, laughing still, said:

"You did not want to do what I asked you?"

M. Dubuis replied:

"No, monsieur."

The train had just left the station.

The officer said:

"I'll cut off your mustache to fill my pipe with."

And he put out his hand toward the Frenchman's face.

The Englishmen stared at them, retaining their previous impassive manner.

The German had already pulled out a few hairs, and was still tugging at the mustache, when M. Dubuis, with a back stroke of his hand, flung aside the officer's arm, and, seizing him by the collar, threw him down on the seat. Then, excited to a pitch of fury, his temples swollen and his eyes glaring, he kept throttling the officer with one hand, while with the other clenched he began to strike him violent blows in the face. The Prussian struggled, tried to draw his sword, to clinch with his adversary, who was on top of him. But M. Dubuis crushed him with his enormous weight and kept punching him without taking breath or knowing where his blows fell. Blood flowed down the face of the German, who, choking and with a rattling in his throat, spat out his broken teeth and vainly strove to shake off this infuriated man who was killing him.

The Englishmen had got on their feet and came closer in order to see better. They remained standing, full of mirth and curiosity, ready to bet for, or against, either combatant.

Suddenly M. Dubuis, exhausted by his violent efforts, rose and resumed his seat without uttering a word.

The Prussian did not attack him, for the savage assault had terrified and astonished the officer as well as causing him suffering. When he was able to breathe freely, he said:

"Unless you give me satisfaction with pistols I will kill you."

M. Dubuis replied:

"Whenever you like. I'm quite ready."

The German said:

"Here is the town of Strasbourg. I'll get two officers to be my seconds, and there will be time before the train leaves the station."

M. Dubuis, who was puffing as hard as the engine, said to the Englishmen:

"Will you be my seconds?" They both answered together:

"Oh, yes!"

And the train stopped.

In a minute the Prussian had found two comrades, who brought pistols, and they made their way toward the ramparts.

The Englishmen were continually looking at their watches, shuffling their feet and hurrying on with the preparations, uneasy lest they should be too late for the train.

M. Dubuis had never fired a pistol in his life.

They made him stand twenty paces away from his enemy. He was asked:

"Are you ready?"

While he was answering, "Yes, monsieur," he noticed that one of the Englishmen had opened his umbrella in order to keep off the rays of the sun.

A voice gave the signal:

"Fire!"

M. Dubuis fired at random without delay, and he was amazed to see the Prussian opposite him stagger, lift up his arms and fall forward, dead. He had killed the officer.

One of the Englishmen exclaimed: "Ah!" He was quivering with delight, with satisfied curiosity and joyous impatience. The other, who still kept his watch in his hand, seized M. Dubuis' arm and hurried him in double-quick time toward the station, his fellow-countryman marking time as he ran beside them, with closed fists, his elbows at his sides, "One, two; one, two!"

And all three, running abreast rapidly, made their way to the station like three grotesque figures in a comic newspaper.

The train was on the point of starting. They sprang into their carriage. Then the Englishmen, taking off their travelling caps, waved them three times over their heads, exclaiming:

"Hip! hip! hip! hurrah!"

And gravely, one after the other, they extended their right hands to M. Dubuis and then went back and sat down in their own corner.

VOLUME II

THE COLONEL'S IDEAS

"Upon my word," said Colonel Laporte, "although I am old and gouty, my legs as stiff as two pieces of wood, yet if a pretty woman were to tell me to go through the eye of a needle, I believe I should take a jump at it, like a clown through a hoop. I shall die like that; it is in the blood. I am an old beau, one of the old school, and the sight of a woman, a pretty woman, stirs me to the tips of my toes. There!

"We are all very much alike in France in this respect; we still remain knights, knights of love and fortune, since God has been abolished whose bodyguard we really were. But nobody can ever get woman out of our hearts; there she is, and there she will remain, and we love her, and shall continue to love her, and go on committing all kinds of follies on her account as long as there is a France on the map of Europe; and even if France were to be wiped off the map, there would always be Frenchmen left.

"When I am in the presence of a woman, of a pretty woman, I feel capable of anything. By Jove! when I feel her looks penetrating me, her confounded looks which set your blood on fire, I should like to do I don't know what; to fight a duel, to have a row, to smash the furniture, in order to show that I am the strongest, the bravest, the most daring and the most devoted of men.

"But I am not the only one, certainly not; the whole French army is like me, I swear to you. From the common soldier to the general, we all start out, from the van to the rear guard, when there is a woman in the case, a pretty woman. Do you remember what

Joan of Arc made us do formerly? Come. I will make a bet that if a pretty woman had taken command of the army on the eve of Sedan, when Marshal MacMahon was wounded, we should have broken through the Prussian lines, by Jove! and had a drink out of their guns.

"It was not a Trochu, but a Sainte-Genevieve, who was needed in Paris; and I remember a little anecdote of the war which proves that we are capable of everything in presence of a woman.

"I was a captain, a simple captain, at the time, and I was in command of a detachment of scouts, who were retreating through a district which swarmed with Prussians. We were surrounded, pursued, tired out and half dead with fatigue and hunger, but we were bound to reach Bar-sur-Tain before the morrow, otherwise we should be shot, cut down, massacred. I do not know how we managed to escape so far. However, we had ten leagues to go during the night, ten leagues through the night, ten leagues through the snow, and with empty stomachs, and I thought to myself:

"'It is all over; my poor devils of fellows will never be able to do it.'

"We had eaten nothing since the day before, and the whole day long we remained hidden in a barn, huddled close together, so as not to feel the cold so much, unable to speak or even move, and sleeping by fits and starts, as one does when worn out with fatigue.

"It was dark by five o'clock, that wan darkness of the snow, and I shook my men. Some of them would not get up; they were almost incapable of moving or of standing upright; their joints were stiff from cold and hunger.

"Before us there was a large expanse of flat, bare country; the snow was still falling like a curtain, in large, white flakes, which concealed everything under a thick, frozen coverlet, a coverlet of frozen wool One might have thought that it was the end of the world.

"'Come, my lads, let us start.'

"They looked at the thick white flakes that were coming down, and they seemed to think: 'We have had enough of this; we may just as well die here!' Then I took out my revolver and said:

"'I will shoot the first man who flinches.' And so they set off, but very slowly, like men whose legs were of very little use to them, and I sent four of them three hundred yards ahead to scout, and the others followed pell-mell, walking at random and without any order. I put the strongest in the rear, with orders to quicken the pace of the sluggards with the points of their bayonets in the back.

"The snow seemed as if it were going to bury us alive; it powdered our kepis and cloaks without melting, and made phantoms of us, a kind of spectres of dead, weary soldiers. I said to myself: 'We shall never get out of this except by a miracle.'

"Sometimes we had to stop for a few minutes, on account of those who could not follow us, and then we heard nothing except the falling snow, that vague, almost undiscernible sound made by the falling flakes. Some of the men shook themselves, others did not move, and so I gave the order to set off again. They shouldered their rifles, and with weary feet we resumed our march, when suddenly the scouts fell back. Something had alarmed them; they had heard voices in front of them. I sent forward six men and a sergeant and waited.

"All at once a shrill cry, a woman's cry, pierced through the heavy silence of the snow, and in a few minutes they brought back two prisoners, an old man and a girl, whom I questioned in a low voice. They were escaping from the Prussians, who had occupied their house during the evening and had got drunk. The father was alarmed on his daughter's account, and, without even telling their servants, they had made their escape in the darkness. I saw immediately that they belonged to the better class. I invited them to accompany us, and we started off again, the old man who knew the road acting as our guide.

"It had ceased snowing, the stars appeared and the cold became intense. The girl, who was leaning on her father's arm, walked unsteadily as though in pain, and several times she murmured:

"'I have no feeling at all in my feet'; and I suffered more than she did to see that poor little woman dragging herself like that through the snow. But suddenly she stopped and said:

"'Father, I am so tired that I cannot go any further.'

"The old man wanted to carry her, but he could not even lift her up, and she sank to the ground with a deep sigh. We all gathered round her, and, as for me, I stamped my foot in perplexity, not knowing what to do, and being unwilling to abandon that man and girl like that, when suddenly one of the soldiers, a Parisian whom they had nicknamed Pratique, said:

"'Come, comrades, we must carry the young lady, otherwise we shall not show ourselves Frenchmen, confound it!'

"I really believe that I swore with pleasure. 'That is very good of you, my children,' I said; 'and I will take my share of the burden.'

"We could indistinctly see, through the darkness, the trees of a little wood on the left. Several of the men went into it, and soon came back with a bundle of branches made into a litter.

"'Who will lend his cape? It is for a pretty girl, comrades,' Pratique said, and ten cloaks were thrown to him. In a moment the girl was lying, warm and comfortable, among them, and was raised upon six shoulders. I placed myself at their head, on the right, well pleased with my position.

"We started off much more briskly, as if we had had a drink of wine, and I even heard some jokes. A woman is quite enough to electrify Frenchmen, you see. The soldiers, who had become cheerful and warm, had almost reformed their ranks, and an old 'franc-tireur' who was following the litter, waiting for his turn to replace the first of his comrades who might give out, said to one of his neighbors, loud enough for me to hear: "'I am not a young man now, but by—-, there is nothing like the women to put courage into you!'

"We went on, almost without stopping, until three o'clock in the morning, when suddenly our scouts fell back once more, and soon the whole detachment showed nothing but a vague shadow on the ground, as the men lay on the snow. I gave my orders in a low voice, and heard the harsh, metallic sound of the cocking, of rifles. For there, in the middle of the plain, some strange object was moving about. It looked like some enormous animal running about, now stretching out like a serpent, now coiling itself into a ball, darting to the right, then to the left, then stopping, and presently starting off again. But presently that wandering shape came nearer, and I saw a dozen lancers at full gallop, one behind the other. They had lost their way and were trying to find it.

"They were so near by that time that I could hear the loud breathing of their horses, the clinking of their swords and the creaking of their saddles, and cried: 'Fire!'

"Fifty rifle shots broke the stillness of the night, then there were four or five reports, and at last one single shot was heard, and when the smoke had cleared away, we saw that the twelve men and nine horses had fallen. Three of the animals were galloping away at a furious pace, and one of them was dragging the dead body of its rider, which rebounded violently from the ground; his foot had caught in the stirrup.

"One of the soldiers behind me gave a terrible laugh and said: 'There will be some widows there!'

"Perhaps he was married. A third added: 'It did not take long!'

"A head emerged from the litter.

"'What is the matter?' she asked; 'are you fighting?'

"'It is nothing, mademoiselle,' I replied; 'we have got rid of a dozen Prussians!'

"'Poor fellows!' she said. But as she was cold, she quickly disappeared beneath the cloaks again, and we started off once more. We marched on for a long time, and at last the sky began to grow lighter. The snow became quite clear, luminous and glistening, and a rosy tint appeared in the east. Suddenly a voice in the distance cried:

"'Who goes there?'

"The whole detachment halted, and I advanced to give the countersign. We had reached the French lines, and, as my men defiled before the outpost, a commandant on horseback, whom I had informed of what had taken place, asked in a sonorous voice, as he saw the litter pass him: 'What have you in there?'

"And immediately a small head covered with light hair appeared, dishevelled and smiling, and replied:

"'It is I, monsieur.'

"At this the men raised a hearty laugh, and we felt quite light-hearted, while Pratique, who was walking by the side of the litter, waved his kepi and shouted:

"'Vive la France!' And I felt really affected. I do not know why, except that I thought it a pretty and gallant thing to say.

"It seemed to me as if we had just saved the whole of France and had done something that other men could not have done, something simple and really patriotic. I shall never forget that little face, you may be sure; and if I had to give my opinion about abolishing drums, trumpets and bugles, I should propose to replace them in every regiment by a pretty girl, and that would be even better than playing the 'Marseillaise: By Jove! it would put some spirit into a trooper to have a Madonna like that, a live Madonna, by the colonel's side."

He was silent for a few moments and then continued, with an air of conviction, and nodding his head:

"All the same, we are very fond of women, we Frenchmen!"

MOTHER SAUVAGE

Fifteen years had passed since I was at Virelogne. I returned there in the autumn to shoot with my friend Serval, who had at last rebuilt his chateau, which the Prussians had destroyed.

I loved that district. It is one of those delightful spots which have a sensuous charm for the eyes. You love it with a physical love. We, whom the country enchants, keep tender memories of certain springs, certain woods, certain pools, certain hills seen very often which have stirred us like joyful events. Sometimes our thoughts turn back to a corner in a forest, or the end of a bank, or an orchard filled with flowers, seen but a single time on some bright day, yet remaining in our hearts like the image of certain women met in the street on a spring morning in their light, gauzy dresses, leaving in soul and body an unsatisfied desire which is not to be forgotten, a feeling that you have just passed by happiness.

At Virelogne I loved the whole countryside, dotted with little woods and crossed by brooks which sparkled in the sun and looked like veins carrying blood to the earth. You fished in them for crawfish, trout and eels. Divine happiness! You could bathe in places and you often found snipe among the high grass which grew along the borders of these small water courses.

I was stepping along light as a goat, watching my two dogs running ahead of me, Serval, a hundred metres to my right, was beating a field of lucerne. I turned round by the thicket which forms the boundary of the wood of Sandres and I saw a cottage in ruins.

Suddenly I remembered it as I had seen it the last time, in 1869, neat, covered with vines, with chickens before the door. What is sadder than a dead house, with its skeleton standing bare and sinister?

I also recalled that inside its doors, after a very tiring day, the good woman had given me a glass of wine to drink and that Serval had told me the history of its people. The father, an old poacher, had been killed by the gendarmes. The son, whom I had once seen, was a tall, dry fellow who also passed for a fierce slayer of game. People called them "Les Sauvage."

Was that a name or a nickname?

I called to Serval. He came up with his long strides like a crane.

I asked him:

"What's become of those people?"

This was his story:

When war was declared the son Sauvage, who was then thirty-three years old, enlisted, leaving his mother alone in the house. People did not pity the old woman very much because she had money; they knew it.

She remained entirely alone in that isolated dwelling, so far from the village, on the edge of the wood. She was not afraid, however, being of the same strain as the men folk—a hardy old woman, tall and thin, who seldom laughed and with whom one never jested. The women of the fields laugh but little in any case, that is men's business. But they themselves have sad and narrowed hearts, leading a melancholy, gloomy life. The peasants imbibe a little noisy merriment at the tavern, but their helpmates always have grave, stern countenances. The muscles of their faces have never learned the motions of laughter.

Mother Sauvage continued her ordinary existence in her cottage, which was soon covered by the snows. She came to the village once a week to get bread and a little meat. Then she returned to her house. As there was talk of wolves, she went out with a gun upon her shoulder—her son's gun, rusty and with the butt worn by the rubbing of the hand—and she was a strange sight, the tall "Sauvage," a little bent, going with slow strides over the snow, the muzzle of the piece extending beyond the black headdress, which confined her head and imprisoned her white hair, which no one had ever seen.

One day a Prussian force arrived. It was billeted upon the inhabitants, according to the property and resources of each. Four were allotted to the old woman, who was known to be rich.

They were four great fellows with fair complexion, blond beards and blue eyes, who had not grown thin in spite of the fatigue which they had endured already and who also, though in a conquered country, had remained kind and gentle. Alone with this aged woman, they showed themselves full of consideration, sparing her, as much as they could, all expense and fatigue. They could be seen, all four of them, making their toilet at the well in their shirt-sleeves in the gray dawn, splashing with great swishes of water their pink-white northern skin, while La Mere Sauvage went and came, preparing their soup. They would be seen cleaning the kitchen, rubbing the tiles, splitting wood, peeling potatoes, doing up all the housework like four good sons around their mother.

But the old woman thought always of her own son, so tall and thin, with his hooked nose and his brown eyes and his heavy mustache which made a roll of black hair upon his lip. She asked every day of each of the soldiers who were installed beside her hearth: "Do you know where the French marching regiment, No. 23, was sent? My boy is in it."

They invariably answered, "No, we don't know, don't know a thing at all." And, understanding her pain and her uneasiness—they who had mothers, too, there at home—they rendered her a thousand little services. She loved them well, moreover, her four enemies, since the peasantry have no patriotic hatred; that belongs to the upper class alone. The humble, those who pay the most because they are poor and because every new burden crushes them down; those who are killed in masses, who make the true cannon's prey because they are so many; those, in fine, who suffer most cruelly the atrocious miseries of war because they are the feeblest and offer least resistance—they hardly understand at all those bellicose ardors, that excitable sense of honor or those pretended political combinations which in six months exhaust two nations, the conqueror with the conquered.

They said in the district, in speaking of the Germans of La Mere Sauvage:

"There are four who have found a soft place."

Now, one morning, when the old woman was alone in the house, she observed, far off on the plain, a man coming toward her dwelling. Soon she recognized him; it was the postman to distribute the letters. He gave her a folded paper and she drew out of her case the spectacles which she used for sewing. Then she read:

MADAME SAUVAGE: This letter is to tell you sad news. Your boy

Victor was killed yesterday by a shell which almost cut him in two.

I was near by, as we stood next each other in the company, and he told me about you and asked me to let you know on the same day if anything happened to him.

I took his watch, which was in his pocket, to bring it back to you when the war is done.

CESAIRE RIVOT,

Soldier of the 2d class, March. Reg. No. 23.

The letter was dated three weeks back.

She did not cry at all. She remained motionless, so overcome and stupefied that she did not even suffer as yet. She thought: "There's Victor killed now." Then little by little the tears came to her eyes and the sorrow filled her heart. Her thoughts came, one by one, dreadful, torturing. She would never kiss him again, her child, her big boy, never again! The gendarmes had killed the father, the Prussians had killed the son. He had been cut in two by a cannon-ball. She seemed to see the thing, the horrible thing: the head falling, the eyes open, while he chewed the corner of his big mustache as he always did in moments of anger.

What had they done with his body afterward? If they had only let her have her boy back as they had brought back her husband—with the bullet in the middle of the forehead!

But she heard a noise of voices. It was the Prussians returning from the village. She hid her letter very quickly in her pocket, and she received them quietly, with her ordinary face, having had time to wipe her eyes.

They were laughing, all four, delighted, for they brought with them a fine rabbit—stolen, doubtless—and they made signs to the old woman that there was to be something good to east.

She set herself to work at once to prepare breakfast, but when it came to killing the rabbit, her heart failed her. And yet it was not the first. One of the soldiers struck it down with a blow of his fist behind the ears.

The beast once dead, she skinned the red body, but the sight of the blood which she was touching, and which covered her hands, and which she felt cooling and coagulating, made her tremble from head to foot, and she kept seeing her big boy cut in two, bloody, like this still palpitating animal.

She sat down at table with the Prussians, but she could not eat, not even a mouthful. They devoured the rabbit without bothering themselves about her. She looked at them sideways, without speaking, her face so impassive that they perceived nothing.

All of a sudden she said: "I don't even know your names, and here's a whole month that we've been together." They understood, not without difficulty, what she wanted, and told their names.

That was not sufficient; she had them written for her on a paper, with the addresses of their families, and, resting her spectacles on her great nose, she contemplated that strange handwriting, then folded the sheet and put it in her pocket, on top of the letter which told her of the death of her son.

When the meal was ended she said to the men:

"I am going to work for you."

And she began to carry up hay into the loft where they slept.

They were astonished at her taking all this trouble; she explained to them that thus they would not be so cold; and they helped her. They heaped the stacks of hay as high as the straw roof, and in that manner they made a sort of great chamber with four walls of fodder, warm and perfumed, where they should sleep splendidly.

At dinner one of them was worried to see that La Mere Sauvage still ate nothing. She told him that she had pains in her stomach. Then she kindled a good fire to warm herself, and the four Germans ascended to their lodging-place by the ladder which served them every night for this purpose.

As soon as they closed the trapdoor the old woman removed the ladder, then opened the outside door noiselessly and went back to look for more bundles of straw, with which she filled her kitchen. She went barefoot in the snow, so softly that no sound was heard. From time to time she listened to the sonorous and unequal snoring of the four soldiers who were fast asleep.

When she judged her preparations to be sufficient, she threw one of the bundles into the fireplace, and when it was alight she scattered it over all the others. Then she went outside again and looked.

In a few seconds the whole interior of the cottage was illumined with a brilliant light and became a frightful brasier, a gigantic fiery furnace, whose glare streamed out of the narrow window and threw a glittering beam upon the snow.

Then a great cry issued from the top of the house; it was a clamor of men shouting heartrending calls of anguish and of terror. Finally the trapdoor having given way, a whirlwind of fire shot up into the loft, pierced the straw roof, rose to the sky like the immense flame of a torch, and all the cottage flared.

Nothing more was heard therein but the crackling of the fire, the cracking of the walls, the falling of the rafters. Suddenly the roof fell in and the burning carcass of the dwelling hurled a great plume of sparks into the air, amid a cloud of smoke.

The country, all white, lit up by the fire, shone like a cloth of silver tinted with red.

A bell, far off, began to toll.

The old "Sauvage" stood before her ruined dwelling, armed with her gun, her son's gun, for fear one of those men might escape.

When she saw that it was ended, she threw her weapon into the brasier. A loud report followed.

People were coming, the peasants, the Prussians.

They found the woman seated on the trunk of a tree, calm and satisfied.

A German officer, but speaking French like a son of France, demanded:

"Where are your soldiers?"

She reached her bony arm toward the red heap of fire which was almost out and answered with a strong voice:

"There!"

They crowded round her. The Prussian asked:

"How did it take fire?"

"It was I who set it on fire."

They did not believe her, they thought that the sudden disaster had made her crazy. While all pressed round and listened, she told the story from beginning to end, from the arrival of the letter to the last shriek of the men who were burned with her house, and never omitted a detail.

When she had finished, she drew two pieces of paper from her pocket, and, in order to distinguish them by the last gleams of the fire, she again adjusted her spectacles. Then she said, showing one:

"That, that is the death of Victor." Showing the other, she added, indicating the red ruins with a bend of the head: "Here are their names, so that you can write home." She quietly held a sheet of paper out to the officer, who held her by the shoulders, and she continued:

"You must write how it happened, and you must say to their mothers that it was I who did that, Victoire Simon, la Sauvage! Do not forget."

The officer shouted some orders in German. They seized her, they threw her against the walls of her house, still hot. Then twelve men drew quickly up before her, at twenty paces. She did not move. She had understood; she waited.

An order rang out, followed instantly by a long report. A belated shot went off by itself, after the others.

The old woman did not fall. She sank as though they had cut off her legs.

The Prussian officer approached. She was almost cut in two, and in her withered hand she held her letter bathed with blood.

My friend Serval added:

"It was by way of reprisal that the Germans destroyed the chateau of the district, which belonged to me."

I thought of the mothers of those four fine fellows burned in that house and of the horrible heroism of that other mother shot against the wall.

And I picked up a little stone, still blackened by the flames.

EPIPHANY

I should say I did remember that Epiphany supper during the war! exclaimed Count de Garens, an army captain.

I was quartermaster of cavalry at the time, and for a fortnight had been scouting in front of the German advance guard. The evening before we had cut down a few Uhlans and had lost three men, one of whom was that poor little Raudeville. You remember Joseph de Raudeville, of course.

Well, on that day my commanding officer ordered me to take six troopers and to go and occupy the village of Porterin, where there had been five skirmishes in three weeks, and to hold it all night. There were not twenty houses left standing, not a dozen houses in that wasps' nest. So I took ten troopers and set out about four o'clock, and at five o'clock, while it was still pitch dark, we reached the first houses of Porterin. I halted and ordered Marchas—you know Pierre de Marchas, who afterward married little Martel-Auvelin, the daughter of the Marquis de Martel-Auvelin—to go alone into the village, and to report to me what he saw.

I had selected nothing but volunteers, all men of good family. It is pleasant when on duty not to be forced to be on intimate terms with unpleasant fellows. This Marchas was as smart as possible, cunning as a fox and supple as a serpent. He could scent the Prussians as a dog can scent a hare, could discover food where we should have died of hunger without him, and obtained information from everybody, and information which was always reliable, with incredible cleverness.

In ten minutes he returned. "All right," he said; "there have been no Prussians here for three days. It is a sinister place, is this village. I have been talking to a Sister of Mercy, who is caring for four or five wounded men in an abandoned convent."

I ordered them to ride on, and we entered the principal street. On the right and left we could vaguely see roofless walls, which were hardly visible in the profound darkness. Here and there a light was burning in a room; some family had remained to keep its house standing as well as they were able; a family of brave or of poor people. The rain began to fall, a fine, icy cold rain, which froze as it fell on our cloaks. The horses stumbled against stones, against beams, against furniture. Marchas guided us, going before us on foot, and leading his horse by the bridle.

"Where are you taking us to?" I asked him. And he replied: "I have a place for us to lodge in, and a rare good one." And we presently stopped before a small house, evidently belonging to some proprietor of the middle class. It stood on the street, was quite inclosed, and had a garden in the rear.

Marchas forced open the lock by means of a big stone which he picked up near the garden gate; then he mounted the steps, smashed in the front door with his feet and shoulders, lit a bit of wax candle, which he was never without, and went before us into the comfortable apartments of some rich private individual, guiding us with admirable assurance, as if he lived in this house which he now saw for the first time.

Two troopers remained outside to take care of our horses, and Marchas said to stout Ponderel, who followed him: "The stables must be on the left; I saw that as we came in; go and put the animals up there, for we do not need them"; and then, turning to me, he said: "Give your orders, confound it all!"

This fellow always astonished me, and I replied with a laugh: "I will post my sentinels at the country approaches and will return to you here."

"How many men are you going to take?"

"Five. The others will relieve them at five o'clock in the evening."

"Very well. Leave me four to look after provisions, to do the cooking and to set the table. I will go and find out where the wine is hidden."

I went off, to reconnoitre the deserted streets until they ended in the open country, so as to post my sentries there.

Half an hour later I was back, and found Marchas lounging in a great easy-chair, the covering of which he had taken off, from love of luxury, as he said. He was warming his feet at the fire and smoking an excellent cigar, whose perfume filled the room. He was alone, his elbows resting on the arms of the chair, his head sunk between his shoulders, his cheeks flushed, his eyes bright, and looking delighted.

I heard the noise of plates and dishes in the next room, and Marchas said to me, smiling in a contented manner: "This is famous; I found the champagne under the flight of steps outside, the brandy—fifty bottles of the very finest in the kitchen garden under a pear tree, which did not seem to me to be quite straight when I looked at it by the light of my lantern. As for solids, we have two fowls, a goose, a duck, and three pigeons. They are being cooked at this moment. It is a delightful district."

I sat down opposite him, and the fire in the grate was burning my nose and cheeks. "Where did you find this wood?" I asked. "Splendid wood," he replied. "The owner's carriage. It is the paint which is causing all this flame, an essence of punch and varnish. A capital house!"

I laughed, for I saw the creature was funny, and he went on: "Fancy this being the Epiphany! I have had a bean put into the goose dressing; but there is no queen; it is really very annoying!" And I repeated like an echo: "It is annoying, but what do you want me to do in the matter?" "To find some, of course." "Some women. Women?—you must be mad?" "I managed to find the brandy under the pear tree, and the champagne under the steps; and yet there was nothing to guide me, while as for you, a petticoat is a sure bait. Go and look, old fellow."

He looked so grave, so convinced, that I could not tell whether he was joking or not, and so I replied: "Look here, Marchas, are you having a joke with me?" "I never joke on duty." "But where the devil do you expect me to find any women?" "Where you like; there must be two or three remaining in the neighborhood, so ferret them out and bring them here."

I got up, for it was too hot in front of the fire, and Marchas went off:

"Do you want an idea?" "Yes." "Go and see the priest." "The priest? What for?" "Ask him to supper, and beg him to bring a woman with him." "The priest! A woman! Ha! ha! ha!"

But Marchas continued with extraordinary gravity: "I am not laughing; go and find the priest and tell him how we are situated, and, as he must be horribly dull, he will come. But tell him that we want one woman at least, a lady, of course, since we, are all men of the world. He is sure to know his female parishioners on the tips of his fingers, and if there is one to suit us, and you manage it well, he will suggest her to you."

"Come, come, Marchas, what are you thinking of?" "My dear Garens, you can do this quite well. It will even be very funny. We are well bred, by Jove! and we will put on our most distinguished manners and our grandest style. Tell the abbe who we are, make him laugh, soften his heart, coax him and persuade him!" "No, it is impossible."

He drew his chair close to mine, and as he knew my special weakness, the scamp continued: "Just think what a swaggering thing it will be to do and how amusing to tell about; the whole army will talk about it, and it will give you a famous reputation."

I hesitated, for the adventure rather tempted me, and he persisted: "Come, my little Garens. You are the head of this detachment, and you alone can go and call on the head of the church in this neighborhood. I beg of you to go, and I promise you that after the war I will relate the whole affair in verse in the Revue de Deux Mondes. You owe this much to your men, for you have made them march enough during the last month."

I got up at last and asked: "Where is the priest's house?" "Take the second turning at the end of the street, you will see an avenue, and at the end of the avenue you will find the church. The parsonage is beside it." As I went out, he called out: "Tell him the bill of fare, to make him hungry!"

I discovered the ecclesiastic's little house without any difficulty; it was by the side of a large, ugly brick church. I knocked at the door with my fist, as there was neither bell nor knocker, and a loud voice from inside asked: "Who is there?" To which I replied: "A quartermaster of hussars."

I heard the noise of bolts and of a key being turned, and found myself face to face with a tall priest with a large stomach, the chest of a prizefighter, formidable hands projecting from turned-up sleeves, a red face, and the look of a kind man. I gave him a military salute and said: "Good-day, Monsieur le Cure."

He had feared a surprise, some marauders' ambush, and he smiled as he replied: "Good-day, my friend; come in." I followed him into a small room with a red tiled floor, in which a small fire was burning, very different to Marchas' furnace, and he gave me a chair and said: "What can I do for you?" "Monsieur, allow me first of all to introduce myself"; and I gave him my card, which he took and read half aloud: "Le Comte de Garens."

I continued: "There are eleven of us here, Monsieur l'Abbe, five on picket duty, and six installed at the house of an unknown inhabitant. The names of the six are: Garens, myself; Pierre de Marchas, Ludovic de Ponderel, Baron d'Streillis, Karl Massouligny, the painter's son, and Joseph Herbon, a young musician. I have come to ask you, in their name and my own, to do us the honor of supping with us. It is an Epiphany supper, Monsieur le Cure, and we should like to make it a little cheerful."

The priest smiled and murmured: "It seems to me to be hardly a suitable occasion for amusing one's self." And I replied: "We are fighting during the day, monsieur. Fourteen of our comrades have been killed in a month, and three fell as late as yesterday. It is war time. We stake our life at every moment; have we not, therefore, the right to amuse ourselves freely? We are Frenchmen, we like to laugh, and we can laugh everywhere. Our fathers laughed on the scaffold! This evening we should like to cheer ourselves up a little, like gentlemen, and not like soldiers; you understand me, I hope. Are we wrong?"

He replied quickly: "You are quite right, my friend, and I accept your invitation with great pleasure." Then he called out: "Hermance!"

An old bent, wrinkled, horrible peasant woman appeared and said: "What do you want?" "I shall not dine at home, my daughter." "Where are you going to dine then?" "With some gentlemen, the hussars."

I felt inclined to say: "Bring your servant with you," just to see Marchas' face, but I did not venture, and continued: "Do you know any one among your parishioners, male or female, whom I could invite as well?" He hesitated, reflected, and then said: "No, I do not know anybody!"

I persisted: "Nobody! Come, monsieur, think; it would be very nice to have some ladies, I mean to say, some married couples! I know nothing about your parishioners. The baker and his wife, the grocer, the—the—the—watchmaker—the—shoemaker—the—the druggist with Mrs. Druggist. We have a good spread and plenty of wine, and we should be enchanted to leave pleasant recollections of ourselves with the people here."

The priest thought again for a long time, and then said resolutely: "No, there is nobody." I began to laugh. "By Jove, Monsieur le Cure, it is very annoying not to have an Epiphany queen, for we have the bean. Come, think. Is there not a married mayor, or a married deputy mayor, or a married municipal councillor or a schoolmaster?" "No, all the ladies have gone away." "What, is there not in the whole place some good tradesman's wife with her good tradesman, to whom we might give this pleasure, for it would be a pleasure to them, a great pleasure under present circumstances?"

But, suddenly, the cure began to laugh, and laughed so violently that he fairly shook, and presently exclaimed: "Ha! ha! ha! I have got what you want, yes. I have got what you want! Ha! ha! ha! We will laugh and enjoy ourselves, my children; we will have some fun. How pleased the ladies will be, I say, how delighted they will be! Ha! ha! Where are you staying?"

I described the house, and he understood where it was. "Very good," he said. "It belongs to Monsieur Bertin-Lavaille. I will be there in half an hour, with four ladies! Ha! ha! ha! four ladies!"

He went out with me, still laughing, and left me, repeating: "That is capital; in half an hour at Bertin-Lavaille's house."

I returned quickly, very much astonished and very much puzzled. "Covers for how many?" Marchas asked, as soon as he saw me. "Eleven. There are six of us hussars, besides the priest and four ladies." He was thunderstruck, and I was triumphant. He repeated: "Four ladies! Did you say, four ladies?" "I said four women." "Real women?" "Real women." "Well, accept my compliments!" "I will, for I deserve them."

He got out of his armchair, opened the door, and I saw a beautiful white tablecloth on a long table, round which three hussars in blue aprons were setting out the plates and glasses. "There are some women coming!" Marchas cried. And the three men began to dance and to cheer with all their might.

Everything was ready, and we were waiting. We waited for nearly an hour, while a delicious smell of roast poultry pervaded the whole house. At last, however, a knock against the shutters made us all jump up at the same moment. Stout Ponderel ran to open the door, and in less than a minute a little Sister of Mercy appeared in the doorway. She was thin, wrinkled and timid, and successively greeted the four bewildered hussars who saw her enter. Behind her, the noise of sticks sounded on the tiled floor in the vestibule, and as soon as she had come into the drawing-room, I saw three old heads in white caps, following each other one by one, who came in, swaying with different movements, one inclining to the right, while the other inclined to the left. And three worthy women appeared, limping, dragging their legs behind them, crippled by illness and deformed through old age, three infirm old women, past service, the only three pensioners who were able to walk in the home presided over by Sister Saint-Benedict.

She had turned round to her invalids, full of anxiety for them, and then, seeing my quartermaster's stripes, she said to me: "I am much obliged to you for thinking of these poor women. They have very little pleasure in life, and you are at the same time giving them a great treat and doing them a great honor."

I saw the priest, who had remained in the dark hallway, and was laughing heartily, and I began to laugh in my turn, especially when I saw Marchas' face. Then, motioning the nun to the seats, I said:

"Sit down, sister; we are very proud and very happy that you have accepted our unpretentious invitation."

She took three chairs which stood against the wall, set them before the fire, led her three old women to them, settled them on them, took their sticks and shawls, which she put into a corner, and then, pointing to the first, a thin woman with an enormous stomach, who was evidently suffering from the dropsy, she said: "This is Mother Paumelle; whose husband was killed by falling from a roof, and whose son died in Africa; she is sixty years old." Then she pointed to another, a tall woman, whose head trembled unceasingly: "This is Mother Jean-Jean, who is sixty-seven. She is nearly blind, for her face was terribly singed in a fire, and her right leg was half burned off."

Then she pointed to the third, a sort of dwarf, with protruding, round, stupid eyes, which she rolled incessantly in all directions, "This is La Putois, an idiot. She is only forty-four."

I bowed to the three women as if I were being presented to some royal highnesses, and turning to the priest, I said: "You are an excellent man, Monsieur l'Abbe, to whom all of us here owe a debt of gratitude."

Everybody was laughing, in fact, except Marchas, who seemed furious, and just then Karl Massouligny cried: "Sister Saint-Benedict, supper is on the table!"

I made her go first with the priest, then I helped up Mother Paumelle, whose arm I took and dragged her into the next room, which was no easy task, for she seemed heavier than a lump of iron.

Stout Ponderel gave his arm to Mother Jean-Jean, who bemoaned her crutch, and little Joseph Herbon took the idiot, La Putois, to the dining-room, which was filled with the odor of the viands.

As soon as we were opposite our plates, the sister clapped her hands three times, and, with the precision of soldiers presenting arms, the women made a rapid sign of the cross, and then the priest slowly repeated the Benedictus in Latin. Then we sat down, and the two fowls appeared, brought in by Marchas, who chose to wait at table, rather than to sit down as a guest to this ridiculous repast.

But I cried: "Bring the champagne at once!" and a cork flew out with the noise of a pistol, and in spite of the resistance of the priest and of the kind sister, the three hussars, sitting by the side of the three invalids, emptied their three full glasses down their throats by force.

Massouligny, who possessed the faculty of making himself at home, and of being on good terms with every one, wherever he was, made love to Mother Paumelle in the drollest manner. The dropsical woman, who had retained her cheerfulness in spite of her misfortunes, answered him banteringly in a high falsetto voice which appeared as if it were put on, and she laughed so heartily at her neighbor's jokes that it was quite alarming. Little Herbon had seriously undertaken the task of making the idiot drunk, and

Baron d'Streillis, whose wits were not always particularly sharp, was questioning old Jean-Jean about the life, the habits, and the rules of the hospital.

The nun said to Massouligny in consternation:

"Oh! oh! you will make her ill; pray do not make her laugh like that, monsieur. Oh! monsieur—" Then she got up and rushed at Herbon to take from him a full glass which he was hastily emptying down La Putois' throat, while the priest shook with laughter, and said to the sister: "Never mind; just this once, it will not hurt them. Do leave them alone."

After the two fowls they ate the duck, which was flanked by the three pigeons and the blackbird, and then the goose appeared, smoking, golden-brown, and diffusing a warm odor of hot, browned roast meat. La Paumelle, who was getting lively, clapped her hands; La Jean-Jean left off answering the baron's numerous questions, and La Putois uttered grunts of pleasure, half cries and half sighs, as little children do when one shows them candy. "Allow me to take charge of this animal," the cure said. "I understand these sort of operations better than most people." "Certainly, Monsieur l'Abbe," and the sister said: "How would it be to open the window a little? They are too warm, and I am afraid they will be ill."

I turned to Marchas: "Open the window for a minute." He did so; the cold outer air as it came in made the candles flare, and the steam from the goose, which the cure was scientifically carving, with a table napkin round his neck, whirl about. We watched him doing it, without speaking now, for we were interested in his attractive handiwork, and seized with renewed appetite at the sight of that enormous golden-brown bird, whose limbs fell one after another into the brown gravy at the bottom of the dish. At that moment, in the midst of that greedy silence which kept us all attentive, the distant report of a shot came in at the open window.

I started to my feet so quickly that my chair fell down behind me, and I shouted: "To saddle, all of you! You, Marchas, take two men and go and see what it is. I shall expect you back here in five minutes." And while the three riders went off at full gallop through the night, I got into the saddle with my three remaining hussars, in front of the steps of the villa, while the cure, the sister and the three old women showed their frightened faces at the window.

We heard nothing more, except the barking of a dog in the distance. The rain had ceased, and it was cold, very cold, and soon I heard the gallop of a horse, of a single horse, coming back. It was Marchas, and I called out to him: "Well?" "It is nothing; Francois has wounded an old peasant who refused to answer his challenge: 'Who goes there?' and who continued to advance in spite of the order to keep off; but they are bringing him here, and we shall see what is the matter."

I gave orders for the horses to be put back in the stable, and I sent my two soldiers to meet the others, and returned to the house. Then the cure, Marchas, and I took a mattress into the room to lay the wounded man on; the sister tore up a table napkin in order to make lint, while the three frightened women remained huddled up in a corner.

Soon I heard the rattle of sabres on the road, and I took a candle to show a light to the men who were returning; and they soon appeared, carrying that inert, soft, long, sinister object which a human body becomes when life no longer sustains it.

They put the wounded man on the mattress that had been prepared for him, and I saw at the first glance that he was dying. He had the death rattle and was spitting up blood, which ran out of the corners of his mouth at every gasp. The man was covered with blood! His cheeks, his beard, his hair, his neck and his clothes seemed to have been soaked, to have been dipped in a red tub; and that blood stuck to him, and had become a dull color which was horrible to look at.

The wounded man, wrapped up in a large shepherd's cloak, occasionally opened his dull, vacant eyes, which seemed stupid with astonishment, like those of animals wounded by a sportsman, which fall at his feet, more than half dead already, stupefied with terror and surprise.

The cure exclaimed: "Ah, it is old Placide, the shepherd from Les Moulins. He is deaf, poor man, and heard nothing. Ah! Oh, God! they have killed the unhappy man!" The sister had opened his blouse and shirt, and was looking at a little blue hole in his chest, which was not bleeding any more. "There is nothing to be done," she said.

The shepherd was gasping terribly and bringing up blood with every last breath, and in his throat, to the very depth of his lungs, they could hear an ominous and continued gurgling. The cure, standing in front of him, raised his right hand, made the sign of the cross, and in a slow and solemn voice pronounced the Latin words which purify men's souls, but before they were finished, the old man's body trembled violently, as if something had given way inside him, and he ceased to breathe. He was dead.

When I turned round, I saw a sight which was even more horrible than the death struggle of this unfortunate man; the three old women were standing up huddled close together, hideous, and grimacing with fear and horror. I went up to them, and they began to utter shrill screams, while La Jean-Jean, whose burned leg could no longer support her, fell to the ground at full length.

Sister Saint-Benedict left the dead man, ran up to her infirm old women, and without a word or a look for me, wrapped their shawls round them, gave them their crutches, pushed them to the door, made them go out, and disappeared with them into the dark night.

I saw that I could not even let a hussar accompany them, for the mere rattle of a sword would have sent them mad with fear.

The cure was still looking at the dead man; but at last he turned round to me and said:

"Oh! What a horrible thing!"

THE MUSTACHE

CHATEAU DE SOLLES,

July 30, 1883.

My Dear Lucy:

I have no news. We live in the drawing-room, looking out at the rain. We cannot go out in this frightful weather, so we have theatricals. How stupid they are, my dear, these drawing entertainments in the repertory of real life! All is forced, coarse, heavy. The jokes are like cannon balls, smashing everything in their passage. No wit, nothing natural, no sprightliness, no elegance. These literary men, in truth, know nothing of society. They are perfectly ignorant of how people think and talk in our set. I do not mind if they despise our customs, our conventionalities, but I do not forgive them for not knowing them. When they want to be humorous they make puns that would do for a barrack; when they try to be jolly, they give us jokes that they must have picked up on the outer boulevard in those beer houses artists are supposed to frequent, where one has heard the same students' jokes for fifty years.

So we have taken to Theatricals. As we are only two women, my husband takes the part of a soubrette, and, in order to do that, he has shaved off his mustache. You cannot imagine, my dear Lucy, how it changes him! I no longer recognize him-by day or at night. If he did not let it grow again I think I should no longer love him; he looks so horrid like this.

In fact, a man without a mustache is no longer a man. I do not care much for a beard; it almost always makes a man look untidy. But a mustache, oh, a mustache is indispensable to a manly face. No, you would never believe how these little hair bristles on the upper lip are a relief to the eye and good in other ways. I have thought over the matter a great deal but hardly dare to write my thoughts. Words look so different on paper and the subject is so difficult, so delicate, so dangerous that it requires infinite skill to tackle it.

Well, when my husband appeared, shaven, I understood at once that I never could fall in love with a strolling actor nor a preacher, even if it were Father Didon, the most charming of all! Later when I was alone with him (my husband) it was worse still. Oh, my dear Lucy, never let yourself be kissed by a man without a mustache; their kisses have no flavor, none whatever! They no longer have the charm, the mellowness and the snap —yes, the snap—of a real kiss. The mustache is the spice.

Imagine placing to your lips a piece of dry—or moist—parchment. That is the kiss of the man without a mustache. It is not worth while.

Whence comes this charm of the mustache, will you tell me? Do I know myself? It tickles your face, you feel it approaching your mouth and it sends a little shiver through you down to the tips of your toes.

And on your neck! Have you ever felt a mustache on your neck? It intoxicates you, makes you feel creepy, goes to the tips of your fingers. You wriggle, shake your shoulders, toss back your head. You wish to get away and at the same time to remain there; it is delightful, but irritating. But how good it is!

A lip without a mustache is like a body without clothing; and one must wear clothes, very few, if you like, but still some clothing.

I recall a sentence (uttered by a politician) which has been running in my mind for three months. My husband, who keeps up with the newspapers, read me one evening a very singular speech by our Minister of Agriculture, who was called M. Meline. He may have been superseded by this time. I do not know.

I was paying no attention, but the name Meline struck me. It recalled, I do not exactly know why, the 'Scenes de la vie de boheme'. I thought it was about some grisette. That shows how scraps of the speech entered my mind. This M. Meline was making this statement to the people of Amiens, I believe, and I have ever since been trying to understand what he meant: "There is no patriotism without agriculture!" Well, I have just discovered his meaning, and I affirm in my turn that there is no love without a mustache. When you say it that way it sounds comical, does it not?

There is no love without a mustache!

"There is no patriotism without agriculture," said M. Meline, and he was right, that minister; I now understand why.

From a very different point of view the mustache is essential. It gives character to the face. It makes a man look gentle, tender, violent, a monster, a rake, enterprising! The hairy man, who does not shave off his whiskers, never has a refined look, for his features are concealed; and the shape of the jaw and the chin betrays a great deal to those who understand.

The man with a mustache retains his own peculiar expression and his refinement at the same time.

And how many different varieties of mustaches there are! Sometimes they are twisted, curled, coquettish. Those seem to be chiefly devoted to women.

Sometimes they are pointed, sharp as needles, and threatening. That kind prefers wine, horses and war.

Sometimes they are enormous, overhanging, frightful. These big ones generally conceal a fine disposition, a kindliness that borders on weakness and a gentleness that savors of timidity.

But what I adore above all in the mustache is that it is French, altogether French. It came from our ancestors, the Gauls, and has remained the insignia of our national character.

It is boastful, gallant and brave. It sips wine gracefully and knows how to laugh with refinement, while the broad-bearded jaws are clumsy in everything they do.

I recall something that made me weep all my tears and also—I see it now—made me love a mustache on a man's face.

It was during the war, when I was living with my father. I was a young girl then. One day there was a skirmish near the chateau. I had heard the firing of the cannon and of the artillery all the morning, and that evening a German colonel came and took up his abode in our house. He left the following day.

My father was informed that there were a number of dead bodies in the fields. He had them brought to our place so that they might be buried together. They were laid all along the great avenue of pines as fast as they brought them in, on both sides of the avenue, and as they began to smell unpleasant, their bodies were covered with earth until the deep trench could be dug. Thus one saw only their heads which seemed to protrude from the clayey earth and were almost as yellow, with their closed eyes.

I wanted to see them. But when I saw those two rows of frightful faces, I thought I should faint. However, I began to look at them, one by one, trying to guess what kind of men these had been.

The uniforms were concealed beneath the earth, and yet immediately, yes, immediately, my dear, I recognized the Frenchmen by their mustache!

Some of them had shaved on the very day of the battle, as though they wished to be elegant up to the last; others seemed to have a week's growth, but all wore the French mustache, very plain, the proud mustache that seems to say: "Do not take me for my bearded friend, little one; I am a brother."

And I cried, oh, I cried a great deal more than I should if I had not recognized them, the poor dead fellows.

It was wrong of me to tell you this. Now I am sad and cannot chatter any longer. Well, good-by, dear Lucy. I send you a hearty kiss. Long live the mustache! JEANNE.

MADAME BAPTISTE

The first thing I did was to look at the clock as I entered the waiting-room of the station at Loubain, and I found that I had to wait two hours and ten minutes for the Paris express.

I had walked twenty miles and felt suddenly tired. Not seeing anything on the station walls to amuse me, I went outside and stood there racking my brains to think of something to do. The street was a kind of boulevard, planted with acacias, and on either side a row of houses of varying shape and different styles of architecture, houses such as one only sees in a small town, and ascended a slight hill, at the extreme end of which there were some trees, as though it ended in a park.

From time to time a cat crossed the street and jumped over the gutters carefully. A cur sniffed at every tree and hunted for scraps from the kitchens, but I did not see a single human being, and I felt listless and disheartened. What could I do with myself? I was already thinking of the inevitable and interminable visit to the small cafe at the railway station, where I should have to sit over a glass of undrinkable beer and the illegible newspaper, when I saw a funeral procession coming out of a side street into the one in which I was, and the sight of the hearse was a relief to me. It would, at any rate, give me something to do for ten minutes.

Suddenly, however, my curiosity was aroused. The hearse was followed by eight gentlemen, one of whom was weeping, while the others were chatting together, but there was no priest, and I thought to myself:

"This is a non-religious funeral," and then I reflected that a town like Loubain must contain at least a hundred freethinkers, who would have made a point of making a manifestation. What could it be, then? The rapid pace of the procession clearly proved that the body was to be buried without ceremony, and, consequently, without the intervention of the Church.

My idle curiosity framed the most complicated surmises, and as the hearse passed me, a strange idea struck me, which was to follow it, with the eight gentlemen. That would take up my time for an hour, at least, and I accordingly walked with the others, with a sad look on my face, and, on seeing this, the two last turned round in surprise, and then spoke to each other in a low voice.

No doubt they were asking each other whether I belonged to the town, and then they consulted the two in front of them, who stared at me in turn. This close scrutiny annoyed me, and to put an end to it I went up to them, and, after bowing, I said:

"I beg your pardon, gentlemen, for interrupting your conversation, but, seeing a civil funeral, I have followed it, although I did not know the deceased gentleman whom you are accompanying."

"It was a woman," one of them said.

I was much surprised at hearing this, and asked:

"But it is a civil funeral, is it not?"

The other gentleman, who evidently wished to tell me all about it, then said: "Yes and no. The clergy have refused to allow us the use of the church."

On hearing this I uttered a prolonged "A-h!" of astonishment. I could not understand it at all, but my obliging neighbor continued:

"It is rather a long story. This young woman committed suicide, and that is the reason why she cannot be buried with any religious ceremony. The gentleman who is walking first, and who is crying, is her husband."

I replied with some hesitation:

"You surprise and interest me very much, monsieur. Shall I be indiscreet if I ask you to tell me the facts of the case? If I am troubling you, forget that I have said anything about the matter."

The gentleman took my arm familiarly.

"Not at all, not at all. Let us linger a little behind the others, and I will tell it you, although it is a very sad story. We have plenty of time before getting to the cemetery, the trees of which you see up yonder, for it is a stiff pull up this hill."

And he began:

"This young woman, Madame Paul Hamot, was the daughter of a wealthy merchant in the neighborhood, Monsieur Fontanelle. When she was a mere child of eleven, she had a shocking adventure; a footman attacked her and she nearly died. A terrible criminal case was the result, and the man was sentenced to penal servitude for life.

"The little girl grew up, stigmatized by disgrace, isolated, without any companions; and grown-up people would scarcely kiss her, for they thought that they would soil their lips if they touched her forehead, and she became a sort of monster, a phenomenon to all the town. People said to each other in a whisper: 'You know, little Fontanelle,' and everybody turned away in the streets when she passed. Her parents could not even get a nurse to take her out for a walk, as the other servants held aloof from her, as if contact with her would poison everybody who came near her.

"It was pitiable to see the poor child go and play every afternoon. She remained quite by herself, standing by her maid and looking at the other children amusing themselves. Sometimes, yielding to an irresistible desire to mix with the other children, she advanced timidly, with nervous gestures, and mingled with a group, with furtive steps, as if conscious of her own disgrace. And immediately the mothers, aunts and nurses would come running from every seat and take the children entrusted to their care by the hand and drag them brutally away.

"Little Fontanelle remained isolated, wretched, without understanding what it meant, and then she began to cry, nearly heartbroken with grief, and then she used to run and hide her head in her nurse's lap, sobbing.

"As she grew up, it was worse still. They kept the girls from her, as if she were stricken with the plague. Remember that she had nothing to learn, nothing; that she no longer had the right to the symbolical wreath of orange-flowers; that almost before she could read she had penetrated that redoubtable mystery which mothers scarcely allow their daughters to guess at, trembling as they enlighten them on the night of their marriage.

"When she went through the streets, always accompanied by her governess, as if, her parents feared some fresh, terrible adventure, with her eyes cast down under the load of that mysterious disgrace which she felt was always weighing upon her, the other girls, who were not nearly so innocent as people thought, whispered and giggled as they looked at her knowingly, and immediately turned their heads absently, if she happened to look at them. People scarcely greeted her; only a few men bowed to her, and the mothers pretended not to see her, while some young blackguards called her Madame Baptiste, after the name of the footman who had attacked her.

"Nobody knew the secret torture of her mind, for she hardly ever spoke, and never laughed, and her parents themselves appeared uncomfortable in her presence, as if they bore her a constant grudge for some irreparable fault.

"An honest man would not willingly give his hand to a liberated convict, would he, even if that convict were his own son? And Monsieur and Madame Fontanelle looked on their daughter as they would have done on a son who had just been released from the hulks. She was pretty and pale, tall, slender, distinguished-looking, and she would have pleased me very much, monsieur, but for that unfortunate affair.

"Well, when a new sub-prefect was appointed here, eighteen months ago, he brought his private secretary with him. He was a queer sort of fellow, who had lived in the Latin Quarter, it appears. He saw Mademoiselle Fontanelle and fell in love with her, and when told of what occurred, he merely said:

"'Bah! That is just a guarantee for the future, and I would rather it should have happened before I married her than afterward. I shall live tranquilly with that woman.'

"He paid his addresses to her, asked for her hand and married her, and then, not being deficient in assurance, he paid wedding calls, as if nothing had happened. Some people returned them, others did not; but, at last, the affair began to be forgotten, and she took her proper place in society.

"She adored her husband as if he had been a god; for, you must remember, he had restored her to honor and to social life, had braved public opinion, faced insults, and, in a word, performed such a courageous act as few men would undertake, and she felt the most exalted and tender love for him.

"When she became enceinte, and it was known, the most particular people and the greatest sticklers opened their doors to her, as if she had been definitely purified by maternity.

"It is strange, but so it is, and thus everything was going on as well as possible until the other day, which was the feast of the patron saint of our town. The prefect, surrounded by his staff and the authorities, presided at the musical competition, and when he had finished his speech the distribution of medals began, which Paul Hamot, his private secretary, handed to those who were entitled to them.

"As you know, there are always jealousies and rivalries, which make people forget all propriety. All the ladies of the town were there on the platform, and, in his turn, the bandmaster from the village of Mourmillon came up. This band was only to receive a second-class medal, for one cannot give first-class medals to everybody, can one? But when the private secretary handed him his badge, the man threw it in his face and exclaimed:

"'You may keep your medal for Baptiste. You owe him a first-class one, also, just as you do me.'

"There were a number of people there who began to laugh. The common herd are neither charitable nor refined, and every eye was turned toward that poor lady. Have you ever seen a woman going mad, monsieur? Well, we were present at the sight! She got up and fell back on her chair three times in succession, as if she wished to make her escape, but saw that she could not make her way through the crowd, and then another voice in the crowd exclaimed:

"'Oh! Oh! Madame Baptiste!'

"And a great uproar, partly of laughter and partly of indignation, arose. The word was repeated over and over again; people stood on tiptoe to see the unhappy woman's face; husbands lifted their wives up in their arms, so that they might see her, and people asked:

"'Which is she? The one in blue?'

"The boys crowed like cocks, and laughter was heard all over the place.

"She did not move now on her state chair, but sat just as if she had been put there for the crowd to look at. She could not move, nor conceal herself, nor hide her face. Her eyelids blinked quickly, as if a vivid light were shining on them, and she breathed heavily, like a horse that is going up a steep hill, so that it almost broke one's heart to see her. Meanwhile, however, Monsieur Hamot had seized the ruffian by the throat, and they were rolling on the ground together, amid a scene of indescribable confusion, and the ceremony was interrupted.

"An hour later, as the Hamots were returning home, the young woman, who had not uttered a word since the insult, but who was trembling as if all her nerves had been set in motion by springs, suddenly sprang over the parapet of the bridge and threw herself into the river before her husband could prevent her. The water is very deep under the arches, and it was two hours before her body was recovered. Of course, she was dead."

The narrator stopped and then added:

"It was, perhaps, the best thing she could do under the circumstances. There are some things which cannot be wiped out, and now you understand why the clergy refused to have her taken into church. Ah! If it had been a religious funeral the whole town would have been present, but you can understand that her suicide added to the other affair and made families abstain from attending her funeral; and then, it is not an easy matter here to attend a funeral which is performed without religious rites."

We passed through the cemetery gates and I waited, much moved by what I had heard, until the coffin had been lowered into the grave, before I went up to the poor fellow who was sobbing violently, to press his hand warmly. He looked at me in surprise through his tears and then said:

"Thank you, monsieur." And I was not sorry that I had followed the funeral.

THE QUESTION OF LATIN

This subject of Latin that has been dinned into our ears for some time past recalls to my mind a story—a story of my youth.

I was finishing my studies with a teacher, in a big central town, at the Institution Robineau, celebrated through the entire province for the special attention paid there to the study of Latin.

For the past ten years, the Robineau Institute beat the imperial lycee of the town at every competitive examination, and all the colleges of the subprefecture, and these constant successes were due, they said, to an usher, a simple usher, M. Piquedent, or rather Pere Piquedent.

He was one of those middle-aged men quite gray, whose real age it is impossible to tell, and whose history we can guess at first glance. Having entered as an usher at twenty into the first institution that presented itself so that he could proceed to take first his degree of Master of Arts and afterward the degree of Doctor of Laws, he found himself so enmeshed in this routine that he remained an usher all his life. But his love for Latin did not leave him and harassed him like an unhealthy passion. He continued to read the poets, the prose writers, the historians, to interpret them and penetrate their meaning, to comment on them with a perseverance bordering on madness.

One day, the idea came into his head to oblige all the students in his class to answer him in Latin only; and he persisted in this resolution until at last they were capable of sustaining an entire conversation with him just as they would in their mother tongue.

He listened to them, as a leader of an orchestra listens to his musicians rehearsing, and striking his desk every moment with his ruler, he exclaimed:

"Monsieur Lefrere, Monsieur Lefrere, you are committing a solecism! You forget the rule.

"Monsieur Plantel, your way of expressing yourself is altogether French and in no way Latin. You must understand the genius of a language. Look here, listen to me."

Now, it came to pass that the pupils of the Institution Robineau carried off, at the end of the year, all the prizes for composition, translation, and Latin conversation.

Next year, the principal, a little man, as cunning as an ape, whom he resembled in his grinning and grotesque appearance, had had printed on his programmes, on his advertisements, and painted on the door of his institution:

"Latin Studies a Specialty. Five first prizes carried off in the five classes of the lycee.

"Two honor prizes at the general examinations in competition with all the lycees and colleges of France."

For ten years the Institution Robineau triumphed in the same fashion. Now my father, allured by these successes, sent me as a day pupil to Robineau's—or, as we called it, Robinetto or Robinettino's—and made me take special private lessons from Pere Piquedent at the rate of five francs per hour, out of which the usher got two francs and the principal three francs. I was then eighteen, and was in the philosophy class.

These private lessons were given in a little room looking out on the street. It so happened that Pere Piquedent, instead of talking Latin to me, as he did when teaching publicly in the institution, kept telling me his troubles in French. Without relations, without friends, the poor man conceived an attachment to me, and poured out his misery to me.

He had never for the last ten or fifteen years chatted confidentially with any one.

"I am like an oak in a desert," he said—"'sicut quercus in solitudine'."

The other ushers disgusted him. He knew nobody in the town, since he had no time to devote to making acquaintances.

"Not even the nights, my friend, and that is the hardest thing on me. The dream of my life is to have a room with my own furniture, my own books, little things that belong to myself and which others may not touch. And I have nothing of my own, nothing except my trousers and my frock-coat, nothing, not even my mattress and my pillow! I have not four walls to shut myself up in, except when I come to give a lesson in this room. Do you see what this means—a man forced to spend his life without ever having the right, without ever finding the time, to shut himself up all alone, no matter where, to think, to reflect, to work, to dream? Ah! my dear boy, a key, the key of a door which one can lock—this is happiness, mark you, the only happiness!

"Here, all day long, teaching all those restless rogues, and during the night the dormitory with the same restless rogues snoring. And I have to sleep in the bed at the end of two rows of beds occupied by these youngsters whom I must look after. I can never be alone, never! If I go out I find the streets full of people, and, when I am tired of walking, I go into some cafe crowded with smokers and billiard players. I tell you what, it is the life of a galley slave."

I said:

"Why did you not take up some other line, Monsieur Piquedent?"

He exclaimed:

"What, my little friend? I am not a shoemaker, or a joiner, or a hatter, or a baker, or a hairdresser. I only know Latin, and I have no diploma which would enable me to sell my knowledge at a high price. If I were a doctor I would sell for a hundred francs what I now sell for a hundred sous; and I would supply it probably of an inferior quality, for my title would be enough to sustain my reputation."

Sometimes he would say to me:

"I have no rest in life except in the hours spent with you. Don't be afraid! you'll lose nothing by that. I'll make it up to you in the class-room by making you speak twice as much Latin as the others."

One day, I grew bolder, and offered him a cigarette. He stared at me in astonishment at first, then he gave a glance toward the door.

"If any one were to come in, my dear boy?"

"Well, let us smoke at the window," said I.

And we went and leaned our elbows on the windowsill looking on the street, holding concealed in our hands the little rolls of tobacco. Just opposite to us was a laundry. Four women in loose white waists were passing hot, heavy irons over the linen spread out before them, from which a warm steam arose.

Suddenly, another, a fifth, carrying on her arm a large basket which made her stoop, came out to take the customers their shirts, their handkerchiefs, and their sheets. She stopped on the threshold as if she were already fatigued; then, she raised her eyes, smiled as she saw us smoking, flung at us, with her left hand, which was free, the sly kiss characteristic of a free-and-easy working-woman, and went away at a slow place, dragging her feet as she went.

She was a woman of about twenty, small, rather thin, pale, rather pretty, with a roguish air and laughing eyes beneath her ill-combed fair hair.

Pere Piquedent, affected, began murmuring:

"What an occupation for a woman! Really a trade only fit for a horse."

And he spoke with emotion about the misery of the people. He had a heart which swelled with lofty democratic sentiment, and he referred to the fatiguing pursuits of the working class with phrases borrowed from Jean-Jacques Rousseau, and with sobs in his throat.

Next day, as we were leaning our elbows on the same window sill, the same woman perceived us and cried out to us:

"Good-day, scholars!" in a comical sort of tone, while she made a contemptuous gesture with her hands.

I flung her a cigarette, which she immediately began to smoke. And the four other ironers rushed out to the door with outstretched hands to get cigarettes also.

And each day a friendly intercourse was established between the working-women of the pavement and the idlers of the boarding school.

Pere Piquedent was really a comical sight. He trembled at being noticed, for he might lose his position; and he made timid and ridiculous gestures, quite a theatrical display of love signals, to which the women responded with a regular fusillade of kisses.

A perfidious idea came into my mind. One day, on entering our room, I said to the old usher in a low tone:

"You would not believe it, Monsieur Piquedent, I met the little washerwoman! You know the one I mean, the woman who had the basket, and I spoke to her!"

He asked, rather worried at my manner:

"What did she say to you?"

"She said to me—why, she said she thought you were very nice. The fact of the matter is, I believe, I believe, that she is a little in love with you." I saw that he was growing pale.

"She is laughing at me, of course. These things don't happen at my age," he replied.

I said gravely:

"How is that? You are all right."

As I felt that my trick had produced its effect on him, I did not press the matter.

But every day I pretended that I had met the little laundress and that I had spoken to her about him, so that in the end he believed me, and sent her ardent and earnest kisses.

Now it happened that one morning, on my way to the boarding school, I really came across her. I accosted her without hesitation, as if I had known her for the last ten years.

"Good-day, mademoiselle. Are you quite well?"

"Very well, monsieur, thank you."

"Will you have a cigarette?"

"Oh! not in the street."

"You can smoke it at home."

"In that case, I will."

"Let me tell you, mademoiselle, there's something you don't know."

"What is that, monsieur?"

"The old gentleman—my old professor, I mean—"

"Pere Piquedent?"

"Yes, Pere Piquedent. So you know his name?"

"Faith, I do! What of that?"

"Well, he is in love with you!"

She burst out laughing wildly, and exclaimed:

"You are only fooling."

"Oh! no, I am not fooling! He keeps talking of you all through the lesson. I bet that he'll marry you!"

She ceased laughing. The idea of marriage makes every girl serious. Then she repeated, with an incredulous air:

"This is humbug!"

"I swear to you, it's true."

She picked up her basket which she had laid down at her feet.

"Well, we'll see," she said. And she went away.

Presently when I had reached the boarding school, I took Pere Piquedent aside, and said:

"You must write to her; she is infatuated with you."

And he wrote a long letter, tenderly affectionate, full of phrases and circumlocutions, metaphors and similes, philosophy and academic gallantry; and I took on myself the responsibility of delivering it to the young woman.

She read it with gravity, with emotion; then she murmured:

"How well he writes! It is easy to see he has got education! Does he really mean to marry me?"

I replied intrepidly: "Faith, he has lost his head about you!"

"Then he must invite me to dinner on Sunday at the Ile des Fleurs."

I promised that she should be invited.

Pere Piquedent was much touched by everything I told him about her.

I added:

"She loves you, Monsieur Piquedent, and I believe her to be a decent girl. It is not right to lead her on and then abandon her."

He replied in a firm tone:

"I hope I, too, am a decent man, my friend."

I confess I had at the time no plan. I was playing a practical joke a schoolboy joke, nothing more. I had been aware of the simplicity of the old usher, his innocence and his weakness. I amused myself without asking myself how it would turn out. I was eighteen, and I had been for a long time looked upon at the lycee as a sly practical joker.

So it was agreed that Pere Piquedent and I should set out in a hack for the ferry of Queue de Vache, that we should there pick up Angele, and that I should take them into my boat, for in those days I was fond of boating. I would then bring them to the Ile des

Fleurs, where the three of us would dine. I had inflicted myself on them, the better to enjoy my triumph, and the usher, consenting to my arrangement, proved clearly that he was losing his head by thus risking the loss of his position.

When we arrived at the ferry, where my boat had been moored since morning, I saw in the grass, or rather above the tall weeds of the bank, an enormous red parasol, resembling a monstrous wild poppy. Beneath the parasol was the little laundress in her Sunday clothes. I was surprised. She was really pretty, though pale; and graceful, though with a rather suburban grace.

Pere Piquedent raised his hat and bowed. She put out her hand toward him, and they stared at one another without uttering a word. Then they stepped into my boat, and I took the oars. They were seated side by side near the stern.

The usher was the first to speak.

"This is nice weather for a row in a boat."

She murmured:

"Oh! yes."

She dipped her hand into the water, skimming the surface, making a thin, transparent film like a sheet of glass, which made a soft plashing along the side of the boat.

When they were in the restaurant, she took it on herself to speak, and ordered dinner, fried fish, a chicken, and salad; then she led us on toward the isle, which she knew perfectly.

After this, she was gay, romping, and even rather tantalizing.

Until dessert, no question of love arose. I had treated them to champagne, and Pere Piquedent was tipsy. Herself slightly the worse, she called out to him:

"Monsieur Piquenez."

He said abruptly:

"Mademoiselle, Monsieur Raoul has communicated my sentiments to you."

She became as serious as a judge.

"Yes, monsieur."

"What is your reply?"

"We never reply to these questions!"

He puffed with emotion, and went on:

"Well, will the day ever come that you will like me?"

She smiled.

"You big stupid! You are very nice."

"In short, mademoiselle, do you think that, later on, we might—"

She hesitated a second; then in a trembling voice she said:

"Do you mean to marry me when you say that? For on no other condition, you know."

"Yes, mademoiselle!"

"Well, that's all right, Monsieur Piquedent!"

It was thus that these two silly creatures promised marriage to each other through the trick of a young scamp. But I did not believe that it was serious, nor, indeed, did they, perhaps.

"You know, I have nothing, not four sous," she said.

He stammered, for he was as drunk as Silenus:

"I have saved five thousand francs."

She exclaimed triumphantly:

"Then we can set up in business?"

He became restless.

"In what business?"

"What do I know? We shall see. With five thousand francs we could do many things. You don't want me to go and live in your boarding school, do you?"

He had not looked forward so far as this, and he stammered in great perplexity:

"What business could we set up in? That would not do, for all I know is Latin!"

She reflected in her turn, passing in review all her business ambitions.

"You could not be a doctor?"

"No, I have no diploma."

"Or a chemist?"

"No more than the other."

She uttered a cry of joy. She had discovered it.

"Then we'll buy a grocer's shop! Oh! what luck! we'll buy a grocer's shop. Not on a big scale, of course; with five thousand francs one does not go far."

He was shocked at the suggestion.

"No, I can't be a grocer. I am—I am—too well known: I only know Latin, that is all I know."

But she poured a glass of champagne down his throat. He drank it and was silent.

We got back into the boat. The night was dark, very dark. I saw clearly, however, that he had caught her by the waist, and that they were hugging each other again and again.

It was a frightful catastrophe. Our escapade was discovered, with the result that Pere Piquedent was dismissed. And my father, in a fit of anger, sent me to finish my course of philosophy at Ribaudet's school.

Six months later I took my degree of Bachelor of Arts. Then I went to study law in Paris, and did not return to my native town till two years later.

At the corner of the Rue de Serpent a shop caught my eye. Over the door were the words: "Colonial Products—Piquedent"; then underneath, so as to enlighten the most ignorant: "Grocery."

I exclaimed:

"'Quantum mutatus ab illo!'"

Piquedent raised his head, left his female customer, and rushed toward me with outstretched hands.

"Ah! my young friend, my young friend, here you are! What luck! what luck!"

A beautiful woman, very plump, abruptly left the cashier's desk and flung herself on my breast. I had some difficulty in recognizing her, she had grown so stout.

I asked:

"So then you're doing well?"

Piquedent had gone back to weigh the groceries.

"Oh! very well, very well, very well. I have made three thousand francs clear this year!"

"And what about Latin, Monsieur Piquedent?"

"Oh, good heavens! Latin, Latin, Latin—you see it does not keep the pot boiling!"

A MEETING

It was nothing but an accident, an accident pure and simple. On that particular evening the princess' rooms were open, and as they appeared dark after the brilliantly lighted parlors, Baron d'Etraille, who was tired of standing, inadvertently wandered into an empty bedroom.

He looked round for a chair in which to have a doze, as he was sure his wife would not leave before daylight. As soon as he became accustomed to the light of the room he distinguished the big bed with its azure-and-gold hangings, in the middle of the great room, looking like a catafalque in which love was buried, for the princess was no longer young. Behind it, a large bright surface looked like a lake seen at a distance. It was a large mirror, discreetly covered with dark drapery, that was very rarely let down, and seemed to look at the bed, which was its accomplice. One might almost fancy that it had reminiscences, and that one might see in it charming female forms and the gentle movement of loving arms.

The baron stood still for a moment, smiling, almost experiencing an emotion on the threshold of this chamber dedicated to love. But suddenly something appeared in the looking-glass, as if the phantoms which he had evoked had risen up before him. A man and a woman who had been sitting on a low couch concealed in the shadow had arisen, and the polished surface, reflecting their figures, showed that they were kissing each other before separating.

Baron d'Etraille recognized his wife and the Marquis de Cervigne. He turned and went away like a man who is fully master of himself, and waited till it was day before taking away the baroness; but he had no longer any thoughts of sleeping.

As soon as they were alone he said:

"Madame, I saw you just now in Princesse de Raynes' room; I need say no more, and I am not fond either of reproaches, acts of violence, or of ridicule. As I wish to avoid all such things, we shall separate without any scandal. Our lawyers will settle your position according to my orders. You will be free to live as you please when you are no longer under my roof; but, as you will continue to bear my name, I must warn you that should any scandal arise I shall show myself inflexible."

She tried to speak, but he stopped her, bowed, and left the room.

He was more astonished and sad than unhappy. He had loved her dearly during the first period of their married life; but his ardor had cooled, and now he often amused himself elsewhere, either in a theatre or in society, though he always preserved a certain liking for the baroness.

She was very young, hardly four-and-twenty, small, slight—too slight—and very fair. She was a true Parisian doll: clever, spoiled, elegant, coquettish, witty, with more charm than real beauty. He used to say familiarly to his brother, when speaking of her:

"My wife is charming, attractive, but—there is nothing to lay hold of. She is like a glass of champagne that is all froth; when you get to the wine it is very good, but there is too little of it, unfortunately."

He walked up and down the room in great agitation, thinking of a thousand things. At one moment he was furious, and felt inclined to give the marquis a good thrashing, or to slap his face publicly, in the club. But he decided that would not do, it would not be good form; he would be laughed at, and not his rival, and this thought wounded his vanity. So he went to bed, but could not sleep. Paris knew in a few days that the Baron and Baroness d'Etraille had agreed to an amicable separation on account of incompatibility of temper. No one suspected anything, no one laughed, and no one was astonished.

The baron, however, to avoid meeting his wife, travelled for a year, then spent the summer at the seaside, and the autumn in shooting, returning to Paris for the winter. He did not meet the baroness once.

He did not even know what people said about her. In any case, she took care to respect appearances, and that was all he asked for.

He became dreadfully bored, travelled again, restored his old castle of Villebosc, which took him two years; then for over a year he entertained friends there, till at last, tired of all these so-called pleasures, he returned to his mansion in the Rue de Lille, just six years after the separation.

He was now forty-five, with a good crop of gray hair, rather stout, and with that melancholy look characteristic of those who have been handsome, sought after, and liked, but who are deteriorating, daily.

A month after his return to Paris, he took cold on coming out of his club, and had such a bad cough that his medical man ordered him to Nice for the rest of the winter.

He reached the station only a few minutes before the departure of the train on Monday evening, and had barely time to get into a carriage, with only one other occupant, who was sitting in a corner so wrapped in furs and cloaks that he could not even make out whether it was a man or a woman, as nothing of the figure could be seen. When he perceived that he could not find out, he put on his travelling cap, rolled himself up in his rugs, and stretched out comfortably to sleep.

He did not wake until the day was breaking, and looked at once at his fellow-traveller, who had not stirred all night, and seemed still to be sound asleep.

M. d'Etraille made use of the opportunity to brush his hair and his beard, and to try to freshen himself up a little generally, for a night's travel does not improve one's appearance when one has attained a certain age.

A great poet has said:

"When we are young, our mornings are triumphant!"

Then we wake up with a cool skin, a bright eye, and glossy hair.

As one grows older one wakes up in a very different condition. Dull eyes, red, swollen cheeks, dry lips, hair and beard disarranged, impart an old, fatigued, worn-out look to the face.

The baron opened his travelling case, and improved his looks as much as possible.

The engine whistled, the train stopped, and his neighbor moved. No doubt he was awake. They started off again, and then a slanting ray of sunlight shone into the carriage and on the sleeper, who moved again, shook himself, and then his face could be seen.

It was a young, fair, pretty, plump woman, and the baron looked at her in amazement. He did not know what to think. He could really have sworn that it was his wife, but wonderfully changed for the better: stouter —why she had grown as stout as he was, only it suited her much better than it did him.

She looked at him calmly, did not seem to recognize him, and then slowly laid aside her wraps. She had that quiet assurance of a woman who is sure of herself, who feels that on awaking she is in her full beauty and freshness.

The baron was really bewildered. Was it his wife, or else as like her as any sister could be? Not having seen her for six years, he might be mistaken.

She yawned, and this gesture betrayed her. She turned and looked at him again, calmly, indifferently, as if she scarcely saw him, and then looked out of the window again.

He was upset and dreadfully perplexed, and kept looking at her sideways.

Yes; it was surely his wife. How could he possibly have doubted it? There could certainly not be two noses like that, and a thousand recollections flashed through his mind. He felt the old feeling of the intoxication of love stealing over him, and he called to mind the sweet odor of her skin, her smile when she put her arms on to his shoulders, the soft intonations of her voice, all her graceful, coaxing ways.

But how she had changed and improved! It was she and yet not she. She seemed riper, more developed, more of a woman, more seductive, more desirable, adorably desirable.

And this strange, unknown woman, whom he had accidentally met in a railway carriage, belonged to him; he had only to say to her:

"I insist upon it."

He had formerly slept in her arms, existed only in her love, and now he had found her again certainly, but so changed that he scarcely knew her. It was another, and yet it was she herself. It was some one who had been born and had formed and grown since he had left her. It was she, indeed; she whom he had loved, but who was now altered, with a more assured smile and greater self-possession. There were two women in one, mingling a great part of what was new and unknown with many sweet recollections of the past. There was something singular, disturbing, exciting about it—a kind of mystery of love in which there floated a delicious confusion. It was his wife in a new body and in new flesh which lips had never pressed.

And he thought that in a few years nearly every thing changes in us; only the outline can be recognized, and sometimes even that disappears.

The blood, the hair, the skin, all changes and is renewed, and when people have not seen each other for a long time, when they meet they find each other totally different beings, although they are the same and bear the same name.

And the heart also can change. Ideas may be modified and renewed, so that in forty years of life we may, by gradual and constant transformations, become four or five totally new and different beings.

He dwelt on this thought till it troubled him; it had first taken possession of him when he surprised her in the princess' room. He was not the least angry; it was not the same woman that he was looking at—that thin, excitable little doll of those days.

What was he to do? How should he address her? and what could he say to her? Had she recognized him?

The train stopped again. He got up, bowed, and said: "Bertha, do you want anything I could bring you?"

She looked at him from head to foot, and answered, without showing the slightest surprise, or confusion, or anger, but with the most perfect indifference:

"I do not want anything—-thank you."

He got out and walked up and down the platform a little in order to recover himself, and, as it were, to recover his senses after a fall. What should he do now? If he got into another carriage it would look as if he were running away. Should he be polite or importunate? That would look as if he were asking for forgiveness. Should he speak as if he were her master? He would look like a fool, and, besides, he really had no right to do so.

He got in again and took his place.

During his absence she had hastily arranged her dress and hair, and was now lying stretched out on the seat, radiant, and without showing any emotion.

He turned to her, and said: "My dear Bertha, since this singular chance has brought up together after a separation of six years—a quite friendly separation—are we to continue to look upon each other as irreconcilable enemies? We are shut up together, tete-a-tete, which is so much the better or so much the worse. I am not going to get into another carriage, so don't you think it is preferable to talk as friends till the end of our journey?"

She answered, quite calmly again:

"Just as you please."

Then he suddenly stopped, really not knowing what to say; but as he had plenty of assurance, he sat down on the middle seat, and said:

"Well, I see I must pay my court to you; so much the better. It is, however, really a pleasure, for you are charming. You cannot imagine how you have improved in the last six years. I do not know any woman who could give me that delightful sensation which I experienced just now when you emerged from your wraps. I really could not have thought such a change possible."

Without moving her head or looking at him, she said: "I cannot say the same with regard to you; you have certainly deteriorated a great deal."

He got red and confused, and then, with a smile of resignation, he said:

"You are rather hard."

"Why?" was her reply. "I am only stating facts. I don't suppose you intend to offer me your love? It must, therefore, be a matter of perfect indifference to you what I think about you. But I see it is a painful subject, so let us talk of something else. What have you been doing since I last saw you?"

He felt rather out of countenance, and stammered:

"I? I have travelled, done some shooting, and grown old, as you see. And you?"

She said, quite calmly: "I have taken care of appearances, as you ordered me."

He was very nearly saying something brutal, but he checked himself; and kissed his wife's hand:

"And I thank you," he said.

She was surprised. He was indeed diplomatic, and always master of himself.

He went on: "As you have acceded to my first request, shall we now talk without any bitterness?"

She made a little movement of surprise.

"Bitterness? I don't feel any; you are a complete stranger to me; I am only trying to keep up a difficult conversation."

He was still looking at her, fascinated in spite of her harshness, and he felt seized with a brutal Beside, the desire of the master.

Perceiving that she had hurt his feelings, she said:

"How old are you now? I thought you were younger than you look."

"I am forty-five"; and then he added: "I forgot to ask after Princesse de Raynes. Are you still intimate with her?"

She looked at him as if she hated him:

"Yes, I certainly am. She is very well, thank you."

They remained sitting side by side, agitated and irritated. Suddenly he said:

"My dear Bertha, I have changed my mind. You are my wife, and I expect you to come with me to-day. You have, I think, improved both morally and physically, and I am going to take you back again. I am your husband, and it is my right to do so."

She was stupefied, and looked at him, trying to divine his thoughts; but his face was resolute and impenetrable.

"I am very sorry," she said, "but I have made other engagements."

"So much the worse for you," was his reply. "The law gives me the power, and I mean to use it."

They were nearing Marseilles, and the train whistled and slackened speed. The baroness rose, carefully rolled up her wraps, and then, turning to her husband, said:

"My dear Raymond, do not make a bad use of this tete-a tete which I had carefully prepared. I wished to take precautions, according to your advice, so that I might have nothing to fear from you or from other people, whatever might happen. You are going to Nice, are you not?"

"I shall go wherever you go."

"Not at all; just listen to me, and I am sure that you will leave me in peace. In a few moments, when we get to the station, you will see the Princesse de Raynes and Comtesse Henriot waiting for me with their husbands. I wished them to see as, and to know that we had spent the night together in the railway carriage. Don't be alarmed; they will tell it everywhere as a most surprising fact.

"I told you just now that I had most carefully followed your advice and saved appearances. Anything else does not matter, does it? Well, in order to do so, I wished to be seen with you. You told me carefully to avoid any scandal, and I am avoiding it, for, I am afraid—I am afraid—"

She waited till the train had quite stopped, and as her friends ran up to open the carriage door, she said:

"I am afraid"—hesitating—"that there is another reason—je suis enceinte."

The princess stretched out her arms to embrace her,—and the baroness said, painting to the baron, who was dumb with astonishment, and was trying to get at the truth:

"You do not recognize Raymond? He has certainly changed a good deal, and he agreed to come with me so that I might not travel alone. We take little trips like this occasionally, like good friends who cannot live together. We are going to separate here; he has had enough of me already."

She put out her hand, which he took mechanically, and then she jumped out on to the platform among her friends, who were waiting for her.

The baron hastily shut the carriage door, for he was too much disturbed to say a word or come to any determination. He heard his wife's voice and their merry laughter as they went away.

He never saw her again, nor did he ever discover whether she had told him a lie or was speaking the truth.

THE BLIND MAN

How is it that the sunlight gives us such joy? Why does this radiance when it falls on the earth fill us with the joy of living? The whole sky is blue, the fields are green, the houses all white, and our enchanted eyes drink in those bright colors which bring delight to our souls. And then there springs up in our hearts a desire to dance, to run, to sing, a happy lightness of thought, a sort of enlarged tenderness; we feel a longing to embrace the sun.

The blind, as they sit in the doorways, impassive in their eternal darkness, remain as calm as ever in the midst of this fresh gaiety, and, not understanding what is taking place around them, they continually check their dogs as they attempt to play.

When, at the close of the day, they are returning home on the arm of a young brother or a little sister, if the child says: "It was a very fine day!" the other answers: "I could notice that it was fine. Loulou wouldn't keep quiet."

I knew one of these men whose life was one of the most cruel martyrdoms that could possibly be conceived.

He was a peasant, the son of a Norman farmer. As long as his father and mother lived, he was more or less taken care of; he suffered little save from his horrible infirmity; but as soon as the old people were gone, an atrocious life of misery commenced for him. Dependent on a sister of his, everybody in the farmhouse treated him as a beggar who is eating the bread of strangers. At every meal the very food he swallowed was made a subject of reproach against him; he was called a drone, a clown, and although his brother-in-law had taken possession of his portion of the inheritance, he was helped grudgingly to soup, getting just enough to save him from starving.

His face was very pale and his two big white eyes looked like wafers. He remained unmoved at all the insults hurled at him, so reserved that one could not tell whether he felt them.

Moreover, he had never known any tenderness, his mother having always treated him unkindly and caring very little for him; for in country places useless persons are considered a nuisance, and the peasants would be glad to kill the infirm of their species, as poultry do.

As soon as he finished his soup he went and sat outside the door in summer and in winter beside the fireside, and did not stir again all the evening. He made no gesture, no movement; only his eyelids, quivering from some nervous affection, fell down sometimes over his white, sightless orbs. Had he any intellect, any thinking faculty, any consciousness of his own existence? Nobody cared to inquire.

For some years things went on in this fashion. But his incapacity for work as well as his impassiveness eventually exasperated his relatives, and he became a laughingstock, a sort of butt for merriment, a prey to the inborn ferocity, to the savage gaiety of the brutes who surrounded him.

It is easy to imagine all the cruel practical jokes inspired by his blindness. And, in order to have some fun in return for feeding him, they now converted his meals into hours of pleasure for the neighbors and of punishment for the helpless creature himself.

The peasants from the nearest houses came to this entertainment; it was talked about from door to door, and every day the kitchen of the farmhouse was full of people. Sometimes they placed before his plate, when he was beginning to eat his soup, some cat or dog. The animal instinctively perceived the man's infirmity, and, softly approaching, commenced eating noiselessly, lapping up the soup daintily; and, when they lapped the food rather noisily, rousing the poor fellow's attention, they would prudently scamper away to avoid the blow of the spoon directed at random by the blind man!

Then the spectators ranged along the wall would burst out laughing, nudge each other and stamp their feet on the floor. And he, without ever uttering a word, would continue eating with his right hand, while stretching out his left to protect his plate.

Another time they made him chew corks, bits of wood, leaves or even filth, which he was unable to distinguish.

After this they got tired even of these practical jokes, and the brother-in-law, angry at having to support him always, struck him, cuffed him incessantly, laughing at his futile efforts to ward off or return the blows. Then came a new pleasure—the pleasure of smacking his face. And the plough-men, the servant girls and even every passing vagabond were every moment giving him cuffs, which caused his eyelashes to twitch spasmodically. He did not know where to hide himself and remained with his arms always held out to guard against people coming too close to him.

At last he was forced to beg.

He was placed somewhere on the high-road on market-days, and as soon as he heard the sound of footsteps or the rolling of a vehicle, he reached out his hat, stammering:

"Charity, if you please!"

But the peasant is not lavish, and for whole weeks he did not bring back a sou.

Then he became the victim of furious, pitiless hatred. And this is how he died.

One winter the ground was covered with snow, and it was freezing hard. His brother-in-law led him one morning a great distance along the high road in order that he might solicit alms. The blind man was left there all day; and when night came on, the brother-in-law told the people of his house that he could find no trace of the mendicant. Then he added:

"Pooh! best not bother about him! He was cold and got someone to take him away. Never fear! he's not lost. He'll turn up soon enough tomorrow to eat the soup."

Next day he did not come back.

After long hours of waiting, stiffened with the cold, feeling that he was dying, the blind man began to walk. Being unable to find his way along the road, owing to its thick coating of ice, he went on at random, falling into ditches, getting up again, without uttering a sound, his sole object being to find some house where he could take shelter.

But, by degrees, the descending snow made a numbness steal over him, and his feeble limbs being incapable of carrying him farther, he sat down in the middle of an open field. He did not get up again.

The white flakes which fell continuously buried him, so that his body, quite stiff and stark, disappeared under the incessant accumulation of their rapidly thickening mass, and nothing was left to indicate the place where he lay.

His relatives made a pretence of inquiring about him and searching for him for about a week. They even made a show of weeping.

The winter was severe, and the thaw did not set in quickly. Now, one Sunday, on their way to mass, the farmers noticed a great flight of crows, who were whirling incessantly above the open field, and then descending like a shower of black rain at the same spot, ever going and coming.

The following week these gloomy birds were still there. There was a crowd of them up in the air, as if they had gathered from all corners of the horizon, and they swooped down with a great cawing into the shining snow, which they covered like black patches, and in which they kept pecking obstinately. A young fellow went to see what they were doing and discovered the body of the blind man, already half devoured, mangled. His wan eyes had disappeared, pecked out by the long, voracious beaks.

And I can never feel the glad radiance of sunlit days without sadly remembering and pondering over the fate of the beggar who was such an outcast in life that his horrible death was a relief to all who had known him.

INDISCRETION

They had loved each other before marriage with a pure and lofty love. They had first met on the sea-shore. He had thought this young girl charming, as she passed by with her light-colored parasol and her dainty dress amid the marine landscape against the horizon. He had loved her, blond and slender, in these surroundings of blue ocean and spacious sky. He could not distinguish the tenderness which this budding woman awoke in him from the vague and powerful emotion which the fresh salt air and the grand scenery of surf and sunshine and waves aroused in his soul.

She, on the other hand, had loved him because he courted her, because he was young, rich, kind, and attentive. She had loved him because it is natural for young girls to love men who whisper sweet nothings to them.

So, for three months, they had lived side by side, and hand in hand. The greeting which they exchanged in the morning before the bath, in the freshness of the morning, or in the evening on the sand, under the stars, in the warmth of a calm night, whispered low, very low, already had the flavor of kisses, though their lips had never met.

Each dreamed of the other at night, each thought of the other on awaking, and, without yet having voiced their sentiments, each longing for the other, body and soul.

After marriage their love descended to earth. It was at first a tireless, sensuous passion, then exalted tenderness composed of tangible poetry, more refined caresses, and new and foolish inventions. Every glance and gesture was an expression of passion.

But, little by little, without even noticing it, they began to get tired of each other. Love was still strong, but they had nothing more to reveal to each other, nothing more to learn from each other, no new tale of endearment, no unexpected outburst, no new way of expressing the well-known, oft-repeated verb.

They tried, however, to rekindle the dwindling flame of the first love. Every day they tried some new trick or desperate attempt to bring back to their hearts the uncooled ardor of their first days of married life. They tried moonlight walks under the trees, in the sweet warmth of the summer evenings: the poetry of mist-covered beaches; the excitement of public festivals.

One morning Henriette said to Paul:

"Will you take me to a cafe for dinner?"

"Certainly, dearie."

"To some well-known cafe?"

"Of course!"

He looked at her with a questioning glance, seeing that she was thinking of something which she did not wish to tell.

She went on:

"You know, one of those cafes—oh, how can I explain myself?—a sporty cafe!"

He smiled: "Of course, I understand—you mean in one of the cafes which are commonly called bohemian."

"Yes, that's it. But take me to one of the big places, one where you are known, one where you have already supped—no—dined—well, you know—I—I—oh! I will never dare say it!"

"Go ahead, dearie. Little secrets should no longer exist between us."

"No, I dare not."

"Go on; don't be prudish. Tell me."

"Well, I—I—I want to be taken for your sweetheart—there! and I want the boys, who do not know that you are married, to take me for such; and you too—I want you to think that I am your sweetheart for one hour, in that place which must hold so many memories for you. There! And I will play that I am your sweetheart. It's awful, I know—I am abominably ashamed, I am as red as a peony. Don't look at me!"

He laughed, greatly amused, and answered:

"All right, we will go to-night to a very swell place where I am well known."

Toward seven o'clock they went up the stairs of one of the big cafes on the Boulevard, he, smiling, with the look of a conqueror, she, timid, veiled, delighted. They were immediately shown to one of the luxurious private dining-rooms, furnished with four large arm-chairs and a red plush couch. The head waiter entered and brought them the menu. Paul handed it to his wife.

"What do you want to eat?"

"I don't care; order whatever is good."

After handing his coat to the waiter, he ordered dinner and champagne. The waiter looked at the young woman and smiled. He took the order and murmured:

"Will Monsieur Paul have his champagne sweet or dry?"

"Dry, very dry."

Henriette was pleased to hear that this man knew her husband's name. They sat on the couch, side by side, and began to eat.

Ten candles lighted the room and were reflected in the mirrors all around them, which seemed to increase the brilliancy a thousand-fold. Henriette drank glass after glass in order to keep up her courage, although she felt dizzy after the first few glasses. Paul, excited by the memories which returned to him, kept kissing his wife's hands. His eyes were sparkling.

She was feeling strangely excited in this new place, restless, pleased, a little guilty, but full of life. Two waiters, serious, silent, accustomed to seeing and forgetting everything, to entering the room only when it was necessary and to leaving it when they felt they were intruding, were silently flitting hither and thither.

Toward the middle of the dinner, Henriette was well under the influence of champagne. She was prattling along fearlessly, her cheeks flushed, her eyes glistening.

"Come, Paul; tell me everything."

"What, sweetheart?"

"I don't dare tell you."

"Go on!"

"Have you loved many women before me?"

He hesitated, a little perplexed, not knowing whether he should hide his adventures or boast of them.

She continued:

"Oh! please tell me. How many have you loved?"

"A few."

"How many?"

"I don't know. How do you expect me to know such things?"

"Haven't you counted them?"

"Of course not."

"Then you must have loved a good many!"

"Perhaps."

"About how many? Just tell me about how many."

"But I don't know, dearest. Some years a good many, and some years only a few."

"How many a year, did you say?"

"Sometimes twenty or thirty, sometimes only four or five."

"Oh! that makes more than a hundred in all!"

"Yes, just about."

"Oh! I think that is dreadful!"

"Why dreadful?"

"Because it's dreadful when you think of it—all those women—and always—always the same thing. Oh! it's dreadful, just the same—more than a hundred women!"

He was surprised that she should think that dreadful, and answered, with the air of superiority which men take with women when they wish to make them understand that they have said something foolish:

"That's funny! If it is dreadful to have a hundred women, it's dreadful to have one."

"Oh, no, not at all!"

"Why not?"

"Because with one woman you have a real bond of love which attaches you to her, while with a hundred women it's not the same at all. There is no real love. I don't understand how a man can associate with such women."

"But they are all right."

"No, they can't be!"

"Yes, they are!"

"Oh, stop; you disgust me!"

"But then, why did you ask me how many sweethearts I had had?"

"Because——"

"That's no reason!"

"What were they-actresses, little shop-girls, or society women?"

"A few of each."

"It must have been rather monotonous toward the last."

"Oh, no; it's amusing to change."

She remained thoughtful, staring at her champagne glass. It was full—she drank it in one gulp; then putting it back on the table, she threw her arms around her husband's neck and murmured in his ear:

"Oh! how I love you, sweetheart! how I love you!"

He threw his arms around her in a passionate embrace. A waiter, who was just entering, backed out, closing the door discreetly. In about five minutes the head waiter came back, solemn and dignified, bringing the fruit for dessert. She was once more holding between her fingers a full glass, and gazing into the amber liquid as though seeking unknown things. She murmured in a dreamy voice:

"Yes, it must be fun!"

A FAMILY AFFAIR

The small engine attached to the Neuilly steam-tram whistled as it passed the Porte Maillot to warn all obstacles to get out of its way and puffed like a person out of breath as it sent out its steam, its pistons moving rapidly with a noise as of iron legs running. The train was going along the broad avenue that ends at the Seine. The sultry heat at the close of a July day lay over the whole city, and from the road, although there was not a breath of wind stirring, there arose a white, chalky, suffocating, warm dust, which adhered to the moist skin, filled the eyes and got into the lungs. People stood in the doorways of their houses to try and get a breath of air.

The windows of the steam-tram were open and the curtains fluttered in the wind. There were very few passengers inside, because on warm days people preferred the outside or the platforms. They consisted of stout women in peculiar costumes, of those shopkeepers' wives from the suburbs, who made up for the distinguished looks which they did not possess by ill-assumed dignity; of men tired from office-work, with yellow faces, stooped shoulders, and with one shoulder higher than the other, in consequence of, their long hours of writing at a desk. Their uneasy and melancholy faces also spoke of domestic troubles, of constant want of money, disappointed hopes, for they all belonged to the army of poor, threadbare devils who vegetate economically in cheap, plastered houses with a tiny piece of neglected garden on the outskirts of Paris, in the midst of those fields where night soil is deposited.

A short, corpulent man, with a puffy face, dressed all in black and wearing a decoration in his buttonhole, was talking to a tall, thin man, dressed in a dirty, white linen suit, the coat all unbuttoned, with a white Panama hat on his head. The former spoke so slowly and hesitatingly that it occasionally almost seemed as if he stammered; he was Monsieur Caravan, chief clerk in the Admiralty. The other, who had formerly been surgeon on board a merchant ship, had set up in practice in Courbevoie, where he applied the vague remnants of medical knowledge which he had retained after an adventurous life, to the wretched population of that district. His name was Chenet, and strange rumors were current as to his morality.

Monsieur Caravan had always led the normal life of a man in a Government office. For the last thirty years he had invariably gone the same way to his office every morning, and had met the same men going to business at the same time, and nearly on the same spot, and he returned home every evening by the same road, and again met the same faces which he had seen growing old. Every morning, after buying his penny paper at the corner of the Faubourg Saint Honore, he bought two rolls, and then went to his office, like a culprit who is giving himself up to justice, and got to his desk as quickly as possible, always feeling uneasy; as though he were expecting a rebuke for some neglect of duty of which he might have been guilty.

Nothing had ever occurred to change the monotonous order of his existence, for no event affected him except the work of his office, perquisites, gratuities, and promotion. He never spoke of anything but of his duties, either at the office, or at home—he had married the portionless daughter of one of his colleagues. His mind, which was in a state of atrophy from his depressing daily work, had no other thoughts, hopes or dreams than such as related to the office, and there was a constant source of bitterness that spoilt every pleasure that he might have had, and that was the employment of so many naval officials, tinsmiths, as they were called because of their silver-lace as first-class clerks; and every evening at dinner he discussed the matter hotly with his wife, who shared his angry feelings, and proved to their own satisfaction that it was in every way unjust to give places in Paris to men who ought properly to have been employed in the navy.

He was old now, and had scarcely noticed how his life was passing, for school had merely been exchanged for the office without any intermediate transition, and the ushers, at whom he had formerly trembled, were replaced by his chiefs, of whom he was terribly afraid. When he had to go into the rooms of these official despots, it made him tremble from head to foot, and that constant fear had given him a very awkward manner in their presence, a humble demeanor, and a kind of nervous stammering.

He knew nothing more about Paris than a blind man might know who was led to the same spot by his dog every day; and if he read the account of any uncommon events or scandals in his penny paper, they appeared to him like fantastic tales, which some pressman had made up out of his own head, in order to amuse the inferior employees. He did not read the political news, which his paper frequently altered as the cause which subsidized it might require, for he was not fond of innovations, and when he went through the Avenue of the Champs-Elysees every evening, he looked at the surging crowd of pedestrians, and at the stream of carriages, as a traveller might who has lost his way in a strange country.

As he had completed his thirty years of obligatory service that year, on the first of January, he had had the cross of the Legion of Honor bestowed upon him, which, in the semi-military public offices, is a recompense for the miserable slavery—the official phrase is, loyal services—of unfortunate convicts who are riveted to their desk. That unexpected dignity gave him a high and new idea of his own capacities, and altogether changed him. He immediately left off wearing light trousers and fancy waistcoats, and wore black trousers and long coats, on which his ribbon, which was very broad, showed off better. He got shaved every morning, manicured his nails more carefully, changed his linen every two days, from a legitimate sense of what was proper, and out of respect for the national Order, of which he formed a part, and from that day he was another Caravan, scrupulously clean, majestic and condescending.

At home, he said, "my cross," at every moment, and he had become so proud of it, that he could not bear to see men wearing any other ribbon in their button-holes. He became especially angry on seeing strange orders: "Which nobody ought to be allowed to wear in France," and he bore Chenet a particular grudge, as he met him on a tram-car every evening, wearing a decoration of one kind or another, white, blue, orange, or green.

The conversation of the two men, from the Arc de Triomphe to Neuilly, was always the same, and on that day they discussed, first of all, various local abuses which disgusted them both, and the Mayor of Neuilly received his full share of their censure. Then, as invariably happens in the company of medical men, Caravan began to enlarge on the chapter of illness, as in that manner, he hoped to obtain a little gratuitous advice, if he was careful not to show his hand. His mother had been causing him no little anxiety for some time; she had frequent and prolonged fainting fits, and, although she was ninety, she would not take care of herself.

Caravan grew quite tender-hearted when he mentioned her great age, and more than once asked Doctor Chenet, emphasizing the word doctor—although he was not fully qualified, being only an Offcier de Sante—whether he had often met anyone as old as that. And he rubbed his hands with pleasure; not, perhaps, that he cared very much about seeing the good woman last forever here on earth, but because the long duration of his mother's life was, as it were an earnest of old age for himself, and he continued:

"In my family, we last long, and I am sure that, unless I meet with an accident, I shall not die until I am very old."

The doctor looked at him with pity, and glanced for a moment at his neighbor's red face, his short, thick neck, his "corporation," as Chenet called it to himself, his two fat, flabby legs, and the apoplectic rotundity of the old official; and raising the white Panama hat from his head, he said with a snigger:

"I am not so sure of that, old fellow; your mother is as tough as nails, and I should say that your life is not a very good one."

This rather upset Caravan, who did not speak again until the tram put them down at their destination, where the two friends got out, and Chenet asked his friend to have a glass of vermouth at the Cafe du Globe, opposite, which both of them were in the habit of frequenting. The proprietor, who was a friend of theirs, held out to them two fingers, which they shook across the bottles of the counter; and then they joined three of their friends, who were playing dominoes, and who had been there since midday. They exchanged cordial greetings, with the usual question: "Anything new?" And then the three players continued their game, and held out their hands without looking up, when the others wished them "Good-night," and then they both went home to dinner.

Caravan lived in a small two-story house in Courbevaie, near where the roads meet; the ground floor was occupied by a hairdresser. Two bed rooms, a dining-room and a kitchen, formed the whole of their apartments, and Madame Caravan spent nearly her whole time in cleaning them up, while her daughter, Marie-Louise, who was twelve, and her son, Phillip-Auguste, were running about with all the little, dirty, mischievous brats of the neighborhood, and playing in the gutter.

Caravan had installed his mother, whose avarice was notorious in the neighborhood, and who was terribly thin, in the room above them. She was always cross, and she never passed a day without quarreling and flying into furious tempers. She would apostrophize the neighbors, who were standing at their own doors, the coster-mongers, the street-sweepers, and the street-boys, in the most violent language; and the latter, to have their revenge, used to follow her at a distance when she went out, and call out rude things after her.

A little servant from Normandy, who was incredibly giddy and thoughtless, performed the household work, and slept on the second floor in the same room as the old woman, for fear of anything happening to her in the night.

When Caravan got in, his wife, who suffered from a chronic passion for cleaning, was polishing up the mahogany chairs that were scattered about the room with a piece of flannel. She always wore cotton gloves, and adorned her head with a cap ornamented with many colored ribbons, which was always tilted over one ear; and whenever anyone caught her polishing, sweeping, or washing, she used to say:

"I am not rich; everything is very simple in my house, but cleanliness is my luxury, and that is worth quite as much as any other."

As she was gifted with sound, obstinate, practical common sense, she led her husband in everything. Every evening during dinner, and afterwards when they were in their room, they talked over the business of the office for a long time, and although she was twenty years younger than he was, he confided everything to her as if she took the lead, and followed her advice in every matter.

She had never been pretty, and now she had grown ugly; in addition to that, she was short and thin, while her careless and tasteless way of dressing herself concealed her few small feminine attractions, which might have been brought out if she had possessed any taste in dress. Her skirts were always awry, and she frequently scratched herself, no matter on what part of her person, totally indifferent as to who might see her, and so persistently, that anyone who saw her might think that she was suffering from something like the itch. The only adornments that she allowed herself were silk ribbons, which she had in great profusion, and of various colors mixed together, in the pretentious caps which she wore at home.

As soon as she saw her husband she rose and said, as she kissed his whiskers:

"Did you remember Potin, my dear?"

He fell into a chair, in consternation, for that was the fourth time on which he had forgotten a commission that he had promised to do for her.

"It is a fatality," he said; "it is no good for me to think of it all day long, for I am sure to forget it in the evening."

But as he seemed really so very sorry, she merely said, quietly:

"You will think of it to-morrow, I dare say. Anything new at the office?"

"Yes, a great piece of news; another tinsmith has been appointed second chief clerk." She became very serious, and said:

"So he succeeds Ramon; this was the very post that I wanted you to have. And what about Ramon?"

"He retires on his pension."

She became furious, her cap slid down on her shoulder, and she continued:

"There is nothing more to be done in that shop now. And what is the name of the new commissioner?"

"Bonassot."

She took up the Naval Year Book, which she always kept close at hand, and looked him up.

"'Bonassot-Toulon. Born in 1851. Student Commissioner in 1871. Sub-Commissioner in 1875.' Has he been to sea?" she continued. At that question Caravan's looks cleared up, and he laughed until his sides shook.

"As much as Balin—as much as Baffin, his chief." And he added an old office joke, and laughed more than ever:

"It would not even do to send them by water to inspect the Point-du-Jour, for they would be sick on the penny steamboats on the Seine."

But she remained as serious as if she had not heard him, and then she said in a low voice, as she scratched her chin:

"If we only had a Deputy to fall back upon. When the Chamber hears everything that is going on at the Admiralty, the Minister will be turned out——"

She was interrupted by a terrible noise on the stairs. Marie-Louise and Philippe-Auguste, who had just come in from the gutter, were slapping each other all the way upstairs. Their mother rushed at them furiously, and taking each of them by an arm she dragged them into the room, shaking them vigorously; but as soon as they saw their father, they rushed up to him, and he kissed them affectionately, and taking one of them on each knee, began to talk to them.

Philippe-Auguste was an ugly, ill-kempt little brat, dirty from head to foot, with the face of an idiot, and Marie-Louise was already like her mother—spoke like her, repeated her words, and even imitated her movements. She also asked him whether there was anything fresh at the office, and he replied merrily:

"Your friend, Ramon, who comes and dines here every Sunday, is going to leave us, little one. There is a new second head-clerk."

She looked at her father, and with a precocious child's pity, she said:

"Another man has been put over your head again."

He stopped laughing, and did not reply, and in order to create a diversion, he said, addressing his wife, who was cleaning the windows:

"How is mamma, upstairs?"

Madame Caravan left off rubbing, turned round pulled her cap up, as it had fallen quite on to her back, and said with trembling lips:

"Ah! yes; let us talk about your mother, for she has made a pretty scene. Just imagine: a short time ago Madame Lebaudin, the hairdresser's wife, came upstairs to borrow a packet of starch of me, and, as I was not at home, your mother chased her out as though she were a beggar; but I gave it to the old woman. She pretended not to hear, as she always does when one tells her unpleasant truths, but she is no more deaf than I am, as you know. It is all a sham, and the proof of it is, that she went up to her own room immediately, without saying a word."

Caravan, embarrassed, did not utter a word, and at that moment the little servant came in to announce dinner. In order to let his mother know, he took a broom-handle, which always stood in a corner, and rapped loudly on the ceiling three times, and then they went into the dining-room. Madame Caravan, junior, helped the soup, and waited for the old woman, but she did not come, and as the soup was getting cold, they began to eat slowly, and when their plates were empty, they waited again, and Madame Caravan, who was furious, attacked her husband:

"She does it on purpose, you know that as well as I do. But you always uphold her."

Not knowing which side to take, he sent Marie-Louise to fetch her grandmother, and he sat motionless, with his eyes cast down, while his wife tapped her glass angrily with her knife. In about a minute, the door flew open suddenly, and the child came in again, out of breath and very pale, and said hurriedly:

"Grandmamma has fallen on the floor."

Caravan jumped up, threw his table-napkin down, and rushed upstairs, while his wife, who thought it was some trick of her mother-in-law's, followed more slowly, shrugging her shoulders, as if to express her doubt. When they got upstairs, however, they found the old woman lying at full length in the middle of the room; and when they turned her over, they saw that she was insensible and motionless, while her skin looked more wrinkled and yellow than usual, her eyes were closed, her teeth clenched, and her thin body was stiff.

Caravan knelt down by her, and began to moan.

"My poor mother! my poor mother!" he said. But the other Madame Caravan said:

"Bah! She has only fainted again, that is all, and she has done it to prevent us from dining comfortably, you may be sure of that."

They put her on the bed, undressed her completely, and Caravan, his wife, and the servant began to rub her; but, in spite of their efforts, she did not recover consciousness, so they sent Rosalie, the servant, to fetch Doctor Chenet. He lived a long way off, on the quay, going towards Suresnes, and so it was a considerable time before he arrived. He came at last, however, and, after having looked at the old woman, felt her pulse, and listened for a heart beat, he said: "It is all over."

Caravan threw himself on the body, sobbing violently; he kissed his mother's rigid face, and wept so that great tears fell on the dead woman's face like drops of water, and, naturally, Madame Caravan, junior, showed a decorous amount of grief, and uttered feeble moans as she stood behind her husband, while she rubbed her eyes vigorously.

But, suddenly, Caravan raised himself up, with his thin hair in disorder, and, looking very ugly in his grief, said:

"But—are you sure, doctor? Are you quite sure?"

The doctor stooped over the body, and, handling it with professional dexterity, as a shopkeeper might do, when showing off his goods, he said:

"See, my dear friend, look at her eye."

He raised the eyelid, and the old woman's eye appeared altogether unaltered, unless, perhaps, the pupil was rather larger, and Caravan felt a severe shock at the sight. Then Monsieur Chenet took her thin arm, forced the fingers open, and said, angrily, as if he had been contradicted:

"Just look at her hand; I never make a mistake, you may be quite sure of that."

Caravan fell on the bed, and almost bellowed, while his wife, still whimpering, did what was necessary.

She brought the night-table, on which she spread a towel and placed four wax candles on it, which she lighted; then she took a sprig of box, which was hanging over the chimney glass, and put it between the four candles, in a plate, which she filled with clean water, as she had no holy water. But, after a moment's rapid reflection, she threw a pinch of salt into the water, no doubt thinking she was performing some sort of act of consecration by doing that, and when she had finished, she remained standing motionless, and the doctor, who had been helping her, whispered to her:

"We must take Caravan away."

She nodded assent, and, going up to her husband, who was still on his knees, sobbing, she raised him up by one arm, while Chenet took him by the other.

They put him into a chair, and his wife kissed his forehead, and then began to lecture him. Chenet enforced her words and preached firmness, courage, and resignation—the very things which are always wanting in such overwhelming misfortunes—and then both of them took him by the arms again and led him out.

He was crying like a great child, with convulsive sobs; his arms hanging down, and his legs weak, and he went downstairs without knowing what he was doing, and moving his feet mechanically. They put him into the chair which he always occupied at dinner, in front of his empty soup plate. And there he sat, without moving, his eyes fixed on his glass, and so stupefied with grief, that he could not even think.

In a corner, Madame Caravan was talking with the doctor and asking what the necessary formalities were, as she wanted to obtain practical information. At last, Monsieur Chenet, who appeared to be waiting for something, took up his hat and prepared to go, saying that he had not dined yet; whereupon she exclaimed:

"What! you have not dined? Why, stay here, doctor; don't go. You shall have whatever we have, for, of course, you understand that we do not fare sumptuously." He made excuses and refused, but she persisted, and said: "You really must stay; at times like this, people like to have friends near them, and, besides that, perhaps you will be able to persuade my husband to take some nourishment; he must keep up his strength."

The doctor bowed, and, putting down his hat, he said:

"In that case, I will accept your invitation, madame."

She gave Rosalie, who seemed to have lost her head, some orders, and then sat down, "to pretend to eat," as she said, "to keep the doctor company."

The soup was brought in again, and Monsieur Chenet took two helpings. Then there came a dish of tripe, which exhaled a smell of onions, and which Madame Caravan made up her mind to taste.

"It is excellent," the doctor said, at which she smiled, and, turning to her husband, she said:

"Do take a little, my poor Alfred, only just to put something in your stomach. Remember that you have got to pass the night watching by her!"

He held out his plate, docilely, just as he would have gone to bed, if he had been told to, obeying her in everything, without resistance and without reflection, and he ate; the doctor helped himself three times, while Madame Caravan, from time to time, fished out a large piece at the end of her fork, and swallowed it with a sort of studied indifference.

When a salad bowl full of macaroni was brought in, the doctor said:

"By Jove! That is what I am very fond of." And this time, Madame Caravan helped everybody. She even filled the saucers that were being scraped by the children, who, being left to themselves, had been drinking wine without any water, and were now kicking each other under the table.

Chenet remembered that Rossini, the composer, had been very fond of that Italian dish, and suddenly he exclaimed:

"Why! that rhymes, and one could begin some lines like this:

The Maestro Rossini

Was fond of macaroni."

Nobody listened to him, however. Madame Caravan, who had suddenly grown thoughtful, was thinking of all the probable consequences of the event, while her husband made bread pellets, which he put on the table-cloth, and looked at with a fixed, idiotic stare. As he was devoured by thirst, he was continually raising his glass full of wine to his lips, and the consequence was that his mind, which had been upset by the shock and grief, seemed to become vague, and his ideas danced about as digestion commenced.

The doctor, who, meanwhile, had been drinking away steadily, was getting visibly drunk, and Madame Caravan herself felt the reaction which follows all nervous shocks, and was agitated and excited, and, although she had drunk nothing but water, her head felt rather confused.

Presently, Chenet began to relate stories of death that appeared comical to him. For in that suburb of Paris, that is full of people from the provinces, one finds that indifference towards death which all peasants show, were it even their own father or mother; that want of respect, that unconscious brutality which is so common in the country, and so rare in Paris, and he said:

"Why, I was sent for last week to the Rue du Puteaux, and when I went, I found the patient dead and the whole family calmly sitting beside the bed finishing a bottle of aniseed cordial, which had been bought the night before to satisfy the dying man's fancy."

But Madame Caravan was not listening; she was continually thinking of the inheritance, and Caravan was incapable of understanding anything further.

Coffee was presently served, and it had been made very strong to give them courage. As every cup was well flavored with cognac, it made all their faces red, and confused their ideas still more. To make matters still worse, Chenet suddenly seized the brandy bottle and poured out "a drop for each of them just to wash their mouths out with," as he termed it, and then, without speaking any more, overcome in spite of themselves, by that feeling of animal comfort which alcohol affords after dinner, they slowly sipped the sweet cognac, which formed a yellowish syrup at the bottom of their cups.

The children had fallen asleep, and Rosalie carried them off to bed. Caravan, mechanically obeying that wish to forget oneself which possesses all unhappy persons, helped himself to brandy again several times, and his dull eyes grew bright. At last the doctor rose to go, and seizing his friend's arm, he said:

"Come with me; a little fresh air will do you good. When one is in trouble, one must not remain in one spot."

The other obeyed mechanically, put on his hat, took his stick, and went out, and both of them walked arm-in-arm towards the Seine, in the starlight night.

The air was warm and sweet, for all the gardens in the neighborhood were full of flowers at this season of the year, and their fragrance, which is scarcely perceptible during the day, seemed to awaken at the approach of night, and mingled with the light breezes which blew upon them in the darkness.

The broad avenue with its two rows of gas lamps, that extended as far as the Arc de Triomphe, was deserted and silent, but there was the distant roar of Paris, which seemed to have a reddish vapor hanging over it. It was a kind of continual rumbling, which was at times answered by the whistle of a train in the distance, travelling at full speed to the ocean, through the provinces.

The fresh air on the faces of the two men rather overcame them at first, made the doctor lose his equilibrium a little, and increased Caravan's giddiness, from which he had suffered since dinner. He walked as if he were in a dream; his thoughts were paralyzed, although he felt no great grief, for he was in a state of mental torpor that prevented him from suffering, and he even felt a sense of relief which was increased by the mildness of the night.

When they reached the bridge, they turned to the right, and got the fresh breeze from the river, which rolled along, calm and melancholy, bordered by tall poplar trees, while the stars looked as if they were floating on the water and were moving with the current. A slight white mist that floated over the opposite banks, filled their lungs with a sensation of cold, and Caravan stopped suddenly, for he was struck by that smell from the water which brought back old memories to his mind. For, in his mind, he suddenly saw his mother again, in Picardy, as he had seen her years before, kneeling in front of their door, and washing the heaps of linen at her side in the stream that ran through their garden. He almost fancied that he could hear the sound of the wooden paddle with which she beat the linen in the calm silence of the country, and her voice, as she called out to him: "Alfred, bring me some soap." And he smelled that odor of running water, of the mist rising from the wet ground, that marshy smell, which he should never forget, and which came back to him on this very evening on which his mother had died.

He stopped, seized with a feeling of despair. A sudden flash seemed to reveal to him the extent of his calamity, and that breath from the river plunged him into an abyss of hopeless grief. His life seemed cut in half, his youth disappeared, swallowed up by that death. All the former days were over and done with, all the recollections of his youth had been swept away; for the future, there would be nobody to talk to him of what had happened in days gone by, of the people he had known of old, of his own part of the country, and of his past life; that was a part of his existence which existed no longer, and the rest might as well end now.

And then he saw "the mother" as she was when young, wearing well-worn dresses, which he remembered for such a long time that they seemed inseparable from her; he recollected her movements, the different tones of her voice, her habits, her predilections, her fits of anger, the wrinkles on her face, the movements of her thin fingers, and all her well-known attitudes, which she would never have again, and clutching hold of the doctor, he began to moan and weep. His thin legs began to tremble, his whole stout body was shaken by his sobs, all he could say was:

"My mother, my poor mother, my poor mother!"

But his companion, who was still drunk, and who intended to finish the evening in certain places of bad repute that he frequented secretly, made him sit down on the grass by the riverside, and left him almost immediately, under the pretext that he had to see a patient.

Caravan went on crying for some time, and when he had got to the end of his tears, when his grief had, so to say, run out, he again felt relief, repose and sudden tranquillity.

The moon had risen, and bathed the horizon in its soft light.

The tall poplar trees had a silvery sheen on them, and the mist on the plain looked like drifting snow; the river, in which the stars were reflected, and which had a sheen as of mother-of-pearl, was gently rippled by the wind. The air was soft and sweet, and Caravan inhaled it almost greedily, and thought that he could perceive a feeling of freshness, of calm and of superhuman consolation pervading him.

He actually resisted that feeling of comfort and relief, and kept on saying to himself: "My poor mother, my poor mother!" and tried to make himself cry, from a kind of conscientious feeling; but he could not succeed in doing so any longer, and those sad thoughts, which had made him sob so bitterly a shore time before, had almost passed away. In a few moments, he rose to go home, and returned slowly, under the influence of that serene night, and with a heart soothed in spite of himself.

When he reached the bridge, he saw that the last tramcar was ready to start, and behind it were the brightly lighted windows of the Cafe du Globe. He felt a longing to tell somebody of his loss, to excite pity, to make himself interesting. He put on a woeful face, pushed open the door, and went up to the counter, where the landlord still was. He had counted on creating a sensation, and had hoped that everybody would get up and come to him with outstretched hands, and say: "Why, what is the matter with you?" But nobody noticed his disconsolate face, so he rested his two elbows on the counter, and, burying his face in his hands, he murmured: "Mon Dieu! Mon Dieu!"

The landlord looked at him and said: "Are you ill, Monsieur Caravan?"

"No, my friend," he replied, "but my mother has just died."

"Ah!" the other exclaimed, and as a customer at the other end of the establishment asked for a glass of Bavarian beer, he went to attend to him, leaving Caravan dumfounded at his want of sympathy.

The three domino players were sitting at the same table which they had occupied before dinner, totally absorbed in their game, and Caravan went up to them, in search of pity, but as none of them appeared to notice him he made up his mind to speak.

"A great misfortune has happened to me since I was here," he said.

All three slightly raised their heads at the same instant, but keeping their eyes fixed on the pieces which they held in their hands.

"What do you say?"

"My mother has just died"; whereupon one of them said:

"Oh! the devil," with that false air of sorrow which indifferent people assume. Another, who could not find anything to say, emitted a sort of sympathetic whistle, shaking his head at the same time, and the third turned to the game again, as if he were saying to himself: "Is that all!"

Caravan had expected some of these expressions that are said to "come from the heart," and when he saw how his news was received, he left the table, indignant at their calmness at their friend's sorrow, although this sorrow had stupefied him so that he scarcely felt it any longer. When he got home his wife was waiting for him in her nightgown, and sitting in a low chair by the open window, still thinking of the inheritance.

"Undress yourself," she said; "we can go on talking."

He raised his head, and looking at the ceiling, said:

"But—there is nobody upstairs."

"I beg your pardon, Rosalie is with her, and you can go and take her place at three o'clock in the morning, when you have had some sleep."

He only partially undressed, however, so as to be ready for anything that might happen, and after tying a silk handkerchief round his head, he lay down to rest, and for some time neither of them spoke. Madame Caravan was thinking.

Her nightcap was adorned with a red bow, and was pushed rather to one side, as was the way with all the caps she wore, and presently she turned towards him and said:

"Do you know whether your mother made a will?"

He hesitated for a moment, and then replied:

"I—I do not think so. No, I am sure that she did not."

His wife looked at him, and she said, in a low, angry tone:

"I call that infamous; here we have been wearing ourselves out for ten years in looking after her, and have boarded and lodged her! Your sister would not have done so much for her, nor I either, if I had known how I was to be rewarded! Yes, it is a disgrace to her memory! I dare say that you will tell me that she paid us, but one cannot pay one's children in ready money for what they do; that obligation is recognized after death; at any rate, that is how honorable people act. So I have had all my worry and trouble for nothing! Oh, that is nice! that is very nice!"

Poor Caravan, who was almost distracted, kept on repeating:

"My dear, my dear, please, please be quiet."

She grew calmer by degrees, and, resuming her usual voice and manner, she continued:

"We must let your sister know to-morrow."

He started, and said:

"Of course we must; I had forgotten all about it; I will send her a telegram the first thing in the morning."

"No," she replied, like a woman who had foreseen everything; "no, do not send it before ten or eleven o'clock, so that we may have time to turn round before she comes. It does not take more than two hours to get here from Charenton, and we can say that you lost your head from grief. If we let her know in the course of the day, that will be soon enough, and will give us time to look round."

Caravan put his hand to his forehead, and, in the came timid voice in which he always spoke of his chief, the very thought of whom made him tremble, he said:

"I must let them know at the office."

"Why?" she replied. "On occasions like this, it is always excusable to forget. Take my advice, and don't let him know; your chief will not be able to say anything to you, and you will put him in a nice fix.

"Oh! yes, that I shall, and he will be in a terrible rage, too, when he notices my absence. Yes, you are right; it is a capital idea, and when I tell him that my mother is dead, he will be obliged to hold his tongue."

And he rubbed his hands in delight at the joke, when he thought of his chief's face; while upstairs lay the body of the dead old woman, with the servant asleep beside it.

But Madame Caravan grew thoughtful, as if she were preoccupied by something which she did not care to mention, and at last she said:

"Your mother had given you her clock, had she not—the girl playing at cup and ball?"

He thought for a moment, and then replied:

"Yes, yes; she said to me (but it was a long time ago, when she first came here): 'I shall leave the clock to you, if you look after me well.'"

Madame Caravan was reassured, and regained her serenity, and said:

"Well, then, you must go and fetch it out of her room, for if we get your sister here, she will prevent us from taking it."

He hesitated.

"Do you think so?"

That made her angry.

"I certainly think so; once it is in our possession, she will know nothing at all about where it came from; it belongs to us. It is just the same with the chest of drawers with the marble top, that is in her room; she gave it me one day when she was in a good temper. We will bring it down at the same time."

Caravan, however, seemed incredulous, and said:

"But, my dear, it is a great responsibility!"

She turned on him furiously.

"Oh! Indeed! Will you never change? You would let your children die of hunger, rather than make a move. Does not that chest of drawers belong to us, as she gave it to me? And if your sister is not satisfied, let her tell me so, me! I don't care a straw for your sister. Come, get up, and we will bring down what your mother gave us, immediately."

Trembling and vanquished, he got out of bed and began to put on his trousers, but she stopped him:

"It is not worth while to dress yourself; your underwear is quite enough. I mean to go as I am."

They both left the room in their night clothes, went upstairs quite noiselessly, opened the door and went into the room, where the four lighted tapers and the plate with the sprig of box alone seemed to be watching the old woman in her rigid repose, for Rosalie, who was lying back in the easy chair with her legs stretched out, her hands folded in her lap, and her head on one side, was also quite motionless, and was snoring with her mouth wide open.

Caravan took the clock, which was one of those grotesque objects that were produced so plentifully under the Empire. A girl in gilt bronze was holding a cup and ball, and the ball formed the pendulum.

"Give that to me," his wife said, "and take the marble slab off the chest of drawers."

He put the marble slab on his shoulder with considerable effort, and they left the room. Caravan had to stoop in the doorway, and trembled as he went downstairs, while his wife walked backwards, so as to light him, and held the candlestick in one hand, carrying the clock under the other arm.

When they were in their own room, she heaved a sigh.

"We have got over the worst part of the job," she said; "so now let us go and fetch the other things."

But the bureau drawers were full of the old woman's wearing apparel, which they must manage to hide somewhere, and Madame Caravan soon thought of a plan.

"Go and get that wooden packing case in the vestibule; it is hardly worth anything, and we may just as well put it here."

And when he had brought it upstairs they began to fill it. One by one they took out all the collars, cuffs, chemises, caps, all the well-worn things that had belonged to the poor woman lying there behind them, and arranged them methodically in the wooden box in such a manner as to deceive Madame Braux, the deceased woman's other child, who would be coming the next day.

When they had finished, they first of all carried the bureau drawers downstairs, and the remaining portion afterwards, each of them holding an end, and it was some time before they could make up their minds where it would stand best; but at last they decided upon their own room, opposite the bed, between the two windows, and as soon as it was in its place Madame Caravan filled it with her own things. The clock was placed on the chimney-piece in the dining-room, and they looked to see what the effect was, and were both delighted with it and agreed that nothing could be better. Then they retired, she blew out the candle, and soon everybody in the house was asleep.

It was broad daylight when. Caravan opened his eyes again. His mind was rather confused when he woke up, and he did not clearly remember what had happened for a few minutes; when he did, he felt a weight at his heart, and jumped out of bed, almost ready to cry again.

He hastened to the room overhead, where Rosalie was still sleeping in the same position as the night before, not having awakened once. He sent her to do her work, put fresh tapers in the place of those that had burnt out, and then he looked at his mother, revolving in his brain those apparently profound thoughts, those religious and philosophical commonplaces which trouble people of mediocre intelligence in the presence of death.

But, as his wife was calling him, he went downstairs. She had written out a list of what had to be done during the morning, and he was horrified when he saw the memorandum:

1. Report the death at the mayor's office. 2. See the doctor who had attended her. 3. Order the coffin. 4. Give notice at the church. 5. Go to the undertaker. 6. Order the notices of her death at the printer's. 7. Go to the lawyer. 8. Telegraph the news to all the family.

Besides all this, there were a number of small commissions; so he took his hat and went out. As the news had spread abroad, Madame Caravan's female friends and neighbors soon began to come in and begged to be allowed to see the body. There had been a scene between husband and wife at the hairdresser's on the ground floor about the matter, while a customer was being shaved. The wife, who was knitting steadily, said: "Well, there is one less, and as great a miser as one ever meets with. I certainly did not care for her; but, nevertheless, I must go and have a look at her."

The husband, while lathering his patient's chin, said: "That is another queer fancy! Nobody but a woman would think of such a thing. It is not enough for them to worry you during life, but they cannot even leave you at peace when you are dead:" But his wife, without being in the least disconcerted, replied: "The feeling is stronger than I am, and I must go. It has been on me since the morning. If I were not to see her, I should think about it all my life; but when I have had a good look at her, I shall be satisfied."

The knight of the razor shrugged his shoulders and remarked in a low voice to the gentleman whose cheek he was scraping: "I just ask you, what sort of ideas do you think these confounded females have? I should not amuse myself by going to see a corpse!" But his wife had heard him and replied very quietly: "But it is so, it is so." And then, putting her knitting on the counter, she went upstairs to the first floor, where she met two other neighbors, who had just come, and who were discussing the event with Madame Caravan, who was giving them the details, and they all went together to the death chamber. The four women went in softly, and, one after the other, sprinkled the bed clothes with the salt water, knelt down, made the sign of the cross while they mumbled a prayer. Then they rose from their knees and looked for some time at the corpse with round, wide-open eyes and mouths partly open, while the daughter-in-law of the dead woman, with her handkerchief to her face, pretended to be sobbing piteously.

When she turned about to walk away whom should she perceive standing close to the door but Marie-Louise and Philippe-Auguste, who were curiously taking stock of all that was going on. Then, forgetting her pretended grief, she threw herself upon them with uplifted hands, crying out in a furious voice, "Will you get out of this, you horrid brats!"

Ten minutes later, going upstairs again with another contingent of neighbors, she prayed, wept profusely, performed all her duties, and found once more her two children, who had followed her upstairs. She again boxed their ears soundly, but the next time she paid no heed to them, and at each fresh arrival of visitors the two urchins always followed in the wake, kneeling down in a corner and imitating slavishly everything they saw their mother do.

When the afternoon came the crowds of inquisitive people began to diminish, and soon there were no more visitors. Madame Caravan, returning to her own apartments, began to make the necessary preparations for the funeral ceremony, and the deceased was left alone.

The window of the room was open. A torrid heat entered, along with clouds of dust; the flames of the four candles were flickering beside the immobile corpse, and upon the cloth which covered the face, the closed eyes, the two stretched-out hands, small flies alighted, came, went and careered up and down incessantly, being the only companions of the old woman for the time being.

Marie-Louise and Philippe-Auguste, however, had now left the house and were running up and down the street. They were soon surrounded by their playmates, by little girls especially, who were older and who were much more interested in all the mysteries of life, asking questions as if they were grown people.

"Then your grandmother is dead?" "Yes, she died yesterday evening." "What does a dead person look like?"

Then Marie began to explain, telling all about the candles, the sprig of box and the face of the corpse. It was not long before great curiosity was aroused in the minds of all the children, and they asked to be allowed to go upstairs to look at the departed.

Marie-Louise at once organized a first expedition, consisting of five girls and two boys—the biggest and the most courageous. She made them take off their shoes so that they might not be discovered. The troupe filed into the house and mounted the stairs as stealthily as an army of mice.

Once in the chamber, the little girl, imitating her mother, regulated the ceremony. She solemnly walked in advance of her comrades, went down on her knees, made the sign of the cross, moved her lips as in prayer, rose, sprinkled the bed, and while the children, all crowded together, were approaching—frightened and curious and eager to look at the face and hands of the deceased—she began suddenly to simulate sobbing and to bury her eyes in her little handkerchief. Then, becoming instantly consoled, on thinking of the other children who were downstairs waiting at the door, she ran downstairs followed by the rest, returning in a minute with another group, then a third; for all the little ragamuffins of the countryside, even to the little beggars in rags, had congregated in order to participate in this new pleasure; and each time she repeated her mother's grimaces with absolute perfection.

At length, however, she became tired. Some game or other drew the children away from the house, and the old grandmother was left alone, forgotten suddenly by everybody.

The room was growing dark, and upon the dry and rigid features of the corpse the fitful flames of the candles cast patches of light.

Towards 8 o'clock Caravan ascended to the chamber of death, closed the windows and renewed the candles. He was now quite composed on entering the room, accustomed already to regard the corpse as though it had been there for months. He even went the length of declaring that, as yet, there were no signs of decomposition, making this remark just at the moment when he and his wife were about to sit down at table. "Pshaw!" she responded, "she is now stark and stiff; she will keep for a year."

The soup was eaten in silence. The children, who had been left to themselves all day, now worn out by fatigue, were sleeping soundly on their chairs, and nobody ventured to break the silence.

Suddenly the flame of the lamp went down. Madame Caravan immediately turned up the wick, a hollow sound ensued, and the light went out. They had forgotten to buy oil. To send for it now to the grocer's would keep back the dinner, and they began to look for candles, but none were to be found except the tapers which had been placed upon the table upstairs in the death chamber.

Madame Caravan, always prompt in her decisions, quickly despatched Marie-Louise to fetch two, and her return was awaited in total darkness.

The footsteps of the girl who had ascended the stairs were distinctly heard. There was silence for a few seconds and then the child descended precipitately. She threw open the door and in a choking voice murmured: "Oh! papa, grandmamma is dressing herself!"

Caravan bounded to his feet with such precipitance that his chair fell over against the wall. He stammered out: "You say? . . . . What are you saying?"

But Marie-Louise, gasping with emotion, repeated: "Grand—grand—grandmamma is putting on her clothes, she is coming downstairs."

Caravan rushed boldly up the staircase, followed by his wife, dumfounded; but he came to a standstill before the door of the second floor, overcome with terror, not daring to enter. What was he going to see? Madame Caravan, more courageous, turned the handle of the door and stepped forward into the room.

The old woman was standing up. In awakening from her lethargic sleep, before even regaining full consciousness, in turning upon her side and raising herself on her elbow, she had extinguished three of the candles which burned near the bed. Then, gaining strength, she got off the bed and began to look for her clothes. The absence of her chest of drawers had at first worried her, but, after a little, she had succeeded in finding her things at the bottom of the wooden box, and was now quietly dressing. She emptied the plateful of water, replaced the sprig of box behind the looking-glass, and arranged the chairs in their places, and was ready to go downstairs when there appeared before her her son and daughter-in-law.

Caravan rushed forward, seized her by the hands, embraced her with tears in his eyes, while his wife, who was behind him, repeated in a hypocritical tone of voice: "Oh, what a blessing! oh, what a blessing!"

But the old woman, without being at all moved, without even appearing to understand, rigid as a statue, and with glazed eyes, simply asked: "Will dinner soon be ready?"

He stammered out, not knowing what he said:

"Oh, yes, mother, we have been waiting for you."

And with an alacrity unusual in him, he took her arm, while Madame Caravan, the younger, seized the candle and lighted them downstairs, walking backwards in front of them, step by step, just as she had done the previous night for her husband, who was carrying the marble.

On reaching the first floor, she almost ran against people who were ascending the stairs. It was the Charenton family, Madame Braux, followed by her husband.

The wife, tall and stout, with a prominent stomach, opened wide her terrified eyes and was ready to make her escape. The husband, a socialist shoemaker, a little hairy man, the perfect image of a monkey, murmured quite unconcerned: "Well, what next? Is she resurrected?"

As soon as Madame Caravan recognized them, she made frantic gestures to them; then, speaking aloud, she said: "Why, here you are! What a pleasant surprise!"

But Madame Braux, dumfounded, understood nothing. She responded in a low voice: "It was your telegram that brought us; we thought that all was over."

Her husband, who was behind her, pinched her to make her keep silent. He added with a sly laugh, which his thick beard concealed: "It was very kind of you to invite us here. We set out post haste," which remark showed the hostility which had for a long time reigned between the households. Then, just as the old woman reached the last steps, he pushed forward quickly and rubbed his hairy face against her cheeks, shouting in her ear, on account of her deafness: "How well you look, mother; sturdy as usual, hey!"

Madame Braux, in her stupefaction at seeing the old woman alive, whom they all believed to be dead, dared not even embrace her; and her enormous bulk blocked up the passageway and hindered the others from advancing. The old woman, uneasy and suspicious, but without speaking, looked at everyone around her; and her little gray eyes, piercing and hard, fixed themselves now on one and now on the other, and they were so full of meaning that the children became frightened.

Caravan, to explain matters, said: "She has been somewhat ill, but she is better now; quite well, indeed, are you not, mother?"

Then the good woman, continuing to walk, replied in a husky voice, as though it came from a distance: "It was syncope. I heard you all the while."

An embarrassing silence followed. They entered the dining-room, and in a few minutes all sat down to an improvised dinner.

Only M. Braux had retained his self-possession. His gorilla features grinned wickedly, while he let fall some words of double meaning which painfully disconcerted everyone.

But the door bell kept ringing every second, and Rosalie, distracted, came to call Caravan, who rushed out, throwing down his napkin. His brother-in-law even asked him whether it was not one of his reception days, to which he stammered out in answer: "No, only a few packages; nothing more."

A parcel was brought in, which he began to open carelessly, and the mourning announcements with black borders appeared unexpectedly. Reddening up to the very eyes, he closed the package hurriedly and pushed it under his waistcoat.

His mother had not seen it! She was looking intently at her clock which stood on the mantelpiece, and the embarrassment increased in midst of a dead silence. Turning her wrinkled face towards her daughter, the old woman, in whose eyes gleamed malice, said: "On Monday you must take me away from here, so that I can see your little girl. I want so much to see her." Madame Braux, her features all beaming, exclaimed: "Yes, mother, that I will," while Madame Caravan, the younger, who had turned pale, was ready to faint with annoyance. The two men, however, gradually drifted into conversation and soon became embroiled in a political discussion. Braux maintained the most revolutionary and communistic doctrines, his eyes glowing, and gesticulating and throwing about his arms. "Property, sir," he said, "is a robbery perpetrated on the working classes; the land is the common property of every man; hereditary rights are an infamy and a disgrace." But here he suddenly stopped, looking as if he had just said something foolish, then added in softer tones: "But this is not the proper moment to discuss such things."

The door was opened and Dr. Chenet appeared. For a moment he seemed bewildered, but regaining his usual smirking expression of countenance, he jauntily approached the old woman and said: "Aha! mamma; you are better to-day. Oh! I never had any doubt but you would come round again; in fact, I said to myself as I was mounting the staircase, 'I have an idea that I shall find the old lady on her feet once more';" and as he patted her gently on the back: "Ah! she is as solid as the Pont-Neuf, she will bury us all; see if she does not."

He sat down, accepted the coffee that was offered him, and soon began to join in the conversation of the two men, backing up Braux, for he himself had been mixed up in the Commune.

The old woman, now feeling herself fatigued, wished to retire. Caravan rushed forward. She looked him steadily in the eye and said: "You, you must carry my clock and chest of drawers upstairs again without a moment's delay." "Yes, mamma," he replied, gasping; "yes, I will do so." The old woman then took the arm of her daughter and withdrew from the room. The two Caravans remained astounded, silent, plunged in the deepest despair, while Braux rubbed his hands and sipped his coffee gleefully.

Suddenly Madame Caravan, consumed with rage, rushed at him, exclaiming: "You are a thief, a footpad, a cur! I would spit in your face! I—I —would—" She could find nothing further to say, suffocating as she was with rage, while he went on sipping his coffee with a smile.

His wife returning just then, Madame Caravan attacked her sister-in-law, and the two women—the one with her enormous bulk, the other epileptic and spare, with changed voices and trembling hands flew at one another with words of abuse.

Chenet and Braux now interposed, and the latter, taking his better half by the shoulders, pushed her out of the door before him, shouting: "Go on, you slut; you talk too much"; and the two were heard in the street quarrelling until they disappeared from sight.

M. Chenet also took his departure, leaving the Caravans alone, face to face. The husband fell back on his chair, and with the cold sweat standing out in beads on his temples, murmured: "What shall I say to my chief to-morrow?"

BESIDE SCHOPENHAUER'S CORPSE

He was slowly dying, as consumptives die. I saw him each day, about two o'clock, sitting beneath the hotel windows on a bench in the promenade, looking out on the calm sea. He remained for some time without moving, in the heat of the sun, gazing mournfully at the Mediterranean. Every now and then, he cast a glance at the lofty mountains with beclouded summits that shut in Mentone; then, with a very slow movement, he would cross his long legs, so thin that they seemed like two bones, around which fluttered the cloth of his trousers, and he would open a book, always the same book. And then he did not stir any more, but read on, read on with his eye and his mind; all his wasting body seemed to read, all his soul plunged, lost, disappeared, in this book, up to the hour when the cool air made him cough a little. Then, he got up and reentered the hotel.

He was a tall German, with fair beard, who breakfasted and dined in his own room, and spoke to nobody.

A vague, curiosity attracted me to him. One day, I sat down by his side, having taken up a book, too, to keep up appearances, a volume of Musset's poems.

And I began to look through "Rolla."

Suddenly, my neighbor said to me, in good French:

"Do you know German, monsieur?"

"Not at all, monsieur."

"I am sorry for that. Since chance has thrown us side by side, I could have lent you, I could have shown you, an inestimable thing—this book which I hold in my hand."

"What is it, pray?"

"It is a copy of my master, Schopenhauer, annotated with his own hand. All the margins, as you may see, are covered with his handwriting."

I took the book from him reverently, and I gazed at these forms incomprehensible to me, but which revealed the immortal thoughts of the greatest shatterer of dreams who had ever dwelt on earth.

And Musset's verses arose in my memory:

"Hast thou found out, Voltaire, that it is bliss to die,
And does thy hideous smile over thy bleached bones fly?"

And involuntarily I compared the childish sarcasm, the religious sarcasm of Voltaire with the irresistible irony of the German philosopher whose influence is henceforth ineffaceable.

Let us protest and let us be angry, let us be indignant, or let us be enthusiastic, Schopenhauer has marked humanity with the seal of his disdain and of his disenchantment.

A disabused pleasure-seeker, he overthrew beliefs, hopes, poetic ideals and chimeras, destroyed the aspirations, ravaged the confidence of souls, killed love, dragged down the chivalrous worship of women, crushed the illusions of hearts, and accomplished the most gigantic task ever attempted by scepticism. He spared nothing with his mocking spirit, and exhausted everything. And even to-day those who execrate him seem to carry in their own souls particles of his thought.

"So, then, you were intimately acquainted with Schopenhauer?" I said to the German.

He smiled sadly.

"Up to the time of his death, monsieur."

And he spoke to me about the philosopher and told me about the almost supernatural impression which this strange being made on all who came near him.

He gave me an account of the interview of the old iconoclast with a French politician, a doctrinaire Republican, who wanted to get a glimpse of this man, and found him in a noisy tavern, seated in the midst of his disciples, dry, wrinkled, laughing with an unforgettable laugh, attacking and tearing to pieces ideas and beliefs with a single word, as a dog tears with one bite of his teeth the tissues with which he plays.

He repeated for me the comment of this Frenchman as he went away, astonished and terrified: "I thought I had spent an hour with the devil."

Then he added:

"He had, indeed, monsieur, a frightful smile, which terrified us even after his death. I can tell you an anecdote about it that is not generally known, if it would interest you."

And he began, in a languid voice, interrupted by frequent fits of coughing.

"Schopenhauer had just died, and it was arranged that we should watch, in turn, two by two, till morning.

"He was lying in a large apartment, very simple, vast and gloomy. Two wax candles were burning on the stand by the bedside.

"It was midnight when I went on watch, together with one of our comrades. The two friends whom we replaced had left the apartment, and we came and sat down at the foot of the bed.

"The face was not changed. It was laughing. That pucker which we knew so well lingered still around the corners of the lips, and it seemed to us that he was about to open his eyes, to move and to speak. His thought, or rather his thoughts, enveloped us. We felt ourselves more than ever in the atmosphere of his genius, absorbed, possessed by him. His domination seemed to be even more sovereign now that he was dead. A feeling of mystery was blended with the power of this incomparable spirit.

"The bodies of these men disappear, but they themselves remain; and in the night which follows the cessation of their heart's pulsation I assure you, monsieur, they are terrifying.

"And in hushed tones we talked about him, recalling to mind certain sayings, certain formulas of his, those startling maxims which are like jets of flame flung, in a few words, into the darkness of the Unknown Life.

"'It seems to me that he is going to speak,' said my comrade. And we stared with uneasiness bordering on fear at the motionless face, with its eternal laugh. Gradually, we began to feel ill at ease, oppressed, on the point of fainting. I faltered:

"'I don't know what is the matter with me, but, I assure you I am not well.'

"And at that moment we noticed that there was an unpleasant odor from the corpse.

"Then, my comrade suggested that we should go into the adjoining room, and leave the door open; and I assented to his proposal.

"I took one of the wax candles which burned on the stand, and I left the second behind. Then we went and sat down at the other end of the adjoining apartment, in such a position that we could see the bed and the corpse, clearly revealed by the light.

"But he still held possession of us. One would have said that his immaterial essence, liberated, free, all-powerful and dominating, was flitting around us. And sometimes, too, the dreadful odor of the decomposed body came toward us and penetrated us, sickening and indefinable.

"Suddenly a shiver passed through our bones: a sound, a slight sound, came from the death-chamber. Immediately we fixed our glances on him, and we saw, yes, monsieur, we saw distinctly, both of us, something white pass across the bed, fall on the carpet, and vanish under an armchair.

"We were on our feet before we had time to think of anything, distracted by stupefying terror, ready to run away. Then we stared at each other. We were horribly pale. Our hearts throbbed fiercely enough to have raised the clothing on our chests. I was the first to speak:

"'Did you see?'

"'Yes, I saw.'

"'Can it be that he is not dead?'

"'Why, when the body is putrefying?'

"'What are we to do?'

"My companion said in a hesitating tone:

"'We must go and look.'

"I took our wax candle and entered first, glancing into all the dark corners in the large apartment. Nothing was moving now, and I approached the bed. But I stood transfixed with stupor and fright:

"Schopenhauer was no longer laughing! He was grinning in a horrible fashion, with his lips pressed together and deep hollows in his cheeks. I stammered out:

"'He is not dead!'

"But the terrible odor ascended to my nose and stifled me. And I no longer moved, but kept staring fixedly at him, terrified as if in the presence of an apparition.

"Then my companion, having seized the other wax candle, bent forward. Next, he touched my arm without uttering a word. I followed his glance, and saw on the ground, under the armchair by the side of the bed, standing out white on the dark carpet, and open as if to bite, Schopenhauer's set of artificial teeth.

"The work of decomposition, loosening the jaws, had made it jump out of the mouth.

"I was really frightened that day, monsieur."

And as the sun was sinking toward the glittering sea, the consumptive German rose from his seat, gave me a parting bow, and retired into the hotel.

VOLUME III

MISS HARRIET

There were seven of us on a drag, four women and three men; one of the latter sat on the box seat beside the coachman. We were ascending, at a snail's pace, the winding road up the steep cliff along the coast.

Setting out from Etretat at break of day in order to visit the ruins of Tancarville, we were still half asleep, benumbed by the fresh air of the morning. The women especially, who were little accustomed to these early excursions, half opened and closed their eyes every moment, nodding their heads or yawning, quite insensible to the beauties of the dawn.

It was autumn. On both sides of the road stretched the bare fields, yellowed by the stubble of wheat and oats which covered the soil like a beard that had been badly shaved. The moist earth seemed to steam. Larks were singing high up in the air, while other birds piped in the bushes.

The sun rose at length in front of us, bright red on the plane of the horizon, and in proportion as it ascended, growing clearer from minute to minute, the country seemed to awake, to smile, to shake itself like a young girl leaving her bed in her white robe of vapor. The Comte d'Etraille, who was seated on the box, cried:

"Look! look! a hare!" and he extended his arm toward the left, pointing to a patch of clover. The animal scurried along, almost hidden by the clover, only its large ears showing. Then it swerved across a furrow, stopped, started off again at full speed, changed its course, stopped anew, uneasy, spying out every danger, uncertain what route to take, when suddenly it began to run with great bounds, disappearing finally in a large patch of beet-root. All the men had waked up to watch the course of the animal.

Rene Lamanoir exclaimed:

"We are not at all gallant this morning," and; regarding his neighbor, the little Baroness de Serennes, who struggled against sleep, he said to her in a low tone: "You are thinking of your husband, baroness. Reassure yourself; he will not return before Saturday, so you have still four days."

She answered with a sleepy smile:

"How stupid you are!" Then, shaking off her torpor, she added: "Now, let somebody say something to make us laugh. You, Monsieur Chenal, who have the reputation of having had more love affairs than the Duc de Richelieu, tell us a love story in which you have played a part; anything you like."

Leon Chenal, an old painter, who had once been very handsome, very strong, very proud of his physique and very popular with women, took his long white beard in his hand and smiled. Then, after a few moments' reflection, he suddenly became serious.

"Ladies, it will not be an amusing tale, for I am going to relate to you the saddest love affair of my life, and I sincerely hope that none of my friends may ever pass through a similar experience.

"I was twenty-five years of age and was pillaging along the coast of Normandy. I call 'pillaging' wandering about, with a knapsack on one's back, from inn to inn, under the pretext of making studies and sketching landscapes. I knew nothing more enjoyable than that happy-go-lucky wandering life, in which one is perfectly free, without shackles of any kind, without care, without preoccupation, without thinking even of the morrow. One goes in any direction one pleases, without any guide save his fancy, without any counsellor save his eyes. One stops because a running brook attracts one, because the smell of potatoes frying tickles one's olfactories on passing an inn. Sometimes it is the perfume of clematis which decides one in his choice or the roguish glance of the servant at an inn. Do not despise me for my affection for these rustics. These girls have a soul as well as senses, not to mention firm cheeks and fresh lips; while their hearty and willing kisses have the flavor of wild fruit. Love is always love, come whence it may. A heart that beats at your approach, an eye that weeps when you go away are things so rare, so sweet, so precious that they must never be despised.

"I have had rendezvous in ditches full of primroses, behind the cow stable and in barns among the straw, still warm from the heat of the day. I have recollections of coarse gray cloth covering supple peasant skin and regrets for simple, frank kisses, more delicate in their unaffected sincerity than the subtle favors of charming and distinguished women.

"But what one loves most amid all these varied adventures is the country, the woods, the rising of the sun, the twilight, the moonlight. These are, for the painter, honeymoon trips with Nature. One is alone with her in that long and quiet association. You go to sleep in the fields, amid marguerites and poppies, and when you open your eyes in the full glare of the sunlight you descry in the distance the little village with its pointed clock tower which sounds the hour of noon.

"You sit down by the side of a spring which gushes out at the foot of an oak, amid a growth of tall, slender weeds, glistening with life. You go down on your knees, bend forward and drink that cold, pellucid water which wets your mustache and nose; you drink it with a physical pleasure, as though you kissed the spring, lip to lip. Sometimes, when you find a deep hole along the course of these tiny brooks, you plunge in quite naked, and you feel on your skin, from head to foot, as it were, an icy and delicious caress, the light and gentle quivering of the stream.

"You are gay on the hills, melancholy on the edge of ponds, inspired when the sun is setting in an ocean of blood-red clouds and casts red reflections or the river. And at night, under the moon, which passes across the vault of heaven, you think of a thousand strange things which would never have occurred to your mind under the brilliant light of day.

"So, in wandering through the same country where we, are this year, I came to the little village of Benouville, on the cliff between Yport and Etretat. I came from Fecamp, following the coast, a high coast as straight as a wall, with its projecting chalk cliffs descending perpendicularly into the sea. I had walked since early morning on the short grass, smooth and yielding as a carpet, that grows on the edge of the cliff. And, singing lustily, I walked with long strides, looking sometimes at the slow circling flight of a gull with its white curved wings outlined on the blue sky, sometimes at the brown sails of a fishing bark on the green sea. In short, I had passed a happy day, a day of liberty and of freedom from care.

"A little farmhouse where travellers were lodged was pointed out to me, a kind of inn, kept by a peasant woman, which stood in the centre of a Norman courtyard surrounded by a double row of beeches.

"Leaving the coast, I reached the hamlet, which was hemmed in by great trees, and I presented myself at the house of Mother Lecacheur.

"She was an old, wrinkled and stern peasant woman, who seemed always to receive customers under protest, with a kind of defiance.

"It was the month of May. The spreading apple trees covered the court with a shower of blossoms which rained unceasingly both upon people and upon the grass.

"I said: 'Well, Madame Lecacheur, have you a room for me?'

"Astonished to find that I knew her name, she answered:

"'That depends; everything is let, but all the same I can find out."

"In five minutes we had come to an agreement, and I deposited my bag upon the earthen floor of a rustic room, furnished with a bed, two chairs, a table and a washbowl. The room looked into the large, smoky kitchen, where the lodgers took their meals with the people of the farm and the landlady, who was a widow.

"I washed my hands, after which I went out. The old woman was making a chicken fricassee for dinner in the large fireplace in which hung the iron pot, black with smoke.

"'You have travellers, then, at the present time?' said I to her.

"She answered in an offended tone of voice:

"'I have a lady, an English lady, who has reached years of maturity. She occupies the other room.'

"I obtained, by means of an extra five sous a day, the privilege of dining alone out in the yard when the weather was fine.

"My place was set outside the door, and I was beginning to gnaw the lean limbs of the Normandy chicken, to drink the clear cider and to munch the hunk of white bread, which was four days old but excellent.

"Suddenly the wooden gate which gave on the highway was opened, and a strange lady directed her steps toward the house. She was very thin, very tall, so tightly enveloped in a red Scotch plaid shawl that one might have supposed she had no arms, if one had not seen a long hand appear just above the hips, holding a white tourist umbrella. Her face was like that of a mummy, surrounded with curls of gray hair, which tossed about at every step she took and made me think, I know not why, of a pickled herring in curl papers. Lowering her eyes, she passed quickly in front of me and entered the house.

"That singular apparition cheered me. She undoubtedly was my neighbor, the English lady of mature age of whom our hostess had spoken.

"I did not see her again that day. The next day, when I had settled myself to commence painting at the end of that beautiful valley which you know and which extends as far as Etretat, I perceived, on lifting my eyes suddenly, something singular standing on the crest of the cliff, one might have said a pole decked out with flags. It was she. On seeing me, she suddenly disappeared. I reentered the house at midday for lunch and took my seat at the general table, so as to make the acquaintance of this odd character. But she did not respond to my polite advances, was insensible even to my little attentions. I poured out water for her persistently, I passed her the dishes with great eagerness. A slight, almost imperceptible, movement of the head and an English word, murmured so low that I did not understand it, were her only acknowledgments.

"I ceased occupying myself with her, although she had disturbed my thoughts.

"At the end of three days I knew as much about her as did Madame Lecacheur herself.

"She was called Miss Harriet. Seeking out a secluded village in which to pass the summer, she had been attracted to Benouville some six months before and did not seem disposed to leave it. She never spoke at table, ate rapidly, reading all the while a small book of the Protestant propaganda. She gave a copy of it to everybody. The cure himself had received no less than four copies, conveyed by an urchin to whom she had paid two sous commission. She said sometimes to our hostess abruptly, without preparing her in the least for the declaration:

"'I love the Saviour more than all. I admire him in all creation; I adore him in all nature; I carry him always in my heart.'

"And she would immediately present the old woman with one of her tracts which were destined to convert the universe.

"In, the village she was not liked. In fact, the schoolmaster having pronounced her an atheist, a kind of stigma attached to her. The cure, who had been consulted by Madame Lecacheur, responded:

"'She is a heretic, but God does not wish the death of the sinner, and I believe her to be a person of pure morals.'

"These words, 'atheist,' 'heretic,' words which no one can precisely define, threw doubts into some minds. It was asserted, however, that this English woman was rich and that she had passed her life in travelling through every country in the world because her family had cast her off. Why had her family cast her off? Because of her impiety, of course!

"She was, in fact, one of those people of exalted principles; one of those opinionated puritans, of which England produces so many; one of those good and insupportable old maids who haunt the tables d'hote of every hotel in Europe, who spoil Italy, poison Switzerland, render the charming cities of the Mediterranean uninhabitable, carry everywhere their fantastic manias their manners of petrified vestals, their indescribable toilets and a certain odor of india-rubber which makes one believe that at night they are slipped into a rubber casing.

"Whenever I caught sight of one of these individuals in a hotel I fled like the birds who see a scarecrow in a field.

"This woman, however, appeared so very singular that she did not displease me.

"Madame Lecacheur, hostile by instinct to everything that was not rustic, felt in her narrow soul a kind of hatred for the ecstatic declarations of the old maid. She had found a phrase by which to describe her, a term of contempt that rose to her lips, called forth by I know not what confused and mysterious mental ratiocination. She said: 'That woman is a demoniac.' This epithet, applied to that austere and sentimental creature, seemed to me irresistibly droll. I myself never called her anything now but 'the demoniac,' experiencing a singular pleasure in pronouncing aloud this word on perceiving her.

"One day I asked Mother Lecacheur: 'Well, what is our demoniac about to-day?'

"To which my rustic friend replied with a shocked air:

"'What do you think, sir? She picked up a toad which had had its paw crushed and carried it to her room and has put it in her washbasin and bandaged it as if it were a man. If that is not profanation I should like to know what is!'

"On another occasion, when walking along the shore she bought a large fish which had just been caught, simply to throw it back into the sea again. The sailor from whom she had bought it, although she paid him handsomely, now began to swear, more exasperated, indeed, than if she had put her hand into his pocket and taken his money. For more than a month he could not speak of the circumstance without becoming furious and denouncing it as an outrage. Oh, yes! She was indeed a demoniac, this Miss Harriet, and Mother Lecacheur must have had an inspiration in thus christening her.

"The stable boy, who was called Sapeur, because he had served in Africa in his youth, entertained other opinions. He said with a roguish air: 'She is an old hag who has seen life.'

"If the poor woman had but known!

"The little kind-hearted Celeste did not wait upon her willingly, but I was never able to understand why. Probably her only reason was that she was a stranger, of another race; of a different tongue and of another religion. She was, in fact, a demoniac!

"She passed her time wandering about the country, adoring and seeking God in nature. I found her one evening on her knees in a cluster of bushes. Having discovered something red through the leaves, I brushed aside the branches, and Miss Harriet at once rose to her feet, confused at having been found thus, fixing on me terrified eyes like those of an owl surprised in open day.

"Sometimes, when I was working among the rocks, I would suddenly descry her on the edge of the cliff like a lighthouse signal. She would be gazing in rapture at the vast sea glittering in the sunlight and the boundless sky with its golden tints. Sometimes I would distinguish her at the end of the valley, walking quickly with her elastic English step, and I would go toward her, attracted by I know not what, simply to see her illuminated visage, her dried-up, ineffable features, which seemed to glow with inward and profound happiness.

"I would often encounter her also in the corner of a field, sitting on the grass under the shadow of an apple tree, with her little religious booklet lying open on her knee while she gazed out at the distance.

"I could not tear myself away from that quiet country neighborhood, to which I was attached by a thousand links of love for its wide and peaceful landscape. I was happy in this sequestered farm, far removed from everything, but in touch with the earth, the good, beautiful, green earth. And—must I avow it?—there was, besides, a little curiosity which retained me at the residence of Mother Lecacheur. I wished to become acquainted a little with this strange Miss Harriet and to know what transpires in the solitary souls of those wandering old English women.

"We became acquainted in a rather singular manner. I had just finished a study which appeared to me to be worth something, and so it was, as it sold for ten thousand francs fifteen years later. It was as simple, however, as two and two make four and was not according to academic rules. The whole right side of my canvas represented a rock, an enormous rock, covered with sea-wrack, brown, yellow and red, across which the sun poured like a stream of oil. The light fell upon the rock as though it were aflame without the sun, which was at my back, being visible. That was all. A first bewildering study of blazing, gorgeous light.

"On the left was the sea, not the blue sea, the slate-colored sea, but a sea of jade, greenish, milky and solid beneath the deep-colored sky.

"I was so pleased with my work that I danced from sheer delight as I carried it back to the inn. I would have liked the whole world to see it at once. I can remember that I showed it to a cow that was browsing by the wayside, exclaiming as I did so: 'Look at that, my old beauty; you will not often see its like again.'

"When I had reached the house I immediately called out to Mother Lecacheur, shouting with all my might:

"'Hullo, there! Mrs. Landlady, come here and look at this.'

"The rustic approached and looked at my work with her stupid eyes which distinguished nothing and could not even tell whether the picture represented an ox or a house.

"Miss Harriet just then came home, and she passed behind me just as I was holding out my canvas at arm's length, exhibiting it to our landlady. The demoniac could not help but see it, for I took care to exhibit the thing in such a way that it could not escape her notice. She stopped abruptly and stood motionless, astonished. It was her rock which was depicted, the one which she climbed to dream away her time undisturbed.

"She uttered a British 'Aoh,' which was at once so accentuated and so flattering that I turned round to her, smiling, and said:

"'This is my latest study, mademoiselle.'

"She murmured rapturously, comically and tenderly:

"'Oh! monsieur, you understand nature as a living thing.'

"I colored and was more touched by that compliment than if it had come from a queen. I was captured, conquered, vanquished. I could have embraced her, upon my honor.

"I took my seat at table beside her as usual. For the first time she spoke, thinking aloud:

"'Oh! I do love nature.'

"I passed her some bread, some water, some wine. She now accepted these with a little smile of a mummy. I then began to talk about the scenery.

"After the meal we rose from the table together and walked leisurely across the courtyard; then, attracted doubtless by the fiery glow which the setting sun cast over the surface of the sea, I opened the gate which led to the cliff, and we walked along side by side, as contented as two persons might be who have just learned to understand and penetrate each other's motives and feelings.

"It was one of those warm, soft evenings which impart a sense of ease to flesh and spirit alike. All is enjoyment, everything charms. The balmy air, laden with the perfume of grasses and the smell of seaweed, soothes the olfactory sense with its wild fragrance, soothes the palate with its sea savor, soothes the mind with its pervading sweetness.

"We were now walking along the edge of the cliff, high above the boundless sea which rolled its little waves below us at a distance of a hundred metres. And we drank in with open mouth and expanded chest that fresh breeze, briny from kissing the waves, that came from the ocean and passed across our faces.

"Wrapped in her plaid shawl, with a look of inspiration as she faced the breeze, the English woman gazed fixedly at the great sun ball as it descended toward the horizon. Far off in the distance a three-master in full sail was outlined on the blood-red sky and a steamship, somewhat nearer, passed along, leaving behind it a trail of smoke on the horizon. The red sun globe sank slowly lower and lower and presently touched the water just behind the motionless vessel, which, in its dazzling effulgence, looked as though framed in a flame of fire. We saw it plunge, grow smaller and disappear, swallowed up by the ocean.

"Miss Harriet gazed in rapture at the last gleams of the dying day. She seemed longing to embrace the sky, the sea, the whole landscape.

"She murmured: 'Aoh! I love—I love' I saw a tear in her eye. She continued: 'I wish I were a little bird, so that I could mount up into the firmament.'

"She remained standing as I had often before seen her, perched on the cliff, her face as red as her shawl. I should have liked to have sketched her in my album. It would have been a caricature of ecstasy.

"I turned away so as not to laugh.

"I then spoke to her of painting as I would have done to a fellow artist, using the technical terms common among the devotees of the profession. She listened attentively, eagerly seeking to divine the meaning of the terms, so as to understand my thoughts. From time to time she would exclaim:

"'Oh! I understand, I understand. It is very interesting.'

"We returned home.

"The next day, on seeing me, she approached me, cordially holding out her hand; and we at once became firm friends.

"She was a good creature who had a kind of soul on springs, which became enthusiastic at a bound. She lacked equilibrium like all women who are spinsters at the age of fifty. She seemed to be preserved in a pickle of innocence, but her heart still retained something very youthful and inflammable. She loved both nature and animals with a fervor, a love like old wine fermented through age, with a sensuous love that she had never bestowed on men.

"One thing is certain, that the sight of a bitch nursing her puppies, a mare roaming in a meadow with a foal at its side, a bird's nest full of young ones, screaming, with their open mouths and their enormous heads, affected her perceptibly.

"Poor, solitary, sad, wandering beings! I love you ever since I became acquainted with Miss Harriet.

"I soon discovered that she had something she would like to tell me, but dare not, and I was amused at her timidity. When I started out in the morning with my knapsack on my back, she would accompany me in silence as far as the end of the village, evidently struggling to find words with which to begin a conversation. Then she would leave me abruptly and walk away quickly with her springy step.

"One day, however, she plucked up courage:

"I would like to see how you paint pictures. Are you willing? I have been very curious.'

"And she blushed as if she had said something very audacious.

"I conducted her to the bottom of the Petit-Val, where I had begun a large picture.

"She remained standing behind me, following all my gestures with concentrated attention. Then, suddenly, fearing perhaps that she was disturbing me, she said: 'Thank you,' and walked away.

"But she soon became more friendly, and accompanied me every day, her countenance exhibiting visible pleasure. She carried her camp stool under her arm, not permitting me to carry it. She would remain there for hours, silent and motionless, following with her eyes the point of my brush, in its every movement. When I obtained unexpectedly just the effect I wanted by a dash of color put on with the palette knife, she involuntarily uttered a little 'Ah!' of astonishment, of joy, of admiration. She had the most tender respect for my canvases, an almost religious respect for that human reproduction of a part of nature's work divine. My studies appeared to her a kind of religious pictures, and sometimes she spoke to me of God, with the idea of converting me.

"Oh, he was a queer, good-natured being, this God of hers! He was a sort of village philosopher without any great resources and without great power, for she always figured him to herself as inconsolable over injustices committed under his eyes, as though he were powerless to prevent them.

"She was, however, on excellent terms with him, affecting even to be the confidante of his secrets and of his troubles. She would say:

"'God wills' or 'God does not will,' just like a sergeant announcing to a recruit: 'The colonel has commanded.'

"At the bottom of her heart she deplored my ignorance of the intentions of the Eternal, which she endeavored to impart to me.

"Almost every day I found in my pockets, in my hat when I lifted it from the ground, in my paintbox, in my polished shoes, standing in front of my door in the morning, those little pious tracts which she no doubt, received directly from Paradise.

"I treated her as one would an old friend, with unaffected cordiality. But I soon perceived that she had changed somewhat in her manner, though, for a while, I paid little attention to it.

"When I was painting, whether in my valley or in some country lane, I would see her suddenly appear with her rapid, springy walk. She would then sit down abruptly, out of breath, as though she had been running or were overcome by some profound emotion. Her face would be red, that English red which is denied to the people of all other countries; then, without any reason, she would turn ashy pale and seem about to faint away. Gradually, however, her natural color would return and she would begin to speak.

"Then, without warning, she would break off in the middle of a sentence, spring up from her seat and walk away so rapidly and so strangely that I was at my wits' ends to discover whether I had done or said anything to displease or wound her.

"I finally came to the conclusion that those were her normal manners, somewhat modified no doubt in my honor during the first days of our acquaintance.

"When she returned to the farm, after walking for hours on the windy coast, her long curls often hung straight down, as if their springs had been broken. This had hitherto seldom given her any concern, and she would come to dinner without embarrassment all dishevelled by her sister, the breeze.

"But now she would go to her room and arrange the untidy locks, and when I would say, with familiar gallantry, which, however, always offended her:

"'You are as beautiful as a star to-day, Miss Harriet,' a blush would immediately rise to her cheeks, the blush of a young girl, of a girl of fifteen.

"Then she would suddenly become quite reserved and cease coming to watch me paint. I thought, 'This is only a fit of temper; it will blow over.' But it did not always blow over, and when I spoke to her she would answer me either with affected indifference or with sullen annoyance.

"She became by turns rude, impatient and nervous. I never saw her now except at meals, and we spoke but little. I concluded at length that I must have offended her in some way, and, accordingly, I said to her one evening:

"'Miss Harriet, why is it that you do not act toward me as formerly? What have I done to displease you? You are causing me much pain!'

"She replied in a most comical tone of anger:

"'I am just the same with you as formerly. It is not true, not true,' and she ran upstairs and shut herself up in her room.

"Occasionally she would look at me in a peculiar manner. I have often said to myself since then that those who are condemned to death must look thus when they are informed that their last day has come. In her eye there lurked a species of insanity, an insanity at once mystical and violent; and even more, a fever, an aggravated longing, impatient and impotent, for the unattained and unattainable.

"Nay, it seemed to me there was also going on within her a struggle in which her heart wrestled with an unknown force that she sought to master, and even, perhaps, something else. But what do I know? What do I know?

"It was indeed a singular revelation.

"For some time I had commenced to work, as soon as daylight appeared, on a picture the subject of which was as follows:

"A deep ravine, enclosed, surmounted by two thickets of trees and vines, extended into the distance and was lost, submerged in that milky vapor, in that cloud like cotton down that sometimes floats over valleys at daybreak. And at the extreme end of that heavy, transparent fog one saw, or, rather, surmised, that a couple of human beings were approaching, a human couple, a youth and a maiden, their arms interlaced, embracing each other, their heads inclined toward each other, their lips meeting.

"A first ray of the sun, glistening through the branches, pierced that fog of the dawn, illuminated it with a rosy reflection just behind the rustic lovers, framing their vague shadows in a silvery background. It was well done; yes, indeed, well done.

"I was working on the declivity which led to the Valley of Etretat. On this particular morning I had, by chance, the sort of floating vapor which I needed. Suddenly something rose up in front of me like a phantom; it was Miss Harriet. On seeing me she was about to flee. But I called after her, saying: 'Come here, come here, mademoiselle. I have a nice little picture for you.'

"She came forward, though with seeming reluctance. I handed her my sketch. She said nothing, but stood for a long time, motionless, looking at it, and suddenly she burst into tears. She wept spasmodically, like men who have striven hard to restrain their tears, but who can do so no longer and abandon themselves to grief, though still resisting. I sprang to my feet, moved at the sight of a sorrow I did not comprehend, and I took her by the hand with an impulse of brusque affection, a true French impulse which acts before it reflects.

"She let her hands rest in mine for a few seconds, and I felt them quiver as if all her nerves were being wrenched. Then she withdrew her hands abruptly, or, rather, snatched them away.

"I recognized that tremor, for I had felt it, and I could not be deceived. Ah! the love tremor of a woman, whether she be fifteen or fifty years of age, whether she be of the people or of society, goes so straight to my heart that I never have any hesitation in understanding it!

"Her whole frail being had trembled, vibrated, been overcome. I knew it. She walked away before I had time to say a word, leaving me as surprised as if I had witnessed a miracle and as troubled as if I had committed a crime.

"I did not go in to breakfast. I went to take a turn on the edge of the cliff, feeling that I would just as lief weep as laugh, looking on the adventure as both comic and deplorable and my position as ridiculous, believing her unhappy enough to go insane.

"I asked myself what I ought to do. It seemed best for me to leave the place, and I immediately resolved to do so.

"Somewhat sad and perplexed, I wandered about until dinner time and entered the farmhouse just when the soup had been served up.

"I sat down at the table as usual. Miss Harriet was there, eating away solemnly, without speaking to any one, without even lifting her eyes. Her manner and expression were, however, the same as usual.

"I waited patiently till the meal had been finished, when, turning toward the landlady, I said: 'Well, Madame Lecacheur, it will not be long now before I shall have to take my leave of you.'

"The good woman, at once surprised and troubled, replied in her drawling voice: 'My dear sir, what is it you say? You are going to leave us after I have become so accustomed to you?'

"I glanced at Miss Harriet out of the corner of my eye. Her countenance did not change in the least. But Celeste, the little servant, looked up at me. She was a fat girl, of about eighteen years of age, rosy, fresh, as strong as a horse, and possessing the rare attribute of cleanliness. I had kissed her at odd times in out-of-the-way corners, after the manner of travellers—nothing more.

"The dinner being at length over, I went to smoke my pipe under the apple trees, walking up and down from one end of the enclosure to the other. All the reflections which I had made during the day, the strange discovery of the morning, that passionate and grotesque attachment for me, the recollections which that revelation had suddenly called up, recollections at once charming and perplexing, perhaps also that look which the servant had cast on me at the announcement of my departure—all these things, mixed up and combined, put me now in a reckless humor, gave me a tickling sensation of kisses on the lips and in my veins a something which urged me on to commit some folly.

"Night was coming on, casting its dark shadows under the trees, when I descried Celeste, who had gone to fasten up the poultry yard at the other end of the enclosure. I darted toward her, running so noiselessly that she heard nothing, and as she got up from closing the small trapdoor by which the chickens got in and out, I clasped her in my arms and rained on her coarse, fat face a shower of kisses. She struggled, laughing all the time, as she was accustomed to do in such circumstances. Why did I suddenly loose my grip of her? Why did I at once experience a shock? What was it that I heard behind me?

"It was Miss Harriet, who had come upon us, who had seen us and who stood in front of us motionless as a spectre. Then she disappeared in the darkness.

"I was ashamed, embarrassed, more desperate at having been thus surprised by her than if she had caught me committing some criminal act.

"I slept badly that night. I was completely unnerved and haunted by sad thoughts. I seemed to hear loud weeping, but in this I was no doubt deceived. Moreover, I thought several times that I heard some one walking up and down in the house and opening the hall door.

"Toward morning I was overcome by fatigue and fell asleep. I got up late and did not go downstairs until the late breakfast, being still in a bewildered state, not knowing what kind of expression to put on.

"No one had seen Miss Harriet. We waited for her at table, but she did not appear. At length Mother Lecacheur went to her room. The English woman had gone out. She must have set out at break of day, as she was wont to do, in order to see the sun rise.

"Nobody seemed surprised at this, and we began to eat in silence.

"The weather was hot, very hot, one of those broiling, heavy days when not a leaf stirs. The table had been placed out of doors, under an apple tree, and from time to time Sapeur had gone to the cellar to draw a jug of cider, everybody was so thirsty. Celeste brought the dishes from the kitchen, a ragout of mutton with potatoes, a cold rabbit and a salad. Afterward she placed before us a dish of strawberries, the first of the season.

"As I wished to wash and freshen these, I begged the servant to go and draw me a pitcher of cold water.

"In about five minutes she returned, declaring that the well was dry. She had lowered the pitcher to the full extent of the cord and had touched the bottom, but on drawing the pitcher up again it was empty. Mother Lecacheur, anxious to examine the thing for herself, went and looked down the hole. She returned, announcing that one could see clearly something in the well, something altogether unusual. But this no doubt was bundles of straw, which a neighbor had thrown in out of spite.

"I wished to look down the well also, hoping I might be able to clear up the mystery, and I perched myself close to the brink. I perceived indistinctly a white object. What could it be? I then conceived the idea of lowering a lantern at the end of a cord. When I did so the yellow flame danced on the layers of stone and gradually became clearer. All four of us were leaning over the opening, Sapeur and Celeste having now joined us. The lantern rested on a black-and-white indistinct mass, singular, incomprehensible. Sapeur exclaimed:

"'It is a horse. I see the hoofs. It must have got out of the meadow during the night and fallen in headlong.'

"But suddenly a cold shiver froze me to the marrow. I first recognized a foot, then a leg sticking up; the whole body and the other leg were completely under water.

"I stammered out in a loud voice, trembling so violently that the lantern danced hither and thither over the slipper:

"'It is a woman! Who-who-can it be? It is Miss Harriet!'

"Sapeur alone did not manifest horror. He had witnessed many such scenes in Africa.

"Mother Lecacheur and Celeste began to utter piercing screams and ran away.

"But it was necessary to recover the corpse of the dead woman. I attached the young man securely by the waist to the end of the pulley rope and lowered him very slowly, watching him disappear in the darkness. In one hand he held the lantern and a rope in the other. Soon I recognized his voice, which seemed to come from the centre of the earth, saying:

"'Stop!'

"I then saw him fish something out of the water. It was the other leg. He then bound the two feet together and shouted anew:

"'Haul up!'

"I began to wind up, but I felt my arms crack, my muscles twitch, and I was in terror lest I should let the man fall to the bottom. When his head appeared at the brink I asked:

"'Well?' as if I expected he had a message from the drowned woman.

"We both got on the stone slab at the edge of the well and from opposite sides we began to haul up the body.

"Mother Lecacheur and Celeste watched us from a distance, concealed from view behind the wall of the house. When they saw issuing from the hole the black slippers and white stockings of the drowned person they disappeared.

"Sapeur seized the ankles, and we drew up the body of the poor woman. The head was shocking to look at, being bruised and lacerated, and the long gray hair, out of curl forevermore, hanging down tangled and disordered.

"'In the name of all that is holy! how lean she is,' exclaimed Sapeur in a contemptuous tone.

"We carried her into the room, and as the women did not put in an appearance I, with the assistance of the stable lad, dressed the corpse for burial.

"I washed her disfigured face. Under the touch of my finger an eye was slightly opened and regarded me with that pale, cold look, that terrible look of a corpse which seems to come from the beyond. I braided as well as I could her dishevelled hair and with my clumsy hands arranged on her head a novel and singular coiffure. Then I took off her dripping wet garments, baring, not without a feeling of shame, as though I had been guilty of some profanation, her shoulders and her chest and her long arms, as slim as the twigs of a tree.

"I next went to fetch some flowers, poppies, bluets, marguerites and fresh, sweet-smelling grass with which to strew her funeral couch.

"I then had to go through the usual formalities, as I was alone to attend to everything. A letter found in her pocket, written at the last moment, requested that her body be buried in the village in which she had passed the last days of her life. A sad suspicion weighed on my heart. Was it not on my account that she wished to be laid to rest in this place?

"Toward evening all the female gossips of the locality came to view the remains of the defunct, but I would not allow a single person to enter. I wanted to be alone, and I watched beside her all night.

"I looked at the corpse by the flickering light of the candles, at this unhappy woman, unknown to us all, who had died in such a lamentable manner and so far away from home. Had she left no friends, no relations behind her? What had her infancy been? What had been her life? Whence had she come thither alone, a wanderer, lost like a dog driven from home? What secrets of sufferings and of despair were sealed up in that unprepossessing body, in that poor body whose outward appearance had driven from her all affection, all love?

"How many unhappy beings there are! I felt that there weighed upon that human creature the eternal injustice of implacable nature! It was all over with her, without her ever having experienced, perhaps, that which sustains the greatest outcasts to wit, the hope of being loved once! Otherwise why should she thus have concealed herself, fled from the face of others? Why did she love everything so tenderly and so passionately, everything living that was not a man?

"I recognized the fact that she believed in a God, and that she hoped to receive compensation from the latter for all the miseries she had endured. She would now disintegrate and become, in turn, a plant. She would blossom in the sun, the cattle would browse on her leaves, the birds would bear away the seeds, and through these changes she would become again human flesh. But that which is called the soul had been extinguished at the bottom of the dark well. She suffered no longer. She had given her life for that of others yet to come.

"Hours passed away in this silent and sinister communion with the dead. A pale light at length announced the dawn of a new day; then a red ray streamed in on the bed, making a bar of light across the coverlet and across her hands. This was the hour she had so much loved. The awakened birds began to sing in the trees.

"I opened the window to its fullest extent and drew back the curtains that the whole heavens might look in upon us, and, bending over the icy corpse, I took in my hands the mutilated head and slowly, without terror or disgust, I imprinted a kiss, a long kiss, upon those lips which had never before been kissed."

Leon Chenal remained silent. The women wept. We heard on the box seat the Count d'Atraille blowing his nose from time to time. The coachman alone had gone to sleep. The horses, who no longer felt the sting of the whip, had slackened their pace and moved along slowly. The drag, hardly advancing at all, seemed suddenly torpid, as if it had been freighted with sorrow.

[Miss Harriet appeared in Le Gaulois, July 9, 1883, under the title of Miss Hastings. The story was later revised, enlarged; and partly reconstructed. This is what De Maupassant wrote to Editor Havard March 15, 1884, in an unedited letter, in regard to the title of the story that was to give its name to the volume:

"I do not believe that Hastings is a bad name, inasmuch as it is known all over the world, and recalls the greatest facts in English history. Besides, Hastings is as much a name as Duval is with us.

"The name Cherbuliez selected, Miss Revel, is no more like an English name than like a Turkish name. But here is another name as English as Hastings, and more euphonious; it is Miss Harriet. I will ask you therefore to substitute Harriet for Hastings."

It was in regard to this very tittle that De Maupassant had a disagreement with Audran and Boucheron director of the Bouffes Parisiens in October, 1890. They had given this title to an operetta about to be played at the Bouffes. It ended however, by their ceding to De Maupassant, and the title of the operetta was changed to Miss Helyett.]

LITTLE LOUISE ROQUE

The former soldier, Mederic Rompel, familiarly called Mederic by the country folks, left the post office of Roily-le-Tors at the usual hour. After passing through the village with his long stride, he cut across the meadows of Villaume and reached the bank of the Brindille, following the path along the water's edge to the village of Carvelin, where he commenced to deliver his letters. He walked quickly, following the course of the narrow river, which frothed, murmured and boiled in its grassy bed beneath an arch of willows.

Mederic went on without stopping, with only this thought in his mind: "My first letter is for the Poivron family, then I have one for Monsieur Renardet; so I must cross the wood."

His blue blouse, fastened round his waist by a black leather belt, moved in a quick, regular fashion above the green hedge of willow trees, and his stout stick of holly kept time with his steady tread.

He crossed the Brindille on a bridge consisting of a tree trunk, with a handrail of rope, fastened at either end to a stake driven into the ground.

The wood, which belonged to Monsieur Renardet, the mayor of Carvelin and the largest landowner in the district, consisted of huge old trees, straight as pillars and extending for about half a league along the left bank of the stream which served as a boundary to this immense dome of foliage. Alongside the water large shrubs had grown up in the sunlight, but under the trees one found nothing but moss, thick, soft and yielding, from which arose, in the still air, an odor of dampness and of dead wood.

Mederic slackened his pace, took off his black cap adorned with red lace and wiped his forehead, for it was by this time hot in the meadows, though it was not yet eight o'clock in the morning.

He had just recovered from the effects of the heat and resumed his quick pace when he noticed at the foot of a tree a knife, a child's small knife. When he picked it up he discovered a thimble and also a needlecase not far away.

Having taken up these objects, he thought: "I'll entrust them to the mayor," and he resumed his journey, but now he kept his eyes open, expecting to find something else.

All of a sudden he stopped short, as if he had struck against a wooden barrier. Ten paces in front of him lay stretched on her back on the moss a little girl, perfectly nude, her face covered with a handkerchief. She was about twelve years old.

Meredic advanced on tiptoe, as if he apprehended some danger, and he glanced toward the spot uneasily.

What was this? No doubt she was asleep. Then he reflected that a person does not go to sleep naked at half-past seven in the morning under the cool trees. So, then, she must be dead, and he must be face to face with a crime. At this thought a cold shiver ran through his frame, although he was an old soldier. And then a murder was such a rare thing in the country, and, above all, the murder of a child, that he could not believe his eyes. But she had no wound-nothing save a spot of blood on her leg. How, then, had she been killed?

He stopped close to her and gazed at her, while he leaned on his stick. Certainly he must know her, for he knew all the inhabitants of the district; but, not being able to get a look at her face, he could not guess her name. He stooped forward in order to take off the handkerchief which covered her face, then paused, with outstretched hand, restrained by an idea that occurred to him.

Had he the right to disarrange anything in the condition of the corpse before the official investigation? He pictured justice to himself as a kind of general whom nothing escapes and who attaches as much importance to a lost button as to the stab of a knife in the stomach. Perhaps under this handkerchief evidence could be found to sustain a charge of murder; in fact, if such proof were there it might lose its value if touched by an awkward hand.

Then he raised himself with the intention of hastening toward the mayor's residence, but again another thought held him back. If the little girl were still alive, by any chance, he could not leave her lying there in this way. He sank on his knees very gently, a little distance from her, through precaution, and extended his hand toward her foot. It was icy cold, with the terrible coldness of death which leaves us no longer in doubt. The letter carrier, as he touched her, felt his heart in his mouth, as he said himself afterward, and his mouth parched. Rising up abruptly, he rushed off under the trees toward Monsieur Renardet's house.

He walked on faster than ever, with his stick under his arm, his hands clenched and his head thrust forward, while his leathern bag, filled with letters and newspapers, kept flapping at his side.

The mayor's residence was at the end of the wood which served as a park, and one side of it was washed by the Brindille.

It was a big square house of gray stone, very old, and had stood many a siege in former days, and at the end of it was a huge tower, twenty metres high, rising out of the water.

From the top of this fortress one could formerly see all the surrounding country. It was called the Fox's tower, without any one knowing exactly why; and from this appellation, no doubt, had come the name Renardet, borne by the owners of this fief, which had remained in the same family, it was said, for more than two hundred years. For the Renardets formed part of the upper middle class, all but noble, to be met with so often in the province before the Revolution.

The postman dashed into the kitchen, where the servants were taking breakfast, and exclaimed:

"Is the mayor up? I want to speak to him at once."

Mederic was recognized as a man of standing and authority, and they understood that something serious had happened.

As soon as word was brought to Monsieur Renardet, he ordered the postman to be sent up to him. Pale and out of breath, with his cap in his hand, Mederic found the mayor seated at a long table covered with scattered papers.

He was a large, tall man, heavy and red-faced, strong as an ox, and was greatly liked in the district, although of an excessively violent disposition. Almost forty years old and a widower for the past six months, he lived on his estate like a country gentleman. His choleric temperament had often brought him into trouble from which the magistrates of Roily-le-Tors, like indulgent and prudent friends, had extricated him. Had he not one day thrown the conductor of the diligence from the top of his seat because he came near running over his retriever, Micmac? Had he not broken the ribs of a gamekeeper who abused him for having, gun in hand, passed through a neighbor's property? Had he not even caught by the collar the sub-prefect, who stopped over in the village during an administrative circuit, called by Monsieur Renardet an electioneering circuit, for he was opposed to the government, in accordance with family traditions.

The mayor asked:

"What's the matter now, Mederic?"

"I found a little girl dead in your wood."

Renardet rose to his feet, his face the color of brick.

"What do you say—a little girl?"

"Yes, m'sieu, a little girl, quite naked, on her back, with blood on her, dead—quite dead!"

The mayor gave vent to an oath:

"By God, I'd make a bet it is little Louise Roque! I have just learned that she did not go home to her mother last night. Where did you find her?"

The postman described the spot, gave full details and offered to conduct the mayor to the place.

But Renardet became brusque:

"No, I don't need you. Send the watchman, the mayor's secretary and the doctor to me at once, and resume your rounds. Quick, quick, go and tell them to meet me in the wood."

The letter carrier, a man used to discipline, obeyed and withdrew, angry and grieved at not being able to be present at the investigation.

The mayor, in his turn, prepared to go out, took his big soft hat and paused for a few seconds on the threshold of his abode. In front of him stretched a wide sward, in which were three large beds of flowers in full bloom, one facing the house and the others at either side of it. Farther on the outlying trees of the wood rose skyward, while at the left, beyond the Brindille, which at that spot widened into a pond, could be seen long meadows, an entirely green flat sweep of country, intersected by trenches and hedges of pollard willows.

To the right, behind the stables, the outhouses and all the buildings connected with the property, might be seen the village, which was wealthy, being mainly inhabited by cattle breeders.

Renardet slowly descended the steps in front of his house, and, turning to the left, gained the water's edge, which he followed at a slow pace, his hand behind his back. He walked on, with bent head, and from time to time glanced round in search of the persons he had sent for.

When he stood beneath the trees he stopped, took off his hat and wiped his forehead as Mederic had done, for the burning sun was darting its fiery rays on the earth. Then the mayor resumed his journey, stopped once more and retraced his steps. Suddenly, stooping down, he steeped his handkerchief in the stream that glided along at his feet and spread it over his head, under his hat. Drops of water flowed down his temples over his ears, which were always purple, over his strong red neck, and made their way, one after the other, under his white shirt collar.

As nobody had appeared, he began tapping with his foot, then he called out:

"Hello! Hello!"

A voice at his right answered:

"Hello! Hello!"

And the doctor appeared under the trees. He was a thin little man, an ex-military surgeon, who passed in the neighborhood for a very skillful practitioner. He limped, having been wounded while in the service, and had to use a stick to assist him in walking.

Next came the watchman and the mayor's secretary, who, having been sent for at the same time, arrived together. They looked scared, and hurried forward, out of breath, walking and running alternately to hasten their progress, and moving their arms up and down so vigorously that they seemed to do more work with them than with their legs.

Renardet said to the doctor:

"You know what the trouble is about?"

"Yes, a child found dead in the wood by Mederic."

"That's quite correct. Come on!"

They walked along, side by side, followed by the two men.

Their steps made no sound on the moss. Their eyes were gazing ahead in front of them.

Suddenly the doctor, extending his arm, said:

"See, there she is!"

Far ahead of them under the trees they saw something white on which the sun gleamed down through the branches. As they approached they gradually distinguished a human form lying there, its head toward the river, the face covered and the arms extended as though on a crucifix.

"I am fearfully warm," said the mayor, and stooping down, he again soaked his handkerchief in the water and placed it round his forehead.

The doctor hastened his steps, interested by the discovery. As soon as they were near the corpse, he bent down to examine it without touching it. He had put on his pince-nez, as one does in examining some curious object, and turned round very quietly.

He said, without rising:

"Violated and murdered, as we shall prove presently. This little girl, moreover, is almost a woman—look at her throat."

The doctor lightly drew away the handkerchief which covered her face, which looked black, frightful, the tongue protruding, the eyes bloodshot. He went on:

"By heavens! She was strangled the moment the deed was done."

He felt her neck.

"Strangled with the hands without leaving any special trace, neither the mark of the nails nor the imprint of the fingers. Quite right. It is little Louise Roque, sure enough!"

He carefully replaced the handkerchief.

"There's nothing for me to do. She's been dead for the last hour at least. We must give notice of the matter to the authorities."

Renardet, standing up, with his hands behind his back, kept staring with a stony look at the little body exposed to view on the grass. He murmured:

"What a wretch! We must find the clothes."

The doctor felt the hands, the arms, the legs. He said:

"She had been bathing no doubt. They ought to be at the water's edge."

The mayor thereupon gave directions:

"Do you, Principe" (this was his secretary), "go and find those clothes for me along the stream. You, Maxime" (this was the watchman), "hurry on toward Rouy-le-Tors and bring with you the magistrate with the gendarmes. They must be here within an hour. You understand?"

The two men started at once, and Renardet said to the doctor:

"What miscreant could have done such a deed in this part of the country?"

The doctor murmured:

"Who knows? Any one is capable of that. Every one in particular and nobody in general. No matter, it must be some prowler, some workman out of employment. Since we have become a Republic we meet only this kind of person along the roads."

Both of them were Bonapartists.

The mayor went on:

"Yes, it can only be a stranger, a passer-by, a vagabond without hearth or home."

The doctor added, with the shadow of a smile on his face:

"And without a wife. Having neither a good supper nor a good bed, he became reckless. You can't tell how many men there may be in the world capable of a crime at a given moment. Did you know that this little girl had disappeared?"

And with the end of his stick he touched one after the other the stiffened fingers of the corpse, resting on them as on the keys of a piano.

"Yes, the mother came last night to look for me about nine o'clock, the child not having come home at seven to supper. We looked for her along the roads up to midnight, but we did not think of the wood. However, we needed daylight to carry out a thorough search."

"Will you have a cigar?" said the doctor.

"Thanks, I don't care to smoke. This thing affects me so."

They remained standing beside the corpse of the young girl, so pale on the dark moss. A big blue fly was walking over the body with his lively, jerky movements. The two men kept watching this wandering speck.

The doctor said:

"How pretty it is, a fly on the skin! The ladies of the last century had good reason to paste them on their faces. Why has this fashion gone out?"

The mayor seemed not to hear, plunged as he was in deep thought.

But, all of a sudden, he turned round, surprised by a shrill noise. A woman in a cap and blue apron was running toward them under the trees. It was the mother, La Roque. As soon as she saw Renardet she began to shriek:

"My little girl! Where's my little girl?" so distractedly that she did not glance down at the ground. Suddenly she saw the corpse, stopped short, clasped her hands and raised both her arms while she uttered a sharp, heartrending cry—the cry of a wounded animal. Then she rushed toward the body, fell on her knees and snatched away the handkerchief that covered the face. When she saw that frightful countenance, black and distorted, she rose to her feet with a shudder, then sinking to the ground, face downward, she pressed her face against the ground and uttered frightful, continuous screams on the thick moss.

Her tall, thin frame, with its close-clinging dress, was palpitating, shaken with spasms. One could see her bony ankles and her dried-up calves covered with coarse blue stockings shaking horribly. She was digging the soil with her crooked fingers, as though she were trying to make a hole in which to hide herself.

The doctor, much affected, said in a low tone:

"Poor old woman!"

Renardet felt a strange sensation. Then he gave vent to a sort of loud sneeze, and, drawing his handkerchief from his pocket, he began to weep internally, coughing, sobbing and blowing his nose noisily.

He stammered:

"Damn—damn—damned pig to do this! I would like to see him guillotined."

Principe reappeared with his hands empty. He murmured:

"I have found nothing, M'sieu le Maire, nothing at all anywhere."

The mayor, alarmed, replied in a thick voice, drowned in tears:

"What is that you could not find?"

"The little girl's clothes."

"Well—well—look again, and find them—or you 'll have to answer to me."

The man, knowing that the mayor would not brook opposition, set forth again with hesitating steps, casting a timid side glance at the corpse.

Distant voices were heard under the trees, a confused sound, the noise of an approaching crowd, for Mederic had, in the course of his rounds, carried the news from door to door. The people of the neighborhood, dazed at first, had gossiped about it in the street, from one threshold to another. Then they gathered together. They talked over, discussed and commented on the event for some minutes and had now come to see for themselves.

They arrived in groups, a little faltering and uneasy through fear of the first impression of such a scene on their minds. When they saw the body they stopped, not daring to advance, and speaking low. Then they grew bolder, went on a few steps, stopped again, advanced once more, and presently formed around the dead girl, her mother, the doctor and Renardet a close circle, restless and noisy, which crowded forward at the sudden impact of newcomers. And now they touched the corpse. Some of them even bent down to feel it with their fingers. The doctor kept them back. But the mayor, waking abruptly out of his torpor, flew into a rage, and seizing Dr. Labarbe's stick, flung himself on his townspeople, stammering:

"Clear out—clear out—you pack of brutes—clear out!"

And in a second the crowd of sightseers had fallen back two hundred paces.

Mother La Roque had risen to a sitting posture and now remained weeping, with her hands clasped over her face.

The crowd was discussing the affair, and young lads' eager eyes curiously scrutinized this nude young form. Renardet perceived this, and, abruptly taking off his coat, he flung it over the little girl, who was entirely hidden from view beneath the large garment.

The secretary drew near quietly. The wood was filled with people, and a continuous hum of voices rose up under the tangled foliage of the tall trees.

The mayor, in his shirt sleeves, remained standing, with his stick in his hands, in a fighting attitude. He seemed exasperated by this curiosity on the part of the people and kept repeating:

"If one of you come nearer I'll break his head just as I would a dog's."

The peasants were greatly afraid of him. They held back. Dr. Labarbe, who was smoking, sat down beside La Roque and spoke to her in order to distract her attention. The old woman at once removed her hands from her face and replied with a flood of tearful words, emptying her grief in copious talk. She told the whole story of her life, her marriage, the death of her man, a cattle drover, who had been gored to death, the infancy of her daughter, her wretched existence as a widow without resources and with a child to support. She had only this one, her little Louise, and the child had been killed—killed in this wood. Then she felt anxious to see her again, and, dragging herself on her knees toward the corpse, she raised up one corner of the garment that covered her; then she let it fall again and began wailing once more. The crowd remained silent, eagerly watching all the mother's gestures.

But suddenly there was a great commotion at the cry of "The gendarmes! the gendarmes!"

Two gendarmes appeared in the distance, advancing at a rapid trot, escorting their captain and a little gentleman with red whiskers, who was bobbing up and down like a monkey on a big white mare.

The watchman had just found Monsieur Putoin, the magistrate, at the moment when he was mounting his horse to take his daily ride, for he posed as a good horseman, to the great amusement of the officers.

He dismounted, along with the captain, and pressed the hands of the mayor and the doctor, casting a ferret-like glance on the linen coat beneath which lay the corpse.

When he was made acquainted with all the facts, he first gave orders to disperse the crowd, whom the gendarmes drove out of the wood, but who soon reappeared in the meadow and formed a hedge, a big hedge of excited and moving heads, on the other side of the stream.

The doctor, in his turn, gave explanations, which Renardet noted down in his memorandum book. All the evidence was given, taken down and commented on without leading to any discovery. Maxime, too, came back without having found any trace of the clothes.

This disappearance surprised everybody; no one could explain it except on the theory of theft, and as her rags were not worth twenty sous, even this theory was inadmissible.

The magistrate, the mayor, the captain and the doctor set to work searching in pairs, putting aside the smallest branch along the water.

Renardet said to the judge:

"How does it happen that this wretch has concealed or carried away the clothes, and has thus left the body exposed, in sight of every one?"

The other, crafty and sagacious, answered:

"Ha! ha! Perhaps a dodge? This crime has been committed either by a brute or by a sly scoundrel. In any case, we'll easily succeed in finding him."

The noise of wheels made them turn their heads round. It was the deputy magistrate, the doctor and the registrar of the court who had arrived in their turn. They resumed their search, all chatting in an animated fashion.

Renardet said suddenly:

"Do you know that you are to take luncheon with me?"

Every one smilingly accepted the invitation, and the magistrate, thinking that the case of little Louise Roque had occupied enough attention for one day, turned toward the mayor.

"I can have the body brought to your house, can I not? You have a room in which you can keep it for me till this evening?"

The other became confused and stammered:

"Yes—no—no. To tell the truth, I prefer that it should not come into my house on account of—on account of my servants, who are already talking about ghosts in—in my tower, in the Fox's tower. You know—I could no longer keep a single one. No—I prefer not to have it in my house."

The magistrate began to smile.

"Good! I will have it taken at once to Roily for the legal examination." And, turning to his deputy, he said:

"I can make use of your trap, can I not?"

"Yes, certainly."

They all came back to the place where the corpse lay. Mother La Roque, now seated beside her daughter, was holding her hand and was staring right before her with a wandering, listless eye.

The two doctors endeavored to lead her away, so that she might not witness the dead girl's removal, but she understood at once what they wanted to do, and, flinging herself on the body, she threw both arms round it. Lying on top of the corpse, she exclaimed:

"You shall not have it—it's mine—it's mine now. They have killed her for me, and I want to keep her—you shall not have her——"

All the men, affected and not knowing how to act, remained standing around her. Renardet fell on his knees and said to her:

"Listen, La Roque, it is necessary, in order to find out who killed her. Without this, we could not find out. We must make a search for the man in order to punish him. When we have found him we'll give her up to you. I promise you this."

This explanation bewildered the woman, and a feeling of hatred manifested itself in her distracted glance.

"So then they'll arrest him?"

"Yes, I promise you that."

She rose up, deciding to let them do as they liked, but when the captain remarked:

"It is surprising that her clothes were not found," a new idea, which she had not previously thought of, abruptly entered her mind, and she asked:

"Where are her clothes? They're mine. I want them. Where have they been put?"

They explained to her that they had not been found. Then she demanded them persistently, crying and moaning.

"They're mine—I want them. Where are they? I want them!"

The more they tried to calm her the more she sobbed and persisted in her demands. She no longer wanted the body, she insisted on having the clothes, as much perhaps through the unconscious cupidity of a wretched being to whom a piece of silver represents a fortune as through maternal tenderness.

And when the little body, rolled up in blankets which had been brought out from Renardet's house, had disappeared in the vehicle, the old woman standing under the trees, sustained by the mayor and the captain, exclaimed:

"I have nothing, nothing, nothing in the world, not even her little cap—her little cap."

The cure, a young priest, had just arrived. He took it on himself to accompany the mother, and they went away together toward the village. The mother's grief was modified by the sugary words of the clergyman, who promised her a thousand compensations. But she kept repeating: "If I had only her little cap." This idea now dominated every other.

Renardet called from the distance:

"You will lunch with us, Monsieur l'Abbe—in an hour's time."

The priest turned his head round and replied:

"With pleasure, Monsieur le Maire. I'll be with you at twelve."

And they all directed their steps toward the house, whose gray front, with the large tower built on the edge of the Brindille, could be seen through the branches.

The meal lasted a long time. They talked about the crime. Everybody was of the same opinion. It had been committed by some tramp passing there by mere chance while the little girl was bathing.

Then the magistrates returned to Rouy, announcing that they would return next day at an early hour. The doctor and the cure went to their respective homes, while Renardet, after a long walk through the meadows, returned to the wood, where he remained walking till nightfall with slow steps, his hands behind his back.

He went to bed early and was still asleep next morning when the magistrate entered his room. He was rubbing his hands together with a self-satisfied air.

"Ha! ha! You are still sleeping! Well, my dear fellow, we have news this morning."

The mayor sat up in his bed.

"What, pray?"

"Oh! Something strange. You remember well how the mother clamored yesterday for some memento of her daughter, especially her little cap? Well, on opening her door this morning she found on the threshold her child's two little wooden shoes. This proves that the crime was perpetrated by some one from the district, some one who felt pity for her. Besides, the postman, Mederic, brought me the thimble, the knife and the needle case of the dead girl. So, then, the man in carrying off the clothes to hide them must have let fall the articles which were in the pocket. As for me, I attach special importance to the wooden shoes, as they indicate a certain moral culture and a faculty for tenderness on the part of the assassin. We will, therefore, if you have no objection, go over together the principal inhabitants of your district."

The mayor got up. He rang for his shaving water and said:

"With pleasure, but it will take some time, and we may begin at once."

M. Putoin sat astride a chair.

Renardet covered his chin with a white lather while he looked at himself in the glass. Then he sharpened his razor on the strop and continued:

"The principal inhabitant of Carvelin bears the name of Joseph Renardet, mayor, a rich landowner, a rough man who beats guards and coachmen—"

The examining magistrate burst out laughing.

"That's enough. Let us pass on to the next."

"The second in importance is Pelledent, his deputy, a cattle breeder, an equally rich landowner, a crafty peasant, very sly, very close-fisted on every question of money, but incapable in my opinion of having perpetrated such a crime."

"Continue," said M. Putoin.

Renardet, while proceeding with his toilet, reviewed the characters of all the inhabitants of Carvelin. After two hours' discussion their suspicions were fixed on three individuals who had hitherto borne a shady reputation—a poacher named Cavalle, a fisherman named Paquet, who caught trout and crabs, and a cattle drover named Clovis. II

The search for the perpetrator of the crime lasted all summer, but he was not discovered. Those who were suspected and arrested easily proved their innocence, and the authorities were compelled to abandon the attempt to capture the criminal.

But this murder seemed to have moved the entire country in a singular manner. There remained in every one's mind a disquietude, a vague fear, a sensation of mysterious terror, springing not merely from the impossibility of discovering any trace of the assassin, but also and above all from that strange finding of the wooden shoes in front of La Roque's door the day after the crime. The certainty that the murderer had assisted at the investigation, that he was still, doubtless, living in the village, possessed all minds and seemed to brood over the neighborhood like a constant menace.

The wood had also become a dreaded spot, a place to be avoided and supposed to be haunted.

Formerly the inhabitants went there to spend every Sunday afternoon. They used to sit down on the moss at the feet of the huge tall trees or walk along the water's edge watching the trout gliding among the weeds. The boy's used to play bowls, hide-and-seek and other games where the ground had been cleared and levelled, and the girls, in rows of four or five, would trip along, holding one another by the arms and screaming songs with their shrill voices. Now nobody ventured there for fear of finding some corpse lying on the ground.

Autumn arrived, the leaves began to fall from the tall trees, whirling round and round to the ground, and the sky could be seen through the bare branches. Sometimes, when a gust of wind swept over the tree tops, the slow, continuous rain suddenly grew heavier and became a rough storm that covered the moss with a thick yellow carpet that made a kind of creaking sound beneath one's feet.

And the sound of the falling leaves seemed like a wail and the leaves themselves like tears shed by these great, sorrowful trees, that wept in the silence of the bare and empty wood, this dreaded and deserted wood where wandered lonely the soul, the little soul of little Louise Roque.

The Brindille, swollen by the storms, rushed on more quickly, yellow and angry, between its dry banks, bordered by two thin, bare, willow hedges.

And here was Renardet suddenly resuming his walks under the trees. Every day, at sunset, he came out of his house, descended the front steps slowly and entered the wood in a dreamy fashion, with his hands in his pockets, and paced over the damp soft moss, while a legion of rooks from all the neighboring haunts came thither to rest in the tall trees and then flew off like a black cloud uttering loud, discordant cries.

Night came on, and Renardet was still strolling slowly under the trees; then, when the darkness prevented him from walking any longer, he would go back to the house and sink into his armchair in front of the glowing hearth, stretching his damp feet toward the fire.

One morning an important bit of news was circulated through the district; the mayor was having his wood cut down.

Twenty woodcutters were already at work. They had commenced at the corner nearest to the house and worked rapidly in the master's presence.

And each day the wood grew thinner, losing its trees, which fell down one by one, as an army loses its soldiers.

Renardet no longer walked up, and down. He remained from morning till night, contemplating, motionless, with his hands behind his back, the slow destruction of his wood. When a tree fell he placed his foot on it as if it were a corpse. Then he raised his eyes to the next with a kind of secret, calm impatience, as if he expected, hoped for something at the end of this slaughter.

Meanwhile they were approaching the place where little Louise Roque had been found. They came to it one evening in the twilight.

As it was dark, the sky being overcast, the woodcutters wanted to stop their work, putting off till next day the fall of an enormous beech tree, but the mayor objected to this and insisted that they should at once lop and cut down this giant, which had sheltered the crime.

When the lopper had laid it bare and the woodcutters had sapped its base, five men commenced hauling at the rope attached to the top.

The tree resisted; its powerful trunk, although notched to the centre, was as rigid as iron. The workmen, all together, with a sort of simultaneous motion, strained at the rope, bending backward and uttering a cry which timed and regulated their efforts.

Two woodcutters standing close to the giant remained with axes in their grip, like two executioners ready to strike once more, and Renardet, motionless, with his hand on the trunk, awaited the fall with an uneasy, nervous feeling.

One of the men said to him:

"You are too near, Monsieur le Maire. When it falls it may hurt you."

He did not reply and did not move away. He seemed ready to catch the beech tree in his open arms and to cast it on the ground like a wrestler.

All at once, at the base of the tall column of wood there was a rent which seemed to run to the top, like a painful shock; it bent slightly, ready to fall, but still resisting. The men, in a state of excitement, stiffened their arms, renewed their efforts with greater vigor, and, just as the tree came crashing down, Renardet suddenly made a forward step, then stopped, his shoulders raised to receive the irresistible shock, the mortal shock which would crush him to the earth.

But the beech tree, having deviated a little, only rubbed against his loins, throwing him on his face, five metres away.

The workmen dashed forward to lift him up. He had already arisen to his knees, stupefied, with bewildered eyes and passing his hand across his forehead, as if he were awaking from an attack of madness.

When he had got to his feet once more the men, astonished, questioned him, not being able to understand what he had done. He replied in faltering tones that he had been dazed for a moment, or, rather, he had been thinking of his childhood days; that he thought he would have time to run under the tree, just as street boys rush in front of vehicles driving rapidly past; that he had played at danger; that for the past eight days he felt this desire growing stronger within him, asking himself each time a tree began to fall whether he could pass beneath it without being touched. It was a piece of stupidity, he confessed, but every one has these moments of insanity and these temptations to boyish folly.

He made this explanation in a slow tone, searching for his words, and speaking in a colorless tone.

Then he went off, saying:

"Till to-morrow, my friends-till to-morrow."

As soon as he got back to his room he sat down at his table which his lamp lighted up brightly, and, burying his head in his hands, he began to cry.

He remained thus for a long time, then wiped his eyes, raised his head and looked at the clock. It was not yet six o'clock.

He thought:

"I have time before dinner."

And he went to the door and locked it. He then came back, and, sitting down at his table, pulled out the middle drawer. Taking from it a revolver, he laid it down on his papers in full view. The barrel of the firearm glittered, giving out gleams of light.

Renardet gazed at it for some time with the uneasy glance of a drunken man. Then he rose and began to pace up and down the room.

He walked from one end of the apartment to the other, stopping from time to time, only to pace up and down again a moment afterward. Suddenly he opened the door of his dressing-room, steeped a towel in the water pitcher and moistened his forehead, as he had done on the morning of the crime.

Then he, began walking up and down again. Each time he passed the table the gleaming revolver attracted his glance, tempted his hand, but he kept watching the clock and reflected:

"I have still time."

It struck half-past six. Then he took up the revolver, opened his mouth wide with a frightful grimace and stuck the barrel into it as if he wanted to swallow it. He remained in this position for some seconds without moving, his finger on the trigger. Then, suddenly seized with a shudder of horror, he dropped the pistol on the carpet.

He fell back on his armchair, sobbing:

"I cannot. I dare not! My God! my God! How can I have the courage to kill myself?'"

There was a knock at the door. He rose up, bewildered. A servant said:

"Monsieur's dinner is ready."

He replied:

"All right. I'm coming down."

Then he picked up the revolver, locked it up again in the drawer and looked at himself in the mirror over the mantelpiece to see whether his face did not look too much troubled. It was as red as usual, a little redder perhaps. That was all. He went down and seated himself at table.

He ate slowly, like a man who wants to prolong the meal, who does not want to be alone.

Then he smoked several pipes in the hall while the table was being cleared. After that he went back to his room.

As soon as he had locked himself in he looked, under the bed, opened all the closets, explored every corner, rummaged through all the furniture. Then he lighted the candles on the mantelpiece, and, turning round several times, ran his eye all over the apartment with an anguish of terror that distorted his face, for he knew well that he would see her, as he did every night—little Louise Roque, the little girl he had attacked and afterward strangled.

Every night the odious vision came back again. First he seemed to hear a kind of roaring sound, such as is made by a threshing machine or the distant passage of a train over a bridge. Then he commenced to gasp, to suffocate, and he had to unbutton his collar and his belt. He moved about to make his blood circulate, he tried to read, he attempted to sing. It was in vain. His thoughts, in spite of himself, went back to the day of the murder and made him begin it all over again in all its most secret details, with all the violent emotions he had experienced from the first minute to the last.

He had felt on rising that morning, the morning of the horrible day, a little dizziness and headache, which he attributed to the heat, so that he remained in his room until breakfast time.

After the meal he had taken a siesta, then, toward the close of the afternoon, he had gone out to breathe the fresh, soothing breeze under the trees in the wood.

But, as soon as he was outside, the heavy, scorching air of the plain oppressed him still more. The sun, still high in the heavens, poured down on the parched soil waves of burning light. Not a breath of wind stirred the leaves. Every beast and bird, even the grasshoppers, were silent. Renardet reached the tall trees and began to walk over the moss where the Brindille produced a slight freshness of the air beneath the immense roof of branches. But he felt ill at ease. It seemed to him that an unknown, invisible hand was strangling him, and he scarcely thought of anything, having usually few ideas in his head. For the last three months only one thought haunted him, the thought of marrying again. He suffered from living alone, suffered from it morally and physically. Accustomed for ten years past to feeling a woman near him, habituated to her presence every moment, he had need, an imperious and perplexing need of such association. Since Madame Renardet's death he had suffered continually without knowing why, he had suffered at not feeling her dress brushing past him, and, above all, from no longer being able to calm and rest himself in her arms. He had been scarcely six months a widower and he was already looking about in the district for some young girl or some widow he might marry when his period of mourning was at an end.

He had a chaste soul, but it was lodged in a powerful, herculean body, and carnal imaginings began to disturb his sleep and his vigils. He drove them away; they came back again; and he murmured from time to time, smiling at himself:

"Here I am, like St. Anthony."

Having this special morning had several of these visions, the desire suddenly came into his breast to bathe in the Brindille in order to refresh himself and cool his blood.

He knew of a large deep pool, a little farther down, where the people of the neighborhood came sometimes to take a dip in summer. He went there.

Thick willow trees hid this clear body of water where the current rested and went to sleep for a while before starting on its way again. Renardet, as he appeared, thought he heard a light sound, a faint plashing which was not that of the stream on the banks. He softly put aside the leaves and looked. A little girl, quite naked in the transparent water, was beating the water with both hands, dancing about in it and dipping herself with pretty movements. She was not a child nor was she yet a woman. She was plump and developed, while preserving an air of youthful precocity, as of one who had grown rapidly. He no longer moved, overcome with surprise, with desire, holding his breath with a strange, poignant emotion. He remained there, his heart beating as if one of his sensuous dreams had just been realized, as if an impure fairy had conjured up before him this young creature, this little rustic Venus, rising from the eddies of the stream as the real Venus rose from the waves of the sea.

Suddenly the little girl came out of the water, and, without seeing him, came over to where he stood, looking for her clothes in order to dress herself. As she approached gingerly, on account of the sharp-pointed stones, he felt himself pushed toward her by an irresistible force, by a bestial transport of passion, which stirred his flesh, bewildered his mind and made him tremble from head to foot.

She remained standing some seconds behind the willow tree which concealed him from view. Then, losing his reason entirely, he pushed aside the branches, rushed on her and seized her in his arms. She fell, too terrified to offer any resistance, too terror-stricken to cry out. He seemed possessed, not understanding what he was doing.

He woke from his crime as one wakes from a nightmare. The child burst out weeping.

"Hold your tongue! Hold your tongue!" he said. "I'll give you money."

But she did not hear him and went on sobbing.

"Come now, hold your tongue! Do hold your tongue! Keep quiet!" he continued.

She kept shrieking as she tried to free herself. He suddenly realized that he was ruined, and he caught her by the neck to stop her mouth from uttering these heartrending, dreadful screams. As she continued to struggle with the desperate strength of a being who is seeking to fly from death, he pressed his enormous hands on the little throat swollen with screaming, and in a few seconds he had strangled her, so furiously did he grip her. He had not intended to kill her, but only to make her keep quiet.

Then he stood up, overwhelmed with horror.

She lay before him, her face bleeding and blackned. He was about to rush away when there sprang up in his agitated soul the mysterious and undefined instinct that guides all beings in the hour of danger.

He was going to throw the body into the water, but another impulse drove him toward the clothes, which he made into a small package. Then, as he had a piece of twine in his pocket, he tied it up and hid it in a deep portion of the stream, beneath the trunk of a tree that overhung the Brindille.

Then he went off at a rapid pace, reached the meadows, took a wide turn in order to show himself to some peasants who dwelt some distance away at the opposite side of the district, and came back to dine at the usual hour, telling his servants all that was supposed to have happened during his walk.

He slept, however, that night; he slept with a heavy, brutish sleep like the sleep of certain persons condemned to death. He did not open his eyes until the first glimmer of dawn, and he waited till his usual hour for riding, so as to excite no suspicion.

Then he had to be present at the inquiry as to the cause of death. He did so like a somnambulist, in a kind of vision which showed him men and things as in a dream, in a cloud of intoxication, with that sense of unreality which perplexes the mind at the time of the greatest catastrophes.

But the agonized cry of Mother Roque pierced his heart. At that moment he had felt inclined to cast himself at the old woman's feet and to exclaim:

"I am the guilty one!"

But he had restrained himself. He went back, however, during the night to fish up the dead girl's wooden shoes, in order to place them on her mother's threshold.

As long as the inquiry lasted, as long as it was necessary to lead justice astray he was calm, master of himself, crafty and smiling. He discussed quietly with the magistrates all the suppositions that passed through their minds, combated their opinions and demolished their arguments. He even took a keen and mournful pleasure in disturbing their investigations, in embroiling their ideas, in showing the innocence of those whom they suspected.

But as soon as the inquiry was abandoned he became gradually nervous, more excitable than he had been before, although he mastered his irritability. Sudden noises made him start with fear; he shuddered at the slightest thing and trembled sometimes from head to foot when a fly alighted on his forehead. Then he was seized with an imperious desire for motion, which impelled him to take long walks and to remain up whole nights pacing up and down his room.

It was not that he was goaded by remorse. His brutal nature did not lend itself to any shade of sentiment or of moral terror. A man of energy and even of violence, born to make war, to ravage conquered countries and to massacre the vanquished, full of the savage instincts of the hunter and the fighter, he scarcely took count of human life. Though he respected the Church outwardly, from policy, he believed neither in God nor the devil, expecting neither chastisement nor recompense for his acts in another life. His sole belief was a vague philosophy drawn from all the ideas of the encyclopedists of the last century, and he regarded religion as a moral sanction of the law, the one and the other having been invented by men to regulate social relations. To kill any one in a duel, or in war, or in a quarrel, or by accident, or for the sake of revenge, or even through bravado would have seemed to him an amusing and clever thing and would not have left more impression on his mind than a shot fired at a hare; but he had experienced a profound emotion at the murder of this child. He had, in the first place, perpetrated it in the heat of an irresistible gust of passion, in a sort of tempest of the senses that had overpowered his reason. And he had cherished in his heart, in his flesh, on his lips, even to the very tips of his murderous fingers a kind of bestial love, as well as a feeling of terrified horror, toward this little girl surprised by him and basely killed. Every moment his thoughts returned to that horrible scene, and, though he endeavored to drive this picture from his mind, though he put it aside with terror, with disgust, he felt it surging through his soul, moving about in him, waiting incessantly for the moment to reappear.

Then, as evening approached, he was afraid of the shadow falling around him. He did not yet know why the darkness seemed frightful to him, but he instinctively feared it, he felt that it was peopled with terrors. The bright daylight did not lend itself to fears. Things and beings were visible then, and only natural things and beings could exhibit themselves in the light of day. But the night, the impenetrable night, thicker than walls and empty; the infinite night, so black, so vast, in which one might brush against frightful things; the night, when one feels that a mysterious terror is wandering, prowling about, appeared to him to conceal an unknown threatening danger, close beside him.

What was it?

He knew ere long. As he sat in his armchair, rather late one evening when he could not sleep, he thought he saw the curtain of his window move. He waited, uneasily, with beating heart. The drapery did not stir; then, all of a sudden, it moved once more. He did not venture to rise; he no longer ventured to breathe, and yet he was brave. He had often fought, and he would have liked to catch thieves in his house.

Was it true that this curtain did move? he asked himself, fearing that his eyes had deceived him. It was, moreover, such a slight thing, a gentle flutter of drapery, a kind of trembling in its folds, less than an undulation caused by the wind.

Renardet sat still, with staring eyes and outstretched neck. He sprang to his feet abruptly, ashamed of his fear, took four steps, seized the drapery with both hands and pulled it wide apart. At first he saw nothing but darkened glass, resembling plates of glittering ink. The night, the vast, impenetrable night, stretched beyond as far as the invisible horizon. He remained standing in front of this illimitable shadow, and suddenly he perceived a light, a moving light, which seemed some distance away.

Then he put his face close to the window pane, thinking that a person looking for crabs might be poaching in the Brindille, for it was past midnight, and this light rose up at the edge of the stream, under the trees. As he was not yet able to see clearly, Renardet placed his hands over his eyes, and suddenly this light became an illumination, and he beheld little Louise Roque naked and bleeding on the moss. He recoiled, frozen with horror, knocked over his chair and fell over on his back. He remained there some minutes in anguish of mind; then he sat up and began to reflect. He had had a hallucination—that was all, a hallucination due to the fact that a night marauder was walking with a lantern in his hand near the water's edge. What was there astonishing, besides, in the circumstance that the recollection of his crime should sometimes bring before him the vision of the dead girl?

He rose from the ground, swallowed a glass of wine and sat down again. He was thinking:

"What am I to do if this occurs again?"

And it would occur; he felt it; he was sure of it. Already his glance was drawn toward the window; it called him; it attracted him. In order to avoid looking at it, he turned his chair round. Then he took a book and tried to read, but it seemed to him that he presently heard something stirring behind him, and he swung round his armchair on one foot.

The curtain was moving again; unquestionably, it moved this time. He could no longer have any doubt about it.

He rushed forward and grasped it so violently that he pulled it down with its pole. Then he eagerly glued his face to the glass. He saw nothing. All was black outside, and he breathed with the joy of a man whose life has just been saved.

Then he went back to his chair and sat down again, but almost immediately he felt a longing to look out once more through the window. Since the curtain had fallen down, the window made a sort of gap, fascinating and terrible, on the dark landscape. In order not to yield to this dangerous temptation, he undressed, blew out the light and closed his eyes.

Lying on his back motionless, his skin warm and moist, he awaited sleep. Suddenly a great gleam of light flashed across his eyelids. He opened them, believing that his dwelling was on fire. All was black as before, and he leaned on his elbow to try to distinguish the window which had still for him an unconquerable attraction. By dint of, straining his eyes he could perceive some stars, and he rose, groped his way across the room, discovered the panes with his outstretched hands, and placed his forehead close to them. There below, under the trees, lay the body of the little girl gleaming like phosphorus, lighting up the surrounding darkness.

Renardet uttered a cry and rushed toward his bed, where he lay till morning, his head hidden under the pillow.

From that moment his life became intolerable. He passed his days in apprehension of each succeeding night, and each night the vision came back again. As soon as he had locked himself up in his room he strove to resist it, but in vain. An irresistible force lifted him up and pushed him against the window, as if to call the phantom, and he saw it at once, lying first in the spot where the crime was committed in the position in which it had been found.

Then the dead girl rose up and came toward him with little steps just as the child had done when she came out of the river. She advanced quietly, passing straight across the grass and over the bed of withered flowers. Then she rose up in the air toward Renardet's window. She came toward him as she had come on the day of the crime. And the man recoiled before the apparition—he retreated to his bed and sank down upon it, knowing well that the little one had entered the room and that she now was standing behind the curtain, which presently moved. And until daybreak he kept staring at this curtain with a fixed glance, ever waiting to see his victim depart.

But she did not show herself any more; she remained there behind the curtain, which quivered tremulously now and then.

And Renardet, his fingers clutching the clothes, squeezed them as he had squeezed the throat of little Louise Roque.

He heard the clock striking the hours, and in the stillness the pendulum kept ticking in time with the loud beating of his heart. And he suffered, the wretched man, more than any man had ever suffered before.

Then, as soon as a white streak of light on the ceiling announced the approaching day, he felt himself free, alone at last, alone in his room; and he went to sleep. He slept several hours—a restless, feverish sleep in which he retraced in dreams the horrible vision of the past night.

When he went down to the late breakfast he felt exhausted as after unusual exertion, and he scarcely ate anything, still haunted as he was by the fear of what he had seen the night before.

He knew well, however, that it was not an apparition, that the dead do not come back, and that his sick soul, his soul possessed by one thought alone, by an indelible remembrance, was the only cause of his torture, was what brought the dead girl back to life and raised her form before his eyes, on which it was ineffaceably imprinted. But he knew, too, that there was no cure, that he would never escape from the savage persecution of his memory, and he resolved to die rather than to endure these tortures any longer.

Then he thought of how he would kill himself, It must be something simple and natural, which would preclude the idea of suicide. For he clung to his reputation, to the name bequeathed to him by his ancestors; and if his death awakened any suspicion people's thoughts might be, perhaps, directed toward the mysterious crime, toward the murderer who could not be found, and they would not hesitate to accuse him of the crime.

A strange idea came into his head, that of allowing himself to be crushed by the tree at the foot of which he had assassinated little Louise Roque. So he determined to have the wood cut down and to simulate an accident. But the beech tree refused to crush his ribs.

Returning to his house, a prey to utter despair, he had snatched up his revolver, and then did not dare to fire it.

The dinner bell summoned him. He could eat nothing, and he went upstairs again. And he did not know what to do. Now that he had escaped the first time, he felt himself a coward. Presently he would be ready, brave, decided, master of his courage and of his resolution; now he was weak and feared death as much as he did the dead girl.

He faltered:

"I dare not venture it again—I dare not venture it."

Then he glanced with terror, first at the revolver on the table and next at the curtain which hid his window. It seemed to him, moreover, that something horrible would occur as soon as his life was ended. Something? What? A meeting with her, perhaps. She was watching for him; she was waiting for him; she was calling him; and it was in order to seize him in her turn, to draw him toward the doom that would avenge her, and to lead him to die, that she appeared thus every night.

He began to cry like a child, repeating:

"I will not venture it again—I will not venture it."

Then he fell on his knees and murmured:

"My God! my God!" without believing, nevertheless, in God. And he no longer dared, in fact, to look at his window, where he knew the apparition was hiding, nor at his table, where his revolver gleamed. When he had risen up he said:

"This cannot last; there must be an end of it"

The sound of his voice in the silent room made a chill of fear pass through his limbs, but as he could not bring himself to come to a determination, as he felt certain that his finger would always refuse to pull the trigger of his revolver, he turned round to hide his head under the bedclothes and began to reflect.

He would have to find some way in which he could force himself to die, to play some trick on himself which would not permit of any hesitation on his part, any delay, any possible regrets. He envied condemned criminals who are led to the scaffold surrounded by soldiers. Oh! if he could only beg of some one to shoot him; if after confessing his crime to a true friend who would never divulge it he could procure death at his hand. But from whom could he ask this terrible service? From whom? He thought of all the people he knew. The doctor? No, he would talk about it afterward, most probably. And suddenly a fantastic idea entered his mind. He would write to the magistrate, who was on terms of close friendship with him, and would denounce himself as the perpetrator of the crime. He would in this letter confess everything, revealing how his soul had been tortured, how he had resolved to die, how he had hesitated about carrying out his resolution and what means he had employed to strengthen his failing courage. And in the name of their old friendship he would implore of the other to destroy the letter as soon as he had ascertained that the culprit had inflicted justice on himself. Renardet could rely on this magistrate; he knew him to be true, discreet, incapable of even an idle word. He was one of those men who have an inflexible conscience, governed, directed, regulated by their reason alone.

Scarcely had he formed this project when a strange feeling of joy took possession of his heart. He was calm now. He would write his letter slowly, then at daybreak he would deposit it in the box nailed to the outside wall of his office; then he would ascend his tower to watch for the postman's arrival; and when the man in the blue blouse had gone away, he would cast himself head foremost on the rocks on which the foundations rested, He would take care to be seen first by the workmen who had cut down his wood. He could climb to the projecting stone which bore the flagstaff displayed on festivals, He would smash this pole with a shake and carry it along with him as he fell.

Who would suspect that it was not an accident? And he would be killed outright, owing to his weight and the height of the tower.

Presently he got out of bed, went over to the table and began to write. He omitted nothing, not a single detail of the crime, not a single detail of the torments of his heart, and he ended by announcing that he had passed sentence on himself, that he was going to execute the criminal, and begged his friend, his old friend, to be careful that there should never be any stain on his memory.

When he had finished this letter he saw that the day had dawned.

He closed, sealed it and wrote the address. Then he descended with light steps, hurried toward the little white box fastened to the outside wall in the corner of the farmhouse, and when he had thrown into it this letter, which made his hand tremble, he came back quickly, drew the bolts of the great door and climbed up to his tower to wait for the passing of the postman, who was to bear away his death sentence.

He felt self-possessed now. Liberated! Saved!

A cold dry wind, an icy wind passed across his face. He inhaled it eagerly with open mouth, drinking in its chilling kiss. The sky was red, a wintry red, and all the plain, whitened with frost, glistened under the first rays of the sun, as if it were covered with powdered glass.

Renardet, standing up, his head bare, gazed at the vast tract of country before him, the meadows to the left and to the right the village whose chimneys were beginning to smoke in preparation for the morning meal. At his feet he saw the Brindille flowing amid the rocks, where he would soon be crushed to death. He felt new life on that beautiful frosty morning. The light bathed him, entered his being like a new-born hope. A thousand recollections assailed him, recollections of similar mornings, of rapid walks on the hard earth which rang beneath his footsteps, of happy days of shooting on the edges of pools where wild ducks sleep. All the good things that he loved, the good things of existence, rushed to his memory, penetrated him with fresh desires, awakened all the vigorous appetites of his active, powerful body.

And he was about to die! Why? He was going to kill himself stupidly because he was afraid of a shadow-afraid of nothing! He was still rich and in the prime of life. What folly! All he needed was distraction, absence, a voyage in order to forget.

This night even he had not seen the little girl because his mind was preoccupied and had wandered toward some other subject. Perhaps he would not see her any more? And even if she still haunted him in this house, certainly she would not follow him elsewhere! The earth was wide, the future was long.

Why should he die?

His glance travelled across the meadows, and he perceived a blue spot in the path which wound alongside the Brindille. It was Mederic coming to bring letters from the town and to carry away those of the village.

Renardet gave a start, a sensation of pain shot through his breast, and he rushed down the winding staircase to get back his letter, to demand it back from the postman. Little did it matter to him now whether he was seen, He hurried across the grass damp from the light frost of the previous night and arrived in front of the box in the corner of the farmhouse exactly at the same time as the letter carrier.

The latter had opened the little wooden door and drew forth the four papers deposited there by the inhabitants of the locality.

Renardet said to him:

"Good-morrow, Mederic."

"Good-morrow, Monsieur le Maire."

"I say, Mederic, I threw a letter into the box that I want back again. I came to ask you to give it back to me."

"That's all right, Monsieur le Maire—you'll get it."

And the postman raised his eyes. He stood petrified at the sight of Renardet's face. The mayor's cheeks were purple, his eyes were anxious and sunken, with black circles round them, his hair was unbrushed, his beard untrimmed, his necktie unfastened. It was evident that he had not been in bed.

The postman asked:

"Are you ill, Monsieur le Maire?"

The other, suddenly comprehending that his appearance must be unusual, lost countenance and faltered:

"Oh! no-oh! no. Only I jumped out of bed to ask you for this letter. I was asleep. You understand?"

He said in reply:

"What letter?"

"The one you are going to give back to me."

Mederic now began to hesitate. The mayor's attitude did not strike him as natural. There was perhaps a secret in that letter, a political secret. He knew Renardet was not a Republican, and he knew all the tricks and chicanery employed at elections.

He asked:

"To whom is it addressed, this letter of yours?"

"To Monsieur Putoin, the magistrate—you know, my friend, Monsieur Putoin!"

The postman searched through the papers and found the one asked for. Then he began looking at it, turning it round and round between his fingers, much perplexed, much troubled by the fear of either committing a grave offence or of making an enemy of the mayor.

Seeing his hesitation, Renardet made a movement for the purpose of seizing the letter and snatching it away from him. This abrupt action convinced Mederic that some important secret was at stake and made him resolve to do his duty, cost what it may.

So he flung the letter into his bag and fastened it up, with the reply:

"No, I can't, Monsieur le Maire. As long as it is for the magistrate, I can't."

A dreadful pang wrung Renardet's heart and he murmured:

"Why, you know me well. You are even able to recognize my handwriting. I tell you I want that paper."

"I can't."

"Look here, Mederic, you know that I'm incapable of deceiving you—I tell you I want it."

"No, I can't."

A tremor of rage passed through Renardet's soul.

"Damn it all, take care! You know that I never trifle and that I could get you out of your job, my good fellow, and without much delay, either, And then, I am the mayor of the district, after all; and I now order you to give me back that paper."

The postman answered firmly:

"No, I can't, Monsieur le Maire."

Thereupon Renardet, losing his head, caught hold of the postman's arms in order to take away his bag; but, freeing himself by a strong effort, and springing backward, the letter carrier raised his big holly stick. Without losing his temper, he said emphatically:

"Don't touch me, Monsieur le Maire, or I'll strike. Take care, I'm only doing my duty!"

Feeling that he was lost, Renardet suddenly became humble, gentle, appealing to him like a whimpering child:

"Look here, look here, my friend, give me back that letter and I'll recompense you—I'll give you money. Stop! stop! I'll give you a hundred francs, you understand—a hundred francs!"

The postman turned on his heel and started on his journey.

Renardet followed him, out of breath, stammering:

"Mederic, Mederic, listen! I'll give you a thousand francs, you understand—a thousand francs."

The postman still went on without giving any answer.

Renardet went on:

"I'll make your fortune, you understand—whatever you wish—fifty thousand francs—fifty thousand francs for that letter! What does it matter to you? You won't? Well, a hundred thousand—I say—a hundred thousand francs. Do you understand? A hundred thousand francs—a hundred thousand francs."

The postman turned back, his face hard, his eye severe:

"Enough of this, or else I'll repeat to the magistrate everything you have just said to me."

Renardet stopped abruptly. It was all over. He turned back and rushed toward his house, running like a hunted animal.

Then, in his turn, Mederic stopped and watched his flight with stupefaction. He saw the mayor reenter his house, and he waited still, as if something astonishing were about to happen.

In fact, presently the tall form of Renardet appeared on the summit of the Fox's tower. He ran round the platform like a madman. Then he seized the flagstaff and shook it furiously without succeeding in breaking it; then, all of a sudden, like a diver, with his two hands before him, he plunged into space.

Mederic rushed forward to his assistance. He saw the woodcutters going to work and called out to them, telling them an accident had occurred. At the foot of the walls they found a bleeding body, its head crushed on a rock. The Brindille surrounded this rock, and over its clear, calm waters could be seen a long red thread of mingled brains and blood.

THE DONKEY

There was not a breath of air stirring; a heavy mist was lying over the river. It was like a layer of cotton placed on the water. The banks themselves were indistinct, hidden behind strange fogs. But day was breaking and the hill was becoming visible. In the dawning light of day the plaster houses began to appear like white spots. Cocks were crowing in the barnyard.

On the other side of the river, hidden behind the fogs, just opposite Frette, a slight noise from time to time broke the dead silence of the quiet morning. At times it was an indistinct plashing, like the cautious advance of a boat, then again a sharp noise like the rattle of an oar and then the sound of something dropping in the water. Then silence.

Sometimes whispered words, coming perhaps from a distance, perhaps from quite near, pierced through these opaque mists. They passed by like wild birds which have slept in the rushes and which fly away at the first light of day, crossing the mist and uttering a low and timid sound which wakes their brothers along the shores.

Suddenly along the bank, near the village, a barely perceptible shadow appeared on the water. Then it grew, became more distinct and, coming out of the foggy curtain which hung over the river, a flatboat, manned by two men, pushed up on the grass.

The one who was rowing rose and took a pailful of fish from the bottom of the boat, then he threw the dripping net over his shoulder. His companion, who had not made a motion, exclaimed:

"Say, Mailloche, get your gun and see if we can't land some rabbit along the shore."

The other one answered: "All right. I'll be with you in a minute." Then he disappeared, in order to hide their catch.

The man who had stayed in the boat slowly filled his pipe and lighted it. His name was Labouise, but he was called Chicot, and was in partnership with Maillochon, commonly called Mailloche, to practice the doubtful and undefined profession of junk-gatherers along the shore.

They were a low order of sailors and they navigated regularly only in the months of famine. The rest of the time they acted as junk-gatherers. Rowing about on the river day and night, watching for any prey, dead or alive, poachers on the water and nocturnal hunters, sometimes ambushing venison in the Saint-Germain forests, sometimes looking for drowned people and searching their clothes, picking up floating rags and empty bottles; thus did Labouise and Maillochon live easily.

At times they would set out on foot about noon and stroll along straight ahead. They would dine in some inn on the shore and leave again side by side. They would remain away for a couple of days; then one morning they would be seen rowing about in the tub which they called their boat.

At Joinville or at Nogent some boatman would be looking for his boat, which had disappeared one night, probably stolen, while twenty or thirty miles from there, on the Oise, some shopkeeper would be rubbing his hands, congratulating himself on the bargain he had made when he bought a boat the day before for fifty francs, which two men offered him as they were passing.

Maillochon reappeared with his gun wrapped up in rags. He was a man of forty or fifty, tall and thin, with the restless eye of people who are worried by legitimate troubles and of hunted animals. His open shirt showed his hairy chest, but he seemed never to have had any more hair on his face than a short brush of a mustache and a few stiff hairs under his lower lip. He was bald around the temples. When he took off the dirty cap that he wore his scalp seemed to be covered with a fluffy down, like the body of a plucked chicken.

Chicot, on the contrary, was red, fat, short and hairy. He looked like a raw beefsteak. He continually kept his left eye closed, as if he were aiming at something or at somebody, and when people jokingly cried to him, "Open your eye, Labouise!" he would answer quietly: "Never fear, sister, I open it when there's cause to."

He had a habit of calling every one "sister," even his scavenger companion.

He took up the oars again, and once more the boat disappeared in the heavy mist, which was now turned snowy white in the pink-tinted sky.

"What kind of lead did you take, Maillochon?" Labouise asked.

"Very small, number nine; that's the best for rabbits."

They were approaching the other shore so slowly, so quietly that no noise betrayed them. This bank belongs to the Saint-Germain forest and is the boundary line for rabbit hunting. It is covered with burrows hidden under the roots of trees, and the creatures at daybreak frisk about, running in and out of the holes.

Maillochon was kneeling in the bow, watching, his gun hidden on the floor. Suddenly he seized it, aimed, and the report echoed for some time throughout the quiet country.

Labouise, in a few strokes, touched the beach, and his companion, jumping to the ground, picked up a little gray rabbit, not yet dead.

Then the boat once more disappeared into the fog in order to get to the other side, where it could keep away from the game wardens.

The two men seemed to be riding easily on the water. The weapon had disappeared under the board which served as a hiding place and the rabbit was stuffed into Chicot's loose shirt.

After about a quarter of an hour Labouise asked: "Well, sister, shall we get one more?"

"It will suit me," Maillochon answered.

The boat started swiftly down the current. The mist, which was hiding both shores, was beginning to rise. The trees could be barely perceived, as through a veil, and the little clouds of fog were floating up from the water. When they drew near the island, the end of which is opposite Herblay, the two men slackened their pace and began to watch. Soon a second rabbit was killed.

Then they went down until they were half way to Conflans. Here they stopped their boat, tied it to a tree and went to sleep in the bottom of it.

From time to time Labouise would sit up and look over the horizon with his open eye. The last of the morning mist had disappeared and the large summer sun was climbing in the blue sky.

On the other side of the river the vineyard-covered hill stretched out in a semicircle. One house stood out alone at the summit. Everything was silent.

Something was moving slowly along the tow-path, advancing with difficulty. It was a woman dragging a donkey. The stubborn, stiff-jointed beast occasionally stretched out a leg in answer to its companion's efforts, and it proceeded thus, with outstretched neck and ears lying flat, so slowly that one could not tell when it would ever be out of sight.

The woman, bent double, was pulling, turning round occasionally to strike the donkey with a stick.

As soon as he saw her, Labouise exclaimed: "Say, Mailloche!"

Mailloche answered: "What's the matter?"

"Want to have some fun?"

"Of course!"

"Then hurry, sister; we're going to have a laugh."

Chicot took the oars. When he had crossed the river he stopped opposite the woman and called:

"Hey, sister!"

The woman stopped dragging her donkey and looked.

Labouise continued: "What are you doing—going to the locomotive show?"

The woman made no reply. Chicot continued:

"Say, your trotter's prime for a race. Where are you taking him at that speed?"

At last the woman answered: "I'm going to Macquart, at Champioux, to have him killed. He's worthless."

Labouise answered: "You're right. How much do you think Macquart will give you for him?"

The woman wiped her forehead on the back of her hand and hesitated, saying: "How do I know? Perhaps three francs, perhaps four."

Chicot exclaimed: "I'll give you five francs and your errand's done! How's that?"

The woman considered the matter for a second and then exclaimed: "Done!"

The two men landed. Labouise grasped the animal by the bridle. Maillochon asked in surprise:

"What do you expect to do with that carcass?"

Chicot this time opened his other eye in order to express his gaiety. His whole red face was grinning with joy. He chuckled: "Don't worry, sister. I've got my idea."

He gave five francs to the woman, who then sat down by the road to see what was going to happen. Then Labouise, in great humor, got the gun and held it out to Maillochon, saying: "Each one in turn; we're going after big game, sister. Don't get so near or you'll kill it right away! You must make the pleasure last a little."

He placed his companion about forty paces from the victim. The ass, feeling itself free, was trying to get a little of the tall grass, but it was so exhausted that it swayed on its legs as if it were about to fall.

Maillochon aimed slowly and said: "A little pepper for the ears; watch, Ghicot!" And he fired.

The tiny shot struck the donkey's long ears and he began to shake them in order to get rid of the stinging sensation. The two men were doubled up with laughter and stamped their feet with joy. The woman, indignant, rushed forward; she did not want her donkey to be tortured, and she offered to return the five francs. Labouise threatened her with a thrashing and pretended to roll up his sleeves. He had paid, hadn't he? Well, then, he would take a shot at her skirts, just to show that it didn't hurt. She went away, threatening to call the police. They could hear her protesting indignantly and cursing as she went her way.

Maillochon held out the gun to his comrade, saying: "It's your turn, Chicot."

Labouise aimed and fired. The donkey received the charge in his thighs, but the shot was so small and came from such a distance that he thought he was being stung by flies, for he began to thrash himself with his tail.

Labouise sat down to laugh more comfortably, while Maillochon reloaded the weapon, so happy that he seemed to sneeze into the barrel. He stepped forward a few paces, and, aiming at the same place that his friend had shot at, he fired again. This time the beast started, tried to kick and turned its head. At last a little blood was running. It had been wounded and felt a sharp pain, for it tried to run away with a slow, limping, jerky gallop.

Both men darted after the beast, Maillochon with a long stride, Labouise with the short, breathless trot of a little man. But the donkey, tired out, had stopped, and, with a bewildered look, was watching his two murderers approach. Suddenly he stretched his neck and began to bray.

Labouise, out of breath, had taken the gun. This time he walked right up close, as he did not wish to begin the chase over again.

When the poor beast had finished its mournful cry, like a last call for help, the man called: "Hey, Mailloche! Come here, sister; I'm going to give him some medicine." And while the other man was forcing the animal's mouth open, Chicot stuck the barrel of his gun down its throat, as if he were trying to make it drink a potion. Then he said: "Look out, sister, here she goes!"

He pressed the trigger. The donkey stumbled back a few steps, fell down, tried to get up again and finally lay on its side and closed its eyes: The whole body was trembling, its legs were kicking as if it were, trying to run. A stream of blood was oozing through its teeth. Soon it stopped moving. It was dead.

The two men went along, laughing. It was over too quickly; they had not had their money's worth. Maillochon asked: "Well, what are we going to do now?"

Labouise answered: "Don't worry, sister. Get the thing on the boat; we're going to have some fun when night comes."

They went and got the boat. The animal's body was placed on the bottom, covered with fresh grass, and the two men stretched out on it and went to sleep.

Toward noon Labouise drew a bottle of wine, some bread and butter and raw onions from a hiding place in their muddy, worm-eaten boat, and they began to eat.

When the meal was over they once more stretched out on the dead donkey and slept. At nightfall Labouise awoke and shook his comrade, who was snoring like a buzzsaw. "Come on, sister," he ordered.

Maillochon began to row. As they had plenty of time they went up the Seine slowly. They coasted along the reaches covered with water-lilies, and the heavy, mud-covered boat slipped over the lily pads and bent the flowers, which stood up again as soon as they had passed.

When they reached the wall of the Eperon, which separates the Saint-Germain forest from the Maisons-Laffitte Park, Labouise stopped his companion and explained his idea to him. Maillochon was moved by a prolonged, silent laugh.

They threw into the water the grass which had covered the body, took the animal by the feet and hid it behind some bushes. Then they got into their boat again and went to Maisons-Laffitte.

The night was perfectly black when they reached the wine shop of old man Jules. As soon as the dealer saw them he came up, shook hands with them and sat down at their table. They began to talk of one thing and another. By eleven o'clock the last customer had left and old man Jules winked at Labouise and asked: "Well, have you got any?"

Labouise made a motion with his head and answered: "Perhaps so, perhaps not!"

The dealer insisted: "Perhaps you've not nothing but gray ones?"

Chicot dug his hands into his flannel shirt, drew out the ears of a rabbit and declared: "Three francs a pair!"

Then began a long discussion about the price. Two francs sixty-five and the two rabbits were delivered. As the two men were getting up to go, old man Jules, who had been watching them, exclaimed:

"You have something else, but you won't say what."

Labouise answered: "Possibly, but it is not for you; you're too stingy."

The man, growing eager, kept asking: "What is it? Something big? Perhaps we might make a deal."

Labouise, who seemed perplexed, pretended to consult Maillochon with a glance. Then he answered in a slow voice: "This is how it is. We were in the bushes at Eperon when something passed right near us, to the left, at the end of the wall. Mailloche takes a shot and it drops. We skipped on account of the game people. I can't tell you what it is, because I don't know. But it's big enough. But what is it? If I told you I'd be lying, and you know, sister, between us everything's above-board."

Anxiously the man asked: "Think it's venison?"

Labouise answered: "Might be and then again it might not! Venison?—uh! uh!—might be a little big for that! Mind you, I don't say it's a doe, because I don't know, but it might be."

Still the dealer insisted: "Perhaps it's a buck?"

Labouise stretched out his hand, exclaiming: "No, it's not that! It's not a buck. I should have seen the horns. No, it's not a buck!"

"Why didn't you bring it with you?" asked the man.

"Because, sister, from now on I sell from where I stand. Plenty of people will buy. All you have to do is to take a walk over there, find the thing and take it. No risk for me."

The innkeeper, growing suspicious, exclaimed "Supposing he wasn't there!"

Labouise once more raised his hand and said:

"He's there, I swear!—first bush to the left. What it is, I don't know. But it's not a buck, I'm positive. It's for you to find out what it is. Twenty-five francs, cash down!"

Still the man hesitated: "Couldn't you bring it?"

Maillochon exclaimed: "No, indeed! You know our price! Take it or leave it!"

The dealer decided: "It's a bargain for twenty francs!"

And they shook hands over the deal.

Then he took out four big five-franc pieces from the cash drawer, and the two friends pocketed the money. Labouise arose, emptied his glass and left. As he was disappearing in the shadows he turned round to exclaim: "It isn't a buck. I don't know what it is!—but it's there. I'll give you back your money if you find nothing!"

And he disappeared in the darkness. Maillochon, who was following him, kept punching him in the back to express his joy.

MOIRON

As we were still talking about Pranzini, M. Maloureau, who had been attorney general under the Empire, said: "Oh! I formerly knew a very curious affair, curious for several reasons, as you will see.

"I was at that time imperial attorney in one of the provinces. I had to take up the case which has remained famous under the name of the Moiron case.

"Monsieur Moiron, who was a teacher in the north of France, enjoyed an excellent reputation throughout the whole country. He was a person of intelligence, quiet, very religious, a little taciturn; he had married in the district of Boislinot, where he exercised his profession. He had had three children, who had died of consumption, one after the other. From this time he seemed to bestow upon the youngsters confided to his care all the tenderness of his heart. With his own money he bought toys for his best scholars and for the good boys; he gave them little dinners and stuffed them with delicacies, candy and cakes: Everybody loved this good man with his big heart, when suddenly five of his pupils died, in a strange manner, one after the other. It was supposed that there was an epidemic due to the condition of the water, resulting from drought; they looked for the causes without being able to discover them, the more so that the symptoms were so peculiar. The children seemed to be attacked by a feeling of lassitude; they would not eat, they complained of pains in their stomachs, dragged along for a short time, and died in frightful suffering.

"A post-mortem examination was held over the last one, but nothing was discovered. The vitals were sent to Paris and analyzed, and they revealed the presence of no toxic substance.

"For a year nothing new developed; then two little boys, the best scholars in the class, Moiron's favorites, died within four days of each other. An examination of the bodies was again ordered, and in both of them were discovered tiny fragments of crushed glass. The conclusion arrived at was that the two youngsters must imprudently have eaten from some carelessly cleaned receptacle. A glass broken over a pail of milk could have produced this frightful accident, and the affair would have been pushed no further if Moiron's servant had not been taken sick at this time. The physician who was called in noticed the same symptoms he had seen in the children. He questioned her and obtained the admission that she had stolen and eaten some candies that had been bought by the teacher for his scholars.

"On an order from the court the schoolhouse was searched, and a closet was found which was full of toys and dainties destined for the children. Almost all these delicacies contained bits of crushed glass or pieces of broken needles!

"Moiron was immediately arrested; but he seemed so astonished and indignant at the suspicion hanging over him that he was almost released. How ever, indications of his guilt kept appearing, and baffled in my mind my first conviction, based on his excellent reputation, on his whole life, on the complete absence of any motive for such a crime.

"Why should this good, simple, religious man have killed little children, and the very children whom he seemed to love the most, whom he spoiled and stuffed with sweet things, for whom he spent half his salary in buying toys and bonbons?

"One must consider him insane to believe him guilty of this act. Now, Moiron seemed so normal, so quiet, so rational and sensible that it seemed impossible to adjudge him insane.

"However, the proofs kept growing! In none of the candies that were bought at the places where the schoolmaster secured his provisions could the slightest trace of anything suspicious be found.

"He then insisted that an unknown enemy must have opened his cupboard with a false key in order to introduce the glass and the needles into the eatables. And he made up a whole story of an inheritance dependent on the death of a child, determined on and sought by some peasant, and promoted thus by casting suspicions on the schoolmaster. This brute, he claimed, did not care about the other children who were forced to die as well.

"The story was possible. The man appeared to be so sure of himself and in such despair that we should undoubtedly have acquitted him, notwithstanding the charges against him, if two crushing discoveries had not been made, one after the other.

"The first one was a snuffbox full of crushed glass; his own snuffbox, hidden in the desk where he kept his money!

"He explained this new find in an acceptable manner, as the ruse of the real unknown criminal. But a mercer from Saint-Marlouf came to the presiding judge and said that a gentleman had several times come to his store to buy some needles; and he always asked for the thinnest needles he could find, and would break them to see whether they pleased him. The man was brought forward in the presence of a dozen or more persons, and immediately recognized Moiron. The inquest revealed that the schoolmaster had indeed gone into Saint-Marlouf on the days mentioned by the tradesman.

"I will pass over the terrible testimony of children on the choice of dainties and the care which he took to have them eat the things in his presence, and to remove the slightest traces.

"Public indignation demanded capital punishment, and it became more and more insistent, overturning all objections.

"Moiron was condemned to death, and his appeal was rejected. Nothing was left for him but the imperial pardon. I knew through my father that the emperor would not grant it.

"One morning, as I was working in my study, the visit of the prison almoner was announced. He was an old priest who knew men well and understood the habits of criminals. He seemed troubled, ill at ease, nervous. After talking for a few minutes about one thing and another, he arose and said suddenly: 'If Moiron is executed, monsieur, you will have put an innocent man to death.'

"Then he left without bowing, leaving me behind with the deep impression made by his words. He had pronounced them in such a sincere and solemn manner, opening those lips, closed and sealed by the secret of confession, in order to save a life.

"An hour later I left for Paris, and my father immediately asked that I be granted an audience with the emperor.

"The following day I was received. His majesty was working in a little reception room when we were introduced. I described the whole case, and I was just telling about the priest's visit when a door opened behind the sovereign's chair and the empress, who supposed he was alone, appeared. His majesty, Napoleon, consulted her. As soon as she had heard the matter, she exclaimed: 'This man must be pardoned. He must, since he is innocent.'

"Why did this sudden conviction of a religious woman cast a terrible doubt in my mind?

"Until then I had ardently desired a change of sentence. And now I suddenly felt myself the toy, the dupe of a cunning criminal who had employed the priest and confession as a last means of defence.

"I explained my hesitancy to their majesties. The emperor remained undecided, urged on one side by his natural kindness and held back on the other by the fear of being deceived by a criminal; but the empress, who was convinced that the priest had obeyed a divine inspiration, kept repeating: 'Never mind! It is better to spare a criminal than to kill an innocent man!' Her advice was taken. The death sentence was commuted to one of hard labor.

"A few years later I heard that Moiron had again been called to the emperor's attention on account of his exemplary conduct in the prison at Toulon and was now employed as a servant by the director of the penitentiary.

"For a long time I heard nothing more of this man. But about two years ago, while I was spending a summer near Lille with my cousin, De Larielle, I was informed one evening, just as we were sitting down to dinner, that a young priest wished to speak to me.

"I had him shown in and he begged me to come to a dying man who desired absolutely to see me. This had often happened to me in my long career as a magistrate, and, although I had been set aside by the Republic, I was still often called upon in similar circumstances. I therefore followed the priest, who led me to a miserable little room in a large tenement house.

"There I found a strange-looking man on a bed of straw, sitting with his back against the wall, in order to get his breath. He was a sort of skeleton, with dark, gleaming eyes.

"As soon as he saw me, he murmured: 'Don't you recognize me?'

"'No.'

"'I am Moiron.'

"I felt a shiver run through me, and I asked 'The schoolmaster?'

"'Yes.'

"'How do you happen to be here?'

"'The story is too long. I haven't time to tell it. I was going to die —and that priest was brought to me—and as I knew that you were here I sent for you. It is to you that I wish to confess—since you were the one who once saved my life.'

"His hands clutched the straw of his bed through the sheet and he continued in a hoarse, forcible and low tone: 'You see—I owe you the truth—I owe it to you—for it must be told to some one before I leave this earth.

"'It is I who killed the children—all of them. I did it—for revenge!

"'Listen. I was an honest, straightforward, pure man—adoring God—this good Father—this Master who teaches us to love, and not the false God, the executioner, the robber, the murderer who governs the earth. I had never done any harm; I had never committed an evil act. I was as good as it is possible to be, monsieur.

"'I married and had children, and I loved them as no father or mother ever loved their children. I lived only for them. I was wild about them. All three of them died! Why? why? What had I done? I was rebellious, furious; and suddenly my eyes were opened as if I were waking up out of a sleep. I understood that God is bad. Why had He killed my children? I opened my eyes and saw that He loves to kill. He loves only that, monsieur. He gives life but to destroy it! God, monsieur, is a murderer! He needs death every day. And He makes it of every variety, in order the better to be amused. He has invented sickness and accidents in order to give Him diversion all through the months and the years; and when He grows tired of this, He has epidemics, the plague, cholera, diphtheria, smallpox, everything possible! But this does not satisfy Him; all these things are too similar; and so from time to time He has wars, in order to see two hundred thousand soldiers killed at once, crushed in blood and in the mud, blown apart, their arms and legs torn off, their heads smashed by bullets, like eggs that fall on the ground.

"'But this is not all. He has made men who eat each other. And then, as men become better than He, He has made beasts, in order to see men hunt them, kill them and eat them. That is not all. He has made tiny little animals which live one day, flies who die by the millions in one hour, ants which we are continually crushing under our feet, and so many, many others that we cannot even imagine. And all these things are continually killing each other and dying. And the good Lord looks on and is amused, for He sees everything, the big ones as well as the little ones, those who are in the drops of water and those in the other firmaments. He watches them and is amused. Wretch!

"'Then, monsieur, I began to kill children. I played a trick on Him. He did not get those. It was not He, but I! And I would have killed many others, but you caught me. There!

"'I was to be executed. I! How He would have laughed! Then I asked for a priest, and I lied. I confessed to him. I lied and I lived.

"'Now, all is over. I can no longer escape from Him. I no longer fear Him, monsieur; I despise Him too much.'

"This poor wretch was frightful to see as he lay there gasping, opening an enormous mouth in order to utter words which could scarcely be heard, his breath rattling, picking at his bed and moving his thin legs under a grimy sheet as though trying to escape.

"Oh! The mere remembrance of it is frightful!

"'You have nothing more to say?' I asked.

"'No, monsieur.'

"'Then, farewell.'

"'Farewell, monsieur, till some day——'

"I turned to the ashen-faced priest, whose dark outline stood out against the wall, and asked: 'Are you going to stay here, Monsieur l'Abbe?'

"'Yes.'

"Then the dying man sneered: 'Yes, yes, He sends His vultures to the corpses.'

"I had had enough of this. I opened the door and ran away."

THE DISPENSER OF HOLY WATER

He lived formerly in a little house beside the high road outside the village. He had set up in business as a wheelwright, after marrying the daughter of a farmer of the neighborhood, and as they were both industrious, they managed to save up a nice little fortune. But they had no children, and this caused them great sorrow. Finally a son was born, whom they named Jean. They both loved and petted him, enfolding him with their affection, and were unwilling to let him be out of their sight.

When he was five years old some mountebanks passed through the country and set up their tent in the town hall square.

Jean, who had seen them pass by, made his escape from the house, and after his father had made a long search for him, he found him among the learned goats and trick dogs, uttering shouts of laughter and sitting on the knees of an old clown.

Three days later, just as they were sitting down to dinner, the wheelwright and his wife noticed that their son was not in the house. They looked for him in the garden, and as they did not find him, his father went out into the road and shouted at the top of his voice, "Jean!"

Night came on. A brown vapor arose making distant objects look still farther away and giving them a dismal, weird appearance. Three tall pines, close at hand, seemed to be weeping. Still there was no reply, but the air appeared to be full of indistinct sighing. The father listened for some time, thinking he heard a sound first in one direction, then in another, and, almost beside himself, he ran, out into the night, calling incessantly "Jean! Jean!"

He ran along thus until daybreak, filling the, darkness with his shouts, terrifying stray animals, torn by a terrible anguish and fearing that he was losing his mind. His wife, seated on the stone step of their home, sobbed until morning.

They did not find their son. They both aged rapidly in their inconsolable sorrow. Finally they sold their house and set out to search together.

They inquired of the shepherds on the hillsides, of the tradesmen passing by, of the peasants in the villages and of the authorities in the towns. But their boy had been lost a long time and no one knew anything about him. He had probably forgotten his own name by this time and also the name of his village, and his parents wept in silence, having lost hope.

Before long their money came to an end, and they worked out by the day in the farms and inns, doing the most menial work, eating what was left from the tables, sleeping on the ground and suffering from cold. Then as they became enfeebled by hard work no one would employ them any longer, and they were forced to beg along the high roads. They accosted passers-by in an entreating voice and with sad, discouraged faces; they begged a morsel of bread from the harvesters who were dining around a tree in the fields at noon, and they ate in silence seated on the edge of a ditch. An innkeeper to whom they told their story said to them one day:

"I know some one who had lost their daughter, and they found her in Paris."

They at once set out for Paris.

When they entered the great city they were bewildered by its size and by the crowds that they saw. But they knew that Jean must be in the midst of all these people, though they did not know how to set about looking for him. Then they feared that they might not recognize him, for he was only five years old when they last saw him.

They visited every place, went through all the streets, stopping whenever they saw a group of people, hoping for some providential meeting, some extraordinary luck, some compassionate fate.

They frequently walked at haphazard straight ahead, leaning one against the other, looking so sad and poverty-stricken that people would give them alms without their asking.

They spent every Sunday at the doors of the churches, watching the crowds entering and leaving, trying to distinguish among the faces one that might be familiar. Several times they thought they recognized him, but always found they had made a mistake.

In the vestibule of one of the churches which they visited the most frequently there was an old dispenser of holy Water who had become their friend. He also had a very sad history, and their sympathy for him had established a bond of close friendship between them. It ended by them all three living together in a poor lodging on the top floor of a large house situated at some distance, quite on the outskirts of the city, and the wheelwright would sometimes take his new friend's place at the church when the latter was ill.

Winter came, a very severe winter. The poor holy water sprinkler died and the parish priest appointed the wheelwright, whose misfortunes had come to his knowledge, to replace him. He went every morning and sat in the same place, on the same chair, wearing away the old stone pillar by continually leaning against it. He would gaze steadily at every man who entered the church and looked forward to Sunday with as much impatience as a schoolboy, for on that day the church was filled with people from morning till night.

He became very old, growing weaker each day from the dampness of the church, and his hope oozed away gradually.

He now knew by sight all the people who came to the services; he knew their hours, their manners, could distinguish their step on the stone pavement.

His interests had become so contracted that the entrance of a stranger in the church was for him a great event. One day two ladies came in; one was old, the other young—a mother and daughter probably. Behind them came a man who was following them. He bowed to them as they came out, and after offering them some holy water, he took the arm of the elder lady.

"That must be the fiance of the younger one," thought the wheelwright. And until evening he kept trying to recall where he had formerly seen a young man who resembled this one. But the one he was thinking of must be an old man by this time, for it seemed as if he had known him down home in his youth.

The same man frequently came again to walk home with the ladies, and this vague, distant, familiar resemblance which he could not place worried the old man so much that he made his wife come with him to see if she could help his impaired memory.

One evening as it was growing dusk the three strangers entered together. When they had passed the old man said:

"Well, do you know him?"

His wife anxiously tried to ransack her memory. Suddenly she said in a low tone:

"Yes—yes—but he is darker, taller, stouter and is dressed like a gentleman, but, father, all the same, it is your face when you were young!"

The old man started violently.

It was true. He looked like himself and also like his brother who was dead, and like his father, whom he remembered while he was yet young. The old couple were so affected that they could not speak. The three persons came out and were about to leave the church.

The man touched his finger to the holy water sprinkler. Then the old man, whose hand was trembling so that he was fairly sprinkling the ground with holy water, exclaimed:

"Jean!"

The young man stopped and looked at him.

He repeated in a lower tone:

"Jean!"

The two women looked at them without understanding.

He then said for the third time, sobbing as he did so:

"Jean!"

The man stooped down, with his face close to the old man's, and as a memory of his childhood dawned on him he replied:

"Papa Pierre, Mamma Jeanne!"

He had forgotten everything, his father's surname and the name of his native place, but he always remembered those two words that he had so often repeated: "Papa Pierre, Mamma Jeanne."

He sank to the floor, his face on the old man's knees, and he wept, kissing now his father and then his mother, while they were almost breathless from intense joy.

The two ladies also wept, understanding as they did that some great happiness had come to pass.

Then they all went to the young man's house and he told them his history. The circus people had carried him off. For three years he traveled with them in various countries. Then the troupe disbanded, and one day an old lady in a chateau had paid to have him stay with her because she liked his appearance. As he was intelligent, he was sent to school, then to college, and the old lady having no children, had left him all her money. He, for his part, had tried to find his parents, but as he could remember only the two names, "Papa Pierre, Mamma Jeanne," he had been unable to do so. Now he was about to be married, and he introduced his fiancee, who was very good and very pretty.

When the two old people had told their story in their turn he kissed them once more. They sat up very late that night, not daring to retire lest the happiness they had so long sought should escape them again while they were asleep.

But misfortune had lost its hold on them and they were happy for the rest of their lives.

A PARRICIDE

The lawyer had presented a plea of insanity. How could anyone explain this strange crime otherwise?

One morning, in the grass near Chatou, two bodies had been found, a man and a woman, well known, rich, no longer young and married since the preceding year, the woman having been a widow for three years before.

They were not known to have enemies; they had not been robbed. They seemed to have been thrown from the roadside into the river, after having been struck, one after the other, with a long iron spike.

The investigation revealed nothing. The boatmen, who had been questioned, knew nothing. The matter was about to be given up, when a young carpenter from a neighboring village, Georges Louis, nicknamed "the Bourgeois," gave himself up.

To all questions he only answered this:

"I had known the man for two years, the woman for six months. They often had me repair old furniture for them, because I am a clever workman."

And when he was asked:

"Why did you kill them?"

He would obstinately answer:

"I killed them because I wanted to kill them."

They could get nothing more out of him.

This man was undoubtedly an illegitimate child, put out to nurse and then abandoned. He had no other name than

Georges Louis, but as on growing up he became particularly intelligent, with the good taste and native refinement which his acquaintances did not have, he was nicknamed "the Bourgeois," and he was never called otherwise. He had become remarkably clever in the trade of a carpenter, which he had taken up. He was also said to be a socialist fanatic, a believer in communistic and nihilistic doctrines, a great reader of bloodthirsty novels, an influential political agitator and a clever orator in the public meetings of workmen or of farmers.

His lawyer had pleaded insanity.

Indeed, how could one imagine that this workman should kill his best customers, rich and generous (as he knew), who in two years had enabled him to earn three thousand francs (his books showed it)? Only one explanation could be offered: insanity, the fixed idea of the unclassed individual who reeks vengeance on two bourgeois, on all the bourgeoisie, and the lawyer made a clever allusion to this nickname of "The Bourgeois," given throughout the neighborhood to this poor wretch. He exclaimed:

"Is this irony not enough to unbalance the mind of this poor wretch, who has neither father nor mother? He is an ardent republican. What am I saying? He even belongs to the same political party, the members of which, formerly shot or exiled by the government, it now welcomes with open arms this party to which arson is a principle and murder an ordinary occurrence.

"These gloomy doctrines, now applauded in public meetings, have ruined this man. He has heard republicans—even women, yes, women—ask for the blood of M. Gambetta, the blood of M. Grevy; his weakened mind gave way; he wanted blood, the blood of a bourgeois!

"It is not he whom you should condemn, gentlemen; it is the Commune!"

Everywhere could be heard murmurs of assent. Everyone felt that the lawyer had won his case. The prosecuting attorney did not oppose him.

Then the presiding judge asked the accused the customary question:

"Prisoner, is there anything that you wish to add to your defense?"

The man stood up.

He was a short, flaxen blond, with calm, clear, gray eyes. A strong, frank, sonorous voice came from this frail-looking boy and, at the first words, quickly changed the opinion which had been formed of him.

He spoke loud in a declamatory manner, but so distinctly that every word could be understood in the farthest corners of the big hall:

"Your honor, as I do not wish to go to an insane asylum, and as I even prefer death to that, I will tell everything.

"I killed this man and this woman because they were my parents.

"Now, listen, and judge me.

"A woman, having given birth to a boy, sent him out, somewhere, to a nurse. Did she even know where her accomplice carried this innocent little being, condemned to eternal misery, to the shame of an illegitimate birth; to more than that—to death, since he was abandoned and the nurse, no longer receiving the monthly pension, might, as they often do, let him die of hunger and neglect!

"The woman who nursed me was honest, better, more noble, more of a mother than my own mother. She brought me up. She did wrong in doing her duty. It is more humane to let them die, these little wretches who are cast away in suburban villages just as garbage is thrown away.

"I grew up with the indistinct impression that I was carrying some burden of shame. One day the other children called me a 'b——-'. They did not know the meaning of this word, which one of them had heard at home. I was also ignorant of its meaning, but I felt the sting all the same.

"I was, I may say, one of the cleverest boys in the school. I would have been a good man, your honor, perhaps a man of superior intellect, if my parents had not committed the crime of abandoning me.

"This crime was committed against me. I was the victim, they were the guilty ones. I was defenseless, they were pitiless. Their duty was to love me, they rejected me.

"I owed them life—but is life a boon? To me, at any rate, it was a misfortune. After their shameful desertion, I owed them only vengeance. They committed against me the most inhuman, the most infamous, the most monstrous crime which can be committed against a human creature.

"A man who has been insulted, strikes; a man who has been robbed, takes back his own by force. A man who has been deceived, played upon, tortured, kills; a man who has been slapped, kills; a man who has been dishonored, kills. I have been robbed, deceived, tortured, morally slapped, dishonored, all this to a greater degree than those whose anger you excuse.

"I revenged myself, I killed. It was my legitimate right. I took their happy life in exchange for the terrible one which they had forced on me.

"You will call me parricide! Were these people my parents, for whom I was an abominable burden, a terror, an infamous shame; for whom my birth was a calamity and my life a threat of disgrace? They sought a selfish pleasure; they got an unexpected child. They suppressed the child. My turn came to do the same for them.

"And yet, up to quite recently, I was ready to love them.

"As I have said, this man, my father, came to me for the first time two years ago. I suspected nothing. He ordered two pieces of furniture. I found out, later on, that, under the seal of secrecy, naturally, he had sought information from the priest.

"He returned often. He gave me a lot of work and paid me well. Sometimes he would even talk to me of one thing or another. I felt a growing affection for him.

"At the beginning of this year he brought with him his wife, my mother. When she entered she was trembling so that I thought her to be suffering from some nervous disease. Then she asked for a seat and a glass of water. She said nothing; she looked around abstractedly at my work and only answered 'yes' and 'no,' at random, to all the questions which he asked her. When she had left I thought her a little unbalanced.

"The following month they returned. She was calm, self-controlled. That day they chattered for a long time, and they left me a rather large order. I saw her three more times, without suspecting anything. But one day she began to talk to me of my life, of my childhood, of my parents. I answered: 'Madame, my parents were wretches who deserted me.' Then she clutched at her heart and fell, unconscious. I immediately thought: 'She is my mother!' but I took care not to let her notice anything. I wished to observe her.

"I, in turn, sought out information about them. I learned that they had been married since last July, my mother having been a widow for only three years. There had been rumors that they had loved each other during the lifetime of the first husband, but there was no proof of it. I was the proof—the proof which they had at first hidden and then hoped to destroy.

"I waited. She returned one evening, escorted as usual by my father. That day she seemed deeply moved, I don't know why. Then, as she was leaving, she said to me: 'I wish you success, because you seem to me to be honest and a hard worker; some day you will undoubtedly think of getting married. I have come to help you to choose freely the woman who may suit you. I was married against my inclination once and I know what suffering it causes. Now I am rich, childless, free, mistress of my fortune. Here is your dowry.'

"She held out to me a large, sealed envelope.

"I looked her straight in the eyes and then said: 'Are you my mother?'

"She drew back a few steps and hid her face in her hands so as not to see me. He, the man, my father, supported her in his arms and cried out to me: 'You must be crazy!'

"I answered: 'Not in the least. I know that you are my parents. I cannot be thus deceived. Admit it and I will keep the secret; I will bear you no ill will; I will remain what I am, a carpenter.'

"He retreated towards the door, still supporting his wife who was beginning to sob. Quickly I locked the door, put the key in my pocket and continued: 'Look at her and dare to deny that she is my mother.'

"Then he flew into a passion, very pale, terrified at the thought that the scandal, which had so far been avoided, might suddenly break out; that their position, their good name, their honor might all at once be lost. He stammered out: 'You are a rascal, you wish to get money from us! That's the thanks we get for trying to help such common people!'

"My mother, bewildered, kept repeating: 'Let's get out of here, let's get out!'

"Then, when he found the door locked, he exclaimed: 'If you do not open this door immediately, I will have you thrown into prison for blackmail and assault!'

"I had remained calm; I opened the door and saw them disappear in the darkness.

"Then I seemed to have been suddenly orphaned, deserted, pushed to the wall. I was seized with an overwhelming sadness, mingled with anger, hatred, disgust; my whole being seemed to rise up in revolt against the injustice, the meanness, the dishonor, the rejected love. I began to run, in order to overtake them along the Seine, which they had to follow in order to reach the station of Chaton.

"I soon caught up with them. It was now pitch dark. I was creeping up behind them softly, that they might not hear me. My mother was still crying. My father was saying: 'It's all your own fault. Why did you wish to see him? It was absurd in our position. We could have helped him from afar, without showing ourselves. Of what use are these dangerous visits, since we can't recognize him?'

"Then I rushed up to them, beseeching. I cried:

"'You see! You are my parents. You have already rejected me once; would you repulse me again?'

"Then, your honor, he struck me. I swear it on my honor, before the law and my country. He struck me, and as I seized him by the collar, he drew from his pocket a revolver.

"The blood rushed to my head, I no longer knew what I was doing, I had my compass in my pocket; I struck him with it as often as I could.

"Then she began to cry: 'Help! murder!' and to pull my beard. It seems that I killed her also. How do I know what I did then?

"Then, when I saw them both lying on the ground, without thinking, I threw them into the Seine.

"That's all. Now sentence me."

The prisoner sat down. After this revelation the case was carried over to the following session. It comes up very soon. If we were jurymen, what would we do with this parricide?

BERTHA

Dr. Bonnet, my old friend—one sometimes has friends older than one's self—had often invited me to spend some time with him at Riom, and, as I did not know Auvergne, I made up my mind to visit him in the summer of 1876.

I arrived by the morning train, and the first person I saw on the platform was the doctor. He was dressed in a gray suit, and wore a soft, black, wide-brimmed, high-crowned felt hat, narrow at the top like a chimney pot, a hat which hardly any one except an Auvergnat would wear, and which reminded one of a charcoal burner. Dressed like that, the doctor had the appearance of an old young man, with his spare body under his thin coat, and his large head covered with white hair.

He embraced me with that evident pleasure which country people feel when they meet long-expected friends, and, stretching out his arm, he said proudly:

"This is Auvergne!" I saw nothing before me except a range of mountains, whose summits, which resembled truncated cones, must have been extinct volcanoes.

Then, pointing to the name of the station, he said:

"Riom, the fatherland of magistrates, the pride of the magistracy, and which ought rather to be the fatherland of doctors."

"Why?" I, asked.

"Why?" he replied with a laugh. "If you transpose the letters, you have the Latin word 'mori', to die. That is the reason why I settled here, my young friend."

And, delighted at his own joke, he carried me off, rubbing his hands.

As soon as I had swallowed a cup of coffee, he made me go and see the town. I admired the druggist's house, and the other noted houses, which were all black, but as pretty as bric-a-brac, with their facades of sculptured stone. I admired the statue of the Virgin, the patroness of butchers, and he told me an amusing story about this, which I will relate some other time, and then Dr. Bonnet said to me:

"I must beg you to excuse me for a few minutes while I go and see a patient, and then I will take you to Chatel-Guyon, so as to show you the general aspect of the town, and all the mountain chain of the Puy-de-Dome before lunch. You can wait for me outside; I shall only go upstairs and come down immediately."

He left me outside one of those old, gloomy, silent, melancholy houses, which one sees in the provinces, and this one appeared to look particularly sinister, and I soon discovered the reason. All the large windows on the first floor were boarded half way up. The upper part of them alone could be opened, as if one had wished to prevent the people who were locked up in that huge stone box from looking into the street.

When the doctor came down again, I told him how it struck me, and he replied:

"You are quite right; the poor creature who is living there must never see what is going on outside. She is a madwoman, or rather an idiot, what you Normans would call a Niente. It is a miserable story, but a very singular pathological case at the same time. Shall I tell you?"

I begged him to do so, and he continued:

"Twenty years ago the owners of this house, who were my patients, had a daughter who was like all other girls, but I soon discovered that while her body became admirably developed, her intellect remained stationary.

"She began to walk very early, but she could not talk. At first I thought she was deaf, but I soon discovered that, although she heard perfectly, she did not understand anything that was said to her. Violent noises made her start and frightened her, without her understanding how they were caused.

"She grew up into a superb woman, but she was dumb, from an absolute want of intellect. I tried all means to introduce a gleam of intelligence into her brain, but nothing succeeded. I thought I noticed that she knew her nurse, though as soon as she was weaned, she failed to recognize her mother. She could never pronounce that word which is the first that children utter and the last which soldiers murmur when they are dying on the field of battle. She sometimes tried to talk, but she produced nothing but incoherent sounds.

"When the weather was fine, she laughed continually, and emitted low cries which might be compared to the twittering of birds; when it rained she cried and moaned in a mournful, terrifying manner, which sounded like the howling of a dog before a death occurs in a house.

"She was fond of rolling on the grass, as young animals do, and of running about madly, and she would clap her hands every morning, when the sun shone into her room, and would insist, by signs, on being dressed as quickly as possible, so that she might get out.

"She did not appear to distinguish between people, between her mother and her nurse, or between her father and me, or between the coachman and the cook. I particularly liked her parents, who were very unhappy on her account, and went to see them nearly every day. I dined with them quite frequently, which enabled me to remark that Bertha (they had called her Bertha) seemed to recognize the various dishes, and to prefer some to others. At that time she was twelve years old, but as fully formed in figure as a girl of eighteen, and taller than I was. Then the idea struck me of developing her greediness, and by this means of cultivating some slight power of discrimination in her mind, and to force her, by the diversity of flavors, if not to reason, at any rate to arrive at instinctive distinctions, which would of themselves constitute a kind of process that was necessary to thought. Later on, by appealing to her passions, and by carefully making use of those which could serve our purpose, we might hope to obtain a kind of reaction on her intellect, and by degrees increase the unconscious action of her brain.

"One day I put two plates before her, one of soup, and the other of very sweet vanilla cream. I made her taste each of them successively, and then I let her choose for herself, and she ate the plate of cream. In a short time I made her very greedy, so greedy that it appeared as if the only idea she had in her head was the desire for eating. She perfectly recognized the various dishes, and stretched out her hands toward those that she liked, and took hold of them eagerly, and she used to cry when they were taken from her. Then I thought I would try and teach her to come to the dining-room when the dinner bell rang. It took a long time, but I succeeded in the end. In her vacant intellect a vague correlation was established between sound and taste, a correspondence between the two senses, an appeal from one to the other, and consequently a sort of connection of ideas—if one can call that kind of instinctive hyphen between two organic functions an idea—and so I carried my experiments further, and taught her, with much difficulty, to recognize meal times by the clock.

"It was impossible for me for a long time to attract her attention to the hands, but I succeeded in making her remark the clockwork and the striking apparatus. The means I employed were very simple; I asked them not to have the bell rung for lunch, and everybody got up and went into the dining-room when the little brass hammer struck twelve o'clock, but I found great difficulty in making her learn to count the strokes. She ran to the door each time she heard the clock strike, but by degrees she learned that all the strokes had not the same value as far as regarded meals, and she frequently fixed her eyes, guided by her ears, on the dial of the clock.

"When I noticed that, I took care every day at twelve, and at six o'clock, to place my fingers on the figures twelve and six, as soon as the moment she was waiting for had arrived, and I soon noticed that she attentively followed the motion of the small brass hands, which I had often turned in her presence.

"She had understood! Perhaps I ought rather to say that she had grasped the idea. I had succeeded in getting the knowledge, or, rather, the sensation, of the time into her, just as is the case with carp, who certainly have no clocks, when they are fed every day exactly at the same time.

"When once I had obtained that result all the clocks and watches in the house occupied her attention almost exclusively. She spent her time in looking at them, listening to them, and in waiting for meal time, and once something very funny happened. The striking apparatus of a pretty little Louis XVI clock that hung at the head of her bed having got out of order, she noticed it. She sat for twenty minutes with her eyes on the hands, waiting for it to strike ten, but when the hands passed the figure she was astonished at not hearing anything; so stupefied was she, indeed, that she sat down, no doubt overwhelmed by a feeling of violent emotion such as attacks us in the face of some terrible catastrophe. And she had the wonderful patience to wait until eleven o'clock in order to see what would happen, and as she naturally heard nothing, she was suddenly either seized with a wild fit of rage at having been deceived and imposed upon by appearances, or else overcome by that fear which some frightened creature feels at some terrible mystery, and by the furious impatience of a passionate individual who meets with some obstacle; she took up the tongs from the fireplace and struck the clock so violently that she broke it to pieces in a moment.

"It was evident, therefore, that her, brain did act and calculate, obscurely it is true, and within very restricted limits, for I could never succeed in making her distinguish persons as she distinguished the time; and to stir her intellect, it was necessary to appeal to her passions, in the material sense of the word, and we soon had another, and alas! a very terrible proof of this!

"She had grown up into a splendid girl, a perfect type of a race, a sort of lovely and stupid Venus. She was sixteen, and I have rarely seen such perfection of form, such suppleness and such regular features. I said she was a Venus; yes, a fair, stout, vigorous Venus, with large, bright, vacant eyes, which were as blue as the flowers of the flax plant; she had a large mouth with full lips, the mouth of a glutton, of a sensualist, a mouth made for kisses. Well, one morning her father came into my consulting room with a strange look on his face, and, sitting down without even replying to my greeting, he said:

"'I want to speak to you about a very serious matter. Would it be possible—would it be possible for Bertha to marry?'

"'Bertha to marry! Why, it is quite impossible!'

"'Yes, I know, I know,' he replied. 'But reflect, doctor. Don't you think—perhaps—we hoped—if she had children—it would be a great shock to her, but a great happiness, and—who knows whether maternity might not rouse her intellect?'

"I was in a state of great perplexity. He was right, and it was possible that such a new situation, and that wonderful instinct of maternity, which beats in the hearts of the lower animals as it does in the heart of a woman, which makes the hen fly at a dog's jaws to defend her chickens, might bring about a revolution, an utter change in her vacant mind, and set the motionless mechanism of her thoughts in motion. And then, moreover, I immediately remembered a personal instance. Some years previously I had owned a spaniel bitch who was so stupid that I could do nothing with her, but when she had had puppies she became, if not exactly intelligent, yet almost like many other dogs who had not been thoroughly broken.

"As soon as I foresaw the possibility of this, the wish to get Bertha married grew in me, not so much out of friendship for her and her poor parents as from scientific curiosity. What would happen? It was a singular problem. I said in reply to her father:

"'Perhaps you are right. You might make the attempt, but you will never find a man to consent to marry her.'

"'I have found somebody,' he said, in a low voice.

"I was dumfounded, and said: 'Somebody really suitable? Some one of your own rank and position in society?'

"'Decidedly,' he replied.

"'Oh! And may I ask his name?'

"'I came on purpose to tell you, and to consult you. It is Monsieur Gaston du Boys de Lucelles.'

"I felt inclined to exclaim: 'The wretch!' but I held my tongue, and after a few moments' silence I said:

"'Oh! Very good. I see nothing against it.'

"The poor man shook me heartily by the hand.

"'She is to be married next month,' he said.

"Monsieur Gaston du Boys de Lucelles was a scapegrace of good family, who, after having spent all that he had inherited from his father, and having incurred debts in all kinds of doubtful ways, had been trying to discover some other means of obtaining money, and he had discovered this method. He was a good-looking young fellow, and in capital health, but fast; one of that odious race of provincial fast men, and he appeared to me to be as suitable as anyone, and could be got rid of later by making him an allowance. He came to the house to pay his addresses and to strut about before the idiot girl, who, however, seemed to please him. He brought her flowers, kissed her hands, sat at her feet, and looked at her with affectionate eyes; but she took no notice of any of his attentions, and did not make any distinction between him and the other persons who were about her.

"However, the marriage took place, and you may guess how my curiosity was aroused. I went to see Bertha the next day to try and discover from her looks whether any feelings had been awakened in her, but I found her just the same as she was every day, wholly taken up with the clock and dinner, while he, on the contrary, appeared really in love, and tried to rouse his wife's spirits and affection by little endearments and such caresses as one bestows on a kitten. He could think of nothing better.

"I called upon the married couple pretty frequently, and I soon perceived that the young woman knew her husband, and gave him those eager looks which she had hitherto only bestowed on sweet dishes.

"She followed his movements, knew his step on the stairs or in the neighboring rooms, clapped her hands when he came in, and her face was changed and brightened by the flames of profound happiness and of desire.

"She loved him with her whole body and with all her soul to the very depths of her poor, weak soul, and with all her heart, that poor heart of some grateful animal. It was really a delightful and innocent picture of simple passion, of carnal and yet modest passion, such as nature had implanted in mankind, before man had complicated and disfigured it by all the various shades of sentiment. But he soon grew tired of this ardent, beautiful, dumb creature, and did not spend more than an hour during the day with her, thinking it sufficient if he came home at night, and she began to suffer in consequence. She used to wait for him from morning till night with her eyes on the clock; she did not even look after the meals now, for he took all his away from home, Clermont, Chatel-Guyon, Royat, no matter where, as long as he was not obliged to come home.

"She began to grow thin; every other thought, every other wish, every other expectation, and every confused hope disappeared from her mind, and the hours during which she did not see him became hours of terrible suffering to her. Soon he ceased to come home regularly of nights; he spent them with women at the casino at Royat and did not come home until daybreak. But she never went to bed before he returned. She remained sitting motionless in an easy-chair, with her eyes fixed on the hands of the clock, which turned so slowly and regularly round the china face on which the hours were painted.

"She heard the trot of his horse in the distance and sat up with a start, and when he came into the room she got up with the movements of an automaton and pointed to the clock, as if to say: 'Look how late it is!'

"And he began to be afraid of this amorous and jealous, half-witted woman, and flew into a rage, as brutes do; and one night he even went so far as to strike her, so they sent for me. When I arrived she was writhing and screaming in a terrible crisis of pain, anger, passion, how do I know what? Can one tell what goes on in such undeveloped brains?

"I calmed her by subcutaneous injections of morphine, and forbade her to see that man again, for I saw clearly that marriage would infallibly kill her by degrees.

"Then she went mad! Yes, my dear friend, that idiot went mad. She is always thinking of him and waiting for him; she waits for him all day and night, awake or asleep, at this very moment, ceaselessly. When I saw her getting thinner and thinner, and as she persisted in never taking her eyes off the clocks, I had them removed from the house. I thus made it impossible for her to count the hours, and to try to remember, from her indistinct reminiscences, at what time he used to come home formerly. I hope to destroy the recollection of it in time, and to extinguish that ray of thought which I kindled with so much difficulty.

"The other day I tried an experiment. I offered her my watch; she took it and looked at it for some time; then she began to scream terribly, as if the sight of that little object had suddenly awakened her memory, which was beginning to grow indistinct. She is pitiably thin now, with hollow and glittering eyes, and she walks up and down ceaselessly, like a wild beast in its cage; I have had gratings put on the windows, boarded them up half way, and have had the seats fixed to the floor so as to prevent her from looking to see whether he is coming.

"Oh! her poor parents! What a life they must lead!"

We had got to the top of the hill, and the doctor turned round and said to me:

"Look at Riom from here."

The gloomy town looked like some ancient city. Behind it a green, wooded plain studded with towns and villages, and bathed in a soft blue haze, extended until it was lost in the distance. Far away, on my right, there was a range of lofty mountains with round summits, or else cut off flat, as if with a sword, and the doctor began to enumerate the villages, towns and hills, and to give me the history of all of them. But I did not listen to him; I was thinking of nothing but the madwoman, and I only saw her. She seemed to be hovering over that vast extent of country like a mournful ghost, and I asked him abruptly:

"What has become of the husband?"

My friend seemed rather surprised, but after a few moments' hesitation, he replied:

"He is living at Royat, on an allowance that they made him, and is quite happy; he leads a very fast life."

As we were slowly going back, both of us silent and rather low-spirited, an English dogcart, drawn by a thoroughbred horse, came up behind us and passed us rapidly. The doctor took me by the arm.

"There he is," he said.

I saw nothing except a gray felt hat, cocked over one ear above a pair of broad shoulders, driving off in a cloud of dust.

THE PATRON

We never dreamed of such good fortune! The son of a provincial bailiff, Jean Marin had come, as do so many others, to study law in the Quartier Latin. In the various beer-houses that he had frequented he had made friends with several talkative students who spouted politics as they drank their beer. He had a great admiration for them and followed them persistently from cafe to cafe, even paying for their drinks when he had the money.

He became a lawyer and pleaded causes, which he lost. However, one morning he read in the papers that one of his former comrades of the Quartier had just been appointed deputy.

He again became his faithful hound, the friend who does the drudgery, the unpleasant tasks, for whom one sends when one has need of him and with whom one does not stand on ceremony. But it chanced through some parliamentary incident that the deputy became a minister. Six months later Jean Marin was appointed a state councillor.

He was so elated with pride at first that he lost his head. He would walk through the streets just to show himself off, as though one could tell by his appearance what position he occupied. He managed to say to the shopkeepers as soon as he entered a store, bringing it in somehow in the course of the most insignificant remarks and even to the news vendors and the cabmen:

"I, who am a state councillor—"

Then, in consequence of his position as well as for professional reasons and as in duty bound through being an influential and generous man, he felt an imperious need of patronizing others. He offered his support to every one on all occasions and with unbounded generosity.

When he met any one he recognized on the boulevards he would advance to meet them with a charmed air, would take their hand, inquire after their health, and, without waiting for any questions, remark:

"You know I am state councillor, and I am entirely at your service. If I can be of any use to you, do not hesitate to call on me. In my position one has great influence."

Then he would go into some cafe with the friend he had just met and ask for a pen and ink and a sheet of paper. "Just one, waiter; it is to write a letter of recommendation."

And he wrote ten, twenty, fifty letters of recommendation a day. He wrote them to the Cafe Americain, to Bignon's, to Tortoni's, to the Maison Doree, to the Cafe Riche, to the Helder, to the Cafe Anglais, to the Napolitain, everywhere, everywhere. He wrote them to all the officials of the republican government, from the magistrates to the ministers. And he was happy, perfectly happy.

One morning as he was starting out to go to the council it began to rain. He hesitated about taking a cab, but decided not to do so and set out on foot.

The rain came down in torrents, swamping the sidewalks and inundating the streets. M. Marin was obliged to take shelter in a doorway. An old priest was standing there—an old priest with white hair. Before he became a councillor M. Marin did not like the clergy. Now he treated them with consideration, ever since a cardinal had consulted him on an important matter. The rain continued to pour down in floods and obliged the two men to take shelter in the porter's lodge so as to avoid getting wet. M. Marin, who was always itching to talk so as to let people know who he was, remarked:

"This is horrible weather, Monsieur l'Abbe."

The old priest bowed:

"Yes indeed, sir, it is very unpleasant when one comes to Paris for only a few days."

"Ah! You come from the provinces?"

"Yes, monsieur. I am only passing through on my journey."

"It certainly is very disagreeable to have rain during the few days one spends in the capital. We officials who stay here the year round, we think nothing of it."

The priest did not reply. He was looking at the street where the rain seemed to be falling less heavily. And with a sudden resolve he raised his cassock just as women raise their skirts in stepping across water.

M. Marin, seeing him start away, exclaimed:

"You will get drenched, Monsieur l'Abbe. Wait a few moments longer; the rain will be over."

The good man stopped irresistibly and then said:

"But I am in a great hurry. I have an important engagement."

M. Marin seemed quite worried.

"But you will be absolutely drenched. Might I ask in which direction you are going?"

The priest appeared to hesitate. Then he said:

"I am going in the direction of the Palais Royal."

"In that case, if you will allow me, Monsieur l'Abbe, I will offer you the shelter of my umbrella: As for me, I am going to the council. I am a councillor of state."

The old priest raised his head and looked at his neighbor and then exclaimed:

"I thank you, monsieur. I shall be glad to accept your offer."

M. Marin then took his arm and led him away. He directed him, watched over him and advised him.

"Be careful of that stream, Monsieur l'Abbe. And be very careful about the carriage wheels; they spatter you with mud sometimes from head to foot. Look out for the umbrellas of the people passing by; there is nothing more dangerous to the eyes than the tips of the ribs. Women especially are unbearable; they pay no heed to where they are going and always jab you in the face with the point of their parasols or umbrellas. And they never move aside for anybody. One would suppose the town belonged to them. They monopolize the pavement and the street. It is my opinion that their education has been greatly neglected."

And M. Marin laughed.

The priest did not reply. He walked along, slightly bent over, picking his steps carefully so as not to get mud on his boots or his cassock.

M. Marin resumed:

"I suppose you have come to Paris to divert your mind a little?"

The good man replied:

"No, I have some business to attend to."

"Ali! Is it important business? Might I venture to ask what it is? If I can be of any service to you, you may command me."

The priest seemed embarrassed. He murmured:

"Oh, it is a little personal matter; a little difficulty with—with my bishop. It would not interest you. It is a matter of internal regulation—an ecclesiastical affair."

M. Marin was eager.

"But it is precisely the state council that regulates all those things. In that case, make use of me."

"Yes, monsieur, it is to the council that I am going. You are a thousand times too kind. I have to see M. Lerepere and M. Savon and also perhaps M. Petitpas."

M. Marin stopped short.

"Why, those are my friends, Monsieur l'Abbe, my best friends, excellent colleagues, charming men. I will speak to them about you, and very highly. Count upon me."

The cure thanked him, apologizing for troubling him, and stammered out a thousand grateful promises.

M. Marin was enchanted.

"Ah, you may be proud of having made a stroke of luck, Monsieur l'Abbe. You will see—you will see that, thanks to me, your affair will go along swimmingly."

They reached the council hall. M. Marin took the priest into his office, offered him a chair in front of the fire and sat down himself at his desk and began to write.

"My dear colleague, allow me to recommend to you most highly a venerable and particularly worthy and deserving priest, M. L'Abbe——"

He stopped and asked:

"Your name, if you please?"

"L'Abbe Ceinture."

"M. l'Abbe Ceinture, who needs your good office in a little matter which he will communicate to you.

"I am pleased at this incident which gives me an opportunity, my dear colleague——"

And he finished with the usual compliments.

When he had written the three letters he handed them to his protege, who took his departure with many protestations of gratitude.

M. Marin attended to some business and then went home, passed the day quietly, slept well, woke in a good humor and sent for his newspapers.

The first he opened was a radical sheet. He read:

"OUR CLERGY AND OUR GOVERNMENT OFFICIALS

"We shall never make an end of enumerating the misdeeds of the clergy. A certain priest, named Ceinture, convicted of conspiracy against the present government, accused of base actions to which we will not even allude, suspected besides of being a former Jesuit, metamorphosed into a simple priest, suspended by a bishop for causes that are said to be unmentionable and summoned to Paris to give an explanation of his conduct, has found an ardent defender in the man named Marin, a councillor of state, who was not afraid to give this frocked malefactor the warmest letters of recommendation to all the republican officials, his colleagues.

"We call the, attention of the ministry to the unheard of attitude of this councillor of state——"

M. Marin bounded out of bed, dressed himself and hastened to his colleague, Petitpas, who said to him:

"How now? You were crazy to recommend to me that old conspirator!"

M. Marin, bewildered, stammered out:

"Why no—you see—I was deceived. He looked such an honest man. He played me a trick—a disgraceful trick! I beg that you will sentence him severely, very severely. I am going to write. Tell me to whom I should write about having him punished. I will go and see the attorney-general and the archbishop of Paris—yes, the archbishop."

And seating himself abruptly at M. Petitpas' desk, he wrote:

"Monseigneur, I have the honor to bring to your grace's notice the fact that I have recently been made a victim of the intrigues and lies of a certain Abbe Ceinture, who imposed on my kind-heartedness.

"Deceived by the representations of this ecclesiastic, I was led——"

Then, having signed and sealed his letter, he turned to his colleague and exclaimed:

"See here; my dear friend, let this be a warning to you never to recommend any one again."

THE DOOR

"Bah!" exclaimed Karl Massouligny, "the question of complaisant husbands is a difficult one. I have seen many kinds, and yet I am unable to give an opinion about any of them. I have often tried to determine whether they are blind, weak or clairvoyant. I believe that there are some which belong to each of these categories.

"Let us quickly pass over the blind ones. They cannot rightly be called complaisant, since they do not know, but they are good creatures who cannot see farther than their nose. It is a curious and interesting thing to notice the ease with which men and women can, be deceived. We are taken in by the slightest trick of those who surround us, by our children, our friends, our servants, our tradespeople. Humanity is credulous, and in order to discover deceit in others, we do not display one-tenth the shrewdness which we use when we, in turn, wish to deceive some one else.

"Clairvoyant husbands may be divided into three classes: Those who have some interest, pecuniary, ambitious or otherwise, in their wife's having love affairs. These ask only to safeguard appearances as much as possible, and they are satisfied.

"Next come those who get angry. What a beautiful novel one could write about them!

"Finally the weak ones! Those who are afraid of scandal.

"There are also those who are powerless, or, rather, tired, who flee from the duties of matrimony through fear of ataxia or apoplexy, who are satisfied to see a friend run these risks.

"But I once met a husband of a rare species, who guarded against the common accident in a strange and witty manner.

"In Paris I had made the acquaintance of an elegant, fashionable couple. The woman, nervous, tall, slender, courted, was supposed to have had many love adventures. She pleased me with her wit, and I believe that I pleased her also. I courted her, a trial courting to which she answered with evident provocations. Soon we got to tender glances, hand pressures, all the little gallantries which precede the final attack.

"Nevertheless, I hesitated. I consider that, as a rule, the majority of society intrigues, however short they may be, are not worth the trouble which they give us and the difficulties which may arise. I therefore mentally compared the advantages and disadvantages which I might expect, and I thought I noticed that the husband suspected me.

"One evening, at a ball, as I was saying tender things to the young woman in a little parlor leading from the big hall where the dancing was going on, I noticed in a mirror the reflection of some one who was watching me. It was he. Our looks met and then I saw him turn his head and walk away.

"I murmured: 'Your husband is spying on us.'

"She seemed dumbfounded and asked: 'My husband?'

"'Yes, he has been watching us for some time:

"'Nonsense! Are you sure?'

"'Very sure.'

"'How strange! He is usually extraordinarily pleasant to all my friends.'

"'Perhaps he guessed that I love you!'

"'Nonsense! You are not the first one to pay attention to me. Every woman who is a little in view drags behind her a herd of admirers.'

"'Yes. But I love you deeply.'

"'Admitting that that is true, does a husband ever guess those things?'

"'Then he is not jealous?'

"'No-no!'

"She thought for an instant and then continued: 'No. I do not think that I ever noticed any jealousy on his part.'

"'Has he never watched you?'

"'No. As I said, he is always agreeable to my friends.'

"From that day my courting became much more assiduous. The woman did not please me any more than before, but the probable jealousy of her husband tempted me greatly.

"As for her, I judged her coolly and clearly. She had a certain worldly charm, due to a quick, gay, amiable and superficial mind, but no real, deep attraction. She was, as I have already said, an excitable little being, all on the surface, with rather a showy elegance. How can I explain myself? She was an ornament, not a home.

"One day, after taking dinner with her, her husband said to me, just as I was leaving: 'My dear friend' (he now called me 'friend'), 'we soon leave for the country. It is a great pleasure to my wife and myself to entertain people whom we like. We would be very pleased to have you spend a month with us. It would be very nice of you to do so.'

"I was dumbfounded, but I accepted.

"A month later I arrived at their estate of Vertcresson, in Touraine. They were waiting for me at the station, five miles from the chateau. There were three of them, she, the husband and a gentleman unknown to me, the Comte de Morterade, to whom I was introduced. He appeared to be delighted to make my acquaintance, and the strangest ideas passed through my mind while we trotted along the beautiful road between two hedges. I was saying to myself: 'Let's see, what can this mean? Here is a husband who cannot doubt that his wife and I are on more than friendly terms, and yet he invites me to his house, receives me like an old friend and seems to say: "Go ahead, my friend, the road is clear!"'

"Then I am introduced to a very pleasant gentleman, who seems already to have settled down in the house, and—and who is perhaps trying to get out of it, and who seems as pleased at my arrival as the husband himself.

"Is it some former admirer who wishes to retire? One might think so. But, then, would these two men tacitly have come to one of these infamous little agreements so common in society? And it is proposed to me that I should quietly enter into the pact and carry it out. All hands and arms are held out to me. All doors and hearts are open to me.

"And what about her? An enigma. She cannot be ignorant of everything. However—however—Well, I cannot understand it.

"The dinner was very gay and cordial. On leaving the table the husband and his friend began to play cards, while I went out on the porch to look at the moonlight with madame. She seemed to be greatly affected by nature, and I judged that the moment for my happiness was near. That evening she was really delightful. The country had seemed to make her more tender. Her long, slender waist looked pretty on this stone porch beside a great vase in which grew some flowers. I felt like dragging her out under the trees, throwing myself at her feet and speaking to her words of love.

"Her husband's voice called 'Louise!'

"'Yes, dear.'

"'You are forgetting the tea.'

"'I'll go and see about it, my friend.'

"We returned to the house, and she gave us some tea. When the two men had finished playing cards, they were visibly tired. I had to go to my room. I did not get to sleep till late, and then I slept badly.

"An excursion was decided upon for the following afternoon, and we went in an open carriage to visit some ruins. She and I were in the back of the vehicle and they were opposite us, riding backward. The conversation was sympathetic and agreeable. I am an orphan, and it seemed to me as though I had just found my family, I felt so at home with them.

"Suddenly, as she had stretched out her foot between her husband's legs, he murmured reproachfully: 'Louise, please don't wear out your old shoes yourself. There is no reason for being neater in Paris than in the country.'

"I lowered my eyes. She was indeed wearing worn-out shoes, and I noticed that her stockings were not pulled up tight.

"She had blushed and hidden her foot under her dress. The friend was looking out in the distance with an indifferent and unconcerned look.

"The husband offered me a cigar, which I accepted. For a few days it was impossible for me to be alone with her for two minutes; he was with us everywhere. He was delightful to me, however.

"One morning he came to get me to take a walk before breakfast, and the conversation happened to turn on marriage. I spoke a little about solitude and about how charming life can be made by the affection of a woman. Suddenly he interrupted me, saying: 'My friend, don't talk about things you know nothing about. A woman who has no other reason for loving you will not love you long. All the little coquetries which make them so exquisite when they do not definitely belong to us cease as soon as they become ours. And then—the respectable women—that is to say our wives—are—are not—in fact do not understand their profession of wife. Do you understand?'

"He said no more, and I could not guess his thoughts.

"Two days after this conversation he called me to his room quite early, in order to show me a collection of engravings. I sat in an easy chair opposite the big door which separated his apartment from his wife's, and behind this door I heard some one walking and moving, and I was thinking very little of the engravings, although I kept exclaiming: 'Oh, charming! delightful! exquisite!'

"He suddenly said: 'Oh, I have a beautiful specimen in the next room. I'll go and get it.'

"He ran to the door quickly, and both sides opened as though for a theatrical effect.

"In a large room, all in disorder, in the midst of skirts, collars, waists lying around on the floor, stood a tall, dried-up creature. The lower part of her body was covered with an old, worn-out silk petticoat, which was hanging limply on her shapeless form, and she was standing in front of a mirror brushing some short, sparse blond hairs. Her arms formed two acute angles, and as she turned around in astonishment I saw under a common cotton chemise a regular cemetery of ribs, which were hidden from the public gaze by well-arranged pads.

"The husband uttered a natural exclamation and came back, closing the doors, and said: 'Gracious! how stupid I am! Oh, how thoughtless! My wife will never forgive me for that!'

"I already felt like thanking him. I left three days later, after cordially shaking hands with the two men and kissing the lady's fingers. She bade me a cold good-by."

Karl Massouligny was silent. Some one asked: "But what was the friend?"

"I don't know—however—however he looked greatly distressed to see me leaving so soon."

A SALE

The defendants, Cesaire-Isidore Brument and Prosper-Napoleon Cornu, appeared before the Court of Assizes of the Seine-Inferieure, on a charge of attempted murder, by drowning, of Mme. Brument, lawful wife of the first of the aforenamed.

The two prisoners sat side by side on the traditional bench. They were two peasants; the first was small and stout, with short arms, short legs, and a round head with a red pimply face, planted directly on his trunk, which was also round and short, and with apparently no neck. He was a raiser of pigs and lived at Cacheville-la-Goupil, in the district of Criquetot.

Cornu (Prosper-Napoleon) was thin, of medium height, with enormously long arms. His head was on crooked, his jaw awry, and he squinted. A blue blouse, as long as a shirt, hung down to his knees, and his yellow hair, which was scanty and plastered down on his head, gave his face a worn-out, dirty look, a dilapidated look that was frightful. He had been nicknamed "the cure" because he could imitate to perfection the chanting in church, and even the sound of the serpent. This talent attracted to his cafe—for he was a saloon keeper at Criquetot—a great many customers who preferred the "mass at Cornu" to the mass in church.

Mme. Brument, seated on the witness bench, was a thin peasant woman who seemed to be always asleep. She sat there motionless, her hands crossed on her knees, gazing fixedly before her with a stupid expression.

The judge continued his interrogation.

"Well, then, Mme. Brument, they came into your house and threw you into a barrel full of water. Tell us the details. Stand up."

She rose. She looked as tall as a flag pole with her cap which looked like a white skull cap. She said in a drawling tone:

"I was shelling beans. Just then they came in. I said to myself, 'What is the matter with them? They do not seem natural, they seem up to some mischief.' They watched me sideways, like this, especially Cornu, because he squints. I do not like to see them together, for they are two good-for-nothings when they are in company. I said: 'What do you want with me?' They did not answer. I had a sort of mistrust——"

The defendant Brument interrupted the witness hastily, saying:

"I was full."

Then Cornu, turning towards his accomplice said in the deep tones of an organ:

"Say that we were both full, and you will be telling no lie."

The judge, severely:

"You mean by that that you were both drunk?"

Brument: "There can be no question about it."

Cornu: "That might happen to anyone."

The judge to the victim: "Continue your testimony, woman Brument."

"Well, Brument said to me, 'Do you wish to earn a hundred sous?' 'Yes,' I replied, seeing that a hundred sous are not picked up in a horse's tracks. Then he said: 'Open your eyes and do as I do,' and he went to fetch the large empty barrel which is under the rain pipe in the corner, and he turned it over and brought it into my kitchen, and stuck it down in the middle of the floor, and then he said to me: 'Go and fetch water until it is full.'

"So I went to the pond with two pails and carried water, and still more water for an hour, seeing that the barrel was as large as a vat, saving your presence, m'sieu le president.

"All this time Brument and Cornu were drinking a glass, and then another glass, and then another. They were finishing their drinks when I said to them: 'You are full, fuller than this barrel.' And Brument answered me. 'Do not worry, go on with your work, your turn will come, each one has his share.' I paid no attention to what he said as he was full.

"When the barrel was full to the brim, I said: 'There, that's done.'

"And then Cornu gave me a hundred sous, not Brument, Cornu; it was Cornu gave them to me. And Brument said: 'Do you wish to earn a hundred sous more?' 'Yes,' I said, for I am not accustomed to presents like that. Then he said: 'Take off your clothes!

"'Take off my clothes?'

"'Yes,' he said.

"'How many shall I take off?'

"'If it worries you at all, keep on your chemise, that won't bother us.'

"A hundred sous is a hundred sous, and I have to undress myself; but I did not fancy undressing before those two good-for-nothings. I took off my cap, and then my jacket, and then my skirt, and then my sabots. Brument said, 'Keep on your stockings, also; we are good fellows.'

"And Cornu said, too, 'We are good fellows.'

"So there I was, almost like mother Eve. And they got up from their chairs, but could not stand straight, they were so full, saving your presence, M'sieu le president.

"I said to myself: 'What are they up to?'

"And Brument said: 'Are you ready?'

"And Cornu said: 'I'm ready!'

"And then they took me, Brument by the head, and Cornu by the feet, as one might take, for instance, a sheet that has been washed. Then I began to bawl.

"And Brument said: 'Keep still, wretched creature!'

"And they lifted me up in the air and put me into the barrel, which was full of water, so that I had a check of the circulation, a chill to my very insides.

"And Brument said: 'Is that all?'

"Cornu said: 'That is all.'

"Brument said: 'The head is not in, that will make a difference in the measure.'

"Cornu said: 'Put in her head.'

"And then Brument pushed down my head as if to drown me, so that the water ran into my nose, so that I could already see Paradise. And he pushed it down, and I disappeared.

"And then he must have been frightened. He pulled me out and said: 'Go and get dry, carcass.'

"As for me, I took to my heels and ran as far as M. le cure's. He lent me a skirt belonging to his servant, for I was almost in a state of nature, and he went to fetch Maitre Chicot, the country watchman who went to Criquetot to fetch the police who came to my house with me.

"Then we found Brument and Cornu fighting each other like two rams.

"Brument was bawling: 'It isn't true, I tell you that there is at least a cubic metre in it. It is the method that was no good.'

"Cornu bawled: 'Four pails, that is almost half a cubic metre. You need not reply, that's what it is.'

"The police captain put them both under arrest. I have no more to tell."

She sat down. The audience in the court room laughed. The jurors looked at one another in astonishment. The judge said:

"Defendant Cornu, you seem to have been the instigator of this infamous plot. What have you to say?"

And Cornu rose in his turn.

"Judge," he replied, "I was full."

The Judge answered gravely:

"I know it. Proceed."

"I will. Well, Brument came to my place about nine o'clock, and ordered two drinks, and said: 'There's one for you, Cornu.' I sat down opposite him and drank, and out of politeness, I offered him a glass. Then he returned the compliment and so did I, and so it went on from glass to glass until noon, when we were full.

"Then Brument began to cry. That touched me. I asked him what was the matter. He said: 'I must have a thousand francs by Thursday.' That cooled me off a little, you understand. Then he said to me all at once: 'I will sell you my wife.'

"I was full, and I was a widower. You understand, that stirred me up. I did not know his wife, but she was a woman, wasn't she? I asked him: 'How much would you sell her for?'

"He reflected, or pretended to reflect. When one is full one is not very clear-headed, and he replied: 'I will sell her by the cubic metre.'

"That did not surprise me, for I was as drunk as he was, and I knew what a cubic metre is in my business. It is a thousand litres, that suited me.

"But the price remained to be settled. All depends on the quality. I said: 'How much do you want a cubic metre?'

"He answered: 'Two thousand francs.'

"I gave a bound like a rabbit, and then I reflected that a woman ought not to measure more than three hundred litres. So I said: 'That's too dear.'

"He answered: 'I cannot do it for less. I should lose by it.'

"You understand, one is not a dealer in hogs for nothing. One understands one's business. But, if he is smart, the seller of bacon, I am smarter, seeing that I sell them also. Ha, Ha, Ha! So I said to him: 'If she were new, I would not say anything, but she has been married to you for some time, so she is not as fresh as she was. I will give you fifteen hundred francs a cubic metre, not a sou more. Will that suit you?'

"He answered: 'That will do. That's a bargain!'

"I agreed, and we started out, arm in arm. We must help each other in this world.

"But a fear came to me: 'How can you measure her unless you put her into the liquid?'

"Then he explained his idea, not without difficulty for he was full. He said to me: 'I take a barrel, and fill it with water to the brim. I put her in it. All the water that comes out we will measure, that is the way to fix it.'

"I said: 'I see, I understand. But this water that overflows will run away; how are you going to gather it up?'

"Then he began stuffing me and explained to me that all we should have to do would be to refill the barrel with the water his wife had displaced as soon as she should have left. All the water we should pour in would be the measure. I supposed about ten pails; that would be a cubic metre. He isn't a fool, all the same, when he is drunk, that old horse.

"To be brief, we reached his house and I took a look at its mistress. A beautiful woman she certainly was not. Anyone can see her, for there she is. I said to myself: 'I am disappointed, but never mind, she will be of value; handsome or ugly, it is all the same, is it not, monsieur le president?' And then I saw that she was as thin as a rail. I said to myself: 'She will not measure four hundred litres.' I understand the matter, it being in liquids.

"She told you about the proceeding. I even let her keep on her chemise and stockings, to my own disadvantage.

"When that was done she ran away. I said: 'Look out, Brument! she is escaping.'

"He replied: 'Do not be afraid. I will catch her all right. She will have to come back to sleep, I will measure the deficit.'

"We measured. Not four pailfuls. Ha, Ha, Ha!"

The witness began to laugh so persistently that a gendarme was obliged to punch him in the back. Having quieted down, he resumed:

"In short, Brument exclaimed: 'Nothing doing, that is not enough.' I bawled and bawled, and bawled again, he punched me, I hit back. That would have kept on till the Day of judgment, seeing we were both drunk.

"Then came the gendarmes! They swore at us, they took us off to prison. I want damages."

He sat down.

Brument confirmed in every particular the statements of his accomplice. The jury, in consternation, retired to deliberate.

At the end of an hour they returned a verdict of acquittal for the defendants, with some severe strictures on the dignity of marriage, and establishing the precise limitations of business transactions.

Brument went home to the domestic roof accompanied by his wife.

Cornu went back to his business.

THE IMPOLITE SEX

Madame de X. to Madame de L
ETRETAT, Friday.
My Dear Aunt:

I am coming to see you without anyone knowing it. I shall be at Les Fresnes on the 2d of September, the day before the hunting season opens, as I do not want to miss it, so that I may tease these gentlemen. You are too good, aunt, and you will allow them, as you usually do when there are no strange guests, to come to table, under pretext of fatigue, without dressing or shaving for the occasion.

They are delighted, of course, when I am not present. But I shall be there and will hold a review, like a general, at dinner time; and, if I find a single one of them at all careless in dress, no matter how little, I mean to send them down to the kitchen with the servants.

The men of to-day have so little consideration for others and so little good manners that one must be always severe with them. We live indeed in an age of vulgarity. When they quarrel, they insult each other in terms worthy of longshoremen, and, in our presence, they do not conduct themselves even as well as our servants. It is at the seaside that you see this most clearly. They are to be found there in battalions, and you can judge them in the lump. Oh! what coarse beings they are!

Just imagine, in a train, a gentleman who looked well, as I thought at first sight, thanks to his tailor, carefully took off his boots in order to put on a pair of old shoes! Another, an old man who was probably some wealthy upstart (these are the most ill-bred), while sitting opposite to me, had the delicacy to place his two feet on the seat quite close to me. This is a positive fact.

At the watering-places the vulgarity is unrestrained. I must here make one admission—that my indignation is perhaps due to the fact that I am not accustomed to associate, as a rule, with the sort of people one comes across here, for I should be less shocked by their manners if I had the opportunity of observing them oftener. In the office of the hotel I was nearly thrown down by a young man who snatched the key over my head. Another knocked against me so violently without begging my pardon or lifting his hat, coming away from a ball at the Casino, that it gave me a pain in the chest. It is the same way with all of them. Watch them addressing ladies on the terrace; they scarcely ever bow. They merely raise their hands to their headgear. But, indeed, as they are all more or less bald, it is the best plan.

But what exasperates and disgusts me particularly is the liberty they take of talking in public, without any kind of precaution, about the most revolting adventures. When two men are together, they relate to each other, in the broadest language and with the most abominable comments really horrible stories, without caring in the slightest degree whether a woman's ear is within reach of their voices. Yesterday, on the beach, I was forced to leave the place where I was sitting in order not to be any longer the involuntary confidante of an obscene anecdote, told in such immodest language that I felt just as humiliated as indignant at having heard it. Would not the most elementary good-breeding teach them to speak in a lower tone about such matters when we are near at hand. Etretat is, moreover, the country of gossip and scandal. From five to seven o'clock you can see people wandering about in quest of scandal, which they retail from group to group. As you remarked to me, my dear aunt, tittle-tattle is the mark of petty individuals and petty minds. It is also the consolation of women who are no longer loved or sought after. It is enough for me to observe the women who are fondest of gossiping to be persuaded that you are quite right.

The other day I was present at a musical evening at the Casino, given by a remarkable artist, Madame Masson, who sings in a truly delightful manner. I took the opportunity of applauding the admirable Coquelin, as well as two charming vaudeville performers, M——and Meillet. I met, on this occasion, all the bathers who were at the beach. It is no great distinction this year.

Next day I went to lunch at Yport. I noticed a tall man with a beard, coming out of a large house like a castle. It was the painter, Jean Paul Laurens. He is not satisfied apparently with imprisoning the subjects of his pictures, he insists on imprisoning himself.

Then I found myself seated on the shingle close to a man still young, of gentle and refined appearance, who was reading poetry. But he read it with such concentration, with such passion, I may say, that he did not even raise his eyes towards me. I was somewhat astonished and asked the proprietor of the baths, without appearing to be much concerned, the name of this gentleman. I laughed to myself a little at this reader of rhymes; he seemed behind the age, for a man. This person, I thought, must be a simpleton. Well, aunt, I am now infatuated about this stranger. Just fancy, his name is Sully Prudhomme! I went back and sat down beside him again so as to get a good look at him. His face has an expression of calmness and of penetration. Somebody came to look for him, and I heard his voice, which is sweet and almost timid. He would certainly not tell obscene stories aloud in public or knock up against ladies without apologizing. He is assuredly a man of refinement, but his refinement is of an almost morbid, sensitive character, I will try this winter to get an introduction to him.

I have no more news, my dear aunt, and I must finish this letter in haste, as the mail will soon close. I kiss your hands and your cheeks. Your devoted niece,

BERTHE DE X.

P. S.—I should add, however, by way of justification of French politeness, that our fellow-countrymen are, when travelling, models of good manners in comparison with the abominable English, who seem to have been brought up in a stable, so careful are they not to discommode themselves in any way, while they always discommode their neighbors.

Madame de L. to Madame de X.

LES FRESNES, Saturday.

My Dear Child:

Many of the things you have said to me are very sensible, but that does not prevent you from being wrong. Like you, I used formerly to feel very indignant at the impoliteness of men, who, as I supposed, constantly treated me with neglect; but, as I grew older and reflected on everything, putting aside coquetry, and observing things without taking any part in them myself, I perceived this much—that if men are not always polite, women are always indescribably rude.

We imagine that we should be permitted to do anything, my darling, and at the same time we consider that we have a right to the utmost respect, and in the most flagrant manner we commit actions devoid of that elementary good-breeding of which you speak so feelingly.

I find, on the contrary, that men consider us much more than we consider them. Besides, darling, men must needs be, and are, what we make them. In a state of society, where women are all true gentlewomen, all men would become gentlemen.

Come now; just observe and reflect.

Look at two women meeting in the street. What an attitude each assumes towards the other! What disparaging looks! What contempt they throw into each glance! How they toss their heads while they inspect each other to find something to condemn! And, if the footpath is narrow, do you think one woman would make room for another, or would beg pardon as she sweeps by? Never! When two men jostle each other by accident in some narrow lane, each of them bows and at the same time gets out of the other's way, while we women press against each other stomach to stomach, face to face, insolently staring each other out of countenance.

Look at two women who are acquaintances meeting on a staircase outside the door of a friend's drawing-room, one of them just leaving, the other about to go in. They begin to talk to each other and block up all the landing. If anyone happens to be coming up behind them, man or woman, do you imagine that they will put themselves half an inch out of their way? Never! never!

I was waiting myself, with my watch in my hands, one day last winter at a certain drawing-room door. And, behind me, two gentlemen were also waiting without showing any readiness, as I did, to lose their temper. The reason was that they had long grown accustomed to our unconscionable insolence.

The other day, before leaving Paris, I went to dine with no less a person than your husband, in the Champs Elysees, in order to enjoy the fresh air. Every table was occupied. The waiter asked us to wait and there would soon be a vacant table.

At that moment I noticed an elderly lady of noble figure, who, having paid for her dinner, seemed on the point of going away. She saw me, scanned me from head to foot, and did not budge. For more than a quarter of an hour she sat there, immovable, putting on her gloves, and calmly staring at those who were waiting like myself. Now, two young men who were just finishing their dinner, having seen me in their turn, hastily summoned the waiter, paid what they owed, and at once offered me their seats, even insisting on standing while waiting for their change. And, bear in mind, my fair niece, that I am no longer pretty, like you, but old and white-haired.

It is we, you see, who should be taught politeness, and the task would be such a difficult one that Hercules himself would not be equal to it. You speak to me about Etretat and about the people who indulged in "tittle-tattle" along the beach of that delightful watering-place. It is a spot now lost to me, a thing of the past, but I found much amusement therein days gone by.

There were only a few of us, people in good society, really good society, and a few artists, and we all fraternized. We paid little attention to gossip in those days.

As we had no monotonous Casino, where people only gather for show, where they whisper, where they dance stupidly, where they succeed in thoroughly boring one another, we sought some other way of passing our evenings pleasantly. Now, just guess what came into the head of one of our husbands? Nothing less than to go and dance each night in one of the farm-houses in the neighborhood.

We started out in a group with a street-organ, generally played by Le Poittevin, the painter, with a cotton nightcap on his head. Two men carried lanterns. We followed in procession, laughing and chattering like a pack of fools.

We woke up the farmer and his servant-maids and farm hands. We got them to make onion soup (horror!), and we danced under the apple trees, to the sound of the barrel-organ. The cocks waking up began to crow in the darkness of the out-houses; the horses began prancing on the straw of their stables. The cool air of the country caressed our cheeks with the smell of grass and of new-mown hay.

How long ago it is! How long ago it is! It is thirty years since then!

I do not want you, my darling, to come for the opening of the hunting season. Why spoil the pleasure of our friends by inflicting on them fashionable toilettes on this day of vigorous exercise in the country? This is the way, child, that men are spoiled. I embrace you. Your old aunt,

GENEVIEVE DE L.

A WEDDING GIFT

For a long time Jacques Bourdillere had sworn that he would never marry, but he suddenly changed his mind. It happened suddenly, one summer, at the seashore.

One morning as he lay stretched out on the sand, watching the women coming out of the water, a little foot had struck him by its neatness and daintiness. He raised his eyes and was delighted with the whole person, although in fact he could see nothing but the ankles and the head emerging from a flannel bathrobe carefully held closed. He was supposed to be sensual and a fast liver. It was therefore by the mere grace of the form that he was at first captured. Then he was held by the charm of the young girl's sweet mind, so simple and good, as fresh as her cheeks and lips.

He was presented to the family and pleased them. He immediately fell madly in love. When he saw Berthe Lannis in the distance, on the long yellow stretch of sand, he would tingle to the roots of his hair. When he was near her he would become silent, unable to speak or even to think, with a kind of throbbing at his heart, and a buzzing in his ears, and a bewilderment in his mind. Was that love?

He did not know or understand, but he had fully decided to have this child for his wife.

Her parents hesitated for a long time, restrained by the young man's bad reputation. It was said that he had an old sweetheart, one of these binding attachments which one always believes to be broken off and yet which always hold.

Besides, for a shorter or longer period, he loved every woman who came within reach of his lips.

Then he settled down and refused, even once, to see the one with whom he had lived for so long. A friend took care of this woman's pension and assured her an income. Jacques paid, but he did not even wish to hear of her, pretending even to ignore her name. She wrote him letters which he never opened. Every week he would recognize the clumsy writing of the abandoned woman, and every week a greater anger surged within him against her, and he would quickly tear the envelope and the paper, without opening it, without reading one single line, knowing in advance the reproaches and complaints which it contained.

As no one had much faith in his constancy, the test was prolonged through the winter, and Berthe's hand was not granted him until the spring. The wedding took place in Paris at the beginning of May.

The young couple had decided not to take the conventional wedding trip, but after a little dance for the younger cousins, which would not be prolonged after eleven o'clock, in order that this day of lengthy ceremonies might not be too tiresome, the young pair were to spend the first night in the parental home and then, on the following morning, to leave for the beach so dear to their hearts, where they had first known and loved each other.

Night had come, and the dance was going on in the large parlor. 'The two had retired into a little Japanese boudoir hung with bright silks and dimly lighted by the soft rays of a large colored lantern hanging from the ceiling like a gigantic egg. Through the open window the fresh air from outside passed over their faces like a caress, for the night was warm and calm, full of the odor of spring.

They were silent, holding each other's hands and from time to time squeezing them with all their might. She sat there with a dreamy look, feeling a little lost at this great change in her life, but smiling, moved, ready to cry, often also almost ready to faint from joy, believing the whole world to be changed by what had just happened to her, uneasy, she knew not why, and feeling her whole body and soul filled with an indefinable and delicious lassitude.

He was looking at her persistently with a fixed smile. He wished to speak, but found nothing to say, and so sat there, expressing all his ardor by pressures of the hand. From time to time he would murmur: "Berthe!" And each time she would raise her eyes to him with a look of tenderness; they would look at each other for a second and then her look, pierced and fascinated by his, would fall.

They found no thoughts to exchange. They had been left alone, but occasionally some of the dancers would cast a rapid glance at them, as though they were the discreet and trusty witnesses of a mystery.

A door opened and a servant entered, holding on a tray a letter which a messenger had just brought. Jacques, trembling, took this paper, overwhelmed by a vague and sudden fear, the mysterious terror of swift misfortune.

He looked for a longtime at the envelope, the writing on which he did not know, not daring to open it, not wishing to read it, with a wild desire to put it in his pocket and say to himself: "I'll leave that till to-morrow, when I'm far away!" But on one corner two big words, underlined, "Very urgent," filled him with terror. Saying, "Please excuse me, my dear," he tore open the envelope. He read the paper, grew frightfully pale, looked over it again, and, slowly, he seemed to spell it out word for word.

When he raised his head his whole expression showed how upset he was. He stammered: "My dear, it's—it's from my best friend, who has had a very great misfortune. He has need of me immediately—for a matter of life or death. Will you excuse me if I leave you for half an hour? I'll be right back."

Trembling and dazed, she stammered: "Go, my dear!" not having been his wife long enough to dare to question him, to demand to know. He disappeared. She remained alone, listening to the dancing in the neighboring parlor.

He had seized the first hat and coat he came to and rushed downstairs three steps at a time. As he was emerging into the street he stopped under the gas-jet of the vestibule and reread the letter. This is what it said:

SIR: A girl by the name of Ravet, an old sweetheart of yours, it seems, has just given birth to a child that she says is yours. The mother is about to die and is begging for you. I take the liberty to write and ask you if you can grant this last request to a woman who seems to be very unhappy and worthy of pity.

Yours truly, DR. BONNARD.

When he reached the sick-room the woman was already on the point of death. He did not recognize her at first. The doctor and two nurses were taking care of her. And everywhere on the floor were pails full of ice and rags covered with blood. Water flooded the carpet; two candles were burning on a bureau; behind the bed, in a little wicker crib, the child was crying, and each time it would moan the mother, in torture, would try to move, shivering under her ice bandages.

She was mortally wounded, killed by this birth. Her life was flowing from her, and, notwithstanding the ice and the care, the merciless hemorrhage continued, hastening her last hour.

She recognized Jacques and wished to raise her arms. They were so weak that she could not do so, but tears coursed down her pallid cheeks. He dropped to his knees beside the bed, seized one of her hands and kissed it frantically. Then, little by little, he drew close to the thin face, which started at the contact. One of the nurses was lighting them with a candle, and the doctor was watching them from the back of the room.

Then she said in a voice which sounded as though it came from a distance: "I am going to die, dear. Promise to stay to the end. Oh! don't leave me now. Don't leave me in my last moments!"

He kissed her face and her hair, and, weeping, he murmured: "Do not be uneasy; I will stay."

It was several minutes before she could speak again, she was so weak. She continued: "The little one is yours. I swear it before God and on my soul. I swear it as I am dying! I have never loved another man but you —promise to take care of the child."

He was trying to take this poor pain-racked body in his arms. Maddened by remorse and sorrow, he stammered: "I swear to you that I will bring him up and love him. He shall never leave me."

Then she tried to kiss Jacques. Powerless to lift her head, she held out her white lips in an appeal for a kiss. He approached his lips to respond to this piteous entreaty.

As soon as she felt a little calmer, she murmured: "Bring him here and let me see if you love him."

He went and got the child. He placed him gently on the bed between them, and the little one stopped crying. She murmured: "Don't move any more!" And he was quiet. And he stayed there, holding in his burning hand this other hand shaking in the chill of death, just as, a while ago, he had been holding a hand trembling with love. From time to time he would cast a quick glance at the clock, which marked midnight, then one o'clock, then two.

The physician had returned. The two nurses, after noiselessly moving about the room for a while, were now sleeping on chairs. The child was asleep, and the mother, with eyes shut, appeared also to be resting.

Suddenly, just as pale daylight was creeping in behind the curtains, she stretched out her arms with such a quick and violent motion that she almost threw her baby on the floor. A kind of rattle was heard in her throat, then she lay on her back motionless, dead.

The nurses sprang forward and declared: "All is over!"

He looked once more at this woman whom he had so loved, then at the clock, which pointed to four, and he ran away, forgetting his overcoat, in the evening dress, with the child in his arms.

After he had left her alone the young wife had waited, calmly enough at first, in the little Japanese boudoir. Then, as she did not see him return, she went back to the parlor with an indifferent and calm appearance, but terribly anxious. When her mother saw her alone she asked: "Where is your husband?" She answered: "In his room; he is coming right back."

After an hour, when everybody had questioned her, she told about the letter, Jacques' upset appearance and her fears of an accident.

Still they waited. The guests left; only the nearest relatives remained. At midnight the bride was put to bed, sobbing bitterly. Her mother and two aunts, sitting around the bed, listened to her crying, silent and in despair. The father had gone to the commissary of police to see if he could obtain some news.

At five o'clock a slight noise was heard in the hall. A door was softly opened and closed. Then suddenly a little cry like the mewing of a cat was heard throughout the silent house.

All the women started forward and Berthe sprang ahead of them all, pushing her way past her aunts, wrapped in a bathrobe.

Jacques stood in the middle of the room, pale and out of breath, holding an infant in his arms. The four women looked at him, astonished; but Berthe, who had suddenly become courageous, rushed forward with anguish in her heart, exclaiming: "What is it? What's the matter?"

He looked about him wildly and answered shortly:

"I—I have a child and the mother has just died."

And with his clumsy hands he held out the screaming infant.

Without saying a word, Berthe seized the child, kissed it and hugged it to her. Then she raised her tear-filled eyes to him, asking: "Did you say that the mother was dead?" He answered: "Yes—just now—in my arms. I had broken with her since summer. I knew nothing. The physician sent for me."

Then Berthe murmured: "Well, we will bring up the little one."

THE RELIC

"To the Abbe Louis d'Ennemare, at Soissons.

"My Dear Abbe.

"My marriage with your cousin is broken off in the most stupid way, all on account of an idiotic trick which I almost involuntarily played my intended. In my perplexity I turn to you, my old school chum, for you may be able to help me out of the difficulty. If you can, I shall be grateful to you until I die.

"You know Gilberte, or, rather, you think you know her, but do we ever understand women? All their opinions, their ideas, their creeds, are a surprise to us. They are all full of twists and turns, cf the unforeseen, of unintelligible arguments, of defective logic and of obstinate ideas, which seem final, but which they alter because a little bird came and perched on the window ledge.

"I need not tell you that your cousin is very religious, as she was brought up by the White (or was it the Black?) Ladies at Nancy. You know that better than I do, but what you perhaps do not know is, that she is just as excitable about other matters as she is about religion. Her head flies away, just as a leaf is whirled away by the wind; and she is a true woman, or, rather, girl, for she is moved or made angry in a moment, starting off at a gallop in affection, just as she does in hatred, and returning in the same manner; and she is pretty—as you know, and more charming than I can say—as you will never know.

"Well, we became engaged, and I adored her, as I adore her still, and she appeared to love me.

"One evening, I received a telegram summoning me to Cologne for a consultation, which might be followed by a serious and difficult operation, and as I had to start the next morning, I went to wish Gilberte good-by, and tell her why I could not dine with them on Wednesday, but would do so on Friday, the day of my return. Ah! Beware of Fridays, for I assure you they are unlucky!

"When I told her that I had to go to Germany, I saw that her eyes filled with tears, but when I said I should be back very soon, she clapped her hands, and said:

"'I am very glad you are going, then! You must bring me back something; a mere trifle, just a souvenir, but a souvenir that you have chosen for me. You must guess what I should like best, do you hear? And then I shall see whether you have any imagination.'

"She thought for a few moments, and then added:

"'I forbid you to spend more than twenty francs on it. I want it for the intention, and for a remembrance of your penetration, and not for its intrinsic value:

"And then, after another moment's silence, she said, in a low voice, and with downcast eyes:

"'If it costs you nothing in money, but is something very ingenious and pretty, I will—I will kiss you.'

"The next day I was in Cologne. It was a case of a terrible accident, which had plunged a whole family into despair, and a difficult amputation was necessary. They lodged me in the house; I might say, they almost locked me up, and I saw nobody but people in tears, who almost deafened me with their lamentations; I operated on a man who appeared to be in a moribund state, and who nearly died under my hands, and with whom I remained two nights; and then, when I saw that there was a chance of his recovery, I drove to the station. I had, however, made a mistake in the trains, and I had an hour to wait, and so I wandered about the streets, still thinking of my poor patient, when a man accosted me. I do not know German, and he was totally ignorant of French, but at last I made out that he was offering me some relics. I thought of Gilberte, for I knew her fanatical devotion, and here was my present ready to hand, so I followed the man into a shop where religious objects were for sale, and I bought a small piece of a bone of one of the Eleven Thousand Virgins.

"The pretended relic was inclosed in a charming old silver box, and that determined my choice, and, putting my purchase into my pocket, I went to the railway station, and so on to Paris.

"As soon as I got home, I wished to examine my purchase again, and on taking hold of it, I found that the box was open, and the relic missing! I searched in vain in my pocket, and turned it inside out; the small bit of bone, which was no bigger than half a pin, had disappeared.

"You know, my dear little Abbe, that my faith is not very fervent, but, as my friend, you are magnanimous enough to put up with my lukewarmness, and to leave me alone, and to wait for the future, so you say. But I absolutely disbelieve in the relics of secondhand dealers in piety, and you share my doubts in that respect. Therefore, the loss of that bit of sheep's carcass did not grieve me, and I easily procured a similar fragment, which I carefully fastened inside my jewel-box, and then I went to see my intended.

"As soon as she saw me, she ran up to me, smiling and eager, and, said to me:

"'What have you brought me?'

"I pretended to have forgotten, but she did not believe me, and I made her beg, and even beseech me. But when I saw that she was devoured by curiosity, I gave her the sacred silver box. She appeared overjoyed.

"'A relic! Oh! A relic!'

"And she kissed the box passionately, so that I was ashamed of my deception. She was not quite satisfied, however, and her uneasiness soon turned to terrible fear, and looking straight into my eyes, she said:

"'Are you sure-that it is genuine?'

"'Absolutely certain.'

"'How can you be so certain?'

"I was trapped; for to say that I had bought it of a man in the streets would be my destruction. What was I to say? A wild idea struck me, and I said, in a low, mysterious voice:

"'I stole it for you.'

"She looked at me with astonishment and delight in her large eyes.

"'Oh! You stole it? Where?'

"'In the cathedral; in the very shrine of the Eleven Thousand Virgins.'

"Her heart beat with pleasure, and she murmured:

"'Oh! Did you really do that-for me? Tell me-all about it!'

"That was the climax; I could not retract what I had said. I made up a fanciful story; with precise details: I had given the custodian of the building a hundred francs to be allowed to go about the building by myself; the shrine was being repaired, but I happened to be there at the breakfast hour of the workmen and clergy; by removing a small panel, I had been enabled to seize a small piece of bone (oh! so small), among a quantity of others (I said a quantity, as I thought of the amount that the remains of the skeletons of eleven thousand virgins must produce). Then I went to a goldsmith's and bought a casket worthy of the relic; and I was not sorry to let her know that the silver box cost me five hundred francs.

"But she did not think of that; she listened to me, trembling, in an ecstasy, and whispering: 'How I love you!' she threw herself into my arms.

"Just note this: I had committed sacrilege for her sake. I had committed a theft; I had violated a church; I had violated a shrine; violated and stolen holy relics, and for that she adored me, thought me perfect, tender, divine. Such is woman, my dear Abbe, every woman.

"For two months I was the most admirable of lovers. In her room, she had made a kind of magnificent chapel in which to keep this bit of mutton chop, which, as she thought, had made me commit that divine love-crime, and she worked up her religious enthusiasm in front of it every morning and evening. I had asked her to keep the matter secret, for fear, as I said, that I might be arrested, condemned, and given over to Germany, and she kept her promise.

"Well, at the beginning of the summer, she was seized with an irresistible desire to see the scene of my exploit, and she teased her father so persistently (without telling him her secret reason), that he took her to Cologne, but without telling me of their trip, according to his daughter's wish.

"I need not tell you that I had not seen the interior of the cathedral. I do not know where the tomb (if there be a tomb) of the Eleven Thousand Virgins is; and then, it appears, it is unapproachable, alas!

"A week afterward, I received ten lines, breaking off our engagement, and then an explanatory letter from her father, whom she had, somewhat late, taken into her confidence.

"At the sight of the shrine, she had suddenly seen through my trickery and my lie, and at the same time discovered my real innocence of any crime. Having asked the keeper of the relics whether any robbery had been committed, the man began to laugh, and pointed out to them how impossible such a crime was. But, from the moment that I had not plunged my profane hand into venerable relics, I was no longer worthy of my fair-haired, sensitive betrothed.

"I was forbidden the house; I begged and prayed in vain; nothing could move the fair devotee, and I became ill from grief. Well, last week, her cousin, Madame d'Arville, who is your cousin also, sent me word that she should like to see me, and when I called, she told me on what conditions I might obtain my pardon, and here they are. I must bring her a relic, a real, authentic relic of some virgin and martyr, certified to be such by our Holy Father, the Pope, and I am going mad from embarrassment and anxiety.

"I will go to Rome, if needful, but I cannot call on the Pope unexpectedly, to tell him my stupid misadventure; and, besides, I doubt whether they allow private individuals to have relics. Could not you give me an introduction to some cardinal, or even to some French prelate who possesses some remains of a female saint? Or, perhaps, you may have the precious object she wants in your collection?

"Help me out of my difficulty, my dear Abbe, and I promise you that I will be converted ten years sooner than I otherwise should be!

"Madame d'Arville, who takes the matter seriously, said to me the other day:

"'Poor Gilberte will never marry.'

"My dear old schoolmate, will you allow your cousin to die the victim of a stupid piece of subterfuge on my part? Pray prevent her from being virgin eleven thousand and one.

"Pardon me, I am unworthy, but I embrace you, and love you with all my heart.

"Your old friend,

"HENRI FONTAL."

VOLUME IV

THE MORIBUND

The warm autumn sun was beating down on the farmyard. Under the grass, which had been cropped close by the cows, the earth soaked by recent rains, was soft and sank in under the feet with a soggy noise, and the apple trees, loaded with apples, were dropping their pale green fruit in the dark green grass.

Four young heifers, tied in a line, were grazing and at times looking toward the house and lowing. The fowls made a colored patch on the dung-heap before the stable, scratching, moving about and cackling, while two roosters crowed continually, digging worms for their hens, whom they were calling with a loud clucking.

The wooden gate opened and a man entered. He might have been forty years old, but he looked at least sixty, wrinkled, bent, walking slowly, impeded by the weight of heavy wooden shoes full of straw. His long arms hung down on both sides of his body. When he got near the farm a yellow cur, tied at the foot of an enormous pear tree, beside a barrel which served as his kennel, began at first to wag his tail and then to bark for joy. The man cried:

"Down, Finot!"

The dog was quiet.

A peasant woman came out of the house. Her large, flat, bony body was outlined under a long woollen jacket drawn in at the waist. A gray skirt, too short, fell to the middle of her legs, which were encased in blue stockings. She, too, wore wooden shoes, filled with straw. The white cap, turned yellow, covered a few hairs which were plastered to the scalp, and her brown, thin, ugly, toothless face had that wild, animal expression which is often to be found on the faces of the peasants.

The man asked:

"How is he gettin' along?"

The woman answered:

"The priest said it's the end—that he will never live through the night."

Both of them went into the house.

After passing through the kitchen, they entered a low, dark room, barely lighted by one window, in front of which a piece of calico was hanging. The big beams, turned brown with age and smoke, crossed the room from one side to the other, supporting the thin floor of the garret, where an army of rats ran about day and night.

The moist, lumpy earthen floor looked greasy, and, at the back of the room, the bed made an indistinct white spot. A harsh, regular noise, a difficult, hoarse, wheezing breathing, like the gurgling of water from a broken pump, came from the darkened couch where an old man, the father of the peasant woman, was dying.

The man and the woman approached the dying man and looked at him with calm, resigned eyes.

The son-in-law said:

"I guess it's all up with him this time; he will not last the night."

The woman answered:

"He's been gurglin' like that ever since midday." They were silent. The father's eyes were closed, his face was the color of the earth and so dry that it looked like wood. Through his open mouth came his harsh, rattling breath, and the gray linen sheet rose and fell with each respiration.

The son-in-law, after a long silence, said:

"There's nothing more to do; I can't help him. It's a nuisance, just the same, because the weather is good and we've got a lot of work to do."

His wife seemed annoyed at this idea. She reflected a few moments and then said:

"He won't be buried till Saturday, and that will give you all day tomorrow."

The peasant thought the matter over and answered:

"Yes, but to-morrow I'll have to invite the people to the funeral. That means five or six hours to go round to Tourville and Manetot, and to see everybody."

The woman, after meditating two or three minutes, declared:

"It isn't three o'clock yet. You could begin this evening and go all round the country to Tourville. You can just as well say that he's dead, seem' as he's as good as that now."

The man stood perplexed for a while, weighing the pros and cons of the idea. At last he declared:

"Well, I'll go!"

He was leaving the room, but came back after a minute's hesitation:

"As you haven't got anythin' to do you might shake down some apples to bake and make four dozen dumplings for those who come to the funeral, for one must have something to cheer them. You can light the fire with the wood that's under the shed. It's dry."

He left the room, went back into the kitchen, opened the cupboard, took out a six-pound loaf of bread, cut off a slice, and carefully gathered the crumbs in the palm of his hand and threw them into his mouth, so as not to lose anything. Then, with the end of his knife, he scraped out a little salt butter from the bottom of an earthen jar, spread it on his bread and began to eat slowly, as he did everything.

He recrossed the farmyard, quieted the dog, which had started barking again, went out on the road bordering on his ditch, and disappeared in the direction of Tourville.

As soon as she was alone, the woman began to work. She uncovered the meal-bin and made the dough for the dumplings. She kneaded it a long time, turning it over and over again, punching, pressing, crushing it. Finally she made a big, round, yellow-white ball, which she placed on the corner of the table.

Then she went to get her apples, and, in order not to injure the tree with a pole, she climbed up into it by a ladder. She chose the fruit with care, only taking the ripe ones, and gathering them in her apron.

A voice called from the road:

"Hey, Madame Chicot!"

She turned round. It was a neighbor, Osime Favet, the mayor, on his way to fertilize his fields, seated on the manure-wagon, with his feet hanging over the side. She turned round and answered:

"What can I do for you, Maitre Osime?"

"And how is the father?"

She cried:

"He is as good as dead. The funeral is Saturday at seven, because there's lots of work to be done."

The neighbor answered:

"So! Good luck to you! Take care of yourself."

To his kind remarks she answered:"

"Thanks; the same to you."

And she continued picking apples.

When she went back to the house, she went over to look at her father, expecting to find him dead. But as soon as she reached the door she heard his monotonous, noisy rattle, and, thinking it a waste of time to go over to him, she began to prepare her dumplings. She wrapped up the fruit, one by one, in a thin layer of paste, then she lined them up on the edge of the table. When she had made forty-eight dumplings, arranged in dozens, one in front of the other, she began to think of preparing supper, and she hung her kettle over the fire to cook potatoes, for she judged it useless to heat the oven that day, as she had all the next day in which to finish the preparations.

Her husband returned at about five. As soon as he had crossed the threshold he asked:

"Is it over?"

She answered:

"Not yet; he's still gurglin'."

They went to look at him. The old man was in exactly the same condition. His hoarse rattle, as regular as the ticking of a clock, was neither quicker nor slower. It returned every second, the tone varying a little, according as the air entered or left his chest.

His son-in-law looked at him and then said:

"He'll pass away without our noticin' it, just like a candle."

They returned to the kitchen and started to eat without saying a word. When they had swallowed their soup, they ate another piece of bread and butter. Then, as soon as the dishes were washed, they returned to the dying man.

The woman, carrying a little lamp with a smoky wick, held it in front of her father's face. If he had not been breathing, one would certainly have thought him dead.

The couple's bed was hidden in a little recess at the other end of the room. Silently they retired, put out the light, closed their eyes, and soon two unequal snores, one deep and the other shriller, accompanied the uninterrupted rattle of the dying man.

The rats ran about in the garret.

The husband awoke at the first streaks of dawn. His father-in-law was still alive. He shook his wife, worried by the tenacity of the old man.

"Say, Phemie, he don't want to quit. What would you do?"

He knew that she gave good advice.

She answered:

"You needn't be afraid; he can't live through the day. And the mayor won't stop our burying him to-morrow, because he allowed it for Maitre Renard's father, who died just during the planting season."

He was convinced by this argument, and left for the fields.

His wife baked the dumplings and then attended to her housework.

At noon the old man was not dead. The people hired for the day's work came by groups to look at him. Each one had his say. Then they left again for the fields.

At six o'clock, when the work was over, the father was still breathing. At last his son-in-law was frightened.

"What would you do now, Phemie?"

She no longer knew how to solve the problem. They went to the mayor. He promised that he would close his eyes and authorize the funeral for the following day. They also went to the health officer, who likewise promised, in order to oblige Maitre Chicot, to antedate the death certificate. The man and the woman returned, feeling more at ease.

They went to bed and to sleep, just as they did the preceding day, their sonorous breathing blending with the feeble breathing of the old man.

When they awoke, he was not yet dead.

Then they began to be frightened. They stood by their father, watching him with distrust, as though he had wished to play them a mean trick, to deceive them, to annoy them on purpose, and they were vexed at him for the time which he was making them lose.

The son-in-law asked:

"What am I goin' to do?"

She did not know. She answered:

"It certainly is annoying!"

The guests who were expected could not be notified. They decided to wait and explain the case to them.

Toward a quarter to seven the first ones arrived. The women in black, their heads covered with large veils, looking very sad. Then men, ill at ease in their homespun coats, were coming forward more slowly, in couples, talking business.

Maitre Chicot and his wife, bewildered, received them sorrowfully, and suddenly both of them together began to cry as they approached the first group. They explained the matter, related their difficulty, offered chairs, bustled about, tried to make excuses, attempting to prove that everybody would have done as they did, talking continually and giving nobody a chance to answer.

They were going from one person to another:

"I never would have thought it; it's incredible how he can last this long!"

The guests, taken aback, a little disappointed, as though they had missed an expected entertainment, did not know what to do, some remaining seated others standing. Several wished to leave. Maitre Chicot held them back:

"You must take something, anyhow! We made some dumplings; might as well make use of 'em."

The faces brightened at this idea. The yard was filling little by little; the early arrivals were telling the news to those who had arrived later. Everybody was whispering. The idea of the dumplings seemed to cheer everyone up.

The women went in to take a look at the dying man. They crossed themselves beside the bed, muttered a prayer and went out again. The men, less anxious for this spectacle, cast a look through the window, which had been opened.

Madame Chicot explained her distress:

"That's how he's been for two days, neither better nor worse. Doesn't he sound like a pump that has gone dry?"

When everybody had had a look at the dying man, they thought of the refreshments; but as there were too many people for the kitchen to hold, the table was moved out in front of the door. The four dozen golden dumplings, tempting and appetizing, arranged in two big dishes, attracted the eyes of all. Each one reached out to take his, fearing that there would not be enough. But four remained over.

Maitre Chicot, his mouth full, said:

"Father would feel sad if he were to see this. He loved them so much when he was alive."

A big, jovial peasant declared:

"He won't eat any more now. Each one in his turn."

This remark, instead of making the guests sad, seemed to cheer them up. It was their turn now to eat dumplings.

Madame Chicot, distressed at the expense, kept running down to the cellar continually for cider. The pitchers were emptied in quick succession. The company was laughing and talking loud now. They were beginning to shout as they do at feasts.

Suddenly an old peasant woman who had stayed beside the dying man, held there by a morbid fear of what would soon happen to herself, appeared at the window and cried in a shrill voice:

"He's dead! he's dead!"

Everybody was silent. The women arose quickly to go and see. He was indeed dead. The rattle had ceased. The men looked at each other, looking down, ill at ease. They hadn't finished eating the dumplings. Certainly the rascal had not chosen a propitious moment. The Chicots were no longer weeping. It was over; they were relieved.

They kept repeating:

"I knew it couldn't 'last. If he could only have done it last night, it would have saved us all this trouble."

Well, anyhow, it was over. They would bury him on Monday, that was all, and they would eat some more dumplings for the occasion.

The guests went away, talking the matter over, pleased at having had the chance to see him and of getting something to eat.

And when the husband and wife were alone, face to face, she said, her face distorted with grief:

"We'll have to bake four dozen more dumplings! Why couldn't he have made up his mind last night?"

The husband, more resigned, answered:

"Well, we'll not have to do this every day."

THE GAMEKEEPER

It was after dinner, and we were talking about adventures and accidents which happened while out shooting.

An old friend, known to all of us, M. Boniface, a great sportsman and a connoisseur of wine, a man of wonderful physique, witty and gay, and endowed with an ironical and resigned philosophy, which manifested itself in caustic humor, and never in melancholy, suddenly exclaimed:

"I know a story, or rather a tragedy, which is somewhat peculiar. It is not at all like those which one hears of usually, and I have never told it, thinking that it would interest no one.

"It is not at all sympathetic. I mean by that, that it does not arouse the kind of interest which pleases or which moves one agreeably.

"Here is the story:

"I was then about thirty-five years of age, and a most enthusiastic sportsman.

"In those days I owned a lonely bit of property in the neighborhood of Jumieges, surrounded by forests and abounding in hares and rabbits. I was accustomed to spending four or five days alone there each year, there not being room enough to allow of my bringing a friend with me.

"I had placed there as gamekeeper, an old retired gendarme, a good man, hot-tempered, a severe disciplinarian, a terror to poachers and fearing nothing. He lived all alone, far from the village, in a little house, or rather hut, consisting of two rooms downstairs, with kitchen and store-room, and two upstairs. One of them, a kind of box just large enough to accommodate a bed, a cupboard and a chair, was reserved for my use.

"Old man Cavalier lived in the other one. When I said that he was alone in this place, I was wrong. He had taken his nephew with him, a young scamp about fourteen years old, who used to go to the village and run errands for the old man.

"This young scapegrace was long and lanky, with yellow hair, so light that it resembled the fluff of a plucked chicken, so thin that he seemed bald. Besides this, he had enormous feet and the hands of a giant.

"He was cross-eyed, and never looked at anyone. He struck me as being in the same relation to the human race as ill-smelling beasts are to the animal race. He reminded me of a polecat.

"He slept in a kind of hole at the top of the stairs which led to the two rooms.

"But during my short sojourns at the Pavilion—so I called the hut —Marius would give up his nook to an old woman from Ecorcheville, called Celeste, who used to come and cook for me, as old man Cavalier's stews were not sufficient for my healthy appetite.

"You now know the characters and the locality. Here is the story:

"It was on the fifteenth of October, 1854—I shall remember that date as long as I live.

"I left Rouen on horseback, followed by my dog Bock, a big Dalmatian hound from Poitou, full-chested and with a heavy jaw, which could retrieve among the bushes like a Pont-Andemer spaniel.

"I was carrying my satchel slung across my back and my gun diagonally across my chest. It was a cold, windy, gloomy day, with clouds scurrying across the sky.

"As I went up the hill at Canteleu, I looked over the broad valley of the Seine, the river winding in and out along its course as far as the eye could see. To the right the towers of Rouen stood out against the sky, and to the left the landscape was bounded by the distant slopes covered with trees. Then I crossed the forest of Roumare and, toward five o'clock, reached the Pavilion, where Cavalier and Celeste were expecting me.

"For ten years I had appeared there at the same time, in the same manner; and for ten years the same faces had greeted me with the same words:

"'Welcome, master! We hope your health is good.'

"Cavalier had hardly changed. He withstood time like an old tree; but Celeste, especially in the past four years, had become unrecognizable.

"She was bent almost double, and, although still active, when she walked her body was almost at right angles to her legs.

"The old woman, who was very devoted to me, always seemed affected at seeing me again, and each time, as I left, she would say:

"'This may be the last time, master.'

"The sad, timid farewell of this old servant, this hopeless resignation to the inevitable fate which was not far off for her, moved me strangely each year.

"I dismounted, and while Cavalier, whom I had greeted, was leading my horse to the little shed which served as a stable, I entered the kitchen, which also served as dining-room, followed by Celeste.

"Here the gamekeeper joined us. I saw at first glance that something was the matter. He seemed preoccupied, ill at ease, worried.

"I said to him:

"'Well, Cavalier, is everything all right?'

"He muttered:

"'Yes and no. There are things I don't like.'

"I asked:

"'What? Tell me about it.'

"But he shook his head.

"'No, not yet, monsieur. I do not wish to bother you with my little troubles so soon after your arrival.'

"I insisted, but he absolutely refused to give me any information before dinner. From his expression, I could tell that it was something very serious.

"Not knowing what to say to him, I asked:

"'How about game? Much of it this year?'

"'Oh, yes! You'll find all you want. Thank heaven, I looked out for that.'

"He said this with so much seriousness, with such sad solemnity, that it was really almost funny. His big gray mustache seemed almost ready to drop from his lips.

"Suddenly I remembered that I had not yet seen his nephew.

"'Where is Marius? Why does he not show himself?'

"The gamekeeper started, looking me suddenly in the face:

"'Well, monsieur, I had rather tell you the whole business right away; it's on account of him that I am worrying.'

"'Ah! Well, where is he?'

"'Over in the stable, monsieur. I was waiting for the right time to bring him out.'

"'What has he done?'

"'Well, monsieur——'

"The gamekeeper, however, hesitated, his voice altered and shaky, his face suddenly furrowed by the deep lines of an old man.

"He continued slowly:

"'Well, I found out, last winter, that someone was poaching in the woods of Roseraies, but I couldn't seem to catch the man. I spent night after night on the lookout for him. In vain. During that time they began poaching over by Ecorcheville. I was growing thin from vexation. But as for catching the trespasser, impossible! One might have thought that the rascal was forewarned of my plans.

"'But one day, while I was brushing Marius' Sunday trousers, I found forty cents in his pocket. Where did he get it?

"'I thought the matter over for about a week, and I noticed that he used to go out; he would leave the house just as I was coming home to go to bed—yes, monsieur.

"'Then I started to watch him, without the slightest suspicion of the real facts. One morning, just after I had gone to bed before him, I got right up again, and followed him. For shadowing a man, there is nobody like me, monsieur.

"'And I caught him, Marius, poaching on your land, monsieur; he my nephew, I your keeper!

"'The blood rushed to my head, and I almost killed him on the spot, I hit him so hard. Oh! yes, I thrashed him all right. And I promised him that he would get another beating from my hand, in your presence, as an example.

"'There! I have grown thin from sorrow. You know how it is when one is worried like that. But tell me, what would you have done? The boy has no father or mother, and I am the last one of his blood; I kept him, I couldn't drive him out, could I?

"'I told him that if it happened again I would have no more pity for him, all would be over. There! Did I do right, monsieur?'

"I answered, holding out my hand:

"'You did well, Cavalier; you are an honest man.'

"He rose.

"'Thank you, monsieur. Now I am going to fetch him. I must give him his thrashing, as an example.'

"I knew that it was hopeless to try and turn the old man from his idea. I therefore let him have his own way.

"He got the rascal and brought him back by the ear.

"I was seated on a cane chair, with the solemn expression of a judge.

"Marius seemed to have grown; he was homelier even than the year before, with his evil, sneaking expression.

"His big hands seemed gigantic.

"His uncle pushed him up to me, and, in his soldierly voice, said:

"'Beg the gentleman's pardon.'

"The boy didn't say a word.

"Then putting one arm round him, the former gendarme lifted him right off the ground, and began to whack him with such force that I rose to stop the blows.

"The boy was now howling: 'Mercy! mercy! mercy! I promise——'

"Cavalier put him back on the ground and forced him to his knees:

"'Beg for pardon,' he said.

"With eyes lowered, the scamp murmured:

"'I ask for pardon!'

"Then his uncle lifted him to his feet, and dismissed him with a cuff which almost knocked him down again.

"He made his escape, and I did not see him again that evening.

"Cavalier appeared overwhelmed.'

"'He is a bad egg,' he said.

"And throughout the whole dinner, he kept repeating:

"'Oh! that worries me, monsieur, that worries me.'

"I tried to comfort him, but in vain.

"I went to bed early, so that I might start out at daybreak.

"My dog was already asleep on the floor, at the foot of my bed, when I put out the light.

"I was awakened toward midnight by the furious barking of my dog Bock. I immediately noticed that my room was full of smoke. I jumped out of bed, struck a light, ran to the door and opened it. A cloud of flames burst in. The house was on fire.

"I quickly closed the heavy oak door and, drawing on my trousers, I first lowered the dog through the window, by means of a rope made of my sheets; then, having thrown out the rest of my clothes, my game-bag and my gun, I in turn escaped the same way.

"I began to shout with all my might: 'Cavalier! Cavalier! Cavalier!'

"But the gamekeeper did not wake up. He slept soundly like an old gendarme.

"However, I could see through the lower windows that the whole ground-floor was nothing but a roaring furnace; I also noticed that it had been filled with straw to make it burn readily.

"Somebody must purposely have set fire to the place!

"I continued shrieking wildly: 'Cavalier!'

"Then the thought struck me that the smoke might be suffocating him. An idea came to me. I slipped two cartridges into my gun, and shot straight at his window.

"The six panes of glass shattered into the room in a cloud of glass. This time the old man had heard me, and he appeared, dazed, in his nightshirt, bewildered by the glare which illumined the whole front of his 'house.

"I cried to him:

"'Your house is on fire! Escape through the window! Quick! Quick!'

"The flames were coming out through all the cracks downstairs, were licking along the wall, were creeping toward him and going to surround him. He jumped and landed on his feet, like a cat.

"It was none too soon. The thatched roof cracked in the middle, right over the staircase, which formed a kind of flue for the fire downstairs; and an immense red jet jumped up into the air, spreading like a stream of water and sprinkling a shower of sparks around the hut. In a few seconds it was nothing but a pool of flames.

"Cavalier, thunderstruck, asked:

"'How did the fire start?'

"I answered:

"'Somebody lit it in the kitchen.'

"He muttered:

"'Who could have started the fire?'

"And I, suddenly guessing, answered:

"'Marius!'

"The old man understood. He stammered:

"'Good God! That is why he didn't return.'

"A terrible thought flashed through my mind. I cried:

"'And Celeste! Celeste!'

"He did not answer. The house caved in before us, forming only an enormous, bright, blinding brazier, an awe-inspiring funeral-pile, where the poor woman could no longer be anything but a glowing ember, a glowing ember of human flesh.

"We had not heard a single cry.

"As the fire crept toward the shed, I suddenly bethought me of my horse, and Cavalier ran to free it.

"Hardly had he opened the door of the stable, when a supple, nimble body darted between his legs, and threw him on his face. It was Marius, running for all he was worth.

"The man was up in a second. He tried to run after the wretch, but, seeing that he could not catch him, and maddened by an irresistible anger, yielding to one of those thoughtless impulses which we cannot foresee or prevent, he picked up my gun, which was lying on the ground. near him, put it to his shoulder, and, before I could make a motion, he pulled the trigger without even noticing whether or not the weapon was loaded.

"One of the cartridges which I had put in to announce the fire was still intact, and the charge caught the fugitive right in the back,—throwing him forward on the ground, bleeding profusely. He immediately began to claw the earth with his hands and with his knees, as though trying to run on all fours like a rabbit who has been mortally wounded, and sees the hunter approaching.

"I rushed forward to the boy, but I could already hear the death-rattle. He passed away before the fire was extinguished, without having said a word.

"Cavalier, still in his shirt, his legs bare, was standing near us, motionless, dazed.

"When the people from the village arrived, my gamekeeper was taken away, like an insane man.

"I appeared at the trial as witness, and related the facts in detail, without changing a thing. Cavalier was acquitted. He disappeared that very day, leaving the country.

"I have never seen him since.

"There, gentlemen, that is my story."

THE STORY OF A FARM GIRL

PART I

As the weather was very fine, the people on the farm had hurried through their dinner and had returned to the fields.

The servant, Rose, remained alone in the large kitchen, where the fire was dying out on the hearth beneath the large boiler of hot water. From time to time she dipped out some water and slowly washed her dishes, stopping occasionally to look at the two streaks of light which the sun threw across the long table through the window, and which showed the defects in the glass.

Three venturesome hens were picking up the crumbs under the chairs, while the smell of the poultry yard and the warmth from the cow stall came in through the half-open door, and a cock was heard crowing in the distance.

When she had finished her work, wiped down the table, dusted the mantelpiece and put the plates on the high dresser close to the wooden clock with its loud tick-tock, she drew a long breath, as she felt rather oppressed, without exactly knowing why. She looked at the black clay walls, the rafters that were blackened with smoke and from which hung spiders' webs, smoked herrings and strings of onions, and then she sat down, rather overcome by the stale odor from the earthen floor, on which so many things had been continually spilled and which the heat brought out. With this there was mingled the sour smell of the pans of milk which were set out to raise the cream in the adjoining dairy.

She wanted to sew, as usual, but she did not feel strong enough, and so she went to the door to get a mouthful of fresh air, which seemed to do her good.

The fowls were lying on the steaming dunghill; some of them were scratching with one claw in search of worms, while the cock stood up proudly in their midst. When he crowed, the cocks in all the neighboring farmyards replied to him, as if they were uttering challenges from farm to farm.

The girl looked at them without thinking, and then she raised her eyes and was almost dazzled at the sight of the apple trees in blossom. Just then a colt, full of life and friskiness, jumped over the ditches and then stopped suddenly, as if surprised at being alone.

She also felt inclined to run; she felt inclined to move and to stretch her limbs and to repose in the warm, breathless air. She took a few undecided steps and closed her eyes, for she was seized with a feeling of animal comfort, and then she went to look for eggs in the hen loft. There were thirteen of them, which she took in and put into the storeroom; but the smell from the kitchen annoyed her again, and she went out to sit on the grass for a time.

The farmyard, which was surrounded by trees, seemed to be asleep. The tall grass, amid which the tall yellow dandelions rose up like streaks of yellow light, was of a vivid, fresh spring green. The apple trees cast their shade all round them, and the thatched roofs, on which grew blue and yellow irises, with their sword-like leaves, steamed as if the moisture of the stables and barns were coming through the straw. The girl went to the shed, where the carts and buggies were kept. Close to it, in a ditch, there was a large patch of violets, whose fragrance was spread abroad, while beyond the slope the open country could be seen, where grain was growing, with clumps of trees in places, and groups of laborers here and there, who looked as small as dolls, and white horses like toys, who were drawing a child's cart, driven by a man as tall as one's finger.

She took up a bundle of straw, threw it into the ditch and sat down upon it. Then, not feeling comfortable, she undid it, spread it out and lay down upon it at full length on her back, with both arms under her head and her legs stretched out.

Gradually her eyes closed, and she was falling into a state of delightful languor. She was, in fact, almost asleep when she felt two hands on her bosom, and she sprang up at a bound. It was

Jacques, one of the farm laborers, a tall fellow from Picardy, who had been making love to her for a long time. He had been herding the sheep, and, seeing her lying down in the shade, had come up stealthily and holding his breath, with glistening eyes and bits of straw in his hair.

He tried to kiss her, but she gave him a smack in the face, for she was as strong as he, and he was shrewd enough to beg her pardon; so they sat down side by side and talked amicably. They spoke about the favorable weather, of their master, who was a good fellow, then of their neighbors, of all the people in the country round, of themselves, of their village, of their youthful days, of their recollections, of their relations, who had left them for a long time, and it might be forever. She grew sad as she thought of it, while he, with one fixed idea in his head, drew closer to her.

"I have not seen my mother for a long time," she said. "It is very hard to be separated like that," and she directed her looks into the distance, toward the village in the north which she had left.

Suddenly, however, he seized her by the neck and kissed her again, but she struck him so violently in the face with her clenched fist that his nose began to bleed, and he got up and laid his head against the stem of a tree. When she saw that, she was sorry, and going up to him, she said: "Have I hurt you?" He, however, only laughed. "No, it was a mere nothing; only she had hit him right on the middle of the nose. What a devil!" he said, and he looked at her with admiration, for she had inspired him with a feeling of respect and of a very different kind of admiration which was the beginning of a real love for that tall, strong wench. When the bleeding had stopped, he proposed a walk, as he was afraid of his neighbor's heavy hand, if they remained side by side like that much longer; but she took his arm of her own accord, in the avenue, as if they had been out for an evening's walk, and said: "It is not nice of you to despise me like that, Jacques." He protested, however. No, he did not despise her. He was in love with her, that was all.

"So you really want to marry me?" she asked.

He hesitated and then looked at her sideways, while she looked straight ahead of her. She had fat, red cheeks, a full bust beneath her cotton jacket; thick, red lips; and her neck, which was almost bare, was covered with small beads of perspiration. He felt a fresh access of desire, and, putting his lips to her ear, he murmured: "Yes, of course I do."

Then she threw her arms round his neck and kissed him till they were both out of breath. From that moment the eternal story of love began between them. They plagued one another in corners; they met in the moonlight beside the haystack and gave each other bruises on the legs, under the table, with their heavy nailed boots. By degrees, however, Jacques seemed to grow tired of her; he avoided her, scarcely spoke to her, and did not try any longer to meet her alone, which made her sad and anxious; and soon she found that she was enceinte.

At first she was in a state of consternation, but then she got angry, and her rage increased every day because she could not meet him, as he avoided her most carefully. At last, one night, when every one in the farmhouse was asleep, she went out noiselessly in her petticoat, with bare feet, crossed the yard and opened the door of the stable where Jacques was lying in a large box of straw above his horses. He pretended to snore when he heard her coming, but she knelt down by his side and shook him until he sat up.

"What do you want?" he then asked her. And with clenched teeth, and trembling with anger, she replied: "I want—I want you to marry me, as you promised." But he only laughed and replied: "Oh! if a man were to marry all the girls with whom he has made a slip, he would have more than enough to do."

Then she seized him by the throat, threw him or his back, so that he could not get away from her, and, half strangling him, she shouted into his face:

"I am enceinte, do you hear? I am enceinte!"

He gasped for breath, as he was almost choked, and so they remained, both of them, motionless and without speaking, in the dark silence, which was only broken by the noise made by a horse as he, pulled the hay out of the manger and then slowly munched it.

When Jacques found that she was the stronger, he stammered out: "Very well, I will marry you, as that is the case." But she did not believe his promises. "It must be at once," she said. "You must have the banns put up." "At once," he replied. "Swear solemnly that you will." He hesitated for a few moments and then said: "I swear it, by Heaven!"

Then she released her grasp and went away without another word.

She had no chance of speaking to him for several days; and, as the stable was now always locked at night, she was afraid to make any noise, for fear of creating a scandal. One morning, however, she saw another man come in at dinner time, and she said: "Has Jacques left?" "Yes;" the man replied; "I have got his place."

This made her tremble so violently that she could not take the saucepan off the fire; and later, when they were all at work, she went up into her room and cried, burying her head in the bolster, so that she might not be heard. During the day, however, she tried to obtain some information without exciting any suspicion, but she was so overwhelmed by the thoughts of her misfortune that she fancied that all the people whom she asked laughed maliciously. All she learned, however, was that he had left the neighborhood altogether.

PART II

Then a cloud of constant misery began for her. She worked mechanically, without thinking of what she was doing, with one fixed idea in her head:

"Suppose people were to know."

This continual feeling made her so incapable of reasoning that she did not even try to think of any means of avoiding the disgrace that she knew must ensue, which was irreparable and drawing nearer every day, and which was as sure as death itself. She got up every morning long before the others and persistently tried to look at her figure in a piece of broken looking-glass, before which she did her hair, as she was very anxious to know whether anybody would notice a change in her, and, during the day, she stopped working every few minutes to look at herself from top to toe, to see whether her apron did not look too short.

The months went on, and she scarcely spoke now, and when she was asked a question, did not appear to understand; but she had a frightened look, haggard eyes and trembling hands, which made her master say to her occasionally: "My poor girl, how stupid you have grown lately."

In church she hid behind a pillar, and no longer ventured to go to confession, as she feared to face the priest, to whom she attributed superhuman powers, which enabled him to read people's consciences; and at meal times the looks of her fellow servants almost made her faint with mental agony; and she was always fancying that she had been found out by the cowherd, a precocious and cunning little lad, whose bright eyes seemed always to be watching her.

One morning the postman brought her a letter, and as she had never received one in her life before she was so upset by it that she was obliged to sit down. Perhaps it was from him? But, as she could not read, she sat anxious and trembling with that piece of paper, covered with ink, in her hand. After a time, however, she put it into her pocket, as she did not venture to confide her secret to any one. She often stopped in her work to look at those lines written at regular intervals, and which terminated in a signature, imagining vaguely that she would suddenly discover their meaning, until at last, as she felt half mad with impatience and anxiety, she went to the schoolmaster, who told her to sit down and read to her as follows:

"MY DEAR DAUGHTER: I write to tell you that I am very ill. Our neighbor, Monsieur Dentu, begs you to come, if you can.

"From your affectionate mother,

"CESAIRE DENTU, Deputy Mayor."

She did not say a word and went away, but as soon as she was alone her legs gave way under her, and she fell down by the roadside and remained there till night.

When she got back, she told the farmer her bad news, and he allowed her to go home for as long as she liked, and promised to have her work done by a charwoman and to take her back when she returned.

Her mother died soon after she got there, and the next day Rose gave birth to a seven-months child, a miserable little skeleton, thin enough to make anybody shudder, and which seemed to be suffering continually, to judge from the painful manner in which it moved its poor little hands, which were as thin as a crab's legs; but it lived for all that. She said she was married, but could not be burdened with the child, so she left it with some neighbors, who promised to take great care of it, and she went back to the farm.

But now in her heart, which had been wounded so long, there arose something like brightness, an unknown love for that frail little creature which she had left behind her, though there was fresh suffering in that very love, suffering which she felt every hour and every minute, because she was parted from her child. What pained her most, however, was the mad longing to kiss it, to press it in her arms, to feel the warmth of its little body against her breast. She could not sleep at night; she thought of it the whole day long, and in the evening, when her work was done, she would sit in front of the fire and gaze at it intently, as people do whose thoughts are far away.

They began to talk about her and to tease her about her lover. They asked her whether he was tall, handsome and rich. When was the wedding to be and the christening? And often she ran away to cry by herself, for these questions seemed to hurt her like the prick of a pin; and, in order to forget their jokes, she began to work still more energetically, and, still thinking of her child, she sought some way of saving up money for it, and determined to work so that her master would be obliged to raise her wages.

By degrees she almost monopolized the work and persuaded him to get rid of one servant girl, who had become useless since she had taken to working like two; she economized in the bread, oil and candles; in the corn, which they gave to the chickens too extravagantly, and in the fodder for the horses and cattle, which was rather wasted. She was as miserly about her master's money as if it had been her own; and, by dint of making good bargains, of getting high prices for all their produce, and by baffling the peasants' tricks when they offered anything for sale, he, at last, entrusted her with buying and selling everything, with the direction of all the laborers, and with the purchase of provisions necessary for the household; so that, in a short time, she became. indispensable to him. She kept such a strict eye on everything about her that, under her direction, the farm prospered wonderfully, and for five miles around people talked of "Master Vallin's servant," and the farmer himself said everywhere: "That girl is worth more than her weight in gold."

But time passed by, and her wages remained the same. Her hard work was accepted as something that was due from every good servant, and as a mere token of good will; and she began to think rather bitterly that if the farmer could put fifty or a hundred crowns extra into the bank every month, thanks to her, she was still only earning her two hundred francs a year, neither more nor less; and so she made up her mind to ask for an increase of wages. She went to see the schoolmaster three times about it, but when she got there, she spoke about something else. She felt a kind of modesty in asking for money, as if it were something disgraceful; but, at last, one day, when the farmer was having breakfast by himself in the kitchen, she said to him, with some embarrassment, that she wished to speak to him particularly. He raised his head in surprise, with both his hands on the table, holding his knife, with its point in the air, in one, and a piece of bread in the other, and he looked fixedly at, the girl, who felt uncomfortable under his gaze, but asked for a week's holiday, so that she might get away, as she was not very well. He acceded to her request immediately, and then added, in some embarrassment himself:

"When you come back, I shall have something to say to you myself."

PART III

The child was nearly eight months old, and she did not recognize it. It had grown rosy and chubby all over, like a little roll of fat. She threw herself on it, as if it had been some prey, and kissed it so violently that it began to scream with terror; and then she began to cry herself, because it did not know her, and stretched out its arms to its nurse as soon as it saw her. But the next day it began to know her, and laughed when it saw her, and she took it into the fields, and ran about excitedly with it, and sat down under the shade of the trees; and then, for the first time in her life, she opened her heart to somebody, although he could not understand her, and told him her troubles; how hard her work was, her anxieties and her hopes, and she quite tired the child with the violence of her caresses.

She took the greatest pleasure in handling it, in washing and dressing it, for it seemed to her that all this was the confirmation of her maternity; and she would look at it, almost feeling surprised 'that it was hers, and would say to herself in a low voice as she danced it in her arms: "It is my baby, it's my baby."

She cried all the way home as she returned to the farm and had scarcely got in before her master called her into his room; and she went, feeling astonished and nervous, without knowing why.

"Sit down there," he said. She sat down, and for some moments they remained side by side, in some embarrassment, with their arms hanging at their sides, as if they did not know what to do with them, and looking each other in the face, after the manner of peasants.

The farmer, a stout, jovial, obstinate man of forty-five, who had lost two wives, evidently felt embarrassed, which was very unusual with him; but, at last, he made up his mind, and began to speak vaguely, hesitating a little, and looking out of the window as he talked. "How is it, Rose," he said, "that you have never thought of settling in life?" She grew as pale as death, and, seeing that she gave him no answer, he went on: "You are a good, steady, active and economical girl; and a wife like you would make a man's fortune."

She did not move, but looked frightened; she did not even try to comprehend his meaning, for her thoughts were in a whirl, as if at the approach of some great danger; so, after waiting for a few seconds, he went on: "You see, a farm without a mistress can never succeed, even with a servant like you." Then he stopped, for he did not know what else to say, and Rose looked at him with the air of a person who thinks that he is face to face with a murderer and ready to flee at the slightest movement he may make; but, after waiting for about five minutes, he asked her: "Well, will it suit you?" "Will what suit me, master?" And he said quickly: "Why, to marry me, by Heaven!"

She jumped up, but fell back on her chair, as if she had been struck, and there she remained motionless, like a person who is overwhelmed by some great misfortune. At last the farmer grew impatient and said: "Come, what more do you want?" She looked at him, almost in terror, then suddenly the tears came into her eyes and she said twice in a choking voice: "I cannot, I cannot!" "Why not?" he asked. "Come, don't be silly; I will give you until tomorrow to think it over."

And he hurried out of the room, very glad to have got through with the matter, which had troubled him a good deal, for he had no doubt that she would the next morning accept a proposal which she could never have expected and which would be a capital bargain for him, as he thus bound a woman to his interests who would certainly bring him more than if she had the best dowry in the district.

Neither could there be any scruples about an unequal match between them, for in the country every one is very nearly equal; the farmer works with his laborers, who frequently become masters in their turn, and the female servants constantly become the mistresses of the establishments without its making any change in their life or habits.

Rose did not go to bed that night. She threw herself, dressed as she was, on her bed, and she had not even the strength to cry left in her, she was so thoroughly dumfounded. She remained quite inert, scarcely knowing that she had a body, and without being at all able to collect her thoughts, though, at moments, she remembered something of what had happened, and then she was frightened at the idea of what might happen. Her terror increased, and every time the great kitchen clock struck the hour she broke out in a perspiration from grief. She became bewildered, and had the nightmare; her candle went out, and then she began to imagine that some one had cast a spell over her, as country people so often imagine, and she felt a mad inclination to run away, to escape and to flee before her misfortune, like a ship scudding before the wind. An owl hooted; she shivered, sat up, passed her hands over her face, her hair, and all over her body, and then she went downstairs, as if she were walking in her sleep. When she got into the yard she stooped down, so as not to be seen by any prowling scamp, for the moon, which was setting, shed a bright light over the fields. Instead of opening the gate she scrambled over the fence, and as soon as she was outside she started off. She went on straight before her, with a quick, springy trot, and from time to time she unconsciously uttered a piercing cry. Her long shadow accompanied her, and now and then some night bird flew over her head, while the dogs in the farmyards barked as they heard her pass; one even jumped over the ditch, and followed her and tried to bite her, but she turned round and gave such a terrible yell that the frightened animal ran back and cowered in silence in its kennel.

The stars grew dim, and the birds began to twitter; day was breaking. The girl was worn out and panting; and when the sun rose in the purple sky, she stopped, for her swollen feet refused to go any farther; but she saw a pond in the distance, a large pond whose stagnant water looked like blood under the reflection of this new day, and she limped on slowly with her hand on her heart, in order to dip both her feet in it. She sat down on a tuft of grass, took off her heavy shoes, which were full of dust, pulled off her stockings and plunged her legs into the still water, from which bubbles were rising here and there.

A feeling of delicious coolness pervaded her from head to foot, and suddenly, while she was looking fixedly at the deep pool, she was seized with dizziness, and with a mad longing to throw herself into it. All her sufferings would be over in there, over forever. She no longer thought of her child; she only wanted peace, complete rest, and to sleep forever, and she got up with raised arms and took two steps forward. She was in the water up to her thighs, and she was just about to throw her self in when sharp, pricking pains in her ankles made her jump back, and she uttered a cry of despair, for, from her knees to the tips of her feet, long black leeches were sucking her lifeblood, and were swelling as they adhered to her flesh. She did not dare to touch them, and screamed with horror, so that her cries of despair attracted a peasant, who was driving along at some distance, to the spot. He pulled off the leeches one by one, applied herbs to the wounds, and drove the girl to her master's farm in his gig.

She was in bed for a fortnight, and as she was sitting outside the door on the first morning that she got up, the farmer suddenly came and planted himself before her. "Well," he said, "I suppose the affair is settled isn't it?" She did not reply at first, and then, as he remained standing and looking at her intently with his piercing eyes, she said with difficulty: "No, master, I cannot." He immediately flew into a rage.

"You cannot, girl; you cannot? I should just like to know the reason why?" She began to cry, and repeated: "I cannot." He looked at her, and then exclaimed angrily: "Then I suppose you have a lover?" "Perhaps that is it," she replied, trembling with shame.

The man got as red as a poppy, and stammered out in a rage: "Ah! So you confess it, you slut! And pray who is the fellow? Some penniless, half-starved ragamuffin, without a roof to his head, I suppose? Who is it, I say?" And as she gave him no answer, he continued: "Ah! So you will not tell me. Then I will tell you; it is Jean Baudu?"—"No, not he," she exclaimed. "Then it is Pierre Martin?"—"Oh! no, master."

And he angrily mentioned all the young fellows in the neighborhood, while she denied that he had hit upon the right one, and every moment wiped her eyes with the corner of her blue apron. But he still tried to find it out, with his brutish obstinacy, and, as it were, scratching at her heart to discover her secret, just as a terrier scratches at a hole to try and get at the animal which he scents inside it. Suddenly, however, the man shouted: "By George! It is Jacques, the man who was here last year. They used to say that you were always talking together, and that you thought about getting married."

Rose was choking, and she grew scarlet, while her tears suddenly stopped and dried up on her cheeks, like drops of water on hot iron, and she exclaimed: "No, it is not he, it is not he!" "Is that really a fact?" asked the cunning peasant, who partly guessed the truth; and she replied, hastily: "I will swear it; I will swear it to you—" She tried to think of something by which to swear, as she did not venture to invoke sacred things, but he interrupted her: "At any rate, he used to follow you into every corner and devoured you with his eyes at meal times. Did you ever give him your promise, eh?"

This time she looked her master straight in the face. "No, never, never; I will solemnly swear to you that if he were to come to-day and ask me to marry him I would have nothing to do with him." She spoke with such an air of sincerity that the farmer hesitated, and then he continued, as if speaking to himself: "What, then? You have not had a misfortune, as they call it, or it would have been known, and as it has no consequences, no girl would refuse her master on that account. There must be something at the bottom of it, however."

She could say nothing; she had not the strength to speak, and he asked her again: "You will not?" "I cannot, master," she said, with a sigh, and he turned on his heel.

She thought she had got rid of him altogether and spent the rest of the day almost tranquilly, but was as exhausted as if she had been turning the thrashing machine all day in the place of the old white horse, and she went to bed as soon as she could and fell asleep immediately. In the middle of the night, however, two hands touching the bed woke her. She trembled with fear, but immediately recognized the farmer's voice, when he said to her: "Don't be frightened, Rose; I have come to speak to you." She was surprised at first, but when he tried to take liberties with her she understood and began to tremble violently, as she felt quite alone in the darkness, still heavy from sleep, and quite unprotected, with that man standing near her. She certainly did not consent, but she resisted carelessly struggling against that instinct which is always strong in simple natures and very imperfectly protected by the undecided will of inert and gentle races. She turned her head now to the wall, and now toward the room, in order to avoid the attentions which the farmer tried to press on her, but she was weakened by fatigue, while he became brutal, intoxicated by desire.

They lived together as man and wife, and one morning he said to her: "I have put up our banns, and we will get married next month."

She did not reply, for what could she say? She did not resist, for what could she do?

PART IV

She married him. She felt as if she were in a pit with inaccessible sides from which she could never get out, and all kinds of misfortunes were hanging over her head, like huge rocks, which would fall on the first occasion. Her husband gave her the impression of a man whom she had robbed, and who would find it out some day or other. And then she thought of her child, who was the cause of her misfortunes, but who was also the cause of all her happiness on earth, and whom she went to see twice a year, though she came back more unhappy each time.

But she gradually grew accustomed to her life, her fears were allayed, her heart was at rest, and she lived with an easier mind, though still with some vague fear floating in it. And so years went on, until the child was six. She was almost happy now, when suddenly the farmer's temper grew very bad.

For two or three years he seemed to have been nursing some secret anxiety, to be troubled by some care, some mental disturbance, which was gradually increasing. He remained sitting at table after dinner, with his head in his hands, sad and devoured by sorrow. He always spoke hastily, sometimes even brutally, and it even seemed as if he had a grudge against his wife, for at times he answered her roughly, almost angrily.

One day, when a neighbor's boy came for some eggs, and she spoke rather crossly to him, as she was very busy, her husband suddenly came in and said to her in his unpleasant voice: "If that were your own child you would not treat him so." She was hurt and did not reply, and then she went back into the house, with all her grief awakened afresh; and at dinner the farmer neither spoke to her nor looked at her, and he seemed to hate her, to despise her, to know something about the affair at last. In consequence she lost her composure, and did not venture to remain alone with him after the meal was over, but left the room and hastened to the church.

It was getting dusk; the narrow nave was in total darkness, but she heard footsteps in the choir, for the sacristan was preparing the tabernacle lamp for the night. That spot of trembling light, which was lost in the darkness of the arches, looked to Rose like her last hope, and with her eyes fixed on it, she fell on her knees. The chain rattled as the little lamp swung up into the air, and almost immediately the small bell rang out the Angelus through the increasing mist. She went up to him, as he was going out.

"Is Monsieur le Cure at home?" she asked. "Of course he is; this is his dinnertime." She trembled as she rang the bell of the parsonage. The priest was just sitting down to dinner, and he made her sit down also. "Yes, yes, I know all about it; your husband has mentioned the matter to me that brings you here." The poor woman nearly fainted, and the priest continued: "What do you want, my child?" And he hastily swallowed several spoonfuls of soup, some of which dropped on to his greasy cassock. But Rose did not venture to say anything more, and she got up to go, but the priest said: "Courage."

And she went out and returned to the farm without knowing what she was doing. The farmer was waiting for her, as the laborers had gone away during her absence, and she fell heavily at his feet, and, shedding a flood of tears, she said to him: "What have you got against me?"

He began to shout and to swear: "What have I got against you? That I have no children, by—-. When a man takes a wife it is not that they may live alone together to the end of their days. That is what I have against you. When a cow has no calves she is not worth anything, and when a woman has no children she is also not worth anything."

She began to cry, and said: "It is not my fault! It is not my fault!" He grew rather more gentle when he heard that, and added: "I do not say that it is, but it is very provoking, all the same."

PART V

From that day forward she had only one thought: to have a child another child; she confided her wish to everybody, and, in consequence of this, a neighbor told her of an infallible method. This was, to make her husband drink a glass of water with a pinch of ashes in it every evening. The farmer consented to try it, but without success; so they said to each other: "Perhaps there are some secret ways?" And they tried to find out. They were told of a shepherd who lived ten leagues off, and so Vallin one day drove off to consult him. The shepherd gave him a loaf on which he had made some marks; it was kneaded up with herbs, and each of them was to eat a piece of it, but they ate the whole loaf without obtaining any results from it.

Next, a schoolmaster unveiled mysteries and processes of love which were unknown in the country, but infallible, so he declared; but none of them had the desired effect. Then the priest advised them to make a pilgrimage to the shrine at Fecamp. Rose went with the crowd and prostrated herself in the abbey, and, mingling her prayers with the coarse desires of the peasants around her, she prayed that she might be fruitful a second time; but it was in vain, and then she thought that she was being punished for her first fault, and she was seized by terrible grief. She was wasting away with sorrow; her husband was also aging prematurely, and was wearing himself out in useless hopes.

Then war broke out between them; he called her names and beat her. They quarrelled all day long, and when they were in their room together at night he flung insults and obscenities at her, choking with rage, until one night, not being able to think of any means of making her suffer more he ordered her to get up and go and stand out of doors in the rain until daylight. As she did not obey him, he seized her by the neck and began to strike her in the face with his fists, but she said nothing and did not move. In his exasperation he knelt on her stomach, and with clenched teeth, and mad with rage, he began to beat her. Then in her despair she rebelled, and flinging him against the wall with a furious gesture, she sat up, and in an altered voice she hissed: "I have had a child, I have had one! I had it by Jacques; you know Jacques. He promised to marry me, but he left this neighborhood without keeping his word."

The man was thunderstruck and could hardly speak, but at last he stammered out: "What are you saying? What are you saying?" Then she began to sob, and amid her tears she continued: "That was the reason why I did not want to marry you. I could not tell you, for you would have left me without any bread for my child. You have never had any children, so you cannot understand, you cannot understand!"

He said again, mechanically, with increasing surprise: "You have a child? You have a child?"

"You took me by force, as I suppose you know? I did not want to marry you," she said, still sobbing.

Then he got up, lit the candle, and began to walk up and down, with his arms behind him. She was cowering on the bed and crying, and suddenly he stopped in front of her, and said: "Then it is my fault that you have no children?" She gave him no answer, and he began to walk up and down again, and then, stopping again, he continued: "How old is your child?" "Just six," she whispered. "Why did you not tell me about it?" he asked. "How could I?" she replied, with a sigh.

He remained standing, motionless. "Come, get up," he said. She got up with some difficulty, and then, when she was standing on the floor, he suddenly began to laugh with the hearty laugh of his good days, and, seeing how surprised she was, he added: "Very well, we will go and fetch the child, as you and I can have none together."

She was so scared that if she had had the strength she would assuredly have run away, but the farmer rubbed his hands and said: "I wanted to adopt one, and now we have found one. I asked the cure about an orphan some time ago."

Then, still laughing, he kissed his weeping and agitated wife on both cheeks, and shouted out, as though she could not hear him:

"Come along, mother, we will go and see whether there is any soup left; I should not mind a plateful."

She put on her petticoat and they went downstairs; and while she was kneeling in front of the fireplace and lighting the fire under the saucepan, he continued to walk up and down the kitchen with long strides, repeating:

"Well, I am really glad of this; I am not saying it for form's sake, but I am glad, I am really very glad."

THE WRECK

It was yesterday, the 31st of December.

I had just finished breakfast with my old friend Georges Garin when the servant handed him a letter covered with seals and foreign stamps.

Georges said:

"Will you excuse me?"

"Certainly."

And so he began to read the letter, which was written in a large English handwriting, crossed and recrossed in every direction. He read them slowly, with serious attention and the interest which we only pay to things which touch our hearts.

Then he put the letter on the mantelpiece and said:

"That was a curious story! I've never told you about it, I think. Yet it was a sentimental adventure, and it really happened to me. That was a strange New Year's Day, indeed! It must have been twenty years ago, for I was then thirty and am now fifty years old.

"I was then an inspector in the Maritime Insurance Company, of which I am now director. I had arranged to pass New Year's Day in Paris—since it is customary to make that day a fete—when I received a letter from the manager, asking me to proceed at once to the island of Re, where a three-masted vessel from Saint-Nazaire, insured by us, had just been driven ashore. It was then eight o'clock in the morning. I arrived at the office at ten to get my advices, and that evening I took the express, which put me down in La Rochelle the next day, the 31st of December.

"I had two hours to wait before going aboard the boat for Re. So I made a tour of the town. It is certainly a queer city, La Rochelle, with strong characteristics of its own streets tangled like a labyrinth, sidewalks running under endless arcaded galleries like those of the Rue de Rivoli, but low, mysterious, built as if to form a suitable setting for conspirators and making a striking background for those old-time wars, the savage heroic wars of religion. It is indeed the typical old Huguenot city, conservative, discreet, with no fine art to show, with no wonderful monuments, such as make Rouen; but it is remarkable for its severe, somewhat sullen look; it is a city of obstinate fighters, a city where fanaticism might well blossom, where the faith of the Calvinists became enthusiastic and which gave birth to the plot of the 'Four Sergeants.'

"After I had wandered for some time about these curious streets, I went aboard the black, rotund little steamboat which was to take me to the island of Re. It was called the Jean Guiton. It started with angry puffings, passed between the two old towers which guard the harbor, crossed the roadstead and issued from the mole built by Richelieu, the great stones of which can be seen at the water's edge, enclosing the town like a great necklace. Then the steamboat turned to the right.

"It was one of those sad days which give one the blues, tighten the heart and take away all strength and energy and force-a gray, cold day, with a heavy mist which was as wet as rain, as cold as frost, as bad to breathe as the steam of a wash-tub.

"Under this low sky of dismal fog the shallow, yellow, sandy sea of all practically level beaches lay without a wrinkle, without a movement, without life, a sea of turbid water, of greasy water, of stagnant water. The Jean Guiton passed over it, rolling a little from habit, dividing the smooth, dark blue water and leaving behind a few waves, a little splashing, a slight swell, which soon calmed down.

"I began to talk to the captain, a little man with small feet, as round as his boat and rolling in the same manner. I wanted some details of the disaster on which I was to draw up a report. A great square-rigged three-master, the Marie Joseph, of Saint-Nazaire, had gone ashore one night in a hurricane on the sands of the island of Re.

"The owner wrote us that the storm had thrown the ship so far ashore that it was impossible to float her and that they had to remove everything which could be detached with the utmost possible haste. Nevertheless I must examine the situation of the wreck, estimate what must have been her condition before the disaster and decide whether all efforts had been used to get her afloat. I came as an agent of the company in order to give contradictory testimony, if necessary, at the trial.

"On receipt of my report, the manager would take what measures he might think necessary to protect our interests.

"The captain of the Jean Guiton knew all about the affair, having been summoned with his boat to assist in the attempts at salvage.

"He told me the story of the disaster. The Marie Joseph, driven by a furious gale lost her bearings completely in the night, and steering by chance over a heavy foaming sea—'a milk-soup sea,' said the captain—had gone ashore on those immense sand banks which make the coasts of this country look like limitless Saharas when the tide is low.

"While talking I looked around and ahead. Between the ocean and the lowering sky lay an open space where the eye could see into the distance. We were following a coast. I asked:

"'Is that the island of Re?'

"'Yes, sir.'

"And suddenly the captain stretched his right hand out before us, pointed to something almost imperceptible in the open sea, and said:

"'There's your ship!'

"'The Marie Joseph!'

"'Yes.'

"I was amazed. This black, almost imperceptible speck, which looked to me like a rock, seemed at least three miles from land.

"I continued:

"'But, captain, there must be a hundred fathoms of water in that place.'

"He began to laugh.

"'A hundred fathoms, my child! Well, I should say about two!'

"He was from Bordeaux. He continued:

"'It's now nine-forty, just high tide. Go down along the beach with your hands in your pockets after you've had lunch at the

Hotel du Dauphin, and I'll wager that at ten minutes to three, or three o'clock, you'll reach the wreck without wetting your feet, and have from an hour and three-quarters to two hours aboard of her; but not more, or you'll be caught. The faster the sea goes out the faster it comes back. This coast is as flat as a turtle! But start away at ten minutes to five, as I tell you, and at half-past seven you will be again aboard of the Jean Guiton, which will put you down this same evening on the quay at La Rochelle.'

"I thanked the captain and I went and sat down in the bow of the steamer to get a good look at the little city of Saint-Martin, which we were now rapidly approaching.

"It was just like all small seaports which serve as capitals of the barren islands scattered along the coast—a large fishing village, one foot on sea and one on shore, subsisting on fish and wild fowl, vegetables and shell-fish, radishes and mussels. The island is very low and little cultivated, yet it seems to be thickly populated. However, I did not penetrate into the interior.

"After breakfast I climbed across a little promontory, and then, as the tide was rapidly falling, I started out across the sands toward a kind of black rock which I could just perceive above the surface of the water, out a considerable distance.

"I walked quickly over the yellow plain. It was elastic, like flesh and seemed to sweat beneath my tread. The sea had been there very lately. Now I perceived it at a distance, escaping out of sight, and I no longer could distinguish the line which separated the sands from ocean. I felt as though I were looking at a gigantic supernatural work of enchantment. The Atlantic had just now been before me, then it had disappeared into the sands, just as scenery disappears through a trap; and I was now walking in the midst of a desert. Only the feeling, the breath of the salt-water, remained in me. I perceived the smell of the wrack, the smell of the sea, the good strong smell of sea coasts. I walked fast; I was no longer cold. I looked at the stranded wreck, which grew in size as I approached, and came now to resemble an enormous shipwrecked whale.

"It seemed fairly to rise out of the ground, and on that great, flat, yellow stretch of sand assumed wonderful proportions. After an hour's walk I at last reached it. It lay upon its side, ruined and shattered, its broken bones showing as though it were an animal, its bones of tarred wood pierced with great bolts. The sand had already invaded it, entering it by all the crannies, and held it and refused to let it go. It seemed to have taken root in it. The bow had entered deep into this soft, treacherous beach, while the stern, high in air, seemed to cast at heaven, like a cry of despairing appeal, the two white words on the black planking, Marie Joseph.

"I climbed upon this carcass of a ship by the lowest side; then, having reached the deck, I went below. The daylight, which entered by the stove-in hatches and the cracks in the sides, showed me dimly long dark cavities full of demolished woodwork. They contained nothing but sand, which served as foot-soil in this cavern of planks.

"I began to take some notes about the condition of the ship. I was seated on a broken empty cask, writing by the light of a great crack, through which I could perceive the boundless stretch of the strand. A strange shivering of cold and loneliness ran over my skin from time to time, and I would often stop writing for a moment to listen to the mysterious noises in the derelict: the noise of crabs scratching the planking with their crooked claws; the noise of a thousand little creatures of the sea already crawling over this dead body or else boring into the wood.

"Suddenly, very near me, I heard human voices. I started as though I had seen a ghost. For a second I really thought I was about to see drowned men rise from the sinister depths of the hold, who would tell me about their death. At any rate, it did not take me long to swing myself on deck. There, standing by the bows, was a tall Englishman with three young misses. Certainly they were a good deal more frightened at seeing this sudden apparition on the abandoned three-master than I was at seeing them. The youngest girl turned and ran, the two others threw their arms round their father. As for him, he opened his mouth—that was the only sign of emotion which he showed.

"Then, after several seconds, he spoke:

"'Mosieu, are you the owner of this ship?'

"'I am.'

"'May I go over it?'

"'You may.'

"Then he uttered a long sentence in English, in which I only distinguished the word 'gracious,' repeated several times.

"As he was looking for a place to climb up I showed him the easiest way, and gave him a hand. He climbed up. Then we helped up the three girls, who had now quite recovered their composure. They were charming, especially the oldest, a blonde of eighteen, fresh as a flower, and very dainty and pretty! Ah, yes! the pretty Englishwomen have indeed the look of tender sea fruit. One would have said of this one that she had just risen out of the sands and that her hair had kept their tint. They all, with their exquisite freshness, make you think of the delicate colors of pink sea-shells and of shining pearls hidden in the unknown depths of the ocean.

"She spoke French a little better than her father and acted as interpreter. I had to tell all about the shipwreck, and I romanced as though I had been present at the catastrophe. Then the whole family descended into the interior of the wreck. As soon as they had penetrated into this sombre, dimly lit cavity they uttered cries of astonishment and admiration. Suddenly the father and his three daughters were holding sketch-books in their hands, which they had doubtless carried hidden somewhere in their heavy weather-proof clothes, and were all beginning at once to make pencil sketches of this melancholy and weird place.

"They had seated themselves side by side on a projecting beam, and the four sketch-books on the eight knees were being rapidly covered with little black lines which were intended to represent the half-opened hulk of the Marie Joseph.

"I continued to inspect the skeleton of the ship, and the oldest girl talked to me while she worked.

"They had none of the usual English arrogance; they were simple honest hearts of that class of continuous travellers with which England covers the globe. The father was long and thin, with a red face framed in white whiskers, and looking like a living sandwich, a piece of ham carved like a face between two wads of hair. The daughters, who had long legs like young storks, were also thin-except the oldest. All three were pretty, especially the tallest.

"She had such a droll way of speaking, of laughing, of understanding and of not understanding, of raising her eyes to ask a question (eyes blue as the deep ocean), of stopping her drawing a moment to make a guess at what you meant, of returning once more to work, of saying 'yes' or 'no'—that I could have listened and looked indefinitely.

"Suddenly she murmured:

"'I hear a little sound on this boat.'

"I listened and I immediately distinguished a low, steady, curious sound. I rose and looked out of the crack and gave a scream. The sea had come up to us; it would soon surround us!

"We were on deck in an instant. It was too late. The water circled us about and was running toward the coast at tremendous speed. No, it did not run, it glided, crept, spread like an immense, limitless blot. The water was barely a few centimeters deep, but the rising flood had gone so far that we no longer saw the vanishing line of the imperceptible tide.

"The Englishman wanted to jump. I held him back. Flight was impossible because of the deep places which we had been obliged to go round on our way out and into which we should fall on our return.

"There was a minute of horrible anguish in our hearts. Then the little English girl began to smile and murmured:

"'It is we who are shipwrecked.'

"I tried to laugh, but fear held me, a fear which was cowardly and horrid and base and treacherous like the tide. All the danger which we ran appeared to me at once. I wanted to shriek: 'Help!' But to whom?

"The two younger girls were clinging to their father, who looked in consternation at the measureless sea which hedged us round about.

"The night fell as swiftly as the ocean rose—a lowering, wet, icy night.

"I said:

"'There's nothing to do but to stay on the ship:

"The Englishman answered:

"'Oh, yes!'

"And we waited there a quarter of an hour, half an hour, indeed I don't know how long, watching that creeping water growing deeper as it swirled around us, as though it were playing on the beach, which it had regained.

"One of the young girls was cold, and we went below to shelter ourselves from the light but freezing wind that made our skins tingle.

"I leaned over the hatchway. The ship was full of water. So we had to cower against the stern planking, which shielded us a little.

"Darkness was now coming on, and we remained huddled together. I felt the shoulder of the little English girl trembling against mine, her teeth chattering from time to time. But I also felt the gentle warmth of her body through her ulster, and that warmth was as delicious to me as a kiss. We no longer spoke; we sat motionless, mute, cowering down like animals in a ditch when a hurricane is raging. And, nevertheless, despite the night, despite the terrible and increasing danger, I began to feel happy that I was there, glad of the cold and the peril, glad of the long hours of darkness and anguish that I must pass on this plank so near this dainty, pretty little girl.

"I asked myself, 'Why this strange sensation of well-being and of joy?'

"Why! Does one know? Because she was there? Who? She, a little unknown English girl? I did not love her, I did not even know her. And for all that, I was touched and conquered. I wanted to save her, to sacrifice myself for her, to commit a thousand follies! Strange thing! How does it happen that the presence of a woman overwhelms us so? Is it the power of her grace which enfolds us? Is it the seduction of her beauty and youth, which intoxicates one like wine?

"Is it not rather the touch of Love, of Love the Mysterious, who seeks constantly to unite two beings, who tries his strength the instant he has put a man and a woman face to face?

"The silence of the darkness became terrible, the stillness of the sky dreadful, because we could hear vaguely about us a slight, continuous sound, the sound of the rising tide and the monotonous plashing of the water against the ship.

"Suddenly I heard the sound of sobs. The youngest of the girls was crying. Her father tried to console her, and they began to talk in their own tongue, which I did not understand. I guessed that he was reassuring her and that she was still afraid.

"I asked my neighbor:

"'You are not too cold, are you, mademoiselle?'

"'Oh, yes. I am very cold.'

"I offered to give her my cloak; she refused it.

"But I had taken it off and I covered her with it against her will. In the short struggle her hand touched mine. It made a delicious thrill run through my body.

"For some minutes the air had been growing brisker, the dashing of the water stronger against the flanks of the ship. I raised myself; a great gust of wind blew in my face. The wind was rising!

"The Englishman perceived this at the same time that I did and said simply:

"'This is bad for us, this——'

"Of course it was bad, it was certain death if any breakers, however feeble, should attack and shake the wreck, which was already so shattered and disconnected that the first big sea would carry it off.

"So our anguish increased momentarily as the squalls grew stronger and stronger. Now the sea broke a little, and I saw in the darkness white lines appearing and disappearing, lines of foam, while each wave struck the Marie Joseph and shook her with a short quiver which went to our hearts.

"The English girl was trembling. I felt her shiver against me. And I had a wild desire to take her in my arms.

"Down there, before and behind us, to the left and right, lighthouses were shining along the shore—lighthouses white, yellow and red, revolving like the enormous eyes of giants who were watching us, waiting eagerly for us to disappear. One of them in especial irritated me. It went out every thirty seconds and it lit up again immediately. It was indeed an eye, that one, with its lid incessantly lowered over its fiery glance.

"From time to time the Englishman struck a match to see the hour; then he put his watch back in his pocket. Suddenly he said to me, over the heads of his daughters, with tremendous gravity:

"'I wish you a happy New Year, Mosieu.'

"It was midnight. I held out my hand, which he pressed. Then he said something in English, and suddenly he and his daughters began to sing 'God Save the Queen,' which rose through the black and silent air and vanished into space.

"At first I felt a desire to laugh; then I was seized by a powerful, strange emotion.

"It was something sinister and superb, this chant of the shipwrecked, the condemned, something like a prayer and also like something grander, something comparable to the ancient 'Ave Caesar morituri te salutant.'

"When they had finished I asked my neighbor to sing a ballad alone, anything she liked, to make us forget our terrors. She consented, and immediately her clear young voice rang out into the night. She sang something which was doubtless sad, because the notes were long drawn out and hovered, like wounded birds, above the waves.

"The sea was rising now and beating upon our wreck. As for me, I thought only of that voice. And I thought also of the sirens. If a ship had passed near by us what would the sailors have said? My troubled spirit lost itself in the dream! A siren! Was she not really a siren, this daughter of the sea, who had kept me on this worm-eaten ship and who was soon about to go down with me deep into the waters?

"But suddenly we were all five rolling on the deck, because the Marie Joseph had sunk on her right side. The English girl had fallen upon me, and before I knew what I was doing, thinking that my last moment was come, I had caught her in my arms and kissed her cheek, her temple and her hair.

"The ship did not move again, and we, we also, remained motionless.

"The father said, 'Kate!' The one whom I was holding answered 'Yes' and made a movement to free herself. And at that moment I should have wished the ship to split in two and let me fall with her into the sea.

"The Englishman continued:

"'A little rocking; it's nothing. I have my three daughters safe.'

"Not having seen the oldest, he had thought she was lost overboard!

"I rose slowly, and suddenly I made out a light on the sea quite close to us. I shouted; they answered. It was a boat sent out in search of us by the hotelkeeper, who had guessed at our imprudence.

"We were saved. I was in despair. They picked us up off our raft and they brought us back to Saint-Martin.

"The Englishman began to rub his hand and murmur:

"'A good supper! A good supper!'

"We did sup. I was not gay. I regretted the Marie Joseph.

"We had to separate the next day after much handshaking and many promises to write. They departed for Biarritz. I wanted to follow them.

"I was hard hit. I wanted to ask this little girl to marry me. If we had passed eight days together, I should have done so! How weak and incomprehensible a man sometimes is!

"Two years passed without my hearing a word from them. Then I received a letter from New York. She was married and wrote to tell me. And since then we write to each other every year, on New Year's Day. She tells me about her life, talks of her children, her sisters, never of her husband! Why? Ah! why? And as for me, I only talk of the Marie Joseph. That was perhaps the only woman I have ever loved—no—that I ever should have loved. Ah, well! who can tell? Circumstances rule one. And then—and then—all passes. She must be old now; I should not know her. Ah! she of the bygone time, she of the wreck! What a creature! Divine! She writes me her hair is white. That caused me terrible pain. Ah! her yellow hair. No, my English girl exists no longer. How sad it all is!"

THEODULE SABOT'S CONFESSION

When Sabot entered the inn at Martinville it was a signal for laughter. What a rogue he was, this Sabot! There was a man who did not like priests, for instance! Oh, no, oh, no! He did not spare them, the scamp.

Sabot (Theodule), a master carpenter, represented liberal thought in Martinville. He was a tall, thin man, with gray, cunning eyes, and thin lips, and wore his hair plastered down on his temples. When he said: "Our holy father, the pope" in a certain manner, everyone laughed. He made a point of working on Sunday during the hour of mass. He killed his pig each year on Monday in Holy Week in order to have enough black pudding to last till Easter, and when the priest passed by, he always said by way of a joke: "There goes one who has just swallowed his God off a salver."

The priest, a stout man and also very tall, dreaded him on account of his boastful talk which attracted followers. The Abbe Maritime was a politic man, and believed in being diplomatic. There had been a rivalry between them for ten years, a secret, intense, incessant rivalry. Sabot was municipal councillor, and they thought he would become mayor, which would inevitably mean the final overthrow of the church.

The elections were about to take place. The church party was shaking in its shoes in Martinville.

One morning the cure set out for Rouen, telling his servant that he was going to see the archbishop. He returned in two days with a joyous, triumphant air. And everyone knew the following day that the chancel of the church was going to be renovated. A sum of six hundred francs had been contributed by the archbishop out of his private fund. All the old pine pews were to be removed, and replaced by new pews made of oak. It would be a big carpentering job, and they talked about it that very evening in all the houses in the village.

Theodule Sabot was not laughing.

When he went through the village the following morning, the neighbors, friends and enemies, all asked him, jokingly:

"Are you going to do the work on the chancel of the church?"

He could find nothing to say, but he was furious, he was good and angry.

Ill-natured people added:

"It is a good piece of work; and will bring in not less than two or three per cent. profit."

Two days later, they heard that the work of renovation had been entrusted to Celestin Chambrelan, the carpenter from Percheville. Then this was denied, and it was said that all the pews in the church were going to be changed. That would be well worth the two thousand francs that had been demanded of the church administration.

Theodule Sabot could not sleep for thinking about it. Never, in all the memory of man, had a country carpenter undertaken a similar piece of work. Then a rumor spread abroad that the cure felt very grieved that he had to give this work to a carpenter who was a stranger in the community, but that Sabot's opinions were a barrier to his being entrusted with the job.

Sabot knew it well. He called at the parsonage just as it was growing dark. The servant told him that the cure was at church. He went to the church.

Two attendants on the altar of the Virgin, two sour old maids, were decorating the altar for the month of Mary, under the direction of the priest, who stood in the middle of the chancel with his portly paunch, directing the two women who, mounted on chairs, were placing flowers around the tabernacle.

Sabot felt ill at ease in there, as though he were in the house of his greatest enemy, but the greed of gain was gnawing at his heart.

He drew nearer, holding his cap in his hand, and not paying any attention to the "demoiselles de la Vierge," who remained standing startled, astonished, motionless on their chairs.

He faltered:

"Good morning, monsieur le cure."

The priest replied without looking at him, all occupied as he was with the altar:

"Good morning, Mr. Carpenter."

Sabot, nonplussed, knew not what to say next. But after a pause he remarked:

"You are making preparations?"

Abbe Maritime replied:

"Yes, we are near the month of Mary."

"Why, why," remarked Sabot and then was silent. He would have liked to retire now without saying anything, but a glance at the chancel held him back. He saw sixteen seats that had to be remade, six to the right and eight to the left, the door of the sacristy occupying the place of two. Sixteen oak seats, that would be worth at most three hundred francs, and by figuring carefully one might certainly make two hundred francs on the work if one were not clumsy.

Then he stammered out:

"I have come about the work."

The cure appeared surprised. He asked:

"What work?"

"The work to be done," murmured Sabot, in dismay.

Then the priest turned round and looking him straight in the eyes, said:

"Do you mean the repairs in the chancel of my church?"

At the tone of the abbe, Theodule Sabot felt a chill run down his back and he once more had a longing to take to his heels. However, he replied humbly:

"Why, yes, monsieur le cure."

Then the abbe folded his arms across his large stomach and, as if filled with amazement, said:

"Is it you—you—you, Sabot—who have come to ask me for this . . . You—the only irreligious man in my parish! Why, it would be a scandal, a public scandal! The archbishop would give me a reprimand, perhaps transfer me."

He stopped a few seconds, for breath, and then resumed in a calmer tone: "I can understand that it pains you to see a work of such importance entrusted to a carpenter from a neighboring parish. But I cannot do otherwise, unless—but no—it is impossible—you would not consent, and unless you did, never."

Sabot now looked at the row of benches in line as far as the entrance door. Christopher, if they were going to change all those!

And he asked:

"What would you require of me? Tell me."

The priest, in a firm tone replied:

"I must have an extraordinary token of your good intentions."

"I do not say—I do not say; perhaps we might come to an understanding," faltered Sabot.

"You will have to take communion publicly at high mass next Sunday," declared the cure.

The carpenter felt he was growing pale, and without replying, he asked:

"And the benches, are they going to be renovated?"

The abbe replied with confidence:

"Yes, but later on."

Sabot resumed:

"I do not say, I do not say. I am not calling it off, I am consenting to religion, for sure. But what rubs me the wrong way is, putting it in practice; but in this case I will not be refractory."

The attendants of the Virgin, having got off their chairs had concealed themselves behind the altar; and they listened pale with emotion.

The cure, seeing he had gained the victory, became all at once very friendly, quite familiar.

"That is good, that is good. That was wisely said, and not stupid, you understand. You will see, you will see."

Sabot smiled and asked with an awkward air:

"Would it not be possible to put off this communion just a trifle?"

But the priest replied, resuming his severe expression:

"From the moment that the work is put into your hands, I want to be assured of your conversion."

Then he continued more gently:

"You will come to confession to-morrow; for I must examine you at least twice."

"Twice?" repeated Sabot.

"Yes."

The priest smiled.

"You understand perfectly that you must have a general cleaning up, a thorough cleansing. So I will expect you to-morrow."

The carpenter, much agitated, asked:

"Where do you do that?"

"Why—in the confessional."

"In—that box, over there in the corner? The fact is—is—that it does not suit me, your box."

"How is that?"

"Seeing that—seeing that I am not accustomed to that, and also I am rather hard of hearing."

The cure was very affable and said:

"Well, then! you shall come to my house and into my parlor. We will have it just the two of us, tete-a-tete. Does that suit you?"

"Yes, that is all right, that will suit me, but your box, no."

"Well, then, to-morrow after the days work, at six o'clock."

"That is understood, that is all right, that is agreed on. To-morrow, monsieur le cure. Whoever draws back is a skunk!"

And he held out his great rough hand which the priest grasped heartily with a clap that resounded through the church.

Theodule Sabot was not easy in his mind all the following day. He had a feeling analogous to the apprehension one experiences when a tooth has to be drawn. The thought recurred to him at every moment: "I must go to confession this evening." And his troubled mind, the mind of an atheist only half convinced, was bewildered with a confused and overwhelming dread of the divine mystery.

As soon as he had finished his work, he betook himself to the parsonage. The cure was waiting for him in the garden, reading his breviary as he walked along a little path. He appeared radiant and greeted him with a good-natured laugh.

"Well, here we are! Come in, come in, Monsieur Sabot, no one will eat you."

And Sabot preceded him into the house. He faltered:

"If you do not mind I should like to get through with this little matter at once."

The cure replied:

"I am at your service. I have my surplice here. One minute and I will listen to you."

The carpenter, so disturbed that he had not two ideas in his head, watched him as he put on the white vestment with its pleated folds. The priest beckoned to him and said:

"Kneel down on this cushion."

Sabot remained standing, ashamed of having to kneel. He stuttered:

"Is it necessary?"

But the abbe had become dignified.

"You cannot approach the penitent bench except on your knees."

And Sabot knelt down.

"Repeat the confiteor," said the priest.

"What is that?" asked Sabot.

"The confiteor. If you do not remember it, repeat after me, one by one, the words I am going to say." And the cure repeated the sacred prayer, in a slow tone, emphasizing the words which the carpenter repeated after him. Then he said:

"Now make your confession."

But Sabot was silent, not knowing where to begin. The abbe then came to his aid.

"My child, I will ask you questions, since you don't seem familiar with these things. We will take, one by one, the commandments of God. Listen to me and do not be disturbed. Speak very frankly and never fear that you may say too much.

"'One God alone, thou shalt adore,
And love him perfectly.'

"Have you ever loved anything, or anybody, as well as you loved God? Have you loved him with all your soul, all your heart, all the strength of your love?"

Sabot was perspiring with the effort of thinking. He replied:

"No. Oh, no, m'sieu le cure. I love God as much as I can. That is —yes—I love him very much. To say that I do not love my children, no—I cannot say that. To say that if I had to choose between them and God, I could not be sure. To say that if I had to lose a hundred francs for the love of God, I could not say about that. But I love him well, for sure, I love him all the same." The priest said gravely "You must love Him more than all besides." And Sabot, meaning well, declared "I will do what I possibly can, m'sieu le cure." The abbe resumed:

"'God's name in vain thou shalt not take
Nor swear by any other thing.'

"Did you ever swear?"

"No-oh, that, no! I never swear, never. Sometimes, in a moment of anger, I may say sacre nom de Dieu! But then, I never swear."

"That is swearing," cried the priest, and added seriously:

"Do not do it again.

"'Thy Sundays thou shalt keep
In serving God devoutly.'

"What do you do on Sunday?"

This time Sabot scratched his ear.

"Why, I serve God as best I can, m'sieu le cure. I serve him—at home. I work on Sunday."

The cure interrupted him, saying magnanimously:

"I know, you will do better in future. I will pass over the following commandments, certain that you have not transgressed the two first. We will take from the sixth to the ninth. I will resume:

"'Others' goods thou shalt not take
Nor keep what is not thine.'

"Have you ever taken in any way what belonged to another?"

But Theodule Sabot became indignant.

"Of course not, of course not! I am an honest man, m'sieu le cure, I swear it, for sure. To say that I have not sometimes charged for a few more hours of work to customers who had means, I could not say that. To say that I never add a few centimes to bills, only a few, I would not say that. But to steal, no! Oh, not that, no!"

The priest resumed severely:

"To take one single centime constitutes a theft. Do not do it again.

'False witness thou shalt not bear,
Nor lie in any way.'

"Have you ever told a lie?"

"No, as to that, no. I am not a liar. That is my quality. To say that I have never told a big story, I would not like to say that. To say that I have never made people believe things that were not true when it was to my own interest, I would not like to say that. But as for lying, I am not a liar."

The priest simply said:

"Watch yourself more closely." Then he continued:

"'The works of the flesh thou shalt not desire
Except in marriage only.'

"Did you ever desire, or live with, any other woman than your wife?"

Sabot exclaimed with sincerity:

"As to that, no; oh, as to that, no, m'sieu le Cure. My poor wife, deceive her! No, no! Not so much as the tip of a finger, either in thought or in act. That is the truth."

They were silent a few seconds, then, in a lower tone, as though a doubt had arisen in his mind, he resumed:

"When I go to town, to say that I never go into a house, you know, one of the licensed houses, just to laugh and talk and see something different, I could not say that. But I always pay, monsieur le cure, I always pay. From the moment you pay, without anyone seeing or knowing you, no one can get you into trouble."

The cure did not insist, and gave him absolution.

Theodule Sabot did the work on the chancel, and goes to communion every month.

THE WRONG HOUSE

Quartermaster Varajou had obtained a week's leave to go and visit his sister, Madame Padoie. Varajou, who was in garrison at Rennes and was leading a pretty gay life, finding himself high and dry, wrote to his sister saying that he would devote a week to her. It was not that he cared particularly for Mme. Padoie, a little moralist, a devotee, and always cross; but he needed money, needed it very badly, and he remembered that, of all his relations, the Padoies were the only ones whom he had never approached on the subject.

Pere Varajou, formerly a horticulturist at Angers, but now retired from business, had closed his purse strings to his scapegrace son and had hardly seen him for two years. His daughter had married Padoie, a former treasury clerk, who had just been appointed tax collector at Vannes.

Varajou, on leaving the train, had some one direct him to the house of his brother-in-law, whom he found in his office arguing with the Breton peasants of the neighborhood. Padoie rose from his seat, held out his hand across the table littered with papers, murmured, "Take a chair. I will be at liberty in a moment," sat down again and resumed his discussion.

The peasants did not understand his explanations, the collector did not understand their line of argument. He spoke French, they spoke Breton, and the clerk who acted as interpreter appeared not to understand either.

It lasted a long time, a very long time. Varajou looked at his brother-in-law and thought: "What a fool!" Padoie must have been almost fifty. He was tall, thin, bony, slow, hairy, with heavy arched eyebrows. He wore a velvet skull cap with a gold cord vandyke design round it. His look was gentle, like his actions. His speech, his gestures, his thoughts, all were soft. Varajou said to himself, "What a fool!"

He, himself, was one of those noisy roysterers for whom the greatest pleasures in life are the cafe and abandoned women. He understood nothing outside of these conditions of existence.

A boisterous braggart, filled with contempt for the rest of the world, he despised the entire universe from the height of his ignorance. When he said: "Nom d'un chien, what a spree!" he expressed the highest degree of admiration of which his mind was capable.

Having finally got rid of his peasants, Padoie inquired:

"How are you?"

"Pretty well, as you see. And how are you?"

"Quite well, thank you. It is very kind of you to have thought of coming to see us."

"Oh, I have been thinking of it for some time; but, you know, in the military profession one has not much freedom."

"Oh, I know, I know. All the same, it is very kind of you."

"And Josephine, is she well?"

"Yes, yes, thank you; you will see her presently." "Where is she?"

"She is making some calls. We have a great many friends here; it is a very nice town."

"I thought so."

The door opened and Mme. Padoie appeared. She went over to her brother without any eagerness, held her cheek for him to kiss, and asked:

"Have you been here long?"

"No, hardly half an hour."

"Oh, I thought the train would be late. Will you come into the parlor?"

They went into the adjoining room, leaving Padoie to his accounts and his taxpayers. As soon as they were alone, she said:

"I have heard nice things about you!"

"What have you heard?"

"It seems that you are behaving like a blackguard, getting drunk and contracting debts."

He appeared very much astonished.

"I! never in the world!"

"Oh, do not deny it, I know it."

He attempted to defend himself, but she gave him such a lecture that he could say nothing more.

She then resumed:

"We dine at six o'clock, and you can amuse yourself until then. I cannot entertain you, as I have so many things to do."

When he was alone he hesitated as to whether he should sleep or take a walk. He looked first at the door leading to his room and then at the hall door, and decided to go out. He sauntered slowly through the quiet Breton town, so sleepy, so calm, so dead, on the shores of its inland bay that is called "le Morbihan." He looked at the little gray houses, the occasional pedestrians, the empty stores, and he murmured:

"Vannes is certainly not gay, not lively. It was a sad idea, my coming here."

He reached the harbor, the desolate harbor, walked back along a lonely, deserted boulevard, and got home before five o'clock. Then he threw himself on his bed to sleep till dinner time. The maid woke him, knocking at the door.

"Dinner is ready, sir."

He went downstairs. In the damp dining-room with the paper peeling from the walls near the floor, he saw a soup tureen on a round table without any table cloth, on which were also three melancholy soup-plates.

M. and Mme. Padoie entered the room at the same time as Varajou. They all sat down to table, and the husband and wife crossed themselves over the pit of their stomachs, after which Padoie helped the soup, a meat soup. It was the day for pot-roast.

After the soup, they had the beef, which was done to rags, melted, greasy, like pap. The officer ate slowly, with disgust, weariness and rage.

Mme. Padoie said to her husband:

"Are you going to the judge's house this evening?"

"Yes, dear."

"Do not stay late. You always get so tired when you go out. You are not made for society, with your poor health."

She then talked about society in Vannes, of the excellent social circle in which the Padoies moved, thanks to their religious sentiments.

A puree of potatoes and a dish of pork were next served, in honor of the guest. Then some cheese, and that was all. No coffee.

When Varajou saw that he would have to spend the evening tete-a-tete with his sister, endure her reproaches, listen to her sermons, without even a glass of liqueur to help him to swallow these remonstrances, he felt that he could not stand the torture, and declared that he was obliged to go to the police station to have something attended to regarding his leave of absence. And he made his escape at seven o'clock.

He had scarcely reached the street before he gave himself a shake like a dog coming out of the water. He muttered:

"Heavens, heavens, heavens, what a galley slave's life!"

And he set out to look for a cafe, the best in the town. He found it on a public square, behind two gas lamps. Inside the cafe, five or six men, semi-gentlemen, and not noisy, were drinking and chatting quietly, leaning their elbows on the small tables, while two billiard players walked round the green baize, where the balls were hitting each other as they rolled.

One heard them counting:

"Eighteen-nineteen. No luck. Oh, that's a good stroke! Well played! Eleven. You should have played on the red. Twenty. Froze! Froze! Twelve. Ha! Wasn't I right?"

Varajou ordered:

"A demi-tasse and a small decanter of brandy, the best." Then he sat down and waited for it.

He was accustomed to spending his evenings off duty with his companions, amid noise and the smoke of pipes. This silence, this quiet, exasperated him. He began to drink; first the coffee, then the brandy, and asked for another decanter. He now wanted to laugh, to shout, to sing, to fight some one. He said to himself:

"Gee, I am half full. I must go and have a good time."

And he thought he would go and look for some girls to amuse him. He called the waiter:

"Hey, waiter."

"Yes, sir."

"Tell me, where does one amuse oneself here?"

The man looked stupid, and replied:

"I do not know, sir. Here, I suppose!"

"How do you mean here? What do you call amusing oneself, yourself?"

"I do not know, sir, drinking good beer or good wine."

"Ah, go away, dummy, how about the girls?"

"The girls, ah! ah!"

"Yes, the girls, where can one find any here?"

"Girls?"

"Why, yes, girls!"

The boy approached and lowering his voice, said: "You want to know where they live?"

"Why, yes, the devil!"

"You take the second street to the left and then the first to the right. It is number fifteen."

"Thank you, old man. There is something for you."

"Thank you, sir."

And Varajou went out of the cafe, repeating, "Second to the left, first to the right, number 15." But at the end of a few seconds he thought, "second to the left yes. But on leaving the cafe must I walk to the right or the left? Bah, it cannot be helped, we shall see."

And he walked on, turned down the second street to the left, then the first to the right and looked for number 15. It was a nice looking house, and one could see behind the closed blinds that the windows were lighted up on the first floor. The hall door was left partly open, and a lamp was burning in the vestibule. The non-commissioned officer thought to himself:

"This looks all right."

He went in and, as no one appeared, he called out:

"Hallo there, hallo!"

A little maid appeared and looked astonished at seeing a soldier. He said:

"Good-morning, my child. Are the ladies upstairs?"

"Yes, sir."

"In the parlor?"

"Yes, sir."

"May I go up?"

"Yes, sir."

"The door opposite the stairs?"

"Yes, sir."

He ascended the stairs, opened a door and saw sitting in a room well lighted up by two lamps, a chandelier, and two candelabras with candles in them, four ladies in evening dress, apparently expecting some one.

Three of them, the younger ones, remained seated, with rather a formal air, on some crimson velvet chairs; while the fourth, who was about forty-five, was arranging some flowers in a vase. She was very stout, and wore a green silk dress with low neck and short sleeves, allowing her red neck, covered with powder, to escape as a huge flower might from its corolla.

The officer saluted them, saying:

"Good-day, ladies."

The older woman turned round, appeared surprised, but bowed.

"Good-morning, sir."

He sat down. But seeing that they did not welcome him eagerly, he thought that possibly only commissioned officers were admitted to the house, and this made him uneasy. But he said:

"Bah, if one comes in, we can soon tell."

He then remarked:

"Are you all well?"

The large lady, no doubt the mistress of the house, replied:

"Very well, thank you!"

He could think of nothing else to say, and they were all silent. But at last, being ashamed of his bashfulness, and with an awkward laugh, he said:

"Do not people have any amusement in this country? I will pay for a bottle of wine."

He had not finished his sentence when the door opened, and in walked Padoie dressed in a black suit.

Varajou gave a shout of joy, and rising from his seat, he rushed at his brother-in-law, put his arms round him and waltzed him round the room, shouting:

"Here is Padoie! Here is Padoie! Here is Padoie!"

Then letting go of the tax collector he exclaimed as he looked him in the face:

"Oh, oh, oh, you scamp, you scamp! You are out for a good time, too. Oh, you scamp! And my sister! Are you tired of her, say?"

As he thought of all that he might gain through this unexpected situation, the forced loan, the inevitable blackmail, he flung himself on the lounge and laughed so heartily that the piece of furniture creaked all over.

The three young ladies, rising simultaneously, made their escape, while the older woman retreated to the door looking as though she were about to faint.

And then two gentlemen appeared in evening dress, and wearing the ribbon of an order. Padoie rushed up to them.

"Oh, judge—he is crazy, he is crazy. He was sent to us as a convalescent. You can see that he is crazy."

Varajou was sitting up now, and not being able to understand it all, he guessed that he had committed some monstrous folly. Then he rose, and turning to his brother-in-law, said:

"What house is this?"

But Padoie, becoming suddenly furious, stammered out:

"What house—what—what house is this? Wretch—scoundrel—villain—what house, indeed? The house of the judge—of the judge of the Supreme Court—of the Supreme Court—of the Supreme Court—Oh, oh—rascal! —rascal!—rascal!"

THE DIAMOND NECKLACE

The girl was one of those pretty and charming young creatures who sometimes are born, as if by a slip of fate, into a family of clerks. She had no dowry, no expectations, no way of being known, understood, loved, married by any rich and distinguished man; so she let herself be married to a little clerk of the Ministry of Public Instruction.

She dressed plainly because she could not dress well, but she was unhappy as if she had really fallen from a higher station; since with women there is neither caste nor rank, for beauty, grace and charm take the place of family and birth. Natural ingenuity, instinct for what is elegant, a supple mind are their sole hierarchy, and often make of women of the people the equals of the very greatest ladies.

Mathilde suffered ceaselessly, feeling herself born to enjoy all delicacies and all luxuries. She was distressed at the poverty of her dwelling, at the bareness of the walls, at the shabby chairs, the ugliness of the curtains. All those things, of which another woman of her rank would never even have been conscious, tortured her and made her angry. The sight of the little Breton peasant who did her humble housework aroused in her despairing regrets and bewildering dreams. She thought of silent antechambers hung with Oriental tapestry, illumined by tall bronze candelabra, and of two great footmen in knee breeches who sleep in the big armchairs, made drowsy by the oppressive heat of the stove. She thought of long reception halls hung with ancient silk, of the dainty cabinets containing priceless curiosities and of the little coquettish perfumed reception rooms made for chatting at five o'clock with intimate friends, with men famous and sought after, whom all women envy and whose attention they all desire.

When she sat down to dinner, before the round table covered with a tablecloth in use three days, opposite her husband, who uncovered the soup tureen and declared with a delighted air, "Ah, the good soup! I don't know anything better than that," she thought of dainty dinners, of shining silverware, of tapestry that peopled the walls with ancient personages and with strange birds flying in the midst of a fairy forest; and she thought of delicious dishes served on marvellous plates and of the whispered gallantries to which you listen with a sphinxlike smile while you are eating the pink meat of a trout or the wings of a quail.

She had no gowns, no jewels, nothing. And she loved nothing but that. She felt made for that. She would have liked so much to please, to be envied, to be charming, to be sought after.

She had a friend, a former schoolmate at the convent, who was rich, and whom she did not like to go to see any more because she felt so sad when she came home.

But one evening her husband reached home with a triumphant air and holding a large envelope in his hand.

"There," said he, "there is something for you."

She tore the paper quickly and drew out a printed card which bore these words:

The Minister of Public Instruction and Madame Georges Ramponneau request the honor of M. and Madame Loisel's company at the palace of the Ministry on Monday evening, January 18th.

Instead of being delighted, as her husband had hoped, she threw the invitation on the table crossly, muttering:

"What do you wish me to do with that?"

"Why, my dear, I thought you would be glad. You never go out, and this is such a fine opportunity. I had great trouble to get it. Every one wants to go; it is very select, and they are not giving many invitations to clerks. The whole official world will be there."

She looked at him with an irritated glance and said impatiently:

"And what do you wish me to put on my back?"

He had not thought of that. He stammered:

"Why, the gown you go to the theatre in. It looks very well to me."

He stopped, distracted, seeing that his wife was weeping. Two great tears ran slowly from the corners of her eyes toward the corners of her mouth.

"What's the matter? What's the matter?" he answered.

By a violent effort she conquered her grief and replied in a calm voice, while she wiped her wet cheeks:

"Nothing. Only I have no gown, and, therefore, I can't go to this ball. Give your card to some colleague whose wife is better equipped than I am."

He was in despair. He resumed:

"Come, let us see, Mathilde. How much would it cost, a suitable gown, which you could use on other occasions—something very simple?"

She reflected several seconds, making her calculations and wondering also what sum she could ask without drawing on herself an immediate refusal and a frightened exclamation from the economical clerk.

Finally she replied hesitating:

"I don't know exactly, but I think I could manage it with four hundred francs."

He grew a little pale, because he was laying aside just that amount to buy a gun and treat himself to a little shooting next summer on the plain of Nanterre, with several friends who went to shoot larks there of a Sunday.

But he said:

"Very well. I will give you four hundred francs. And try to have a pretty gown."

The day of the ball drew near and Madame Loisel seemed sad, uneasy, anxious. Her frock was ready, however. Her husband said to her one evening:

"What is the matter? Come, you have seemed very queer these last three days."

And she answered:

"It annoys me not to have a single piece of jewelry, not a single ornament, nothing to put on. I shall look poverty-stricken. I would almost rather not go at all."

"You might wear natural flowers," said her husband. "They're very stylish at this time of year. For ten francs you can get two or three magnificent roses."

She was not convinced.

"No; there's nothing more humiliating than to look poor among other women who are rich."

"How stupid you are!" her husband cried. "Go look up your friend, Madame Forestier, and ask her to lend you some jewels. You're intimate enough with her to do that."

She uttered a cry of joy:

"True! I never thought of it."

The next day she went to her friend and told her of her distress.

Madame Forestier went to a wardrobe with a mirror, took out a large jewel box, brought it back, opened it and said to Madame Loisel:

"Choose, my dear."

She saw first some bracelets, then a pearl necklace, then a Venetian gold cross set with precious stones, of admirable workmanship. She tried on the ornaments before the mirror, hesitated and could not make up her mind to part with them, to give them back. She kept asking:

"Haven't you any more?"

"Why, yes. Look further; I don't know what you like."

Suddenly she discovered, in a black satin box, a superb diamond necklace, and her heart throbbed with an immoderate desire. Her hands trembled as she took it. She fastened it round her throat, outside her high-necked waist, and was lost in ecstasy at her reflection in the mirror.

Then she asked, hesitating, filled with anxious doubt:

"Will you lend me this, only this?"

"Why, yes, certainly."

She threw her arms round her friend's neck, kissed her passionately, then fled with her treasure.

The night of the ball arrived. Madame Loisel was a great success. She was prettier than any other woman present, elegant, graceful, smiling and wild with joy. All the men looked at her, asked her name, sought to be introduced. All the attaches of the Cabinet wished to waltz with her. She was remarked by the minister himself.

She danced with rapture, with passion, intoxicated by pleasure, forgetting all in the triumph of her beauty, in the glory of her success, in a sort of cloud of happiness comprised of all this homage, admiration, these awakened desires and of that sense of triumph which is so sweet to woman's heart.

She left the ball about four o'clock in the morning. Her husband had been sleeping since midnight in a little deserted anteroom with three other gentlemen whose wives were enjoying the ball.

He threw over her shoulders the wraps he had brought, the modest wraps of common life, the poverty of which contrasted with the elegance of the ball dress. She felt this and wished to escape so as not to be remarked by the other women, who were enveloping themselves in costly furs.

Loisel held her back, saying: "Wait a bit. You will catch cold outside. I will call a cab."

But she did not listen to him and rapidly descended the stairs. When they reached the street they could not find a carriage and began to look for one, shouting after the cabmen passing at a distance.

They went toward the Seine in despair, shivering with cold. At last they found on the quay one of those ancient night cabs which, as though they were ashamed to show their shabbiness during the day, are never seen round Paris until after dark.

It took them to their dwelling in the Rue des Martyrs, and sadly they mounted the stairs to their flat. All was ended for her. As to him, he reflected that he must be at the ministry at ten o'clock that morning.

She removed her wraps before the glass so as to see herself once more in all her glory. But suddenly she uttered a cry. She no longer had the necklace around her neck!

"What is the matter with you?" demanded her husband, already half undressed.

She turned distractedly toward him.

"I have—I have—I've lost Madame Forestier's necklace," she cried.

He stood up, bewildered.

"What!—how? Impossible!"

They looked among the folds of her skirt, of her cloak, in her pockets, everywhere, but did not find it.

"You're sure you had it on when you left the ball?" he asked.

"Yes, I felt it in the vestibule of the minister's house."

"But if you had lost it in the street we should have heard it fall. It must be in the cab."

"Yes, probably. Did you take his number?"

"No. And you—didn't you notice it?"

"No."

They looked, thunderstruck, at each other. At last Loisel put on his clothes.

"I shall go back on foot," said he, "over the whole route, to see whether I can find it."

He went out. She sat waiting on a chair in her ball dress, without strength to go to bed, overwhelmed, without any fire, without a thought.

Her husband returned about seven o'clock. He had found nothing.

He went to police headquarters, to the newspaper offices to offer a reward; he went to the cab companies—everywhere, in fact, whither he was urged by the least spark of hope.

She waited all day, in the same condition of mad fear before this terrible calamity.

Loisel returned at night with a hollow, pale face. He had discovered nothing.

"You must write to your friend," said he, "that you have broken the clasp of her necklace and that you are having it mended. That will give us time to turn round."

She wrote at his dictation.

At the end of a week they had lost all hope. Loisel, who had aged five years, declared:

"We must consider how to replace that ornament."

The next day they took the box that had contained it and went to the jeweler whose name was found within. He consulted his books.

"It was not I, madame, who sold that necklace; I must simply have furnished the case."

Then they went from jeweler to jeweler, searching for a necklace like the other, trying to recall it, both sick with chagrin and grief.

They found, in a shop at the Palais Royal, a string of diamonds that seemed to them exactly like the one they had lost. It was worth forty thousand francs. They could have it for thirty-six.

So they begged the jeweler not to sell it for three days yet. And they made a bargain that he should buy it back for thirty-four thousand francs, in case they should find the lost necklace before the end of February.

Loisel possessed eighteen thousand francs which his father had left him. He would borrow the rest.

He did borrow, asking a thousand francs of one, five hundred of another, five louis here, three louis there. He gave notes, took up ruinous obligations, dealt with usurers and all the race of lenders. He compromised all the rest of his life, risked signing a note without even knowing whether he could meet it; and, frightened by the trouble yet to come, by the black misery that was about to fall upon him, by the prospect of all the physical privations and moral tortures that he was to suffer, he went to get the new necklace, laying upon the jeweler's counter thirty-six thousand francs.

When Madame Loisel took back the necklace Madame Forestier said to her with a chilly manner:

"You should have returned it sooner; I might have needed it."

She did not open the case, as her friend had so much feared. If she had detected the substitution, what would she have thought, what would she have said? Would she not have taken Madame Loisel for a thief?

Thereafter Madame Loisel knew the horrible existence of the needy. She bore her part, however, with sudden heroism. That dreadful debt must be paid. She would pay it. They dismissed their servant; they changed their lodgings; they rented a garret under the roof.

She came to know what heavy housework meant and the odious cares of the kitchen. She washed the dishes, using her dainty fingers and rosy nails on greasy pots and pans. She washed the soiled linen, the shirts and the dishcloths, which she dried upon a line; she carried the slops down to the street every morning and carried up the water, stopping for breath at every landing. And dressed like a woman of the people, she went to the fruiterer, the grocer, the butcher, a basket on her arm, bargaining, meeting with impertinence, defending her miserable money, sou by sou.

Every month they had to meet some notes, renew others, obtain more time.

Her husband worked evenings, making up a tradesman's accounts, and late at night he often copied manuscript for five sous a page.

This life lasted ten years.

At the end of ten years they had paid everything, everything, with the rates of usury and the accumulations of the compound interest.

Madame Loisel looked old now. She had become the woman of impoverished households—strong and hard and rough. With frowsy hair, skirts askew and red hands, she talked loud while washing the floor with great swishes of water. But sometimes, when her husband was at the office, she sat down near the window and she thought of that gay evening of long ago, of that ball where she had been so beautiful and so admired.

What would have happened if she had not lost that necklace? Who knows? who knows? How strange and changeful is life! How small a thing is needed to make or ruin us!

But one Sunday, having gone to take a walk in the Champs Elysees to refresh herself after the labors of the week, she suddenly perceived a woman who was leading a child. It was Madame Forestier, still young, still beautiful, still charming.

Madame Loisel felt moved. Should she speak to her? Yes, certainly. And now that she had paid, she would tell her all about it. Why not?

She went up.

"Good-day, Jeanne."

The other, astonished to be familiarly addressed by this plain good-wife, did not recognize her at all and stammered:

"But—madame!—I do not know—You must have mistaken."

"No. I am Mathilde Loisel."

Her friend uttered a cry.

"Oh, my poor Mathilde! How you are changed!"

"Yes, I have had a pretty hard life, since I last saw you, and great poverty—and that because of you!"

"Of me! How so?"

"Do you remember that diamond necklace you lent me to wear at the ministerial ball?"

"Yes. Well?"

"Well, I lost it."

"What do you mean? You brought it back."

"I brought you back another exactly like it. And it has taken us ten years to pay for it. You can understand that it was not easy for us, for us who had nothing. At last it is ended, and I am very glad."

Madame Forestier had stopped.

"You say that you bought a necklace of diamonds to replace mine?"

"Yes. You never noticed it, then! They were very similar."

And she smiled with a joy that was at once proud and ingenuous.

Madame Forestier, deeply moved, took her hands.

"Oh, my poor Mathilde! Why, my necklace was paste! It was worth at most only five hundred francs!"

THE MARQUIS DE FUMEROL

Roger de Tourneville was whiffing a cigar and blowing out small clouds of smoke every now and then, as he sat astride a chair amid a party of friends. He was talking.

"We were at dinner when a letter was brought in which my father opened. You know my father, who thinks that he is king of France ad interim. I call him Don Quixote, because for twelve years he has been running a tilt against the windmill of the Republic, without quite knowing whether it was in the cause of the Bourbons or the Orleanists. At present he is bearing the lance in the cause of the Orleanists alone, because there is no one else left. In any case, he thinks himself the first gentleman of France, the best known, the most influential, the head of the party; and as he is an irremovable senator, he thinks that the thrones of the neighboring kings are very insecure.

"As for my mother, she is my father's soul, she is the soul of the kingdom and of religion, and the scourge of all evil-thinkers.

"Well, a letter was brought in while we were at dinner, and my father opened and read it, and then he said to mother: 'Your brother is dying.' She grew very pale. My uncle was scarcely ever mentioned in the house, and I did not know him at all; all I knew from public talk was, that he had led, and was still leading, a gay life. After having spent his fortune in fast living, he was now in small apartments in the Rue des Martyrs.

"An ancient peer of France and former colonel of cavalry, it was said that he believed in neither God nor devil. Not believing, therefore, in a future life he had abused the present life in every way, and had become a live wound in my mother's heart.

"'Give me that letter, Paul,' she said, and when she read it, I asked for it in my turn. Here it is:

'Monsieur le Comte, I think I ought to let you know that your brother-in-law, the Comte Fumerol, is going to die. Perhaps you would like to make some arrangements, and do not forget I told you.

Your servant,

'MELANIE.'

"'We must take counsel,' papa murmured. 'In my position, I ought to watch over your brother's last moments.'

"Mamma continued: 'I will send for Abbe Poivron and ask his advice, and then I will go to my brother with the abbe and Roger. Remain here, Paul, for you must not compromise yourself; but a woman can, and ought to do these things. For a politician in your position, it is another matter. It would be a fine thing for one of your opponents to be able to bring one of your most laudable actions up against you.' 'You are right,' my father said. 'Do as you think best, my dear wife.'

"A quarter of an hour, later, the Abbe Poivron came into the drawing-room, and the situation was explained to him, analyzed and discussed in all its bearings. If the Marquis de Fumerol, one of the greatest names in France, were to die without the ministrations of religion, it would assuredly be a terrible blow to the nobility in general, and to the Count de Tourneville in particular, and the freethinkers would be triumphant. The liberal newspapers would sing songs of victory for six months; my mother's name would be dragged through the mire and brought into the prose of Socialistic journals, and my father's name would be smirched. It was impossible that such a thing should be.

"A crusade was therefore immediately decided upon, which was to be led by the Abbe Poivron, a little, fat, clean, priest with a faint perfume about him, a true vicar of a large church in a noble and rich quarter.

"The landau was ordered and we all three set out, my mother, the cure and I, to administer the last sacraments to my uncle.

"It had been decided first of all we should see Madame Melanie who had written the letter, and who was most likely the porter's wife, or my uncle's servant, and I dismounted, as an advance guard, in front of a seven-story house and went into a dark passage, where I had great difficulty in finding the porter's den. He looked at me distrustfully, and I said:

"'Madame Melanie, if you please.' 'Don't know her!' 'But I have received a letter from her.' 'That may be, but I don't know her. Are you asking for a lodger?' 'No, a servant probably. She wrote me about a place.' 'A servant?—a servant? Perhaps it is the marquis'. Go and see, the fifth story on the left.'

"As soon as he found I was not asking for a doubtful character he became more friendly and came as far as the corridor with me. He was a tall, thin man with white whiskers, the manners of a beadle and majestic gestures.

"I climbed up a long spiral staircase, the railing of which I did not venture to touch, and I gave three discreet knocks at the left-hand door on the fifth story. It opened immediately, and an enormous dirty woman appeared before me. She barred the entrance with her extended arms which she placed against the two doorposts, and growled:

"'What do you want?' 'Are you Madame Melanie?' 'Yes.' 'I am the Visconte de Tourneville.' 'Ah! All right! Come in.' 'Well, the fact is, my mother is downstairs with a priest.' 'Oh! All right; go and bring them up; but be careful of the porter.'

"I went downstairs and came up again with my mother, who was followed by the abbe, and I fancied that I heard other footsteps behind us. As soon as we were in the kitchen, Melanie offered us chairs, and we all four sat down to deliberate.

"'Is he very ill?' my mother asked. 'Oh! yes, madame; he will not be here long.' 'Does he seem disposed to receive a visit from a priest?' 'Oh! I do not think so.' 'Can I see him?' 'Well—yes madame—only —only—those young ladies are with him.' 'What young ladies?' 'Why—why—his lady friends, of course.' 'Oh!' Mamma had grown scarlet, and the Abbe Poivron had lowered his eyes.

"The affair began to amuse me, and I said: 'Suppose I go in first? I shall see how he receives me, and perhaps I shall be able to prepare him to receive you.'

"My mother, who did not suspect any trick, replied: 'Yes, go, my dear.' But a woman's voice cried out: 'Melanie!'

"The servant ran out and said: 'What do you want, Mademoiselle Claire?' 'The omelette; quickly.' 'In a minute, mademoiselle.' And coming back to us, she explained this summons.

"They had ordered a cheese omelette at two o'clock as a slight collation. And she at once began to break the eggs into a salad bowl, and to whip them vigorously, while I went out on the landing and pulled the bell, so as to formally announce my arrival. Melanie opened the door to me, and made me sit down in an ante-room, while she went to tell my uncle that I had come; then she came back and asked me to go in, while the abbe hid behind the door, so that he might appear at the first signal.

"I was certainly very much surprised at the sight of my uncle, for he was very handsome, very solemn and very elegant, the old rake.

"Sitting, almost lying, in a large armchair, his legs wrapped in blankets, his hands, his long, white hands, over the arms of the chair, he was waiting for death with the dignity of a patriarch. His white beard fell on his chest, and his hair, which was also white, mingled with it on his cheeks.

"Standing behind his armchair, as if to defend him against me, were two young women, who looked at me with bold eyes. In their petticoats and morning wrappers, with bare arms, with coal black hair twisted in a knot on the nape of their neck, with embroidered, Oriental slippers, which showed their ankles and silk stockings, they looked like the figures in some symbolical painting, by the side of the dying man. Between the easy-chair and the bed, there was a table covered with a white cloth, on which two plates, two glasses, two forks and two knives, were waiting for the cheese omelette which had been ordered some time before of Melanie.

"My uncle said in a weak, almost breathless, but clear voice:

"'Good-morning, my child; it is rather late in the day to come and see me; our acquaintanceship will not last long.' I stammered out, 'It was not my fault, uncle:' 'No; I know that,' he replied. 'It is your father and mother's fault more than yours. How are they?' 'Pretty well, thank you. When they heard that you were ill, they sent me to ask after you.' 'Ah! Why did they not come themselves?'

"I looked up at the two girls and said gently: 'It is not their fault if they could not come, uncle. But it would be difficult for my father, and impossible for my mother to come in here.' The old man did not reply, but raised his hand toward mine, and I took the pale, cold hand and held it in my own.

"The door opened, Melanie came in with the omelette and put it on the table, and the two girls immediately sat down at the table, and began to eat without taking their eyes off me. Then I said: 'Uncle, it would give great pleasure to my mother to embrace you.' 'I also,' he murmured, 'should like——' He said no more, and I could think of nothing to propose to him, and there was silence except for the noise of the plates and that vague sound of eating.

"Now, the abbe, who was listening behind the door, seeing our embarrassment, and thinking we had won the game, thought the time had come to interpose, and showed himself. My uncle was so stupefied at sight of him that at first he remained motionless; and then he opened his mouth as if he meant to swallow up the priest, and shouted to him in a strong, deep, furious voice: 'What are you doing here?'

"The abbe, who was used to difficult situations, came forward into the room, murmuring: 'I have come in your sister's name, Monsieur le Marquis; she has sent me. She would be happy, monsieur—'

"But the marquis was not listening. Raising one hand, he pointed to the door with a proud, tragic gesture, and said angrily and breathing hard: 'Leave this room—go out—robber of souls. Go out from here, you violator of consciences. Go out from here, you pick-lock of dying men's doors!'

"The abbe retreated, and I also went to the door, beating a retreat with the priest; the two young women, who had the best of it, got up, leaving their omelette only half eaten, and went and stood on either side of my uncle's easy-chair, putting their hands on his arms to calm him, and to protect him against the criminal enterprises of the Family, and of Religion.

"The abbe and I rejoined my mother in the kitchen, and Melanie again offered us chairs. 'I knew quite well that this method would not work; we must try some other means, otherwise he will escape us.' And they began deliberating afresh, my mother being of one opinion and the abbe of another, while I held a third.

"We had been discussing the matter in a low voice for half an hour, perhaps, when a great noise of furniture being moved and of cries uttered by my uncle, more vehement and terrible even than the former had been, made us all four jump up.

"Through the doors and walls we could hear him shouting: 'Go out—out —rascals—humbugs, get out, scoundrels—get out—get out!'

"Melanie rushed in, but came back immediately to call me to help her, and I hastened in. Opposite to my uncle, who was terribly excited by anger, almost standing up and vociferating, stood two men, one behind the other, who seemed to be waiting till he should be dead with rage.

"By his ridiculous long coat, his long English shoes, his manners of a tutor out of a position, his high collar, white necktie and straight hair, his humble face of a false priest of a bastard religion, I immediately recognized the first as a Protestant minister.

"The second was the porter of the house, who belonged to the reformed religion and had followed us, and having seen our defeat, had gone to fetch his own pastor, in hopes that he might meet a better reception. My uncle seemed mad with rage! If the sight of the Catholic priest, of the priest of his ancestors, had irritated the Marquis de Fumerol, who had become a freethinker, the sight of his porter's minister made him altogether beside himself. I therefore took the two men by the arm and threw them out of the room so roughly that they bumped against each other twice, between the two doors which led to the staircase; and then I disappeared in my turn and returned to the kitchen, which was our headquarters in order to take counsel with my mother and the abbe.

"But Melanie came back in terror, sobbing out:

"'He is dying—he is dying—come immediately—he is dying.'

"My mother rushed out. My uncle had fallen to the ground, and lay full length along the floor, without moving. I fancy he was already dead. My mother was superb at that moment! She went straight up to the two girls who were kneeling by the body and trying to raise it up, and pointing to the door with irresistible authority, dignity and majesty, she said: 'Now it is time for you to leave the room.'

"And they went out without a word of protest. I must add, that I was getting ready to turn them out as unceremoniously as I had done the parson and the porter.

"Then the Abbe Poivron administered the last sacraments to my uncle with all the customary prayers, and remitted all his sins, while my mother sobbed as she knelt near her brother. Suddenly, however, she exclaimed: 'He recognized me; he pressed my hand; I am sure he recognized me!!!—and that he thanked me! Oh, God, what happiness!'

"Poor mamma! If she had known or guessed for whom those thanks were intended!

"They laid my uncle on his bed; he was certainly dead this time.

"'Madame,' Melanie said, 'we have no sheets to bury him in; all the linen belongs to these two young ladies,' and when I looked at the omelette which they had not finished, I felt inclined to laugh and to cry at the same time. There are some humorous moments and some humorous situations in life, occasionally!

"We gave my uncle a magnificent funeral, with five speeches at the grave. Baron de Croiselles, the senator, showed in admirable terms that God always returns victorious into well-born souls which have temporarily been led into error. All the members of the Royalist and Catholic party followed the funeral procession with the enthusiasm of victors, as they spoke of that beautiful death after a somewhat troublous life."

Viscount Roger ceased speaking; his audience was laughing. Then somebody said: "Bah! That is the story of all conversions in extremis."

THE TRIP OF LE HORLA

On the morning of July 8th I received the following telegram: "Fine day. Always my predictions. Belgian frontier. Baggage and servants left at noon at the social session. Beginning of manoeuvres at three. So I will wait for you at the works from five o'clock on. Jovis."

At five o'clock sharp I entered the gas works of La Villette. It might have been mistaken for the colossal ruins of an old town inhabited by Cyclops. There were immense dark avenues separating heavy gasometers standing one behind another, like monstrous columns, unequally high and, undoubtedly, in the past the supports of some tremendous, some fearful iron edifice.

The balloon was lying in the courtyard and had the appearance of a cake made of yellow cloth, flattened on the ground under a rope. That is called placing a balloon in a sweep-net, and, in fact, it appeared like an enormous fish.

Two or three hundred people were looking at it, sitting or standing, and some were examining the basket, a nice little square basket for a human cargo, bearing on its side in gold letters on a mahogany plate the words: Le Horla.

Suddenly the people began to stand back, for the gas was beginning to enter into the balloon through a long tube of yellow cloth, which lay on the soil, swelling and undulating like an enormous worm. But another thought, another picture occurs to every mind. It is thus that nature itself nourishes beings until their birth. The creature that will rise soon begins to move, and the attendants of Captain Jovis, as Le Horla grew larger, spread and put in place the net which covers it, so that the pressure will be regular and equally distributed at every point.

The operation is very delicate and very important, for the resistance of the cotton cloth of which the balloon is made is figured not in proportion to the contact surface of this cloth with the net, but in proportion to the links of the basket.

Le Horla, moreover, has been designed by M. Mallet, constructed under his own eyes and made by himself. Everything had been made in the shops of M. Jovis by his own working staff and nothing was made outside.

We must add that everything was new in this balloon, from the varnish to the valve, those two essential parts of a balloon. Both must render the cloth gas-proof, as the sides of a ship are waterproof. The old varnishes, made with a base of linseed oil, sometimes fermented and thus burned the cloth, which in a short time would tear like a piece of paper.

The valves were apt to close imperfectly after being opened and when the covering called "cataplasme" was injured. The fall of M. L'Hoste in the open sea during the night proved the imperfection of the old system.

The two discoveries of Captain Jovis, the varnish principally, are of inestimable value in the art of ballooning.

The crowd has begun to talk, and some men, who appear to be specialists, affirm with authority that we shall come down before reaching the fortifications. Several other things have been criticized in this novel type of balloon with which we are about to experiment with so much pleasure and success.

It is growing slowly but surely. Some small holes and scratches made in transit have been discovered, and we cover them and plug them with a little piece of paper applied on the cloth while wet. This method of repairing alarms and mystifies the public.

While Captain Jovis and his assistants are busy with the last details, the travellers go to dine in the canteen of the gas-works, according to the established custom.

When we come out again the balloon is swaying, enormous and transparent, a prodigious golden fruit, a fantastic pear which is still ripening, covered by the last rays of the setting sun. Now the basket is attached, the barometers are brought, the siren, which we will blow to our hearts' content, is also brought, also the two trumpets, the eatables, the overcoats and raincoats, all the small articles that can go with the men in that flying basket.

As the wind pushes the balloon against the gasometers, it is necessary to steady it now and then, to avoid an accident at the start.

Captain Jovis is now ready and calls all the passengers.

Lieutenant Mallet jumps aboard, climbing first on the aerial net between the basket and the balloon, from which he will watch during the night the movements of Le Horla across the skies, as the officer on watch, standing on starboard, watches the course of a ship.

M. Etierine Beer gets in after him, then comes M. Paul Bessand, then M. Patrice Eyries and I get in last.

But the basket is too heavy for the balloon, considering the long trip to be taken, and M. Eyries has to get out, not without great regret.

M. Joliet, standing erect on the edge of the basket, begs the ladies, in very gallant terms, to stand aside a little, for he is afraid he might throw sand on their hats in rising. Then he commands:

"Let it loose," and, cutting with one stroke of his knife the ropes that hold the balloon to the ground, he gives Le Horla its liberty.

In one second we fly skyward. Nothing can be heard; we float, we rise, we fly, we glide. Our friends shout with glee and applaud, but we hardly hear them, we hardly see them. We are already so far, so high! What? Are we really leaving these people down there? Is it possible? Paris spreads out beneath us, a dark bluish patch, cut by its streets, from which rise, here and there, domes, towers, steeples, then around it the plain, the country, traversed by long roads, thin and white, amidst green fields of a tender or dark green, and woods almost black.

The Seine appears like a coiled snake, asleep, of which we see neither head nor tail; it crosses Paris, and the entire field resembles an immense basin of prairies and forests dotted here and there by mountains, hardly visible in the horizon.

The sun, which we could no longer see down below, now reappears as though it were about to rise again, and our balloon seems to be lighted; it must appear like a star to the people who are looking up. M. Mallet every few seconds throws a cigarette paper intospace and says quietly: "We are rising, always rising," while Captain Jovis, radiant with joy, rubs his hands together and repeats: "Eh? this varnish? Isn't it good?"

In fact, we can see whether we are rising or sinking only by throwing a cigarette paper out of the basket now and then. If this paper appears to fall down like a stone, it means that the balloon is rising; if it appears to shoot skyward the balloon is descending.

The two barometers mark about five hundred meters, and we gaze with enthusiastic admiration at the earth we are leaving and to which we are not attached in any way; it looks like a colored map, an immense plan of the country. All its noises, however, rise to our ears very distinctly, easily recognizable. We hear the sound of the wheels rolling in the streets, the snap of a whip, the cries of drivers, the rolling and whistling of trains and the laughter of small boys running after one another. Every time we pass over a village the noise of children's voices is heard above the rest and with the greatest distinctness. Some men are calling us; the locomotives whistle; we answer with the siren, which emits plaintive, fearfully shrill wails like the voice of a weird being wandering through the world.

We perceive lights here and there, some isolated fire in the farms, and lines of gas in the towns. We are going toward the northwest, after roaming for some time over the little lake of Enghien. Now we see a river; it is the Oise, and we begin to argue about the exact spot we are passing. Is that town Creil or Pontoise—the one with so many lights? But if we were over Pontoise we could see the junction of the Seine and the Oise; and that enormous fire to the left, isn't it the blast furnaces of Montataire? So then we are above Creil. The view is superb; it is dark on the earth, but we are still in the light, and it is now past ten o'clock. Now we begin to hear slight country noises, the double cry of the quail in particular, then the mewing of cats and the barking of dogs. Surely the dogs have scented the balloon; they have seen it and have given the alarm. We can hear them barking all over the plain and making the identical noise they make when baying at the moon. The cows also seem to wake up in the barns, for we can hear them lowing; all the beasts are scared and moved before the aerial monster that is passing.

The delicious odors of the soil rise toward us, the smell of hay, of flowers, of the moist, verdant earth, perfuming the air-a light air, in fact, so light, so sweet, so delightful that I realize I never was so fortunate as to breathe before. A profound sense of well-being, unknown to me heretofore, pervades me, a well-being of body and spirit, composed of supineness, of infinite rest, of forgetfulness, of indifference to everything and of this novel sensation of traversing space without any of the sensations that make motion unbearable, without noise, without shocks and without fear.

At times we rise and then descend. Every few minutes Lieutenant Mallet, suspended in his cobweb of netting, says to Captain Jovis: "We are descending; throw down half a handful." And the captain, who is talking and laughing with us, with a bag of ballast between his legs, takes a handful of sand out of the bag and throws it overboard.

Nothing is more amusing, more delicate, more interesting than the manoeuvring of a balloon. It is an enormous toy, free and docile, which obeys with surprising sensitiveness, but it is also, and before all, the slave of the wind, which we cannot control. A pinch of sand, half a sheet of paper, one or two drops of water, the bones of a chicken which we had just eaten, thrown overboard, makes it go up quickly.

A breath of cool, damp air rising from the river or the wood we are traversing makes the balloon descend two hundred metres. It does not vary when passing over fields of ripe grain, and it rises when it passes over towns.

The earth sleeps now, or, rather, men sleep on the earth, for the beasts awakened by the sight of our balloon announce our approach everywhere. Now and then the rolling of a train or the whistling of a locomotive is plainly distinguishable. We sound our siren as we pass over inhabited places; and the peasants, terrified in their beds, must surely tremble and ask themselves if the Angel Gabriel is not passing by.

A strong and continuous odor of gas can be plainly observed. We must have encountered a current of warm air, and the balloon expands, losing its invisible blood by the escape-valve, which is called the appendix, and which closes of itself as soon as the expansion ceases.

We are rising. The earth no longer gives back the echo of our trumpets; we have risen almost two thousand feet. It is not light enough for us to consult the instruments; we only know that the rice paper falls from us like dead butterflies, that we are rising, always rising. We can no longer see the earth; a light mist separates us from it; and above our head twinkles a world of stars.

A silvery light appears before us and makes the sky turn pale, and suddenly, as if it were rising from unknown depths behind the horizon below us rises the moon on the edge of a cloud. It seems to be coming from below, while we are looking down upon it from a great height, leaning on the edge of our basket like an audience on a balcony. Clear and round, it emerges from the clouds and slowly rises in the sky.

The earth no longer seems to exist, it is buried in milky vapors that resemble a sea. We are now alone in space with the moon, which looks like another balloon travelling opposite us; and our balloon, which shines in the air, appears like another, larger moon, a world wandering in the sky amid the stars, through infinity. We no longer speak, think nor live; we float along through space in delicious inertia. The air which is bearing us up has made of us all beings which resemble itself, silent, joyous, irresponsible beings, intoxicated by this stupendous flight, peculiarly alert, although motionless. One is no longer conscious of one's flesh or one's bones; one's heart seems to have ceased beating; we have become something indescribable, birds who do not even have to flap their wings.

All memory has disappeared from our minds, all trouble from our thoughts; we have no more regrets, plans nor hopes. We look, we feel, we wildly enjoy this fantastic journey; nothing in the sky but the moon and ourselves! We are a wandering, travelling world, like our sisters, the planets; and this little world carries five men who have left the earth and who have almost forgotten it. We can now see as plainly as in daylight; we look at each other, surprised at this brightness, for we have nothing to look at but ourselves and a few silvery clouds floating below us. The barometers mark twelve hundred metres, then thirteen, fourteen, fifteen hundred; and the little rice papers still fall about us.

Captain Jovis claims that the moon has often made balloons act thus, and that the upward journey will continue.

We are now at two thousand metres; we go up to two thousand three hundred and fifty; then the balloon stops: We blow the siren and are surprised that no one answers us from the stars.

We are now going down rapidly. M. Mallet keeps crying: "Throw out more ballast! throw out more ballast!" And the sand and stones that we throw over come back into our faces, as if they were going up, thrown from below toward the stars, so rapid is our descent.

Here is the earth! Where are we? It is now past midnight, and we are crossing a broad, dry, well-cultivated country, with many roads and well populated.

To the right is a large city and farther away to the left is another. But suddenly from the earth appears a bright fairy light; it disappears, reappears and once more disappears. Jovis, intoxicated by space, exclaims: "Look, look at this phenomenon of the moon in the water. One can see nothing more beautiful at night!"

Nothing indeed can give one an idea of the wonderful brightness of these spots of light which are not fire, which do not look like reflections, which appear quickly here or there and immediately go out again. These shining lights appear on the winding rivers at every turn, but one hardly has time to see them as the balloon passes as quickly as the wind.

We are now quite near the earth, and Beer exclaims:—"Look at that! What is that running over there in the fields? Isn't it a dog?" Indeed, something is running along the ground with great speed, and this something seems to jump over ditches, roads, trees with such ease that we could not understand what it might be. The captain laughed: "It is the shadow of our balloon. It will grow as we descend."

I distinctly hear a great noise of foundries in the distance. And, according to the polar star, which we have been observing all night, 'and which I have so often watched and consulted from the bridge of my little yacht on the Mediterranean, we are heading straight for Belgium.

Our siren and our two horns are continually calling. A few cries from some truck driver or belated reveler answer us. We bellow: "Where are we?" But the balloon is going so rapidly that the bewildered man has not even time to answer us. The growing shadow of Le Horla, as large as a child's ball, is fleeing before us over the fields, roads and woods. It goes along steadily, preceding us by about a quarter of a mile; and now I am leaning out of the basket, listening to the roaring of the wind in the trees and across the harvest fields. I say to Captain Jovis: "How the wind blows!"

He answers: "No, those are probably waterfalls." I insist, sure of my ear that knows the sound of the wind, from hearing it so often whistle through the rigging. Then Jovis nudges me; he fears to frighten his happy, quiet passengers, for he knows full well that a storm is pursuing us.

At last a man manages to understand us; he answers: "Nord!" We get the same reply from another.

Suddenly the lights of a town, which seems to be of considerable size, appear before us. Perhaps it is Lille. As we approach it, such a wonderful flow of fire appears below us that I think myself transported into some fairyland where precious stones are manufactured for giants.

It seems that it is a brick factory. Here are others, two, three. The fusing material bubbles, sparkles, throws out blue, red, yellow, green sparks, reflections from giant diamonds, rubies, emeralds, turquoises, sapphires, topazes. And near by are great foundries roaring like apocalyptic lions; high chimneys belch forth their clouds of smoke and flame, and we can hear the noise of metal striking against metal.

"Where are we?"

The voice of some joker or of a crazy person answers: "In a balloon!"

"Where are we?"

"At Lille!"

We were not mistaken. We are already out of sight of the town, and we see Roubaix to the right, then some well-cultivated, rectangular fields, of different colors according to the crops, some yellow, some gray or brown. But the clouds are gathering behind us, hiding the moon, whereas toward the east the sky is growing lighter, becoming a clear blue tinged with red. It is dawn. It grows rapidly, now showing us all the little details of the earth, the trains, the brooks, the cows, the goats. And all this passes beneath us with surprising speed. One hardly has time to notice that other fields, other meadows, other houses have already disappeared. Cocks are crowing, but the voice of ducks drowns everything. One might think the world to be peopled, covered with them, they make so much noise.

The early rising peasants are waving their arms and crying to us: "Let yourselves drop!" But we go along steadily, neither rising nor falling, leaning over the edge of the basket and watching the world fleeing under our feet.

Jovis sights another city far off in the distance. It approaches; everywhere are old church spires. They are delightful, seen thus from above. Where are we? Is this Courtrai? Is it Ghent?

We are already very near it, and we see that it is surrounded by water and crossed in every direction by canals. One might think it a Venice of the north. Just as we are passing so near to a church tower that our long guy-rope almost touches it, the chimes begin to ring three o'clock. The sweet, clear sounds rise to us from this frail roof which we have almost touched in our wandering course. It is a charming greeting, a friendly welcome from Holland. We answer with our siren, whose raucous voice echoes throughout the streets.

It was Bruges. But we have hardly lost sight of it when my neighbor, Paul Bessand, asks me: "Don't you see something over there, to the right, in front of us? It looks like a river."

And, indeed, far ahead of us stretches a bright highway, in the light of the dawning day. Yes, it looks like a river, an immense river full of islands.

"Get ready for the descent," cried the captain. He makes M. Mallet leave his net and return to the basket; then we pack the barometers and everything that could be injured by possible shocks. M. Bessand exclaims: "Look at the masts over there to the left! We are at the sea!"

Fogs had hidden it from us until then. The sea was everywhere, to the left and opposite us, while to our right the Scheldt, which had joined the Moselle, extended as far as the sea, its mouths vaster than a lake.

It was necessary to descend within a minute or two. The rope to the escape-valve, which had been religiously enclosed in a little white bag and placed in sight of all so that no one would touch it, is unrolled, and M. Mallet holds it in his hand while Captain Jovis looks for a favorable landing.

Behind us the thunder was rumbling and not a single bird followed our mad flight.

"Pull!" cried Jovis.

We were passing over a canal. The basket trembled and tipped over slightly. The guy-rope touched the tall trees on both banks. But our speed is so great that the long rope now trailing does not seem to slow down, and we pass with frightful rapidity over a large farm, from which the bewildered chickens, pigeons and ducks fly away, while the cows, cats and dogs run, terrified, toward the house.

Just one-half bag of ballast is left. Jovis throws it overboard, and Le Horla flies lightly across the roof.

The captain once more cries: "The escape-valve!"

M. Mallet reaches for the rope and hangs to it, and we drop like an arrow. With a slash of a knife the cord which retains the anchor is cut, and we drag this grapple behind us, through a field of beets. Here are the trees.

"Take care! Hold fast! Look out for your heads!"

We pass over them. Then a strong shock shakes us. The anchor has taken hold.

"Look out! Take a good hold! Raise yourselves by your wrists. We are going to touch ground."

The basket does indeed strike the earth. Then it flies up again. Once more it falls and bounds upward again, and at last it settles on the ground, while the balloon struggles madly, like a wounded beast.

Peasants run toward us, but they do not dare approach. They were a long time before they decided to come and deliver us, for one cannot set foot on the ground until the bag is almost completely deflated.

Then, almost at the same time as the bewildered men, some of whom showed their astonishment by jumping, with the wild gestures of savages, all the cows that were grazing along the coast came toward us, surrounding our balloon with a strange and comical circle of horns, big eyes and blowing nostrils.

With the help of the accommodating and hospitable Belgian peasants, we were able in a short time to pack up all our material and carry it to the station at Heyst, where at twenty minutes past eight we took the train for Paris.

The descent occurred at three-fifteen in the morning, preceding by only a few seconds the torrent of rain and the blinding lightning of the storm which had been chasing us before it.

Thanks to Captain Jovis, of whom I had heard much from my colleague, Paul Ginisty—for both of them had fallen together and voluntarily into the sea opposite Mentone—thanks to this brave man, we were able to see, in a single night, from far up in the sky, the setting of the sun, the rising of the moon and the dawn of day and to go from Paris to the mouth of the Scheldt through the skies.

[This story appeared in "Figaro" on July 16, 1887, under the title:

"From Paris to Heyst."]

FAREWELL!

The two friends were getting near the end of their dinner. Through the cafe windows they could see the Boulevard, crowded with people. They could feel the gentle breezes which are wafted over Paris on warm summer evenings and make you feel like going out somewhere, you care not where, under the trees, and make you dream of moonlit rivers, of fireflies and of larks.

One of the two, Henri Simon, heaved a deep sigh and said:

"Ah! I am growing old. It's sad. Formerly, on evenings like this, I felt full of life. Now, I only feel regrets. Life is short!"

He was perhaps forty-five years old, very bald and already growing stout.

The other, Pierre Carnier, a trifle older, but thin and lively, answered:

"Well, my boy, I have grown old without noticing it in the least. I have always been merry, healthy, vigorous and all the rest. As one sees oneself in the mirror every day, one does not realize the work of age, for it is slow, regular, and it modifies the countenance so gently that the changes are unnoticeable. It is for this reason alone that we do not die of sorrow after two or three years of excitement. For we cannot understand the alterations which time produces. In order to appreciate them one would have to remain six months without seeing one's own face —then, oh, what a shock!

"And the women, my friend, how I pity the poor beings! All their joy, all their power, all their life, lies in their beauty, which lasts ten years.

"As I said, I aged without noticing it; I thought myself practically a youth, when I was almost fifty years old. Not feeling the slightest infirmity, I went about, happy and peaceful.

"The revelation of my decline came to me in a simple and terrible manner, which overwhelmed me for almost six months—then I became resigned.

"Like all men, I have often been in love, but most especially once.

"I met her at the seashore, at Etretat, about twelve years ago, shortly after the war. There is nothing prettier than this beach during the morning bathing hour. It is small, shaped like a horseshoe, framed by high white cliffs, which are pierced by strange holes called the 'Portes,' one stretching out into the ocean like the leg of a giant, the other short and dumpy. The women gather on the narrow strip of sand in this frame of high rocks, which they make into a gorgeous garden of beautiful gowns. The sun beats down on the shores, on the multicolored parasols, on the blue-green sea; and all is gay, delightful, smiling. You sit down at the edge of the water and you watch the bathers. The women come down, wrapped in long bath robes, which they throw off daintily when they reach the foamy edge of the rippling waves; and they run into the water with a rapid little step, stopping from time to time for a delightful little thrill from the cold water, a short gasp.

"Very few stand the test of the bath. It is there that they can be judged, from the ankle to the throat. Especially on leaving the water are the defects revealed, although water is a powerful aid to flabby skin.

"The first time that I saw this young woman in the water, I was delighted, entranced. She stood the test well. There are faces whose charms appeal to you at first glance and delight you instantly. You seem to have found the woman whom you were born to love. I had that feeling and that shock.

"I was introduced, and was soon smitten worse than I had ever been before. My heart longed for her. It is a terrible yet delightful thing thus to be dominated by a young woman. It is almost torture, and yet infinite delight. Her look, her smile, her hair fluttering in the wind, the little lines of her face, the slightest movement of her features, delighted me, upset me, entranced me. She had captured me, body and soul, by her gestures, her manners, even by her clothes, which seemed to take on a peculiar charm as soon as she wore them. I grew tender at the sight of her veil on some piece of furniture, her gloves thrown on a chair. Her gowns seemed to me inimitable. Nobody had hats like hers.

"She was married, but her husband came only on Saturday, and left on Monday. I didn't cencern myself about him, anyhow. I wasn't jealous of him, I don't know why; never did a creature seem to me to be of less importance in life, to attract my attention less than this man.

"But she! how I loved her! How beautiful, graceful and young she was! She was youth, elegance, freshness itself! Never before had I felt so strongly what a pretty, distinguished, delicate, charming, graceful being woman is. Never before had I appreciated the seductive beauty to be found in the curve of a cheek, the movement of a lip, the pinkness of an ear, the shape of that foolish organ called the nose.

"This lasted three months; then I left for America, overwhelmed with sadness. But her memory remained in me, persistent, triumphant. From far away I was as much hers as I had been when she was near me. Years passed by, and I did not forget her. The charming image of her person was ever before my eyes and in my heart. And my love remained true to her, a quiet tenderness now, something like the beloved memory of the most beautiful and the most enchanting thing I had ever met in my life.

"Twelve years are not much in a lifetime! One does not feel them slip by. The years follow each other gently and quickly, slowly yet rapidly, each one is long and yet so soon over! They add up so rapidly, they leave so few traces behind them, they disappear so completely, that, when one turns round to look back over bygone years, one sees nothing and yet one does not understand how one happens to be so old. It seemed to me, really, that hardly a few months separated me from that charming season on the sands of Etretat.

"Last spring I went to dine with some friends at Maisons-Laffitte.

"Just as the train was leaving, a big, fat lady, escorted by four little girls, got into my car. I hardly looked at this mother hen, very big, very round, with a face as full as the moon framed in an enormous, beribboned hat.

"She was puffing, out of breath from having been forced to walk quickly. The children began to chatter. I unfolded my paper and began to read.

"We had just passed Asnieres, when my neighbor suddenly turned to me and said:

"'Excuse me, sir, but are you not Monsieur Garnier?'

"'Yes, madame.'

"Then she began to laugh, the pleased laugh of a good woman; and yet it was sad.

"'You do not seem to recognize me.'

"I hesitated. It seemed to me that I had seen that face somewhere; but where? when? I answered:

"'Yes—and no. I certainly know you, and yet I cannot recall your name.'

"She blushed a little:

"'Madame Julie Lefevre.'

"Never had I received such a shock. In a second it seemed to me as though it were all over with me! I felt that a veil had been torn from my eyes and that I was going to make a horrible and heartrending discovery.

"So that was she! That big, fat, common woman, she! She had become the mother of these four girls since I had last her. And these little beings surprised me as much as their mother. They were part of her; they were big girls, and already had a place in life. Whereas she no longer counted, she, that marvel of dainty and charming gracefulness. It seemed to me that I had seen her but yesterday, and this is how I found her again! Was it possible? A poignant grief seized my heart; and also a revolt against nature herself, an unreasoning indignation against this brutal, infarious act of destruction.

"I looked at her, bewildered. Then I took her hand in mine, and tears came to my eyes. I wept for her lost youth. For I did not know this fat lady.

"She was also excited, and stammered:

"'I am greatly changed, am I not? What can you expect—everything has its time! You see, I have become a mother, nothing but a good mother. Farewell to the rest, that is over. Oh! I never expected you to recognize me if we met. You, too, have changed. It took me quite a while to be sure that I was not mistaken. Your hair is all white. Just think! Twelve years ago! Twelve years! My oldest girl is already ten.'

"I looked at the child. And I recognized in her something of her mother's old charm, but something as yet unformed, something which promised for the future. And life seemed to me as swift as a passing train.

"We had reached. Maisons-Laffitte. I kissed my old friend's hand. I had found nothing but the most commonplace remarks. I was too much upset to talk.

"At night, alone, at home, I stood in front of the mirror for a long time, a very long time. And I finally remembered what I had been, finally saw in my mind's eye my brown mustache, my black hair and the youthful expression of my face. Now I was old. Farewell!"

THE WOLF

This is what the old Marquis d'Arville told us after St. Hubert's dinner at the house of the Baron des Ravels.

We had killed a stag that day. The marquis was the only one of the guests who had not taken part in this chase. He never hunted.

During that long repast we had talked about hardly anything but the slaughter of animals. The ladies themselves were interested in bloody and exaggerated tales, and the orators imitated the attacks and the combats of men against beasts, raised their arms, romanced in a thundering voice.

M. d Arville talked well, in a certain flowery, high-sounding, but effective style. He must have told this story frequently, for he told it fluently, never hesitating for words, choosing them with skill to make his description vivid.

Gentlemen, I have never hunted, neither did my father, nor my grandfather, nor my great-grandfather. This last was the son of a man who hunted more than all of you put together. He died in 1764. I will tell you the story of his death.

His name was Jean. He was married, father of that child who became my great-grandfather, and he lived with his younger brother, Francois d'Arville, in our castle in Lorraine, in the midst of the forest.

Francois d'Arville had remained a bachelor for love of the chase.

They both hunted from one end of the year to the other, without stopping and seemingly without fatigue. They loved only hunting, understood nothing else, talked only of that, lived only for that.

They had at heart that one passion, which was terrible and inexorable. It consumed them, had completely absorbed them, leaving room for no other thought.

They had given orders that they should not be interrupted in the chase for any reason whatever. My great-grandfather was born while his father was following a fox, and Jean d'Arville did not stop the chase, but exclaimed: "The deuce! The rascal might have waited till after the view—halloo!"

His brother Francois was still more infatuated. On rising he went to see the dogs, then the horses, then he shot little birds about the castle until the time came to hunt some large game.

In the countryside they were called M. le Marquis and M. le Cadet, the nobles then not being at all like the chance nobility of our time, which wishes to establish an hereditary hierarchy in titles; for the son of a marquis is no more a count, nor the son of a viscount a baron, than a son of a general is a colonel by birth. But the contemptible vanity of today finds profit in that arrangement.

My ancestors were unusually tall, bony, hairy, violent and vigorous. The younger, still taller than the older, had a voice so strong that, according to a legend of which he was proud, all the leaves of the forest shook when he shouted.

When they were both mounted to set out hunting, it must have been a superb sight to see those two giants straddling their huge horses.

Now, toward the midwinter of that year, 1764, the frosts were excessive, and the wolves became ferocious.

They even attacked belated peasants, roamed at night outside the houses, howled from sunset to sunrise, and robbed the stables.

And soon a rumor began to circulate. People talked of a colossal wolf with gray fur, almost white, who had eaten two children, gnawed off a woman's arm, strangled all the watch dogs in the district, and even come without fear into the farmyards. The people in the houses affirmed that they had felt his breath, and that it made the flame of the lights flicker. And soon a panic ran through all the province. No one dared go out any more after nightfall. The darkness seemed haunted by the image of the beast.

The brothers d'Arville determined to find and kill him, and several times they brought together all the gentlemen of the country to a great hunt.

They beat the forests and searched the coverts in vain; they never met him. They killed wolves, but not that one. And every night after a battue the beast, as if to avenge himself, attacked some traveller or killed some one's cattle, always far from the place where they had looked for him.

Finally, one night he stole into the pigpen of the Chateau d'Arville and ate the two fattest pigs.

The brothers were roused to anger, considering this attack as a direct insult and a defiance. They took their strong bloodhounds, used to pursue dangerous animals, and they set off to hunt, their hearts filled with rage.

From dawn until the hour when the empurpled sun descended behind the great naked trees, they beat the woods without finding anything.

At last, furious and disgusted, both were returning, walking their horses along a lane bordered with hedges, and they marvelled that their skill as huntsmen should be baffled by this wolf, and they were suddenly seized with a mysterious fear.

The elder said:

"That beast is not an ordinary one. You would say it had a mind like a man."

The younger answered:

"Perhaps we should have a bullet blessed by our cousin, the bishop, or pray some priest to pronounce the words which are needed."

Then they were silent.

Jean continued:

"Look how red the sun is. The great wolf will do some harm to-night."

He had hardly finished speaking when his horse reared; that of Franqois began to kick. A large thicket covered with dead leaves opened before them, and a mammoth beast, entirely gray, jumped up and ran off through the wood.

Both uttered a kind of grunt of joy, and bending over the necks of their heavy horses, they threw them forward with an impulse from all their body, hurling them on at such a pace, urging them, hurrying them away, exciting them so with voice and with gesture and with spur that the experienced riders seemed to be carrying the heavy beasts between their thighs and to bear them off as if they were flying.

Thus they went, plunging through the thickets, dashing across the beds of streams, climbing the hillsides, descending the gorges, and blowing the horn as loud as they could to attract their people and the dogs.

And now, suddenly, in that mad race, my ancestor struck his forehead against an enormous branch which split his skull; and he fell dead on the ground, while his frightened horse took himself off, disappearing in the gloom which enveloped the woods.

The younger d'Arville stopped quick, leaped to the earth, seized his brother in his arms, and saw that the brains were escaping from the wound with the blood.

Then he sat down beside the body, rested the head, disfigured and red, on his knees, and waited, regarding the immobile face of his elder brother. Little by little a fear possessed him, a strange fear which he had never felt before, the fear of the dark, the fear of loneliness, the fear of the deserted wood, and the fear also of the weird wolf who had just killed his brother to avenge himself upon them both.

The gloom thickened; the acute cold made the trees crack. Francois got up, shivering, unable to remain there longer, feeling himself growing faint. Nothing was to be heard, neither the voice of the dogs nor the sound of the horns-all was silent along the invisible horizon; and this mournful silence of the frozen night had something about it terrific and strange.

He seized in his immense hands the great body of Jean, straightened it, and laid it across the saddle to carry it back to the chateau; then he went on his way softly, his mind troubled as if he were in a stupor, pursued by horrible and fear-giving images.

And all at once, in the growing darkness a great shape crossed his path. It was the beast. A shock of terror shook the hunter; something cold, like a drop of water, seemed to glide down his back, and, like a monk haunted of the devil, he made a great sign of the cross, dismayed at this abrupt return of the horrible prowler. But his eyes fell again on the inert body before him, and passing abruptly from fear to anger, he shook with an indescribable rage.

Then he spurred his horse and rushed after the wolf.

He followed it through the copses, the ravines, and the tall trees, traversing woods which he no longer recognized, his eyes fixed on the white speck which fled before him through the night.

His horse also seemed animated by a force and strength hitherto unknown. It galloped straight ahead with outstretched neck, striking against trees, and rocks, the head and the feet of the dead man thrown across the saddle. The limbs tore out his hair; the brow, beating the huge trunks, spattered them with blood; the spurs tore their ragged coats of bark. Suddenly the beast and the horseman issued from the forest and rushed into a valley, just as the moon appeared above the mountains. The valley here was stony, inclosed by enormous rocks.

Francois then uttered a yell of joy which the echoes repeated like a peal of thunder, and he leaped from his horse, his cutlass in his hand.

The beast, with bristling hair, the back arched, awaited him, its eyes gleaming like two stars. But, before beginning battle, the strong hunter, seizing his brother, seated him on a rock, and, placing stones under his head, which was no more than a mass of blood, he shouted in the ears as if he was talking to a deaf man: "Look, Jean; look at this!"

Then he attacked the monster. He felt himself strong enough to overturn a mountain, to bruise stones in his hands. The beast tried to bite him, aiming for his stomach; but he had seized the fierce animal by the neck, without even using his weapon, and he strangled it gently, listening to the cessation of breathing in its throat and the beatings of its heart. He laughed, wild with joy, pressing closer and closer his formidable embrace, crying in a delirium of joy, "Look, Jean, look!" All resistance ceased; the body of the wolf became limp. He was dead.

Francois took him up in his arms and carried him to the feet of the elder brother, where he laid him, repeating, in a tender voice: "There, there, there, my little Jean, see him!"

Then he replaced on the saddle the two bodies, one upon the other, and rode away.

He returned to the chateau, laughing and crying, like Gargantua at the birth of Pantagruel, uttering shouts of triumph, and boisterous with joy as he related the death of the beast, and grieving and tearing his beard in telling of that of his brother.

And often, later, when he talked again of that day, he would say, with tears in his eyes: "If only poor Jean could have seen me strangle the beast, he would have died content, that I am sure!"

The widow of my ancestor inspired her orphan son with that horror of the chase which has transmitted itself from father to son as far down as myself.

The Marquis d'Arville was silent. Some one asked:

"That story is a legend, isn't it?"

And the story teller answered:

"I swear to you that it is true from beginning to end."

Then a lady declared, in a little, soft voice

"All the same, it is fine to have passions like that."

THE INN

Resembling in appearance all the wooden hostelries of the High Alps situated at the foot of glaciers in the barren rocky gorges that intersect the summits of the mountains, the Inn of Schwarenbach serves as a resting place for travellers crossing the Gemini Pass.

It remains open for six months in the year and is inhabited by the family of Jean Hauser; then, as soon as the snow begins to fall and to fill the valley so as to make the road down to Loeche impassable, the father and his three sons go away and leave the house in charge of the old guide, Gaspard Hari, with the young guide, Ulrich Kunsi, and Sam, the great mountain dog.

The two men and the dog remain till the spring in their snowy prison, with nothing before their eyes except the immense white slopes of the Balmhorn, surrounded by light, glistening summits, and are shut in, blocked up and buried by the snow which rises around them and which envelops, binds and crushes the little house, which lies piled on the roof, covering the windows and blocking up the door.

It was the day on which the Hauser family were going to return to Loeche, as winter was approaching, and the descent was becoming dangerous. Three mules started first, laden with baggage and led by the three sons. Then the mother, Jeanne Hauser, and her daughter Louise mounted a fourth mule and set off in their turn and the father followed them, accompanied by the two men in charge, who were to escort the family as far as the brow of the descent. First of all they passed round the small lake, which was now frozen over, at the bottom of the mass of rocks which stretched in front of the inn, and then they followed the valley, which was dominated on all sides by the snow-covered summits.

A ray of sunlight fell into that little white, glistening, frozen desert and illuminated it with a cold and dazzling flame. No living thing appeared among this ocean of mountains. There was no motion in this immeasurable solitude and no noise disturbed the profound silence.

By degrees the young guide, Ulrich Kunsi, a tall, long-legged Swiss, left old man Hauser and old Gaspard behind, in order to catch up the mule which bore the two women. The younger one looked at him as he approached and appeared to be calling him with her sad eyes. She was a young, fairhaired little peasant girl, whose milk-white cheeks and pale hair looked as if they had lost their color by their long abode amid the ice. When he had got up to the animal she was riding he put his hand on the crupper and relaxed his speed. Mother Hauser began to talk to him, enumerating with the minutest details all that he would have to attend to during the winter. It was the first time that he was going to stay up there, while old Hari had already spent fourteen winters amid the snow, at the inn of Schwarenbach.

Ulrich Kunsi listened, without appearing to understand and looked incessantly at the girl. From time to time he replied: "Yes, Madame Hauser," but his thoughts seemed far away and his calm features remained unmoved.

They reached Lake Daube, whose broad, frozen surface extended to the end of the valley. On the right one saw the black, pointed, rocky summits of the Daubenhorn beside the enormous moraines of the Lommern glacier, above which rose the Wildstrubel. As they approached the Gemmi pass, where the descent of Loeche begins, they suddenly beheld the immense horizon of the Alps of the Valais, from which the broad, deep valley of the Rhone separated them.

In the distance there was a group of white, unequal, flat, or pointed mountain summits, which glistened in the sun; the Mischabel with its two peaks, the huge group of the Weisshorn, the heavy Brunegghorn, the lofty and formidable pyramid of Mount Cervin, that slayer of men, and the Dent-Blanche, that monstrous coquette.

Then beneath them, in a tremendous hole, at the bottom of a terrific abyss, they perceived Loeche, where houses looked as grains of sand which had been thrown into that enormous crevice that is ended and closed by the Gemmi and which opens, down below, on the Rhone.

The mule stopped at the edge of the path, which winds and turns continually, doubling backward, then, fantastically and strangely, along the side of the mountain as far as the almost invisible little village at its feet. The women jumped into the snow and the two old men joined them. "Well," father Hauser said, "good-by, and keep up your spirits till next year, my friends," and old Hari replied: "Till next year."

They embraced each other and then Madame Hauser in her turn offered her cheek, and the girl did the same.

When Ulrich Kunsi's turn came, he whispered in Louise's ear, "Do not forget those up yonder," and she replied, "No," in such a low voice that he guessed what she had said without hearing it. "Well, adieu," Jean Hauser repeated, "and don't fall ill." And going before the two women, he commenced the descent, and soon all three disappeared at the first turn in the road, while the two men returned to the inn at Schwarenbach.

They walked slowly, side by side, without speaking. It was over, and they would be alone together for four or five months. Then Gaspard Hari began to relate his life last winter. He had remained with Michael Canol, who was too old now to stand it, for an accident might happen during that long solitude. They had not been dull, however; the only thing was to make up one's mind to it from the first, and in the end one would find plenty of distraction, games and other means of whiling away the time.

Ulrich Kunsi listened to him with his eyes on the ground, for in his thoughts he was following those who were descending to the village. They soon came in sight of the inn, which was, however, scarcely visible, so small did it look, a black speck at the foot of that enormous billow of snow, and when they opened the door Sam, the great curly dog, began to romp round them.

"Come, my boy," old Gaspard said, "we have no women now, so we must get our own dinner ready. Go and peel the potatoes." And they both sat down on wooden stools and began to prepare the soup.

The next morning seemed very long to Kunsi. Old Hari smoked and spat on the hearth, while the young man looked out of the window at the snow-covered mountain opposite the house.

In the afternoon he went out, and going over yesterday's ground again, he looked for the traces of the mule that had carried the two women. Then when he had reached the Gemmi Pass, he laid himself down on his stomach and looked at Loeche.

The village, in its rocky pit, was not yet buried under the snow, from which it was sheltered by the pine woods which protected it on all sides. Its low houses looked like paving stones in a large meadow from above. Hauser's little daughter was there now in one of those gray-colored houses. In which? Ulrich Kunsi was too far away to be able to make them out separately. How he would have liked to go down while he was yet able!

But the sun had disappeared behind the lofty crest of the Wildstrubel and the young man returned to the chalet. Daddy Hari was smoking, and when he saw his mate come in he proposed a game of cards to him, and they sat down opposite each other, on either side of the table. They played for a long time a simple game called brisque and then they had supper and went to bed.

The following days were like the first, bright and cold, without any fresh snow. Old Gaspard spent his afternoons in watching the eagles and other rare birds which ventured on those frozen heights, while Ulrich returned regularly to the Gemmi Pass to look at the village. Then they played cards, dice or dominoes and lost and won a trifle, just to create an interest in the game.

One morning Hari, who was up first, called his companion. A moving, deep and light cloud of white spray was falling on them noiselessly and was by degrees burying them under a thick, heavy coverlet of foam. That lasted four days and four nights. It was necessary to free the door and the windows, to dig out a passage and to cut steps to get over this frozen powder, which a twelve hours' frost had made as hard as the granite of the moraines.

They lived like prisoners and did not venture outside their abode. They had divided their duties, which they performed regularly. Ulrich Kunsi undertook the scouring, washing and everything that belonged to cleanliness. He also chopped up the wood while Gaspard Hari did the cooking and attended to the fire. Their regular and monotonous work was interrupted by long games at cards or dice, and they never quarrelled, but were always calm and placid. They were never seen impatient or ill-humored, nor did they ever use hard words, for they had laid in a stock of patience for their wintering on the top of the mountain.

Sometimes old Gaspard took his rifle and went after chamois, and occasionally he killed one. Then there was a feast in the inn at Schwarenbach and they revelled in fresh meat. One morning he went out as usual. The thermometer outside marked eighteen degrees of frost, and as the sun had not yet risen, the hunter hoped to surprise the animals at the approaches to the Wildstrubel, and Ulrich, being alone, remained in bed until ten o'clock. He was of a sleepy nature, but he would not have dared to give way like that to his inclination in the presence of the old guide, who was ever an early riser. He breakfasted leisurely with Sam, who also spent his days and nights in sleeping in front of the fire; then he felt low-spirited and even frightened at the solitude, and was seized by a longing for his daily game of cards, as one is by the craving of a confirmed habit, and so he went out to meet his companion, who was to return at four o'clock.

The snow had levelled the whole deep valley, filled up the crevasses, obliterated all signs of the two lakes and covered the rocks, so that between the high summits there was nothing but an immense, white, regular, dazzling and frozen surface. For three weeks Ulrich had not been to the edge of the precipice from which he had looked down on the village, and he wanted to go there before climbing the slopes which led to Wildstrubel. Loeche was now also covered by the snow and the houses could scarcely be distinguished, covered as they were by that white cloak.

Then, turning to the right, he reached the Loemmern glacier. He went along with a mountaineer's long strides, striking the snow, which was as hard as a rock, with his iron-pointed stick, and with his piercing eyes he looked for the little black, moving speck in the distance, on that enormous, white expanse.

When he reached the end of the glacier he stopped and asked himself whether the old man had taken that road, and then he began to walk along the moraines with rapid and uneasy steps. The day was declining, the snow was assuming a rosy tint, and a dry, frozen wind blew in rough gusts over its crystal surface. Ulrich uttered a long, shrill, vibrating call. His voice sped through the deathlike silence in which the mountains were sleeping; it reached the distance, across profound and motionless waves of glacial foam, like the cry of a bird across the waves of the sea. Then it died away and nothing answered him.

He began to walk again. The sun had sunk yonder behind the mountain tops, which were still purple with the reflection from the sky, but the depths of the valley were becoming gray, and suddenly the young man felt frightened. It seemed to him as if the silence, the cold, the solitude, the winter death of these mountains were taking possession of him, were going to stop and to freeze his blood, to make his limbs grow stiff and to turn him into a motionless and frozen object, and he set off running, fleeing toward his dwelling. The old man, he thought, would have returned during his absence. He had taken another road; he would, no doubt, be sitting before the fire, with a dead chamois at his feet. He soon came in sight of the inn, but no smoke rose from it. Ulrich walked faster and opened the door. Sam ran up to him to greet him, but Gaspard Hari had not returned. Kunsi, in his alarm, turned round suddenly, as if he had expected to find his comrade hidden in a corner. Then he relighted the fire and made the soup, hoping every moment to see the old man come in. From time to time he went out to see if he were not coming. It was quite night now, that wan, livid night of the mountains, lighted by a thin, yellow crescent moon, just disappearing behind the mountain tops.

Then the young man went in and sat down to warm his hands and feet, while he pictured to himself every possible accident. Gaspard might have broken a leg, have fallen into a crevasse, taken a false step and dislocated his ankle. And, perhaps, he was lying on the snow, overcome and stiff with the cold, in agony of mind, lost and, perhaps, shouting for help, calling with all his might in the silence of the night.. But where? The mountain was so vast, so rugged, so dangerous in places, especially at that time of the year, that it would have required ten or twenty guides to walk for a week in all directions to find a man in that immense space. Ulrich Kunsi, however, made up his mind to set out with Sam if Gaspard did not return by one in the morning, and he made his preparations.

He put provisions for two days into a bag, took his steel climbing iron, tied a long, thin, strong rope round his waist, and looked to see that his iron-shod stick and his axe, which served to cut steps in the ice, were in order. Then he waited. The fire was burning on the hearth, the great dog was snoring in front of it, and the clock was ticking, as regularly as a heart beating, in its resounding wooden case. He waited, with his ears on the alert for distant sounds, and he shivered when the wind blew against the roof and the walls. It struck twelve and he trembled: Then, frightened and shivering, he put some water on the fire, so that he might have some hot coffee before starting, and when the clock struck one he got up, woke Sam, opened the door and went off in the direction of the Wildstrubel. For five hours he mounted, scaling the rocks by means of his climbing irons, cutting into the ice, advancing continually, and occasionally hauling up the dog, who remained below at the foot of some slope that was too steep for him, by means of the rope. It was about six o'clock when he reached one of the summits to which old Gaspard often came after chamois, and he waited till it should be daylight.

The sky was growing pale overhead, and a strange light, springing nobody could tell whence, suddenly illuminated the immense ocean of pale mountain summits, which extended for a hundred leagues around him. One might have said that this vague brightness arose from the snow itself and spread abroad in space. By degrees the highest distant summits assumed a delicate, pink flesh color, and the red sun appeared behind the ponderous giants of the Bernese Alps.

Ulrich Kunsi set off again, walking like a hunter, bent over, looking for tracks, and saying to his dog: "Seek, old fellow, seek!"

He was descending the mountain now, scanning the depths closely, and from time to time shouting, uttering aloud, prolonged cry, which soon died away in that silent vastness. Then he put his ear to the ground to listen. He thought he could distinguish a voice, and he began to run and shouted again, but he heard nothing more and sat down, exhausted and in despair. Toward midday he breakfasted and gave Sam, who was as tired as himself, something to eat also, and then he recommenced his search.

When evening came he was still walking, and he had walked more than thirty miles over the mountains. As he was too far away to return home and too tired to drag himself along any further, he dug a hole in the snow and crouched in it with his dog under a blanket which he had brought with him. And the man and the dog lay side by side, trying to keep warm, but frozen to the marrow nevertheless. Ulrich scarcely slept, his mind haunted by visions and his limbs shaking with cold.

Day was breaking when he got up. His legs were as stiff as iron bars and his spirits so low that he was ready to cry with anguish, while his heart was beating so that he almost fell over with agitation, when he thought he heard a noise.

Suddenly he imagined that he also was going to die of cold in the midst of this vast solitude, and the terror of such a death roused his energies and gave him renewed vigor. He was descending toward the inn, falling down and getting up again, and followed at a distance by Sam, who was limping on three legs, and they did not reach Schwarenbach until four o'clock in the afternoon. The house was empty and the young man made a fire, had something to eat and went to sleep, so worn out that he did not think of anything more.

He slept for a long time, for a very long time, an irresistible sleep. But suddenly a voice, a cry, a name, "Ulrich!" aroused him from his profound torpor and made him sit up in bed. Had he been dreaming? Was it one of those strange appeals which cross the dreams of disquieted minds? No, he heard it still, that reverberating cry-which had entered his ears and remained in his flesh-to the tips of his sinewy fingers. Certainly somebody had cried out and called "Ulrich!" There was somebody there near the house, there could be no doubt of that, and he opened the door and shouted, "Is it you, Gaspard?" with all the strength of his lungs. But there was no reply, no murmur, no groan, nothing. It was quite dark and the snow looked wan.

The wind had risen, that icy wind that cracks the rocks and leaves nothing alive on those deserted heights, and it came in sudden gusts, which were more parching and more deadly than the burning wind of the desert, and again Ulrich shouted: "Gaspard! Gaspard! Gaspard." And then he waited again. Everything was silent on the mountain.

Then he shook with terror and with a bound he was inside the inn, when he shut and bolted the door, and then he fell into a chair trembling all over, for he felt certain that his comrade had called him at the moment he was expiring.

He was sure of that, as sure as one is of being alive or of eating a piece of bread. Old Gaspard Hari had been dying for two days and three nights somewhere, in some hole, in one of those deep, untrodden ravines whose whiteness is more sinister than subterranean darkness. He had been dying for two days and three nights and he had just then died, thinking of his comrade. His soul, almost before it was released, had taken its flight to the inn where Ulrich was sleeping, and it had called him by that terrible and mysterious power which the spirits of the dead have to haunt the living. That voiceless soul had cried to the worn-out soul of the sleeper; it had uttered its last farewell, or its reproach, or its curse on the man who had not searched carefully enough.

And Ulrich felt that it was there, quite close to him, behind the wall, behind the door which he had just fastened. It was wandering about, like a night bird which lightly touches a lighted window with his wings, and the terrified young man was ready to scream with horror. He wanted to run away, but did not dare to go out; he did not dare, and he should never dare to do it in the future, for that phantom would remain there day and night, round the inn, as long as the old man's body was not recovered and had not been deposited in the consecrated earth of a churchyard.

When it was daylight Kunsi recovered some of his courage at the return of the bright sun. He prepared his meal, gave his dog some food and then remained motionless on a chair, tortured at heart as he thought of the old man lying on the snow, and then, as soon as night once more covered the mountains, new terrors assailed him. He now walked up and down the dark kitchen, which was scarcely lighted by the flame of one candle, and he walked from one end of it to the other with great strides, listening, listening whether the terrible cry of the other night would again break the dreary silence outside. He felt himself alone, unhappy man, as no man had ever been alone before! He was alone in this immense desert of Snow, alone five thousand feet above the inhabited earth, above human habitation, above that stirring, noisy, palpitating life, alone under an icy sky! A mad longing impelled him to run away, no matter where, to get down to Loeche by flinging himself over the precipice; but he did not even dare to open the door, as he felt sure that the other, the dead man, would bar his road, so that he might not be obliged to remain up there alone:

Toward midnight, tired with walking, worn out by grief and fear, he at last fell into a doze in his chair, for he was afraid of his bed as one is of a haunted spot. But suddenly the strident cry of the other evening pierced his ears, and it was so shrill that Ulrich stretched out his arms to repulse the ghost, and he fell backward with his chair.

Sam, who was awakened by the noise, began to howl as frightened dogs do howl, and he walked all about the house trying to find out where the danger came from. When he got to the door, he sniffed beneath it, smelling vigorously, with his coat bristling and his tail stiff, while he growled angrily. Kunsi, who was terrified, jumped up, and, holding his chair by one leg, he cried: "Don't come in, don't come in, or I shall kill you." And the dog, excited by this threat, barked angrily at that invisible enemy who defied his master's voice. By degrees, however, he quieted down and came back and stretched himself in front of the fire, but he was uneasy and kept his head up and growled between his teeth.

Ulrich, in turn, recovered his senses, but as he felt faint with terror, he went and got a bottle of brandy out of the sideboard, and he drank off several glasses, one after anther, at a gulp. His ideas became vague, his courage revived and a feverish glow ran through his veins.

He ate scarcely anything the next day and limited himself to alcohol, and so he lived for several days, like a drunken brute. As soon as he thought of Gaspard Hari, he began to drink again, and went on drinking until he fell to the ground, overcome by intoxication. And there he remained lying on his face, dead drunk, his limbs benumbed, and snoring loudly. But scarcely had he digested the maddening and burning liquor than the same cry, "Ulrich!" woke him like a bullet piercing his brain, and he got up, still staggering, stretching out his hands to save himself from falling, and calling to Sam to help him. And the dog, who appeared to be going mad like his master, rushed to the door, scratched it with his claws and gnawed it with his long white teeth, while the young man, with his head thrown back drank the brandy in draughts, as if it had been cold water, so that it might by and by send his thoughts, his frantic terror, and his memory to sleep again.

In three weeks he had consumed all his stock of ardent spirits. But his continual drunkenness only lulled his terror, which awoke more furiously than ever as soon as it was impossible for him to calm it. His fixed idea then, which had been intensified by a month of drunkenness, and which was continually increasing in his absolute solitude, penetrated him like a gimlet. He now walked about the house like a wild beast in its cage, putting his ear to the door to listen if the other were there and defying him through the wall. Then, as soon as he dozed, overcome by fatigue, he heard the voice which made him leap to his feet.

At last one night, as cowards do when driven to extremities, he sprang to the door and opened it, to see who was calling him and to force him to keep quiet, but such a gust of cold wind blew into his face that it chilled him to the bone, and he closed and bolted the door again immediately, without noticing that Sam had rushed out. Then, as he was shivering with cold, he threw some wood on the fire and sat down in front of it to warm himself, but suddenly he started, for somebody was scratching at the wall and crying. In desperation he called out: "Go away!" but was answered by another long, sorrowful wail.

Then all his remaining senses forsook him from sheer fright. He repeated: "Go away!" and turned round to try to find some corner in which to hide, while the other person went round the house still crying and rubbing against the wall. Ulrich went to the oak sideboard, which was full of plates and dishes and of provisions, and lifting it up with superhuman strength, he dragged it to the door, so as to form a barricade. Then piling up all the rest of the furniture, the mattresses, palliasses and chairs, he stopped up the windows as one does when assailed by an enemy.

But the person outside now uttered long, plaintive, mournful groans, to which the young man replied by similar groans, and thus days and nights passed without their ceasing to howl at each other. The one was continually walking round the house and scraped the walls with his nails so vigorously that it seemed as if he wished to destroy them, while the other, inside, followed all his movements, stooping down and holding his ear to the walls and replying to all his appeals with terrible cries. One evening, however, Ulrich heard nothing more, and he sat down, so overcome by fatigue, that he went to sleep immediately and awoke in the morning without a thought, without any recollection of what had happened, just as if his head had been emptied during his heavy sleep, but he felt hungry, and he ate.

The winter was over and the Gemmi Pass was practicable again, so the Hauser family started off to return to their inn. As soon as they had reached the top of the ascent the women mounted their mule and spoke about the two men whom they would meet again shortly. They were, indeed, rather surprised that neither of them had come down a few days before, as soon as the road was open, in order to tell them all about their long winter sojourn. At last, however, they saw the inn, still covered with snow, like a quilt. The door and the window were closed, but a little smoke was coming out of the chimney, which reassured old Hauser. On going up to the door, however, he saw the skeleton of an animal which had been torn to pieces by the eagles, a large skeleton lying on its side.

They all looked close at it and the mother said:

"That must be Sam," and then she shouted: "Hi, Gaspard!" A cry from the interior of the house answered her and a sharp cry that one might have thought some animal had uttered it. Old Hauser repeated, "Hi, Gaspard!" and they heard another cry similar to the first.

Then the three men, the father and the two sons, tried to open the door, but it resisted their efforts. From the empty cow-stall they took a beam to serve as a battering-ram and hurled it against the door with all their might. The wood gave way and the boards flew into splinters. Then the house was shaken by a loud voice, and inside, behind the side board which was overturned, they saw a man standing upright, with his hair falling on his shoulders and a beard descending to his breast, with shining eyes, and nothing but rags to cover him. They did not recognize him, but Louise Hauser exclaimed:

"It is Ulrich, mother." And her mother declared that it was Ulrich, although his hair was white.

He allowed them to go up to him and to touch him, but he did not reply to any of their questions, and they were obliged to take him to Loeche, where the doctors found that he was mad, and nobody ever found out what had become of his companion.

Little Louise Hauser nearly died that summer of decline, which the physicians attributed to the cold air of the mountains.

VOLUME V

MONSIEUR PARENT

George's father was sitting in an iron chair, watching his little son with concentrated affection and attention, as little George piled up the sand into heaps during one of their walks. He would take up the sand with both hands, make a mound of it, and put a chestnut leaf on top. His father saw no one but him in that public park full of people.

The sun was just disappearing behind the roofs of the Rue Saint-Lazare, but still shed its rays obliquely on that little, overdressed crowd. The chestnut trees were lighted up by its yellow rays, and the three fountains before the lofty porch of the church had the appearance of liquid silver.

Monsieur Parent, accidentally looking up at the church clock, saw that he was five minutes late. He got up, took the child by the arm, shook his dress, which was covered with sand, wiped his hands, and led him in the direction of the Rue Blanche. He walked quickly, so as not to get in after his wife, and the child could not keep up with him. He took him up and carried him, though it made him pant when he had to walk up the steep street. He was a man of forty, already turning gray, and rather stout. At last he reached his house. An old servant who had brought him up, one of those trusted servants who are the tyrants of families, opened the door to him.

"Has madame come in yet?" he asked anxiously.

The servant shrugged her shoulders:

"When have you ever known madame to come home at half-past six, monsieur?"

"Very well; all the better; it will give me time to change my things, for I am very warm."

The servant looked at him with angry and contemptuous pity. "Oh, I can see that well enough," she grumbled. "You are covered with perspiration, monsieur. I suppose you walked quickly and carried the child, and only to have to wait until half-past seven, perhaps, for madame. I have made up my mind not to have dinner ready on time. I shall get it for eight o'clock, and if, you have to wait, I cannot help it; roast meat ought not to be burnt!"

Monsieur Parent pretended not to hear, but went into his own room, and as soon as he got in, locked the door, so as to be alone, quite alone. He was so used now to being abused and badly treated that he never thought himself safe except when he was locked in.

What could he do? To get rid of Julie seemed to him such a formidable thing to do that he hardly ventured to think of it, but it was just as impossible to uphold her against his wife, and before another month the situation would become unbearable between the two. He remained sitting there, with his arms hanging down, vaguely trying to discover some means to set matters straight, but without success. He said to himself: "It is lucky that I have George; without him I should-be very miserable."

Just then the clock struck seven, and he started up. Seven o'clock, and he had not even changed his clothes. Nervous and breathless, he undressed, put on a clean shirt, hastily finished his toilet, as if he had been expected in the next room for some event of extreme importance, and went into the drawing-room, happy at having nothing to fear. He glanced at the newspaper, went and looked out of the window, and then sat down again, when the door opened, and the boy came in, washed, brushed, and smiling. Parent took him up in his arms and kissed him passionately; then he tossed him into the air, and held him up to the ceiling, but soon sat down again, as he was tired with all his exertion. Then, taking George on his knee, he made him ride a-cock-horse. The child laughed and clapped his hands and shouted with pleasure, as did his father, who laughed until his big stomach shook, for it amused him almost more than it did the child.

Parent loved him with all the heart of a weak, resigned, ill-used man. He loved him with mad bursts of affection, with caresses and with all the bashful tenderness which was hidden in him, and which had never found an outlet, even at the early period of his married life, for his wife had always shown herself cold and reserved.

Just then Julie came to the door, with a pale face and glistening eyes, and said in a voice which trembled with exasperation: "It is half-past seven, monsieur."

Parent gave an uneasy and resigned look at the clock and replied: "Yes, it certainly is half-past seven."

"Well, my dinner is quite ready now."

Seeing the storm which was coming, he tried to turn it aside. "But did you not tell me when I came in that it would not be ready before eight?"

"Eight! what are you thinking about? You surely do not mean to let the child dine at eight o'clock? It would ruin his stomach. Just suppose that he only had his mother to look after him! She cares a great deal about her child. Oh, yes, we will speak about her; she is a mother! What a pity it is that there should be any mothers like her!"

Parent thought it was time to cut short a threatened scene. "Julie," he said, "I will not allow you to speak like that of your mistress. You understand me, do you not? Do not forget it in the future."

The old servant, who was nearly choked with surprise, turned and went out, slamming the door so violently after her that the lustres on the chandelier rattled, and for some seconds it sounded as if a number of little invisible bells were ringing in the drawing-room.

Eight o'clock struck, the door opened, and Julie came in again. She had lost her look of exasperation, but now she put on an air of cold and determined resolution, which was still more formidable.

"Monsieur," she said, "I served your mother until the day of her death, and I have attended to you from your birth until now, and I think it may be said that I am devoted to the family." She waited for a reply, and Parent stammered:

"Why, yes, certainly, my good Julie."

"You know quite well," she continued, "that I have never done anything for the sake of money, but always for your sake; that I have never deceived you nor lied to you, that you have never had to find fault with me—"

"Certainly, my good Julie."

"Very well, then, monsieur; it cannot go on any longer like this. I have said nothing, and left you in your ignorance, out of respect and liking for you, but it is too much, and every one in the neighborhood is laughing at you. Everybody knows about it, and so I must tell you also, although I do not like to repeat it. The reason why madame comes in at any time she chooses is that she is doing abominable things."

He seemed stupefied and not to understand, and could only stammer out:

"Hold your tongue; you know I have forbidden you——"

But she interrupted him with irresistible resolution. "No, monsieur, I must tell you everything now. For a long time madame has been carrying on with Monsieur Limousin. I have seen them kiss scores of times behind the door. Ah! you may be sure that if Monsieur Limousin had been rich, madame would never have married Monsieur Parent. If you remember how the marriage was brought about, you would understand the matter from beginning to end."

Parent had risen, and stammered out, his face livid: "Hold your tongue—hold your tongue, or——"

She went on, however: "No, I mean to tell you everything. She married you from interest, and she deceived you from the very first day. It was all settled between them beforehand. You need only reflect for a few moments to understand it, and then, as she was not satisfied with having married you, as she did not love you, she has made your life miserable, so miserable that it has almost broken my heart when I have seen it."

He walked up and down the room with hands clenched, repeating: "Hold your tongue—hold your tongue——" For he could find nothing else to say. The old servant, however, would not yield; she seemed resolved on everything.

George, who had been at first astonished and then frightened at those angry voices, began to utter shrill screams, and remained behind his father, with his face puckered up and his mouth open, roaring.

His son's screams exasperated Parent, and filled him with rage and courage. He rushed at Julie with both arms raised, ready to strike her, exclaiming: "Ah! you wretch. You will drive the child out of his senses." He already had his hand on her, when she screamed in his face:

"Monsieur, you may beat me if you like, me who reared you, but that will not prevent your wife from deceiving you, or alter the fact that your child is not yours——"

He stopped suddenly, let his arms fall, and remained standing opposite to her, so overwhelmed that he could understand nothing more.

"You need only to look at the child," she added, "to know who is its father! He is the very image of Monsieur Limousin. You need only look at his eyes and forehead. Why, a blind man could not be mistaken in him."

He had taken her by the shoulders, and was now shaking her with all his might. "Viper, viper!" he said. "Go out the room, viper! Go out, or I shall kill you! Go out! Go out!"

And with a desperate effort he threw her into the next room. She fell across the table, which was laid for dinner, breaking the glasses. Then, rising to her feet, she put the table between her master and herself. While he was pursuing her, in order to take hold of her again, she flung terrible words at him.

"You need only go out this evening after dinner, and come in again immediately, and you will see! You will see whether I have been lying! Just try it, and you will see." She had reached the kitchen door and escaped, but he ran after her, up the back stairs to her bedroom, into which she had locked herself, and knocking at the door, he said:

"You will leave my house this very instant!"

"You may be certain of that, monsieur," was her reply. "In an hour's time I shall not be here any longer."

He then went slowly downstairs again, holding on to the banister so as not to fall, and went back to the drawing-room, where little George was sitting on the floor, crying. He fell into a chair, and looked at the child with dull eyes. He understood nothing, knew nothing more; he felt dazed, stupefied, mad, as if he had just fallen on his head, and he scarcely even remembered the dreadful things the servant had told him. Then, by degrees, his mind, like muddy water, became calmer and clearer, and the abominable revelations began to work in his heart.

He was no longer thinking of George. The child was quiet now and sitting on the carpet; but, seeing that no notice was being taken of him, he began to cry. His father ran to him, took him in his arms, and covered him with kisses. His child remained to him, at any rate! What did the rest matter? He held him in his arms and pressed his lips to his light hair, and, relieved and composed, he whispered:

"George—my little George—my dear little George——" But he suddenly remembered what Julie had said! Yes, she had said that he was Limousin's child. Oh! it could not be possible, surely. He could not believe it, could not doubt, even for a moment, that he was his own child. It was one of those low scandals which spring from servants' brains! And he repeated: "George—my dear little George." The youngster was quiet again, now that his father was fondling him.

Parent felt the warmth of the little chest penetrate through his clothes, and it filled him with love, courage, and happiness; that gentle warmth soothed him, fortified him and saved him. Then he put the small, curly head away from him a little, and looked at it affectionately, still repeating: "George! Oh, my little George!" But suddenly he thought:

"Suppose he were to resemble Limousin, after all!" He looked at him with haggard, troubled eyes, and tried to discover whether there was any likeness in his forehead, in his nose, mouth, or cheeks. His thoughts wandered as they do when a person is going mad, and his child's face changed in his eyes, and assumed a strange look and improbable resemblances.

The hall bell rang. Parent gave a bound as if a bullet had gone through him. "There she is," he said. "What shall I do?" And he ran and locked himself up in his room, to have time to bathe his eyes. But in a few moments another ring at the bell made him jump again, and then he remembered that Julie had left, without the housemaid knowing it, and so nobody would go to open the door. What was he to do? He went himself, and suddenly he felt brave, resolute, ready for dissimulation and the struggle. The terrible blow had matured him in a few moments. He wished to know the truth, he desired it with the rage of a timid man, and with the tenacity of an easy-going man who has been exasperated.

Nevertheless, he trembled. Does one know how much excited cowardice there often is in boldness? He went to the door with furtive steps, and stopped to listen; his heart beat furiously. Suddenly, however, the noise of the bell over his head startled him like an explosion. He seized the lock, turned the key, and opening the door, saw his wife and Limousin standing before him on the stairs.

With an air of astonishment, which also betrayed a little irritation, she said:

"So you open the door now? Where is Julie?"

His throat felt tight and his breathing was labored as he tried to. reply, without being able to utter a word.

"Are you dumb?" she continued. "I asked you where Julie is?"

"She—she—has—gone——" he managed to stammer.

His wife began to get angry. "What do you mean by gone? Where has she gone? Why?"

By degrees he regained his coolness. He felt an intense hatred rise up in him for that insolent woman who was standing before him.

"Yes, she has gone altogether. I sent her away."

"You have sent away Julie? Why, you must be mad."

"Yes, I sent her away because she was insolent, and because—because she was ill-using the child."

"Julie?"

"Yes—Julie."

"What was she insolent about?"

"About you."

"About me?"

"Yes, because the dinner was burnt, and you did not come in."

"And she said——"

"She said—offensive things about you—which I ought not—which I could not listen to——"

"What did she, say?"

"It is no good repeating them."

"I want to hear them."

"She said it was unfortunate for a man like me to be married to a woman like you, unpunctual, careless, disorderly, a bad mother, and a bad wife."

The young woman had gone into the anteroom, followed by Limousin, who did not say a word at this unexpected condition of things. She shut the door quickly, threw her cloak on a chair, and going straight up to her husband, she stammered out:

"You say? You say? That I am——"

Very pale and calm, he replied: "I say nothing, my dear. I am simply repeating what Julie said to me, as you wanted to know what it was, and I wish you to remark that I turned her off just on account of what she said."

She trembled with a violent longing to tear out his beard and scratch his face. In his voice and manner she felt that he was asserting his position as master. Although she had nothing to say by way of reply, she tried to assume the offensive by saying something unpleasant. "I suppose you have had dinner?" she asked.

"No, I waited for you."

She shrugged her shoulders impatiently. "It is very stupid of you to wait after half-past seven," she said. "You might have guessed that I was detained, that I had a good many things to do, visits and shopping,"

And then, suddenly, she felt that she wanted to explain how she had spent her time, and told him in abrupt, haughty words that, having to buy some furniture in a shop a long distance off, very far off, in the Rue de Rennes, she had met Limousin at past seven o'clock on the Boulevard Saint-Germain, and that then she had gone with him to have something to eat in a restaurant, as she did not like to go to one by herself, although she was faint with hunger. That was how she had dined with Limousin, if it could be called dining, for they had only some soup and half a chicken, as they were in a great hurry to get back.

Parent replied simply: "Well, you were quite right. I am not finding fault with you."

Then Limousin, who, had not spoken till then, and who had been half hidden behind Henriette, came forward and put out his hand, saying: "Are you very well?"

Parent took his hand, and shaking it gently, replied: "Yes, I am very well."

But the young woman had felt a reproach in her husband's last words. "Finding fault! Why do you speak of finding fault? One might think that you meant to imply something."

"Not at all," he replied, by way of excuse. "I simply meant that I was not at all anxious although you were late, and that I did not find fault with you for it."

She, however, took the high hand, and tried to find a pretext for a quarrel. "Although I was late? One might really think that it was one o'clock in the morning, and that I spent my nights away from home."

"Certainly not, my dear. I said late because I could find no other word. You said you should be back at half-past six, and you returned at half-past eight. That was surely being late. I understand it perfectly well. I am not at all surprised, even. But—but—I can hardly use any other word."

"But you pronounce them as if I had been out all night."

"Oh, no-oh, no!"

She saw that he would yield on every point, and she was going into her own room, when at last she noticed that George was screaming, and then she asked, with some feeling: "What is the matter with the child?"

"I told you that Julie had been rather unkind to him."

"What has the wretch been doing to him?"

"Oh nothing much. She gave him a push, and he fell down."

She wanted to see her child, and ran into the dining room, but stopped short at the sight of the table covered with spilt wine, with broken decanters and glasses and overturned saltcellars. "Who did all that mischief?" she asked.

"It was Julie, who——" But she interrupted him furiously:

"That is too much, really! Julie speaks of me as if I were a shameless woman, beats my child, breaks my plates and dishes, turns my house upside down, and it appears that you think it all quite natural."

"Certainly not, as I have got rid of her."

"Really! You have got rid of her! But you ought to have given her in charge. In such cases, one ought to call in the Commissary of Police!"

"But—my dear—I really could not. There was no reason. It would have been very difficult——"

She shrugged her shoulders disdainfully. "There! you will never be anything but a poor, wretched fellow, a man without a will, without any firmness or energy. Ah! she must have said some nice things to you, your Julie, to make you turn her off like that. I should like to have been here for a minute, only for a minute." Then she opened the drawing-room door and ran to George, took him into her arms and kissed him, and said: "Georgie, what is it, my darling, my pretty one, my treasure?"

Then, suddenly turning to another idea, she said: "But the child has had no dinner? You have had nothing to eat, my pet?"

"No, mamma."

Then she again turned furiously upon her husband. "Why, you must be mad, utterly mad! It is half-past eight, and George has had no dinner!"

He excused himself as best he could, for he had nearly lost his wits through the overwhelming scene and the explanation, and felt crushed by this ruin of his life. "But, my dear, we were waiting for you, as I did not wish to dine without you. As you come home late every day, I expected you every moment."

She threw her bonnet, which she had kept on till then, into an easy-chair, and in an angry voice she said: "It is really intolerable to have to do with people who can understand nothing, who can divine nothing and do nothing by themselves. So, I suppose, if I were to come in at twelve o'clock at night, the child would have had nothing to eat? Just as if you could not have understood that, as it was after half-past seven, I was prevented from coming home, that I had met with some hindrance!"

Parent trembled, for he felt that his anger was getting the upper hand, but Limousin interposed, and turning toward the young woman, said:

"My dear friend, you, are altogether unjust. Parent could not guess that you would come here so late, as you never do so, and then, how could you expect him to get over the difficulty all by himself, after having sent away Julie?"

But Henriette was very angry, and replied:

"Well, at any rate, he must get over the difficulty himself, for I will not help him," she replied. "Let him settle it!" And she went into her own room, quite forgetting that her child had not had anything to eat.

Limousin immediately set to work to help his friend. He picked up the broken glasses which strewed the table and took them out, replaced the plates and knives and forks, and put the child into his high chair, while Parent went to look for the chambermaid to wait at table. The girl came in, in great astonishment, as she had heard nothing in George's room, where she had been working. She soon, however, brought in the soup, a burnt leg of mutton, and mashed potatoes.

Parent sat by the side of the child, very much upset and distressed at all that had happened. He gave the boy his dinner, and endeavored to eat something himself, but he could only swallow with an effort, as his throat felt paralyzed. By degrees he was seized with an insane desire to look at Limousin, who was sitting opposite to him, making bread pellets, to see whether George was like him, but he did not venture to raise his eyes for some time. At last, however, he made up his mind to do so, and gave a quick, sharp look at the face which he knew so well, although he almost fancied that he had never examined it carefully. It looked so different to what he had imagined. From time to time he looked at Limousin, trying to recognize a likeness in the smallest lines of his face, in the slightest features, and then he looked at his son, under the pretext of feeding him.

Two words were sounding in his ears: "His father! his father! his father!" They buzzed in his temples at every beat of his heart. Yes, that man, that tranquil man who was sitting on the other side of the table, was, perhaps, the father of his son, of George, of his little George. Parent left off eating; he could not swallow any more. A terrible pain, one of those attacks of pain which make men scream, roll on the ground, and bite the furniture, was tearing at his entrails, and he felt inclined to take a knife and plunge it into his stomach. He started when he heard the door open. His wife came in. "I am hungry," she said; "are not you, Limousin?"

He hesitated a little, and then said: "Yes, I am, upon my word." She had the leg of mutton brought in again. Parent asked himself "Have they had dinner? Or are they late because they have had a lovers' meeting?"

They both ate with a very good appetite. Henriette was very calm, but laughed and joked. Her husband watched her furtively. She had on a pink teagown trimmed with white lace, and her fair head, her white neck and her plump hands stood out from that coquettish and perfumed dress as though it were a sea shell edged with foam.

What fun they must be making of him, if he had been their dupe since the first day! Was it possible to make a fool of a man, of a worthy man, because his father had left him a little money? Why could one not see into people's souls? How was it that nothing revealed to upright hearts the deceits of infamous hearts? How was it that voices had the same sound for adoring as for lying? Why was a false, deceptive look the same as a sincere one? And he watched them, waiting to catch a gesture, a word, an intonation. Then suddenly he thought: "I will surprise them this evening," and he said:

"My dear, as I have dismissed Julie, I will see about getting another girl this very day. I will go at once to procure one by to-morrow morning, so I may not be in until late."

"Very well," she replied; "go. I shall not stir from here. Limousin will keep me company. We will wait for you." Then, turning to the maid, she said: "You had better put George to bed, and then you can clear away and go up to your room."

Parent had got up; he was unsteady on his legs, dazed and bewildered, and saying, "I shall see you again later on," he went out, holding on to the wall, for the floor seemed to roll like a ship. George had been carried out by his nurse, while Henriette and Limousin went into the drawing-room.

As soon as the door was shut, he said: "You must be mad, surely, to torment your husband as you do?"

She immediately turned on him: "Ah! Do you know that I think the habit you have got into lately, of looking upon Parent as a martyr, is very unpleasant?"

Limousin threw himself into an easy-chair and crossed his legs. "I am not setting him up as a martyr in the least, but I think that, situated as we are, it is ridiculous to defy this man as you do, from morning till night."

She took a cigarette from the mantelpiece, lighted it, and replied: "But I do not defy him; quite the contrary. Only he irritates me by his stupidity, and I treat him as he deserves."

Limousin continued impatiently: "What you are doing is very foolish! I am only asking you to treat your husband gently, because we both of us require him to trust us. I think that you ought to see that."

They were close together: he, tall, dark, with long whiskers and the rather vulgar manners of a good-looking man who is very well satisfied with himself; she, small, fair, and pink, a little Parisian, born in the back room of a shop, half cocotte and half bourgeoise, brought up to entice customers to the store by her glances, and married, in consequence, to a simple, unsophisticated man, who saw her outside the door every morning when he went out and every evening when he came home.

"But do you not understand; you great booby," she said, "that I hate him just because he married me, because he bought me, in fact; because everything that he says and does, everything that he thinks, acts on my nerves? He exasperates me every moment by his stupidity, which you call his kindness; by his dullness, which you call his confidence, and then, above all, because he is my husband, instead of you. I feel him between us, although he does not interfere with us much. And then—-and then! No, it is, after all, too idiotic of him not to guess anything! I wish he would, at any rate, be a little jealous. There are moments when I feel inclined to say to him: 'Do you not see, you stupid creature, that Paul is my lover?'

"It is quite incomprehensible that you cannot understand how hateful he is to me, how he irritates me. You always seem to like him, and you shake hands with him cordially. Men are very extraordinary at times."

"One must know how to dissimulate, my dear."

"It is no question of dissimulation, but of feeling. One might think that, when you men deceive one another, you like each other better on that account, while we women hate a man from the moment that we have betrayed him."

"I do not see why one should hate an excellent fellow because one is friendly with his wife."

"You do not see it? You do not see it? You all of you are wanting in refinement of feeling. However, that is one of those things which one feels and cannot express. And then, moreover, one ought not. No, you would not understand; it is quite useless! You men have no delicacy of feeling."

And smiling, with the gentle contempt of an impure woman, she put both her hands on his shoulders and held up her lips to him. He stooped down and clasped her closely in his arms, and their lips met. And as they stood in front of the mantel mirror, another couple exactly like them embraced behind the clock.

They had heard nothing, neither the noise of the key nor the creaking of the door, but suddenly Henriette, with a loud cry, pushed Limousin away with both her arms, and they saw Parent looking at them, livid with rage, without his shoes on and his hat over his forehead. He looked at each, one after the other, with a quick glance of his eyes and without moving his head. He appeared beside himself. Then, without saying a word, he threw himself on Limousin, seized him as if he were going to strangle him, and flung him into the opposite corner of the room so violently that the other lost his balance, and, beating the air with his hand, struck his head violently against the wall.

When Henriette saw that her husband was going to murder her lover, she threw herself on Parent, seized him by the neck, and digging her ten delicate, rosy fingers into his neck, she squeezed him so tightly, with all the vigor of a desperate woman, that the blood spurted out under her nails, and she bit his shoulder, as if she wished to tear it with her teeth. Parent, half-strangled and choking, loosened his hold on Limousin, in order to shake off his wife, who was hanging to his neck. Putting his arms round her waist, he flung her also to the other end of the drawing-room.

Then, as his passion was short-lived, like that of most good-tempered men, and his strength was soon exhausted, he remained standing between the two, panting, worn out, not knowing what to do next. His brutal fury had expended itself in that effort, like the froth of a bottle of champagne, and his unwonted energy ended in a gasping for breath. As soon as he could speak, however, he said:

"Go away—both of you—immediately! Go away!"

Limousin remained motionless in his corner, against the wall, too startled to understand anything as yet, too frightened to move a finger; while Henriette, with her hands resting on a small, round table, her head bent forward, her hair hanging down, the bodice of her dress unfastened, waited like a wild animal which is about to spring. Parent continued in a stronger voice: "Go away immediately. Get out of the house!"

His wife, however, seeing that he had got over his first exasperation grew bolder, drew herself up, took two steps toward him, and, grown almost insolent, she said: "Have you lost your head? What is the matter with you? What is the meaning of this unjustifiable violence?"

But he turned toward her, and raising his fist to strike her, he stammered out: "Oh—oh—this is too much, too much! I heard everything! Everything—do you understand? Everything! You wretch—you wretch! You are two wretches! Get out of the house, both of you! Immediately, or I shall kill you! Leave the house!"

She saw that it was all over, and that he knew everything; that she could not prove her innocence, and that she must comply. But all her impudence had returned to her, and her hatred for the man, which was aggravated now, drove her to audacity, made her feel the need of bravado, and of defying him, and she said in a clear voice: "Come, Limousin; as he is going to turn me out of doors, I will go to your lodgings with you."

But Limousin did not move, and Parent, in a fresh access of rage, cried out: "Go, will you? Go, you wretches! Or else—or else——" He seized a chair and whirled it over his head.

Henriette walked quickly across the room, took her lover by the arm, dragged him from the wall, to which he appeared fixed, and led him toward the door, saying: "Do come, my friend—you see that the man is mad. Do come!"

As she went out she turned round to her husband, trying to think of something that she could do, something that she could invent to wound him to the heart as she left the house, and an idea struck her, one of those venomous, deadly ideas in which all a woman's perfidy shows itself, and she said resolutely: "I am going to take my child with me."

Parent was stupefied, and stammered: "Your—your—child? You dare to talk of your child? You venture—you venture to ask for your child—after-after—Oh, oh, that is too much! Go, you vile creature! Go!"

She went up to him again, almost smiling, almost avenged already, and defying him, standing close to him, and face to face, she said: "I want my child, and you have no right to keep him, because he is not yours—do you understand? He is not yours! He is Limousin's!"

And Parent cried out in bewilderment: "You lie—you lie—worthless woman!"

But she continued: "You fool! Everybody knows it except you. I tell you, this is his father. You need only look at him to see it."

Parent staggered backward, and then he suddenly turned round, took a candle, and rushed into the next room; returning almost immediately, carrying little George wrapped up in his bedclothes. The child, who had been suddenly awakened, was crying from fright. Parent threw him into his wife's arms, and then, without speaking, he pushed her roughly out toward the stairs, where Limousin was waiting, from motives of prudence.

Then he shut the door again, double-locked and bolted it, but had scarcely got back into the drawing-room when he fell to the floor at full length.

Parent lived alone, quite alone. During the five weeks that followed their separation, the feeling of surprise at his new life prevented him from thinking much. He had resumed his bachelor life, his habits of lounging, about, and took his meals at a restaurant, as he had done formerly. As he wished to avoid any scandal, he made his wife an allowance, which was arranged by their lawyers. By degrees, however, the thought of the child began to haunt him. Often, when he was at home alone at night, he suddenly thought he heard George calling out "Papa," and his heart would begin to beat, and he would get up quickly and open the door, to see whether, by chance, the child might have returned, as dogs or pigeons do. Why should a child have less instinct than an animal? On finding that he was mistaken, he would sit down in his armchair again and think of the boy. He would think of him for hours and whole days. It was not only a moral, but still more a physical obsession, a nervous longing to kiss him, to hold and fondle him, to take him on his knees and dance him. He felt the child's little arms around his neck, his little mouth pressing a kiss on his beard, his soft hair tickling his cheeks, and the remembrance of all those childish ways made him suffer as a man might for some beloved woman who has left him. Twenty or a hundred times a day he asked himself the question whether he was or was not George's father, and almost before he was in bed every night he recommenced the same series of despairing questionings.

He especially dreaded the darkness of the evening, the melancholy feeling of the twilight. Then a flood of sorrow invaded his heart, a torrent of despair which seemed to overwhelm him and drive him mad. He was as afraid of his own thoughts as men are of criminals, and he fled before them as one does from wild beasts. Above all things, he feared his empty, dark, horrible dwelling and the deserted streets, in which, here and there, a gas lamp flickered, where the isolated foot passenger whom one hears in the distance seems to be a night prowler, and makes one walk faster or slower, according to whether he is coming toward you or following you.

And in spite of himself, and by instinct, Parent went in the direction of the broad, well-lighted, populous streets. The light and the crowd attracted him, occupied his mind and distracted his thoughts, and when he was tired of walking aimlessly about among the moving crowd, when he saw the foot passengers becoming more scarce and the pavements less crowded, the fear of solitude and silence drove him into some large cafe full of drinkers and of light. He went there as flies go to a candle, and he would sit down at one of the little round tables and ask for a "bock," which he would drink slowly, feeling uneasy every time a customer got up to go. He would have liked to take him by the arm, hold him back, and beg him to stay a little longer, so much did he dread the time when the waiter should come up to him and say sharply: "Come, monsieur, it is closing time!"

He thus got into the habit of going to the beer houses, where the continual elbowing of the drinkers brings you in contact with a familiar and silent public, where the heavy clouds of tobacco smoke lull disquietude, while the heavy beer dulls the mind and calms the heart. He almost lived there. He was scarcely up before he went there to find people to distract his glances and his thoughts, and soon, as he felt too lazy to move, he took his meals there.

After every meal, during more than an hour, he sipped three or four small glasses of brandy, which stupefied him by degrees, and then his head drooped on his chest, he shut his eyes, and went to sleep. Then, awaking, he raised himself on the red velvet seat, straightened his waistcoat, pulled down his cuffs, and took up the newspapers again, though he had already seen them in the morning, and read them all through again, from beginning to end. Between four and five o'clock he went for a walk on the boulevards, to get a little fresh air, as he used to say, and then came back to the seat which had been reserved for him, and asked for his absinthe. He would talk to the regular customers whose acquaintance he had made. They discussed the news of the day and political events, and that carried him on till dinner time; and he spent the evening as he had the afternoon, until it was time to close. That was a terrible moment for him when he was obliged to go out into the dark, into his empty room full of dreadful recollections, of horrible thoughts, and of mental agony. He no longer saw any of his old friends, none of his relatives, nobody who might remind him of his past life. But as his apartments were a hell to him, he took a room in a large hotel, a good room on the ground floor, so as to see the passers-by. He was no longer alone in that great building. He felt people swarming round him, he heard voices in the adjoining rooms, and when his former sufferings tormented him too much at the sight of his bed, which was turned down, and of his solitary fireplace, he went out into the wide passages and walked up and down them like a sentinel, before all the closed doors, and looked sadly at the shoes standing in couples outside them, women's little boots by the side of men's thick ones, and he thought that, no doubt, all these people were happy, and were sleeping in their warm beds. Five years passed thus; five miserable years. But one day, when he was taking his usual walk between the Madeleine and the Rue Drouot, he suddenly saw a lady whose bearing struck him. A tall gentleman and a child were with her, and all three were walking in front of him. He asked himself where he had seen them before, when suddenly he recognized a movement of her hand; it was his wife, his wife with Limousin and his child, his little George.

His heart beat as if it would suffocate him, but he did not stop, for he wished to see them, and he followed them. They looked like a family of the better middle class. Henriette was leaning on Paul's arm, and speaking to him in a low voice, and looking at him sideways occasionally. Parent got a side view of her and recognized her pretty features, the movements of her lips, her smile, and her coaxing glances. But the child chiefly took up his attention. How tall and strong he was! Parent could not see his face, but only his long, fair curls. That tall boy with bare legs, who was walking by his mother's side like a little man, was George. He saw them suddenly, all three, as they stopped in front of a shop. Limousin had grown very gray, had aged and was thinner; his wife, on the contrary, was as young looking as ever, and had grown stouter. George he would not have recognized, he was so different from what he had been formerly.

They went on again and Parent followed them. He walked on quickly, passed them, and then turned round, so as to meet them face to face. As he passed the child he felt a mad longing to take him into his arms and run off with him, and he knocked against him as if by accident. The boy turned round and looked at the clumsy man angrily, and Parent hurried away, shocked, hurt, and pursued by that look. He went off like a thief, seized with a horrible fear lest he should have been seen and recognized by his wife and her lover. He went to his cafe without stopping, and fell breathless into his chair. That evening he drank three absinthes. For four months he felt the pain of that meeting in his heart. Every night he saw the three again, happy and tranquil, father, mother, and child walking on the boulevard before going in to dinner, and that new vision effaced the old one. It was another matter, another hallucination now, and also a fresh pain. Little George, his little George, the child he had so much loved and so often kissed, disappeared in the far distance, and he saw a new one, like a brother of the first, a little boy with bare legs, who did not know him! He suffered terribly at that thought. The child's love was dead; there was no bond between them; the child would not have held out his arms when he saw him. He had even looked at him angrily.

Then, by degrees he grew calmer, his mental torture diminished, the image that had appeared to his eyes and which haunted his nights became more indistinct and less frequent. He began once more to live nearly like everybody else, like all those idle people who drink beer off marble-topped tables and wear out their clothes on the threadbare velvet of the couches.

He grew old amid the smoke from pipes, lost his hair under the gas lights, looked upon his weekly bath, on his fortnightly visit to the barber's to have his hair cut, and on the purchase of a new coat or hat as an event. When he got to his cafe in a new hat he would look at himself in the glass for a long time before sitting down, and take it off and put it on again several times, and at last ask his friend, the lady at the bar, who was watching him with interest, whether she thought it suited him.

Two or three times a year he went to the theatre, and in the summer he sometimes spent his evenings at one of the open-air concerts in the Champs Elysees. And so the years followed each other slow, monotonous, and short, because they were quite uneventful.

He very rarely now thought of the dreadful drama which had wrecked his life; for twenty years had passed since that terrible evening. But the life he had led since then had worn him out.

The landlord of his cafe would often say to him: "You ought to pull yourself together a little, Monsieur Parent; you should get some fresh air and go into the country. I assure you that you have changed very much within the last few months." And when his customer had gone out be used to say to the barmaid: "That poor Monsieur Parent is booked for another world; it is bad never to get out of Paris. Advise him to go out of town for a day occasionally; he has confidence in you. Summer will soon be here; that will put him straight."

And she, full of pity and kindness for such a regular customer, said to Parent every day: "Come, monsieur, make up your mind to get a little fresh air. It is so charming in the country when the weather is fine. Oh, if I could, I would spend my life there!"

By degrees he was seized with a vague desire to go just once and see whether it was really as pleasant there as she said, outside the walls of the great city. One morning he said to her:

"Do you know where one can get a good luncheon in the neighborhood of Paris?"

"Go to the Terrace at Saint-Germain; it is delightful there!"

He had been there formerly, just when he became engaged. He made up his mind to go there again, and he chose a Sunday, for no special reason, but merely because people generally do go out on Sundays, even when they have nothing to do all the week; and so one Sunday morning he went to Saint-Germain. He felt low-spirited and vexed at having yielded to that new longing, and at having broken through his usual habits. He was thirsty; he would have liked to get out at every station and sit down in the cafe which he saw outside and drink a "bock" or two, and then take the first train back to Paris. The journey seemed very long to him. He could remain sitting for whole days, as long as he had the same motionless objects before his eyes, but he found it very trying and fatiguing to remain sitting while he was being whirled along, and to see the whole country fly by, while he himself was motionless.

However, he found the Seine interesting every time he crossed it. Under the bridge at Chatou he saw some small boats going at great speed under the vigorous strokes of the bare-armed oarsmen, and he thought: "There are some fellows who are certainly enjoying themselves!" The train entered the tunnel just before you get to the station at Saint-Germain, and presently stopped at the platform.

Parent got out, and walked slowly, for he already felt tired, toward the Terrace, with his hands behind his back, and when he got to the iron balustrade, stopped to look at the distant horizon. The immense plain spread out before him vast as the sea, green and studded with large villages, almost as populous as towns. The sun bathed the whole landscape in its full, warm light. The Seine wound like an endless serpent through the plain, flowed round the villages and along the slopes. Parent inhaled the warm breeze, which seemed to make his heart young again, to enliven his spirits, and to vivify his blood, and said to himself:

"Why, it is delightful here."

Then he went on a few steps, and stopped again to look about him. The utter misery of his existence seemed to be brought into full relief by the intense light which inundated the landscape. He saw his twenty years of cafe life—dull, monotonous, heartbreaking. He might have traveled as others did, have gone among foreigners, to unknown countries beyond the sea, have interested himself somewhat in everything which other men are passionately devoted to, in arts and science; he might have enjoyed life in a thousand forms, that mysterious life which is either charming or painful, constantly changing, always inexplicable and strange. Now, however, it was too late. He would go on drinking "bock" after "bock" until he died, without any family, without friends, without hope, without any curiosity about anything, and he was seized with a feeling of misery and a wish to run away, to hide himself in Paris, in his cafe and his lethargy! All the thoughts, all the dreams, all the desires which are dormant in the slough of stagnating hearts had reawakened, brought to life by those rays of sunlight on the plain.

Parent felt that if he were to remain there any longer he should lose his reason, and he made haste to get to the Pavilion Henri IV for lunch, to try and forget his troubles under—the influence of wine and alcohol, and at any rate to have some one to speak to.

He took a small table in one of the arbors, from which one can see all the surrounding country, ordered his lunch, and asked to be served at once. Then some more people arrived and sat down at tables near him. He felt more comfortable; he was no longer alone. Three persons were eating luncheon near him. He looked at them two or three times without seeing them clearly, as one looks at total strangers. Suddenly a woman's voice sent a shiver through him which seemed to penetrate to his very marrow. "George," it said, "will you carve the chicken?"

And another voice replied: "Yes, mamma."

Parent looked up, and he understood; he guessed immediately who those people were! He should certainly not have known them again. His wife had grown quite white and very stout, an elderly, serious, respectable lady, and she held her head forward as she ate for fear of spotting her dress, although she had a table napkin tucked under her chin. George had become a man. He had a slight beard, that uneven and almost colorless beard which adorns the cheeks of youths. He wore a high hat, a white waistcoat, and a monocle, because it looked swell, no doubt. Parent looked at him in astonishment. Was that George, his son? No, he did not know that young man; there could be nothing in common between them. Limousin had his back to him, and was eating; with his shoulders rather bent.

All three of them seemed happy and satisfied; they came and took luncheon in the country at well-known restaurants. They had had a calm and pleasant existence, a family existence in a warm and comfortable house, filled with all those trifles which make life agreeable, with affection, with all those tender words which people exchange continually when they love each other. They had lived thus, thanks to him, Parent, on his money, after having deceived him, robbed him, ruined him! They had condemned him, the innocent, simple-minded, jovial man, to all the miseries of solitude, to that abominable life which he had led, between the pavement and a bar-room, to every mental torture and every physical misery! They had made him a useless, aimless being, a waif in the world, a poor old man without any pleasures, any prospects, expecting nothing from anybody or anything. For him, the world was empty, because he loved nothing in the world. He might go among other nations, or go about the streets, go into all the houses in Paris, open every room, but he would not find inside any door the beloved face, the face of wife or child which smiles when it sees you. This idea worked upon him more than any other, the idea of a door which one opens, to see and to embrace somebody behind it.

And that was the fault of those three wretches! The fault of that worthless woman, of that infamous friend, and of that tall, light-haired lad who put on insolent airs. Now he felt as angry with the child as he did with the other two. Was he not Limousin's son? Would Limousin have kept him and loved him otherwise? Would not Limousin very quickly have got rid of the mother and of the child if he had not felt sure that it was his, positively his? Does anybody bring up other people's children? And now they were there, quite close to him, those three who had made him suffer so much.

Parent looked at them, irritated and excited at the recollection of all his sufferings and of his despair, and was especially exasperated at their placid and satisfied looks. He felt inclined to kill them, to throw his siphon of Seltzer water at them, to split open Limousin's head as he every moment bent it over his plate, raising it again immediately.

He would have his revenge now, on the spot, as he had them under his hand. But how? He tried to think of some means, he pictured such dreadful things as one reads of in the newspapers occasionally, but could not hit on anything practical. And he went on drinking to excite himself, to give himself courage not to allow such an opportunity to escape him, as he might never have another.

Suddenly an idea struck him, a terrible idea; and he left off drinking to mature it. He smiled as he murmured: "I have them, I have them! We will see; we will see!"

They finished their luncheon slowly, conversing with perfect unconcern. Parent could not hear what they were saying, but he saw their quiet gestures. His wife's face especially exasperated him. She had assumed a haughty air, the air of a comfortable, devout woman, of an unapproachable, devout woman, sheathed in principles, iron-clad in virtue. They paid their bill and got up from table. Parent then noticed Limousin. He might have been taken for a retired diplomat, for he looked a man of great importance, with his soft white whiskers, the tips of which touched his coat collar.

They walked away. Parent rose and followed them. First they went up and down the terrace, and calmly admired the landscape, and then they went into the forest. Parent followed them at a distance, hiding himself so as not to excite their suspicion too soon.

Parent came up to them by degrees, breathing hard with emotion and fatigue, for he was unused to walking now. He soon came up to them, but was seized with fear, an inexplicable fear, and he passed them, so as to turn round and meet them face to face.

He walked on, his heart beating, feeling that they were just behind him now, and he said to himself: "Come, now is the time. Courage! courage! Now is the moment!"

He turned round. They were all three sitting on the grass, at the foot of a huge tree, and were still chatting. He made up his mind, and walked back rapidly; stopping in front of them in the middle of the road, he said abruptly, in a voice broken by emotion:

"It is I! Here I am! I suppose you did not expect me?"

They all three stared at this man, who seemed to be insane. He continued:

"One would suppose that you did not know me again. Just look at me! I am Parent, Henri Parent. You thought it was all over, and that you would never see me again. Ah! but here I am once more, you see, and now we will have an explanation."

Henriette, terrified, hid her face in her hands, murmuring: "Oh! Good heavens!"

Seeing this stranger, who seemed to be threatening his mother, George sprang up, ready to seize him by the collar. Limousin, thunderstruck, looked in horror at this apparition, who, after gasping for breath, continued:

"So now we will have an explanation; the proper moment has come! Ah! you deceived me, you condemned me to the life of a convict, and you thought that I should never catch you!"

The young man took him by the shoulders and pushed him back.

"Are you mad?" he asked. "What do you want? Go on your way immediately, or I shall give you a thrashing!"

"What do I want?" replied Parent. "I want to tell you who these people are."

George, however, was in a rage, and shook him; and was even going to strike him.

"Let me go," said Parent. "I am your father. There, see whether they recognize me now, the wretches!"

The young man, thunderstruck, unclenched his fists and turned toward his mother. Parent, as soon as he was released, approached her.

"Well," he said, "tell him yourself who I am! Tell him that my name is Henri Parent, that I am his father because his name is George Parent, because you are my wife, because you are all three living on my money, on the allowance of ten thousand francs which I have made you since I drove you out of my house. Will you tell him also why I drove you out? Because I surprised you with this beggar, this wretch, your lover! Tell him what I was, an honorable man, whom you married for money, and whom you deceived from the very first day. Tell him who you are, and who I am——"

He stammered and gasped for breath in his rage. The woman exclaimed in a heartrending voice:

"Paul, Paul, stop him; make him be quiet! Do not let him say this before my son!"

Limousin had also risen to his feet. He said in a very low voice: "Hold your tongue! Hold your tongue! Do you understand what you are doing?"

"I quite know what I am doing," resumed Parent, "and that is not all. There is one thing that I will know, something that has tormented me for twenty years." Then, turning to George, who was leaning against a tree in consternation, he said:

"Listen to me. When she left my house she thought it was not enough to have deceived me, but she also wanted to drive me to despair. You were my only consolation, and she took you with her, swearing that I was not your father, but, that he was your father. Was she lying? I do not know. I have been asking myself the question for the last twenty years." He went close up to her, tragic and terrible, and, pulling away her hands, with which she had covered her face, he continued:

"Well, now! I call upon you to tell me which of us two is the father of this young man; he or I, your husband or your lover. Come! Come! tell us."

Limousin rushed at him. Parent pushed him back, and, sneering in his fury, he said: "Ah! you are brave now! You are braver than you were that day when you ran downstairs because you thought I was going to murder you. Very well! If she will not reply, tell me yourself. You ought to know as well as she. Tell me, are you this young fellow's father? Come! Come! Tell me!"

He turned to his wife again. "If you will not tell me, at any rate tell your son. He is a man, now, and he has the right to know who his father is. I do not know, and I never did know, never, never! I cannot tell you, my boy."

He seemed to be losing his senses; his voice grew shrill and he worked his arms about as if he had an epileptic 'fit.

"Come! . . . Give me an answer. She does not know . . . I will make a bet that she does not know . . . No . . . she does not know, by Jove! Ha! ha! ha! Nobody knows . . . nobody . . . How can one know such things?

"You will not know either, my boy, you will not know any more than I do . . . never. . . . Look here . . . Ask her you will find that she does not know . . . I do not know either . . . nor does he, nor do you, nobody knows. You can choose . . . You can choose . . . yes, you can choose him or me. . . Choose.

"Good evening . . . It is all over. If she makes up her mind to tell you, you will come and let me know, will you not? I am living at the Hotel des Continents . . . I should be glad to know . . . Good evening . . . I hope you will enjoy yourselves very much . . ."

And he went away gesticulating, talking to himself under the tall trees, in the quiet, the cool air, which was full of the fragrance of growing plants. He did not turn round to look at them, but went straight on, walking under the stimulus of his rage, under a storm of passion, with that one fixed idea in his mind. All at once he found himself outside the station. A train was about to start and he got in. During the journey his anger calmed down, he regained his senses and returned to Paris, astonished at his own boldness, full of aches and pains as if he had broken some bones. Nevertheless, he went to have a "bock" at his brewery.

When she saw him come in, Mademoiselle Zoe asked in surprise: "What! back already? are you tired?"

"Yes—yes, I am tired . . . very tired . . . You know, when one is not used to going out. . . I've had enough of it. I shall not go into the country again. It would have been better to have stayed here. For the future, I shall not stir out."

She could not persuade him to tell her about his little excursion, much as she wished to.

For the first time in his life he got thoroughly drunk that night, and had to be carried home.

QUEEN HORTENSE

In Argenteuil she was called Queen Hortense. No one knew why. Perhaps it was because she had a commanding tone of voice; perhaps because she was tall, bony, imperious; perhaps because she governed a kingdom of servants, chickens, dogs, cats, canaries, parrots, all so dear to an old maid's heart. But she did not spoil these familiar friends; she had for them none of those endearing names, none of the foolish tenderness which women seem to lavish on the soft fur of a purring cat. She governed these beasts with authority; she reigned.

She was indeed an old maid—one of those old maids with a harsh voice and angular motions, whose very soul seems to be hard. She never would stand contradiction, argument, hesitation, indifference, laziness nor fatigue. She had never been heard to complain, to regret anything, to envy anyone. She would say: "Everyone has his share," with the conviction of a fatalist. She did not go to church, she had no use for priests, she hardly believed in God, calling all religious things "weeper's wares."

For thirty years she had lived in her little house, with its tiny garden running along the street; she had never changed her habits, only changing her servants pitilessly, as soon as they reached twenty-one years of age.

When her dogs, cats and birds would die of old age, or from an accident, she would replace them without tears and without regret; with a little spade she would bury the dead animal in a strip of ground, throwing a few shovelfuls of earth over it and stamping it down with her feet in an indifferent manner.

She had a few friends in town, families of clerks who went to Paris every day. Once in a while she would be invited out, in the evening, to tea. She would inevitably fall asleep, and she would have to be awakened, when it was time for her to go home. She never allowed anyone to accompany her, fearing neither light nor darkness. She did not appear to like children.

She kept herself busy doing countless masculine tasks—carpentering, gardening, sawing or chopping wood, even laying bricks when it was necessary.

She had relatives who came to see her twice a year, the Cimmes and the Colombels, her two sisters having married, one of them a florist and the other a retired merchant. The Cimmes had no children; the Colombels had three: Henri, Pauline and Joseph. Henri was twenty, Pauline seventeen and Joseph only three.

There was no love lost between the old maid and her relatives.

In the spring of the year 1882 Queen Hortense suddenly fell sick. The neighbors called in a physician, whom she immediately drove out. A priest then having presented himself, she jumped out of bed, in order to throw him out of the house.

The young servant, in despair, was brewing her some tea.

After lying in bed for three days the situation appeared so serious that the barrel-maker, who lived next door, to the right, acting on advice from the doctor, who had forcibly returned to the house, took it upon himself to call together the two families.

They arrived by the same train, towards ten in the morning, the Colombels bringing little Joseph with them.

When they got to the garden gate, they saw the servant seated in the chair against the wall, crying.

The dog was sleeping on the door mat in the broiling sun; two cats, which looked as though they might be dead, were stretched out in front of the two windows, their eyes closed, their paws and tails stretched out at full length.

A big clucking hen was parading through the garden with a whole regiment of yellow, downy chicks, and a big cage hanging from the wall and covered with pimpernel, contained a population of birds which were chirping away in the warmth of this beautiful spring morning.

In another cage, shaped like a chalet, two lovebirds sat motionless side by side on their perch.

M. Cimme, a fat, puffing person, who always entered first everywhere, pushing aside everyone else, whether man or woman, when it was necessary, asked:

"Well, Celeste, aren't things going well?"

The little servant moaned through her tears:

"She doesn't even recognize me any more. The doctor says it's the end."

Everybody looked around.

Mme. Cimme and Mme. Colombel immediately embraced each other, without saying a word. They looked very much alike, having always worn their hair in Madonna bands, and loud red French cashmere shawls.

Cimme turned to his brother-in-law, a pale, sallow-complexioned, thin man, wasted by stomach complaints, who limped badly, and said in a serious tone of voice:

"Gad! It was high time."

But no one dared to enter the dying woman's room on the ground floor. Even Cimme made way for the others. Colombel was the first to make up his mind, and, swaying from side to side like the mast of a ship, the iron ferule of his cane clattering on the paved hall, he entered.

The two women were the next to venture, and M. Cimmes closed the procession.

Little Joseph had remained outside, pleased at the sight of the dog.

A ray of sunlight seemed to cut the bed in two, shining just on the hands, which were moving nervously, continually opening and closing. The fingers were twitching as though moved by some thought, as though trying to point out a meaning or idea, as though obeying the dictates of a will. The rest of the body lay motionless under the sheets. The angular frame showed not a single movement. The eyes remained closed.

The family spread out in a semi-circle and, without a word, they began to watch the contracted chest and the short, gasping breathing. The little servant had followed them and was still crying.

At last Cimme asked:

"Exactly what did the doctor say?"

The girl stammered:

"He said to leave her alone, that nothing more could be done for her."

But suddenly the old woman's lips began to move. She seemed to be uttering silent words, words hidden in the brain of this dying being, and her hands quickened their peculiar movements.

Then she began to speak in a thin, high voice, which no one had ever heard, a voice which seemed to come from the distance, perhaps from the depths of this heart which had always been closed.

Cimme, finding this scene painful, walked away on tiptoe. Colombel, whose crippled leg was growing tired, sat down.

The two women remained standing.

Queen Hortense was now babbling away, and no one could understand a word. She was pronouncing names, many names, tenderly calling imaginary people.

"Come here, Philippe, kiss your mother. Tell me, child, do you love your mamma? You, Rose, take care of your little sister while I am away. And don't leave her alone. Don't play with matches!"

She stopped for a while, then, in a louder voice, as though she were calling someone: "Henriette!" then waited a moment and continued:

"Tell your father that I wish to speak to him before he goes to business." And suddenly: "I am not feeling very well to-day, darling; promise not to come home late. Tell your employer that I am sick. You know, it isn't safe to leave the children alone when I am in bed. For dinner I will fix you up a nice dish of rice. The little ones like that very much. Won't Claire be happy?"

And she broke into a happy, joyous laugh, such as they had never heard: "Look at Jean, how funny he looks! He has smeared jam all over his face, the little pig! Look, sweetheart, look; isn't he funny?"

Colombel, who was continually lifting his tired leg from place to place, muttered:

"She is dreaming that she has children and a husband; it is the beginning of the death agony."

The two sisters had not yet moved, surprised, astounded.

The little maid exclaimed:

"You must take off your shawls and your hats! Would you like to go into the parlor?"

They went out without having said a word. And Colombel followed them, limping, once more leaving the dying woman alone.

When they were relieved of their travelling garments, the women finally sat down. Then one of the cats left its window, stretched, jumped into the room and on to Mme. Cimme's knees. She began to pet it.

In the next room could be heard the voice of the dying woman, living, in this last hour, the life for which she had doubtless hoped, living her dreams themselves just when all was over for her.

Cimme, in the garden, was playing with little Joseph and the dog, enjoying himself in the whole hearted manner of a countryman, having completely forgotten the dying woman.

But suddenly he entered the house and said to the girl:

"I say, my girl, are we not going to have luncheon? What do you ladies wish to eat?"

They finally agreed on an omelet, a piece of steak with new potatoes, cheese and coffee.

As Mme. Colombel was fumbling in her pocket for her purse, Cimme stopped her, and, turning to the maid: "Have you got any money?"

She answered:

"Yes, monsieur."

"How much?"

"Fifteen francs."

"That's enough. Hustle, my girl, because I am beginning to get very hungry."

Mme. Cimme, looking out over the climbing vines bathed in sunlight, and at the two turtle-doves on the roof opposite, said in an annoyed tone of voice:

"What a pity to have had to come for such a sad occasion. It is so nice in the country to-day."

Her sister sighed without answering, and Colombel mumbled, thinking perhaps of the walk ahead of him:

"My leg certainly is bothering me to-day."

Little Joseph and the dog were making a terrible noise; one was shrieking with pleasure, the other was barking wildly. They were playing hide-and-seek around the three flower beds, running after each other like mad.

The dying woman continued to call her children, talking with each one, imagining that she was dressing them, fondling them, teaching them how to read: "Come on! Simon repeat: A, B, C, D. You are not paying attention, listen—D, D, D; do you hear me? Now repeat—"

Cimme exclaimed: "Funny what people say when in that condition."

Mme. Colombel then asked:

"Wouldn't it be better if we were to return to her?"

But Cimme dissuaded her from the idea:

"What's the use? You can't change anything. We are just as comfortable here."

Nobody insisted. Mme. Cimme observed the two green birds called love-birds. In a few words she praised this singular faithfulness and blamed the men for not imitating these animals. Cimme began to laugh, looked at his wife and hummed in a teasing way: "Tra-la-la, tra-la-la" as though to cast a good deal of doubt on his own, Cimme's, faithfulness:

Colombel was suffering from cramps and was rapping the floor with his cane.

The other cat, its tail pointing upright to the sky, now came in.

They sat down to luncheon at one o'clock.

As soon as he had tasted the wine, Colombel, for whom only the best of Bordeaux had been prescribed, called the servant back:

"I say, my girl, is this the best stuff that you have in the cellar?"

"No, monsieur; there is some better wine, which was only brought out when you came."

"Well, bring us three bottles of it."

They tasted the wine and found it excellent, not because it was of a remarkable vintage, but because it had been in the cellar fifteen years. Cimme declared:

"That is regular invalid's wine."

Colombel, filled with an ardent desire to gain possession of this Bordeaux, once more questioned the girl:

"How much of it is left?"

"Oh! Almost all, monsieur; mamz'elle never touched it. It's in the bottom stack."

Then he turned to his brother-in-law:

"If you wish, Cimme, I would be willing to exchange something else for this wine; it suits my stomach marvellously."

The chicken had now appeared with its regiment of young ones. The two women were enjoying themselves throwing crumbs to them.

Joseph and the dog, who had eaten enough, were sent back to the garden.

Queen Hortense was still talking, but in a low, hushed voice, so that the words could no longer be distinguished.

When they had finished their coffee all went in to observe the condition of the sick woman. She seemed calm.

They went outside again and seated themselves in a circle in the garden, in order to complete their digestion.

Suddenly the dog, who was carrying something in his mouth, began to run around the chairs at full speed. The child was chasing him wildly. Both disappeared into the house.

Cimme fell asleep, his well-rounded paunch bathed in the glow of the shining sun.

The dying woman once more began to talk in a loud voice. Then suddenly she shrieked.

The two women and Colombel rushed in to see what was the matter. Cimme, waking up, did not budge, because, he did not wish to witness such a scene.

She was sitting up, with haggard eyes. Her dog, in order to escape being pursued by little Joseph, had jumped up on the bed, run over the sick woman, and entrenched behind the pillow, was looking down at his playmate with snapping eyes, ready to jump down and begin the game again. He was holding in his mouth one of his mistress' slippers, which he had torn to pieces and with which he had been playing for the last hour.

The child, frightened by this woman who had suddenly risen in front of him, stood motionless before the bed.

The hen had also come in, and frightened by the noise, had jumped up on a chair and was wildly calling her chicks, who were chirping distractedly around the four legs of the chair.

Queen Hortense was shrieking:

"No, no, I don't want to die, I don't want to! I don't want to! Who will bring up my children? Who will take care of them? Who will love them? No, I don't want to!—I don't——"

She fell back. All was over.

The dog, wild with excitement, jumped about the room, barking.

Colombel ran to the window, calling his brother-in-law:

"Hurry up, hurry up! I think that she has just gone."

Then Cimme, resigned, arose and entered the room, mumbling

"It didn't take as long as I thought it would!"

TIMBUCTOO

The boulevard, that river of humanity, was alive with people in the golden light of the setting sun. The whole sky was red, blinding, and behind the Madeleine an immense bank of flaming clouds cast a shower of light the whole length of the boulevard, vibrant as the heat from a brazier.

The gay, animated crowd went by in this golden mist and seemed to be glorified. Their faces were gilded, their black hats and clothes took on purple tints, the patent leather of their shoes cast bright reflections on the asphalt of the sidewalk.

Before the cafes a mass of men were drinking opalescent liquids that looked like precious stones dissolved in the glasses.

In the midst of the drinkers two officers in full uniform dazzled all eyes with their glittering gold lace. They chatted, happy without asking why, in this glory of life, in this radiant light of sunset, and they looked at the crowd, the leisurely men and the hurrying women who left a bewildering odor of perfume as they passed by.

All at once an enormous negro, dressed in black, with a paunch beneath his jean waistcoat, which was covered with charms, his face shining as if it had been polished, passed before them with a triumphant air. He laughed at the passers-by, at the news venders, at the dazzling sky, at the whole of Paris. He was so tall that he overtopped everyone else, and when he passed all the loungers turned round to look at his back.

But he suddenly perceived the officers and darted towards them, jostling the drinkers in his path. As soon as he reached their table he fixed his gleaming and delighted eyes upon them and the corners of his mouth expanded to his ears, showing his dazzling white teeth like a crescent moon in a black sky. The two men looked in astonishment at this ebony giant, unable to understand his delight.

With a voice that made all the guests laugh, he said:

"Good-day, my lieutenant."

One of the officers was commander of a battalion, the other was a colonel. The former said:

"I do not know you, sir. I am at a loss to know what you want of me."

"Me like you much, Lieutenant Vedie, siege of Bezi, much grapes, find me."

The officer, utterly bewildered, looked at the man intently, trying to refresh his memory. Then he cried abruptly:

"Timbuctoo?"

The negro, radiant, slapped his thigh as he uttered a tremendous laugh and roared:

"Yes, yes, my lieutenant; you remember Timbuctoo, ya. How do you do?"

The commandant held out his hand, laughing heartily as he did so. Then Timbuctoo became serious. He seized the officer's hand and, before the other could prevent it, he kissed it, according to negro and Arab custom. The officer embarrassed, said in a severe tone:

"Come now, Timbuctoo, we are not in Africa. Sit down there and tell me how it is I find you here."

Timbuctoo swelled himself out and, his words falling over one another, replied hurriedly:

"Make much money, much, big restaurant, good food; Prussians, me, much steal, much, French cooking; Timbuctoo cook to the emperor; two thousand francs mine. Ha, ha, ha, ha!"

And he laughed, doubling himself up, roaring, with wild delight in his glances.

When the officer, who understood his strange manner of expressing himself, had questioned him he said:

"Well, au revoir, Timbuctoo. I will see you again."

The negro rose, this time shaking the hand that was extended to him and, smiling still, cried:

"Good-day, good-day, my lieutenant!"

He went off so happy that he gesticulated as he walked, and people thought he was crazy.

"Who is that brute?" asked the colonel.

"A fine fellow and a brave soldier. I will tell you what I know about him. It is funny enough.

"You know that at the commencement of the war of 1870 I was shut up in Bezieres, that this negro calls Bezi. We were not besieged, but blockaded. The Prussian lines surrounded us on all sides, outside the reach of cannon, not firing on us, but slowly starving us out.

"I was then lieutenant. Our garrison consisted of soldier of all descriptions, fragments of slaughtered regiments, some that had run away, freebooters separated from the main army, etc. We had all kinds, in fact even eleven Turcos [Algerian soldiers in the service of France], who arrived one evening no one knew whence or how. They appeared at the gates of the city, exhausted, in rags, starving and dirty. They were handed over to me.

"I saw very soon that they were absolutely undisciplined, always in the street and always drunk. I tried putting them in the police station, even in prison, but nothing was of any use. They would disappear, sometimes for days at a time, as if they had been swallowed up by the earth, and then come back staggering drunk. They had no money. Where did they buy drink and how and with what?

"This began to worry me greatly, all the more as these savages interested me with their everlasting laugh and their characteristics of overgrown frolicsome children.

"I then noticed that they blindly obeyed the largest among them, the one you have just seen. He made them do as he pleased, planned their mysterious expeditions with the all-powerful and undisputed authority of a leader. I sent for him and questioned him. Our conversation lasted fully three hours, for it was hard for me to understand his remarkable gibberish. As for him, poor devil, he made unheard-of efforts to make himself intelligible, invented words, gesticulated, perspired in his anxiety, mopping his forehead, puffing, stopping and abruptly beginning again when he thought he had found a new method of explaining what he wanted to say.

"I gathered finally that he was the son of a big chief, a sort of negro king of the region around Timbuctoo. I asked him his name. He repeated something like 'Chavaharibouhalikranafotapolara.' It seemed simpler to me to give him the name of his native place, 'Timbuctoo.' And a week later he was known by no other name in the garrison.

"But we were all wildly anxious to find out where this African ex-prince procured his drinks. I discovered it in a singular manner.

"I was on the ramparts one morning, watching the horizon, when I perceived something moving about in a vineyard. It was near the time of vintage, the grapes were ripe, but I was not thinking of that. I thought that a spy was approaching the town, and I organized a complete expedition to catch the prowler. I took command myself, after obtaining permission from the general.

"I sent out by three different gates three little companies, which were to meet at the suspected vineyard and form a cordon round it. In order to cut off the spy's retreat, one of these detachments had to make at least an hour's march. A watch on the walls signalled to me that the person I had seen had not left the place. We went along in profound silence, creeping, almost crawling, along the ditches. At last we reached the spot assigned.

"I abruptly disbanded my soldiers, who darted into the vineyard and found Timbuctoo on hands and knees travelling around among the vines and eating grapes, or rather devouring them as a dog eats his sop, snatching them in mouthfuls from the vine with his teeth.

"I wanted him to get up, but he could not think of it. I then understood why he was crawling on his hands and knees. As soon as we stood him on his feet he began to wabble, then stretched out his arms and fell down on his nose. He was more drunk than I have ever seen anyone.

"They brought him home on two poles. He never stopped laughing all the way back, gesticulating with his arms and legs.

"This explained the mystery. My men also drank the juice of the grapes, and when they were so intoxicated they could not stir they went to sleep in the vineyard. As for Timbuctoo, his love of the vineyard was beyond all belief and all bounds. He lived in it as did the thrushes, whom he hated with the jealous hate of a rival. He repeated incessantly: 'The thrushes eat all the grapes, captain!'

"One evening I was sent for. Something had been seen on the plain coming in our direction. I had not brought my field-glass and I could not distinguish things clearly. It looked like a great serpent uncoiling itself—a convoy. How could I tell?

"I sent some men to meet this strange caravan, which presently made its triumphal entry. Timbuctoo and nine of his comrades were carrying on a sort of altar made of camp stools eight severed, grinning and bleeding heads. The African was dragging along a horse to whose tail another head was fastened, and six other animals followed, adorned in the same manner.

"This is what I learned: Having started out to the vineyard, my Africans had suddenly perceived a detachment of Prussians approaching a village. Instead of taking to their heels, they hid themselves, and as soon as the Prussian officers dismounted at an inn to refresh themselves, the eleven rascals rushed on them, put to flight the lancers, who thought they were being attacked by the main army, killed the two sentries, then the colonel and the five officers of his escort.

"That day I kissed Timbuctoo. I saw, however, that he walked with difficulty and thought he was wounded. He laughed and said: "'Me provisions for my country.'

"Timbuctoo was not fighting for glory, but for gain. Everything he found that seemed to him to be of the slightest value, especially anything that glistened, he put in his pocket. What a pocket! An abyss that began at his hips and reached to his ankles. He had retained an old term used by the troopers and called it his 'profonde,' and it was his 'profonde' in fact.

"He had taken the gold lace off the Prussian uniforms, the brass off their helmets, detached their buttons, etc., and had thrown them all into his 'profonde,' which was full to overflowing.

"Each day he pocketed every glistening object that came beneath his observation, pieces of tin or pieces of silver, and sometimes his contour was very comical.

"He intended to carry all that back to the land of ostriches, whose brother he might have been, this son of a king, tormented with the longing to gobble up all objects that glistened. If he had not had his 'profonde' what would he have done? He doubtless would have swallowed them.

"Each morning his pocket was empty. He had, then, some general store where his riches were piled up. But where? I could not discover it.

"The general, on being informed of Timbuctoo's mighty act of valor, had the headless bodies that had been left in the neighboring village interred at once, that it might not be discovered that they were decapitated. The Prussians returned thither the following day. The mayor and seven prominent inhabitants were shot on the spot, by way of reprisal, as having denounced the Prussians.

"Winter was here. We were exhausted and desperate. There were skirmishes now every day. The famished men could no longer march. The eight 'Turcos' alone (three had been killed) remained fat and shiny, vigorous and always ready to fight. Timbuctoo was even getting fatter. He said to me one day:

"'You much hungry; me good meat.'

"And he brought me an excellent filet. But of what? We had no more cattle, nor sheep, nor goats, nor donkeys, nor pigs. It was impossible to get a horse. I thought of all this after I had devoured my meat. Then a horrible idea came to me. These negroes were born close to a country where they eat human beings! And each day such a number of soldiers were killed around the town! I questioned Timbuctoo. He would not answer. I did not insist, but from that time on I declined his presents.

"He worshipped me. One night snow took us by surprise at the outposts. We were seated, on the ground. I looked with pity at those poor negroes shivering beneath this white frozen shower. I was very cold and began to cough. At once I felt something fall on me like a large warm quilt. It was Timbuctoo's cape that he had thrown on my shoulders.

"I rose and returned his garment, saying:

"'Keep it, my boy; you need it more than I do.'

"'Non, my lieutenant, for you; me no need. Me hot, hot!'

"And he looked at me entreatingly.

"'Come, obey orders. Keep your cape; I insist,' I replied.

"He then stood up, drew his sword, which he had sharpened to an edge like a scythe, and holding in his other hand the large cape which I had refused, said:

"'If you not keep cape, me cut. No one cape.'

"And he would have done it. So I yielded.

"Eight days later we capitulated. Some of us had been able to escape, the rest were to march out of the town and give themselves up to the conquerors.

"I went towards the exercising ground, where we were all to meet, when I was dumfounded at the sight of a gigantic negro dressed in white duck and wearing a straw hat. It was Timbuctoo. He was beaming and was walking with his hands in his pockets in front of a little shop where two plates and two glasses were displayed.

"'What are you doing?' I said.

"'Me not go. Me good cook; me make food for Colonel Algeria. Me eat Prussians; much steal, much.'

"There were ten degrees of frost. I shivered at sight of this negro in white duck. He took me by the arm and made me go inside. I noticed an immense flag that he was going to place outside his door as soon as we had left, for he had some shame."

I read this sign, traced by the hand of some accomplice

"'ARMY KITCHEN OF M. TIMBUCTOO,

"'Formerly Cook to H. M. the Emperor.

"'A Parisian Artist. Moderate Prices.'

"In spite of the despair that was gnawing at my heart, I could not help laughing, and I left my negro to his new enterprise.

"Was not that better than taking him prisoner?

"You have just seen that he made a success of it, the rascal.

"Bezieres to-day belongs to the Germans. The 'Restaurant Timbuctoo' is the beginning of a retaliation."

TOMBSTONES

The five friends had finished dinner, five men of the world, mature, rich, three married, the two others bachelors. They met like this every month in memory of their youth, and after dinner they chatted until two o'clock in the morning. Having remained intimate friends, and enjoying each other's society, they probably considered these the pleasantest evenings of their lives. They talked on every subject, especially of what interested and amused Parisians. Their conversation was, as in the majority of salons elsewhere, a verbal rehash of what they had read in the morning papers.

One of the most lively of them was Joseph de Bardon, a celibate living the Parisian life in its fullest and most whimsical manner. He was not a debauche nor depraved, but a singular, happy fellow, still young, for he was scarcely forty. A man of the world in its widest and best sense, gifted with a brilliant, but not profound, mind, with much varied knowledge, but no true erudition, ready comprehension without true understanding, he drew from his observations, his adventures, from everything he saw, met with and found, anecdotes at once comical and philosophical, and made humorous remarks that gave him a great reputation for cleverness in society.

He was the after dinner speaker and had his own story each time, upon which they counted, and he talked without having to be coaxed.

As he sat smoking, his elbows on the table, a petit verre half full beside his plate, half torpid in an atmosphere of tobacco blended with steaming coffee, he seemed to be perfectly at home. He said between two whiffs:

"A curious thing happened to me some time ago."

"Tell it to us," they all exclaimed at once.

"With pleasure. You know that I wander about Paris a great deal, like book collectors who ransack book stalls. I just look at the sights, at the people, at all that is passing by and all that is going on.

"Toward the middle of September—it was beautiful weather—I went out one afternoon, not knowing where I was going. One always has a vague wish to call on some pretty woman or other. One chooses among them in one's mental picture gallery, compares them in one's mind, weighs the interest with which they inspire you, their comparative charms and finally decides according to the influence of the day. But when the sun is very bright and the air warm, it takes away from you all desire to make calls.

"The sun was bright, the air warm. I lighted a cigar and sauntered aimlessly along the outer boulevard. Then, as I strolled on, it occurred to me to walk as far as Montmartre and go into the cemetery.

"I am very fond of cemeteries. They rest me and give me a feeling of sadness; I need it. And, besides, I have good friends in there, those that one no longer goes to call on, and I go there from time to time.

"It is in this cemetery of Montmartre that is buried a romance of my life, a sweetheart who made a great impression on me, a very emotional, charming little woman whose memory, although it causes me great sorrow, also fills me with regrets—regrets of all kinds. And I go to dream beside her grave. She has finished with life.

"And then I like cemeteries because they are immense cities filled to overflowing with inhabitants. Think how many dead people there are in this small space, think of all the generations of Parisians who are housed there forever, veritable troglodytes enclosed in their little vaults, in their little graves covered with a stone or marked by a cross, while living beings take up so much room and make so much noise—imbeciles that they are!

"Then, again, in cemeteries there are monuments almost as interesting as in museums. The tomb of Cavaignac reminded me, I must confess without making any comparison, of the chef d'oeuvre of Jean Goujon: the recumbent statue of Louis de Breze in the subterranean chapel of the Cathedral of Rouen. All modern and realistic art has originated there, messieurs. This dead man, Louis de Breze, is more real, more terrible, more like inanimate flesh still convulsed with the death agony than all the tortured corpses that are distorted to-day in funeral monuments.

"But in Montmartre one can yet admire Baudin's monument, which has a degree of grandeur; that of Gautier, of Murger, on which I saw the other day a simple, paltry wreath of immortelles, yellow immortelles, brought thither by whom? Possibly by the last grisette, very old and now janitress in the neighborhood. It is a pretty little statue by Millet, but ruined by dirt and neglect. Sing of youth, O Murger!

"Well, there I was in Montmartre Cemetery, and was all at once filled with sadness, a sadness that is not all pain, a kind of sadness that makes you think when you are in good health, 'This place is not amusing, but my time has not come yet.'

"The feeling of autumn, of the warm moisture which is redolent of the death of the leaves, and the weakened, weary, anaemic sun increased, while rendering it poetical, the sensation of solitude and of finality that hovered over this spot which savors of human mortality.

"I walked along slowly amid these streets of tombs, where the neighbors do not visit each other, do not sleep together and do not read the newspapers. And I began to read the epitaphs. That is the most amusing thing in the world. Never did Labiche or Meilhac make me laugh as I have laughed at the comical inscriptions on tombstones. Oh, how much superior to the books of Paul de Kock for getting rid of the spleen are these marble slabs and these crosses where the relatives of the deceased have unburdened their sorrow, their desires for the happiness of the vanished ones and their hope of rejoining them—humbugs!

"But I love above all in this cemetery the deserted portion, solitary, full of great yews and cypresses, the older portion, belonging to those dead long since, and which will soon be taken into use again; the growing trees nourished by the human corpses cut down in order to bury in rows beneath little slabs of marble those who have died more recently.

"When I had sauntered about long enough to refresh my mind I felt that I would soon have had enough of it and that I must place the faithful homage of my remembrance on my little friend's last resting place. I felt a tightening of the heart as I reached her grave. Poor dear, she was so dainty, so loving and so white and fresh—and now—if one should open the grave—

"Leaning over the iron grating, I told her of my sorrow in a low tone, which she doubtless did not hear, and was moving away when I saw a woman in black, in deep mourning, kneeling on the next grave. Her crape veil was turned back, uncovering a pretty fair head, the hair in Madonna bands looking like rays of dawn beneath her sombre headdress. I stayed.

"Surely she must be in profound grief. She had covered her face with her hands and, standing there in meditation, rigid as a statue, given up to her grief, telling the sad rosary of her remembrances within the shadow of her concealed and closed eyes, she herself seemed like a dead person mourning another who was dead. All at once a little motion of her back, like a flutter of wind through a willow, led me to suppose that she was going to cry. She wept softly at first, then louder, with quick motions of her neck and shoulders. Suddenly she uncovered her eyes. They were full of tears and charming, the eyes of a bewildered woman, with which she glanced about her as if awaking from a nightmare. She looked at me, seemed abashed and hid her face completely in her hands. Then she sobbed convulsively, and her head slowly bent down toward the marble. She leaned her forehead on it, and her veil spreading around her, covered the white corners of the beloved tomb, like a fresh token of mourning. I heard her sigh, then she sank down with her cheek on the marble slab and remained motionless, unconscious.

"I darted toward her, slapped her hands, blew on her eyelids, while I read this simple epitaph: 'Here lies Louis-Theodore Carrel, Captain of Marine Infantry, killed by the enemy at Tonquin. Pray for him.'

"He had died some months before. I was affected to tears and redoubled my attentions. They were successful. She regained consciousness. I appeared very much moved. I am not bad looking, I am not forty. I saw by her first glance that she would be polite and grateful. She was, and amid more tears she told me her history in detached fragments as well as her gasping breath would allow, how the officer was killed at Tonquin when they had been married a year, how she had married him for love, and being an orphan, she had only the usual dowry.

"I consoled her, I comforted her, raised her and lifted her on her feet. Then I said:

"'Do not stay here. Come.'

"'I am unable to walk,' she murmured.

"'I will support you.'

"'Thank you, sir; you are good. Did you also come to mourn for some one?'

"'Yes, madame.'

"'A dead friend?'

"'Yes, madame.'

"'Your wife?'

"'A friend.'

"'One may love a friend as much as they love their wife. Love has no law.'

"'Yes, madame.'

"And we set off together, she leaning on my arm, while I almost carried her along the paths of the cemetery. When we got outside she faltered:

"'I feel as if I were going to be ill.'

"'Would you like to go in anywhere, to take something?'

"'Yes, monsieur.'

"I perceived a restaurant, one of those places where the mourners of the dead go to celebrate the funeral. We went in. I made her drink a cup of hot tea, which seemed to revive her. A faint smile came to her lips. She began to talk about herself. It was sad, so sad to be always alone in life, alone in one's home, night and day, to have no one on whom one can bestow affection, confidence, intimacy.

"That sounded sincere. It sounded pretty from her mouth. I was touched. She was very young, perhaps twenty. I paid her compliments, which she took in good part. Then, as time was passing, I suggested taking her home in a carriage. She accepted, and in the cab we sat so close that our shoulders touched.

"When the cab stopped at her house she murmured: 'I do not feel equal to going upstairs alone, for I live on the fourth floor. You have been so good. Will you let me take your arm as far as my own door?'

"I agreed with eagerness. She ascended the stairs slowly, breathing hard. Then, as we stood at her door, she said:

"'Come in a few moments so that I may thank you.'

"And, by Jove, I went in. Everything was modest, even rather poor, but simple and in good taste.

"We sat down side by side on a little sofa and she began to talk again about her loneliness. She rang for her maid, in order to offer me some wine. The maid did not come. I was delighted, thinking that this maid probably came in the morning only, what one calls a charwoman.

"She had taken off her hat. She was really pretty, and she gazed at me with her clear eyes, gazed so hard and her eyes were so clear that I was terribly tempted. I caught her in my arms and rained kisses on her eyelids, which she closed suddenly.

"She freed herself and pushed me away, saying:

"'Have done, have done.'

"But I next kissed her on the mouth and she did not resist, and as our glances met after thus outraging the memory of the captain killed in Tonquin, I saw that she had a languid, resigned expression that set my mind at rest.

"I became very attentive and, after chatting for some time, I said:

"'Where do you dine?'

"'In a little restaurant in the neighborhood:

"'All alone?'

"'Why, yes.'

"'Will you dine with me?'

"'Where?'

"'In a good restaurant on the Boulevard.'

"She demurred a little. I insisted. She yielded, saying by way of apology to herself: 'I am so lonely—so lonely.' Then she added:

"'I must put on something less sombre, and went into her bedroom. When she reappeared she was dressed in half-mourning, charming, dainty and slender in a very simple gray dress. She evidently had a costume for the cemetery and one for the town.

"The dinner was very enjoyable. She drank some champagne, brightened up, grew lively and I went home with her.

"This friendship, begun amid the tombs, lasted about three weeks. But one gets tired of everything, especially of women. I left her under pretext of an imperative journey. She made me promise that I would come and see her on my return. She seemed to be really rather attached to me.

"Other things occupied my attention, and it was about a month before I thought much about this little cemetery friend. However, I did not forget her. The recollection of her haunted me like a mystery, like a psychological problem, one of those inexplicable questions whose solution baffles us.

"I do not know why, but one day I thought I might possibly meet her in the Montmartre Cemetery, and I went there.

"I walked about a long time without meeting any but the ordinary visitors to this spot, those who have not yet broken off all relations with their dead. The grave of the captain killed at Tonquin had no mourner on its marble slab, no flowers, no wreath.

"But as I wandered in another direction of this great city of the dead I perceived suddenly, at the end of a narrow avenue of crosses, a couple in deep mourning walking toward me, a man and a woman. Oh, horrors! As they approached I recognized her. It was she!

"She saw me, blushed, and as I brushed past her she gave me a little signal, a tiny little signal with her eye, which meant: 'Do not recognize me!' and also seemed to say, 'Come back to see me again, my dear!'

"The man was a gentleman, distingue, chic, an officer of the Legion of Honor, about fifty years old. He was supporting her as I had supported her myself when we were leaving the cemetery.

"I went my way, filled with amazement, asking myself what this all meant, to what race of beings belonged this huntress of the tombs? Was she just a common girl, one who went to seek among the tombs for men who were in sorrow, haunted by the recollection of some woman, a wife or a sweetheart, and still troubled by the memory of vanished caresses? Was she unique? Are there many such? Is it a profession? Do they parade the cemetery as they parade the street? Or else was she only impressed with the admirable, profoundly philosophical idea of exploiting love recollections, which are revived in these funereal places?

"And I would have liked to know whose widow she was on that special day."

MADEMOISELLE PEARL

I

What a strange idea it was for me to choose Mademoiselle Pearl for queen that evening!

Every year I celebrate Twelfth Night with my old friend Chantal. My father, who was his most intimate friend, used to take me round there when I was a child. I continued the custom, and I doubtless shall continue it as long as I live and as long as there is a Chantal in this world.

The Chantals lead a peculiar existence; they live in Paris as though they were in Grasse, Evetot, or Pont-a-Mousson.

They have a house with a little garden near the observatory. They live there as though they were in the country. Of Paris, the real Paris, they know nothing at all, they suspect nothing; they are so far, so far away! However, from time to time, they take a trip into it. Mademoiselle Chantal goes to lay in her provisions, as it is called in the family. This is how they go to purchase their provisions:

Mademoiselle Pearl, who has the keys to the kitchen closet (for the linen closets are administered by the mistress herself), Mademoiselle Pearl gives warning that the supply of sugar is low, that the preserves are giving out, that there is not much left in the bottom of the coffee bag. Thus warned against famine, Mademoiselle Chantal passes everything in review, taking notes on a pad. Then she puts down a lot of figures and goes through lengthy calculations and long discussions with Mademoiselle Pearl. At last they manage to agree, and they decide upon the quantity of each thing of which they will lay in a three months' provision; sugar, rice, prunes, coffee, preserves, cans of peas, beans, lobster, salt or smoked fish, etc., etc. After which the day for the purchasing is determined on and they go in a cab with a railing round the top and drive to a large grocery store on the other side of the river in the new sections of the town.

Madame Chantal and Mademoiselle Pearl make this trip together, mysteriously, and only return at dinner time, tired out, although still excited, and shaken up by the cab, the roof of which is covered with bundles and bags, like an express wagon.

For the Chantals all that part of Paris situated on the other side of the Seine constitutes the new quarter, a section inhabited by a strange, noisy population, which cares little for honor, spends its days in dissipation, its nights in revelry, and which throws money out of the windows. From time to time, however, the young girls are taken to the Opera-Comique or the Theatre Francais, when the play is recommended by the paper which is read by M. Chantal.

At present the young ladies are respectively nineteen and seventeen. They are two pretty girls, tall and fresh, very well brought up, in fact, too well brought up, so much so that they pass by unperceived like two pretty dolls. Never would the idea come to me to pay the slightest attention or to pay court to one of the young Chantal ladies; they are so immaculate that one hardly dares speak to them; one almost feels indecent when bowing to them.

As for the father, he is a charming man, well educated, frank, cordial, but he likes calm and quiet above all else, and has thus contributed greatly to the mummifying of his family in order to live as he pleased in stagnant quiescence. He reads a lot, loves to talk and is readily affected. Lack of contact and of elbowing with the world has made his moral skin very tender and sensitive. The slightest thing moves him, excites him, and makes him suffer.

The Chantals have limited connections carefully chosen in the neighborhood. They also exchange two or three yearly visits with relatives who live in the distance.

As for me, I take dinner with them on the fifteenth of August and on Twelfth Night. That is as much one of my duties as Easter communion is for a Catholic.

On the fifteenth of August a few friends are invited, but on Twelfth Night I am the only stranger.

Well, this year, as every former year, I went to the Chantals' for my Epiphany dinner.

According to my usual custom, I kissed M. Chantal, Madame Chantal and Mademoiselle Pearl, and I made a deep bow to the Misses Louise and Pauline. I was questioned about a thousand and one things, about what had happened on the boulevards, about politics, about how matters stood in Tong-King, and about our representatives in Parliament. Madame Chantal, a fat lady, whose ideas always gave me the impression of being carved out square like building stones, was accustomed to exclaiming at the end of every political discussion: "All that is seed which does not promise much for the future!" Why have I always imagined that Madame Chantal's ideas are square? I don't know; but everything that she says takes that shape in my head: a big square, with four symmetrical angles. There are other people whose ideas always strike me as being round and rolling like a hoop. As soon as they begin a sentence on any subject it rolls on and on, coming out in ten, twenty, fifty round ideas, large and small, which I see rolling along, one behind the other, to the end of the horizon. Other people have pointed ideas—but enough of this.

We sat down as usual and finished our dinner without anything out of the ordinary being said. At dessert the Twelfth Night cake was brought on. Now, M. Chantal had been king every year. I don't know whether this was the result of continued chance or a family convention, but he unfailingly found the bean in his piece of cake, and he would proclaim Madame Chantal to be queen. Therefore, I was greatly surprised to find something very hard, which almost made me break a tooth, in a mouthful of cake. Gently I took this thing from my mouth and I saw that it was a little porcelain doll, no bigger than a bean. Surprise caused me to exclaim:

"Ah!" All looked at me, and Chantal clapped his hands and cried: "It's Gaston! It's Gaston! Long live the king! Long live the king!"

All took up the chorus: "Long live the king!" And I blushed to the tip of my ears, as one often does, without any reason at all, in situations which are a little foolish. I sat there looking at my plate, with this absurd little bit of pottery in my fingers, forcing myself to laugh and not knowing what to do or say, when Chantal once more cried out: "Now, you must choose a queen!"

Then I was thunderstruck. In a second a thousand thoughts and suppositions flashed through my mind. Did they expect me to pick out one of the young Chantal ladies? Was that a trick to make me say which one I prefer? Was it a gentle, light, direct hint of the parents toward a possible marriage? The idea of marriage roams continually in houses with grown-up girls, and takes every shape and disguise, and employs every subterfuge. A dread of compromising myself took hold of me as well as an extreme timidity before the obstinately correct and reserved attitude of the Misses Louise and Pauline. To choose one of them in preference to the other seemed to me as difficult as choosing between two drops of water; and then the fear of launching myself into an affair which might, in spite of me, lead me gently into matrimonial ties, by means as wary and imperceptible and as calm as this insignificant royalty—the fear of all this haunted me.

Suddenly I had an inspiration, and I held out to Mademoiselle Pearl the symbolical emblem. At first every one was surprised, then they doubtless appreciated my delicacy and discretion, for they applauded furiously. Everybody was crying: "Long live the queen! Long live the queen!"

As for herself, poor old maid, she was so amazed that she completely lost control of herself; she was trembling and stammering: "No—no—oh! no—not me—please—not me—I beg of you——"

Then for the first time in my life I looked at Mademoiselle Pearl and wondered what she was.

I was accustomed to seeing her in this house, just as one sees old upholstered armchairs on which one has been sitting since childhood without ever noticing them. One day, with no reason at all, because a ray of sunshine happens to strike the seat, you suddenly think: "Why, that chair is very curious"; and then you discover that the wood has been worked by a real artist and that the material is remarkable. I had never taken any notice of Mademoiselle Pearl.

She was a part of the Chantal family, that was all. But how? By what right? She was a tall, thin person who tried to remain in the background, but who was by no means insignificant. She was treated in a friendly manner, better than a housekeeper, not so well as a relative. I suddenly observed several shades of distinction which I had never noticed before. Madame Chantal said: "Pearl." The young ladies: "Mademoiselle Pearl," and Chantal only addressed her as "Mademoiselle," with an air of greater respect, perhaps.

I began to observe her. How old could she be? Forty? Yes, forty. She was not old, she made herself old. I was suddenly struck by this fact. She fixed her hair and dressed in a ridiculous manner, and, notwithstanding all that, she was not in the least ridiculous, she had such simple, natural gracefulness, veiled and hidden. Truly, what a strange creature! How was it I had never observed her before? She dressed her hair in a grotesque manner with little old maid curls, most absurd; but beneath this one could see a large, calm brow, cut by two deep lines, two wrinkles of long sadness, then two blue eyes, large and tender, so timid, so bashful, so humble, two beautiful eyes which had kept the expression of naive wonder of a young girl, of youthful sensations, and also of sorrow, which had softened without spoiling them.

Her whole face was refined and discreet, a face the expression of which seemed to have gone out without being used up or faded by the fatigues and great emotions of life.

What a dainty mouth! and such pretty teeth! But one would have thought that she did not dare smile.

Suddenly I compared her to Madame Chantal! Undoubtedly Mademoiselle Pearl was the better of the two, a hundred times better, daintier, prouder, more noble. I was surprised at my observation. They were pouring out champagne. I held my glass up to the queen and, with a well-turned compliment, I drank to her health. I could see that she felt inclined to hide her head in her napkin. Then, as she was dipping her lips in the clear wine, everybody cried: "The queen drinks! the queen drinks!" She almost turned purple and choked. Everybody was laughing; but I could see that all loved her.

As soon as dinner was over Chantal took me by the arm. It was time for his cigar, a sacred hour. When alone he would smoke it out in the street; when guests came to dinner he would take them to the billiard room and smoke while playing. That evening they had built a fire to celebrate Twelfth Night; my old friend took his cue, a very fine one, and chalked it with great care; then he said:

"You break, my boy!"

He called me "my boy," although I was twenty-five, but he had known me as a young child.

I started the game and made a few carroms. I missed some others, but as the thought of Mademoiselle Pearl kept returning to my mind, I suddenly asked:

"By the way, Monsieur Chantal, is Mademoiselle Pearl a relative of yours?"

Greatly surprised, he stopped playing and looked at me:

"What! Don't you know? Haven't you heard about Mademoiselle Pearl?"

"No."

"Didn't your father ever tell you?"

"No."

"Well, well, that's funny! That certainly is funny! Why, it's a regular romance!"

He paused, and then continued:

"And if you only knew how peculiar it is that you should ask me that to-day, on Twelfth Night!"

"Why?"

"Why? Well, listen. Forty-one years ago to day, the day of the Epiphany, the following events occurred: We were then living at Roily-le-Tors, on the ramparts; but in order that you may understand, I must first explain the house. Roily is built on a hill, or, rather, on a mound which overlooks a great stretch of prairie. We had a house there with a beautiful hanging garden supported by the old battlemented wall; so that the house was in the town on the streets, while the garden overlooked the plain. There was a door leading from the garden to the open country, at the bottom of a secret stairway in the thick wall—the kind you read about in novels. A road passed in front of this door, which was provided with a big bell; for the peasants, in order to avoid the roundabout way, would bring their provisions up this way.

"You now understand the place, don't you? Well, this year, at Epiphany, it had been snowing for a week. One might have thought that the world was coming to an end. When we went to the ramparts to look over the plain, this immense white, frozen country, which shone like varnish, would chill our very souls. One might have thought that the Lord had packed the world in cotton to put it away in the storeroom for old worlds. I can assure you that it was dreary looking.

"We were a very numerous family at that time my father, my mother, my uncle and aunt, my two brothers and four cousins; they were pretty little girls; I married the youngest. Of all that crowd, there are only three of us left: my wife, I, and my sister-in-law, who lives in Marseilles. Zounds! how quickly a family like that dwindles away! I tremble when I think of it! I was fifteen years old then, since I am fifty-six now.

"We were going to celebrate the Epiphany, and we were all happy, very happy! Everybody was in the parlor, awaiting dinner, and my oldest brother, Jacques, said: 'There has been a dog howling out in the plain for about ten minutes; the poor beast must be lost.'

"He had hardly stopped talking when the garden bell began to ring. It had the deep sound of a church bell, which made one think of death. A shiver ran through everybody. My father called the servant and told him to go outside and look. We waited in complete silence; we were thinking of the snow which covered the ground. When the man returned he declared that he had seen nothing. The dog kept up its ceaseless howling, and always from the same spot.

"We sat down to dinner; but we were all uneasy, especially the young people. Everything went well up to the roast, then the bell began to ring again, three times in succession, three heavy, long strokes which vibrated to the tips of our fingers and which stopped our conversation short. We sat there looking at each other, fork in the air, still listening, and shaken by a kind of supernatural fear.

"At last my mother spoke: 'It's surprising that they should have waited so long to come back. Do not go alone, Baptiste; one of these gentlemen will accompany you.'

"My Uncle Francois arose. He was a kind of Hercules, very proud of his strength, and feared nothing in the world. My father said to him: 'Take a gun. There is no telling what it might be.'

"But my uncle only took a cane and went out with the servant.

"We others remained there trembling with fear and apprehension, without eating or speaking. My father tried to reassure us: 'Just wait and see,' he said; 'it will be some beggar or some traveller lost in the snow. After ringing once, seeing that the door was not immediately opened, he attempted again to find his way, and being unable to, he has returned to our door.'

"Our uncle seemed to stay away an hour. At last he came back, furious, swearing: 'Nothing at all; it's some practical joker! There is nothing but that damned dog howling away at about a hundred yards from the walls. If I had taken a gun I would have killed him to make him keep quiet.'

"We sat down to dinner again, but every one was excited; we felt that all was not over, that something was going to happen, that the bell would soon ring again.

"It rang just as the Twelfth Night cake was being cut. All the men jumped up together. My Uncle, Francois, who had been drinking champagne, swore so furiously that he would murder it, whatever it might be, that my mother and my aunt threw themselves on him to prevent his going. My father, although very calm and a little helpless (he limped ever since he had broken his leg when thrown by a horse), declared, in turn, that he wished to find out what was the matter and that he was going. My brothers, aged eighteen and twenty, ran to get their guns; and as no one was paying any attention to me I snatched up a little rifle that was used in the garden and got ready to accompany the expedition.

"It started out immediately. My father and uncle were walking ahead with Baptiste, who was carrying a lantern. My brothers, Jacques and Paul, followed, and I trailed on behind in spite of the prayers of my mother, who stood in front of the house with her sister and my cousins.

"It had been snowing again for the last hour, and the trees were weighted down. The pines were bending under this heavy, white garment, and looked like white pyramids or enormous sugar cones, and through the gray curtains of small hurrying flakes could be seen the lighter bushes which stood out pale in the shadow. The snow was falling so thick that we could hardly see ten feet ahead of us. But the lantern threw a bright light around us. When we began to go down the winding stairway in the wall I really grew frightened. I felt as though some one were walking behind me, were going to grab me by the shoulders and carry me away, and I felt a strong desire to return; but, as I would have had to cross the garden all alone, I did not dare. I heard some one opening the door leading to the plain; my uncle began to swear again, exclaiming: 'By—-! He has gone again! If I can catch sight of even his shadow, I'll take care not to miss him, the swine!'

"It was a discouraging thing to see this great expanse of plain, or, rather, to feel it before us, for we could not see it; we could only see a thick, endless veil of snow, above, below, opposite us, to the right, to the left, everywhere. My uncle continued:

"'Listen! There is the dog howling again; I will teach him how I shoot. That will be something gained, anyhow.'

"But my father, who was kind-hearted, went on:

"'It will be much better to go on and get the poor animal, who is crying for hunger. The poor fellow is barking for help; he is calling like a man in distress. Let us go to him.'

"So we started out through this mist, through this thick continuous fall of snow, which filled the air, which moved, floated, fell, and chilled the skin with a burning sensation like a sharp, rapid pain as each flake melted. We were sinking in up to our knees in this soft, cold mass, and we had to lift our feet very high in order to walk. As we advanced the dog's voice became clearer and stronger. My uncle cried: 'Here he is!' We stopped to observe him as one does when he meets an enemy at night.

"I could see nothing, so I ran up to the others, and I caught sight of him; he was frightful and weird-looking; he was a big black shepherd's dog with long hair and a wolf's head, standing just within the gleam of light cast by our lantern on the snow. He did not move; he was silently watching us.

"My uncle said: 'That's peculiar, he is neither advancing nor retreating. I feel like taking a shot at him.'

"My father answered in a firm voice: 'No, we must capture him.'

"Then my brother Jacques added: 'But he is not alone. There is something behind him."

"There was indeed something behind him, something gray, impossible to distinguish. We started out again cautiously. When he saw us approaching the dog sat down. He did not look wicked. Instead, he seemed pleased at having been able to attract the attention of some one.

"My father went straight to him and petted him. The dog licked his hands. We saw that he was tied to the wheel of a little carriage, a sort of toy carriage entirely wrapped up in three or four woolen blankets. We carefully took off these coverings, and as Baptiste approached his lantern to the front of this little vehicle, which looked like a rolling kennel, we saw in it a little baby sleeping peacefully.

"We were so astonished that we couldn't speak.

"My father was the first to collect his wits, and as he had a warm heart and a broad mind, he stretched his hand over the roof of the carriage and said: 'Poor little waif, you shall be one of us!' And he ordered my brother Jacques to roll the foundling ahead of us. Thinking out loud, my father continued:

"'Some child of love whose poor mother rang at my door on this night of Epiphany in memory of the Child of God.'

"He once more stopped and called at the top of his lungs through the night to the four corners of the heavens: 'We have found it!' Then, putting his hand on his brother's shoulder, he murmured: 'What if you had shot the dog, Francois?'

"My uncle did not answer, but in the darkness he crossed himself, for, notwithstanding his blustering manner, he was very religious.

"The dog, which had been untied, was following us.

"Ah! But you should have seen us when we got to the house! At first we had a lot of trouble in getting the carriage up through the winding stairway; but we succeeded and even rolled it into the vestibule.

"How funny mamma was! How happy and astonished! And my four little cousins (the youngest was only six), they looked like four chickens around a nest. At last we took the child from the carriage. It was still sleeping. It was a girl about six weeks old. In its clothes we found ten thousand francs in gold, yes, my boy, ten thousand francs!—which papa saved for her dowry. Therefore, it was not a child of poor people, but, perhaps, the child of some nobleman and a little bourgeoise of the town—or again—we made a thousand suppositions, but we never found out anything-never the slightest clue. The dog himself was recognized by no one. He was a stranger in the country. At any rate, the person who rang three times at our door must have known my parents well, to have chosen them thus.

"That is how, at the age of six weeks, Mademoiselle Pearl entered the Chantal household.

"It was not until later that she was called Mademoiselle Pearl. She was at first baptized 'Marie Simonne Claire,' Claire being intended, for her family name.

"I can assure you that our return to the diningroom was amusing, with this baby now awake and looking round her at these people and these lights with her vague blue questioning eyes.

"We sat down to dinner again and the cake was cut. I was king, and for queen I took Mademoiselle Pearl, just as you did to-day. On that day she did not appreciate the honor that was being shown her.

"Well, the child was adopted and brought up in the family. She grew, and the years flew by. She was so gentle and loving and minded so well that every one would have spoiled her abominably had not my mother prevented it.

"My mother was an orderly woman with a great respect for class distinctions. She consented to treat little Claire as she did her own sons, but, nevertheless, she wished the distance which separated us to be well marked, and our positions well established. Therefore, as soon as the child could understand, she acquainted her with her story and gently, even tenderly, impressed on the little one's mind that, for the Chantals, she was an adopted daughter, taken in, but, nevertheless, a stranger. Claire understood the situation with peculiar intelligence and with surprising instinct; she knew how to take the place which was allotted her, and to keep it with so much tact, gracefulness and gentleness that she often brought tears to my father's eyes. My mother herself was often moved by the passionate gratitude and timid devotion of this dainty and loving little creature that she began calling her: 'My daughter.' At times, when the little one had done something kind and good, my mother would raise her spectacles on her forehead, a thing which always indicated emotion with her, and she would repeat: 'This child is a pearl, a perfect pearl!' This name stuck to the little Claire, who became and remained for us Mademoiselle Pearl."

II

M. Chantal stopped. He was sitting on the edge of the billiard table, his feet hanging, and was playing with a ball with his left hand, while with his right he crumpled a rag which served to rub the chalk marks from the slate. A little red in the face, his voice thick, he was talking away to himself now, lost in his memories, gently drifting through the old scenes and events which awoke in his mind, just as we walk through old family gardens where we were brought up and where each tree, each walk, each hedge reminds us of some occurrence.

I stood opposite him leaning against the wall, my hands resting on my idle cue.

After a slight pause he continued:

"By Jove! She was pretty at eighteen—and graceful—and perfect. Ah! She was so sweet—and good and true—and charming! She had such eyes—blue-transparent—clear—such eyes as I have never seen since!"

He was once more silent. I asked: "Why did she never marry?"

He answered, not to me, but to the word "marry" which had caught his ear: "Why? why? She never would—she never would! She had a dowry of thirty thousand francs, and she received several offers—but she never would! She seemed sad at that time. That was when I married my cousin, little Charlotte, my wife, to whom I had been engaged for six years."

I looked at M. Chantal, and it seemed to me that I was looking into his very soul, and I was suddenly witnessing one of those humble and cruel tragedies of honest, straightforward, blameless hearts, one of those secret tragedies known to no one, not even the silent and resigned victims. A rash curiosity suddenly impelled me to exclaim:

"You should have married her, Monsieur Chantal!"

He started, looked at me, and said:

"I? Marry whom?"

"Mademoiselle Pearl."

"Why?"

"Because you loved her more than your cousin."

He stared at me with strange, round, bewildered eyes and stammered:

"I loved her—I? How? Who told you that?"

"Why, anyone can see that—and it's even on account of her that you delayed for so long your marriage to your cousin who had been waiting for you for six years."

He dropped the ball which he was holding in his left hand, and, seizing the chalk rag in both hands, he buried his face in it and began to sob. He was weeping with his eyes, nose and mouth in a heartbreaking yet ridiculous manner, like a sponge which one squeezes. He was coughing, spitting and blowing his nose in the chalk rag, wiping his eyes and sneezing; then the tears would again begin to flow down the wrinkles on his face and he would make a strange gurgling noise in his throat. I felt bewildered, ashamed; I wanted to run away, and I no longer knew what to say, do, or attempt.

Suddenly Madame Chantal's voice sounded on the stairs. "Haven't you men almost finished smoking your cigars?"

I opened the door and cried: "Yes, madame, we are coming right down."

Then I rushed to her husband, and, seizing him by the shoulders, I cried: "Monsieur Chantal, my friend Chantal, listen to me; your wife is calling; pull yourself together, we must go downstairs."

He stammered: "Yes—yes—I am coming—poor girl! I am coming—tell her that I am coming."

He began conscientiously to wipe his face on the cloth which, for the last two or three years, had been used for marking off the chalk from the slate; then he appeared, half white and half red, his forehead, nose, cheeks and chin covered with chalk, and his eyes swollen, still full of tears.

I caught him by the hands and dragged him into his bedroom, muttering: "I beg your pardon, I beg your pardon, Monsieur Chantal, for having caused you such sorrow—but—I did not know—you—you understand."

He squeezed my hand, saying: "Yes—yes—there are difficult moments."

Then he plunged his face into a bowl of water. When he emerged from it he did not yet seem to me to be presentable; but I thought of a little stratagem. As he was growing worried, looking at himself in the mirror, I said to him: "All you have to do is to say that a little dust flew into your eye and you can cry before everybody to your heart's content."

He went downstairs rubbing his eyes with his handkerchief. All were worried; each one wished to look for the speck, which could not be found; and stories were told of similar cases where it had been necessary to call in a physician.

I went over to Mademoiselle Pearl and watched her, tormented by an ardent curiosity, which was turning to positive suffering. She must indeed have been pretty, with her gentle, calm eyes, so large that it looked as though she never closed them like other mortals. Her gown was a little ridiculous, a real old maid's gown, which was unbecoming without appearing clumsy.

It seemed to me as though I were looking into her soul, just as I had into Monsieur Chantal's; that I was looking right from one end to the other of this humble life, so simple and devoted. I felt an irresistible longing to question her, to find out whether she, too, had loved him; whether she also had suffered, as he had, from this long, secret, poignant grief, which one cannot see, know, or guess, but which breaks forth at night in the loneliness of the dark room. I was watching her, and I could observe her heart beating under her waist, and I wondered whether this sweet, candid face had wept on the soft pillow and she had sobbed, her whole body shaken by the violence of her anguish.

I said to her in a low voice, like a child who is breaking a toy to see what is inside: "If you could have seen Monsieur Chantal crying a while ago it would have moved you."

She started, asking: "What? He was weeping?"

"Ah, yes, he was indeed weeping!"

"Why?"

She seemed deeply moved. I answered:

"On your account."

"On my account?"

"Yes. He was telling me how much he had loved you in the days gone by; and what a pang it had given him to marry his cousin instead of you."

Her pale face seemed to grow a little longer; her calm eyes, which always remained open, suddenly closed so quickly that they seemed shut forever. She slipped from her chair to the floor, and slowly, gently sank down as would a fallen garment.

I cried: "Help! help! Mademoiselle Pearl is ill."

Madame Chantal and her daughters rushed forward, and while they were looking for towels, water and vinegar, I grabbed my hat and ran away.

I walked away with rapid strides, my heart heavy, my mind full of remorse and regret. And yet sometimes I felt pleased; I felt as though I had done a praiseworthy and necessary act. I was asking myself: "Did I do wrong or right?" They had that shut up in their hearts, just as some people carry a bullet in a closed wound. Will they not be happier now? It was too late for their torture to begin over again and early enough for them to remember it with tenderness.

And perhaps some evening next spring, moved by a beam of moonlight falling through the branches on the grass at their feet, they will join and press their hands in memory of all this cruel and suppressed suffering; and, perhaps, also this short embrace may infuse in their veins a little of this thrill which they would not have known without it, and will give to those two dead souls, brought to life in a second, the rapid and divine sensation of this intoxication, of this madness which gives to lovers more happiness in an instant than other men can gather during a whole lifetime!

THE THIEF

While apparently thinking of something else, Dr. Sorbier had been listening quietly to those amazing accounts of burglaries and daring deeds that might have been taken from the trial of Cartouche. "Assuredly," he exclaimed, "assuredly, I know of no viler fault nor any meaner action than to attack a girl's innocence, to corrupt her, to profit by a moment of unconscious weakness and of madness, when her heart is beating like that of a frightened fawn, and her pure lips seek those of her tempter; when she abandons herself without thinking of the irremediable stain, nor of her fall, nor of the morrow.

"The man who has brought this about slowly, viciously, who can tell with what science of evil, and who, in such a case, has not steadiness and self-restraint enough to quench that flame by some icy words, who has not sense enough for two, who cannot recover his self-possession and master the runaway brute within him, and who loses his head on the edge of the precipice over which she is going to fall, is as contemptible as any man who breaks open a lock, or as any rascal on the lookout for a house left defenceless and unprotected or for some easy and dishonest stroke of business, or as that thief whose various exploits you have just related to us.

"I, for my part, utterly refuse to absolve him, even when extenuating circumstances plead in his favor, even when he is carrying on a dangerous flirtation, in which a man tries in vain to keep his balance, not to exceed the limits of the game, any more than at lawn tennis; even when the parts are inverted and a man's adversary is some precocious, curious, seductive girl, who shows you immediately that she has nothing to learn and nothing to experience, except the last chapter of love, one of those girls from whom may fate always preserve our sons, and whom a psychological novel writer has christened 'The Semi-Virgins.'

"It is, of course, difficult and painful for that coarse and unfathomable vanity which is characteristic of every man, and which might be called 'malism', not to stir such a charming fire, difficult to act the Joseph and the fool, to turn away his eyes, and, as it were, to put wax into his ears, like the companions of Ulysses when they were attracted by the divine, seductive songs of the Sirens, difficult only to touch that pretty table covered with a perfectly new cloth, at which you are invited to take a seat before any one else, in such a suggestive voice, and are requested to quench your thirst and to taste that new wine, whose fresh and strange flavor you will never forget. But who would hesitate to exercise such self-restraint if, when he rapidly examines his conscience, in one of those instinctive returns to his sober self in which a man thinks clearly and recovers his head, he were to measure the gravity of his fault, consider it, think of its consequences, of the reprisals, of the uneasiness which he would always feel in the future, and which would destroy the repose and happiness of his life?

"You may guess that behind all these moral reflections, such as a graybeard like myself may indulge in, there is a story hidden, and, sad as it is, I am sure it will interest you on account of the strange heroism it shows."

He was silent for a few moments, as if to classify his recollections, and, with his elbows resting on the arms of his easy-chair and his eyes looking into space, he continued in the slow voice of a hospital professor who is explaining a case to his class of medical students, at a bedside:

"He was one of those men who, as our grandfathers used to say, never met with a cruel woman, the type of the adventurous knight who was always foraging, who had something of the scamp about him, but who despised danger and was bold even to rashness. He was ardent in the pursuit of pleasure, and had an irresistible charm about him, one of those men in whom we excuse the greatest excesses as the most natural things in the world. He had run through all his money at gambling and with pretty girls, and so became, as it were, a soldier of fortune. He amused himself whenever and however he could, and was at that time quartered at Versailles.

"I knew him to the very depths of his childlike heart, which was only too easily seen through and sounded, and I loved him as some old bachelor uncle loves a nephew who plays him tricks, but who knows how to coax him. He had made me his confidant rather than his adviser, kept me informed of his slightest pranks, though he always pretended to be speaking about one of his friends, and not about himself; and I must confess that his youthful impetuosity, his careless gaiety, and his amorous ardor sometimes distracted my thoughts and made me envy the handsome, vigorous young fellow who was so happy at being alive, that I had not the courage to check him, to show him the right road, and to call out to him: 'Take care!' as children do at blind man's buff.

"And one day, after one of those interminable cotillons, where the couples do not leave each other for hours, and can disappear together without anybody thinking of noticing them, the poor fellow at last discovered what love was, that real love which takes up its abode in the very centre of the heart and in the brain, and is proud of being there, and which rules like a sovereign and a tyrannous master, and he became desperately enamored of a pretty but badly brought up girl, who was as disquieting and wayward as she was pretty.

"She loved him, however, or rather she idolized him despotically, madly, with all her enraptured soul and all her being. Left to do as she pleased by imprudent and frivolous parents, suffering from neurosis, in consequence of the unwholesome friendships which she contracted at the convent school, instructed by what she saw and heard and knew was going on around her, in spite of her deceitful and artificial conduct, knowing that neither her father nor her mother, who were very proud of their race as well as avaricious, would ever agree to let her marry the man whom she had taken a liking to, that handsome fellow who had little besides vision, ideas and debts, and who belonged to the middle-class, she laid aside all scruples, thought of nothing but of becoming his, no matter what might be the cost.

"By degrees, the unfortunate man's strength gave way, his heart softened, and he allowed himself to be carried away by that current which buffeted him, surrounded him, and left him on the shore like a waif and a stray.

"They wrote letters full of madness to each other, and not a day passed without their meeting, either accidentally, as it seemed, or at parties and balls. She had yielded her lips to him in long, ardent caresses, which had sealed their compact of mutual passion."

The doctor stopped, and his eyes suddenly filled with tears, as these former troubles came back to his mind; and then, in a hoarse voice, he went on, full of the horror of what he was going to relate:

"For months he scaled the garden wall, and, holding his breath and listening for the slightest noise, like a burglar who is going to break into a house, he went in by the servants' entrance, which she had left open, slunk barefoot down a long passage and up the broad staircase, which creaked occasionally, to the second story, where his sweetheart's room was, and stayed there for hours.

"One night, when it was darker than usual, and he was hurrying lest he should be later than the time agreed on, he knocked up against a piece of furniture in the anteroom and upset it. It so happened that the girl's mother had not gone to sleep, either because she had a sick headache, or else because she had sat up late over some novel, and, frightened at that unusual noise which disturbed the silence of the house, she jumped out of bed, opened the door, saw some one indistinctly running away and keeping close to the wall, and, immediately thinking that there were burglars in the house, she aroused her husband and the servants by her frantic screams. The unfortunate man understood the situation; and, seeing what a terrible fix he was in, and preferring to be taken for a common thief to dishonoring his adored one's name, he ran into the drawing-room, felt on the tables and what-nots, filled his pockets at random with valuable bric-a-brac, and then cowered down behind the grand piano, which barred the corner of a large room.

"The servants, who had run in with lighted candles, found him, and, overwhelming him with abuse, seized him by the collar and dragged him, panting and apparently half dead with shame and terror, to the nearest police station. He defended himself with intentional awkwardness when he was brought up for trial, kept up his part with the most perfect self-possession and without any signs of the despair and anguish that he felt in his heart, and, condemned and degraded and made to suffer martyrdom in his honor as a man and a soldier—he was an officer—he did not protest, but went to prison as one of those criminals whom society gets rid of like noxious vermin.

"He died there of misery and of bitterness of spirit, with the name of the fair-haired idol, for whom he had sacrificed himself, on his lips, as if it had been an ecstatic prayer, and he intrusted his will 'to the priest who administered extreme unction to him, and requested him to give it to me. In it, without mentioning anybody, and without in the least lifting the veil, he at last explained the enigma, and cleared himself of those accusations the terrible burden of which he had borne until his last breath.

"I have always thought myself, though I do not know why, that the girl married and had several charming children, whom she brought up with the austere strictness and in the serious piety of former days!"

CLAIR DE LUNE

Abbe Marignan's martial name suited him well. He was a tall, thin priest, fanatic, excitable, yet upright. All his beliefs were fixed, never varying. He believed sincerely that he knew his God, understood His plans, desires and intentions.

When he walked with long strides along the garden walk of his little country parsonage, he would sometimes ask himself the question: "Why has God done this?" And he would dwell on this continually, putting himself in the place of God, and he almost invariably found an answer. He would never have cried out in an outburst of pious humility: "Thy ways, O Lord, are past finding out."

He said to himself: "I am the servant of God; it is right for me to know the reason of His deeds, or to guess it if I do not know it."

Everything in nature seemed to him to have been created in accordance with an admirable and absolute logic. The "whys" and "becauses" always balanced. Dawn was given to make our awakening pleasant, the days to ripen the harvest, the rains to moisten it, the evenings for preparation for slumber, and the dark nights for sleep.

The four seasons corresponded perfectly to the needs of agriculture, and no suspicion had ever come to the priest of the fact that nature has no intentions; that, on the contrary, everything which exists must conform to the hard demands of seasons, climates and matter.

But he hated woman—hated her unconsciously, and despised her by instinct. He often repeated the words of Christ: "Woman, what have I to do with thee?" and he would add: "It seems as though God, Himself, were dissatisfied with this work of His." She was the tempter who led the first man astray, and who since then had ever been busy with her work of damnation, the feeble creature, dangerous and mysteriously affecting one. And even more than their sinful bodies, he hated their loving hearts.

He had often felt their tenderness directed toward himself, and though he knew that he was invulnerable, he grew angry at this need of love that is always vibrating in them.

According to his belief, God had created woman for the sole purpose of tempting and testing man. One must not approach her without defensive precautions and fear of possible snares. She was, indeed, just like a snare, with her lips open and her arms stretched out to man.

He had no indulgence except for nuns, whom their vows had rendered inoffensive; but he was stern with them, nevertheless, because he felt that at the bottom of their fettered and humble hearts the everlasting tenderness was burning brightly—that tenderness which was shown even to him, a priest.

He felt this cursed tenderness, even in their docility, in the low tones of their voices when speaking to him, in their lowered eyes, and in their resigned tears when he reproved them roughly. And he would shake his cassock on leaving the convent doors, and walk off, lengthening his stride as though flying from danger.

He had a niece who lived with her mother in a little house near him. He was bent upon making a sister of charity of her.

She was a pretty, brainless madcap. When the abbe preached she laughed, and when he was angry with her she would give him a hug, drawing him to her heart, while he sought unconsciously to release himself from this embrace which nevertheless filled him with a sweet pleasure, awakening in his depths the sensation of paternity which slumbers in every man.

Often, when walking by her side, along the country road, he would speak to her of God, of his God. She never listened to him, but looked about her at the sky, the grass and flowers, and one could see the joy of life sparkling in her eyes. Sometimes she would dart forward to catch some flying creature, crying out as she brought it back: "Look, uncle, how pretty it is! I want to hug it!" And this desire to "hug" flies or lilac blossoms disquieted, angered, and roused the priest, who saw, even in this, the ineradicable tenderness that is always budding in women's hearts.

Then there came a day when the sexton's wife, who kept house for Abbe Marignan, told him, with caution, that his niece had a lover.

Almost suffocated by the fearful emotion this news roused in him, he stood there, his face covered with soap, for he was in the act of shaving.

When he had sufficiently recovered to think and speak he cried: "It is not true; you lie, Melanie!"

But the peasant woman put her hand on her heart, saying: "May our Lord judge me if I lie, Monsieur le Cure! I tell you, she goes there every night when your sister has gone to bed. They meet by the river side; you have only to go there and see, between ten o'clock and midnight."

He ceased scraping his chin, and began to walk up and down impetuously, as he always did when he was in deep thought. When he began shaving again he cut himself three times from his nose to his ear.

All day long he was silent, full of anger and indignation. To his priestly hatred of this invincible love was added the exasperation of her spiritual father, of her guardian and pastor, deceived and tricked by a child, and the selfish emotion shown by parents when their daughter announces that she has chosen a husband without them, and in spite of them.

After dinner he tried to read a little, but could not, growing more and, more angry. When ten o'clock struck he seized his cane, a formidable oak stick, which he was accustomed to carry in his nocturnal walks when visiting the sick. And he smiled at the enormous club which he twirled in a threatening manner in his strong, country fist. Then he raised it suddenly and, gritting his teeth, brought it down on a chair, the broken back of which fell over on the floor.

He opened the door to go out, but stopped on the sill, surprised by the splendid moonlight, of such brilliance as is seldom seen.

And, as he was gifted with an emotional nature, one such as had all those poetic dreamers, the Fathers of the Church, he felt suddenly distracted and moved by all the grand and serene beauty of this pale night.

In his little garden, all bathed in soft light, his fruit trees in a row cast on the ground the shadow of their slender branches, scarcely in full leaf, while the giant honeysuckle, clinging to the wall of his house, exhaled a delicious sweetness, filling the warm moonlit atmosphere with a kind of perfumed soul.

He began to take long breaths, drinking in the air as drunkards drink wine, and he walked along slowly, delighted, marveling, almost forgetting his niece.

As soon as he was outside of the garden, he stopped to gaze upon the plain all flooded with the caressing light, bathed in that tender, languishing charm of serene nights. At each moment was heard the short, metallic note of the cricket, and distant nightingales shook out their scattered notes—their light, vibrant music that sets one dreaming, without thinking, a music made for kisses, for the seduction of moonlight.

The abbe walked on again, his heart failing, though he knew not why. He seemed weakened, suddenly exhausted; he wanted to sit down, to rest there, to think, to admire God in His works.

Down yonder, following the undulations of the little river, a great line of poplars wound in and out. A fine mist, a white haze through which the moonbeams passed, silvering it and making it gleam, hung around and above the mountains, covering all the tortuous course of the water with a kind of light and transparent cotton.

The priest stopped once again, his soul filled with a growing and irresistible tenderness.

And a doubt, a vague feeling of disquiet came over him; he was asking one of those questions that he sometimes put to himself.

"Why did God make this? Since the night is destined for sleep, unconsciousness, repose, forgetfulness of everything, why make it more charming than day, softer than dawn or evening? And why does this seductive planet, more poetic than the sun, that seems destined, so discreet is it, to illuminate things too delicate and mysterious for the light of day, make the darkness so transparent?

"Why does not the greatest of feathered songsters sleep like the others? Why does it pour forth its voice in the mysterious night?

"Why this half-veil cast over the world? Why these tremblings of the heart, this emotion of the spirit, this enervation of the body? Why this display of enchantments that human beings do not see, since they are lying in their beds? For whom is destined this sublime spectacle, this abundance of poetry cast from heaven to earth?"

And the abbe could not understand.

But see, out there, on the edge of the meadow, under the arch of trees bathed in a shining mist, two figures are walking side by side.

The man was the taller, and held his arm about his sweetheart's neck and kissed her brow every little while. They imparted life, all at once, to the placid landscape in which they were framed as by a heavenly hand. The two seemed but a single being, the being for whom was destined this calm and silent night, and they came toward the priest as a living answer, the response his Master sent to his questionings.

He stood still, his heart beating, all upset; and it seemed to him that he saw before him some biblical scene, like the loves of Ruth and Boaz, the accomplishment of the will of the Lord, in some of those glorious stories of which the sacred books tell. The verses of the Song of Songs began to ring in his ears, the appeal of passion, all the poetry of this poem replete with tenderness.

And he said unto himself: "Perhaps God has made such nights as these to idealize the love of men."

He shrank back from this couple that still advanced with arms intertwined. Yet it was his niece. But he asked himself now if he would not be disobeying God. And does not God permit love, since He surrounds it with such visible splendor?

And he went back musing, almost ashamed, as if he had intruded into a temple where he had, no right to enter.

WAITER, A "BOCK"

Why did I go into that beer hall on that particular evening? I do not know. It was cold; a fine rain, a flying mist, veiled the gas lamps with a transparent fog, made the side walks reflect the light that streamed from the shop windows—lighting up the soft slush and the muddy feet of the passers-by.

I was going nowhere in particular; was simply having a short walk after dinner. I had passed the Credit Lyonnais, the Rue Vivienne, and several other streets. I suddenly descried a large beer hall which was more than half full. I walked inside, with no object in view. I was not the least thirsty.

I glanced round to find a place that was not too crowded, and went and sat down by the side of a man who seemed to me to be old, and who was smoking a two-sous clay pipe, which was as black as coal. From six to eight glasses piled up on the table in front of him indicated the number of "bocks" he had already absorbed. At a glance I recognized a "regular," one of those frequenters of beer houses who come in the morning when the place opens, and do not leave till evening when it is about to close. He was dirty, bald on top of his head, with a fringe of iron-gray hair falling on the collar of his frock coat. His clothes, much too large for him, appeared to have been made for him at a time when he was corpulent. One could guess that he did not wear suspenders, for he could not take ten steps without having to stop to pull up his trousers. Did he wear a vest? The mere thought of his boots and of that which they covered filled me with horror. The frayed cuffs were perfectly black at the edges, as were his nails.

As soon as I had seated myself beside him, this individual said to me in a quiet tone of voice:

"How goes it?"

I turned sharply round and closely scanned his features, whereupon he continued:

"I see you do not recognize me."

"No, I do not."

"Des Barrets."

I was stupefied. It was Count Jean des Barrets, my old college chum.

I seized him by the hand, and was so dumbfounded that I could find nothing to say. At length I managed to stammer out:

"And you, how goes it with you?"

He responded placidly:

"I get along as I can."

"What are you doing now?" I asked.

"You see what I am doing," he answered quit resignedly.

I felt my face getting red. I insisted:

"But every day?"

"Every day it is the same thing," was his reply, accompanied with a thick puff of tobacco smoke.

He then tapped with a sou on the top of the marble table, to attract the attention of the waiter, and called out:

"Waiter, two 'bocks.'"

A voice in the distance repeated:

"Two bocks for the fourth table."

Another voice, more distant still, shouted out:

"Here they are!"

Immediately a man with a white apron appeared, carrying two "bocks," which he set down, foaming, on the table, spilling some of the yellow liquid on the sandy floor in his haste.

Des Barrets emptied his glass at a single draught and replaced it on the table, while he sucked in the foam that had been left on his mustache. He next asked:

"What is there new?"

I really had nothing new to tell him. I stammered:

"Nothing, old man. I am a business man."

In his monotonous tone of voice he said:

"Indeed, does it amuse you?"

"No, but what can I do? One must do something!"

"Why should one?"

"So as to have occupation."

"What's the use of an occupation? For my part, I do nothing at all, as you see, never anything. When one has not a sou I can understand why one should work. But when one has enough to live on, what's the use? What is the good of working? Do you work for yourself, or for others? If you work for yourself, you do it for your own amusement, which is all right; if you work for others, you are a fool."

Then, laying his pipe on the marble table, he called out anew:

"Waiter, a 'bock.'" And continued: "It makes me thirsty to keep calling so. I am not accustomed to that sort of thing. Yes, yes, I do nothing. I let things slide, and I am growing old. In dying I shall have nothing to regret. My only remembrance will be this beer hall. No wife, no children, no cares, no sorrows, nothing. That is best."

He then emptied the glass which had been brought him, passed his tongue over his lips, and resumed his pipe.

I looked at him in astonishment, and said:

"But you have not always been like that?"

"Pardon me; ever since I left college."

"That is not a proper life to lead, my dear fellow; it is simply horrible. Come, you must have something to do, you must love something, you must have friends."

"No, I get up at noon, I come here, I have my breakfast, I drink my beer, I remain until the evening, I have my dinner, I drink beer. Then about half-past one in the morning, I go home to bed, because the place closes up; that annoys me more than anything. In the last ten years I have passed fully six years on this bench, in my corner; and the other four in my bed, nowhere else. I sometimes chat with the regular customers."

"But when you came to Paris what did you do at first?"

"I paid my devoirs to the Cafe de Medicis."

"What next?"

"Next I crossed the water and came here."

"Why did you take that trouble?"

"What do you mean? One cannot remain all one's life in the Latin Quarter. The students make too much noise. Now I shall not move again. Waiter, a 'bock.'"

I began to think that he was making fun of me, and I continued:

"Come now, be frank. You have been the victim of some great sorrow; some disappointment in love, no doubt! It is easy to see that you are a man who has had some trouble. What age are you?"

"I am thirty, but I look forty-five, at least."

I looked him straight in the face. His wrinkled, ill-shaven face gave one the impression that he was an old man. On the top of his head a few long hairs waved over a skin of doubtful cleanliness. He had enormous eyelashes, a heavy mustache, and a thick beard. Suddenly I had a kind of vision, I know not why, of a basin filled with dirty water in which all that hair had been washed. I said to him:

"You certainly look older than your age. You surely must have experienced some great sorrow."

He replied:

"I tell you that I have not. I am old because I never go out into the air. Nothing makes a man deteriorate more than the life of a cafe."

I still could not believe him.

"You must surely also have been married? One could not get as bald-headed as you are without having been in love."

He shook his head, shaking dandruff down on his coat as he did so.

"No, I have always been virtuous."

And, raising his eyes toward the chandelier which heated our heads, he said:

"If I am bald, it is the fault of the gas. It destroys the hair. Waiter, a 'bock.' Are you not thirsty?"

"No, thank you. But you really interest me. Since when have you been so morbid? Your life is not normal, it is not natural. There is something beneath it all."

"Yes, and it dates from my infancy. I received a great shock when I was very young, and that turned my life into darkness which will last to the end."

"What was it?"

"You wish to know about it? Well, then, listen. You recall, of course, the castle in which I was brought up, for you used to spend five or six months there during vacation. You remember that large gray building, in the middle of a great park, and the long avenues of oaks which opened to the four points of the compass. You remember my father and mother, both of whom were ceremonious, solemn, and severe.

"I worshipped my mother; I was afraid of my father; but I respected both, accustomed always as I was to see every one bow before them. They were Monsieur le Comte and Madame la Comtesse to all the country round, and our neighbors, the Tannemares, the Ravelets, the Brennevilles, showed them the utmost consideration.

"I was then thirteen years old. I was happy, pleased with everything, as one is at that age, full of the joy of life.

"Well, toward the end of September, a few days before returning to college, as I was playing about in the shrubbery of the park, among the branches and leaves, as I was crossing a path, I saw my father and mother, who were walking along.

"I recall it as though it were yesterday. It was a very windy day. The whole line of trees swayed beneath the gusts of wind, groaning, and seeming to utter cries-those dull, deep cries that forests give out during a tempest.

"The falling leaves, turning yellow, flew away like birds, circling and falling, and then running along the path like swift animals.

"Evening came on. It was dark in the thickets. The motion of the wind and of the branches excited me, made me tear about as if I were crazy, and howl in imitation of the wolves.

"As soon as I perceived my parents, I crept furtively toward them, under the branches, in order to surprise them, as though I had been a veritable prowler. But I stopped in fear a few paces from them. My father, who was in a terrible passion, cried:

"'Your mother is a fool; moreover, it is not a question of your mother. It is you. I tell you that I need this money, and I want you to sign this.'

"My mother replied in a firm voice:

"'I will not sign it. It is Jean's fortune. I shall guard it for him and I will not allow you to squander it with strange women, as you have your own heritage.'

"Then my father, trembling with rage, wheeled round and, seizing his wife by the throat, began to slap her with all his might full in the face with his disengaged hand.

"My mother's hat fell off, her hair became loosened and fell over her shoulders; she tried to parry the blows, but she could not do so. And my father, like a madman, kept on striking her. My mother rolled over on the ground, covering her face with her hands. Then he turned her over on her back in order to slap her still more, pulling away her hands, which were covering her face.

"As for me, my friend, it seemed as though the world was coming to an end, that the eternal laws had changed. I experienced the overwhelming dread that one has in presence of things supernatural, in presence of irreparable disasters. My childish mind was bewildered, distracted. I began to cry with all my might, without knowing why; a prey to a fearful dread, sorrow, and astonishment. My father heard me, turned round, and, on seeing me, started toward me. I believe that he wanted to kill me, and I fled like a hunted animal, running straight ahead into the thicket.

"I ran perhaps for an hour, perhaps for two. I know not. Darkness set in. I sank on the grass, exhausted, and lay there dismayed, frantic with fear, and devoured by a sorrow capable of breaking forever the heart of a poor child. I was cold, hungry, perhaps. At length day broke. I was afraid to get up, to walk, to return home, to run farther, fearing to encounter my father, whom I did not wish to see again.

"I should probably have died of misery and of hunger at the foot of a tree if the park guard had not discovered me and led me home by force.

"I found my parents looking as usual. My mother alone spoke to me "'How you frightened me, you naughty boy. I lay awake the whole night.'

"I did not answer, but began to weep. My father did not utter a single word.

"Eight days later I returned to school.

"Well, my friend, it was all over with me. I had witnessed the other side of things, the bad side. I have not been able to perceive the good side since that day. What has taken place in my mind, what strange phenomenon has warped my ideas, I do not know. But I no longer had a taste for anything, a wish for anything, a love for anybody, a desire for anything whatever, any ambition, or any hope. And I always see my poor mother on the ground, in the park, my father beating her. My mother died some years later; my, father still lives. I have not seen him since. Waiter, a 'bock.'"

A waiter brought him his "bock," which he swallowed at a gulp. But, in taking up his pipe again, trembling as he was, he broke it. "Confound it!" he said, with a gesture of annoyance. "That is a real sorrow. It will take me a month to color another!"

And he called out across the vast hall, now reeking with smoke and full of men drinking, his everlasting: "Garcon, un 'bock'—and a new pipe."

AFTER

"My darlings," said the comtesse, "you might go to bed."

The three children, two girls and a boy, rose and kissed their grandmother. Then they said good-night to M. le Cure, who had dined at the chateau, as was his custom every Thursday.

The Abbe Mauduit lifted two of the children on his knees, passing his long arms clad in black round their necks, and kissing them tenderly on the forehead as he drew their heads toward him as a father might.

Then he set them down on the ground, and the little beings went off, the boy ahead, and the girls following.

"You are fond of children, M. le Cure," said the comtesse.

"Very fond, madame."

The old woman raised her bright eyes toward the priest.

"And—has your solitude never weighed too heavily on you?"

"Yes, sometimes."

He became silent, hesitated, and then added: "But I was never made for ordinary life."

"What do you know about it?"

"Oh! I know very well. I was made to be a priest; I followed my vocation."

The comtesse kept staring at him:

"Come now, M. le Cure, tell me this—tell me how it was you resolved to renounce forever all that makes the rest of us love life—all that consoles and sustains us? What is it that drove you, impelled you, to separate yourself from the great natural path of marriage and the family? You are neither an enthusiast nor a fanatic, neither a gloomy person nor a sad person. Was it some incident, some sorrow, that led you to take life vows?"

The Abbe Mauduit rose and approached the fire, then, holding toward the flame his big shoes, such as country priests generally wear, he seemed still hesitating as to what reply he should make.

He was a tall old man with white hair, and for the last twenty years had been pastor of the parish of Saint-Antoine-du-Rocher. The peasants said of him: "There's a good man for you!" And indeed he was a good man, benevolent, friendly to all, gentle, and, to crown all, generous. Like Saint Martin, he would have cut his cloak in two. He laughed readily, and wept also, on slight provocation, just like a woman—which prejudiced him more or less in the hard minds of the country folk.

The old Comtesse de Saville, living in retirement in her chateau of Rocher, in order to bring up her grandchildren, after the successive deaths of her son and her daughter-in-law, was very much attached to her cure, and used to say of him: "What a heart he has!"

He came every Thursday to spend the evening with the comtesse, and they were close friends, with the frank and honest friendship of old people.

She persisted:

"Look here, M. le Cure! it is your turn now to make a confession!"

He repeated: "I was not made for ordinary life. I saw it fortunately in time, and I have had many proofs since that I made no mistake on the point:

"My parents, who were mercers in Verdiers, and were quite well to do, had great ambitions for me. They sent me to a boarding school while I was very young. No one knows what a boy may suffer at school through the mere fact of separation, of isolation. This monotonous life without affection is good for some, and detestable for others. Young people are often more sensitive than one supposes, and by shutting them up thus too soon, far from those they love, we may develop to an exaggerated extent a sensitiveness which is overwrought and may become sickly and dangerous.

"I scarcely ever played; I had no companions; I passed my hours in homesickness; I spent the whole night weeping in my bed. I sought to bring before my mind recollections of home, trifling memories of little things, little events. I thought incessantly of all I had left behind there. I became almost imperceptibly an over-sensitive youth to whom the slightest annoyances were terrible griefs.

"In this way I remained taciturn, self-absorbed, without expansion, without confidants. This mental excitement was going on secretly and surely. The nerves of children are quickly affected, and one should see to it that they live a tranquil life until they are almost fully developed. But who ever reflects that, for certain boys, an unjust imposition may be as great a pang as the death of a friend in later years? Who can explain why certain young temperaments are liable to terrible emotions for the slightest cause, and may eventually become morbid and incurable?

"This was my case. This faculty of regret developed in me to such an extent that my existence became a martyrdom.

"I did not speak about it; I said nothing about it; but gradually I became so sensitive that my soul resembled an open wound. Everything that affected me gave me painful twitchings, frightful shocks, and consequently impaired my health. Happy are the men whom nature has buttressed with indifference and armed with stoicism.

"I reached my sixteenth year. An excessive timidity had arisen from this abnormal sensitiveness. Feeling myself unprotected from all the attacks of chance or fate, I feared every contact, every approach, every current. I lived as though I were threatened by an unknown and always expected misfortune. I did not venture either to speak or do anything in public. I had, indeed, the feeling that life, is a battle, a dreadful conflict in which one receives terrible blows, grievous, mortal wounds. In place of cherishing, like all men, a cheerful anticipation of the morrow, I had only a confused fear of it, and felt in my own mind a desire to conceal myself to avoid that combat in which I would be vanquished and slain.

"As soon as my studies were finished, they gave me six months' time to choose a career. A very simple occurrence showed me clearly, all of a sudden, the diseased condition of my mind, made me understand the danger, and determined me to flee from it.

"Verdiers is a little town surrounded with plains and woods. In the central street stands my parents' house. I now passed my days far from this dwelling which I had so much regretted, so much desired. Dreams had reawakened in me, and I walked alone in the fields in order to let them escape and fly away. My father and mother, quite occupied with business, and anxious about my future, talked to me only about their profits or about my possible plans. They were fond of me after the manner of hardheaded, practical people; they had more reason than heart in their affection for me. I lived imprisoned in my thoughts, and vibrating with my eternal sensitiveness.

"Now, one evening, after a long walk, as I was making my way home with great strides so as not to be late, I saw a dog trotting toward me. He was a species of red spaniel, very lean, with long curly ears.

"When he was ten paces away from me he stopped. I did the same. Then he began wagging his tail, and came over to me with short steps and nervous movements of his whole body, bending down on his paws as if appealing to me, and softly shaking his head. I spoke to him. He then began to crawl along in such a sad, humble, suppliant manner that I felt the tears coming into my eyes. I approached him; he ran away, then he came back again; and I bent down on one knee trying to coax him to approach me, with soft words. At last, he was within reach of my hands, and I gently and very carefully stroked him.

"He gained courage, gradually rose and, placing his paws on my shoulders, began to lick my face. He followed me to the house.

"This was really the first being I had passionately loved, because he returned my affection. My attachment to this animal was certainly exaggerated and ridiculous. It seemed to me in a confused sort of way that we were two brothers, lost on this earth, and therefore isolated and without defense, one as well as the other. He never again quitted my side. He slept at the foot of my bed, ate at the table in spite of the objections of my parents, and followed me in my solitary walks.

"I often stopped at the side of a ditch, and sat down in the grass. Sam immediately rushed up, lay down at my feet, and lifted up my hand with his muzzle that I might caress him.

"One day toward the end of June, as we were on the road from Saint-Pierre de Chavrol, I saw the diligence from Pavereau coming along. Its four horses were going at a gallop, with its yellow body, and its imperial with the black leather hood. The coachman cracked his whip; a cloud of dust rose up under the wheels of the heavy vehicle, then floated behind, just as a cloud would do.

"Suddenly, as the vehicle came close to me, Sam, perhaps frightened by the noise and wishing to join me, jumped in front of it. A horse's hoof knocked him down. I saw him roll over, turn round, fall back again beneath the horses' feet, then the coach gave two jolts, and behind it I saw something quivering in the dust on the road. He was nearly cut in two; all his intestines were hanging out and blood was spurting from the wound. He tried to get up, to walk, but he could only move his two front paws, and scratch the ground with them, as if to make a hole. The two others were already dead. And he howled dreadfully, mad with pain.

"He died in a few minutes. I cannot describe how much I felt and suffered. I was confined to my room for a month.

"One night, my father, enraged at seeing me so affected by such a trifling occurrence, exclaimed:

"'How will it be when you have real griefs—if you lose your wife or children?'

"His words haunted me and I began to see my condition clearly. I understood why all the small miseries of each day assumed in my eyes the importance of a catastrophe; I saw that I was organized in such a way that I suffered dreadfully from everything, that every painful impression was multiplied by my diseased sensibility, and an atrocious fear of life took possession of me. I was without passions, without ambitions; I resolved to sacrifice possible joys in order to avoid sure sorrows. Existence is short, but I made up my mind to spend it in the service of others, in relieving their troubles and enjoying their happiness. Having no direct experience of either one or the other, I should only experience a milder form of emotion.

"And if you only knew how, in spite of this, misery tortures me, ravages me! But what would formerly have been an intolerable affliction has become commiseration, pity.

"These sorrows which cross my path at every moment, I could not endure if they affected me directly. I could not have seen one of my children die without dying myself. And I have, in spite of everything, preserved such a mysterious, overwhelming fear of events that the sight of the postman entering my house makes a shiver pass every day through my veins, and yet I have nothing to be afraid of now."

The Abbe Mauduit ceased speaking. He stared into the fire in the huge grate, as if he saw there mysterious things, all the unknown of the existence he might have passed had he been more fearless in the face of suffering.

He added, then, in a subdued tone:

"I was right. I was not made for this world."

The comtesse said nothing at first; but at length, after a long silence, she remarked:

"For my part, if I had not my grandchildren, I believe I would not have the courage to live."

And the cure rose up without saying another word.

As the servants were asleep in the kitchen, she accompanied him herself to the door, which looked out on the garden, and she saw his tall shadow, lit up by the reflection of the lamp, disappearing through the gloom of night.

Then she came back and sat down before the fire, and pondered over many things we never think of when we are young.

FORGIVENESS

She had been brought up in one of those families who live entirely to themselves, apart from all the rest of the world. Such families know nothing of political events, although they are discussed at table; for changes in the Government take place at such a distance from them that they are spoken of as one speaks of a historical event, such as the death of Louis XVI or the landing of Napoleon.

Customs are modified in course of time, fashions succeed one another, but such variations are taken no account of in the placid family circle where traditional usages prevail year after year. And if some scandalous episode or other occurs in the neighborhood, the disreputable story dies a natural death when it reaches the threshold of the house. The father and mother may, perhaps, exchange a few words on the subject when alone together some evening, but they speak in hushed tones—for even walls have ears. The father says, with bated breath:

"You've heard of that terrible affair in the Rivoil family?"

And the mother answers:

"Who would have dreamed of such a thing? It's dreadful."

The children suspected nothing, and arrive in their turn at years of discretion with eyes and mind blindfolded, ignorant of the real side of life, not knowing that people do not think as they speak, and do not speak as they act; or aware that they should live at war, or at all events, in a state of armed peace, with the rest of mankind; not suspecting the fact that the simple are always deceived, the sincere made sport of, the good maltreated.

Some go on till the day of their death in this blind probity and loyalty and honor, so pure-minded that nothing can open their eyes.

Others, undeceived, but without fully understanding, make mistakes, are dismayed, and become desperate, believing themselves the playthings of a cruel fate, the wretched victims of adverse circumstances, and exceptionally wicked men.

The Savignols married their daughter Bertha at the age of eighteen. She wedded a young Parisian, George Baron by name, who had dealings on the Stock Exchange. He was handsome, well-mannered, and apparently all that could be desired. But in the depths of his heart he somewhat despised his old-fashioned parents-in-law, whom he spoke of among his intimates as "my dear old fossils."

He belonged to a good family, and the girl was rich. They settled down in Paris.

She became one of those provincial Parisians whose name is legion. She remained in complete ignorance of the great city, of its social side, its pleasures and its customs—just as she remained ignorant also of life, its perfidy and its mysteries.

Devoted to her house, she knew scarcely anything beyond her own street; and when she ventured into another part of Paris it seemed to her that she had accomplished a long and arduous journey into some unknown, unexplored city. She would then say to her husband in the evening:

"I have been through the boulevards to-day."

Two or three times a year her husband took her to the theatre. These were events the remembrance of which never grew dim; they provided subjects of conversation for long afterward.

Sometimes three months afterward she would suddenly burst into laughter, and exclaim:

"Do you remember that actor dressed up as a general, who crowed like a cock?"

Her friends were limited to two families related to her own. She spoke of them as "the Martinets" and "the Michelins."

Her husband lived as he pleased, coming home when it suited him —sometimes not until dawn—alleging business, but not putting himself out overmuch to account for his movements, well aware that no suspicion would ever enter his wife's guileless soul.

But one morning she received an anonymous letter.

She was thunderstruck—too simple-minded to understand the infamy of unsigned information and to despise the letter, the writer of which declared himself inspired by interest in her happiness, hatred of evil, and love of truth.

This missive told her that her husband had had for two years past, a sweetheart, a young widow named Madame Rosset, with whom he spent all his evenings.

Bertha knew neither how to dissemble her grief nor how to spy on her husband. When he came in for lunch she threw the letter down before him, burst into tears, and fled to her room.

He had time to take in the situation and to prepare his reply. He knocked at his wife's door. She opened it at once, but dared not look at him. He smiled, sat down, drew her to his knee, and in a tone of light raillery began:

"My dear child, as a matter of fact, I have a friend named Madame Rosset, whom I have known for the last ten years, and of whom I have a very high opinion. I may add that I know scores of other people whose names I have never mentioned to you, seeing that you do not care for society, or fresh acquaintances, or functions of any sort. But, to make short work of such vile accusations as this, I want you to put on your things after lunch, and we'll go together and call on this lady, who will very soon become a friend of yours, too, I am quite sure."

She embraced her husband warmly, and, moved by that feminine spirit of curiosity which will not be lulled once it is aroused, consented to go and see this unknown widow, of whom she was, in spite of everything, just the least bit jealous. She felt instinctively that to know a danger is to be already armed against it.

She entered a small, tastefully furnished flat on the fourth floor of an attractive house. After waiting five minutes in a drawing-room rendered somewhat dark by its many curtains and hangings, a door opened, and a very dark, short, rather plump young woman appeared, surprised and smiling.

George introduced them:

"My wife—Madame Julie Rosset."

The young widow uttered a half-suppressed cry of astonishment and joy, and ran forward with hands outstretched. She had not hoped, she said, to have this pleasure, knowing that Madame Baron never saw any one, but she was delighted to make her acquaintance. She was so fond of George (she said "George" in a familiar, sisterly sort of way) that, she had been most anxious to know his young wife and to make friends with her, too.

By the end of a month the two new friends were inseparable. They saw each other every day, sometimes twice a day, and dined together every evening, sometimes at one house, sometimes at the other. George no longer deserted his home, no longer talked of pressing business. He adored his own fireside, he said.

When, after a time, a flat in the house where Madame Rosset lived became vacant Madame Baron hastened to take it, in order to be near her friend and spend even more time with her than hitherto.

And for two whole years their friendship was without a cloud, a friendship of heart and mind—absolute, tender, devoted. Bertha could hardly speak without bringing in Julie's name. To her Madame Rosset represented perfection.

She was utterly happy, calm and contented.

But Madame Rosset fell ill. Bertha hardly left her side. She spent her nights with her, distracted with grief; even her husband seemed inconsolable.

One morning the doctor, after leaving the invalid's bedside, took George and his wife aside, and told them that he considered Julie's condition very grave.

As soon as he had gone the grief-stricken husband and wife sat down opposite each other and gave way to tears. That night they both sat up with the patient. Bertha tenderly kissed her friend from time to time, while George stood at the foot of the bed, his eyes gazing steadfastly on the invalid's face.

The next day she was worse.

But toward evening she declared she felt better, and insisted that her friends should go back to their own apartment to dinner.

They were sitting sadly in the dining-room, scarcely even attempting to eat, when the maid gave George a note. He opened it, turned pale as death, and, rising from the table, said to his wife in a constrained voice:

"Wait for me. I must leave you a moment. I shall be back in ten minutes. Don't go away on any account."

And he hurried to his room to get his hat.

Bertha waited for him, a prey to fresh anxiety. But, docile in everything, she would not go back to her friend till he returned.

At length, as he did not reappear, it occurred to her to visit his room and see if he had taken his gloves. This would show whether or not he had had a call to make.

She saw them at the first glance. Beside them lay a crumpled paper, evidently thrown down in haste.

She recognized it at once as the note George had received.

And a burning temptation, the first that had ever assailed her urged her to read it and discover the cause of her husband's abrupt departure. Her rebellious conscience protested but a devouring and fearful curiosity prevailed. She seized the paper, smoothed it out, recognized the tremulous, penciled writing as Julie's, and read:

"Come alone and kiss me, my poor dear. I am dying."

At first she did not understand, the idea of Julie's death being her uppermost thought. But all at once the true meaning of what she read burst in a flash upon her; this penciled note threw a lurid light upon her whole existence, revealed the whole infamous truth, all the treachery and perfidy of which she had been the victim. She understood the long years of deceit, the way in which she had been made their puppet. She saw them again, sitting side by side in the evening, reading by lamplight out of the same book, glancing at each other at the end of each page.

And her poor, indignant, suffering, bleeding heart was cast into the depths of a despair which knew no bounds.

Footsteps drew near; she fled, and shut herself in her own room.

Presently her husband called her:

"Come quickly! Madame Rosset is dying."

Bertha appeared at her door, and with trembling lips replied:

"Go back to her alone; she does not need me."

He looked at her stupidly, dazed with grief, and repeated:

"Come at once! She's dying, I tell you!"

Bertha answered:

"You would rather it were I."

Then at last he understood, and returned alone to the dying woman's bedside.

He mourned her openly, shamelessly, indifferent to the sorrow of the wife who no longer spoke to him, no longer looked at him;

who passed her life in solitude, hedged round with disgust, with indignant anger, and praying night and day to God.

They still lived in the same house, however, and sat opposite each other at table, in silence and despair.

Gradually his sorrow grew less acute; but she did not forgive him.

And so their life went on, hard and bitter for them both.

For a whole year they remained as complete strangers to each other as if they had never met. Bertha nearly lost her reason.

At last one morning she went out very early, and returned about eight o'clock bearing in her hands an enormous bouquet of white roses. And she sent word to her husband that she wanted to speak to him. He came-anxious and uneasy.

"We are going out together," she said. "Please carry these flowers; they are too heavy for me."

A carriage took them to the gate of the cemetery, where they alighted. Then, her eyes filling with tears, she said to George:

"Take me to her grave."

He trembled, and could not understand her motive; but he led the way, still carrying the flowers. At last he stopped before a white marble slab, to which he pointed without a word.

She took the bouquet from him, and, kneeling down, placed it on the grave. Then she offered up a silent, heartfelt prayer.

Behind her stood her husband, overcome by recollections of the past.

She rose, and held out her hands to him.

"If you wish it, we will be friends," she said.

IN THE SPRING

With the first day of spring, when the awakening earth puts on its garment of green, and the warm, fragrant air fans our faces and fills our lungs and appears even to penetrate to our hearts, we experience a vague, undefined longing for freedom, for happiness, a desire to run, to wander aimlessly, to breathe in the spring. The previous winter having been unusually severe, this spring feeling was like a form of intoxication in May, as if there were an overabundant supply of sap.

One morning on waking I saw from my window the blue sky glowing in the sun above the neighboring houses. The canaries hanging in the windows were singing loudly, and so were the servants on every floor; a cheerful noise rose up from the streets, and I went out, my spirits as bright as the day, to go—I did not exactly know where. Everybody I met seemed to be smiling; an air of happiness appeared to pervade everything in the warm light of returning spring. One might almost have said that a breeze of love was blowing through the city, and the sight of the young women whom I saw in the streets in their morning toilets, in the depths of whose eyes there lurked a hidden tenderness, and who walked with languid grace, filled my heart with agitation.

Without knowing how or why, I found myself on the banks of the Seine. Steamboats were starting for Suresnes, and suddenly I was seized by an unconquerable desire to take a walk through the woods. The deck of the Mouche was covered with passengers, for the sun in early spring draws one out of the house, in spite of themselves, and everybody moves about, goes and comes and talks to his neighbor.

I had a girl neighbor; a little work-girl, no doubt, who possessed the true Parisian charm: a little head, with light curly hair, which looked like a shimmer of light as it danced in the wind, came down to her ears, and descended to the nape of her neck, where it became such fine, light-colored clown that one could scarcely see it, but felt an irresistible desire to shower kisses on it.

Under my persistent gaze, she turned her head toward me, and then immediately looked down, while a slight crease at the side of her mouth, that was ready to break out into a smile, also showed a fine, silky, pale down which the sun was gilding a little.

The calm river grew wider; the atmosphere was warm and perfectly still, but a murmur of life seemed to fill all space.

My neighbor raised her eyes again, and this time, as I was still looking at her, she smiled decidedly. She was charming, and in her passing glance I saw a thousand things, which I had hitherto been ignorant of, for I perceived unknown depths, all the charm of tenderness, all the poetry which we dream of, all the happiness which we are continually in search of. I felt an insane longing to open my arms and to carry her off somewhere, so as to whisper the sweet music of words of love into her ears.

I was just about to address her when somebody touched me on the shoulder, and as I turned round in some surprise, I saw an ordinary-looking man, who was neither young nor old, and who gazed at me sadly.

"I should like to speak to you," he said.

I made a grimace, which he no doubt saw, for he added:

"It is a matter of importance."

I got up, therefore, and followed him to the other end of the boat and then he said:

"Monsieur, when winter comes, with its cold, wet and snowy weather, your doctor says to you constantly: 'Keep your feet warm, guard against chills, colds, bronchitis, rheumatism and pleurisy.'

"Then you are very careful, you wear flannel, a heavy greatcoat and thick shoes, but all this does not prevent you from passing two months in bed. But when spring returns, with its leaves and flowers, its warm, soft breezes and its smell of the fields, all of which causes you vague disquiet and causeless emotion, nobody says to you:

"'Monsieur, beware of love! It is lying in ambush everywhere; it is watching for you at every corner; all its snares are laid, all its weapons are sharpened, all its guiles are prepared! Beware of love! Beware of love! It is more dangerous than brandy, bronchitis or pleurisy! It never forgives and makes everybody commit irreparable follies.'

"Yes, monsieur, I say that the French Government ought to put large public notices on the walls, with these words: 'Return of spring. French citizens, beware of love!' just as they put: 'Beware of paint:

"However, as the government will not do this, I must supply its place, and I say to you: 'Beware of love!' for it is just going to seize you, and it is my duty to inform you of it, just as in Russia they inform any one that his nose is frozen."

I was much astonished at this individual, and assuming a dignified manner, I said:

"Really, monsieur, you appear to me to be interfering in a matter which is no concern of yours."

He made an abrupt movement and replied:

"Ah! monsieur, monsieur! If I see that a man is in danger of being drowned at a dangerous spot, ought I to let him perish? So just listen to my story and you will see why I ventured to speak to you like this.

"It was about this time last year that it occurred. But, first of all, I must tell you that I am a clerk in the Admiralty, where our chiefs, the commissioners, take their gold lace as quill-driving officials seriously, and treat us like forecastle men on board a ship. Well, from my office I could see a small bit of blue sky and the swallows, and I felt inclined to dance among my portfolios.

"My yearning for freedom grew so intense that, in spite of my repugnance, I went to see my chief, a short, bad-tempered man, who was always in a rage. When I told him that I was not well, he looked at me and said: 'I do not believe it, monsieur, but be off with you! Do you think that any office can go on with clerks like you?' I started at once and went down the Seine. It was a day like this, and I took the Mouche, to go as far as Saint Cloud. Ah! what a good thing it would have been if my chief had refused me permission to leave the office that day!

"I seemed to myself to expand in the sun. I loved everything—the steamer, the river, the trees, the houses and my fellow-passengers. I felt inclined to kiss something, no matter what; it was love, laying its snare. Presently, at the Trocadero, a girl, with a small parcel in her hand, came on board and sat down opposite me. She was decidedly pretty, but it is surprising, monsieur, how much prettier women seem to us when the day is fine at the beginning of the spring. Then they have an intoxicating charm, something quite peculiar about them. It is just like drinking wine after cheese.

"I looked at her and she also looked at me, but only occasionally, as that girl did at you, just now; but at last, by dint of looking at each other constantly, it seemed to me that we knew each other well enough to enter into conversation, and I spoke to her and she replied. She was decidedly pretty and nice and she intoxicated me, monsieur!

"She got out at Saint-Cloud, and I followed her. She went and delivered her parcel, and when she returned the boat had just started. I walked by her side, and the warmth of the 'air made us both sigh. 'It would be very nice in the woods,' I said. 'Indeed, it would!' she replied. 'Shall we go there for a walk, mademoiselle?'

"She gave me a quick upward look, as if to see exactly what I was like, and then, after a little hesitation, she accepted my proposal, and soon we were there, walking side by side. Under the foliage, which was still rather scanty, the tall, thick, bright green grass was inundated by the sun, and the air was full of insects that were also making love to one another, and birds were singing in all directions. My companion began to jump and to run, intoxicated by the air and the smell of the country, and I ran and jumped, following her example. How silly we are at times, monsieur!

"Then she sang unrestrainedly a thousand things, opera airs and the song of Musette! The song of Musette! How poetical it seemed to me, then! I almost cried over it. Ah! Those silly songs make us lose our heads; and, believe me, never marry a woman who sings in the country, especially if she sings the song of Musette!

"She soon grew tired, and sat down on a grassy slope, and I sat at her feet and took her hands, her little hands, that were so marked with the needle, and that filled me with emotion. I said to myself:

"'These are the sacred marks of toil.' Oh! monsieur, do you know what those sacred marks of toil mean? They mean all the gossip of the workroom, the whispered scandal, the mind soiled by all the filth that is talked; they mean lost chastity, foolish chatter, all the wretchedness of their everyday life, all the narrowness of ideas which belongs to women of the lower orders, combined to their fullest extent in the girl whose fingers bear the sacred marks of toil.

"Then we looked into each other's eyes for a long while. Oh! what power a woman's eye has! How it agitates us, how it invades our very being, takes possession of us, and dominates us! How profound it seems, how full of infinite promises! People call that looking into each other's souls! Oh! monsieur, what humbug! If we could see into each other's souls, we should be more careful of what we did. However, I was captivated and was crazy about her and tried to take her into my arms, but she said: 'Paws off!'. Then I knelt down and opened my heart to her and poured out all the affection that was suffocating me. She seemed surprised at my change of manner and gave me a sidelong glance, as if to say, 'Ah! so that is the way women make a fool of you, old fellow! Very well, we will see.'

"In love, monsieur, we are always novices, and women artful dealers.

"No doubt I could have had her, and I saw my own stupidity later, but what I wanted was not a woman's person, it was love, it was the ideal. I was sentimental, when I ought to have been using my time to a better purpose.

"As soon as she had had enough of my declarations of affection, she got up, and we returned to Saint-Cloud, and I did not leave her until we got to Paris; but she had looked so sad as we were returning, that at last I asked her what was the matter. 'I am thinking,' she replied, 'that this has been one of those days of which we have but few in life.' My heart beat so that it felt as if it would break my ribs.

"I saw her on the following Sunday, and the next Sunday, and every Sunday. I took her to Bougival, Saint-Germain, Maisons-Lafitte, Poissy; to every suburban resort of lovers.

"The little jade, in turn, pretended to love me, until, at last, I altogether lost my head, and three months later I married her.

"What can you expect, monsieur, when a man is a clerk, living alone, without any relations, or any one to advise him? One says to one's self: 'How sweet life would be with a wife!'

"And so one gets married and she calls you names from morning till night, understands nothing, knows nothing, chatters continually, sings the song of Musette at the, top of her voice (oh! that song of Musette, how tired one gets of it!); quarrels with the charcoal dealer, tells the janitor all her domestic details, confides all the secrets of her bedroom to the neighbor's servant, discusses her husband with the tradespeople and has her head so stuffed with stupid stories, with idiotic superstitions, with extraordinary ideas and monstrous prejudices, that I—for what I have said applies more particularly to myself—shed tears of discouragement every time I talk to her."

He stopped, as he was rather out of breath and very much moved, and I looked at him, for I felt pity for this poor, artless devil, and I was just going to give him some sort of answer, when the boat stopped. We were at Saint-Cloud.

The little woman who had so taken my fancy rose from her seat in order to land. She passed close to me, and gave me a sidelong glance and a furtive smile, one of those smiles that drive you wild. Then she jumped on the landing-stage. I sprang forward to follow her, but my neighbor laid hold of my arm. I shook myself loose, however, whereupon he seized the skirt of my coat and pulled me back, exclaiming: "You shall not go! you shall not go!" in such a loud voice that everybody turned round and laughed, and I remained standing motionless and furious, but without venturing to face scandal and ridicule, and the steamboat started.

The little woman on the landing-stage looked at me as I went off with an air of disappointment, while my persecutor rubbed his hands and whispered to me:

"You must acknowledge that I have done you a great service."

A QUEER NIGHT IN PARIS

Mattre Saval, notary at Vernon, was passionately fond of music. Although still young he was already bald; he was always carefully shaven, was somewhat corpulent as was suitable, and wore a gold pince-nez instead of spectacles. He was active, gallant and cheerful and was considered quite an artist in Vernon. He played the piano and the violin, and gave musicals where the new operas were interpreted.

He had even what is called a bit of a voice; nothing but a bit, very little bit of a voice; but he managed it with so much taste that cries of "Bravo!" "Exquisite!" "Surprising!" "Adorable!" issued from every throat as soon as he had murmured the last note.

He subscribed to a music publishing house in Paris, and they sent him the latest music, and from time to time he sent invitations after this fashion to the elite of the town:

"You are invited to be present on Monday evening at the house of M. Saval, notary, Vernon, at the first rendering of 'Sais.'"

A few officers, gifted with good voices, formed the chorus. Two or three lady amateurs also sang. The notary filled the part of leader of the orchestra with so much correctness that the bandmaster of the 190th regiment of the line said of him, one day, at the Cafe de l'Europe.

"Oh! M. Saval is a master. It is a great pity that he did not adopt the career of an artist."

When his name was mentioned in a drawing-room, there was always somebody found to declare: "He is not an amateur; he is an artist, a genuine artist."

And two or three persons repeated, in a tone of profound conviction:

"Oh! yes, a genuine artist," laying particular stress on the word "genuine."

Every time that a new work was interpreted at a big Parisian theatre M. Saval paid a visit to the capital.

Now, last year, according to his custom, he went to hear Henri VIII. He then took the express which arrives in Paris at 4:30 P.M., intending to return by the 12:35 A.M. train, so as not to have to sleep at a hotel. He had put on evening dress, a black coat and white tie, which he concealed under his overcoat with the collar turned up.

As soon as he set foot on the Rue d'Amsterdam, he felt himself in quite jovial mood. He said to himself:

"Decidedly, the air of Paris does not resemble any other air. It has in it something indescribably stimulating, exciting, intoxicating, which fills you with a strange longing to dance about and to do many other things. As soon as I arrive here, it seems to me, all of a sudden, that I have taken a bottle of champagne. What a life one can lead in this city in the midst of artists! Happy are the elect, the great men who make themselves a reputation in such a city! What an existence is theirs!"

And he made plans; he would have liked to know some of these celebrated men, to talk about them in Vernon, and to spend an evening with them from time to time in Paris.

But suddenly an idea struck him. He had heard allusions to little cafes in the outer boulevards at which well-known painters, men of letters, and even musicians gathered, and he proceeded to go up to Montmartre at a slow pace.

He had two hours before him. He wanted to look about him. He passed in front of taverns frequented by belated bohemians, gazing at the different faces, seeking to discover the artists. Finally, he came to the sign of "The Dead Rat," and, allured by the name, he entered.

Five or six women, with their elbows resting on the marble tables, were talking in low tones about their love affairs, the quarrels of Lucie and Hortense, and the scoundrelism of Octave. They were no longer young, were too fat or too thin, tired out, used up. You could see that they were almost bald; and they drank beer like men.

M. Saval sat down at some distance from them and waited, for the hour for taking absinthe was at hand.

A tall young man soon came in and took a seat beside him. The landlady called him M. "Romantin." The notary quivered. Was this the Romantin who had taken a medal at the last Salon?

The young man made a sign to the waiter.

"You will bring up my dinner at once, and then carry to my new studio, 15 Boulevard de Clichy, thirty bottles of beer, and the ham I ordered this morning. We are going to have a housewarming."

M. Saval immediately ordered dinner. Then, he took off his overcoat, so that his dress suit and his white tie could be seen. His neighbor did not seem to notice him. He had taken up a newspaper, and was reading it. M. Saval glanced sideways at him, burning with the desire to speak to him.

Two young men entered, in red vests and with peaked beards, in the fashion of Henry III. They sat down opposite Romantin.

The first of the pair said:

"Is it for this evening?"

Romantin pressed his hand.

"I believe you, old chap, and everyone will be there. I have Bonnat, Guillemet, Gervex, Beraud, Hebert, Duez, Clairin, and Jean-Paul Laurens. It will be a stunning affair! And women, too! Wait till you see! Every actress without exception—of course I mean, you know, all those who have nothing to do this evening."

The landlord of the establishment came across.

"Do you often have this housewarming?"

The painter replied:

"I believe you, every three months, each quarter."

M. Saval could not restrain himself any longer, and in a hesitating voice said:

"I beg your pardon for intruding on you, monsieur, but I heard your name mentioned, and I would be very glad to know if you really are M. Romantin, whose work in the last Salon I have so much admired?"

The painter answered:

"I am the very person, monsieur."

The notary then paid the artist a very well-turned compliment, showing that he was a man of culture.

The painter, gratified, thanked him politely in reply.

Then they chattered. Romantin returned to the subject of his house-warming, going into details as to the magnificence of the forthcoming entertainment.

M. Saval questioned him as to all the men he was going to receive, adding:

"It would be an extraordinary piece of good fortune for a stranger to meet at one time so many celebrities assembled in the studio of an artist of your rank."

Romantin, vanquished, replied:

"If it would be agreeable to you, come."

M. Saval accepted the invitation with enthusiasm, reflecting:

"I shall have time enough to see Henri VIII."

Both of them had finished their meal. The notary insisted on paying the two bills, wishing to repay his neighbor's civilities. He also paid for the drinks of the young fellows in red velvet; then he left the establishment with the painter.

They stopped in front of a very long, low house, the first story having the appearance of an interminable conservatory. Six studios stood in a row with their fronts facing the boulevards.

Romantin was the first to enter, and, ascending the stairs, he opened a door, and lighted a match and then a candle.

They found themselves in an immense apartment, the furniture of which consisted of three chairs, two easels, and a few sketches standing on the ground along the walls. M. Saval remained standing at the door somewhat astonished.

The painter remarked:

"Here you are! we've got to the spot; but everything has yet to be done."

Then, examining the high, bare apartment, its ceiling disappearing in the darkness, he said:

"We might make a great deal out of this studio."

He walked round it, surveying it with the utmost attention, then went on:

"I know someone who might easily give a helping hand. Women are incomparable for hanging drapery. But I sent her to the country for to-day in order to get her off my hands this evening. It is not that she bores me, but she is too much lacking in the ways of good society. It would be embarrassing to my guests."

He reflected for a few seconds, and then added:

"She is a good girl, but not easy to deal with. If she knew that I was holding a reception, she would tear out my eyes."

M. Saval had not even moved; he did not understand.

The artist came over to him.

"Since I have invited you, you will assist me about something."

The notary said emphatically:

"Make any use of me you please. I am at your disposal."

Romantin took off his jacket.

"Well, citizen, to work!' We are first going to clean up."

He went to the back of the easel, on which there was a canvas representing a cat, and seized a very worn-out broom.

"I say! Just brush up while I look after the lighting."

M. Saval took the broom, inspected it, and then began to sweep the floor very awkwardly, raising a whirlwind of dust.

Romantin, disgusted, stopped him: "Deuce take it! you don't know how to sweep the floor! Look at me!"

And he began to roll before him a heap of grayish sweepings, as if he had done nothing else all his life. Then, he gave bark the broom to the notary, who imitated him.

In five minutes, such a cloud of dust filled the studio that Rormantin asked:

"Where are you? I can't see you any longer."

M. Saval, who was coughing, came near to him. The painter said:

"How would you set about making a chandelier?"

The other, surprised, asked:

"What chandelier?"

"Why, a chandelier to light the room—a chandelier with wax-candles."

The notary did not understand.

He answered: "I don't know."

The painter began to jump about, cracking his fingers.

"Well, monseigneur, I have found out a way."

Then he went on more calmly:

"Have you got five francs about you?"

M. Saval replied:

"Why, yes."

The artist said: "Well! you'll go out and buy for me five francs' worth of wax-candles while I go and see the cooper."

And he pushed the notary in his evening coat into the street. At the end of five minutes, they had returned, one of them with the wax-candles and the other with the hoop of a cask. Then Romantin plunged his hand into a cupboard, and drew forth twenty empty bottles, which he fixed in the form of a crown around the hoop.

He then went downstairs to borrow a ladder from the janitress, after having explained that he had made interest with the old woman by painting the portrait of her cat, exhibited on the easel.

When he returned with the ladder, he said to M. Saval:

"Are you active?"

The other, without understanding, answered:

"Why, yes."

"Well, you just climb up there, and fasten this chandelier for me to the ring of the ceiling. Then, you put a wax-candle in each bottle, and light it. I tell you I have a genius for lighting up. But off with your coat, damn it! You are just like a Jeames."

The door was opened brusquely. A woman appeared, her eyes flashing, and remained standing on the threshold.

Romantin gazed at her with a look of terror.

She waited some seconds, crossing her arms over her breast, and then in a shrill, vibrating, exasperated voice said:

"Ha! you dirty scoundrel, is this the way you leave me?"

Romantin made no reply. She went on:

"Ha! you scoundrel! You did a nice thing in parking me off to the country. You'll soon see the way I'll settle your jollification. Yes, I'm going to receive your friends."

She grew warmer.

"I'm going to slap their faces with the bottles and the wax-candles——"

Romantin said in a soft tone:

"Mathilde——"

But she did not pay any attention to him; she went on:

"Wait a little, my fine fellow! wait a little!"

Romantin went over to her, and tried to take her by the hands.

"Mathilde——"

But she was now fairly under way; and on she went, emptying the vials of her wrath with strong words and reproaches. They flowed out of her mouth like, a stream sweeping a heap of filth along with it. The words pouring forth seemed struggling for exit. She stuttered, stammered, yelled, suddenly recovering her voice to cast forth an insult or a curse.

He seized her hands without her having noticed it. She did not seem to see anything, so taken up was she in scolding and relieving her feelings. And suddenly she began to weep. The tears flowed from her eyes, but this did not stop her complaints. But her words were uttered in a screaming falsetto voice with tears in it and interrupted by sobs. She commenced afresh twice or three times, till she stopped as if something were choking her, and at last she ceased with a regular flood of tears.

Then he clasped her in his arms and kissed her hair, affected himself.

"Mathilde, my little Mathilde, listen. You must be reasonable. You know, if I give a supper-party to my friends, it is to thank these gentlemen for the medal I got at the Salon. I cannot receive women. You ought to understand that. It is not the same with artists as with other people."

She stammered, in the midst of her tears:

"Why didn't you tell me this?"

He replied:

"It was in order not to annoy you, not to give you pain. Listen, I'm going to see you home. You will be very sensible, very nice; you will remain quietly waiting for me in bed, and I'll come back as soon as it's over."

She murmured:

"Yes, but you will not begin over again?"

"No, I swear to you!"

He turned towards M. Saval, who had at last hooked on the chandelier:

"My dear friend, I am coming back in five minutes. If anyone arrives in my absence, do the honors for me, will you not?"

And he carried off Mathilde, who kept drying her eyes with her handkerchief as she went along.

Left to himself, M. Saval succeeded in putting everything around him in order. Then he lighted the wax-candles, and waited.

He waited for a quarter of an hour, half an hour, an hour. Romantin did not return. Then, suddenly there was a dreadful noise on the stairs, a song shouted out in chorus by twenty mouths and a regular march like that of a Prussian regiment. The whole house was shaken by the steady tramp of feet. The door flew open, and a motley throng appeared—men and women in file, two and two holding each other by the arm and stamping their heels on the ground to mark time, advanced into the studio like a snake uncoiling itself. They howled:

"Come, and let us all be merry,
Pretty maids and soldiers gay!"

M. Saval, thunderstruck, remained standing in evening dress under the chandelier. The procession of revellers caught sight of him, and uttered a shout:

"A Jeames! A Jeames!"

And they began whirling round him, surrounding him with a circle of vociferations. Then they took each other by the hand and went dancing about madly.

He attempted to explain:

"Messieurs—messieurs—mesdames——"

But they did not listen to him. They whirled about, they jumped, they brawled.

At last, the dancing ceased. M. Saval said:

"Gentlemen——"

A tall young fellow, fair-haired and bearded to the nose, interrupted him:

"What's your name, my friend?"

The notary, quite scared, said:

"I am M. Saval."

A voice exclaimed:

"You mean Baptiste."

A woman said:

"Let the poor waiter alone! You'll end by making him get angry. He's paid to wait on us, and not to be laughed at by us."

Then, M. Saval noticed that each guest had brought his own provisions. One held a bottle of wine, and the other a pie. This one had a loaf of bread, and one a ham.

The tall, fair young fellow placed in his hands an enormous sausage, and gave orders:

"Here, go and arrange the sideboard in the corner over there. Put the bottles at the left and the provisions at the right."

Saval, getting quite distracted, exclaimed: "But, messieurs, I am a notary!"

There was a moment's silence and then a wild outburst of laughter. One suspicious gentleman asked:

"How came you to be here?"

He explained, telling about his project of going to the opera, his departure from Vernon, his arrival in Paris, and the way in which he had spent the evening.

They sat around him to listen to him; they greeted him with words of applause, and called him Scheherazade.

Romantin did not return. Other guests arrived. M. Saval was presented to them so that he might begin his story over again. He declined; they forced him to relate it. They seated and tied him on one of three chairs between two women who kept constantly filling his glass. He drank; he laughed; he talked; he sang, too. He tried to waltz with his chair, and fell on the ground.

From that moment, he forgot everything. It seemed to him, however, that they undressed him, put him to bed, and that he was nauseated.

When he awoke, it was broad daylight, and he lay stretched with his feet against a cupboard, in a strange bed.

An old woman with a broom in her hand was glaring angrily at him. At last, she said:

"Clear out, you blackguard! Clear out! What right has anyone to get drunk like this?"

He sat up in bed, feeling very ill at ease. He asked:

"Where am I?"

"Where are you, you dirty scamp? You are drunk. Take your rotten carcass out of here as quick as you can—and lose no time about it!"

He wanted to get up. He found that he was in no condition to do so. His clothes had disappeared. He blurted out:

"Madame, I——Then he remembered. What was he to do? He asked:

"Did Monsieur Romantin come back?"

The doorkeeper shouted:

"Will you take your dirty carcass out of this, so that he at any rate may not catch you here?"

M. Saval said, in a state of confusion:

"I haven't got my clothes; they have been taken away from me."

He had to wait, to explain his situation, give notice to his friends, and borrow some money to buy clothes. He did not leave Paris till evening. And when people talk about music to him in his beautiful drawing-room in Vernon, he declares with an air of authority that painting is a very inferior art.

VOLUME VI

THAT COSTLY RIDE

The household lived frugally on the meager income derived from the husband's insignificant appointments. Two children had been born of the marriage, and the earlier condition of the strictest economy had become one of quiet, concealed, shamefaced misery, the poverty of a noble family—which in spite of misfortune never forgets its rank.

Hector de Gribelin had been educated in the provinces, under the paternal roof, by an aged priest. His people were not rich, but they managed to live and to keep up appearances.

At twenty years of age they tried to find him a position, and he entered the Ministry of Marine as a clerk at sixty pounds a year. He foundered on the rock of life like all those who have not been early prepared for its rude struggles, who look at life through a mist, who do not know how to protect themselves, whose special aptitudes and faculties have not been developed from childhood, whose early training has not developed the rough energy needed for the battle of life or furnished them with tool or weapon.

His first three years of office work were a martyrdom.

He had, however, renewed the acquaintance of a few friends of his family —elderly people, far behind the times, and poor like himself, who lived in aristocratic streets, the gloomy thoroughfares of the Faubourg Saint-Germain; and he had created a social circle for himself.

Strangers to modern life, humble yet proud, these needy aristocrats lived in the upper stories of sleepy, old-world houses.

From top to bottom of their dwellings the tenants were titled, but money seemed just as scarce on the ground floor as in the attics.

Their eternal prejudices, absorption in their rank, anxiety lest they should lose caste, filled the minds and thoughts of these families once so brilliant, now ruined by the idleness of the men of the family. Hector de Gribelin met in this circle a young girl as well born and as poor as himself and married her.

They had two children in four years.

For four years more the husband and wife, harassed by poverty, knew no other distraction than the Sunday walk in the Champs-Elysees and a few evenings at the theatre (amounting in all to one or two in the course of the winter) which they owed to free passes presented by some comrade or other.

But in the spring of the following year some overtime work was entrusted to Hector de Gribelin by his chief, for which he received the large sum of three hundred francs.

The day he brought the money home he said to his wife:

"My dear Henrietta, we must indulge in some sort of festivity—say an outing for the children."

And after a long discussion it was decided that they should go and lunch one day in the country.

"Well," cried Hector, "once will not break us, so we'll hire a wagonette for you, the children and the maid. And I'll have a saddle horse; the exercise will do me good."

The whole week long they talked of nothing but the projected excursion.

Every evening, on his return from the office, Hector caught up his elder son, put him astride his leg, and, making him bounce up and down as hard as he could, said:

"That's how daddy will gallop next Sunday."

And the youngster amused himself all day long by bestriding chairs, dragging them round the room and shouting:

"This is daddy on horseback!"

The servant herself gazed at her master with awestruck eyes as she thought of him riding alongside the carriage, and at meal-times she listened with all her ears while he spoke of riding and recounted the exploits of his youth, when he lived at home with his father. Oh, he had learned in a good school, and once he felt his steed between his legs he feared nothing—nothing whatever!

Rubbing his hands, he repeated gaily to his wife:

"If only they would give me a restive animal I should be all the better pleased. You'll see how well I can ride; and if you like we'll come back by the Champs-Elysees just as all the people are returning from the Bois. As we shall make a good appearance, I shouldn't at all object to meeting some one from the ministry. That is all that is necessary to insure the respect of one's chiefs."

On the day appointed the carriage and the riding horse arrived at the same moment before the door. Hector went down immediately to examine his mount. He had had straps sewn to his trousers and flourished in his hand a whip he had bought the evening before.

He raised the horse's legs and felt them one after another, passed his hand over the animal's neck, flank and hocks, opened his mouth, examined his teeth, declared his age; and then, the whole household having collected round him, he delivered a discourse on the horse in general and the specimen before him in particular, pronouncing the latter excellent in every respect.

When the rest of the party had taken their seats in the carriage he examined the saddle-girth; then, putting his foot in the stirrup, he sprang to the saddle. The animal began to curvet and nearly threw his rider.

Hector, not altogether at his ease, tried to soothe him:

"Come, come, good horse, gently now!"

Then, when the horse had recovered his equanimity and the rider his nerve, the latter asked:

"Are you ready?"

The occupants of the carriage replied with one voice:

"Yes."

"Forward!" he commanded.

And the cavalcade set out.

All looks were centered on him. He trotted in the English style, rising unnecessarily high in the saddle; looking at times as if he were mounting into space. Sometimes he seemed on the point of falling forward on the horse's mane; his eyes were fixed, his face drawn, his cheeks pale.

His wife, holding one of the children on her knees, and the servant, who was carrying the other, continually cried out:

"Look at papa! look at papa!"

And the two boys, intoxicated by the motion of the carriage, by their delight and by the keen air, uttered shrill cries. The horse, frightened by the noise they made, started off at a gallop, and while Hector was trying to control his steed his hat fell off, and the driver had to get down and pick it up. When the equestrian had recovered it he called to his wife from a distance:

"Don't let the children shout like that! They'll make the horse bolt!"

They lunched on the grass in the Vesinet woods, having brought provisions with them in the carriage.

Although the driver was looking after the three horses, Hector rose every minute to see if his own lacked anything; he patted him on the neck and fed him with bread, cakes and sugar.

"He's an unequal trotter," he declared. "He certainly shook me up a little at first, but, as you saw, I soon got used to it. He knows his master now and won't give any more trouble."

As had been decided, they returned by the Champs-Elysees.

That spacious thoroughfare literally swarmed with vehicles of every kind, and on the sidewalks the pedestrians were so numerous that they looked like two indeterminate black ribbons unfurling their length from the Arc de Triomphe to the Place de la Concorde. A flood of sunlight played on this gay scene, making the varnish of the carriages, the steel of the harness and the handles of the carriage doors shine with dazzling brilliancy.

An intoxication of life and motion seemed to have invaded this assemblage of human beings, carriages and horses. In the distance the outlines of the Obelisk could be discerned in a cloud of golden vapor.

As soon as Hector's horse had passed the Arc de Triomphe he became suddenly imbued with fresh energy, and, realizing that his stable was not far off, began to trot rapidly through the maze of wheels, despite all his rider's efforts to restrain him.

The carriage was now far behind. When the horse arrived opposite the Palais de l'Industrie he saw a clear field before him, and, turning to the right, set off at a gallop.

An old woman wearing an apron was crossing the road in leisurely fashion. She happened to be just in Hector's way as he arrived on the scene riding at full speed. Powerless to control his mount, he shouted at the top of his voice:

"Hi! Look out there! Hi!"

She must have been deaf, for she continued peacefully on her way until the awful moment when, struck by the horse's chest as by a locomotive under full steam, she rolled ten paces off, turning three somersaults on the way.

Voices yelled:

"Stop him!"

Hector, frantic with terror, clung to the horse's mane and shouted:

"Help! help!"

A terrible jolt hurled him, as if shot from a gun, over his horse's ears and cast him into the arms of a policeman who was running up to stop him.

In the space of a second a furious, gesticulating, vociferating group had gathered round him. An old gentleman with a white mustache, wearing a large round decoration, seemed particularly exasperated. He repeated:

"Confound it! When a man is as awkward as all that he should remain at home and not come killing people in the streets, if he doesn't know how to handle a horse."

Four men arrived on the scene, carrying the old woman. She appeared to be dead. Her skin was like parchment, her cap on one side and she was covered with dust.

"Take her to a druggist's," ordered the old gentleman, "and let us go to the commissary of police."

Hector started on his way with a policeman on either side of him, a third was leading his horse. A crowd followed them—and suddenly the wagonette appeared in sight. His wife alighted in consternation, the servant lost her head, the children whimpered. He explained that he would soon be at home, that he had knocked a woman down and that there was not much the matter. And his family, distracted with anxiety, went on their way.

When they arrived before the commissary the explanation took place in few words. He gave his name—Hector de Gribelin, employed at the Ministry of Marine; and then they awaited news of the injured woman. A policeman who had been sent to obtain information returned, saying that she had recovered consciousness, but was complaining of frightful internal pain. She was a charwoman, sixty-five years of age, named Madame Simon.

When he heard that she was not dead Hector regained hope and promised to defray her doctor's bill. Then he hastened to the druggist's. The door way was thronged; the injured woman, huddled in an armchair, was groaning. Her arms hung at her sides, her face was drawn. Two doctors were still engaged in examining her. No bones were broken, but they feared some internal lesion.

Hector addressed her:

"Do you suffer much?"

"Oh, yes!"

"Where is the pain?"

"I feel as if my stomach were on fire."

A doctor approached.

"Are you the gentleman who caused the accident?"

"I am."

"This woman ought to be sent to a home. I know one where they would take her at six francs a day. Would you like me to send her there?"

Hector was delighted at the idea, thanked him and returned home much relieved.

His wife, dissolved in tears, was awaiting him. He reassured her.

"It's all right. This Madame Simon is better already and will be quite well in two or three days. I have sent her to a home. It's all right."

When he left his office the next day he went to inquire for Madame Simon. He found her eating rich soup with an air of great satisfaction.

"Well?" said he.

"Oh, sir," she replied, "I'm just the same. I feel sort of crushed—not a bit better."

The doctor declared they must wait and see; some complication or other might arise.

Hector waited three days, then he returned. The old woman, fresh-faced and clear-eyed, began to whine when she saw him:

"I can't move, sir; I can't move a bit. I shall be like this for the rest of my days."

A shudder passed through Hector's frame. He asked for the doctor, who merely shrugged his shoulders and said:

"What can I do? I can't tell what's wrong with her. She shrieks when they try to raise her. They can't even move her chair from one place to another without her uttering the most distressing cries. I am bound to believe what she tells me; I can't look into her inside. So long as I have no chance of seeing her walk I am not justified in supposing her to be telling lies about herself."

The old woman listened, motionless, a malicious gleam in her eyes.

A week passed, then a fortnight, then a month. Madame Simon did not leave her armchair. She ate from morning to night, grew fat, chatted gaily with the other patients and seemed to enjoy her immobility as if it were the rest to which she was entitled after fifty years of going up and down stairs, of turning mattresses, of carrying coal from one story to another, of sweeping and dusting.

Hector, at his wits' end, came to see her every day. Every day he found her calm and serene, declaring:

"I can't move, sir; I shall never be able to move again."

Every evening Madame de Gribelin, devoured with anxiety, said:

"How is Madame Simon?"

And every time he replied with a resignation born of despair:

"Just the same; no change whatever."

They dismissed the servant, whose wages they could no longer afford. They economized more rigidly than ever. The whole of the extra pay had been swallowed up.

Then Hector summoned four noted doctors, who met in consultation over the old woman. She let them examine her, feel her, sound her, watching them the while with a cunning eye.

"We must make her walk," said one.

"But, sirs, I can't!" she cried. "I can't move!"

Then they took hold of her, raised her and dragged her a short distance, but she slipped from their grasp and fell to the floor, groaning and giving vent to such heartrending cries that they carried her back to her seat with infinite care and precaution.

They pronounced a guarded opinion—agreeing, however, that work was an impossibility to her.

And when Hector brought this news to his wife she sank on a chair, murmuring:

"It would be better to bring her here; it would cost us less."

He started in amazement.

"Here? In our own house? How can you think of such a thing?"

But she, resigned now to anything, replied with tears in her eyes:

"But what can we do, my love? It's not my fault!"

USELESS BEAUTY

I

About half-past five one afternoon at the end of June when the sun was shining warm and bright into the large courtyard, a very elegant victoria with two beautiful black horses drew up in front of the mansion.

The Comtesse de Mascaret came down the steps just as her husband, who was coming home, appeared in the carriage entrance. He stopped for a few moments to look at his wife and turned rather pale. The countess was very beautiful, graceful and distinguished looking, with her long oval face, her complexion like yellow ivory, her large gray eyes and her black hair; and she got into her carriage without looking at him, without even seeming to have noticed him, with such a particularly high-bred air, that the furious jealousy by which he had been devoured for so long again gnawed at his heart. He went up to her and said: "You are going for a drive?"

She merely replied disdainfully: "You see I am!"

"In the Bois de Boulogne?"

"Most probably."

"May I come with you?"

"The carriage belongs to you."

Without being surprised at the tone in which she answered him, he got in and sat down by his wife's side and said: "Bois de

Boulogne." The footman jumped up beside the coachman, and the horses as usual pranced and tossed their heads until they were in the street. Husband and wife sat side by side without speaking. He was thinking how to begin a conversation, but she maintained such an obstinately hard look that he did not venture to make the attempt. At last, however, he cunningly, accidentally as it were, touched the countess' gloved hand with his own, but she drew her arm away with a movement which was so expressive of disgust that he remained thoughtful, in spite of his usual authoritative and despotic character, and he said: "Gabrielle!"

"What do you want?"

"I think you are looking adorable."

She did not reply, but remained lying back in the carriage, looking like an irritated queen. By that time they were driving up the Champs Elysees, toward the Arc de Triomphe. That immense monument, at the end of the long avenue, raised its colossal arch against the red sky and the sun seemed to be descending on it, showering fiery dust on it from the sky.

The stream of carriages, with dashes of sunlight reflected in the silver trappings of the harness and the glass of the lamps, flowed on in a double current toward the town and toward the Bois, and the Comte de Mascaret continued: "My dear Gabrielle!"

Unable to control herself any longer, she replied in an exasperated voice: "Oh! do leave me in peace, pray! I am not even allowed to have my carriage to myself now." He pretended not to hear her and continued: "You never have looked so pretty as you do to-day."

Her patience had come to an end, and she replied with irrepressible anger: "You are wrong to notice it, for I swear to you that I will never have anything to do with you in that way again."

The count was decidedly stupefied and upset, and, his violent nature gaining the upper hand, he exclaimed: "What do you mean by that?" in a tone that betrayed rather the brutal master than the lover. She replied in a low voice, so that the servants might not hear amid the deafening noise of the wheels: "Ah! What do I mean by that? What do I mean by that? Now I recognize you again! Do you want me to tell everything?"

"Yes."

"Everything that has weighed on my heart since I have been the victim of your terrible selfishness?"

He had grown red with surprise and anger and he growled between his closed teeth: "Yes, tell me everything."

He was a tall, broad-shouldered man, with a big red beard, a handsome man, a nobleman, a man of the world, who passed as a perfect husband and an excellent father, and now, for the first time since they had started, she turned toward him and looked him full in the face: "Ah! You will hear some disagreeable things, but you must know that I am prepared for everything, that I fear nothing, and you less than any one to-day."

He also was looking into her eyes and was already shaking with rage as he said in a low voice: "You are mad."

"No, but I will no longer be the victim of the hateful penalty of maternity, which you have inflicted on me for eleven years! I wish to take my place in society as I have the right to do, as all women have the right to do."

He suddenly grew pale again and stammered: "I do not understand you."

"Oh! yes; you understand me well enough. It is now three months since I had my last child, and as I am still very beautiful, and as, in spite of all your efforts you cannot spoil my figure, as you just now perceived, when you saw me on the doorstep, you think it is time that I should think of having another child."

"But you are talking nonsense!"

"No, I am not, I am thirty, and I have had seven children, and we have been married eleven years, and you hope that this will go on for ten years longer, after which you will leave off being jealous."

He seized her arm and squeezed it, saying: "I will not allow you to talk to me like that much longer."

"And I shall talk to you till the end, until I have finished all I have to say to you, and if you try to prevent me, I shall raise my voice so that the two servants, who are on the box, may hear. I only allowed you to come with me for that object, for I have these witnesses who will oblige you to listen to me and to contain yourself, so now pay attention to what I say. I have always felt an antipathy to you, and I have always let you see it, for I have never lied, monsieur. You married me in spite of myself; you forced my parents, who were in embarrassed circumstances, to give me to you, because you were rich, and they obliged me to marry you in spite of my tears.

"So you bought me, and as soon as I was in your power, as soon as I had become your companion, ready to attach myself to you, to forget your coercive and threatening proceedings, in order that I might only remember that I ought to be a devoted wife and to love you as much as it might be possible for me to love you, you became jealous, you, as no man has ever been before, with the base, ignoble jealousy of a spy, which was as degrading to you as it was to me. I had not been married eight months when you suspected me of every perfidiousness, and you even told me so. What a disgrace! And as you could not prevent me from being beautiful and from pleasing people, from being called in drawing-rooms and also in the newspapers one of the most beautiful women in Paris, you tried everything you could think of to keep admirers from me, and you hit upon the abominable idea of making me spend my life in a constant state of motherhood, until the time should come when I should disgust every man. Oh, do not deny it. I did not understand it for some time, but then I guessed it. You even boasted about it to your sister, who told me of it, for she is fond of me and was disgusted at your boorish coarseness.

"Ah! Remember how you have behaved in the past! How for eleven years you have compelled me to give up all society and simply be a mother to your children. And then you would grow disgusted with me and I was sent into the country, the family chateau, among fields and meadows. And when I reappeared, fresh, pretty and unspoiled, still seductive and constantly surrounded by admirers, hoping that at last I should live a little more like a rich young society woman, you were seized with jealousy again, and you began once more to persecute me with that infamous and hateful desire from which you are suffering at this moment by my side. And it is not the desire of possessing me—for I should never have refused myself to you, but it is the wish to make me unsightly.

"And then that abominable and mysterious thing occurred which I was a long time in understanding (but I grew sharp by dint of watching your thoughts and actions): You attached yourself to your children with all the security which they gave you while I bore them. You felt affection for them, with all your aversion to me, and in spite of your ignoble fears, which were momentarily allayed by your pleasure in seeing me lose my symmetry.

"Oh! how often have I noticed that joy in you! I have seen it in your eyes and guessed it. You loved your children as victories, and not because they were of your own blood. They were victories over me, over my youth, over my beauty, over my charms, over the compliments which were paid me and over those that were whispered around me without being paid to me personally. And you are proud of them, you make a parade of them, you take them out for drives in your break in the Bois de Boulogne and you give them donkey rides at Montmorency. You take them to theatrical matinees so that you may be seen in the midst of them, so that the people may say: 'What a kind father' and that it may be repeated——"

He had seized her wrist with savage brutality, and he squeezed it so violently that she was quiet and nearly cried out with the pain and he said to her in a whisper:

"I love my children, do you hear? What you have just told me is disgraceful in a mother. But you belong to me; I am master—your master—I can exact from you what I like and when I like—and I have the law-on my side."

He was trying to crush her fingers in the strong grip of his large, muscular hand, and she, livid with pain, tried in vain to free them from that vise which was crushing them. The agony made her breathe hard and the tears came into her eyes. "You see that I am the master and the stronger," he said. When he somewhat loosened his grip, she asked him: "Do you think that I am a religious woman?"

He was surprised and stammered "Yes."

"Do you think that I could lie if I swore to the truth of anything to you before an altar on which Christ's body is?"

"No."

"Will you go with me to some church?"

"What for?"

"You shall see. Will you?"

"If you absolutely wish it, yes."

She raised her voice and said: "Philippe!" And the coachman, bending down a little, without taking his eyes from his horses, seemed to turn his ear alone toward his mistress, who continued: "Drive to St. Philippe-du-Roule." And the victoria, which had reached the entrance of the Bois de Boulogne returned to Paris.

Husband and wife did not exchange a word further during the drive, and when the carriage stopped before the church Madame de Mascaret jumped out and entered it, followed by the count, a few yards distant. She went, without stopping, as far as the choir-screen, and falling on her knees at a chair, she buried her face in her hands. She prayed for a long time, and he, standing behind her could see that she was crying. She wept noiselessly, as women weep when they are in great, poignant grief. There was a kind of undulation in her body, which ended in a little sob, which was hidden and stifled by her fingers.

But the Comte de Mascaret thought that the situation was lasting too long, and he touched her on the shoulder. That contact recalled her to herself, as if she had been burned, and getting up, she looked straight into his eyes. "This is what I have to say to you. I am afraid of nothing, whatever you may do to me. You may kill me if you like. One of your children is not yours, and one only; that I swear to you before God, who hears me here. That was the only revenge that was possible for me in return for all your abominable masculine tyrannies, in return for the penal servitude of childbearing to which you have condemned me. Who was my lover? That you never will know! You may suspect every one, but you never will find out. I gave myself to him, without love and without pleasure, only for the sake of betraying you, and he also made me a mother. Which is the child? That also you never will know. I have seven; try to find out! I intended to tell you this later, for one has not avenged oneself on a man by deceiving him, unless he knows it. You have driven me to confess it today. I have now finished."

She hurried through the church toward the open door, expecting to hear behind her the quick step: of her husband whom she had defied and to be knocked to the ground by a blow of his fist, but she heard nothing and reached her carriage. She jumped into it at a bound, overwhelmed with anguish and breathless with fear. So she called out to the coachman: "Home!" and the horses set off at a quick trot.

II

The Comtesse de Mascaret was waiting in her room for dinner time as a criminal sentenced to death awaits the hour of his execution. What was her husband going to do? Had he come home? Despotic, passionate, ready for any violence as he was, what was he meditating, what had he made up his mind to do? There was no sound in the house, and every moment she looked at the clock. Her lady's maid had come and dressed her for the evening and had then left the room again. Eight o'clock struck and almost at the same moment there were two knocks at the door, and the butler came in and announced dinner.

"Has the count come in?"

"Yes, Madame la Comtesse. He is in the diningroom."

For a little moment she felt inclined to arm herself with a small revolver which she had bought some time before, foreseeing the tragedy which was being rehearsed in her heart. But she remembered that all the children would be there, and she took nothing except a bottle of smelling salts. He rose somewhat ceremoniously from his chair. They exchanged a slight bow and sat down. The three boys with their tutor, Abbe Martin, were on her right and the three girls, with Miss Smith, their English governess, were on her left. The youngest child, who was only three months old, remained upstairs with his nurse.

The abbe said grace as usual when there was no company, for the children did not come down to dinner when guests were present. Then they began dinner. The countess, suffering from emotion, which she had not calculated upon, remained with her eyes cast down, while the count scrutinized now the three boys and now the three girls with an uncertain, unhappy expression, which travelled from one to the other. Suddenly pushing his wineglass from him, it broke, and the wine was spilt on the tablecloth, and at the slight noise caused by this little accident the countess started up from her chair; and for the first time they looked at each other. Then, in spite of themselves, in spite of the irritation of their nerves caused by every glance, they continued to exchange looks, rapid as pistol shots.

The abbe, who felt that there was some cause for embarrassment which he could not divine, attempted to begin a conversation and tried various subjects, but his useless efforts gave rise to no ideas and did not bring out a word. The countess, with feminine tact and obeying her instincts of a woman of the world, attempted to answer him two or three times, but in vain. She could not find words, in the perplexity of her mind, and her own voice almost frightened her in the silence of the large room, where nothing was heard except the slight sound of plates and knives and forks.

Suddenly her husband said to her, bending forward: "Here, amid your children, will you swear to me that what you told me just now is true?"

The hatred which was fermenting in her veins suddenly roused her, and replying to that question with the same firmness with which she had replied to his looks, she raised both her hands, the right pointing toward the boys and the left toward the girls, and said in a firm, resolute voice and without any hesitation: "On the head of my children, I swear that I have told you the truth."

He got up and throwing his table napkin on the table with a movement of exasperation, he turned round and flung his chair against the wall, and then went out without another word, while she, uttering a deep sigh, as if after a first victory, went on in a calm voice: "You must not pay any attention to what your father has just said, my darlings; he was very much upset a short time ago, but he will be all right again in a few days."

Then she talked with the abbe and Miss Smith and had tender, pretty words for all her children, those sweet, tender mother's ways which unfold little hearts.

When dinner was over she went into the drawing-room, all her children following her. She made the elder ones chatter, and when their bedtime came she kissed them for a long time and then went alone into her room.

She waited, for she had no doubt that the count would come, and she made up her mind then, as her children were not with her, to protect herself as a woman of the world as she would protect her life, and in the pocket of her dress she put the little loaded revolver which she had bought a few days previously. The hours went by, the hours struck, and every sound was hushed in the house. Only the cabs, continued to rumble through the streets, but their noise was only heard vaguely through the shuttered and curtained windows.

She waited, full of nervous energy, without any fear of him now, ready for anything, and almost triumphant, for she had found means of torturing him continually during every moment of his life.

But the first gleam of dawn came in through the fringe at the bottom of her curtain without his having come into her room, and then she awoke to the fact, with much amazement, that he was not coming. Having locked and bolted her door, for greater security, she went to bed at last and remained there, with her eyes open, thinking and barely understanding it all, without being able to guess what he was going to do.

When her maid brought her tea she at the same time handed her a letter from her husband. He told her that he was going to undertake a longish journey and in a postscript added that his lawyer would provide her with any sums of money she might require for all her expenses.

III

It was at the opera, between two acts of "Robert the Devil." In the stalls the men were standing up, with their hats on, their waistcoats cut very low so as to show a large amount of white shirt front, in which gold and jewelled studs glistened, and were looking at the boxes full of ladies in low dresses covered with diamonds and pearls, who were expanding like flowers in that illuminated hothouse, where the beauty of their faces and the whiteness of their shoulders seemed to bloom in order to be gazed at, amid the sound of the music and of human voices.

Two friends, with their backs to the orchestra, were scanning those rows of elegance, that exhibition of real or false charms, of jewels, of luxury and of pretension which displayed itself in all parts of the Grand Theatre, and one of them, Roger de Salnis, said to his companion, Bernard Grandin:

"Just look how beautiful the Comtesse de Mascaret still is."

The older man in turn looked through his opera glasses at a tall lady in a box opposite. She appeared to be still very young, and her striking beauty seemed to attract all eyes in every corner of the house. Her pale complexion, of an ivory tint, gave her the appearance of a statue, while a small diamond coronet glistened on her black hair like a streak of light.

When he had looked at her for some time, Bernard Grandin replied with a jocular accent of sincere conviction: "You may well call her beautiful!"

"How old do you think she is?"

"Wait a moment. I can tell you exactly, for I have known her since she was a child and I saw her make her debut into society when she was quite a girl. She is—she is—thirty—thirty-six."

"Impossible!"

"I am sure of it."

"She looks twenty-five."

"She has had seven children."

"It is incredible."

"And what is more, they are all seven alive, as she is a very good mother. I occasionally go to the house, which is a very quiet and pleasant one, where one may see the phenomenon of the family in the midst of society."

"How very strange! And have there never been any reports about her?"

"Never."

"But what about her husband? He is peculiar, is he not?"

"Yes and no. Very likely there has been a little drama between them, one of those little domestic dramas which one suspects, never finds out exactly, but guesses at pretty closely."

"What is it?"

"I do not know anything about it. Mascaret leads a very fast life now, after being a model husband. As long as he remained a good spouse he had a shocking temper, was crabbed and easily took offence, but since he has been leading his present wild life he has become quite different, But one might surmise that he has some trouble, a worm gnawing somewhere, for he has aged very much."

Thereupon the two friends talked philosophically for some minutes about the secret, unknowable troubles which differences of character or perhaps physical antipathies, which were not perceived at first, give rise to in families, and then Roger de Salnis, who was still looking at Madame de Mascaret through his opera glasses, said: "It is almost incredible that that woman can have had seven children!"

"Yes, in eleven years; after which, when she was thirty, she refused to have any more, in order to take her place in society, which she seems likely to do for many years."

"Poor women!"

"Why do you pity them?"

"Why? Ah! my dear fellow, just consider! Eleven years in a condition of motherhood for such a woman! What a hell! All her youth, all her beauty, every hope of success, every poetical ideal of a brilliant life sacrificed to that abominable law of reproduction which turns the normal woman into a mere machine for bringing children into the world."

"What would you have? It is only Nature!"

"Yes, but I say that Nature is our enemy, that we must always fight against Nature, for she is continually bringing us back to an animal state. You may be sure that God has not put anything on this earth that is clean, pretty, elegant or accessory to our ideal; the human brain has done it. It is man who has introduced a little grace, beauty, unknown charm and mystery into creation by singing about it, interpreting it, by admiring it as a poet, idealizing it as an artist and by explaining it through science, doubtless making mistakes, but finding ingenious reasons, hidden grace and beauty, unknown charm and mystery in the various phenomena of Nature. God created only coarse beings, full of the germs of disease, who, after a few years of bestial enjoyment, grow old and infirm, with all the ugliness and all the want of power of human decrepitude. He seems to have made them only in order that they may reproduce their species in an ignoble manner and then die like ephemeral insects. I said reproduce their species in an ignoble manner and I adhere to that expression. What is there as a matter of fact more ignoble and more repugnant than that act of reproduction of living beings, against which all delicate minds always have revolted and always will revolt? Since all the organs which have been invented by this economical and malicious Creator serve two purposes, why did He not choose another method of performing that sacred mission, which is the noblest and the most exalted of all human functions? The mouth, which nourishes the body by means of material food, also diffuses abroad speech and thought. Our flesh renews itself of its own accord, while we are thinking about it. The olfactory organs, through which the vital air reaches the lungs, communicate all the perfumes of the world to the brain: the smell of flowers, of woods, of trees, of the sea. The ear, which enables us to communicate with our fellow men, has also allowed us to invent music, to create dreams, happiness, infinite and even physical pleasure by means of sound! But one might say that the cynical and cunning Creator wished to prohibit man from ever ennobling and idealizing his intercourse with women. Nevertheless man has found love, which is not a bad reply to that sly Deity, and he has adorned it with so much poetry that woman often forgets the sensual part of it. Those among us who are unable to deceive themselves have invented vice and refined debauchery, which is another way of laughing at God and paying homage, immodest homage, to beauty.

"But the normal man begets children just like an animal coupled with another by law.

"Look at that woman! Is it not abominable to think that such a jewel, such a pearl, born to be beautiful, admired, feted and adored, has spent eleven years of her life in providing heirs for the Comte de Mascaret?"

Bernard Grandin replied with a laugh: "There is a great deal of truth in all that, but very few people would understand you."

Salnis became more and more animated. "Do you know how I picture God myself?" he said. "As an enormous, creative organ beyond our ken, who scatters millions of worlds into space, just as one single fish would deposit its spawn in the sea. He creates because it is His function as God to do so, but He does not know what He is doing and is stupidly prolific in His work and is ignorant of the combinations of all kinds which are produced by His scattered germs. The human mind is a lucky little local, passing accident which was totally unforeseen, and condemned to disappear with this earth and to recommence perhaps here or elsewhere the same or different with fresh combinations of eternally new beginnings. We owe it to this little lapse of intelligence on His part that we are very uncomfortable in this world which was not made for us, which had not been prepared to receive us, to lodge and feed us or to satisfy reflecting beings, and we owe it to Him also that we have to struggle without ceasing against what are still called the designs of Providence, when we are really refined and civilized beings."

Grandin, who was listening to him attentively as he had long known the surprising outbursts of his imagination, asked him: "Then you believe that human thought is the spontaneous product of blind divine generation?"

"Naturally! A fortuitous function of the nerve centres of our brain, like the unforeseen chemical action due to new mixtures and similar also to a charge of electricity, caused by friction or the unexpected proximity of some substance, similar to all phenomena caused by the infinite and fruitful fermentation of living matter.

"But, my dear fellow, the truth of this must be evident to any one who looks about him. If the human mind, ordained by an omniscient Creator, had been intended to be what it has become, exacting, inquiring, agitated, tormented—so different from mere animal thought and resignation—would the world which was created to receive the beings which we now are have been this unpleasant little park for small game, this salad patch, this wooded, rocky and spherical kitchen garden where your improvident Providence had destined us to live naked, in caves or under trees, nourished on the flesh of slaughtered animals, our brethren, or on raw vegetables nourished by the sun and the rain?

"But it is sufficient to reflect for a moment, in order to understand that this world was not made for such creatures as we are. Thought, which is developed by a miracle in the nerves of the cells in our brain, powerless, ignorant and confused as it is, and as it will always remain, makes all of us who are intellectual beings eternal and wretched exiles on earth.

"Look at this earth, as God has given it to those who inhabit it. Is it not visibly and solely made, planted and covered with forests for the sake of animals? What is there for us? Nothing. And for them, everything, and they have nothing to do but to eat or go hunting and eat each other, according to their instincts, for God never foresaw gentleness and peaceable manners; He only foresaw the death of creatures which were bent on destroying and devouring each other. Are not the quail, the pigeon and the partridge the natural prey of the hawk? the sheep, the stag and the ox that of the great flesh-eating animals, rather than meat to be fattened and served up to us with truffles, which have been unearthed by pigs for our special benefit?

"As to ourselves, the more civilized, intellectual and refined we are, the more we ought to conquer and subdue that animal instinct, which represents the will of God in us. And so, in order to mitigate our lot as brutes, we have discovered and made everything, beginning with houses, then exquisite food, sauces, sweetmeats, pastry, drink, stuffs, clothes, ornaments, beds, mattresses, carriages, railways and innumerable machines, besides arts and sciences, writing and poetry. Every ideal comes from us as do all the amenities of life, in order to make our existence as simple reproducers, for which divine Providence solely intended us, less monotonous and less hard.

"Look at this theatre. Is there not here a human world created by us, unforeseen and unknown to eternal fate, intelligible to our minds alone, a sensual and intellectual distraction, which has been invented solely by and for that discontented and restless little animal, man?

"Look at that woman, Madame de Mascaret. God intended her to live in a cave, naked or wrapped up in the skins of wild animals. But is she not better as she is? But, speaking of her, does any one know why and how her brute of a husband, having such a companion by his side, and especially after having been boorish enough to make her a mother seven times, has suddenly left her, to run after bad women?"

Grandin replied: "Oh! my dear fellow, this is probably the only reason. He found that raising a family was becoming too expensive, and from reasons of domestic economy he has arrived at the same principles which you lay down as a philosopher."

Just then the curtain rose for the third act, and they turned round, took off their hats and sat down.

IV

The Comte and Comtesse Mascaret were sitting side by side in the carriage which was taking them home from the Opera, without speaking but suddenly the husband said to his wife: "Gabrielle!"

"What do you want?"

"Don't you think that this has lasted long enough?"

"What?"

"The horrible punishment to which you have condemned me for the last six years?"

"What do you want? I cannot help it."

"Then tell me which of them it is."

"Never."

"Think that I can no longer see my children or feel them round me, without having my heart burdened with this doubt. Tell me which of them it is, and I swear that I will forgive you and treat it like the others."

"I have not the right to do so."

"Do you not see that I can no longer endure this life, this thought which is wearing me out, or this question which I am constantly asking myself, this question which tortures me each time I look at them? It is driving me mad."

"Then you have suffered a great deal?" she said.

"Terribly. Should I, without that, have accepted the horror of living by your side, and the still greater horror of feeling and knowing that there is one among them whom I cannot recognize and who prevents me from loving the others?"

"Then you have really suffered very much?" she repeated.

And he replied in a constrained and sorrowful voice:

"Yes, for do I not tell you every day that it is intolerable torture to me? Should I have remained in that house, near you and them, if I did not love them? Oh! You have behaved abominably toward me. All the affection of my heart I have bestowed upon my children, and that you know. I am for them a father of the olden time, as I was for you a husband of one of the families of old, for by instinct I have remained a natural man, a man of former days. Yes, I will confess it, you have made me terribly jealous, because you are a woman of another race, of another soul, with other requirements. Oh! I shall never forget the things you said to me, but from that day I troubled myself no more about you. I did not kill you, because then I should have had no means on earth of ever discovering which of our—of your children is not mine. I have waited, but I have suffered more than you would believe, for I can no longer venture to love them, except, perhaps, the two eldest; I no longer venture to look at them, to call them to me, to kiss them; I cannot take them on my knee without asking myself, 'Can it be this one?' I have been correct in my behavior toward you for six years, and even kind and complaisant. Tell me the truth, and I swear that I will do nothing unkind."

He thought, in spite of the darkness of the carriage, that he could perceive that she was moved, and feeling certain that she was going to speak at last, he said: "I beg you, I beseech you to tell me" he said.

"I have been more guilty than you think perhaps," she replied, "but I could no longer endure that life of continual motherhood, and I had only one means of driving you from me. I lied before God and I lied, with my hand raised to my children's head, for I never have wronged you."

He seized her arm in the darkness, and squeezing it as he had done on that terrible day of their drive in the Bois de Boulogne, he stammered:

"Is that true?"

"It is true."

But, wild with grief, he said with a groan: "I shall have fresh doubts that will never end! When did you lie, the last time or now? How am I to believe you at present? How can one believe a woman after that? I shall never again know what I am to think. I would rather you had said to me, 'It is Jacques or it is Jeanne.'"

The carriage drove into the courtyard of the house and when it had drawn up in front of the steps the count alighted first, as usual, and offered his wife his arm to mount the stairs. As soon as they reached the first floor he said: "May I speak to you for a few moments longer?" And she replied, "I am quite willing."

They went into a small drawing-room and a footman, in some surprise, lighted the wax candles. As soon as he had left the room and they were alone the count continued: "How am I to know the truth? I have begged you a thousand times to speak, but you have remained dumb, impenetrable, inflexible, inexorable, and now to-day you tell me that you have been lying. For six years you have actually allowed me to believe such a thing! No, you are lying now, I do not know why, but out of pity for me, perhaps?"

She replied in a sincere and convincing manner: "If I had not done so, I should have had four more children in the last six years!"

"Can a mother speak like that?"

"Oh!" she replied, "I do not feel that I am the mother of children who never have been born; it is enough for me to be the mother of those that I have and to love them with all my heart. I am a woman of the civilized world, monsieur—we all are—and we are no longer, and we refuse to be, mere females to restock the earth."

She got up, but he seized her hands. "Only one word, Gabrielle. Tell me the truth!"

"I have just told you. I never have dishonored you."

He looked her full in the face, and how beautiful she was, with her gray eyes, like the cold sky. In her dark hair sparkled the diamond coronet, like a radiance. He suddenly felt, felt by a kind of intuition, that this grand creature was not merely a being destined to perpetuate the race, but the strange and mysterious product of all our complicated desires which have been accumulating in us for centuries but which have been turned aside from their primitive and divine object and have wandered after a mystic, imperfectly perceived and intangible beauty. There are some women like that, who blossom only for our dreams, adorned with every poetical attribute of civilization, with that ideal luxury, coquetry and esthetic charm which surround woman, a living statue that brightens our life.

Her husband remained standing before her, stupefied at his tardy and obscure discovery, confusedly hitting on the cause of his former jealousy and understanding it all very imperfectly, and at last he said: "I believe you, for I feel at this moment that you are not lying, and before I really thought that you were."

She put out her hand to him: "We are friends then?"

He took her hand and kissed it and replied: "We are friends. Thank you, Gabrielle."

Then he went out, still looking at her, and surprised that she was still so beautiful and feeling a strange emotion arising in him.

THE FATHER

I

He was a clerk in the Bureau of Public Education and lived at Batignolles. He took the omnibus to Paris every morning and always sat opposite a girl, with whom he fell in love.

She was employed in a shop and went in at the same time every day. She was a little brunette, one of those girls whose eyes are so dark that they look like black spots, on a complexion like ivory. He always saw her coming at the corner of the same street, and she generally had to run to catch the heavy vehicle, and sprang upon the steps before the horses had quite stopped. Then she got inside, out of breath, and, sitting down, looked round her.

The first time that he saw her, Francois Tessier liked the face. One sometimes meets a woman whom one longs to clasp in one's arms without even knowing her. That girl seemed to respond to some chord in his being, to that sort of ideal of love which one cherishes in the depths of the heart, without knowing it.

He looked at her intently, not meaning to be rude, and she became embarrassed and blushed. He noticed it, and tried to turn away his eyes; but he involuntarily fixed them upon her again every moment, although he tried to look in another direction; and, in a few days, they seemed to know each other without having spoken. He gave up his place to her when the omnibus was full, and got outside, though he was very sorry to do it. By this time she had got so far as to greet him with a little smile; and, although she always dropped her eyes under his looks, which she felt were too ardent, yet she did not appear offended at being looked at in such a manner.

They ended by speaking. A kind of rapid friendship had become established between them, a daily freemasonry of half an hour, and that was certainly one of the most charming half hours in his life to him. He thought of her all the rest of the day, saw her image continually during the long office hours. He was haunted and bewitched by that floating and yet tenacious recollection which the form of a beloved woman leaves in us, and it seemed to him that if he could win that little person it would be maddening happiness to him, almost above human realization.

Every morning she now shook hands with him, and he preserved the sense of that touch and the recollection of the gentle pressure of her little fingers until the next day, and he almost fancied that he preserved the imprint on his palm. He anxiously waited for this short omnibus ride, while Sundays seemed to him heartbreaking days. However, there was no doubt that she loved him, for one Saturday, in spring, she promised to go and lunch with him at Maisons-Laffitte the next day.

II

She was at the railway station first, which surprised him, but she said: "Before going, I want to speak to you. We have twenty minutes, and that is more than I shall take for what I have to say."

She trembled as she hung on his arm, and looked down, her cheeks pale, as she continued: "I do not want you to be deceived in me, and I shall not go there with you, unless you promise, unless you swear not to do—not to do anything—that is at all improper."

She had suddenly become as red as a poppy, and said no more. He did not know what to reply, for he was happy and disappointed at the same time. He should love her less, certainly, if he knew that her conduct was light, but then it would be so charming, so delicious to have a little flirtation.

As he did not say anything, she began to speak again in an agitated voice and with tears in her eyes. "If you do not promise to respect me altogether, I shall return home." And so he squeezed her arm tenderly and replied: "I promise, you shall only do what you like." She appeared relieved in mind, and asked, with a smile: "Do you really mean it?" And he looked into her eyes and replied: "I swear it" "Now you may take the tickets," she said.

During the journey they could hardly speak, as the carriage was full, and when they reached Maisons-Laffite they went toward the Seine. The sun, which shone full on the river, on the leaves and the grass, seemed to be reflected in their hearts, and they went, hand in hand, along the bank, looking at the shoals of little fish swimming near the bank, and they walked on, brimming over with happiness, as if they were walking on air.

At last she said: "How foolish you must think me!"

"Why?" he asked. "To come out like this, all alone with you."

"Certainly not; it is quite natural." "No, no; it is not natural for me —because I do not wish to commit a fault, and yet this is how girls fall. But if you only knew how wretched it is, every day the same thing, every day in the month and every month in the year. I live quite alone with mamma, and as she has had a great deal of trouble, she is not very cheerful. I do the best I can, and try to laugh in spite of everything, but I do not always succeed. But, all the same, it was wrong in me to come, though you, at any rate, will not be sorry."

By way of an answer, he kissed her ardently on the ear that was nearest him, but she moved from him with an abrupt movement, and, getting suddenly angry, exclaimed: "Oh! Monsieur Francois, after what you swore to me!" And they went back to Maisons-Laffitte.

They had lunch at the Petit-Havre, a low house, buried under four enormous poplar trees, by the side of the river. The air, the heat, the weak white wine and the sensation of being so close together made them silent; their faces were flushed and they had a feeling of oppression; but, after the coffee, they regained their high spirits, and, having crossed the Seine, started off along the bank, toward the village of La Frette. Suddenly he asked: "What-is your name?"

"Louise."

"Louise," he repeated and said nothing more.

The girl picked daisies and made them into a great bunch, while he sang vigorously, as unrestrained as a colt that has been turned into a meadow. On their left a vine-covered slope followed the river. Francois stopped motionless with astonishment: "Oh, look there!" he said.

The vines had come to an end, and the whole slope was covered with lilac bushes in flower. It was a purple wood! A kind of great carpet of flowers stretched over the earth, reaching as far as the village, more than two miles off. She also stood, surprised and delighted, and murmured: "Oh! how pretty!" And, crossing a meadow, they ran toward that curious low hill, which, every year, furnishes all the lilac that is drawn through Paris on the carts of the flower venders.

There was a narrow path beneath the trees, so they took it, and when they came to a small clearing, sat down.

Swarms of flies were buzzing around them and making a continuous, gentle sound, and the sun, the bright sun of a perfectly still day, shone over the bright slopes and from that forest of blossoms a powerful fragrance was borne toward them, a breath of perfume, the breath of the flowers.

A church clock struck in the distance, and they embraced gently, then, without the knowledge of anything but that kiss, lay down on the grass. But she soon came to herself with the feeling of a great misfortune, and began to cry and sob with grief, with her face buried in her hands.

He tried to console her, but she wanted to start to return and to go home immediately; and she kept saying, as she walked along quickly: "Good heavens! good heavens!"

He said to her: "Louise! Louise! Please let us stop here." But now her cheeks were red and her eyes hollow, and, as soon as they got to the railway station in Paris, she left him without even saying good-by.

III

When he met her in the omnibus, next day, she appeared to him to be changed and thinner, and she said to him: "I want to speak to you; we will get down at the Boulevard."

As soon as they were on the pavement, she said:

"We must bid each other good-by; I cannot meet you again." "But why?" he asked. "Because I cannot; I have been culpable, and I will not be so again."

Then he implored her, tortured by his love, but she replied firmly: "No, I cannot, I cannot." He, however, only grew all the more excited and promised to marry her, but she said again: "No," and left him.

For a week he did not see her. He could not manage to meet her, and, as he did not know her address, he thought that he had lost her altogether. On the ninth day, however, there was a ring at his bell, and when he opened the door, she was there. She threw herself into his arms and did not resist any longer, and for three months they were close friends. He was beginning to grow tired of her, when she whispered something to him, and then he had one idea and wish: to break with her at any price. As, however, he could not do that, not knowing how to begin, or what to say, full of anxiety through fear of the consequences of his rash indiscretion, he took a decisive step: one night he changed his lodgings and disappeared.

The blow was so heavy that she did not look, for the man who had abandoned her, but threw herself at her mother's knees and confessed her misfortune, and, some months after, gave birth to a boy.

IV

Years passed, and Francois Tessier grew old, without there having been any alteration in his life. He led the dull, monotonous life of an office clerk, without hope and without expectation. Every day he got up at the same time, went through the same streets, went through the same door, past the same porter, went into the same office, sat in the same chair, and did the same work. He was alone in the world, alone during the day in the midst of his different colleagues, and alone at night in his bachelor's lodgings, and he laid by a hundred francs a month against old age.

Every Sunday he went to the Champs-Elysees, to watch the elegant people, the carriages and the pretty women, and the next day he used to say to one of his colleagues: "The return of the carriages from the Bois du Boulogne was very brilliant yesterday."

One fine Sunday morning, however, he went into the Parc Monceau, where the mothers and nurses, sitting on the sides of the walks, watched the children playing, and suddenly Francois Tessier started. A woman passed by, holding two children by the hand, a little boy of about ten and a little girl of four. It was she!

He walked another hundred yards anti then fell into a chair, choking with emotion. She had not recognized him, and so he came back, wishing to see her again. She was sitting down now, and the boy was standing by her side very quietly, while the little girl was making sand castles. It was she, it was certainly she, but she had the reserved appearance of a lady, was dressed simply, and looked self-possessed and dignified. He looked at her from a distance, for he did not venture to go near; but the little boy raised his head, and Francois Tessier felt himself tremble. It was his own son, there could be no doubt of that. And, as he looked at him, he thought he could recognize himself as he appeared in an old photograph taken years ago. He remained hidden behind a tree, waiting for her to go that he might follow her.

He did not sleep that night. The idea of the child especially tormented him. His son! Oh, if he could only have known, have been sure! But what could he have done? However, he went to the house where she lived and asked about her. He was told that a neighbor, an honorable man of strict morals, had been touched by her distress and had married her; he knew the fault she had committed and had married her, and had even recognized the child, his, Francois Tessier's child, as his own.

He returned to the Parc Monceau every Sunday, for then he always saw her, and each time he was seized with a mad, an irresistible longing to take his son into his arms, to cover him with kisses and to steal him, to carry him off.

He suffered horribly in his wretched isolation as an old bachelor, with nobody to care for him, and he also suffered atrocious mental torture, torn by paternal tenderness springing from remorse, longing and jealousy and from that need of loving one's own children which nature has implanted in all. At last he determined to make a despairing attempt, and, going up to her, as she entered the park, he said, standing in the middle of the path, pale and with trembling lips: "You do not recognize me." She raised her eyes, looked at him, uttered an exclamation of horror, of terror, and, taking the two children by the hand, she rushed away, dragging them after her, while he went home and wept inconsolably.

Months passed without his seeing her again, but he suffered, day and night, for he was a prey to his paternal love. He would gladly have died, if he could only have kissed his son; he would have committed murder, performed any task, braved any danger, ventured anything. He wrote to her, but she did not reply, and, after writing her some twenty letters, he saw that there was no hope of altering her determination, and then he formed the desperate resolution of writing to her husband, being quite prepared to receive a bullet from a revolver, if need be. His letter only consisted of a few lines, as follows:

"Monsieur: You must have a perfect horror of my name, but I am so wretched, so overcome by misery that my only hope is in you, and, therefore, I venture to request you to grant me an interview of only five minutes.

"I have the honor, etc."

The next day he received the reply:

"Monsieur: I shall expect you to-morrow, Tuesday, at five o'clock."

As he went up the staircase, Francois Tessier's heart beat so violently that he had to stop several times. There was a dull and violent thumping noise in his breast, as of some animal galloping; and he could breathe only with difficulty, and had to hold on to the banisters, in order not to fall.

He rang the bell on the third floor, and when a maid servant had opened the door, he asked: "Does Monsieur Flamel live here?" "Yes, monsieur. Kindly come in."

He was shown into the drawing-room; he was alone, and waited, feeling bewildered, as in the midst of a catastrophe, until a door opened, and a man came in. He was tall, serious and rather stout, and wore a black frock coat, and pointed to a chair with his hand. Francois Tessier sat down, and then said, with choking breath: "Monsieur—monsieur—I do not know whether you know my name—whether you know——"

Monsieur Flamel interrupted him. "You need not tell it me, monsieur, I know it. My wife has spoken to me about you." He spoke in the dignified tone of voice of a good man who wishes to be severe, and with the commonplace stateliness of an honorable man, and Francois Tessier continued:

"Well, monsieur, I want to say this: I am dying of grief, of remorse, of shame, and I would like once, only once to kiss the child."

Monsieur Flamel got up and rang the bell, and when the servant came in, he said: "Will you bring Louis here?" When she had gone out, they remained face to face, without speaking, as they had nothing more to say to one another, and waited. Then, suddenly, a little boy of ten rushed into the room and ran up to the man whom he believed to be his father, but he stopped when he saw the stranger, and Monsieur Flamel kissed him and said: "Now, go and kiss that gentleman, my dear." And the child went up to the stranger and looked at him.

Francois Tessier had risen. He let his hat fall, and was ready to fall himself as he looked at his son, while Monsieur Flamel had turned away, from a feeling of delicacy, and was looking out of the window.

The child waited in surprise; but he picked up the hat and gave it to the stranger. Then Francois, taking the child up in his arms, began to kiss him wildly all over his face; on his eyes, his cheeks, his mouth, his hair; and the youngster, frightened at the shower of kisses, tried to avoid them, turned away his head, and pushed away the man's face with his little hands. But suddenly Francois Tessier put him down and cried: "Good-by! good-by!" And he rushed out of the room as if he had been a thief.

MY UNCLE SOSTHENES

Some people are Freethinkers from sheer stupidity. My Uncle Sosthenes was one of these. Some people are often religious for the same reason. The very sight of a priest threw my uncle into a violent rage. He would shake his fist and make grimaces at him, and would then touch a piece of iron when the priest's back was turned, forgetting that the latter action showed a belief after all, the belief in the evil eye. Now, when beliefs are unreasonable, one should have all or none at all. I myself am a Freethinker; I revolt at all dogmas, but feel no anger toward places of worship, be they Catholic, Apostolic, Roman, Protestant, Greek, Russian, Buddhist, Jewish, or Mohammedan.

My uncle was a Freemason, and I used to declare that they are stupider than old women devotees. That is my opinion, and I maintain it; if we must have any religion at all, the old one is good enough for me.

What is their object? Mutual help to be obtained by tickling the palms of each other's hands. I see no harm in it, for they put into practice the Christian precept: "Do unto others as ye would they should do unto you." The only difference consists in the tickling, but it does not seem worth while to make such a fuss about lending a poor devil half a crown.

To all my arguments my uncle's reply used to be:

"We are raising up a religion against a religion; Free Thought will kill clericalism. Freemasonry is the stronghold, of those who are demolishing all deities."

"Very well, my dear uncle," I would reply—in my heart I felt inclined to say, "You old idiot! it is just that which I am blaming you for. Instead of destroying, you are organizing competition; it is only a case of lowering prices. And then, if you admitted only Freethinkers among you, I could understand it, but you admit anybody. You have a number of Catholics among you, even the leaders of the party. Pius IX is said to have been one of you before he became pope. If you call a society with such an organization a bulwark against clericalism, I think it is an extremely weak one."

"My dear boy," my uncle would reply, with a wink, "we are most to be dreaded in politics; slowly and surely we are everywhere undermining the monarchical spirit."

Then I broke out: "Yes, you are very clever! If you tell me that Freemasonry is an election machine, I will grant it. I will never deny that it is used as a machine to control candidates of all shades; if you say that it is only used to hoodwink people, to drill them to go to the polls as soldiers are sent under fire, I agree with you; if you declare that it is indispensable to all political ambitions because it changes all its members into electoral agents, I should say to you: 'That is as clear as the sun.' But when you tell me that it serves to undermine the monarchical spirit, I can only laugh in your face.

"Just consider that gigantic and secret democratic association which had Prince Napoleon for its grand master under the Empire; which has the Crown Prince for its grand master in Germany, the Czar's brother in Russia, and to which the Prince of Wales and King Humbert, and nearly all the crowned heads of the globe belong."

"You are quite right," my uncle said; "but all these persons are serving our projects without guessing it."

I felt inclined to tell him he was talking a pack of nonsense.

It was, however, indeed a sight to see my uncle when he had a Freemason to dinner.

On meeting they shook hands in a manner that was irresistibly funny; one could see that they were going through a series of secret, mysterious signs.

Then my uncle would take his friend into a corner to tell him something important, and at dinner they had a peculiar way of looking at each other, and of drinking to each other, in a manner as if to say: "We know all about it, don't we?"

And to think that there are millions on the face of the globe who are amused at such monkey tricks! I would sooner be a Jesuit.

Now, in our town there really was an old Jesuit who was my uncle's detestation. Every time he met him, or if he only saw him at a distance, he used to say: "Get away, you toad." And then, taking my arm, he would whisper to me:

"See here, that fellow will play me a trick some day or other, I feel sure of it."

My uncle spoke quite truly, and this was how it happened, and through my fault.

It was close on Holy Week, and my uncle made up his mind to give a dinner on Good Friday, a real dinner, with his favorite chitterlings and black puddings. I resisted as much as I could, and said:

"I shall eat meat on that day, but at home, quite by myself. Your manifestation, as you call it, is an idiotic idea. Why should you manifest? What does it matter to you if people do not eat any meat?"

But my uncle would not be persuaded. He asked three of his friends to dine with him at one of the best restaurants in the town, and as he was going to pay the bill I had certainly, after all, no scruples about manifesting.

At four o'clock we took a conspicuous place in the most frequented restaurant in the town, and my uncle ordered dinner in a loud voice for six o'clock.

We sat down punctually, and at ten o'clock we had not yet finished. Five of us had drunk eighteen bottles of choice, still wine and four of champagne. Then my uncle proposed what he was in the habit of calling "the archbishop's circuit." Each man put six small glasses in front of him, each of them filled with a different liqueur, and they had all to be emptied at one gulp, one after another, while one of the waiters counted twenty. It was very stupid, but my uncle thought it was very suitable to the occasion.

At eleven o'clock he was as drunk as a fly. So we had to take him home in a cab and put him to bed, and one could easily foresee that his anti-clerical demonstration would end in a terrible fit of indigestion.

As I was going back to my lodgings, being rather drunk myself, with a cheerful drunkenness, a Machiavellian idea struck me which satisfied all my sceptical instincts.

I arranged my necktie, put on a look of great distress, and went and, rang loudly at the old Jesuit's door. As he was deaf he made me wait a longish while, but at length appeared at his window in a cotton nightcap and asked what I wanted.

I shouted out at the top of my voice:

"Make haste, reverend sir, and open the door; a poor, despairing, sick man is in need of your spiritual ministrations."

The good, kind man put on his trousers as quickly as he could, and came down without his cassock. I told him in a breathless voice that my uncle, the Freethinker, had been taken suddenly ill, and fearing it was going to be something serious, he had been seized with a sudden dread of death, and wished to see the priest and talk to him; to have his advice and comfort, to make his peace with the Church, and to confess, so as to be able to cross the dreaded threshold at peace with himself; and I added in a mocking tone:

"At any rate, he wishes it, and if it does him no good it can do him no harm."

The old Jesuit, who was startled, delighted, and almost trembling, said to me:

"Wait a moment, my son; I will come with you." But I replied: "Pardon me, reverend father, if I do not go with you; but my convictions will not allow me to do so. I even refused to come and fetch you, so I beg you not to say that you have seen me, but to declare that you had a presentiment—a sort of revelation of his illness."

The priest consented and went off quickly; knocked at my uncle's door, and was soon let in; and I saw the black cassock disappear within that stronghold of Free Thought.

I hid under a neighboring gateway to wait results. Had he been well, my uncle would have half-murdered the Jesuit, but I knew that he would scarcely be able to move an arm, and I asked myself gleefully what sort of a scene would take place between these antagonists, what disputes, what arguments, what a hubbub, and what would be the issue of the situation, which my uncle's indignation would render still more tragic?

I laughed till my sides ached, and said half aloud: "Oh, what a joke, what a joke!"

Meanwhile it was getting very cold, and I noticed that the Jesuit stayed a long time, and I thought: "They are having an argument, I suppose."

One, two, three hours passed, and still the reverend father did not come out. What had happened? Had my uncle died in a fit when he saw him, or had he killed the cassocked gentleman? Perhaps they had mutually devoured each other? This last supposition appeared very unlikely, for I fancied that my uncle was quite incapable of swallowing a grain more nourishment at that moment.

At last the day broke.

I was very uneasy, and, not venturing to go into the house myself, went to one of my friends who lived opposite. I woke him up, explained matters to him, much to his amusement and astonishment, and took possession of his window.

At nine o'clock he relieved me, and I got a little sleep. At two o'clock I, in my turn, replaced him. We were utterly astonished.

At six o'clock the Jesuit left, with a very happy and satisfied look on his face, and we saw him go away with a quiet step.

Then, timid and ashamed, I went and knocked at the door of my uncle's house; and when the servant opened it I did not dare to ask her any questions, but went upstairs without saying a word.

My uncle was lying, pale and exhausted, with weary, sorrowful eyes and heavy arms, on his bed. A little religious picture was fastened to one of the bed curtains with a pin.

"Why, uncle," I said, "in bed still? Are you not well?"

He replied in a feeble voice:

"Oh, my dear boy, I have been very ill, nearly dead."

"How was that, uncle?"

"I don't know; it was most surprising. But what is stranger still is that the Jesuit priest who has just left—you know, that excellent man whom I have made such fun of—had a divine revelation of my state, and came to see me."

I was seized with an almost uncontrollable desire to laugh, and with difficulty said: "Oh, really!"

"Yes, he came. He heard a voice telling him to get up and come to me, because I was going to die. I was a revelation."

I pretended to sneeze, so as not to burst out laughing; I felt inclined to roll on the ground with amusement.

In about a minute I managed to say indignantly:

"And you received him, uncle? You, a Freethinker, a Freemason? You did not have him thrown out of doors?"

He seemed confused, and stammered:

"Listen a moment, it is so astonishing—so astonishing and providential! He also spoke to me about my father; it seems he knew him formerly."

"Your father, uncle? But that is no reason for receiving a Jesuit."

"I know that, but I was very ill, and he looked after me most devotedly all night long. He was perfect; no doubt he saved my life; those men all know a little of medicine."

"Oh! he looked after you all night? But you said just now that he had only been gone a very short time."

"That is quite true; I kept him to breakfast after all his kindness. He had it at a table by my bedside while I drank a cup of tea."

"And he ate meat?"

My uncle looked vexed, as if I had said something very uncalled for, and then added:

"Don't joke, Gaston; such things are out of place at times. He has shown me more devotion than many a relation would have done, and I expect to have his convictions respected."

This rather upset me, but I answered, nevertheless: "Very well, uncle; and what did you do after breakfast?"

"We played a game of bezique, and then he repeated his breviary while I read a little book which he happened to have in his pocket, and which was not by any means badly written."

"A religious book, uncle?"

"Yes, and no, or, rather—no. It is the history of their missions in Central Africa, and is rather a book of travels and adventures. What these men have done is very grand."

I began to feel that matters were going badly, so I got up. "Well, good-by, uncle," I said, "I see you are going to give up Freemasonry for religion; you are a renegade."

He was still rather confused, and stammered:

"Well, but religion is a sort of Freemasonry."

"When is your Jesuit coming back?" I asked.

"I don't—I don't know exactly; to-morrow, perhaps; but it is not certain."

I went out, altogether overwhelmed.

My joke turned out very badly for me! My uncle became thoroughly converted, and if that had been all I should not have cared so much. Clerical or Freemason, to me it is all the same; six of one and half a dozen of the other; but the worst of it is that he has just made his will—yes, made his will—and he has disinherited me in favor of that rascally Jesuit!

THE BARONESS

"Come with me," said my friend Boisrene, "you will see some very interesting bric-a-brac and works of art there."

He conducted me to the first floor of an elegant house in one of the big streets of Paris. We were welcomed by a very pleasing man, with excellent manners, who led us from room to room, showing us rare things, the price of which he mentioned carelessly. Large sums, ten, twenty, thirty, fifty thousand francs, dropped from his lips with such grace and ease that one could not doubt that this gentleman-merchant had millions shut up in his safe.

I had known him by reputation for a long time. Very bright, clever, intelligent, he acted as intermediary in all sorts of transactions. He kept in touch with all the richest art amateurs in Paris, and even of Europe and America, knowing their tastes and preferences; he apprised them by letter, or by wire if they lived in a distant city, as soon as he knew of some work of art which might suit them.

Men of the best society had had recourse to him in times of difficulty, either to find money for gambling, or to pay off a debt, or to sell a picture, a family jewel, or a tapestry.

It was said that he never refused his services when he saw a chance of gain.

Boisrene seemed very intimate with this strange merchant. They must have worked together in many a deal. I observed the man with great interest.

He was tall, thin, bald, and very elegant. His soft, insinuating voice had a peculiar, tempting charm which seemed to give the objects a special value. When he held anything in his hands, he turned it round and round, looking at it with such skill, refinement, and sympathy that the object seemed immediately to be beautiful and transformed by his look and touch. And its value increased in one's estimation, after the object had passed from the showcase into his hands.

"And your Crucifix," said Boisrene, "that beautiful Renaissance Crucifix which you showed me last year?"

The man smiled and answered:

"It has been sold, and in a very peculiar manner. There is a real Parisian story for you! Would you like to hear it?"

"With pleasure."

"Do you know the Baroness Samoris?"

"Yes and no. I have seen her once, but I know what she is!"

"You know—everything?"

"Yes."

"Would you mind telling me, so that I can see whether you are not mistaken?"

"Certainly. Mme. Samoris is a woman of the world who has a daughter, without anyone having known her husband. At any rate, she is received in a certain tolerant, or blind society. She goes to church and devoutly partakes of Communion, so that everyone may know it, and she never compromises herself. She expects her daughter to marry well. Is that correct?"

"Yes, but I will complete your information. She is a woman who makes herself respected by her admirers in spite of everything. That is a rare quality, for in this manner she can get what she wishes from a man. The man whom she has chosen without his suspecting it courts her for a long time, longs for her timidly, wins her with astonishment and possesses her with consideration. He does not notice that he is paying, she is so tactful; and she maintains her relations on such a footing of reserve and dignity that he would slap the first man who dared doubt her in the least. And all this in the best of faith.

"Several times I have been able to render little services to this woman. She has no secrets from me.

"Toward the beginning of January she came to me in order to borrow thirty thousand francs. Naturally, I did not lend them to her; but, as I wished to oblige her, I told her to explain her situation to me completely, so that I might see whether there was not something I could do for her.

"She told me her troubles in such cautious language that she could not have spoken more delicately of her child's first communion. I finally managed to understand that times were hard, and that she was penniless.

"The commercial crisis, political unrest, rumors of war, had made money scarce even in the hands of her clients. And then, of course, she was very particular.

"She would associate only with a man in the best of society, who could strengthen her reputation as well as help her financially. A reveller, no matter how rich, would have compromised her forever, and would have made the marriage of her daughter quite doubtful.

"She had to maintain her household expenses and continue to entertain, in order not to lose the opportunity of finding, among her numerous visitors, the discreet and distinguished friend for whom she was waiting, and whom she would choose.

"I showed her that my thirty thousand francs would have but little likelihood of returning to me; for, after spending them all, she would have to find at least sixty thousand more, in a lump, to pay me back.

"She seemed very disheartened when she heard this. I did not know just what to do, when an idea, a really fine idea, struck me.

"I had just bought this Renaissance Crucifix which I showed you, an admirable piece of workmanship, one of the finest of its land that I have ever seen.

"'My dear friend,' I said to her, 'I am going to send you that piece of ivory. You will invent some ingenious, touching, poetic story, anything that you wish, to explain your desire for parting with it. It is, of course, a family heirloom left you by your father.

"'I myself will send you amateurs, or will bring them to you. The rest concerns you. Before they come I will drop you a line about their position, both social and financial. This Crucifix is worth fifty thousand francs; but I will let it go for thirty thousand. The difference will belong to you.'

"She considered the matter seriously for several minutes, and then answered: 'Yes, it is, perhaps, a good idea. I thank you very-much.'

"The next day I sent her my Crucifix, and the same evening the Baron de Saint-Hospital.

"For three months I sent her my best clients, from a business point of view. But I heard nothing more from her.

"One day I received a visit from a foreigner who spoke very little French. I decided to introduce him personally to the baroness, in order to see how she was getting along.

"A footman in black livery received us and ushered us into a quiet little parlor, furnished with taste, where we waited for several minutes. She appeared, charming as usual, extended her hand to me and invited us to be seated; and when I had explained the reason of my visit, she rang.

"The footman appeared.

"'See if Mlle. Isabelle can let us go into her oratory.' The young girl herself brought the answer. She was about fifteen years of age, modest and good to look upon in the sweet freshness of her youth. She wished to conduct us herself to her chapel.

"It was a kind of religious boudoir where a silver lamp was burning before the Crucifix, my Crucifix, on a background of black velvet. The setting was charming and very clever. The child crossed herself and then said:

"'Look, gentlemen. Isn't it beautiful?'

"I took the object, examined it and declared it to be remarkable. The foreigner also examined it, but he seemed much more interested in the two women than in the crucifix.

"A delicate odor of incense, flowers and perfume pervaded the whole house. One felt at home there. This really was a comfortable home, where one would have liked to linger.

"When we had returned to the parlor I delicately broached the subject of the price. Mme. Samoris, lowering her eyes, asked fifty thousand francs.

"Then she added: 'If you wish to see it again, monsieur, I very seldom go out before three o'clock; and I can be found at home every day.'

"In the street the stranger asked me for some details about the baroness, whom he had found charming. But I did not hear anything more from either of them.

"Three months passed by.

"One morning, hardly two weeks ago, she came here at about lunch time, and, placing a roll of bills in my hand, said: 'My dear, you are an angel! Here are fifty thousand francs; I am buying your crucifix, and I am paying twenty thousand francs more for it than the price agreed upon, on condition that you always—always send your clients to me—for it is still for sale.'"

MOTHER AND SON

A party of men were chatting in the smoking room after dinner. We were talking of unexpected legacies, strange inheritances. Then M. le Brument, who was sometimes called "the illustrious judge" and at other times "the illustrious lawyer," went and stood with his back to the fire.

"I have," said he, "to search for an heir who disappeared under peculiarly distressing circumstances. It is one of those simple and terrible dramas of ordinary life, a thing which possibly happens every day, and which is nevertheless one of the most dreadful things I know. Here are the facts:

"Nearly six months ago I was called to the bedside of a dying woman. She said to me:

"'Monsieur, I want to intrust to you the most delicate, the most difficult, and the most wearisome mission that can be conceived. Be good enough to notice my will, which is there on the table. A sum of five thousand francs is left to you as a fee if you do not succeed, and of a hundred thousand francs if you do succeed. I want you to find my son after my death.'

"She asked me to assist her to sit up in bed, in order that she might talk with greater ease, for her voice, broken and gasping, was whistling in her throat.

"It was a very wealthy establishment. The luxurious apartment, of an elegant simplicity, was upholstered with materials as thick as walls, with a soft inviting surface.

"The dying woman continued:

"'You are the first to hear my horrible story. I will try to have strength enough to finish it. You must know all, in order that you, whom I know to be a kind-hearted man as well as a man of the world, may have a sincere desire to aid me with all your power.

"'Listen to me:

"'Before my marriage, I loved a young man, whose suit was rejected by my family because he was not rich enough. Not long afterward, I married a man of great wealth. I married him through ignorance, through obedience, through indifference, as young girls do marry.

"'I had a child, a boy. My husband died in the course of a few years.

"'He whom I had loved had married, in his turn. When he saw that I was a widow, he was crushed by grief at knowing he was not free. He came to see me; he wept and sobbed so bitterly, that it was enough to break my heart. He came to see me at first as a friend. Perhaps I ought not to have received him. What could I do? I was alone, so sad, so solitary, so hopeless! And I loved him still. What sufferings we women have sometimes to endure!

"'I had only him in the world, my parents being dead. He came frequently; he spent whole evenings with me. I should not have let him come so often, seeing that he was married. But I had not enough will-power to prevent him from coming.

"'How can I tell it?—he became my lover. How did this come about? Can I explain it? Can any one explain such things? Do you think it could be otherwise when two human beings are drawn to each other by the irresistible force of mutual affection? Do you believe, monsieur, that it is always in our power to resist, that we can keep up the struggle forever, and refuse to yield to the prayers, the supplications, the tears, the frenzied words, the appeals on bended knees, the transports of passion, with which we are pursued by the man we adore, whom we want to gratify even in his slightest wishes, whom we desire to crown with every possible happiness, and whom, if we are to be guided by a worldly code of honor, we must drive to despair? What strength would it not require? What a renunciation of happiness? what self-denial? and even what virtuous selfishness?

"'In short, monsieur, I was his mistress; and I was happy. I became—and this was my greatest weakness and my greatest piece of cowardice-I became his wife's friend.

"'We brought up my son together; we made a man of him, a thorough man, intelligent, full of sense and resolution, of large and generous ideas. The boy reached the age of seventeen.

"'He, the young man, was fond of my—my lover, almost as fond of him as I was myself, for he had been equally cherished and cared for by both of us. He used to call him his 'dear friend,' and respected him immensely, having never received from him anything but wise counsels and an example of integrity, honor, and probity. He looked upon him as an old loyal and devoted comrade of his mother, as a sort of moral father, guardian, protector—how am I to describe it?

"'Perhaps the reason why he never asked any questions was that he had been accustomed from his earliest years to see this man in my house, at my side, and at his side, always concerned about us both.

"'One evening the three of us were to dine together—this was my chief amusement—and I waited for the two men, asking myself which of them would be the first to arrive. The door opened; it was my old friend. I went toward him, with outstretched arms; and he pressed my lips in a long, delicious kiss.

"'All of a sudden, a slight sound, a faint rustling, that mysterious sensation which indicates the presence of another person, made us start and turn round abruptly. Jean, my son, stood there, livid, staring at us.

"'There was a moment of atrocious confusion. I drew back, holding out my hand toward my son as if in supplication; but I could not see him. He had gone.

"'We remained facing each other—my lover and I—crushed, unable to utter a word. I sank into an armchair, and I felt a desire, a vague, powerful desire, to flee, to go out into the night, and to disappear forever. Then convulsive sobs rose in my throat, and I wept, shaken with spasms, my heart breaking, all my nerves writhing with the horrible sensation of an irreparable misfortune, and with that dreadful sense of shame which, in such moments as this, fills a mother's heart.

"'He looked at me in a terrified manner, not venturing to approach, to speak to me, or to touch me, for fear of the boy's return. At last he said:

"'I am going to follow him-to talk to him—to explain matters to him. In short, I must see him and let him know——"

"'And he hurried away.

"'I waited—waited in a distracted frame of mind, trembling at the least sound, starting with fear and with some unutterably strange and intolerable emotion at every slight crackling of the fire in the grate.

"'I waited an hour, two hours, feeling my heart swell with a dread I had never before experienced, such anguish that I would not wish the greatest criminal to endure ten minutes of such misery. Where was my son? What was he doing?

"'About midnight, a messenger brought me a note from my lover. I still know its contents by heart:

"'Has your son returned? I did not find him. I am down here. I do not want to go up at this hour."

"'I wrote in pencil on the same slip of paper:

"'Jean has not returned. You must find him."

"'And I remained all night in the armchair, waiting for him.

"'I felt as if I were going mad. I longed to run wildly about, to roll on the ground. And yet I did not even stir, but kept waiting hour after hour. What was going to happen? I tried to imagine, to guess. But I could form no conception, in spite of my efforts, in spite of the tortures of my soul!

"'And now I feared that they might meet. What would they do in that case? What would my son do? My mind was torn with fearful doubts, with terrible suppositions.

"'You can understand my feelings, can you not, monsieur?

"'My chambermaid, who knew nothing, who understood nothing, came into the room every moment, believing, naturally, that I had lost my reason. I sent her away with a word or a movement of the hand. She went for the doctor, who found me in the throes of a nervous attack.

"'I was put to bed. I had brain fever.

"'When I regained consciousness, after a long illness, I saw beside my bed my—lover—alone.

"'I exclaimed:

"'My son? Where is my son?

"'He made no reply. I stammered:

"'Dead-dead. Has he committed suicide?

"'No, no, I swear it. But we have not found him in spite of all my efforts.

"'Then, becoming suddenly exasperated and even indignant—for women are subject to such outbursts of unaccountable and unreasoning anger—I said:

"'I forbid you to come near me or to see me again unless you find him. Go away!

"He did go away.

"'I have never seen one or the other of them since, monsieur, and thus I have lived for the last twenty years.

"'Can you imagine what all this meant to me? Can you understand this monstrous punishment, this slow, perpetual laceration of a mother's heart, this abominable, endless waiting? Endless, did I say? No; it is about to end, for I am dying. I am dying without ever again seeing either of them—either one or the other!

"'He—the man I loved—has written to me every day for the last twenty years; and I—I have never consented to see him, even for one second; for I had a strange feeling that, if he were to come back here, my son would make his appearance at the same moment. Oh! my son! my son! Is he dead? Is he living? Where is he hiding? Over there, perhaps, beyond the great ocean, in some country so far away that even its very name is unknown to me! Does he ever think of me? Ah! if he only knew! How cruel one's children are! Did he understand to what frightful suffering he condemned me, into what depths of despair, into what tortures, he cast me while I was still in the prime of life, leaving me to suffer until this moment, when I am about to die—me, his mother, who loved him with all the intensity of a mother's love? Oh! isn't it cruel, cruel?

"'You will tell him all this, monsieur—will you not? You will repeat to him my last words:

"'My child, my dear, dear child, be less harsh toward poor women! Life is already brutal and savage enough in its dealings with them. My dear son, think of what the existence of your poor mother has been ever since the day you left her. My dear child, forgive her, and love her, now that she is dead, for she has had to endure the most frightful penance ever inflicted on a woman."

"She gasped for breath, trembling, as if she had addressed the last words to her son and as if he stood by her bedside.

"Then she added:

"'You will tell him also, monsieur, that I never again saw-the other.'

"Once more she ceased speaking, then, in a broken voice, she said:

"'Leave me now, I beg of you. I want to die all alone, since they are not with me.'"

Maitre Le Brument added:

"And I left the house, monsieurs, crying like a fool, so bitterly, indeed, that my coachman turned round to stare at me.

"And to think that, every day, dramas like this are being enacted all around us!

"I have not found the son—that son—well, say what you like about him, but I call him that criminal son!"

THE HAND

All were crowding around M. Bermutier, the judge, who was giving his opinion about the Saint-Cloud mystery. For a month this in explicable crime had been the talk of Paris. Nobody could make head or tail of it.

M. Bermutier, standing with his back to the fireplace, was talking, citing the evidence, discussing the various theories, but arriving at no conclusion.

Some women had risen, in order to get nearer to him, and were standing with their eyes fastened on the clean-shaven face of the judge, who was saying such weighty things. They, were shaking and trembling, moved by fear and curiosity, and by the eager and insatiable desire for the horrible, which haunts the soul of every woman. One of them, paler than the others, said during a pause:

"It's terrible. It verges on the supernatural. The truth will never be known."

The judge turned to her:

"True, madame, it is likely that the actual facts will never be discovered. As for the word 'supernatural' which you have just used, it has nothing to do with the matter. We are in the presence of a very cleverly conceived and executed crime, so well enshrouded in mystery that we cannot disentangle it from the involved circumstances which surround it. But once I had to take charge of an affair in which the uncanny seemed to play a part. In fact, the case became so confused that it had to be given up."

Several women exclaimed at once:

"Oh! Tell us about it!"

M. Bermutier smiled in a dignified manner, as a judge should, and went on:

"Do not think, however, that I, for one minute, ascribed anything in the case to supernatural influences. I believe only in normal causes. But if, instead of using the word 'supernatural' to express what we do not understand, we were simply to make use of the word 'inexplicable,' it would be much better. At any rate, in the affair of which I am about to tell you, it is especially the surrounding, preliminary circumstances which impressed me. Here are the facts:

"I was, at that time, a judge at Ajaccio, a little white city on the edge of a bay which is surrounded by high mountains.

"The majority of the cases which came up before me concerned vendettas. There are some that are superb, dramatic, ferocious, heroic. We find there the most beautiful causes for revenge of which one could dream, enmities hundreds of years old, quieted for a time but never extinguished; abominable stratagems, murders becoming massacres and almost deeds of glory. For two years I heard of nothing but the price of blood, of this terrible Corsican prejudice which compels revenge for insults meted out to the offending person and all his descendants and relatives. I had seen old men, children, cousins murdered; my head was full of these stories.

"One day I learned that an Englishman had just hired a little villa at the end of the bay for several years. He had brought with him a French servant, whom he had engaged on the way at Marseilles.

"Soon this peculiar person, living alone, only going out to hunt and fish, aroused a widespread interest. He never spoke to any one, never went to the town, and every morning he would practice for an hour or so with his revolver and rifle.

"Legends were built up around him. It was said that he was some high personage, fleeing from his fatherland for political reasons; then it was affirmed that he was in hiding after having committed some abominable crime. Some particularly horrible circumstances were even mentioned.

"In my judicial position I thought it necessary to get some information about this man, but it was impossible to learn anything. He called himself Sir John Rowell.

"I therefore had to be satisfied with watching him as closely as I could, but I could see nothing suspicious about his actions.

"However, as rumors about him were growing and becoming more widespread, I decided to try to see this stranger myself, and I began to hunt regularly in the neighborhood of his grounds.

"For a long time I watched without finding an opportunity. At last it came to me in the shape of a partridge which I shot and killed right in front of the Englishman. My dog fetched it for me, but, taking the bird, I went at once to Sir John Rowell and, begging his pardon, asked him to accept it.

"He was a big man, with red hair and beard, very tall, very broad, a kind of calm and polite Hercules. He had nothing of the so-called British stiffness, and in a broad English accent he thanked me warmly for my attention. At the end of a month we had had five or six conversations.

"One night, at last, as I was passing before his door, I saw him in the garden, seated astride a chair, smoking his pipe. I bowed and he invited me to come in and have a glass of beer. I needed no urging.

"He received me with the most punctilious English courtesy, sang the praises of France and of Corsica, and declared that he was quite in love with this country.

"Then, with great caution and under the guise of a vivid interest, I asked him a few questions about his life and his plans. He answered without embarrassment, telling me that he had travelled a great deal in Africa, in the Indies, in America. He added, laughing:

"'I have had many adventures.'

"Then I turned the conversation on hunting, and he gave me the most curious details on hunting the hippopotamus, the tiger, the elephant and even the gorilla.

"I said:

"'Are all these animals dangerous?'

"He smiled:

"'Oh, no! Man is the worst.'

"And he laughed a good broad laugh, the wholesome laugh of a contented Englishman.

"'I have also frequently been man-hunting.'

"Then he began to talk about weapons, and he invited me to come in and see different makes of guns.

"His parlor was draped in black, black silk embroidered in gold. Big yellow flowers, as brilliant as fire, were worked on the dark material.

"He said:

"'It is a Japanese material.'

"But in the middle of the widest panel a strange thing attracted my attention. A black object stood out against a square of red velvet. I went up to it; it was a hand, a human hand. Not the clean white hand of a skeleton, but a dried black hand, with yellow nails, the muscles exposed and traces of old blood on the bones, which were cut off as clean as though it had been chopped off with an axe, near the middle of the forearm.

"Around the wrist, an enormous iron chain, riveted and soldered to this unclean member, fastened it to the wall by a ring, strong enough to hold an elephant in leash.

"I asked:

"'What is that?'

"The Englishman answered quietly:

"'That is my best enemy. It comes from America, too. The bones were severed by a sword and the skin cut off with a sharp stone and dried in the sun for a week.'

"I touched these human remains, which must have belonged to a giant. The uncommonly long fingers were attached by enormous tendons which still had pieces of skin hanging to them in places. This hand was terrible to see; it made one think of some savage vengeance.

"I said:

"'This man must have been very strong.'

"The Englishman answered quietly:

"'Yes, but I was stronger than he. I put on this chain to hold him.'

"I thought that he was joking. I said:

"'This chain is useless now, the hand won't run away.'

"Sir John Rowell answered seriously:

"'It always wants to go away. This chain is needed.'

"I glanced at him quickly, questioning his face, and I asked myself:

"'Is he an insane man or a practical joker?'

"But his face remained inscrutable, calm and friendly. I turned to other subjects, and admired his rifles.

"However, I noticed that he kept three loaded revolvers in the room, as though constantly in fear of some attack.

"I paid him several calls. Then I did not go any more. People had become used to his presence; everybody had lost interest in him.

"A whole year rolled by. One morning, toward the end of November, my servant awoke me and announced that Sir John Rowell had been murdered during the night.

"Half an hour later I entered the Englishman's house, together with the police commissioner and the captain of the gendarmes. The servant, bewildered and in despair, was crying before the door. At first I suspected this man, but he was innocent.

"The guilty party could never be found.

"On entering Sir John's parlor, I noticed the body, stretched out on its back, in the middle of the room.

"His vest was torn, the sleeve of his jacket had been pulled off, everything pointed to, a violent struggle.

"The Englishman had been strangled! His face was black, swollen and frightful, and seemed to express a terrible fear. He held something between his teeth, and his neck, pierced by five or six holes which looked as though they had been made by some iron instrument, was covered with blood.

"A physician joined us. He examined the finger marks on the neck for a long time and then made this strange announcement:

"'It looks as though he had been strangled by a skeleton.'

"A cold chill seemed to run down my back, and I looked over to where I had formerly seen the terrible hand. It was no longer there. The chain was hanging down, broken.

"I bent over the dead man and, in his contracted mouth, I found one of the fingers of this vanished hand, cut—or rather sawed off by the teeth down to the second knuckle.

"Then the investigation began. Nothing could be discovered. No door, window or piece of furniture had been forced. The two watch dogs had not been aroused from their sleep.

"Here, in a few words, is the testimony of the servant:

"For a month his master had seemed excited. He had received many letters, which he would immediately burn.

"Often, in a fit of passion which approached madness, he had taken a switch and struck wildly at this dried hand riveted to the wall, and which had disappeared, no one knows how, at the very hour of the crime.

"He would go to bed very late and carefully lock himself in. He always kept weapons within reach. Often at night he would talk loudly, as though he were quarrelling with some one.

"That night, somehow, he had made no noise, and it was only on going to open the windows that the servant had found Sir John murdered. He suspected no one.

"I communicated what I knew of the dead man to the judges and public officials. Throughout the whole island a minute investigation was carried on. Nothing could be found out.

"One night, about three months after the crime, I had a terrible nightmare. I seemed to see the horrible hand running over my curtains and walls like an immense scorpion or spider. Three times I awoke, three times I went to sleep again; three times I saw the hideous object galloping round my room and moving its fingers like legs.

"The following day the hand was brought me, found in the cemetery, on the grave of Sir John Rowell, who had been buried there because we had been unable to find his family. The first finger was missing.

"Ladies, there is my story. I know nothing more."

The women, deeply stirred, were pale and trembling. One of them exclaimed:

"But that is neither a climax nor an explanation! We will be unable to sleep unless you give us your opinion of what had occurred."

The judge smiled severely:

"Oh! Ladies, I shall certainly spoil your terrible dreams. I simply believe that the legitimate owner of the hand was not dead, that he came to get it with his remaining one. But I don't know how. It was a kind of vendetta."

One of the women murmured:

"No, it can't be that."

And the judge, still smiling, said:

"Didn't I tell you that my explanation would not satisfy you?"

A TRESS OF HAIR

The walls of the cell were bare and white washed. A narrow grated window, placed so high that one could not reach it, lighted this sinister little room. The mad inmate, seated on a straw chair, looked at us with a fixed, vacant and haunted expression. He was very thin, with hollow cheeks and hair almost white, which one guessed might have turned gray in a few months. His clothes appeared to be too large for his shrunken limbs, his sunken chest and empty paunch. One felt that this man's mind was destroyed, eaten by his thoughts, by one thought, just as a fruit is eaten by a worm. His craze, his idea was there in his brain, insistent, harassing, destructive. It wasted his frame little by little. It—the invisible, impalpable, intangible, immaterial idea—was mining his health, drinking his blood, snuffing out his life.

What a mystery was this man, being killed by an ideal! He aroused sorrow, fear and pity, this madman. What strange, tremendous and deadly thoughts dwelt within this forehead which they creased with deep wrinkles which were never still?

"He has terrible attacks of rage," said the doctor to me. "His is one of the most peculiar cases I have ever seen. He has seizures of erotic and macaberesque madness. He is a sort of necrophile. He has kept a journal in which he sets forth his disease with the utmost clearness. In it you can, as it were, put your finger on it. If it would interest you, you may go over this document."

I followed the doctor into his office, where he handed me this wretched man's diary, saying: "Read it and tell me what you think of it." I read as follows:

"Until the age of thirty-two I lived peacefully, without knowing love. Life appeared very simple, very pleasant and very easy. I was rich. I enjoyed so many things that I had no passion for anything in particular. It was good to be alive! I awoke happy every morning and did those things that pleased me during the day and went to bed at night contented, in the expectation of a peaceful tomorrow and a future without anxiety.

"I had had a few flirtations without my heart being touched by any true passion or wounded by any of the sensations of true love. It is good to live like that. It is better to love, but it is terrible. And yet those who love in the ordinary way must experience ardent happiness, though less than mine possibly, for love came to me in a remarkable manner.

"As I was wealthy, I bought all kinds of old furniture and old curiosities, and I often thought of the unknown hands that had touched these objects, of the eyes that had admired them, of the hearts that had loved them; for one does love things! I sometimes remained hours and hours looking at a little watch of the last century. It was so tiny, so pretty with its enamel and gold chasing. And it kept time as on the day when a woman first bought it, enraptured at owning this dainty trinket. It had not ceased to vibrate, to live its mechanical life, and it had kept up its regular tick-tock since the last century. Who had first worn it on her bosom amid the warmth of her clothing, the heart of the watch beating beside the heart of the woman? What hand had held it in its warm fingers, had turned it over and then wiped the enamelled shepherds on the case to remove the slight moisture from her fingers? What eyes had watched the hands on its ornamental face for the expected, the beloved, the sacred hour?

"How I wished I had known her, seen her, the woman who had selected this exquisite and rare object! She is dead! I am possessed with a longing for women of former days. I love, from afar, all those who have loved. The story of those dead and gone loves fills my heart with regrets. Oh, the beauty, the smiles, the youthful caresses, the hopes! Should not all that be eternal?

"How I have wept whole nights-thinking of those poor women of former days, so beautiful, so loving, so sweet, whose arms were extended in an embrace, and who now are dead! A kiss is immortal!

It goes from lips to lips, from century to century, from age to age. Men receive them, give them and die.

"The past attracts me, the present terrifies me because the future means death. I regret all that has gone by. I mourn all who have lived; I should like to check time, to stop the clock. But time goes, it goes, it passes, it takes from me each second a little of myself for the annihilation of to-morrow. And I shall never live again.

"Farewell, ye women of yesterday. I love you!

"But I am not to be pitied. I found her, the one I was waiting for, and through her I enjoyed inestimable pleasure.

"I was sauntering in Paris on a bright, sunny morning, with a happy heart and a high step, looking in at the shop windows with the vague interest of an idler. All at once I noticed in the shop of a dealer in antiques a piece of Italian furniture of the seventeenth century. It was very handsome, very rare. I set it down as being the work of a Venetian artist named Vitelli, who was celebrated in his day.

"I went on my way.

"Why did the remembrance of that piece of furniture haunt me with such insistence that I retraced my steps? I again stopped before the shop, in order to take another look at it, and I felt that it tempted me.

"What a singular thing temptation is! One gazes at an object, and, little by little, it charms you, it disturbs you, it fills your thoughts as a woman's face might do. The enchantment of it penetrates your being, a strange enchantment of form, color and appearance of an inanimate object. And one loves it, one desires it, one wishes to have it. A longing to own it takes possession of you, gently at first, as though it were timid, but growing, becoming intense, irresistible.

"And the dealers seem to guess, from your ardent gaze, your secret and increasing longing.

"I bought this piece of furniture and had it sent home at once. I placed it in my room.

"Oh, I am sorry for those who do not know the honeymoon of the collector with the antique he has just purchased. One looks at it tenderly and passes one's hand over it as if it were human flesh; one comes back to it every moment, one is always thinking of it, wherever one goes, whatever one does.

The dear recollection of it pursues you in the street, in society, everywhere; and when you return home at night, before taking off your gloves or your hat; you go and look at it with the tenderness of a lover.

"Truly, for eight days I worshipped this piece of furniture. I opened its doors and pulled out the drawers every few moments. I handled it with rapture, with all the intense joy of possession.

"But one evening I surmised, while I was feeling the thickness of one of the panels, that there must be a secret drawer in it: My heart began to beat, and I spent the night trying to discover this secret cavity.

"I succeeded on the following day by driving a knife into a slit in the wood. A panel slid back and I saw, spread out on a piece of black velvet, a magnificent tress of hair.

"Yes, a woman's hair, an immense coil of fair hair, almost red, which must have been cut off close to the head, tied with a golden cord.

"I stood amazed, trembling, confused. An almost imperceptible perfume, so ancient that it seemed to be the spirit of a perfume, issued from this mysterious drawer and this remarkable relic.

"I lifted it gently, almost reverently, and took it out of its hiding place. It at once unwound in a golden shower that reached to the floor, dense but light; soft and gleaming like the tail of a comet.

"A strange emotion filled me. What was this? When, how, why had this hair been shut up in this drawer? What adventure, what tragedy did this souvenir conceal? Who had cut it off? A lover on a day of farewell, a husband on a day of revenge, or the one whose head it had graced on the day of despair?

"Was it as she was about to take the veil that they had cast thither that love dowry as a pledge to the world of the living? Was it when they were going to nail down the coffin of the beautiful young corpse that the one who had adored her had cut off her tresses, the only thing that he could retain of her, the only living part of her body that would not suffer decay, the only thing he could still love, and caress, and kiss in his paroxysms of grief?

"Was it not strange that this tress should have remained as it was in life, when not an atom of the body on which it grew was in existence?

"It fell over my fingers, tickled the skin with a singular caress, the caress of a dead woman. It affected me so that I felt as though I should weep.

"I held it in my hands for a long time, then it seemed as if it disturbed me, as though something of the soul had remained in it. And I put it back on the velvet, rusty from age, and pushed in the drawer, closed the doors of the antique cabinet and went out for a walk to meditate.

"I walked along, filled with sadness and also with unrest, that unrest that one feels when in love. I felt as though I must have lived before, as though I must have known this woman.

"And Villon's lines came to my mind like a sob:
Tell me where, and in what place
Is Flora, the beautiful Roman,
Hipparchia and Thais
Who was her cousin-german?

Echo answers in the breeze
O'er river and lake that blows,
Their beauty was above all praise,
But where are last year's snows?

The queen, white as lilies,
Who sang as sing the birds,
Bertha Broadfoot, Beatrice, Alice,
Ermengarde, princess of Maine,
And Joan, the good Lorraine,
Burned by the English at Rouen,
Where are they, Virgin Queen?
And where are last year's snows?

"When I got home again I felt an irresistible longing to see my singular treasure, and I took it out and, as I touched it, I felt a shiver go all through me.

"For some days, however, I was in my ordinary condition, although the thought of that tress of hair was always present to my mind.

"Whenever I came into the house I had to see it and take it in my, hands. I turned the key of the cabinet with the same hesitation that one opens the door leading to one's beloved, for in my hands and my heart I felt a confused, singular, constant sensual longing to plunge my hands in the enchanting golden flood of those dead tresses.

"Then, after I had finished caressing it and had locked the cabinet I felt as if it were a living thing, shut up in there, imprisoned; and I longed to see it again. I felt again the imperious desire to take it in my hands, to touch it, to even feel uncomfortable at the cold, slippery, irritating, bewildering contact.

"I lived thus for a month or two, I forget how long. It obsessed me, haunted me. I was happy and tormented by turns, as when one falls in love, and after the first vows have been exchanged.

"I shut myself in the room with it to feel it on my skin, to bury my lips in it, to kiss it. I wound it round my face, covered my eyes with the golden flood so as to see the day gleam through its gold.

"I loved it! Yes, I loved it. I could not be without it nor pass an hour without looking at it.

"And I waited—I waited—for what? I do not know—For her!

"One night I woke up suddenly, feeling as though I were not alone in my room.

"I was alone, nevertheless, but I could not go to sleep again, and, as I was tossing about feverishly, I got up to look at the golden tress. It seemed softer than usual, more life-like. Do the dead come back? I almost lost consciousness as I kissed it. I took it back with me to bed and pressed it to my lips as if it were my sweetheart.

"Do the dead come back? She came back. Yes, I saw her; I held her in my arms, just as she was in life, tall, fair and round. She came back every evening—the dead woman, the beautiful, adorable, mysterious unknown.

"My happiness was so great that I could not conceal it. No lover ever tasted such intense, terrible enjoyment. I loved her so well that I could not be separated from her. I took her with me always and everywhere. I walked about the town with her as if she were my wife, and took her to the theatre, always to a private box. But they saw her—they guessed—they arrested me. They put me in prison like a criminal. They took her. Oh, misery!"

Here the manuscript stopped. And as I suddenly raised my astonished eyes to the doctor a terrific cry, a howl of impotent rage and of exasperated longing resounded through the asylum.

"Listen," said the doctor. "We have to douse the obscene madman with water five times a day. Sergeant Bertrand was the only one who was in love with the dead."

Filled with astonishment, horror and pity, I stammered out: "But—that tress—did it really exist?"

The doctor rose, opened a cabinet full of phials and instruments and tossed over a long tress of fair hair which flew toward me like a golden bird.

I shivered at feeling its soft, light touch on my hands. And I sat there, my heart beating with disgust and desire, disgust as at the contact of anything accessory to a crime and desire as at the temptation of some infamous and mysterious thing.

The doctor said as he shrugged his shoulders:

"The mind of man is capable of anything."

ON THE RIVER

I rented a little country house last summer on the banks of the Seine, several leagues from Paris, and went out there to sleep every evening. After a few days I made the acquaintance of one of my neighbors, a man between thirty and forty, who certainly was the most curious specimen I ever met. He was an old boating man, and crazy about boating. He was always beside the water, on the water, or in the water. He must have been born in a boat, and he will certainly die in a boat at the last.

One evening as we were walking along the banks of the Seine I asked him to tell me some stories about his life on the water. The good man at once became animated, his whole expression changed, he became eloquent, almost poetical. There was in his heart one great passion, an absorbing, irresistible passion the river.

Ah, he said to me, how many memories I have, connected with that river that you see flowing beside us! You people who live in streets know nothing about the river. But listen to a fisherman as he mentions the word. To him it is a mysterious thing, profound, unknown, a land of mirages and phantasmagoria, where one sees by night things that do not exist, hears sounds that one does not recognize, trembles without knowing why, as in passing through a cemetery—and it is, in fact, the most sinister of cemeteries, one in which one has no tomb.

The land seems limited to the river boatman, and on dark nights, when there is no moon, the river seems limitless. A sailor has not the same feeling for the sea. It is often remorseless and cruel, it is true; but it shrieks, it roars, it is honest, the great sea; while the river is silent and perfidious. It does not speak, it flows along without a sound; and this eternal motion of flowing water is more terrible to me than the high waves of the ocean.

Dreamers maintain that the sea hides in its bosom vast tracts of blue where those who are drowned roam among the big fishes, amid strange forests and crystal grottoes. The river has only black depths where one rots in the slime. It is beautiful, however, when it sparkles in the light of the rising sun and gently laps its banks covered with whispering reeds.

The poet says, speaking of the ocean,

"O waves, what mournful tragedies ye know
—Deep waves, the dread of kneeling mothers' hearts!
Ye tell them to each other as ye roll
On flowing tide, and this it is that gives
The sad despairing tones unto your voice
As on ye roll at eve by mounting tide."

Well, I think that the stories whispered by the slender reeds, with their little soft voices, must be more sinister than the lugubrious tragedies told by the roaring of the waves.

But as you have asked for some of my recollections, I will tell you of a singular adventure that happened to me ten years ago.

I was living, as I am now, in Mother Lafon's house, and one of my closest friends, Louis Bernet who has now given up boating, his low shoes and his bare neck, to go into the Supreme Court, was living in the village of C., two leagues further down the river. We dined together every day, sometimes at his house, sometimes at mine.

One evening as I was coming home along and was pretty tired, rowing with difficulty my big boat, a twelve-footer, which I always took out at night, I stopped a few moments to draw breath near the reed-covered point yonder, about two hundred metres from the railway bridge.

It was a magnificent night, the moon shone brightly, the river gleamed, the air was calm and soft. This peacefulness tempted me. I thought to myself that it would be pleasant to smoke a pipe in this spot. I took up my anchor and cast it into the river.

The boat floated downstream with the current, to the end of the chain, and then stopped, and I seated myself in the stern on my sheepskin and made myself as comfortable as possible. There was not a sound to be heard, except that I occasionally thought I could perceive an almost imperceptible lapping of the water against the bank, and I noticed taller groups of reeds which assumed strange shapes and seemed, at times, to move.

The river was perfectly calm, but I felt myself affected by the unusual silence that surrounded me. All the creatures, frogs and toads, those nocturnal singers of the marsh, were silent.

Suddenly a frog croaked to my right, and close beside me. I shuddered. It ceased, and I heard nothing more, and resolved to smoke, to soothe my mind. But, although I was a noted colorer of pipes, I could not smoke; at the second draw I was nauseated, and gave up trying. I began to sing. The sound of my voice was distressing to me. So I lay still, but presently the slight motion of the boat disturbed me. It seemed to me as if she were making huge lurches, from bank to bank of the river, touching each bank alternately. Then I felt as though an invisible force, or being, were drawing her to the surface of the water and lifting her out, to let her fall again. I was tossed about as in a tempest. I heard noises around me. I sprang to my feet with a single bound. The water was glistening, all was calm.

I saw that my nerves were somewhat shaky, and I resolved to leave the spot. I pulled the anchor chain, the boat began to move; then I felt a resistance. I pulled harder, the anchor did not come up; it had caught on something at the bottom of the river and I could not raise it. I began pulling again, but all in vain. Then, with my oars, I turned the boat with its head up stream to change the position of the anchor. It was no use, it was still caught. I flew into a rage and shook the chain furiously. Nothing budged. I sat down, disheartened, and began to reflect on my situation. I could not dream of breaking this chain, or detaching it from the boat, for it was massive and was riveted at the bows to a piece of wood as thick as my arm. However, as the weather was so fine I thought that it probably would not be long before some fisherman came to my aid. My ill-luck had quieted me. I sat down and was able, at length, to smoke my pipe. I had a bottle of rum; I drank two or three glasses, and was able to laugh at the situation. It was very warm; so that, if need be, I could sleep out under the stars without any great harm.

All at once there was a little knock at the side of the boat. I gave a start, and a cold sweat broke out all over me. The noise was, doubtless, caused by some piece of wood borne along by the current, but that was enough, and I again became a prey to a strange nervous agitation. I seized the chain and tensed my muscles in a desperate effort. The anchor held firm. I sat down again, exhausted.

The river had slowly become enveloped in a thick white fog which lay close to the water, so that when I stood up I could see neither the river, nor my feet, nor my boat; but could perceive only the tops of the reeds, and farther off in the distance the plain, lying white in the moonlight, with big black patches rising up from it towards the sky, which were formed by groups of Italian poplars. I was as if buried to the waist in a cloud of cotton of singular whiteness, and all sorts of strange fancies came into my mind. I thought that someone was trying to climb into my boat which I could no longer distinguish, and that the river, hidden by the thick fog, was full of strange creatures which were swimming all around me. I felt horribly uncomfortable, my forehead felt as if it had a tight band round it, my heart beat so that it almost suffocated me, and, almost beside myself, I thought of swimming away from the place. But then, again, the very idea made me tremble with fear. I saw myself, lost, going by guesswork in this heavy fog, struggling about amid the grasses and reeds which I could not escape, my breath rattling with fear, neither seeing the bank, nor finding my boat; and it seemed as if I would feel myself dragged down by the feet to the bottom of these black waters.

In fact, as I should have had to ascend the stream at least five hundred metres before finding a spot free from grasses and rushes where I could land, there were nine chances to one that I could not find my way in the fog and that I should drown, no matter how well I could swim.

I tried to reason with myself. My will made me resolve not to be afraid, but there was something in me besides my will, and that other thing was afraid. I asked myself what there was to be afraid of. My brave "ego" ridiculed my coward "ego," and never did I realize, as on that day, the existence in us of two rival personalities, one desiring a thing, the other resisting, and each winning the day in turn.

This stupid, inexplicable fear increased, and became terror. I remained motionless, my eyes staring, my ears on the stretch with expectation. Of what? I did not know, but it must be something terrible. I believe if it had occurred to a fish to jump out of the water, as often happens, nothing more would have been required to make me fall over, stiff and unconscious.

However, by a violent effort I succeeded in becoming almost rational again. I took up my bottle of rum and took several pulls. Then an idea came to me, and I began to shout with all my might towards all the points of the compass in succession. When my throat was absolutely paralyzed I listened. A dog was howling, at a great distance.

I drank some more rum and stretched myself out at the bottom of the boat. I remained there about an hour, perhaps two, not sleeping, my eyes wide open, with nightmares all about me. I did not dare to rise, and yet I intensely longed to do so. I delayed it from moment to moment. I said to myself: "Come, get up!" and I was afraid to move. At last I raised myself with infinite caution as though my life depended on the slightest sound that I might make; and looked over the edge of the boat. I was dazzled by the most marvellous, the most astonishing sight that it is possible to see. It was one of those phantasmagoria of fairyland, one of those sights described by travellers on their return from distant lands, whom we listen to without believing.

The fog which, two hours before, had floated on the water, had gradually cleared off and massed on the banks, leaving the river absolutely clear; while it formed on either bank an uninterrupted wall six or seven metres high, which shone in the moonlight with the dazzling brilliance of snow. One saw nothing but the river gleaming with light between these two white mountains; and high above my head sailed the great full moon, in the midst of a bluish, milky sky.

All the creatures in the water were awake. The frogs croaked furiously, while every few moments I heard, first to the right and then to the left, the abrupt, monotonous and mournful metallic note of the bullfrogs. Strange to say, I was no longer afraid. I was in the midst of such an unusual landscape that the most remarkable things would not have astonished me.

How long this lasted I do not know, for I ended by falling asleep. When I opened my eyes the moon had gone down and the sky was full of clouds. The water lapped mournfully, the wind was blowing, it was pitch dark. I drank the rest of the rum, then listened, while I trembled, to the rustling of the reeds and the foreboding sound of the river. I tried to see, but could not distinguish my boat, nor even my hands, which I held up close to my eyes.

Little by little, however, the blackness became less intense. All at once I thought I noticed a shadow gliding past, quite near me. I shouted, a voice replied; it was a fisherman. I called him; he came near and I told him of my ill-luck. He rowed his boat alongside of mine and, together, we pulled at the anchor chain. The anchor did not move. Day came, gloomy gray, rainy and cold, one of those days that bring one sorrows and misfortunes. I saw another boat. We hailed it. The man on board of her joined his efforts to ours, and gradually the anchor yielded. It rose, but slowly, slowly, loaded down by a considerable weight. At length we perceived a black mass and we drew it on board. It was the corpse of an old women with a big stone round her neck.

THE CRIPPLE

The following adventure happened to me about 1882. I had just taken the train and settled down in a corner, hoping that I should be left alone, when the door suddenly opened again and I heard a voice say: "Take care, monsieur, we are just at a crossing; the step is very high."

Another voice answered: "That's all right, Laurent, I have a firm hold on the handle."

Then a head appeared, and two hands seized the leather straps hanging on either side of the door and slowly pulled up an enormous body, whose feet striking on the step, sounded like two canes. When the man had hoisted his torso into the compartment I noticed, at the loose edge of his trousers, the end of a wooden leg, which was soon followed by its mate. A head appeared behind this traveller and asked; "Are you all right, monsieur?"

"Yes, my boy."

"Then here are your packages and crutches."

And a servant, who looked like an old soldier, climbed in, carrying in his arms a stack of bundles wrapped in black and yellow papers and carefully tied; he placed one after the other in the net over his master's head. Then he said: "There, monsieur, that is all. There are five of them—the candy, the doll the drum, the gun, and the pate de foies gras."

"Very well, my boy."

"Thank you, Laurent; good health!"

The man closed the door and walked away, and I looked at my neighbor. He was about thirty-five, although his hair was almost white; he wore the ribbon of the Legion of Honor; he had a heavy mustache and was quite stout, with the stoutness of a strong and active man who is kept motionless on account of some infirmity. He wiped his brow, sighed, and, looking me full in the face, he asked: "Does smoking annoy you, monsieur?"

"No, monsieur."

Surely I knew that eye, that voice, that face. But when and where had I seen them? I had certainly met that man, spoken to him, shaken his hand. That was a long, long time ago. It was lost in the haze wherein the mind seems to feel around blindly for memories and pursues them like fleeing phantoms without being able to seize them. He, too, was observing me, staring me out of countenance, with the persistence of a man who remembers slightly but not completely. Our eyes, embarrassed by this persistent contact, turned away; then, after a few minutes, drawn together again by the obscure and tenacious will of working memory, they met once more, and I said: "Monsieur, instead of staring at each other for an hour or so, would it not be better to try to discover where we have known each other?"

My neighbor answered graciously: "You are quite right, monsieur."

I named myself: "I am Henri Bonclair, a magistrate."

He hesitated for a few minutes; then, with the vague look and voice which accompany great mental tension, he said: "Oh, I remember perfectly. I met you twelve years ago, before the war, at the Poincels!"

"Yes, monsieur. Ah! Ah! You are Lieutenant Revaliere?"

"Yes. I was Captain Revaliere even up to the time when I lost my feet—both of them together from one cannon ball."

Now that we knew each other's identity we looked at each other again. I remembered perfectly the handsome, slender youth who led the cotillons with such frenzied agility and gracefulness that he had been nicknamed "the fury." Going back into the dim, distant past, I recalled a story which I had heard and forgotten, one of those stories to which one listens but forgets, and which leave but a faint impression upon the memory.

There was something about love in it. Little by little the shadows cleared up, and the face of a young girl appeared before my eyes. Then her name struck me with the force of an explosion: Mademoiselle de Mandel. I remembered everything now. It was indeed a love story, but quite commonplace. The young girl loved this young man, and when I had met them there was already talk of the approaching wedding. The youth seemed to be very much in love, very happy.

I raised my eye to the net, where all the packages which had been brought in by the servant were trembling from the motion of the train, and the voice of the servant came back to me, as if he had just finished speaking. He had said: "There, monsieur, that is all. There are five of them: the candy, the doll, the drum, the gun, and the pate de foies gras."

Then, in a second, a whole romance unfolded itself in my head. It was like all those which I had already read, where the young lady married notwithstanding the catastrophe, whether physical or financial; therefore, this officer who had been maimed in the war had returned, after the campaign, to the young girl who had given him her promise, and she had kept her word.

I considered that very beautiful, but simple, just as one, considers simple all devotions and climaxes in books or in plays. It always seems, when one reads or listens to these stories of magnanimity, that one could sacrifice one's self with enthusiastic pleasure and overwhelming joy. But the following day, when an unfortunate friend comes to borrow some money, there is a strange revulsion of feeling.

But, suddenly, another supposition, less poetic and more realistic, replaced the first one. Perhaps he had married before the war, before this frightful accident, and she, in despair and resignation, had been forced to receive, care for, cheer, and support this husband, who had departed, a handsome man, and had returned without his feet, a frightful wreck, forced into immobility, powerless anger, and fatal obesity.

Was he happy or in torture? I was seized with an irresistible desire to know his story, or, at least, the principal points, which would permit me to guess that which he could not or would not tell me. Still thinking the matter over, I began talking to him. We had exchanged a few commonplace words; and I raised my eyes to the net, and thought: "He must have three children: the bonbons are for his wife, the doll for his little girl, the drum and the gun for his sons, and this pate de foies gras for himself."

Suddenly I asked him: "Are you a father, monsieur?"

He answered: "No, monsieur."

I suddenly felt confused, as if I had been guilty of some breach of etiquette, and I continued: "I beg your pardon. I had thought that you were when I heard your servant speaking about the toys. One listens and draws conclusions unconsciously."

He smiled and then murmured: "No, I am not even married. I am still at the preliminary stage."

I pretended suddenly to remember, and said:

"Oh! that's true! When I knew you, you were engaged to Mademoiselle de Mandel, I believe."

"Yes, monsieur, your memory is excellent."

I grew very bold and added: "I also seem to remember hearing that Mademoiselle de Mandel married Monsieur—Monsieur—"

He calmly mentioned the name: "Monsieur de Fleurel."

"Yes, that's it! I remember it was on that occasion that I heard of your wound."

I looked him full in the face, and he blushed. His full face, which was already red from the oversupply of blood, turned crimson. He answered quickly, with a sudden ardor of a man who is pleading a cause which is lost in his mind and in his heart, but which he does not wish to admit.

"It is wrong, monsieur, to couple my name with that of Madame de Fleurel. When I returned from the war-without my feet, alas! I never would have permitted her to become my wife. Was it possible? When one marries, monsieur, it is not in order to parade one's generosity; it is in order to live every day, every hour, every minute, every second beside a man; and if this man is disfigured, as I am, it is a death sentence to marry him! Oh, I understand, I admire all sacrifices and devotions when they have a limit, but I do not admit that a woman should give up her whole life, all joy, all her dreams, in order to satisfy the admiration of the gallery. When I hear, on the floor of my room, the tapping of my wooden legs and of my crutches, I grow angry enough to strangle my servant. Do you think that I would permit a woman to do what

I myself am unable to tolerate? And, then, do you think that my stumps are pretty?"

He was silent. What could I say? He certainly was right. Could I blame her, hold her in contempt, even say that she was wrong? No. However, the end which conformed to the rule, to the truth, did not satisfy my poetic appetite. These heroic deeds demand a beautiful sacrifice, which seemed to be lacking, and I felt a certain disappointment. I suddenly asked: "Has Madame de Fleurel any children?"

"Yes, one girl and two boys. It is for them that I am bringing these toys. She and her husband are very kind to me."

The train was going up the incline to Saint-Germain. It passed through the tunnels, entered the station, and stopped. I was about to offer my arm to the wounded officer, in order to help him descend, when two hands were stretched up to him through the open door.

"Hello! my dear Revaliere!"

"Ah! Hello, Fleurel!"

Standing behind the man, the woman, still beautiful, was smiling and waving her hands to him. A little girl, standing beside her, was jumping for joy, and two young boys were eagerly watching the drum and the gun, which were passing from the car into their father's hands.

When the cripple was on the ground, all the children kissed him. Then they set off, the little girl holding in her hand the small varnished rung of a crutch, just as she might walk beside her big friend and hold his thumb.

A STROLL

When Old Man Leras, bookkeeper for Messieurs Labuze and Company, left the store, he stood for a minute bewildered at the glory of the setting sun. He had worked all day in the yellow light of a small jet of gas, far in the back of the store, on a narrow court, as deep as a well. The little room where he had been spending his days for forty years was so dark that even in the middle of summer one could hardly see without gaslight from eleven until three.

It was always damp and cold, and from this hole on which his window opened came the musty odor of a sewer.

For forty years Monsieur Leras had been arriving every morning in this prison at eight o'clock, and he would remain there until seven at night, bending over his books, writing with the industry of a good clerk.

He was now making three thousand francs a year, having started at fifteen hundred. He had remained a bachelor, as his means did not allow him the luxury of a wife, and as he had never enjoyed anything, he desired nothing. From time to time, however, tired of this continuous and monotonous work, he formed a platonic wish: "Gad! If I only had an income of fifteen thousand francs, I would take life easy."

He had never taken life easy, as he had never had anything but his monthly salary. His life had been uneventful, without emotions, without hopes. The faculty of dreaming with which every one is blessed had never developed in the mediocrity of his ambitions.

When he was twenty-one he entered the employ of Messieurs Labuze and Company. And he had never left them.

In 1856 he had lost his father and then his mother in 1859. Since then the only incident in his life was when he moved, in 1868, because his landlord had tried to raise his rent.

Every day his alarm clock, with a frightful noise of rattling chains, made him spring out of bed at 6 o'clock precisely.

Twice, however, this piece of mechanism had been out of order—once in 1866 and again in 1874; he had never been able to find out the reason why. He would dress, make his bed, sweep his room, dust his chair and the top of his bureau. All this took him an hour and a half.

Then he would go out, buy a roll at the Lahure Bakery, in which he had seen eleven different owners without the name ever changing, and he would eat this roll on the way to the office.

His entire existence had been spent in the narrow, dark office, which was still decorated with the same wall paper. He had entered there as a young man, as assistant to Monsieur Brument, and with the desire to replace him.

He had taken his place and wished for nothing more.

The whole harvest of memories which other men reap in their span of years, the unexpected events, sweet or tragic loves, adventurous journeys, all the occurrences of a free existence, all these things had remained unknown to him.

Days, weeks, months, seasons, years, all were alike to him. He got up every day at the same hour, started out, arrived at the office, ate luncheon, went away, had dinner and went to bed without ever interrupting the regular monotony of similar actions, deeds and thoughts.

Formerly he used to look at his blond mustache and wavy hair in the little round mirror left by his predecessor. Now, every evening before leaving, he would look at his white mustache and bald head in the same mirror. Forty years had rolled by, long and rapid, dreary as a day of sadness and as similar as the hours of a sleepless night. Forty years of which nothing remained, not even a memory, not even a misfortune, since the death of his parents. Nothing.

That day Monsieur Leras stood by the door, dazzled at the brilliancy of the setting sun; and instead of returning home he decided to take a little stroll before dinner, a thing which happened to him four or five times a year.

He reached the boulevards, where people were streaming along under the green trees. It was a spring evening, one of those first warm and pleasant evenings which fill the heart with the joy of life.

Monsieur Leras went along with his mincing old man's step; he was going along with joy in his heart, at peace with the world. He reached the Champs-Elysees, and he continued to walk, enlivened by the sight of the young people trotting along.

The whole sky was aflame; the Arc de Triomphe stood out against the brilliant background of the horizon, like a giant surrounded by fire. As he approached the immense monument, the old bookkeeper noticed that he was hungry, and he went into a wine dealer's for dinner.

The meal was served in front of the store, on the sidewalk. It consisted of some mutton, salad and asparagus. It was the best dinner that Monsieur Leras had had in a long time. He washed down his cheese with a small bottle of burgundy, had his after-dinner cup of coffee, a thing which he rarely took, and finally a little pony of brandy.

When he had paid he felt quite youthful, even a little moved. And he said to himself: "What a fine evening! I will continue my stroll as far as the entrance to the Bois de Boulogne. It will do me good." He set out. An old tune which one of his neighbors used to sing kept returning to his mind. He kept on humming it over and over again. A hot, still night had fallen over Paris. Monsieur Leras walked along the Avenue du Bois de Boulogne and watched the cabs drive by. They kept coming with their shining lights, one behind the other, giving him a glimpse of the couples inside, the women in their light dresses and the men dressed in black.

It was one long procession of lovers, riding under the warm, starlit sky. They kept on coming in rapid succession. They passed by in the carriages, silent, side by side, lost in their dreams, in the emotion of desire, in the anticipation of the approaching embrace. The warm shadows seemed to be full of floating kisses. A sensation of tenderness filled the air. All these carriages full of tender couples, all these people intoxicated with the same idea, with the same thought, seemed to give out a disturbing, subtle emanation.

At last Monsieur Leras grew a little tired of walking, and he sat down on a bench to watch these carriages pass by with their burdens of love. Almost immediately a woman walked up to him and sat down beside him. "Good-evening, papa," she said.

He answered: "Madame, you are mistaken."

She slipped her arm through his, saying: "Come along, now; don't be foolish. Listen——"

He arose and walked away, with sadness in his heart. A few yards away another woman walked up to him and asked: "Won't you sit down beside me?" He said: "What makes you take up this life?"

She stood before him and in an altered, hoarse, angry voice exclaimed:

"Well, it isn't for the fun of it, anyhow!"

He insisted in a gentle voice: "Then what makes you?"

She grumbled: "I've got to live! Foolish question!" And she walked away, humming.

Monsieur Leras stood there bewildered. Other women were passing near him, speaking to him and calling to him. He felt as though he were enveloped in darkness by something disagreeable.

He sat down again on a bench. The carriages were still rolling by. He thought: "I should have done better not to come here; I feel all upset." He began to think of all this venal or passionate love, of all these kisses, sold or given, which were passing by in front of him. Love! He scarcely knew it. In his lifetime he had only known two or three women, his means forcing him to live a quiet life, and he looked back at the life which he had led, so different from everybody else, so dreary, so mournful, so empty.

Some people are really unfortunate. And suddenly, as though a veil had been torn from his eyes, he perceived the infinite misery, the monotony of his existence: the past, present and future misery; his last day similar to his first one, with nothing before him, behind him or about him, nothing in his heart or any place.

The stream of carriages was still going by. In the rapid passage of the open carriage he still saw the two silent, loving creatures. It seemed to him that the whole of humanity was flowing on before him, intoxicated with joy, pleasure and happiness. He alone was looking on. To-morrow he would again be alone, always alone, more so than any one else. He stood up, took a few steps, and suddenly he felt as tired as though he had taken a long journey on foot, and he sat down on the next bench.

What was he waiting for? What was he hoping for? Nothing. He was thinking of how pleasant it must be in old age to return home and find the little children. It is pleasant to grow old when one is surrounded by those beings who owe their life to you, who love you, who caress you, who tell you charming and foolish little things which warm your heart and console you for everything.

And, thinking of his empty room, clean and sad, where no one but himself ever entered, a feeling of distress filled his soul; and the place seemed to him more mournful even than his little office. Nobody ever came there; no one ever spoke in it. It was dead, silent, without the echo of a human voice. It seems as though walls retain something of the people who live within them, something of their manner, face and voice. The very houses inhabited by happy families are gayer than the dwellings of the unhappy. His room was as barren of memories as his life. And the thought of returning to this place, all alone, of getting into his bed, of again repeating all the duties and actions of every evening, this thought terrified him. As though to escape farther from this sinister home, and from the time when he would have to return to it, he arose and walked along a path to a wooded corner, where he sat down on the grass.

About him, above him, everywhere, he heard a continuous, tremendous, confused rumble, composed of countless and different noises, a vague and throbbing pulsation of life: the life breath of Paris, breathing like a giant.

The sun was already high and shed a flood of light on the Bois de Boulogne. A few carriages were beginning to drive about and people were appearing on horseback.

A couple was walking through a deserted alley.

Suddenly the young woman raised her eyes and saw something brown in the branches. Surprised and anxious, she raised her hand, exclaiming: "Look! what is that?"

Then she shrieked and fell into the arms of her companion, who was forced to lay her on the ground.

The policeman who had been called cut down an old man who had hung himself with his suspenders.

Examination showed that he had died the evening before. Papers found on him showed that he was a bookkeeper for Messieurs Labuze and Company and that his name was Leras.

His death was attributed to suicide, the cause of which could not be suspected. Perhaps a sudden access of madness!

ALEXANDRE

At four o'clock that day, as on every other day, Alexandre rolled the three-wheeled chair for cripples up to the door of the little house; then, in obedience to the doctor's orders, he would push his old and infirm mistress about until six o'clock.

When he had placed the light vehicle against the step, just at the place where the old lady could most easily enter it, he went into the house; and soon a furious, hoarse old soldier's voice was heard cursing inside the house: it issued from the master, the retired ex-captain of infantry, Joseph Maramballe.

Then could be heard the noise of doors being slammed, chairs being pushed about, and hasty footsteps; then nothing more. After a few seconds, Alexandre reappeared on the threshold, supporting with all his strength Madame Maramballe, who was exhausted from the exertion of descending the stairs. When she was at last settled in the rolling chair, Alexandre passed behind it, grasped the handle, and set out toward the river.

Thus they crossed the little town every day amid the respectful greeting, of all. These bows were perhaps meant as much for the servant as for the mistress, for if she was loved and esteemed by all, this old trooper, with his long, white, patriarchal beard, was considered a model domestic.

The July sun was beating down unmercifully on the street, bathing the low houses in its crude and burning light. Dogs were sleeping on the sidewalk in the shade of the houses, and Alexandre, a little out of breath, hastened his footsteps in order sooner to arrive at the avenue which leads to the water.

Madame Maramballe was already slumbering under her white parasol, the point of which sometimes grazed along the man's impassive face. As soon as they had reached the Allee des Tilleuls, she awoke in the shade of the trees, and she said in a kindly voice: "Go more slowly, my poor boy; you will kill yourself in this heat."

Along this path, completely covered by arched linden trees, the Mavettek flowed in its winding bed bordered by willows.

The gurgling of the eddies and the splashing of the little waves against the rocks lent to the walk the charming music of babbling water and the freshness of damp air. Madame Maramballe inhaled with deep delight the humid charm of this spot and then murmured: "Ah! I feel better now! But he wasn't in a good humor to-day."

Alexandre answered: "No, madame."

For thirty-five years he had been in the service of this couple, first as officer's orderly, then as simple valet who did not wish to leave his masters; and for the last six years, every afternoon, he had been wheeling his mistress about through the narrow streets of the town. From this long and devoted service, and then from this daily tete-a-tete, a kind of familiarity arose between the old lady and the devoted servant, affectionate on her part, deferential on his.

They talked over the affairs of the house exactly as if they were equals. Their principal subject of conversation and of worry was the bad disposition of the captain, soured by a long career which had begun with promise, run along without promotion, end ended without glory.

Madame Maramballe continued: "He certainly was not in a good humor today. This happens too often since he has left the service."

And Alexandre, with a sigh, completed his mistress's thoughts, "Oh, madame might say that it happens every day and that it also happened before leaving the army."

"That is true. But the poor man has been so unfortunate. He began with a brave deed, which obtained for him the Legion of Honor at the age of twenty; and then from twenty to fifty he was not able to rise higher than captain, whereas at the beginning he expected to retire with at least the rank of colonel."

"Madame might also admit that it was his fault. If he had not always been as cutting as a whip, his superiors would have loved and protected him better. Harshness is of no use; one should try to please if one wishes to advance. As far as his treatment of us is concerned, it is also our fault, since we are willing to remain with him, but with others it's different."

Madame Maramballe was thinking. Oh, for how many years had she thus been thinking of the brutality of her husband, whom she had married long ago because he was a handsome officer, decorated quite young, and full of promise, so they said! What mistakes one makes in life!

She murmured: "Let us stop a while, my poor Alexandre, and you rest on that bench."

It was a little worm-eaten bench, placed at a turn in the alley. Every time they came in this direction Alexandre was accustomed to making a short pause on this seat.

He sat down and with a proud and familiar gesture he took his beautiful white beard in his hand, and, closing his, fingers over it, ran them down to the point, which he held for a minute at the pit of his stomach, as if once more to verify the length of this growth.

Madame Maramballe continued: "I married him; it is only just and natural that I should bear his injustice; but what I do not understand is why you also should have supported it, my good Alexandre!"

He merely shrugged his shoulders and answered: "Oh! I—madame."

She added: "Really. I have often wondered. When I married him you were his orderly and you could hardly do otherwise than endure him. But why did you remain with us, who pay you so little and who treat you so badly, when you could have done as every one else does, settle down, marry, have a family?"

He answered: "Oh, madame! with me it's different."

Then he was silent; but he kept pulling his beard as if he were ringing a bell within him, as if he were trying to pull it out, and he rolled his eyes like a man who is greatly embarrassed.

Madame Maramballe was following her own train of thought: "You are not a peasant. You have an education—"

He interrupted her proudly: "I studied surveying, madame."

"Then why did you stay with us, and blast your prospects?"

He stammered: "That's it! that's it! it's the fault of my dispositton."

"How so, of your disposition?"

"Yes, when I become attached to a person I become attached to him, that's all."

She began to laugh: "You are not going to try to tell me that Maramballe's sweet disposition caused you to become attached to him for life."

He was fidgeting about on his bench visibly embarrassed, and he muttered behind his long beard:

"It was not he, it was you!"

The old lady, who had a sweet face, with a snowy line of curly white hair between her forehead and her bonnet, turned around in her chair and observed her servant with a surprised look, exclaiming: "I, my poor Alexandre! How so?"

He began to look up in the air, then to one side, then toward the distance, turning his head as do timid people when forced to admit shameful secrets. At last he exclaimed, with the courage of a trooper who is ordered to the line of fire: "You see, it's this way—the first time I brought a letter to mademoiselle from the lieutenant, mademoiselle gave me a franc and a smile, and that settled it."

Not understanding well, she questioned him "Explain yourself."

Then he cried out, like a malefactor who is admitting a fatal crime: "I had a sentiment for madame! There!"

She answered nothing, stopped looking at him, hung her head, and thought. She was good, full of justice, gentleness, reason, and tenderness. In a second she saw the immense devotion of this poor creature, who had given up everything in order to live beside her, without saying anything. And she felt as if she could cry. Then, with a sad but not angry expression, she said: "Let us return home."

He rose and began to push the wheeled chair.

As they approached the village they saw Captain Maramballe coming toward them. As soon as he joined them he asked his wife, with a visible desire of getting angry: "What have we for dinner?"

"Some chicken with flageolets."

He lost his temper: "Chicken! chicken! always chicken! By all that's holy, I've had enough chicken! Have you no ideas in your head, that you make me eat chicken every day?"

She answered, in a resigned tone: "But, my dear, you know that the doctor has ordered it for you. It's the best thing for your stomach. If your stomach were well, I could give you many things which I do not dare set before you now."

Then, exasperated, he planted himself in front of Alexandre, exclaiming: "Well, if my stomach is out of order it's the fault of that brute. For thirty-five years he has been poisoning me with his abominable cooking."

Madame Maramballe suddenly turned about completely, in order to see the old domestic. Their eyes met, and in this single glance they both said "Thank you!" to each other.

THE LOG

The drawing-room was small, full of heavy draperies and discreetly fragrant. A large fire burned in the grate and a solitary lamp at one end of the mantelpiece threw a soft light on the two persons who were talking.

She, the mistress of the house, was an old lady with white hair, but one of those old ladies whose unwrinkled skin is as smooth as the finest paper, and scented, impregnated with perfume, with the delicate essences which she had used in her bath for so many years.

He was a very old friend, who had never married, a constant friend, a companion in the journey of life, but nothing more.

They had not spoken for about a minute, and were both looking at the fire, dreaming of no matter what, in one of those moments of friendly silence between people who have no need to be constantly talking in order to be happy together, when suddenly a large log, a stump covered with burning roots, fell out. It fell over the firedogs into the drawing-room and rolled on to the carpet, scattering great sparks around it. The old lady, with a little scream, sprang to her feet to run away, while he kicked the log back on to the hearth and stamped out all the burning sparks with his boots.

When the disaster was remedied, there was a strong smell of burning, and, sitting down opposite to his friend, the man looked at her with a smile and said, as he pointed to the log:

"That is the reason why I never married."

She looked at him in astonishment, with the inquisitive gaze of women who wish to know everything, that eye which women have who are no longer very young,—in which a complex, and often roguish, curiosity is reflected, and she asked:

"How so?"

"Oh, it is a long story," he replied; "a rather sad and unpleasant story.

"My old friends were often surprised at the coldness which suddenly sprang up between one of my best friends whose Christian name was Julien, and myself. They could not understand how two such intimate and inseparable friends, as we had been, could suddenly become almost strangers to one another, and I will tell you the reason of it.

"He and I used to live together at one time. We were never apart, and the friendship that united us seemed so strong that nothing could break it.

"One evening when he came home, he told me that he was going to get married, and it gave me a shock as if he had robbed me or betrayed me. When a man's friend marries, it is all over between them. The jealous affection of a woman, that suspicious, uneasy and carnal affection, will not tolerate the sturdy and frank attachment, that attachment of the mind, of the heart, and that mutual confidence which exists between two men.

"You see, however great the love may be that unites them a man and a woman are always strangers in mind and intellect; they remain belligerents, they belong to different races. There must always be a conqueror and a conquered, a master and a slave; now the one, now the other—they are never two equals. They press each other's hands, those hands trembling with amorous passion; but they never press them with a long, strong, loyal pressure, with that pressure which seems to open hearts and to lay them bare in a burst of sincere, strong, manly affection. Philosophers of old, instead of marrying, and procreating as a consolation for their old age children, who would abandon them, sought for a good, reliable friend, and grew old with him in that communion of thought which can only exist between men.

"Well, my friend Julien married. His wife was pretty, charming, a little, curly-haired blonde, plump and lively, who seemed to worship him. At first I went but rarely to their house, feeling myself de trop. But, somehow, they attracted me to their home;

they were constantly inviting me, and seemed very fond of me. Consequently, by degrees, I allowed myself to be allured by the charm of their life. I often dined with them, and frequently, when I returned home at night, thought that I would do as he had done, and get married, as my empty house now seemed very dull.

"They appeared to be very much in love, and were never apart.

"Well, one evening Julien wrote and asked me to go to dinner, and I naturally went.

"'My dear fellow,' he said, 'I must go out directly afterward on business, and I shall not be back until eleven o'clock; but I shall be back at eleven precisely, and I reckon on you to keep Bertha company.'

"The young woman smiled.

"'It was my idea,' she said, 'to send for you.'

"I held out my hand to her.

"'You are as nice as ever, I said, and I felt a long, friendly pressure of my fingers, but I paid no attention to it; so we sat down to dinner, and at eight o'clock Julien went out.

"As soon as he had gone, a kind of strange embarrassment immediately seemed to arise between his wife and me. We had never been alone together yet, and in spite of our daily increasing intimacy, this tete-a-tete placed us in a new position. At first I spoke vaguely of those indifferent matters with which one fills up an embarrassing silence, but she did not reply, and remained opposite to me with her head down in an undecided manner, as if she were thinking over some difficult subject, and as I was at a loss for small talk, I held my tongue. It is surprising how hard it is at times to find anything to say.

"And then also I felt something in the air, something I could not express, one of those mysterious premonitions that warn one of another person's secret intentions in regard to yourself, whether they be good or evil.

"That painful silence lasted some time, and then Bertha said to me:

"'Will you kindly put a log on the fire for it is going out.'

"So I opened the box where the wood was kept, which was placed just where yours is, took out the largest log and put it on top of the others, which were three parts burned, and then silence again reigned in the room.

"In a few minutes the log was burning so brightly that it scorched our faces, and the young woman raised her eyes to mine—eyes that had a strange look to me.

"'It is too hot now,' she said; 'let us go and sit on the sofa over there.'

"So we went and sat on the sofa, and then she said suddenly, looking me full in the face:

"'What would you do if a woman were to tell you that she was in love with you?'

"'Upon my word,' I replied, very much at a loss for an answer, 'I cannot foresee such a case; but it would depend very much upon the woman.'

"She gave a hard, nervous, vibrating laugh; one of those false laughs which seem as if they must break thin glass, and then she added: 'Men are never either venturesome or spiteful.' And, after a moment's silence, she continued: 'Have you ever been in love, Monsieur Paul?' I was obliged to acknowledge that I certainly had, and she asked me to tell her all about it. Whereupon I made up some story or other. She listened to me attentively, with frequent signs of disapproval and contempt, and then suddenly she said:

"'No, you understand nothing about the subject. It seems to me that real love must unsettle the mind, upset the nerves and distract the head; that it must—how shall I express it?—be dangerous, even terrible, almost criminal and sacrilegious; that it must be a kind of treason; I mean to say that it is bound to break laws, fraternal bonds, sacred obligations; when love is tranquil, easy, lawful and without dangers, is it really love?'

"I did not know what answer to give her, and I made this philosophical reflection to myself: 'Oh! female brain, here; indeed, you show yourself!'

"While speaking, she had assumed a demure saintly air; and, resting on the cushions, she stretched herself out at full length, with her head on my shoulder, and her dress pulled up a little so as to show her red stockings, which the firelight made look still brighter. In a minute or two she continued:

"'I suppose I have frightened you?' I protested against such a notion, and she leaned against my breast altogether, and without looking at me, she said: 'If I were to tell you that I love you, what would you do?'

"And before I could think of an answer, she had thrown her arms around my neck, had quickly drawn my head down, and put her lips to mine.

"Oh! My dear friend, I can tell you that I did not feel at all happy! What! deceive Julien? become the lover of this little, silly, wrong-headed, deceitful woman, who was, no doubt, terribly sensual, and whom her husband no longer satisfied.

"To betray him continually, to deceive him, to play at being in love merely because I was attracted by forbidden fruit, by the danger incurred and the friendship betrayed! No, that did not suit me, but what was I to do? To imitate Joseph would be acting a very stupid and, moreover, difficult part, for this woman was enchanting in her perfidy, inflamed by audacity, palpitating and excited. Let the man who has never felt on his lips the warm kiss of a woman who is ready to give herself to him throw the first stone at me.

"Well, a minute more—you understand what I mean? A minute more, and—I should have been—no, she would have been!—I beg your pardon, he would have been—when a loud noise made us both jump up. The log had fallen into the room, knocking over the fire irons and the fender, and on to the carpet, which it had scorched, and had rolled under an armchair, which it would certainly set alight.

"I jumped up like a madman, and, as I was replacing on the fire that log which had saved me, the door opened hastily, and Julien came in.

"'I am free,' he said, with evident pleasure. 'The business was over two hours sooner than I expected!'

"Yes, my dear friend, without that log, I should have been caught in the very act, and you know what the consequences would have been!

"You may be sure that I took good care never to be found in a similar situation again, never, never. Soon afterward I saw that Julien was giving me the 'cold shoulder,' as they say. His wife was evidently undermining our friendship. By degrees he got rid of me, and we have altogether ceased to meet.

"I never married, which ought not to surprise you, I think."

JULIE ROMAIN

Two years ago this spring I was making a walking tour along the shore of the Mediterranean. Is there anything more pleasant than to meditate while walking at a good pace along a highway? One walks in the sunlight, through the caressing breeze, at the foot of the mountains, along the coast of the sea. And one dreams! What a flood of illusions, loves, adventures pass through a pedestrian's mind during a two hours' march! What a crowd of confused and joyous hopes enter into you with the mild, light air! You drink them in with the breeze, and they awaken in your heart a longing for happiness which increases with the hun ger induced by walking. The fleeting, charming ideas fly and sing like birds.

I was following that long road which goes from Saint Raphael to Italy, or, rather, that long, splendid panoramic highway which seems made for the representation of all the love-poems of earth. And I thought that from Cannes, where one poses, to Monaco, where one gambles, people come to this spot of the earth for hardly any other purpose than to get embroiled or to throw away money on chance games, displaying under this delicious sky and in this garden of roses and oranges all base vanities and foolish pretensions and vile lusts, showing up the human mind such as it is, servile, ignorant, arrogant and full of cupidity.

Suddenly I saw some villas in one of those ravishing bays that one meets at every turn of the mountain; there were only four or five fronting the sea at the foot of the mountains, and behind them a wild fir wood slopes into two great valleys, that were untraversed

by roads. I stopped short before one of these chalets, it was so pretty: a small white house with brown trimmings, overrun with rambler roses up to the top.

The garden was a mass of flowers, of all colors and all kinds, mixed in a coquettish, well-planned disorder. The lawn was full of them, big pots flanked each side of every step of the porch, pink or yellow clusters framed each window, and the terrace with the stone balustrade, which enclosed this pretty little dwelling, had a garland of enormous red bells, like drops of blood. Behind the house I saw a long avenue of orange trees in blossom, which went up to the foot of the mountain.

Over the door appeared the name, "Villa d'Antan," in small gold letters.

I asked myself what poet or what fairy was living there, what inspired, solitary being had discovered this spot and created this dream house, which seemed to nestle in a nosegay.

A workman was breaking stones up the street, and I went to him to ask the name of the proprietor of this jewel.

"It is Madame Julie Romain," he replied.

Julie Romain! In my childhood, long ago, I had heard them speak of this great actress, the rival of Rachel.

No woman ever was more applauded and more loved—especially more loved! What duets and suicides on her account and what sensational adventures! How old was this seductive woman now? Sixty, seventy, seventy-five! Julie Romain here, in this house! The woman who had been adored by the greatest musician and the most exquisite poet of our land! I still remember the sensation (I was then twelve years of age) which her flight to Sicily with the latter, after her rupture with the former, caused throughout France.

She had left one evening, after a premiere, where the audienc[illegible] had applauded her for a whole half hour, and had recalled h[illegible] eleven times in succession. She had gone away with the poet, i[illegible] post-chaise, as was the fashion then; they had crossed the se[illegible] love each other in that antique island, the daughter of Gree[illegible] that immense orange wood which surrounds Palermo, and [illegible] is called the "Shell of Gold."

People told of their ascension of Mount Etna and how [illegible] leaned over the immense crater, arm in arm, cheek to che[illegible] throw themselves into the very abyss.

Now he was dead, that maker of verses so touching and so profound that they turned, the heads of a whole generation, so subtle and so mysterious that they opened a new world to the younger poets.

The other one also was dead—the deserted one, who had attained through her musical periods that are alive in the memories of all, periods of triumph and of despair, intoxicating triumph and heartrending despair.

And she was there, in that house veiled by flowers.

I did not hesitate, but rang the bell.

A small servant answered, a boy of eighteen with awkward mien and clumsy hands. I wrote in pencil on my card a gallant compliment to the actress, begging her to receive me. Perhaps, if she knew my name, she would open her door to me.

The little valet took it in, and then came back, asking me to follow him. He led me to a neat and decorous salon, furnished in the Louis-Philippe style, with stiff and heavy furniture, from which a little maid of sixteen, slender but not pretty, took off the covers in my honor.

Then I was left alone.

On the walls hung three portraits, that of the actress in one of her roles, that of the poet in his close-fitting greatcoat and the ruffled shirt then in style, and that of the musician seated at a piano.

She, blond, charming, but affected, according to the fashion of her day, was smiling, with her pretty mouth and blue eyes; the painting was careful, fine, elegant, but lifeless.

Those faces seemed to be already looking upon posterity.

The whole place had the air of a bygone time, of days that were done and men who had vanished.

A door opened and a little woman entered, old, very old, very small, with white hair and white eyebrows, a veritable white mouse, and as quick and furtive of movement.

She held out her hand to me, saying in a voice still fresh, sonorous and vibrant:

"Thank you, monsieur. How kind it is of the men of to-day to remember the women of yesterday! Sit down."

I told her that her house had attracted me, that I had inquired for the proprietor's name, and that, on learning it, I could not resist the desire to ring her bell.

"This gives me all the more pleasure, monsieur," she replied, "as it is the first time that such a thing has happened. When I received your card, with the gracious note, I trembled as if an old friend who had disappeared for twenty years had been announced to me. I am like a dead body, whom no one remembers, of whom no one will think until the day when I shall actually die; then the newspapers will mention Julie Romain for three days, relating anecdotes and details of my life, reviving memories, and praising me greatly. Then all will be over with me."

After a few moments of silence, she continued:

"And this will not be so very long now. In a few months, in a few days, nothing will remain but a little skeleton of this little woman who is now alive."

She raised her eyes toward her portrait, which smiled down upon this caricature of herself; then she looked at those of the two men, the disdainful poet and the inspired musician, who seemed to say: "What does this ruin want of us?"

An indefinable, poignant, irresistible sadness overwhelmed my heart, the sadness of existences that have had their day, but who are still debating with their memories, like a person drowning in deep water.

From my seat I could see on the highroad the handsome carriages that were whirling from Nice to Monaco; inside them I saw young, pretty, rich and happy women and smiling, satisfied men. Following my eye, she understood my thought and murmured with a smile of resignation:

"One cannot both be and have been."

"How beautiful life must have been for you!" I said.

She heaved a great sigh.

"Beautiful and sweet! And for that reason I regret it so much."

I saw that she was disposed to talk of herself, so I began to question her, gently and discreetly, as one might touch bruised flesh.

She spoke of her successes, her intoxications and her friends, of her whole triumphant existence.

"Was it on the stage that you found your most intense joys, your true happiness?" I asked.

"Oh, no!" she replied quickly.

I smiled; then, raising her eyes to the two portraits, she said, with a sad glance:

"It was with them."

"Which one?" I could not help asking.

"Both. I even confuse them up a little now in my old woman's memory, and then I feel remorse."

"Then, madame, your acknowledgment is not to them, but to Love itself. They were merely its interpreters."

"That is possible. But what interpreters!"

"Are you sure that you have not been, or that you might not have been, loved as well or better by a simple man, but not a great man, who would have offered to you his whole life and heart, all his thoughts, all his days, his whole being, while these gave you two redoubtable rivals, Music and Poetry?"

"No, monsieur, no!" she exclaimed emphatically, with that still youthful voice, which caused the soul to vibrate. "Another one might perhaps have loved me more, but he would not have loved me as these did. Ah! those two sang to me of the music of love as no one else in the world could have sung of it. How they intoxicated me! Could any other man express what they knew so well how to express in tones and in words? Is it enough merely to love if one cannot put all the poetry and all the music of heaven and earth into love? And they knew how to make a woman delirious with songs and with words. Yes, perhaps there was more of illusion than of reality in our passion; but these illusions lift you into the clouds, while realities always leave you trailing in the dust. If others have loved me more, through these two I have understood, felt and worshipped love."

Suddenly she began to weep.

She wept silently, shedding tears of despair.

I pretended not to see, looking off into the distance. She resumed, after a few minutes:

"You see, monsieur, with nearly every one the heart ages with the body. But this has not happened with me. My body is sixty-nine years old, while my poor heart is only twenty. And that is the reason why I live all alone, with my flowers and my dreams."

There was a long silence between us. She grew calmer and continued, smiling:

"How you would laugh at me, if you knew, if you knew how I pass my evenings, when the weather is fine. I am ashamed and I pity myself at the same time."

Beg as I might, she would not tell me what she did. Then I rose to leave.

"Already!" she exclaimed.

And as I said that I wished to dine at Monte Carlo, she asked timidly:

"Will you not dine with me? It would give me a great deal of pleasure."

I accepted at once. She rang, delighted, and after giving some orders to the little maid she took me over her house.

A kind of glass-enclosed veranda, filled with shrubs, opened into the dining-room, revealing at the farther end the long avenue of orange trees extending to the foot of the mountain. A low seat, hidden by plants, indicated that the old actress often came there to sit down.

Then we went into the garden, to look at the flowers. Evening fell softly, one of those calm, moist evenings when the earth breathes forth all her perfumes. Daylight was almost gone when we sat down at table. The dinner was good and it lasted a long time, and we became intimate friends, she and I, when she understood what a profound sympathy she had aroused in my heart. She had taken two thimblefuls of wine, as the phrase goes, and had grown more confiding and expansive.

"Come, let us look at the moon," she said. "I adore the good moon. She has been the witness of my most intense joys. It seems to me that all my memories are there, and that I need only look at her to bring them all back to me. And even—some times—in the evening—I offer to myself a pretty play—yes, pretty—if you only knew! But no, you would laugh at me. I cannot—I dare not—no, no—really—no."

I implored her to tell me what it was.

"Come, now! come, tell me; I promise you that I will not laugh. I swear it to you—come, now!"

She hesitated. I took her hands—those poor little hands, so thin and so cold!—and I kissed them one after the other, several times, as her lovers had once kissed them. She was moved and hesitated.

"You promise me not to laugh?"

"Yes, I swear it to you."

"Well, then, come."

She rose, and as the little domestic, awkward in his green livery, removed the chair behind her, she whispered quickly a few words into his ear.

"Yes, madame, at once," he replied.

She took my arm and led me to the veranda.

The avenue of oranges was really splendid to see. The full moon made a narrow path of silver, a long bright line, which fell on the yellow sand, between the round, opaque crowns of the dark trees.

As these trees were in bloom, their strong, sweet perfume filled the night, and swarming among their dark foliage I saw thousands of fireflies, which looked like seeds fallen from the stars.

"Oh, what a setting for a love scene!" I exclaimed.

She smiled.

"Is it not true? Is it not true? You will see!"

And she made me sit down beside her.

"This is what makes one long for more life. But you hardly think of these things, you men of to-day. You are speculators, merchants and men of affairs.

"You no longer even know how to talk to us. When I say 'you,' I mean young men in general. Love has been turned into a liaison which very often begins with an unpaid dressmaker's bill. If you think the bill is dearer than the woman, you disappear; but if you hold the woman more highly, you pay it. Nice morals—and a nice kind of love!"

She took my hand.

"Look!"

I looked, astonished and delighted. Down there at the end of the avenue, in the moonlight, were two young people, with their arms around each other's waist. They were walking along, interlaced, charming, with short, little steps, crossing the flakes of light; which illuminated them momentarily, and then sinking back into the shadow. The youth was dressed in a suit of white satin, such as men wore in the eighteenth century, and had on a hat with an ostrich plume. The girl was arrayed in a gown with panniers, and the high, powdered coiffure of the handsome dames of the time of the Regency.

They stopped a hundred paces from us, and standing in the middle of the avenue, they kissed each other with graceful gestures.

Suddenly I recognized the two little servants. Then one of those dreadful fits of laughter that convulse you made me writhe in my chair. But I did not laugh aloud. I resisted, convulsed and feeling almost ill, as a man whose leg is cut off resists the impulse to cry out.

As the young pair turned toward the farther end of the avenue they again became delightful. They went farther and farther away, finally disappearing as a dream disappears. I no longer saw them. The avenue seemed a sad place.

I took my leave at once, so as not to see them again, for I guessed that this little play would last a long time, awakening, as it did, a whole past of love and of stage scenery; the artificial past, deceitful and seductive, false but charming, which still stirred the heart of this amorous old comedienne.

THE RONDOLI SISTERS

I

I set out to see Italy thoroughly on two occasions, and each time I was stopped at the frontier and could not get any further. So I do not know Italy, said my friend, Charles Jouvent. And yet my two attempts gave me a charming idea of the manners of that beautiful country. Some time, however, I must visit its cities, as well as the museums and works of art with which it abounds. I will make another attempt to penetrate into the interior, which I have not yet succeeded in doing.

You don't understand me, so I will explain: In the spring of 1874 I was seized with an irresistible desire to see Venice, Florence, Rome and Naples. I am, as you know, not a great traveller; it appears to me a useless and fatiguing business. Nights spent in a train, the disturbed slumbers of the railway carriage, with the attendant headache, and stiffness in every limb, the sudden waking in that rolling box, the unwashed feeling, with your eyes and hair full of dust, the smell of the coal on which one's lungs feed, those bad dinners in the draughty refreshment rooms are, according to my ideas, a horrible way of beginning a pleasure trip.

After this introduction, we have the miseries of the hotel; of some great hotel full of people, and yet so empty; the strange room and the doubtful bed!

I am most particular about my bed; it is the sanctuary of life. We entrust our almost naked and fatigued bodies to it so that they may be reanimated by reposing between soft sheets and feathers.

There we find the most delightful hours of our existence, the hours of love and of sleep. The bed is sacred, and should be respected, venerated and loved by us as the best and most delightful of our earthly possessions.

I cannot lift up the sheets of a hotel bed without a shudder of disgust. Who has occupied it the night before? Perhaps dirty, revolting people have slept in it. I begin, then, to think of all the horrible people with whom one rubs shoulders every day, people with suspicious-looking skin which makes one think of the feet and all the rest! I call to mind those who carry about with them the sickening smell of garlic or of humanity. I think of those who are deformed and unhealthy, of the perspiration emanating from the sick, of everything that is ugly and filthy in man.

And all this, perhaps, in the bed in which I am about to sleep! The mere idea of it makes me feel ill as I get into it.

And then the hotel dinners—those dreary table d'hote dinners in the midst of all sorts of extraordinary people, or else those terrible solitary dinners at a small table in a restaurant, feebly lighted by a wretched composite candle under a shade.

Again, those terribly dull evenings in some unknown town! Do you know anything more wretched than the approach of dusk on such an occasion? One goes about as if almost in a dream, looking at faces that one never has seen before and never will see again; listening to people talking about matters which are quite indifferent to you in a language that perhaps you do not understand. You have a terrible feeling, almost as if you were lost, and you continue to walk on so as not to be obliged to return to the hotel, where you would feel more lost still because you are at home, in a home which belongs to anyone who can pay for it; and at last you sink into a chair of some well-lighted cafe, whose gilding and lights oppress you a thousand times more than the shadows in the streets. Then you feel so abominably lonely sitting in front of the glass of flat bock beer that a kind of madness seizes you, the longing to go somewhere or other, no matter where, as long as you need not remain in front of that marble table amid those dazzling lights.

And then, suddenly, you are aware that you are really alone in the world, always and everywhere, and that in places which we know, the familiar jostlings give us the illusion only of human fraternity. At such moments of self-abandonment and sombre isolation in distant cities one thinks broadly, clearly and profoundly. Then one suddenly sees the whole of life outside the vision of eternal hope, apart from the deceptions of our innate habits, and of our expectations of happiness, which we indulge in dreams never to be realized.

It is only by going a long distance from home that we can fully understand how short-lived and empty everything near at hand is; by searching for the unknown, we perceive how commonplace and evanescent everything is; only by wandering over the face of the earth can we understand how small the world is, and how very much alike it is everywhere.

How well I know, and how I hate and almost fear, those haphazard walks through unknown streets; and this was the reason why, as nothing would induce me to undertake a tour in Italy by myself, I made up my mind to accompany my friend Paul Pavilly.

You know Paul, and how he idealizes women. To him the earth is habitable only because they are there; the sun gives light and is warm because it shines upon them; the air is soft and balmy because it blows upon their skin and ruffles the soft hair on their temples; and the moon is charming because it makes them dream and imparts a languorous charm to love. Every act and action of Paul's has woman for its motive; all his thoughts, all his efforts and hopes are centered in them.

When I mentioned Italy to Paul he at first absolutely refused to leave Paris. I, however, began to tell him of the adventures I had on my travels. I assured him that all Italian women are charming, and I made him hope for the most refined pleasures at Naples, thanks to certain letters of introduction which I had; and so at last he allowed himself to be persuaded.

II

We took the express one Thursday evening, Paul and I. Hardly anyone goes south at that time of the year, so that we had the carriages to ourselves, and both of us were in a bad temper on leaving Paris, sorry for having yielded to the temptation of this journey, and regretting Marly, the Seine, and our lazy boating excursions, and all those pleasures in and near Paris which are so dear to every true Parisian.

As soon as the train started Paul stuck himself in his corner, and said, "It is most idiotic to go all that distance," and as it was too late for him to change his mind then, I said, "Well, you should not have come."

He made no answer, and I felt very much inclined to laugh when I saw how furious he looked. He is certainly always rather like a squirrel, but then every one of us has retained the type of some animal or other as the mark of his primitive origin. How many people have jaws like a bulldog, or heads like goats, rabbits, foxes, horses, or oxen. Paul is a squirrel turned into a man. He has its bright, quick eyes, its hair, its pointed nose, its small, fine, supple, active body, and a certain mysterious resemblance in his general bearing; in fact, a similarity of movement, of gesture, and of bearing which might almost be taken for a recollection.

At last we both went to sleep with that uncomfortable slumber of the railway carriage, which is interrupted by horrible cramps in the arms and neck, and by the sudden stoppages of the train.

We woke up as we were passing along the Rhone. Soon the continued noise of crickets came in through the windows, that cry which seems to be the voice of the warm earth, the song of Provence; and seemed to instill into our looks, our breasts, and our souls the light and happy feeling of the south, that odor of the parched earth, of the stony and light soil of the olive with its gray-green foliage.

When the train stopped again a railway guard ran along the train calling out "Valence" in a sonorous voice, with an accent that again gave us a taste of that Provence which the shrill note of the crickets had already imparted to us.

Nothing fresh happened till we got to Marseilles, where we alighted for breakfast, but when we returned to our carriage we found a woman installed there.

Paul, with a delighted glance at me, gave his short mustache a mechanical twirl, and passed his fingers through his, hair, which had become slightly out of order with the night's journey. Then he sat down opposite the newcomer.

Whenever I happen to see a striking new face, either in travelling or in society, I always have the strongest inclination to find out what character, mind, and intellectual capacities are hidden beneath those features.

She was a young and pretty woman, certainly a native of the south of France, with splendid eyes, beautiful wavy black hair, which was so thick and long that it seemed almost too heavy for her head. She was dressed with a certain southern bad taste which made her look a little vulgar. Her regular features had none of the grace and finish of the refined races, of that slight delicacy which members of the aristocracy inherit from their birth, and which is the hereditary mark of thinner blood.

Her bracelets were too big to be of gold; she wore earrings with large white stones that were certainly not diamonds, and she belonged unmistakably to the People. One surmised that she would talk too loud, and shout on every occasion with exaggerated gestures.

When the train started she remained motionless in her place, in the attitude of a woman who was indignant, without even looking at us.

Paul began to talk to me, evidently with an eye to effect, trying to attract her attention, as shopkeepers expose their choice wares to catch the notice of passersby.

She, however, did not appear to be paying the least attention.

"Toulon! Ten minutes to wait! Refreshment room!" the porters shouted.

Paul motioned to me to get out, and as soon as we had done so, he said:

"I wonder who on earth she can be?"

I began to laugh. "I am sure I don't know, and I don't in the least care."

He was quite excited.

"She is an uncommonly fresh and pretty girl. What eyes she has, and how cross she looks. She must have been dreadfully worried, for she takes no notice of anything."

"You will have all your trouble for nothing," I growled.

He began to lose his temper.

"I am not taking any trouble, my dear fellow. I think her an extremely pretty woman, that is all. If one could only speak to her!

But I don't know how to begin. Cannot you give me an idea? Can't you guess who she is?"

"Upon my word, I cannot. However, I should rather think she is some strolling actress who is going to rejoin her company after a love adventure."

He seemed quite upset, as if I had said something insulting.

"What makes you think that? On the contrary, I think she looks most respectable."

"Just look at her bracelets," I said, "her earrings and her whole dress. I should not be the least surprised if she were a dancer or a circus rider, but most likely a dancer. Her whole style smacks very much of the theatre."

He evidently did not like the idea.

"She is much too young, I am sure; why, she is hardly twenty."

"Well," I replied, "there are many things which one can do before one is twenty; dancing and elocution are among them."

"Take your seats for Nice, Vintimiglia," the guards and porters called.

We got in; our fellow passenger was eating an orange, and certainly she did not do it elegantly. She had spread her pocket-handkerchief on her knees, and the way in which she tore off the peel and opened her mouth to put in the pieces, and then spat the pips out of the window, showed that her training had been decidedly vulgar.

She seemed, also, more put out than ever, and swallowed the fruit with an exceedingly comic air of rage.

Paul devoured her with his eyes, and tried to attract her attention and excite her curiosity; but in spite of his talk, and of the manner in which he brought in well-known names, she did not pay the least attention to him.

After passing Frejus and St. Raphael, the train passed through a veritable garden, a paradise of roses, and groves of oranges and lemons covered with fruits and flowers at the same time. That delightful coast from Marseilles to Genoa is a kingdom of perfumes in a home of flowers.

June is the time to see it in all its beauty, when in every narrow valley and on every slope, the most exquisite flowers are growing luxuriantly. And the roses! fields, hedges, groves of roses. They climb up the walls, blossom on the roofs, hang from the trees, peep out from among the bushes; they are white, red, yellow, large and small, single, with a simple self-colored dress, or full and heavy in brilliant toilettes.

Their breath makes the air heavy and relaxing, and the still more penetrating odor of the orange blossoms sweetens the atmosphere till it might almost be called the refinement of odor.

The shore, with its brown rocks, was bathed by the motionless Mediterranean. The hot summer sun stretched like a fiery cloth over the mountains, over the long expanses of sand, and over the motionless, apparently solid blue sea. The train went on through the tunnels, along the slopes, above the water, on straight, wall-like viaducts, and a soft, vague, saltish smell, a smell of drying seaweed, mingled at times with the strong, heavy perfume of the flowers.

But Paul neither saw, looked at, nor smelled anything, for our fellow traveller engrossed all his attention.

When we reached Cannes, as he wished to speak to me he signed to me to get out, and as soon as I did so, he took me by the arm.

"Do you know, she is really charming. Just look at her eyes; and I never saw anything like her hair."

"Don't excite yourself," I replied, "or else address her, if you have any intentions that way. She does not look unapproachable; I fancy, although she appear to be a little bit grumpy."

"Why don't you speak to her?" he said.

"I don't know what to say, for I am always terribly stupid at first; I can never make advances to a woman in the street. I follow them, go round and round them, and quite close to them, but never know what to say at first. I only once tried to enter into conversation with a woman in that way. As I clearly saw that she was waiting for me to make overtures, and as I felt bound to say something, I stammered out, 'I hope you are quite well, madame?' She laughed in my face, and I made my escape."

I promised Paul to do all I could to bring about a conversation, and when we had taken our places again, I politely asked our neighbor:

"Have you any objection to the smell of tobacco, madame?"

She merely replied, "Non capisco."

So she was an Italian! I felt an absurd inclination to laugh. As Paul did not understand a word of that language, I was obliged to act as his interpreter, so I said in Italian:

"I asked you, madame, whether you had any objection to tobacco smoke?"

With an angry look she replied, "Che mi fa!"

She had neither turned her head nor looked at me, and I really did not know whether to take this "What do I care" for an authorization, a refusal, a real sign of indifference, or for a mere "Let me alone."

"Madame," I replied, "if you mind the smell of tobacco in the least—"

She again said, "Mica," in a tone which seemed to mean, "I wish to goodness you would leave me alone!" It was, however, a kind of permission, so I said to Paul:

"You may smoke."

He looked at me in that curious sort of way that people have when they try to understand others who are talking in a strange language before them, and asked me:

"What did you say to her?"

"I asked whether we might smoke, and she said we might do whatever we liked."

Whereupon I lighted my cigar.

"Did she say anything more?"

"If you had counted her words you would have noticed that she used exactly six, two of which gave me to understand that she knew no French, so four remained, and much can be said in four words."

Paul seemed quite unhappy, disappointed, and at sea, so to speak.

But suddenly the Italian asked me, in that tone of discontent which seemed habitual to her, "Do you know at what time we shall get to Genoa?"

"At eleven o'clock," I replied. Then after a moment I went on:

"My friend and I are also going to Genoa, and if we can be of any service to you, we shall be very happy, as you are quite alone." But she interrupted with such a "Mica!" that I did not venture on another word.

"What did she say?" Paul asked.

"She said she thought you were charming."

But he was in no humor for joking, and begged me dryly not to make fun of him; so I translated her question and my polite offer, which had been so rudely rejected.

Then he really became as restless as a caged squirrel.

"If we only knew," he said, "what hotel she was going to, we would go to the same. Try to find out so as to have another opportunity to make her talk."

It was not particularly easy, and I did not know what pretext to invent, desirous as I was to make the acquaintance of this unapproachable person.

We passed Nice, Monaco, Mentone, and the train stopped at the frontier for the examination of luggage.

Although I hate those ill-bred people who breakfast and dine in railway-carriages, I went and bought a quantity of good things to make one last attack on her by their means. I felt sure that this girl must, ordinarily, be by no means inaccessible. Something had put her out and made her irritable, but very little would suffice, a mere word or some agreeable offer, to decide her and vanquish her.

We started again, and we three were still alone. I spread my eatables on the seat. I cut up the fowl, put the slices of ham neatly on a piece of paper, and then carefully laid out our dessert, strawberries, plums, cherries and cakes, close to the girl.

When she saw that we were about to eat she took a piece of chocolate and two little crisp cakes out of her pocket and began to munch them.

"Ask her to have some of ours," Paul said in a whisper.

"That is exactly what I wish to do, but it is rather a difficult matter."

As she, however, glanced from time to time at our provisions, I felt sure that she would still be hungry when she had finished what she had with her; so, as soon as her frugal meal was over, I said to her:

"It would be very kind of you if you would take some of this fruit."

Again she said "Mica!" but less crossly than before.

"Well, then," I said, "may I offer you a little wine? I see you have not drunk anything. It is Italian wine, and as we are now in your own country, we should be very pleased to see such a pretty Italian mouth accept the offer of its French neighbors."

She shook her head slightly, evidently wishing to refuse, but very desirous of accepting, and her mica this time was almost polite. I took the flask, which was covered with straw in the Italian fashion, and filling the glass, I offered it to her.

"Please drink it," I said, "to bid us welcome to your country."

She took the glass with her usual look, and emptied it at a draught, like a woman consumed with thirst, and then gave it back to me without even saying "Thank you."

I then offered her the cherries. "Please take some," I said; "we shall be so glad if you will."

Out of her corner she looked at all the fruit spread out beside her, and said so rapidly that I could scarcely follow her: "A me non piacciono ne le ciriegie ne le susine; amo soltano le fragole."

"What does she say?" Paul asked.

"That she does riot care for cherries or plums, but only for strawberries."

I put a newspaper full of wild strawberries on her lap, and she ate them quickly, tossing them into her mouth from some distance in a coquettish and charming manner.

When she had finished the little red heap, which soon disappeared under the rapid action of her hands, I asked her:

"What may I offer you now?"

"I will take a little chicken," she replied.

She certainly devoured half of it, tearing it to pieces with the rapid movements of her jaws like some carnivorous animal. Then she made up her mind to have some cherries, which she "did not like," and then some plums, then some little cakes. Then she said, "I have had enough," and sat back in her corner.

I was much amused, and tried to make her eat more, insisting, in fact, till she suddenly flew into a rage, and flung such a furious mica at me, that I would no longer run the risk of spoiling her digestion.

I turned to my friend. "My poor Paul," I said, "I am afraid we have had our trouble for nothing."

The night came on, one of those hot summer nights which extend their warm shade over the burning and exhausted earth. Here and there, in the distance, by the sea, on capes and promontories, bright stars, which I was, at times, almost inclined to confound with lighthouses, began to shine on the dark horizon:

The scent of the orange trees became more penetrating, and we breathed with delight, distending our lungs to inhale it more deeply. The balmy air was soft, delicious, almost divine.

Suddenly I noticed something like a shower of stars under the dense shade of the trees along the line, where it was quite dark. It might have been taken for drops of light, leaping, flying, playing and running among the leaves, or for small stars fallen from the skies in order to have an excursion on the earth; but they were only fireflies dancing a strange fiery ballet in the perfumed air.

One of them happened to come into our carriage, and shed its intermittent light, which seemed to be extinguished one moment and to be burning the next. I covered the carriage-lamp with its blue shade and watched the strange fly careering about in its fiery flight. Suddenly it settled on the dark hair of our neighbor, who was half dozing after dinner. Paul seemed delighted, with his eyes fixed on the bright, sparkling spot, which looked like a living jewel on the forehead of the sleeping woman.

The Italian woke up about eleven o'clock, with the bright insect still in her hair. When I saw her move, I said: "We are just getting to Genoa, madame," and she murmured, without answering me, as if possessed by some obstinate and embarrassing thought:

"What am I going to do, I wonder?"

And then she suddenly asked:

"Would you like me to come with you?"

I was so taken aback that I really did not understand her.

"With us? How do you mean?"

She repeated, looking more and more furious:

"Would you like me to be your guide now, as soon as we get out of the train?"

"I am quite willing; but where do you want to go."

She shrugged her shoulders with an air of supreme indifference.

"Wherever you like; what does it matter to me?" She repeated her "Che mi fa" twice.

"But we are going to the hotel."

"Very well, let us all go to the hotel," she said, in a contemptuous voice.

I turned to Paul, and said:

"She wishes to know whether we should like her to come with us."

My friend's utter surprise restored my self-possession. He stammered:

"With us? Where to? What for? How?"

"I don't know, but she made this strange proposal to me in a most irritated voice. I told her that we were going to the hotel, and she said: 'Very well, let us all go there!' I suppose she is without a penny. She certainly has a very strange way of making acquaintances."

Paul, who 'was very much excited, exclaimed:

"I am quite agreeable. Tell her that we will go wherever she likes." Then, after a moment's hesitation, he said uneasily:

"We must know, however, with whom she wishes to go—with you or with me?"

I turned to the Italian, who did not even seem to be listening to us, and said:

"We shall be very happy to have you with us, but my friend wishes to know whether you will take my arm or his?"

She opened her black eyes wide with vague surprise, and said, "Che ni fa?"

I was obliged to explain myself. "In Italy, I believe, when a man looks after a woman, fulfils all her wishes, and satisfies all her caprices, he is called a patito. Which of us two will you take for your patito?"

Without the slightest hesitation she replied:

"You!"

I turned to Paul. "You see, my friend, she chooses me; you have no chance."

"All the better for you," he replied in a rage. Then, after thinking for a few moments, he went on:

"Do you really care about taking this creature with you? She will spoil our journey. What are we to do with this woman, who looks like I don't know what? They will not take us in at any decent hotel."

I, however, just began to find the Italian much nicer than I had thought her at first, and I was now very desirous to take her with us. The idea delighted me.

I replied, "My dear fellow, we have accepted, and it is too late to recede. You were the first to advise me to say 'Yes.'"

"It is very stupid," he growled, "but do as you please."

The train whistled, slackened speed, and we ran into the station.

I got out of the carriage, and offered my new companion my hand. She jumped out lightly, and I gave her my arm, which she took with an air of seeming repugnance. As soon as we had claimed our luggage we set off into the town, Paul walking in utter silence.

"To what hotel shall we go?" I asked him. "It may be difficult to get into the City of Paris with a woman, especially with this Italian."

Paul interrupted me. "Yes, with an Italian who looks more like a dancer than a duchess. However, that is no business of mine. Do just as you please."

I was in a state of perplexity. I had written to the City of Paris to retain our rooms, and now I did not know what to do.

Two commissionaires followed us with our luggage. I continued: "You might as well go on first, and say that we are coming; and give the landlord to understand that I have a—a friend with me and that we should like rooms quite by themselves for us three, so as not to be brought in contact with other travellers. He will understand, and we will decide according to his answer."

But Paul growled, "Thank you, such commissions and such parts do not suit me, by any means. I did not come here to select your apartments or to minister to your pleasures."

But I was urgent: "Look here, don't be angry. It is surely far better to go to a good hotel than to a bad one, and it is not difficult to ask the landlord for three separate bedrooms and a dining-room."

I put a stress on three, and that decided him.

He went on first, and I saw him go into a large hotel while I remained on the other side of the street, with my fair Italian, who did not say a word, and followed the porters with the luggage.

Paul came back at last, looking as dissatisfied as my companion. "That is settled," he said, "and they will take us in; but here are only two bedrooms. You must settle it as you can."

I followed him, rather ashamed of going in with such a strange companion.

There were two bedrooms separated by a small sitting-room. I ordered a cold supper, and then I turned to the Italian with a perplexed look.

"We have only been able to get two rooms, so you must choose which you like."

She replied with her eternal "Che mi fa!" I thereupon took up her little black wooden trunk, such as servants use, and took it into the room on the right, which I had chosen for her. A bit of paper was fastened to the box, on which was written, Mademoiselle Francesca Rondoli, Genoa.

"Your name is Francesca?" I asked, and she nodded her head, without replying.

"We shall have supper directly," I continued. "Meanwhile, I dare say you would like to arrange your toilette a little?"

She answered with a 'mica', a word which she employed just as frequently as 'Che me fa', but I went on: "It is always pleasant after a journey."

Then I suddenly remembered that she had not, perhaps, the necessary requisites, for she appeared to me in a very singular position, as if she had just escaped from some disagreeable adventure, and I brought her my dressing-case.

I put out all the little instruments for cleanliness and comfort which it contained: a nail-brush, a new toothbrush—I always carry a selection of them about with me—my nail-scissors, a nail-file, and sponges. I uncorked a bottle of eau de cologne, one of lavender-water, and a little bottle of new-mown hay, so that she might have a choice. Then I opened my powder-box, and put out the powder-puff, placed my fine towels over the water-jug, and a piece of new soap near the basin.

She watched my movements with a look of annoyance in her wide-open eyes, without appearing either astonished or pleased at my forethought.

"Here is all that you require," I then said; "I will tell you when supper is ready."

When I returned to the sitting-room I found that Paul had shut himself in the other room, so I sat down to wait.

A waiter went to and fro, bringing plates and glasses. He laid the table slowly, then put a cold chicken on it, and told me that all was ready.

I knocked gently at Mademoiselle Rondoli's door. "Come in," she said, and when I did so I was struck by a strong, heavy smell of perfumes, as if I were in a hairdresser's shop.

The Italian was sitting on her trunk in an attitude either of thoughtful discontent or absent-mindedness. The towel was still folded over the waterjug that was full of water, and the soap, untouched and dry, was lying beside the empty basin; but one would have thought that the young woman had used half the contents of the bottles of perfume. The eau de cologne, however, had been spared, as only about a third of it had gone; but to make up for that she had used a surprising amount of lavender-water and new-mown hay. A cloud of violet powder, a vague white mist, seemed still to be floating in the air, from the effects of her over-powdering her face and neck. It seemed to cover her eyelashes, eyebrows, and the hair on her temples like snow, while her cheeks were plastered with it, and layers of it covered her nostrils, the corners of her eyes, and her chin.

When she got up she exhaled such a strong odor of perfume that it almost made me feel faint.

When we sat down to supper, I found that Paul was in a most execrable temper, and I could get nothing out of him but blame, irritable words, and disagreeable remarks.

Mademoiselle Francesca ate like an ogre, and as soon as she had finished her meal she threw herself upon the sofa in the sitting-room. Sitting down beside her, I said gallantly, kissing her hand:

"Shall I have the bed prepared, or will you sleep on the couch?"

"It is all the same to me. 'Che mi fa'!"

Her indifference vexed me.

"Should you like to retire at once?"

"Yes; I am very sleepy."

She got up, yawned, gave her hand to Paul, who took it with a furious look, and I lighted her into the bedroom. A disquieting feeling haunted me. "Here is all you want," I said again.

The next morning she got up early, like a woman who is accustomed to work. She woke me by doing so, and I watched her through my half-closed eyelids.

She came and went without hurrying herself, as if she were astonished at having nothing to do. At length she went to the dressing-table, and in a moment emptied all my bottles of perfume. She certainly also used some water, but very little.

When she was quite dressed, she sat down on her trunk again, and clasping one knee between her hands, she seemed to be thinking.

At that moment I pretended to first notice her, and said:

"Good-morning, Francesca."

Without seeming in at all a better temper than the previous night, she murmured, "Good-morning!"

When I asked her whether she had slept well, she nodded her head, and jumping out of bed, I went and kissed her.

She turned her face toward me like a child who is being kissed against its will; but I took her tenderly in my arms, and gently pressed my lips on her eyelids, which she closed with evident distaste under my kisses on her fresh cheek and full lips, which she turned away.

"You don't seem to like being kissed," I said to her.

"Mica!" was her only answer.

I sat down on the trunk by her side, and passing my arm through hers, I said: "Mica! mica! mica! in reply to everything. I shall call you Mademoiselle Mica, I think."

For the first time I fancied that I saw the shadow of a smile on her lips, but it passed by so quickly that I may have been mistaken.

"But if you never say anything but Mica, I shall not know what to do to please you. Let me see; what shall we do to-day?"

She hesitated a moment, as if some fancy had flitted through her head, and then she said carelessly: "It is all the same to me; whatever you like."

"Very well, Mademoiselle Mica, we will have a carriage and go for a drive."

"As you please," she said.

Paul was waiting for us in the dining-room, looking as bored as third parties usually do in love affairs. I assumed a delighted air, and shook hands with him with triumphant energy.

"What are you thinking of doing?" he asked.

"First of all, we will go and see a little of the town, and then we might get a carriage and take a drive in the neighborhood."

We breakfasted almost in silence, and then set out. I dragged Francesca from palace to palace, and she either looked at nothing or merely glanced carelessly at the various masterpieces. Paul followed us, growling all sorts of disagreeable things. Then we all three took a drive in silence into the country and returned to dinner.

The next day it was the same thing and the next day again; and on the third Paul said to me: "Look here, I am going to leave you; I am not going to stop here for three weeks watching you make love to this creature."

I was perplexed and annoyed, for to my great surprise I had become singularly attached to Francesca. A man is but weak and foolish, carried away by the merest trifle, and a coward every time that his senses are excited or mastered. I clung to this unknown girl, silent and dissatisfied as she always was. I liked her somewhat ill-tempered face, the dissatisfied droop of her mouth, the weariness of her look; I liked her fatigued movements, the contemptuous way in which she let me kiss her, the very indifference of her caresses. A secret bond, that mysterious bond of physical love, which does not satisfy, bound me to her. I told Paul so, quite frankly. He treated me as if I were a fool, and then said:

"Very well, take her with you."

But she obstinately refused to leave Genoa, without giving any reason. I besought, I reasoned, I promised, but all was of no avail, and so I stayed on.

Paul declared that he would go by himself, and went so far as to pack up his portmanteau; but he remained all the same.

Thus a fortnight passed. Francesca was always silent and irritable, lived beside me rather than with me, responded to all my requirements and all my propositions with her perpetual Che mi fa, or with her no less perpetual Mica.

My friend became more and more furious, but my only answer was, "You can go if you are tired of staying. I am not detaining you."

Then he called me names, overwhelmed me with reproaches, and exclaimed: "Where do you think I can go now? We had three weeks at our disposal, and here is a fortnight gone! I cannot continue my journey now; and, in any case, I am not going to Venice, Florence and Rome all by myself. But you will pay for it, and more dearly than you think, most likely. You are not going to bring a man all the way from Paris in order to shut him up at a hotel in Genoa with an Italian adventuress."

When I told him, very calmly, to return to Paris, he exclaimed that he intended to do so the very next day; but the next day he was still there, still in a rage and swearing.

By this time we began to be known in the streets through which we wandered from morning till night. Sometimes French people would turn round astonished at meeting their fellow-countrymen in the company of this girl with her striking costume, who looked singularly out of place, not to say compromising, beside us.

She used to walk along, leaning on my arm, without looking at anything. Why did she remain with me, with us, who seemed to do so little to amuse her? Who was she? Where did she come from? What was she doing? Had she any plan or idea? Where did she live? As an adventuress, or by chance meetings? I tried in vain to find out and to explain it. The better I knew her the more enigmatical she became. She seemed to be a girl of poor family who had been taken away, and then cast aside and lost. What did she think would become of her, or whom was she waiting for? She certainly did not appear to be trying to make a conquest of me, or to make any real profit out of me.

I tried to question her, to speak to her of her childhood and family; but she never gave me an answer. I stayed with her, my heart unfettered and my senses enchained, never wearied of holding her in my arms, that proud and quarrelsome woman, captivated by my senses, or rather carried away, overcome by a youthful, healthy, powerful charm, which emanated from her fragrant person and from the well-molded lines of her body.

Another week passed, and the term of my journey was drawing on, for I had to be back in Paris by the eleventh of July. By this time Paul had come to take his part in the adventure, though still grumbling at me, while I invented pleasures, distractions and excursions to amuse Francesca and my friend; and in order to do this I gave myself a great amount of trouble.

One day I proposed an excursion to Sta Margarita, that charming little town in the midst of gardens, hidden at the foot of a slope which stretches far into the sea up to the village of Portofino. We three walked along the excellent road which goes along the foot of the mountain. Suddenly Francesca said to me: "I shall not be able to go with you to-morrow; I must go and see some of my relatives."

That was all; I did not ask her any questions, as I was quite sure she would not answer me.

The next morning she got up very early. When she spoke to me it was in a constrained and hesitating voice:

"If I do not come back again, shall you come and fetch me?"

"Most certainly I shall," was my reply. "Where shall I go to find you?"

Then she explained: "You must go into the Street Victor-Emmanuel, down the Falcone road and the side street San-Rafael and into the furniture shop in the building at the right at the end of a court, and there you must ask for Madame Rondoli. That is the place."

And so she went away, leaving me rather astonished.

When Paul saw that I was alone, he stammered out: "Where; is Francesca?" And when I told him what had happened, he exclaimed:

"My dear fellow, let us make use of our opportunity, and bolt; as it is, our time is up. Two days, more or less, make no difference. Let us go at once; go and pack up your things. Off we go!"

But I refused. I could not, as I told him, leave the girl in that manner after such companionship for nearly three weeks. At any rate, I ought to say good-by to her, and make her accept a present; I certainly had no intention of behaving badly to her.

But he would not listen; he pressed and worried me, but I would not give way.

I remained indoors for several hours, expecting Francesca's return, but she did not come, and at last, at dinner, Paul said with a triumphant air:

"She has flown, my dear fellow; it is certainly very strange."

I must acknowledge that I was surprised and rather vexed. He laughed in my face, and made fun of me.

"It is not exactly a bad way of getting rid of you, though rather primitive. 'Just wait for me, I shall be back in a moment,' they often say. How long are you going to wait? I should not wonder if you were foolish enough to go and look for her at the address she gave you. 'Does Madame Rondoli live here, please?' 'No, monsieur.' I'll bet that you are longing to go there."

"Not in the least," I protested, "and I assure you that if she does not come back to-morrow morning I shall leave by the express at eight o'clock. I shall have waited twenty-four hours, and that is enough; my conscience will be quite clear."

I spent an uneasy and unpleasant evening, for I really had at heart a very tender feeling for her. I went to bed at twelve o'clock, and hardly slept at all. I got up at six, called Paul, packed up my things, and two hours later we set out for France together.

III

The next year, at just about the same period, I was seized as one is with a periodical fever, with a new desire to go to Italy, and I immediately made up my mind to carry it into effect. There is no doubt that every really well-educated man ought to see Florence, Venice and Rome. This travel has, also, the additional advantage of providing many subjects of conversation in society, and of giving one an opportunity for bringing forward artistic generalities which appear profound.

This time I went alone, and I arrived at Genoa at the same time as the year before, but without any adventure on the road. I went to the same hotel, and actually happened to have the same room.

I was hardly in bed when the recollection of Francesca which, since the evening before, had been floating vaguely through my mind, haunted me with strange persistency. I thought of her nearly the whole night, and by degrees the wish to see her again seized me, a confused desire at first, which gradually grew stronger and more intense. At last I made up my mind to spend the next day in Genoa to try to find her, and if I should not succeed, to take the evening train.

Early in the morning I set out on my search. I remembered the directions she had given me when she left me, perfectly—Victor-Emmanuel Street, house of the furniture-dealer, at the bottom of the yard on the right.

I found it without the least difficulty, and I knocked at the door of a somewhat dilapidated-looking dwelling. It was opened by a stout woman, who must have been very handsome, but who actually was only very dirty. Although she had too much embonpoint, she still bore the lines of majestic beauty; her untidy hair fell over her forehead and shoulders, and one fancied one could see her floating about in an enormous dressing-gown covered with spots of dirt and grease. Round her neck she wore a great gilt necklace, and on her wrists were splendid bracelets of Genoa filigree work.

In rather a hostile manner she asked me what I wanted, and I replied by requesting her to tell me whether Francesca Rondoli lived there.

"What do you want with her?" she asked.

"I had the pleasure of meeting her last year, and I should like to see her again."

The old woman looked at me suspiciously.

"Where did you meet her?" she asked.

"Why, here in Genoa itself."

"What is your name?"

I hesitated a moment, and then I told her. I had hardly done so when the Italian put out her arms as if to embrace me. "Oh! you are the Frenchman how glad I am to see you! But what grief you caused the poor child! She waited for you a month; yes, a whole month. At first she thought you would come to fetch her. She wanted to see whether you loved her. If you only knew how she cried when she saw that you were not coming! She cried till she seemed to have no tears left. Then she went to the hotel, but you had gone. She thought that most likely you were travelling in Italy, and that you would return by Genoa to fetch her, as she would not go with you. And she waited more than a month, monsieur; and she was so unhappy; so unhappy. I am her mother."

I really felt a little disconcerted, but I regained my self-possession, and asked:

"Where is she now?"

"She has gone to Paris with a painter, a delightful man, who loves her very much, and who gives her everything that she wants. Just look at what she sent me; they are very pretty, are they not?"

And she showed me, with quite southern animation, her heavy bracelets and necklace. "I have also," she continued, "earrings with stones in them, a silk dress, and some rings; but I only wear them on grand occasions. Oh! she is very happy, monsieur, very happy. She will be so pleased when I tell her you have been here. But pray come in and sit down. You will take something or other, surely?"

But I refused, as I now wished to get away by the first train; but she took me by the arm and pulled me in, saying:

"Please, come in; I must tell her that you have been in here."

I found myself in a small, rather dark room, furnished with only a table and a few chairs.

She continued: "Oh, she is very happy now, very happy. When you met her in the train she was very miserable; she had had an unfortunate love affair in Marseilles, and she was coming home, poor child. But she liked you at once, though she was still rather sad, you understand. Now she has all she wants, and she writes and tells me everything that she does. His name is Bellemin, and they say he is a great painter in your country. He fell in love with her at first sight. But you will take a glass of sirup?-it is very good. Are you quite alone, this year?"

"Yes," I said, "quite alone."

I felt an increasing inclination to laugh, as my first disappointment was dispelled by what Mother Rondoli said. I was obliged; however, to drink a glass of her sirup.

"So you are quite alone?" she continued. "How sorry I am that Francesca is not here now; she would have been company for you all the time you stayed. It is not very amusing to go about all by oneself, and she will be very sorry also."

Then, as I was getting up to go, she exclaimed:

"But would you not like Carlotta to go with you? She knows all the walks very well. She is my second daughter, monsieur."

No doubt she took my look of surprise for consent, for she opened the inner door and called out up the dark stairs which I could not see:

"Carlotta! Carlotta! make haste down, my dear child."

I tried to protest, but she would not listen.

"No; she will be very glad to go with you; she is very nice, and much more cheerful than her sister, and she is a good girl, a very good girl, whom I love very much."

In a few moments a tall, slender, dark girl appeared, her hair hanging down, and her youthful figure showing unmistakably beneath an old dress of her mother's.

The latter at once told her how matters stood.

"This is Francesca's Frenchman, you know, the one whom she knew last year. He is quite alone, and has come to look for her, poor fellow; so I told him that you would go with him to keep him company."

The girl looked at me with her handsome dark eyes, and said, smiling:

"I have no objection, if he wishes it"

I could not possibly refuse, and merely said:

"Of course, I shall be very glad of your company."

Her mother pushed her out. "Go and get dressed directly; put on your blue dress and your hat with the flowers, and make haste."

As soon as she had left the room the old woman explained herself: "I have two others, but they are much younger. It costs a lot of money to bring up four children. Luckily the eldest is off my hands at present."

Then she told all about herself, about her husband, who had been an employee on the railway, but who was dead, and she expatiated on the good qualities of Carlotta, her second girl, who soon returned, dressed, as her sister had been, in a striking, peculiar manner.

Her mother examined her from head to foot, and, after finding everything right, she said:

"Now, my children, you can go." Then turning to the girl, she said: "Be sure you are back by ten o'clock to-night; you know the door is locked then." The answer was:

"All right, mamma; don't alarm yourself."

She took my arm and we went wandering about the streets, just as I had wandered the previous year with her sister.

We returned to the hotel for lunch, and then I took my new friend to Santa Margarita, just as I had taken her sister the year previously.

During the whole fortnight which I had at my disposal, I took Carlotta to all the places of interest in and about Genoa. She gave me no cause to regret her sister.

She cried when I left her, and the morning of my departure I gave her four bracelets for her mother, besides a substantial token of my affection for herself.

One of these days I intend to return to Italy, and I cannot help remembering with a certain amount of uneasiness, mingled with hope, that Madame Rondoli has two more daughters.